# Jewish Farmers in Russia Fields (Kherson Region)

## Translation of
### *Khaklaim yehudim b'arvot Russia*

Original Book Edited by: Tzvi Livneh-Lieberman

Originally published by Ha'Kibutz Ha'Artzi, Ha'Shomer Ha'Tzair, Merkhavia, Israel 1965

JewishGen
מרכז עולמי לגנאלוגיה יהודית
The Global Home for Jewish Genealogy

**A Publication of JewishGen**
**Edmond J. Safra Plaza, 36 Battery Place, New York, NY 10280**
**646.494.2972 | info@JewishGen.org | www.jewishgen.org**

MUSEUM OF
JEWISH HERITAGE
A LIVING MEMORIAL
TO THE HOLOCAUST

**Jewish Farmers in Russia Fields (Kherson Region)**
Translation of *Khaklaim yehudim b'arvot Russia*

Copyright © 2024 by JewishGen.  All rights reserved.
First Printing: June 2024, Sivan 5784
Editor of Original Yizkor Book: Tzvi Livneh-Lieberman
Project Coordinator and Translator: Moshe Kutten
Cover Design: Irv Osterer
Layout: Jonathan Wind

Library of Congress Control Number (LCCN): 2024934869

ISBN: 978-1-954176-97-3 (hard cover: 432 pages, alk. paper)

# About JewishGen.org

JewishGen, is a Genealogical Research Division of the Museum of Jewish Heritage - A Living Memorial to the Holocaust, serves as the global home for Jewish genealogy.

Featuring unparalleled access to 30+ million records, it offers unique search tools, along with opportunities for researchers to connect with others who share similar interests. Award winning resources such as the Family Finder, Discussion Groups, and ViewMate, are relied upon by thousands each day.

In addition, JewishGen's extensive informational, educational and historical offerings, such as the Jewish Communities Database, Yizkor Book translations, InfoFiles, Family Tree of the Jewish People, and KehilaLinks, provide critical insights, first-hand accounts, and context about Jewish communal and familial life throughout the world.

Offered as a free resource, JewishGen.org has facilitated thousands of family connections and success stories, and is currently engaged in an intensive expansion effort that will bring many more records, tools, and resources to its collections.

Please visit https://www.jewishgen.org/ to learn more.

**Vice President for JewishGen:** Avraham Groll

## About the JewishGen Yizkor Book Project

Yizkor Books (Memorial Books) were traditionally written to memorialize the names of departed family and martyrs during holiday services in the synagogue (a practice that still exists in many synagogues today).

Over the centuries, as a result of countless persecutions and horrific atrocities committed against the Jews, Yizkor Books (Sefer Zikaron in Hebrew) were expanded to include more historical information, such as biographical sketches of famous personalities and descriptions of daily town life.

Following the Holocaust, the idea of remembrance and learning took on an urgent and crucial importance. Survivors of the Holocaust sought out other surviving residents of their former towns to memorialize and document the names and way of life of those who were ruthlessly murdered by the Nazis. These remembrances were documented in Yizkor Books, hundreds of which were published in the first decades after the Holocaust.

Most of these books were published privately, or through *Landsmanshaftn* (social organizations comprised of members originating from the same European town or region) that still existed, and were often distributed free of charge. The languages used to document these crucial histories and links to our past were Yiddish and Hebrew. JewishGen has undertaken the sacred responsibility of translating these books into English so that the culture and way of life of these communities will be preserved and transmitted to future generations.

In 1986, a group of farsighted JewishGenners started a project to pool their efforts together in groups based upon their ancestors' towns and donate funds to translate the Yizkor books of their ancestral towns into English.  As the translated material became available, it was made accessible for free at https://www.JewishGen.org/Yizkor . Hardcover copies can be purchased by visiting https://www.jewishgen.org/Yizkor/ybip.html  (see below).

It is our hope that the translation of these books into English (and other languages) will assist the countless Jewish family researchers who are so desperately seeking to forge a connection with their heritage.

**Director of JewishGen Yizkor Book Project**: Lance Ackerfeld

## About JewishGen Press

JewishGen Press (formerly the Yizkor Books-in-Print Project) is the publishing division of JewishGen.org, and provides a venue for the publication of non-fiction books pertaining to Jewish genealogy, history, culture, and heritage.

In addition to the Yizkor Book category, publications in the Other Non-Fiction category include Shoah memoirs and research, genealogical research, collections of genealogical and historical materials, biographies, diaries and letters, studies of Jewish experience and cultural life in the past, academic theses, and other books of interest to the Jewish community.

Please visit https://www.jewishgen.org/Yizkor/ybip.html  to learn more.

**Director of JewishGen Press:**  Joel Alpert
**Managing Editor** - Jessica Feinstein
**Publications Manager** - Susan Rosin

## Notes to the Reader

The images in the original book were reproduced from photographs from the time of the first edition.  These reproductions were already of poor quality, being pre-war and at least 30 or more years old. As a result, the images in the book are the best achievable.

A list of all books available from JewishGen Press along with prices is available at: https://www.jewishgen.org/Yizkor/ybip.html

# Dedication

The translation of this book is dedicated to my parents-in-law, David and Rosa Tverdovsky, who survived the harsh life under Stalin, saved themselves by making Aliya to Eretz Israel before WW II and endured the hardships of being pioneers and citizens in Israel.

I began my work on this book by translating the story "Ba'arava" ["On the Prairie"], written by my father-in-law, who was a talented storyteller and Yiddish author. He received the World Jewish Congress [WJC]'s Bimco Award for Yiddish Writing in 1961 for the story, which was first published under the name "Erev Pesakh" ["Passover Eve"] in the Yiddish journal, 'Di Goldene Kyte." It was later translated into Hebrew by the famed author Shimshon Meltzer (See page 145). My wife, Nehama, told me that she saw her father cry for the first time when he received the letter from the WJC. In that letter, the award committee claimed they had never seen such a talented Yiddish writer since Shalom Aleikhem.

The book and the story depict the unique tale of the agricultural settlement of Jews in Southern Ukraine from its forming until the bitter end at the hands of the Nazi oppressors, about 140 years and five generators later. It contains a detailed historical review and first-hand testimonies of the survivors.

Moshe Kutten
Project Coordinator and Translator
Coatesville, PA
June, 2024

# Photo Credits

Cover Design by: Irv Osterer

**Front Cover:**

**Top Photo:**
Yefeh Nahar – The synagogue [Page 192/193]

**Bottom Right:**
Rav Avraham Simongauz, one of the first settlers of Inguletz (one hundred years old) [Page 352/353]

**Bottom Left:**
R' Zalman-Leib Veslnitzki, the patriarch of the large Simkhoni family in Israel - under his cherry tree in his farm in Sdeh-Menukha Ha'Gdola [Page 304/305]

**Back Cover:**

**Top Photo:**
Sdeh Menukah Ha'Ktana —The Vegetable Garden (during the beginning of the 1920's) [Page 176/177]

**Bottom Photo:**
The Harvest in the Field (during the beginning of the 1920's) [Page 336/337]

# Table of Contents

## Memories about the Colonies After the Revolution

## From the Literature

## Appendices

# Jewish Farmers
# in Russia Fields
# (Kherson, Ukraine)

**Translation of**
***Khaklaim yehudim b'arvot Russia***

Edited by Tzvi Livneh-Lieberman

Published by HaKibbutz HaArtzi, HaShomer HaTzair, Merkhavia, Israel 1965

**Acknowledgments:**

**Project Coordinator & Translator**

Moshe Kutten

**Editors:**

**Yocheved Klausner & Rafael Manory**

**Our sincere appreciation to the daughters of Tzvi Livneh-Lieberman *z"l*,
Ms. Rachel Kafri and Ms. Dinka Peled, for permission to put this material on the
JewishGen website**

This is a translation from: *Khaklaim yehudim b'arvot Russia* (Jewish Farmers in Russian
Fields),
Edited by Tzvi Livneh-Lieberman, Published by HaKibbutz HaArtzi, HaShomer HaTzair,
Merkhavia, Israel 1965 (H)

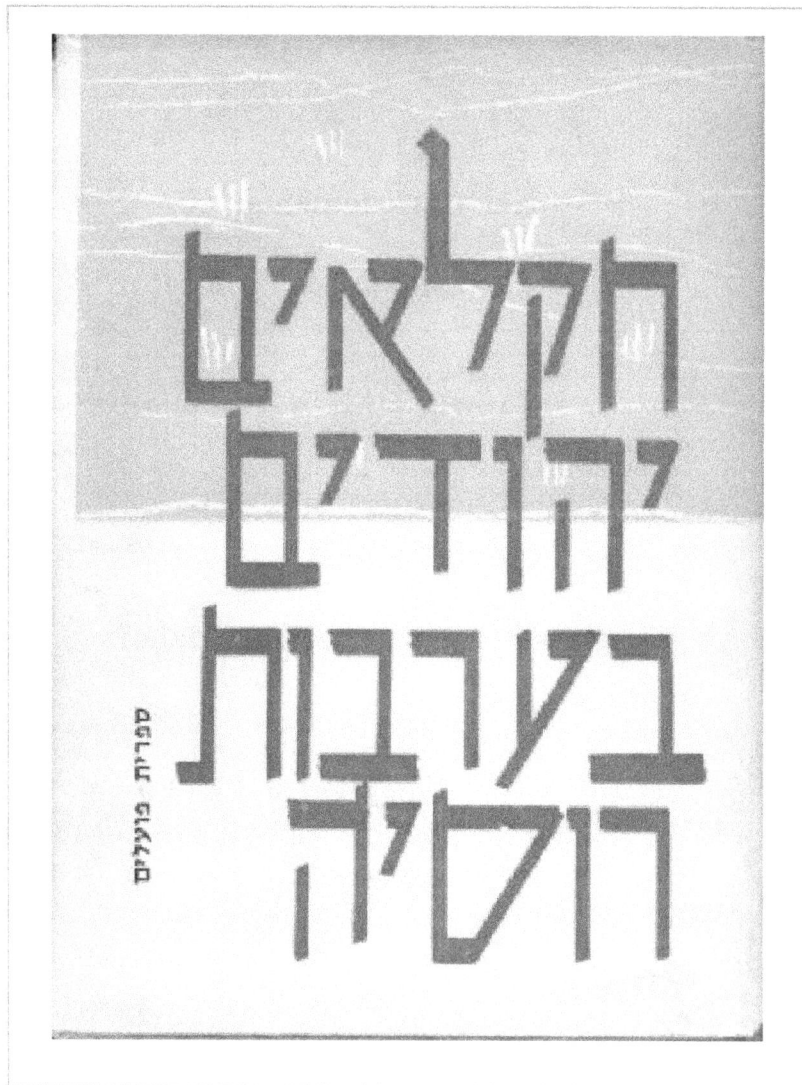

*[Page 3]*

# Jewish

# Farmers

# On Russian

# Fields

**Sifriat HaPoalim**

**Published by the HaKibbutz HaArtzi, HaShomer HaTzair, Merkhavia, Israel**

*[Page 4]*

# Jewish Farmers

# On

# Russian Fields[1]

The chapter: *Toldot* – Historical Review – authored and edited by Tzvi Livneh-Lieberman

The memory chapters –collected and edited by the initiating committee with the involvement of Tzvi Livneh-Lieberman

The Story "Ba'Aravah" ["On the Prairie"] by D. Tverdovsky as well as the article about "A Jewish Colony in the Year 1823" were translated [to Hebrew] by Shimshon Meltzer

The memory poems by Mordekhai Pitkin, were translated [to Hebrew] by Immanuel HaRusi

Helping with the reading and editing of various chapter were:

Diklah Golomb, Yehuda Slutzki and Khayim Halperin

The maps of the region on pages 423–428, were established by Yosi Mestchekin.

The editor: Yosef Wilfned

Graphical editing: Tzvi Zohar

©

Published in Israel, 1965, 5725

*[Page 7]*

# With the Book

## By Israel Ben Eliyahu,
## Mordekhai Khalili and Mordekhai Simkhoni

**Translated by** Moshe Kutten

**Edited by** Rafael Manory

With love and great reverence, we present this book about Jewish agricultural colonies in Southern Ukraine.

We are strongly driven by the feeling of a holy duty toward the tribe of these humble Jews, who worked the land, were honest folks who possessed within them precious virtues of greatness and heroism, and who have molded the image of a Jew who was healthy in his body and spirit amid the sorrowful Jewish diaspora.

We, the descendants–survivors of that tribe, carried for many years the idea of putting in writing the memory of the unique folklore of the agricultural colonies that have raised five generations of farmers and thereby retain and preserve it for the benefit of the future generations in Israel. The objective was also aimed at recording the history of the endeavor; because of the unique circumstances of the period of its demise, i.e. the advent of the Shoah of the entire European Jewry, there are gaps in the remembrance of this unique enterprise in the Jewish historiography of our generations.

The calamity of Hitler, may his name be wiped out, has cut off the existence of all the colonies and their populates (not the least with the help of the Ukrainian neighbors who murdered and inherited…). On the other hand, the existential distress of the Jewish national survival in the USSR is preventing the nourishing of that legacy on the location of its existence and demise.

The three signatories to this article, who served as the de-facto initiative committee, took upon themselves to realize the idea of bringing up from oblivion and muteness the tales of heroism and exploits - the journey and the settlement of the pioneers of Jewish agriculture in Czarist Russia in early 19th century, the struggle and the hardships encountered by the first settlers, the path to substantiation and rooting, and the last struggles to the dying fibrillations during the years of the calamity of the great Shoah.

Our first actions involved finding and organizing the community of the former residents of the colonies and rounding support for gathering the material and writing the articles for the book. We found about one hundred and fifty comrades in all corners of the land–while going from one village to another, from the moshavim to the kibbutzim, as well as to towns and cities. We were fortunate to get a generous response, thus the needed material and spiritual assistance has been secured.

Our first solid step toward the fulfillment of our idea was the agreement made with our comrade Tzvi Livneh (Lieberman), a resident of Nahalal. Tzvi, whose share in expediting and motivating for action was very significant, took upon himself the task

*[Page 8]*

of compiling and authoring the series of historical chapters, as well as participating in the gathering of the articles from the members; these were written or provided to us orally; the material was also gathered from periodicals and archives. Tzvi has also selected and edited material relevant to our subject matter from historical literature in Yiddish and Russian, aiming to write the historical chapters that constitute the first part of the book. For this effort, which he performed with dedication and love, he is thankfully blessed.

It is clear to us that we have not managed to exhaust all options. There is a vast amount of documentary material in repositories in Russia and other archives throughout the world that is waiting for future historians. The material offered here may present a challenge for them to shine a light on this wondrous vision of the Jewish agricultural settlement at the beginning of the 19th century, which enjoyed a magnificent continuation until it fell prey to a malicious enemy.

The folklore and memory chapters were written primarily by people who are not professional writers or authors but are people of labor and accomplishment who told their stories about their experiences and aspirations, actions and feelings, everyone in his or her language and style. As a whole, taken together, the stories form an image of the way of life and conditions of the Jewish farmers in those colonies on Ukraine's prairies. The poets Simon Frugg and Saul Tchernikhovsky wrote poems, at their time, about these lives. They were the weavers of dreams about Jewish plowing land, Jews who breathed nature and about creative work and freedom. More than fifty members contributed their writings to this collection. Some friends guided us with advice and solutions. They all congregated to establish a memorial for the undertaking by five generations of Russian–Jewish agriculturalists and workers.

We like to mention, with appreciation, the contribution of honorable public institutions without whose real assistance, the publication of this book would not have been possible. We also want to thank the publisher– Sifryat HaPoalim, for the fine understanding of this project, which was shown from the time of our first inquiry to the completion of the book.

May all those who landed their hands, cooperated, and took part in our endeavor be blessed. May this book serve as a memorial for our ancestors, our brothers and sisters; thanks to them and their legacy, we have achieved a productive and happy life in our motherland.

*[Page 9]*

# Introduction
## The Historical Role of the Jewish Settlement in Russia

## By Khaim Halperin

**Translated by** Moshe Kutten

**Edited by** Rafi Manory

In the history of Jewish people in the diaspora, the tale of the agricultural settlement of Jews in Russia is unique and distinct. The story of this settlement, with its colonies, enterprises, struggles, and achievements is being told in this book, both in its historical preview chapters and in the folklore and memories chapters, all written either by its participants or by people who cherish its memory.

The historical importance of this settlement movement results primarily from the fact that eighty years before the emergence of the "*Khibat Tzion*" movement ["Lovers of Zion - the precursor to Zionism], and almost one hundred years before Herzl's appearance at the Zionist Congresses, it served as a model and source of inspiration for all the people, institutions, and social movements who have initiated and established agricultural settlements in various countries of the diaspora, in parallel with the Zionist settlement enterprises in Eretz Israel.

The experiments and enterprises of the return of the Jews to village life and agriculture in the diaspora and their faith, during the latest generations, took different forms, whether they have been realized or have not reached fruition in later generations. The biggest of all, in its scope and fortitude, was undoubtedly the enterprise of the Baron de Hirsch in Argentina, which aimed at relieving the distress of Russian Jews by transferring them to an uninhabited and vast land where they would be able to settle as farmers. Baron de Hirsch's vision was immense and daring, however, his henchmen and officials did not share his vision. They were clerks of a charity and philanthropic corporation who treated the settlers with scorn, doubt, and excess harshness (similar to the treatment of the settlers of the first colonies in Eretz Israel by Baron Rothschild's functionaries during the same period). With the clear intention of speeding up the assimilation of the settlers in the new country, the JCA Corporation [the "Jewish Colonization Association" established by Baron de Hirsch] purchased 6 million *dunams* [about 1.5 million acres] that were scattered over many regions, to avoid concentration of the new settlers in one area.

Despite the destructive tendencies among the JCA's officialdom, at the beginning of the 20th century, the enterprise already included close to 4000 families or about 30,000 people. Along with the settlement movement, the organization for cooperative supply and trading was established and developed; banks for common people and credit unions were also established and were concentrated under the umbrella of the union for "Agricultural Brotherhood" ("*Fraternidad Agraria*"), which served as a center for cooperative agriculture federations. A special corporation for the development of Jewish agriculture ("*Formanta Agraria*") was established as well, but the main thing was the unique Jewish atmosphere that was felt in this enterprise.

However, even during the years before World War I, the general trend of migration

*[Page 10]*

"from the village to the city" had penetrated into the Jewish colonies in Argentina. Although the progression was slow, it was continuous. The young generation could not withstand the attraction of Buenos Aires. The growth of the whole enterprise has stagnated. The plots of the people who left were sold to non-Jews and only the owners of cattle herds intended for meat were left. Even among them, many managed their farms from their residence in the city… (Clearly, the low profitability from agriculture has influenced the process of abandonment. Some claimed that the connection between the Jewish farmer and his land was not established and blamed it on the lack of a national ideology related to agricultural settlement). This is how the few remaining colonies lost their Jewish character and the settlement enterprise that has existed for more than 150 years, deteriorated during our time, not because of political events or external pressure, but as a result of the urbanization process in that country.

In connection to our subject, it is worth noting that the foundation for the Jewish settlement in Argentina in 1889, was laid out by settlers who were natives of Kamenetz–Podolsk and its environs, a region that was very near the Jewish colonies in Kherson and Yekaterinoslav. Clearly, the move of these first settlers toward agriculture was influenced by the example of the Jewish farmers in the established colonies in Russia [Southern Ukraine].

The fate of the Jewish settlement in the United States during the same period was different. This settlement continued without intervention by the authorities and in certain aspects, without any significant assistance by public elements.

The initiators and implementers of the US settlement during the 1880s were also immigrants from Russia, many of whom were influenced by the "Am Olam"[1] movement. The movement was established parallel to the "BILU" movement[2], however, unlike BILU, it advocated settlement in America rather than Eretz Israel. The first colony in the US - "Sicily Island Colony" in Louisiana was established by a group of youths from Yelisavetgrad, which was under the influence of the "Am Olam" movement and was received very favorably by the American public, although it did not successfully endure the harsh climate conditions of the southern state. Other experiments, such as the colonies of "New Odesa" and "Bethlehem Yehuda," also agricultural colonies of South Russian natives, did not survive for long.

The "Am Olam" movement established seven colonies in the USA: Karmia, Karmel, Montefiori, Lasker, Gil'ad, Touro, and Liser [?], and we can also add to them the "New Odesa Colony." Altogether, we know about 25 colonies that were established during those years, but none lasted for a long time. The interesting thing about them was that almost all of their founders were Russian natives. There is no doubt that they have been influenced quite a bit by the example of the mother colonies of Jewish agriculture in their native country.

Along these large enterprises, there were also small, less daring

*[Page 11]*

experiments, in Poland, Lithuania, Bessarabia, Brazil, Uruguay, and San Domingo. Some plans have never reached the implementation stage, such as the famed "Uganda Plan," which raised sharp arguments and stormy debates in the Zionist movement at the beginning of the twentieth century. There were also plans for projects in England, Ecuador, Australia, and other places. Among these projects, some lasted a longer time, and there were phenomena of pioneering and heroism; however, none lasted as a permanent settlement of Jews. We are convinced that the Jewish agricultural colonies in Russia served as a prototype, example, and model for all of these experiments and paved the way and gave birth to followers in other diaspora countries.

It can be noted that all the other colonies in the diaspora were abandoned, for objective or subjective reasons, by the settlers themselves, whereas the Jewish agricultural settlement in Russia continued to exist for almost one hundred and fifty years and was not liquidated until it was destroyed from the outside by a hasty and cruel oppressor.

This settlement was the one that contributed from its power and influenced the rebirth of the national settlement in Eretz Israel, during the Second *Aliyah* movement and more than during the Third *Aliyah* movement. More than one hundred and fifty people who came from the Jewish colonies in Russia live today in Israel and continue their life in agriculture in the Israeli moshavim [a form of cooperative village] and kibbutzim [a form of agricultural commune–RM] and some in very prominent roles in society and the state, are a living testimony for that.

Thus, at the 160th anniversary of the establishment of the first colonies, a group from the fifth generation of pioneering settlers, those whose childhood and youth were interwoven with the deeds of their predecessors, rose and initiated this project of commemoration in a form of a book about the villages of their birth. They were the ones who wrote many pages in this book, not as authors but as the children, grandchildren, and great-grandchildren of Jewish cattlemen, yeomen, pioneers, and trailblazers in Russia.

I am not sure why I was found worthy to be invited to serve as an advisor (perhaps because of my connections with the people of the colonies during my initial career in Russia). However, I was very impressed with them during our first discussion and accepted without any argument their generous invitation to author an introduction for the book. However, when I first read what they had written and thought about my introductory words, I felt a storm raging in my soul and was very confused. I could not get rid of the nightmarish picture played in front of my eyes of this huge cemetery filled with gravestones seized by flames. The names kept shining through the flames: Sdeh Menukha HaGdola and Sdeh-Menukha-HaKtana at its side; and near it the name of Nahar-Tov-HaKtana, Yefeh-Nahar, Izraelovka, and Dobroya; Novo- Poltavka and Bobrovy-Kut, Sehaidek, Inguletz, and Mazor[3], and other names that are precious and close to the heart.

And I see the obliterating flames, the weapon of hatred with no reason, malice and evil and blood-thirsty hands that annihilated and demolished, destroyed and exterminated an enterprise of five generations of Jewish pioneering farmers who served as an example for millions of Jews in Russia and throughout the world.

*[Page 12]*

When I reread the notes written by the natives of the colonies, notes that were filled with tears, grief, and longing for their parents, brothers, and sisters who were put on the stake, I see them as Scrolls of Fire. We should take comfort in the fact that the Scrolls of Fire became an eternal flame that would never be extinguished. The one hundred and fifty years of agricultural labor and creation in the Jewish colonies in Russia were not in vain; under their guiding light, generations were taught to live productive lives, love the land, and love humanity. They served as an honorary gate for the Zionist settlement enterprise in Eretz Israel.

The one hundred and fifty natives of the colonies who managed to make *Aliyah* and take roots in Eretz Israel, were privileged to serve as instructors for the many who settled with them in kibbutzim and moshavim and thus ease their absorption difficulties. Their children and descendants in the following generations knew how to preserve in their hearts the memory of the accomplishments of their ancestors in Russia's diaspora. With this book, one generation would tell the story to future generations. This would be the family tree for the descendants; a memorial book for their ancestors, and for future generations - *Pirkei Avot* [Ethics of the Fathers]. The reader and the researcher would be able to find pages and chapters from an important period in the history of the Jewish people, chapters of grief and calamity, but also chapters of exaltation, culture, and accomplishments.

May the name of the Jewish settlement in Russia be exalted and sanctified.

***Translator's Notes:***

1. "Am Olam" (literally means "Eternal People"), established in 1881 in Odesa, was a movement among Russian Jewry aimed at establishing socialist agricultural settlements in America.
2. The "BILU" movement (an acronym in Hebrew for a verse from Isaiah 2:5 "*Beit Ya'akov Lekhu Venelkha*" ("House of Jacob, let us go"). It was established in Russia in 1882 to promote agricultural settlement in Eretz Israel.
3. Jewish Colonies in Southern Ukraine - Kherson province.

[Page 13]

# *Toldot* – An Historical Review

## Authored and edited (in Hebrew) by Tzvi Livneh-Lieberman

### Translated by Moshe Kutten

### Edited by Rafael Manory

[Page 14]

## Untitled poem by Shimon Frugg

And there would come a day
when a great-grandchild and a grandchild will read
the arduous and bitter tale of your torments
and the road you soaked ceaselessly with your tears,
the road you walked bent.

They will drape and adorn it with swards and flowers -
shining flowers that give a fragrant smell.

*[Page 15]*

# A. An Historical Background

## The Jews During the Partitions of Poland

To understand the historical background and the factors that led to the wondrous phenomena of the agricultural settlement by the Jews in Southern Russia at the beginning of the 19ᵗʰ century, we first need to grasp the situation of the Polish Jews during the period of Partitions of Poland in the late18ᵗʰcentury.

The Polish nobility owned most of the old Polish lands. The peasant farmers were enslaved to their estates and plantations. The population as a whole was hungry and poor. The representatives of the Polish Sejm were also nobles and landowners. These representatives – while looking for ways to solve the difficult state of the masses of the peasants, did not really dare to uncover the actual root cause of the problem and thus found the Jews as the scapegoats and described them as the main cause for the disasters and calamities that the peasants were exposed to.

During that period, the Jewish population in Poland, Lithuania, Belarus, and Ukraine amounted to about a million people. About a third resided in the cities and towns and worked in small trade businesses, peddling, bartending, money lending, and crafts. The rest of the Jews were scattered in villages, most leased taverns, flour mills, and inns. The high leasing costs were a major source of income for the nobility. The Jews also served in management roles of the *"Paritsim's"* [noblemen] plantations and as intermediaries for the nobility's crop sales, purchases, shopping, etc. Apart from jobs that were dependent on the village masters, the Jews were also small shopkeepers to provide for the meager needs of the peasant population.

According to the statistical data of those days, 25% of Podolia's Jews made a living as bartenders, whereas in other Ukrainian cities and villages, the percentage of bartenders among the Jews was as high as 39%. The peasants considered these Jewish lessees as blood-sucking parasites while the masters, who were the people who leased the taverns, considered the Jewish lessees as despicable people. The nobles used to abuse them and even evict them from their source of income.

The representatives of the people of the Sejm, most of whom were from the aristocratic class, also considered the Jews as "exploiters"

*[Page 16]*

and the root cause of the people's anger. However, any objective researcher of the state of the Polish Jews during that period should surely note, first and foremost, their poverty, degradation, and lack of confidence, as well as the high leasing costs, the exaggerated government taxes, the need to bribe all officials and the bad-debts of drunken customers, who ruined and destroyed property in their drunken rampages – all these were blows that significantly hurt the standard of living of the Jewish masses.

The degraded state of the Jews, who had been subjects of Poland for hundreds of years, did not trouble the state leaders. Their main concern was how to divert public opinion from the real economic status of the nation's Christian masses and direct the anger of these masses away from the authorities and towards the imaginary enemy.

According to a decision passed in the Polish House of Representatives in 1768, "it was forbidden for Jews, who did not have special rights, to deal in the trade of alcoholic beverages and in leasing or ownership of taverns." This decision resulted in disastrous results for the Jews. Many of the estate owners replaced their Jewish lessees with Christian ones, and the dispossessed Jews were left without a source of income. The competition from the Christian tradesmen, who enjoyed direct and indirect support from the state, was also intensifying. However, the decision by the Sejm was not easy to implement. Taking away the trade profession from the Jews could have led to an economic crisis. The state treasury was very sensitive to the surge in bankruptcies among the dispossessed tradesmen and thereby to a reduction in taxes. The regime witnessed a worsening of the state of the dispossessed and impoverished Jews, and for the first time, liberal public figures started to propose converting the Jews to agricultural work.

However, in the meantime, with the partitions of Poland among its neighbors, the Jewish problem was shifted along with the conquered areas to the Russian and Austro-Hungarian Empires.

In 1775, a constitution concerning the province of Lithuania, which was still part of Poland at that time, was passed in the Polish Sejm. This constitution bestowed the right to acquire lands and hold them permanently to the subjects of this province. A bone was thrown at the Jewish residents as well. They were allowed to lease lands and work them, although only in uninhabited and infertile areas. To encourage them to settle in these deserted areas, they were relieved from paying taxes for six years. The result: only 14 Jewish families settled.

Joseph the 2nd, Emperor of Austria, considered by the people of his generation as a reformist and liberal, abolished the system of leasing of the taverns and inns and thereby destroyed the livelihood of the Jews in Galicia proper. He tried to solve the sustenance problem of these Jews and heal their economy by transferring them to work the land. This was the intention behind the royal decree, which he published on 19 June (1785) – "to establish Jewish agricultural colonies." A year after the decree was published (1786), one Jewish colony was indeed established; however, the implementation of Joseph the 2nd's plans encountered difficulties. Vacant land areas, available for settlement were not found, as it was also necessary to settle landless Christians.

*[Page 17]*

The Jews themselves were not enthusiastic about the idea of the transition to agricultural life. In 1789, the authorities handed the handling of recruiting Jews for settlement to the communities' administrations. These administrations didn't prove their ability and talent for this role, and some considered it a nuisance by a troublesome king and treated it negatively and with contempt.

There were no real results to the plan of the liberal king; however, the very fact that there had been an attempt to solve the Jewish problem by settling them on the land caused several Polish leaders to bother the Sejm with proposals to solve the Jewish problem in Poland similar to the Austrian emperor's plan.

One of these leaders was the Sejm representative from Pinsk, Mateusz Butrymowicz. He published a pamphlet signed by "an unnamed person," which appeared in 1782 (with a second edition to follow in 1785). In 1789, the same pamphlet was published under a new title: "A Way of Transforming the Jews into Useful Citizens of the Country." The essence of this remedy proposal was to instill the art of working the land among the Jews and to distance them from the occupations of tavern-keepers and innkeepers. In looking for ways to enable them more equality and lesser self-segregation from the rest of the population, the representative Mateusz Butrymowicz followed the Western European view. He proposed narrowing the autonomy of the communities, replacing the "jargon" language with the Polish language in schools and businesses, prohibiting special traditional Jewish attire, and placing an embargo on the import of Hebrew books from outside of the country.

This proposal, which appeared in print, and the words of the representative in the Sejm, roused a sharp controversy. Numerous pamphlets and booklets that discussed the solution of the Jewish issue positively were published, and many harsh and unfavorable critical articles appeared in the newspapers against this proposal.

In this sharp controversy between the liberals and the anti-Semites, the voice of the Jews themselves could hardly be heard. Many of the Jews would have certainly agreed to replace their despicable and hopeless occupation with working the land, however, the proposal to narrow the autonomy of the community, replacing the spoken language with the Polish language and the prohibition on the traditional attire, instilled among them fear of assimilation that may also lead to religious conversion.

A few voices among the Jews were heard, nevertheless. Rabbi Tzvi [Herszel] Jozefowicz of Chelm, published a pamphlet in Polish in which he praised the appealing intention of Representative Butrymowicz. However, he rose against the other sections of the proposal that, in his opinion, offended the religious and traditional affairs of Jewish life.

Against the sole outcry of the pious Rabbi, another view was aired. Avraham Hirszowicz, who was most probably, a financier ("a Royal pimp"), submitted to King Stanisław II Augustus a plan similar to the one by Butrymowicz. The main idea behind the plan was to divert the Jews towards crafts and working the land in the prairies of Southern Ukraine, where most of the lands were uncultivated. The plan contained additional sections:

*[Page 18]*

The prohibition on marriage at a young age, the prohibition on silk, atlas, and velvet clothing, as well as the prohibition on wearing pearls and precious stones jewelry, "since the chase after clothing and luxury jewelry impoverishes the middle class." According to Hirszowicz, it was necessary to nominate Rabbis only in big cities but not in small towns, where most of the Rabbis "purchase" their post from the land-owners and burden their congregation by imposing taxes. One paragraph, which stated that the changes must be implemented by the government, is particularly fascinating. The author stated that the reason for that is "because the Jews themselves, due to the differences of opinions among them, would not be able to impose proper orders, so they should yield to the government to uproot their distorted views and false concepts of this stray people."

As mentioned above, Butrymowicz was not alone in his fight to find a humane solution to the Jewish issue. His friend in the fight and view was the famous publicist and historian Tadeusz Czacki, who was also the head of the Sejm finance commission. There were some differences between the proposal of the latter and Butrimowycz's plan, however, essentially the two plans were identical.

Because of the pressure from the liberal Sejm representatives, and under the influence of the riots of Warsaw Christian craftsmen against the Jewish craftsmen, who came to the capital from other towns, the Sejm concluded that it was not possible to postpone the discussion about the Jewish issue any longer. On the 22nd of June 1790, the "General Sejm" [the bicameral parliament] established a committee to discuss a plan of reforms to remedy the state of the Jews. The committee was instructed to process and submit proposals.

Among the members of the committee: were Butrymowicz, Czacki, Jezierski, and others. Jezierski was elected to head the committee. He was considered to be, more than anybody else, the most knowledgeable on the economic problems of the Jews in the country. The committee submitted its proposals to the Sejm at the beginning of 1791. It was based on the plans of Butrymowicz, Czacki, and Jezierski. However, when the proposal was placed on the Sejm's agenda, one of the committee members, Representative Hołowiński, submitted a counter-proposal of his own and the Sejm postponed the discussion. In the end, the Sejm accepted the committee's plan, however, the committee was asked to amend it and generate a final version. There was also the problem of the debt of the Jewish communities to the Polish government, and the issue had to be discussed in the finance committee. In the meantime, a war broke out, which brought the second Polish partition (1793), and the plan was shelved.

At the second Poland partition, the following regions were transferred to Russia: Vohlyn. Podolia, and Minsk provinces, as well as part of the Kiev [Kyiv] province. The following districts were transferred to Prussia: Kalisz, Plock, Danzig, and Toruń.

Two years later (1795), the third and last partition of Poland took place. Russia annexed Lithuania (the provinces of Vilna and Grodno), and with it - masses of Jews in these provinces came under the rule and regime of the Czar. The Sejm's decisions and all the plans for the remedy of the state of the Jews became null and void.

*[Page 19]*

# From the Bad to Worse

Instead of the capital Warsaw, people now had to contact Petersburg. Instead of the Polish King Stanisław August Poniatowski – the ruler was now the Queen Ekaterina the 2nd. However, only the upper regime notables have changed. The rest of the regime remained as it was - the nobility and its wasteful lifestyle. The enslavement of the peasants, the illiteracy of the masses, and the corruption of the officials remained the same as well. Even the Jews continued with their regular lifestyle, despised and hated, and vulnerable to the caprices of the insolent "*Paritz's*" [nobles].

No significant changes have resulted from the transfer of the vast areas from one regime to another. Moshka, the tavern barman, pours and Ivan the peasant, consumes the content of the cup, and both are miserable. The rights of the Polish Grafs and Dukes, the masters of the estates, were honored by the Russian authorities and were not harmed at all. Concerning the Jewish issue, the seismographs showed signs of hypersensitivity. As part of the maze of problems generated by the big Polish inheritance, the Jewish thorn protruded and irritated, from time to time. People called it "The Jewish Issue." In practice, the meaning of the "Jewish Issue" for the people who inherited Poland was decrees and laws that were meant to lessen the rights of the Jewish citizens and to prevent them from the alleged domination over the country. Even before Russia swallowed all of the Polish provinces (during the latest partitions), Ekaterina issued an order that denied the Jews the right to register among the merchants in inner towns and port cities. Only in Belarus, they could enjoy the rights of citizens and townspeople.

This was the first step in establishing a "Pale of Settlement" for the Jews. The tax decree of 1794 stated that the Jews must pay twice the municipal taxes as the citizens and the Christian merchants. Jews who refused to remain in the cities under these conditions were ordered to leave the Russian Empire and pay a penalty amounting to double the tax for three years. One additional step was taken in 1795 when the province ministers were ordered to register all the Jews who resided in villages on municipal lists. They were also ordered to try to move the Jews to the provincial cities.

A harsh drought took place in the province of Minsk in 1797. A directive was issued from Petersburg to Karniov, the province minister of Minsk, to solicit from the Marshals (the heads of the province nobility) [ Marszałek Szlachty in Polish] their opinion about the reasons for the arduous state of the peasants and proposals to improve it. The heads of the nobility, who gathered in Minsk emphasized in their speeches that the Jewish tavernkeepers were the ones who caused the peasants to get drunk, thus causing the situation where the peasants were unable to manage their affairs. They proposed that only the estate owners would be allowed to make alcoholic beverages and only alcoholic beverages produced by the estate owners would be allowed to be traded by the Jews. Czar Pavel [Paul the 1st] issued a decree on 28th July 1797, based on these recommendations, aimed to "limit the rights of the Jews who impoverish the peasants." The province minister of Minsk was ordered to "make an effort to move all the Jews to the provincial cities,

*[Page 20]*

to prevent these people from wandering around and causing damage to the public." In short, the decree stated that Jews should be expelled from the villages.

In 1798, the nobles of Vohlyn were also requested to provide their opinions about the state of the people. In their gathering in Kamenetz, decisions similar to those of Minsk's nobilities were reached. First, a monopoly of the nobility and estate owners in the alcoholic beverages industry was established. As for the Jews - it was decided that some would continue as the nobles' servants in selling the nobles' products abroad, some would serve at the taverns of the estate owners, and a few would become workers of the land and craftsmen.

A similar council of the nobles in Lithuania was held in 1800. Only three of the participants offered to leave the Jews in the existing state. The other sixteen heads of provinces decided on a more extreme plan than the one of the councils in other provinces. Without a doubt, they were influenced by Prizel, the Province Minister of Vilna, a liberal noble of German ancestry, who was considered an expert on the "Jewish Issue." His objective was "to convert the tribe of these illiterate isolationists, who subscribe to superstitions, into useful and productive citizens."

Following the decision about the monopoly of estate owners on the alcoholic beverages industry, the Lithuanian council of nobles established a clause prohibiting the Jews from selling alcoholic beverages in the taverns in the villages. Following that clause, a long line of additional clauses was laid out in detail about the handling of the education and culture of the Jews. For example: prohibition on wearing the unique Jewish wear, the duty of education in state schools, the duty of using the state or Polish language in business documentation (bills, letters, etc.), prohibition of marriage below the age of twenty, elimination and prohibition of the Jewish religious classes and limitations on the autonomic rights of the Jewish communities. In addition, the clauses enforce the division of the Jews into three classes - merchants, craftsmen, and people who work the land, to enable their inclusion in the class regime of the state, thereby eliminating the need for the involvement of community administration in tax collection.

The abovementioned plan was submitted to the high authorities in the name of Lithuania's nobles, with additional clarifcations by the Province Minister Prizel. This was the most extreme and severe plan among the plans for the remedy of the state of the Jews. Despite its negative aspects, in contrast to other plans by the provisional councils, there was one positive aspect, and perhaps a genuine will, to solve the problem of the expelled Jews, who were left without means of subsistence, by allowing them to work the land.

The Russian authorities were not really worried about the one million Jews that were added to them by the partition of Poland. However, there were a few people who tried to find a positive solution to the Jewish issue, albeit by disallowing them to hold "despised occupations" and also by rejecting the way of life imposed on them as a result of their social and economic anomaly. The Jew Neteh Notkin, also called Shklover (after his native town of Shklov) joined these few people. He was a rich merchant, and an army contractor and had connections with people in the regime and the nobility.

*[Page 21]*

# The Mission of the Senator Dyezhavin

According to the decisions by the Polish and the Russian councils of nobles, Czar Pavel instructed the province ministers to expel the [Jewish] alcoholic beverage sellers and innkeepers from the villages. Whether due to his soft style or the apathy of the province ministers, the instructions were not fully implemented, and a catastrophic situation was avoided. If the instructions had been fully followed, the number of expelled Jews from the villages would have reached 300,000 people. They would have wandered to the nearby cities without a roof over their heads, hungry for a piece of bread, infected with infectious diseases, would have competed with the small businesses of the local city population, and would have caused a lowering the wages. This would have forced the authorities to solve the problem of these miserable people urgently.

It is logical to assume that during those days, as during the whole Czarist period, t corruption by the officials and the paid bribes determined the ways the regime operated. The provincial ministers would get orders and instructions and would pass them along to the district ministers for execution. These ministers, in turn, would transfer them to lower-rank officials and these officials would proceed to expel the Jews and their families from the villages, cruelly and with rudeness.

However, during the execution of the expulsion order, the Jew would hurry and approach the province minister and "soften" him up with a personable gift worthy of its name. The province minister – the "*Isperavnik*," considered the additional income more valuable than proving his patriotism in expelling some measly Jews from the villages of his province. Even for the "*Pristav*" (the head of the regional police) and the "*Lauriandnik*" (the local officer), the expulsion order was a source of inexhaustible income... There were times when a Jewish villager would encounter a "miracle" when the estate owner would not find a Christian who could be extorted to pay the exuberant leasing fees and would hint to the *Pristav* to postpone, for the time being, the expulsion of "*Yankale.*"

However, because doing nothing was not acceptable, many of the Jews were expelled from the villages to nearby cities because either the "*Pristav*" was an anti-Semite and gave up on the "side income," or because the village farmers insisted on the expulsion.

The expelled, who became a burden on their relatives in the city, were supported a tad by the community. Under difficult conditions, without a roof over their heads, and infected with disease, they ran around trying to earn a meager penny for their living. A few succeeded with the help of a bribe to sneak back into the villages and continued to live in perpetual fear of expulsion. Despite that, these partial expulsions did not cause a catastrophe as of yet, which could have shaken the complacency of the authorities.

In 1800, The Czar had not yet seen the need to take any steps toward solving the Jewish issue, according to either Prizel's or Notkin's style or, for that matter, any other style. In contrast, the feelings of "compassion by the fatherly Czar" awoke because Belarus cried for help in light of the hunger that took hold there, and the harsh treatment of some of the nobles towards their peasants. On 16th July 1800, the Czar nominated

Senator Dyerzhavin to visit Belarus and investigate. In his nomination letter, given to him by the Czar it was said:

*[Page 22]*

…" Some estate owners who leave their peasants with no help and no bread and send their crops abroad or to the liquor distillers."

The role of Dyerzhavin was to discover the guilty nobles, confiscate their estates, and nominate guardians who would distribute the crops to the hungry peasants.

There was not even one word in this royal directive hinting about the state of the Jews. However, in an addendum directive, given to Dyerzhavin by the attorney general of the senate, Ovolyanov, as if in the name of the Czar, an additional comment was inserted. The comment stated: "Since it is known, that the Jews are a factor in the impoverishment of the peasants in Belarus, by negotiating the money out of them, it is the Czar's utmost will, that Your Excellency would pay a special review and attention to the occupations of the Jews and submit your opinion as to how to prevent this evil from being done to the public." This was a clear hint to Senator Dyerzhavin in what direction he needed to search and where to find the solution to the problem.

Dyerzhavin ended his mission in a very short time. He was quick to discover the flawed treatment of the Polish Duke Ogi ński towards his peasants. He nominated a guardian to his estate, closed down a Jewish liquor distillery in the nearby town of Liozna [Liozno], and made some remarks about the behavior of some other particular nobles. On the issue of hunger and the state of the peasants, he investigated and questioned some people he knew to be reliable: townspeople, Christian merchants, priests, teachers in Jesuit schools, officials, and obviously nobles.

In autumn 1800, Dyerzhavin gave a detailed lecture in Vitebsk, the name of which attests to its content: "Senator Dyerzhavin's opinion concerning the eradication of hunger in Belarus by the restraining and correcting the occupations of greedy Jews, and related matters."

It is clear that the addendum by *Prokuror* [Procurator- Chief Prosecutor] Ovolyanov and the memorandum by the Jew Neteh Notkin, were before his eyes when he prepared his lecture. His language is distinctively anti-Semitic. "The *"kheder"* [Jewish religious school] is a nest of illiteracy and superstitions… The Jews do not have any moral feelings…Love of people and good deeds are far from their hearts…All they want is to extort the wealth out of their neighbors…They are infected with pleasures of the flesh…They dream about rebuilding King Solomon's Temple."

Following his presentation of the Jewish people in this light, he submitted his proposal, containing 88 clauses, for the remedy of the state of the Jews. First and foremost, he requested to deny the Jews the permit to sell alcoholic beverages. He also demanded the division of the Jews into four classes: merchants, townsmen, villagers, and people who worked the land. He proposed abolishing the communities' administrations and appointing commissions of Rabbis and scholars instead, to handle religious matters. Similar to [the proposals by] Russian, Polish, and Lithuanian nobles, he suggested replacing the Jewish wear with the customary wear in the country. He offered to force the Jews to write all of their documents in Russian, Polish, or German, disallow studying in the *"kheders"* and enforce compulsory education in public school beyond the age of 12, forbid Jews from being elected to municipal councils, and prohibit Jews from keeping Christian servants. The only positive clause in Dyerzhavin's plan was his proposal

*[Page 23]*

**to attract Jews towards agriculture.** [Emphasis in the source]. Like Neteh Notkin, he proposed establishing Jewish agricultural colonies on the prairies of Novorossiya [the Southern Ukraine areas taken from the Ottomans] (Kherson and Ekaterinoslav). He emphasized in that clause, that the Jewish farmers would be independent rather than vassals, namely not dependent on estate owners. However, he added that they would need to be under supervision to prevent them from selling alcoholic beverages in Christian villages.

He concluded his lecture with an appeal to the Czar:

"Through these corrections, the intractable and rebellious Jewish people would be regenerated, and Emperor Pavel the 1st, who would implement these corrections, would gain reputation and fame, following what we have been ordered: "Love your enemies and do good to your haters" [Mathews 5:44].

## The Committee for Remedying the State of the Jews and 1804 Regulations

Czar Pavel the 1st was murdered in 1801, and Alexander the 1st ascended to the throne. Many people put their hopes in his progressive and liberal views. During the first few years of his reign, there were indeed some changes in the governing system, and following these changes, the "issue of the Jews" was also on the agenda. In 1802, a "Special Committee for Remedying the State of the Jews" was formed on behalf of the Czar and was named in short, the "Jewish Committee." The following members were elected to serve in the committee: The Interior Minister–Baron Kochubey, Justice Minister, Dyerzhavin, General V.A. Zubov. And two Polish nobles – Adam Czartoryski (Deputy Foreign Minister) and Senator Sivirin-Potoczky.

The rumor about the royal committee, of which Dyerzhavin was a member participating as "an expert on Jewish Affairs," caused panic in the Jewish public, and many communities sent appeals and requested that the ministers not implement the new regulations. Dyerzhavin was indeed removed from the committee for a different reason. However, to calm down the Jewish public, Minister Kochubey found it necessary to announce to the Jews that there was no intention to constrain them but to do quite the opposite:" To advance their remedy and tranquility." At the beginning of 1803, the representatives of the Jewish communities were invited to Petersburg for consultations about the regulations. Not all the communities could afford the expense of sending a delegation to the capital. Only the representatives of Minsk, Mohilev (or Mogilev), Podolia, and Kiev arrived at the capital that summer. In the capital, some Jewish activists, residents of the capital who had good connections with high-ranking regime officials, helped the communities' representatives. The principal activists were: Neteh Notkin from Shklov, the owner of the plans for "productization" [the concept of engaging in productive work.], the rich contractor Avraham Peretz, the scholar Leon Alkon, and the writer Leib Nivokhowitz. In the course of the activity of the so-called "Jewish Committee," it was leaked to the communities' representatives the fact that the committee intended to propose the expulsion of the Jews from the villages. Due to the impossibility of direct action in the elimination of that proposal, the communities' representatives tried to reject the conclusions of the so-called "Jewish Committee" by using the excuse that they needed to consult with the people who had sent them. However,

*[Page 24]*

the "Jewish Committee" did not agree to postpone issuing the conclusions, and the proposed regulations were submitted to the Czar Alexander in October 1804.

Speransky was the only member of the "Jewish Committee" who proposed and demanded recognition of the civil rights of the Jews, to curtail the prohibitions, and to increase their freedom. However, he was alone in his position. The reactionary view triumphed. There was **only one** positive clause aiming to attract Jews to work the land and the proposal to allocate land and budgets for that purpose. The rest of the regulations introduced more prohibitions, ordinances, enslavement, and humiliation for the Jews, such as prohibition to live and work in the inner parts of the country and obliging the Jews to pay double taxes. The cruelest clause was clause number 34, which stated that "It will be forbidden for Jews residing in the provinces of Astrakhan, Kaukaz, Little Russia [Modern day north and central Ukraine], and Novorossiya [modern day southern Ukraine] starting January 1ˢᵗ, 1807, and in the rest of the provinces starting January 1ˢᵗ, 1808, to lease an inn, under their own or in any other name. The clause also prohibited Jews from selling wines in these inns or residing in them except as a temporary shelter." The meaning of this clause was the expulsion of about 60 thousand families, or about 300 hundred thousand people, from the villages of their residence and the elimination of the source of their sustenance, thereby condemning them to a life of hunger and poverty.

As our topic is the Jewish settlement in Russia, we would not expand on all of the clauses and only detail the positive clause, which opened the door for the Jews, albeit for just a tad, for the possibility of replacing their various occupations with working of the land. It is logical to assume that this positive clause was not a result of excess love for the Jews or due to a historical "feeling of guilt" towards them. In our opinion, the reason for this clause comes from three major factors:

1. The expulsion of 300,000 souls from the villages to the cities may cause economic competition and economic crisis. It can also bring diseases and epidemics because of crowdedness in their residences.
2. The expulsion decree without a positive solution by its side, would have painted the leaders of Russia as reactionary in the eyes of the Western nations while the liberalism was still in fashion, both in Russia and Europe.
3. The vast areas around the Black Sea conquered from Turkey were called Novorossiya (New Russia), and were almost uninhabited. To inhabit them, the government encouraged German, Bulgarian, and Greek farmers to immigrate thereby handing them the most fertile plots and even providing them with loans.

Regardless of the factors and even though the regime had doubts as to whether the Jews would be successful in working the land like farmers who were born to do so, for the Jews, this regulation opened a new page in their history in Russia.

These were the clauses of this particular regulation:

1. The Jews would be allowed to permanently acquire untilled lands, in the provinces of Lithuania, White Russia [Belarus], Little Russia [modern north and central Ukraine], Kiev, Minsk Vohlyn, Podol [Podolia], Astrakhan, Kaukaz (Caucasus), Ekaterinoslav, Tabria [Estonia] and Kherson (meaning all the areas of the "Pale of Settlement" with the added provinces of Astrakhan and Kaukaz).

*[Page 25]*

2.  Hired workers could work on these lands, according to contracts signed between the settlers and the workers.
3.  In colonies consisting of no less than 30 households, it would be possible to establish a tavern according to the general state law.
4.  People who would lease lands from estate owners, according to customary contracts, and who would settle together (in one specific colony), would be free of taxes for several years.
5.  Poor Jews, who cannot afford to purchase land with their own money, or even lease land, would be able to settle in the above-mentioned provinces (except Kiev) on available state lands. As a first step, 30 thousand *disiyatins* [81,500 acres. *Disiyatin* was a Russian measure of area equal to 2.7 acres] were allocated for that purpose. The settlers would not need to pay taxes for ten years and would be able to receive an appropriation from the government to establish their farm as a long-term loan according to the conditions provided to foreign subjects' settlers.

To secure a positive attitude by the Jews towards this regulation it was determined that the government would not force those who did not want to work in agriculture to do so and that the Jewish farmers would enjoy the same rights as the other country's citizens. To those who would excel in working the land, prizes, and grants will be granted. The Jews would enjoy the same assistance provided to settlers who were foreign subjects.

The regulations were approved and published as "The Law about the Jews," by the Czar, on 9 December 1804.

## The Atmosphere and Notables

Before we turn to the history of the Jewish settlement in Russia, we will devote here a chapter to describe the atmosphere that surrounded the notables of the Jewish public and the higher echelons of the regime during the initial period of the reign of Alexander the 1st. That was the period when the lines were drawn for the adverse regulations, which laid the foundation for the restrictions on Jewish rights and the discriminatory decrees against Russian Judaism. It started at the beginning of the 19th century and lasted until the fall of the Czarist regime. It would be interesting to mention the notables who acted, for better or worse, about these regulations. We opened with Dyerzhavin and his famous plan for "Remedying the State of the Jews," and mentioned the multiclause plan by the province minister Prizel. It certainly looks like the two plans were developed in coordination with each other, particularly concerning the abolishment of the autonomy of the Jewish communities.

The autonomy regime of the Jewish communities, which crystallized over hundreds of years, started in the German communities and expanded later to Poland. It was very convenient for the authorities because all the state taxes owed by the Jews were collected through the community administration and thus freed the authorities from

*[Page 26]*

handling the problems specific to the Jews. In this way, the community concentrated all of its affairs according to its own points of view, responsibility, and administration. The range of its activities included education, internal justice, Rabbis' administration, slaughtering, synagogues, and public baths, as well as all social activities such as hospitals and poor houses. The disputes between one Jew and another in court were handled by rabbis and *dayanim* [religious judges]. Even approval of state official identity cards was under the jurisdiction of the community. Obviously, the community collected special taxes from its members for its administration and enterprises. Additional funds were secured through the selling of meat, Shabbat candles, etc.

From a democratic point of view, there were certainly flaws and cases of injustice on the part of the community leaders towards the poor classes. However, the authorities did not excel in their democratic and justice values and in treating its citizens either. From a national point of view, the autonomy was certainly of a significant value. The authorities did not intervene in the Jewish internal affairs. During any public event, the representatives of the local communities and the provincial communities would appear in front of the authorities and conduct the negotiations.

Both Dyerzhavin and Prizel united as one with their corresponding plans, assaulted the autonomy rights of the Jews, and proposed to abolish them altogether. They proposed to divide the Jews according to the various classes (merchants, artisans, and farmers) and to have them join the Christian civil associations so that their government taxes, court cases, social activities, etc. could be handled by the economic organizations. Both demanded an absolute prohibition on the sale of alcoholic beverages by the Jews. They also dictated that all businesses owned by Jews would be conducted in the state language or at least using the Polish or German languages. There was also a long list of other clauses meant to remedy the state of the Jews, including compulsory education in state schools and the prohibition of wearing traditional Jewish clothing.

In authoring the clauses of their plans, they meant to implement a comprehensive and revolutionary reform of the Jewish economic, religious-moral, and civil-political way of life. Despite the similarities between their proposals, there was a fundamental difference in their attitude towards the Jews and in their final objective. While Prizel wished to convert the Jews to become citizens with equal rights, Dyerzhavin sought to weaken the "bad influence of these state enemies on its citizens."

In his proposal to abolish the Jewish autonomy and replace it with the inclusion of the Jews according to their status and occupation in the appropriate class of the general population, Prizel proposed to grant the Jews all the rights of their corresponding class. He would have allowed them to elect and be elected to municipal and judicial institutions, credit unions, etc. Dyerzhavin, on the other hand, limited the Jews in their new status. We can cite here from his speech, which hints at his attitude towards the Jews: "It should be forbidden to send any Jewish criminal and his family to Siberia due to the possibility that they would multiply there and spread their corruption onto the local Christian citizens."

We prolonged our treatment of these two notables as their plans concerning the Jews were exceptionally extreme and both had been submitted to the king, the senate, state ministers and

*[Page 27]*

influential notables. Due to the lack of any other material, these two plans served as the foundation for the discussion at the "Jewish Committee," which was appointed by the Czar and the Senate.

Two liberal friends of the Czar, Interior Minister Graf Kochubey and Deputy Foreign Minister Prince Chartorinsky were also appointed members of the "Jewish Committee." However, the same committee included Dyerzhavin, who was the Justice Minister and became famous as the "expert in Jewish affairs."

An active role was assigned to Speransky, although he was not a member of the committee. However, he participated in all of the meetings as the manager of the interior ministry office. He was the only one who dared to propose far-reaching corrections in favor of Jew's rights. He had friendly relationships with the rich contractor, Avraham Peretz. However, according to the historian Julius Gessen, this friendship was not a factor in his daring plan that advocated equal rights for the Jews. Speransky was simply imbued in humanistic consciousness and feelings of friendship towards the Jews.

During the initial meetings of the committee, a liberal atmosphere and goodwill prevailed. The negative influence of Dyerzhavin was not very apparent despite his high status as the justice minister and his "expertise" concerning the Jewish issue. It is reasonable to assume that this liberal spirit was not created only because of the general liberal atmosphere but thanks to the activity of the Jewish lobbyists.

An indication of the positive attitude was the committee's decision to invite representatives of the Jews from throughout Russia to hear from them about their requirements. This was the first time in the history of Russia that representatives of the Jews were invited to voice their concerns and to be consulted about their fate. The following statement appeared in the journal of the Jewish community of Petersburg on 16 Tammuz, 5563 (6 July 1803];" We memorize the fact that in this year, representatives of the Jews, from all the provinces, arrived here to cooperate with the "Committee to Remedy of the State of the Jews" which was established by the order of his majesty the King Alexander the 1st."

Another confirmation of the positive atmosphere that existed within the committee was the fact that [on] 21st January 1803, Interior Minister Graf B. P. Kochubey sent to some province ministers a circular in which he urged them to take steps to calm the fear among the Jews. He stated that they (the province ministers) should "explain to the communities that there is no intention to further burden them or to reduce their rights by the establishment of the "Committee to Remedy the State of the Jews." On the contrary, the committee was established to pursue a remedy for their state and their tranquility."

This circular and the invitation of the Jewish representatives promoted the view among the Jewish public that the committee was standing on the verge of an important decision [in their favor] and urged the Jewish lobbyists in Petersburg to intensify their efforts.

Even though there was a total prohibition on Jews to reside in the capital city - a few managed to penetrate it due to their engagement with the government or due to personal relationships with the nobles. One of them was Avraham Peretz. A son of a Rabbi, he excelled with his talents in his youth, and his teachers predicted great things for him as a student and a scholar of the Torah. He married the daughter of R' Yehoshua Tzeitlin, the manager of the estates of Prince Potyomkin. That family was famous

*[Page 28]*

for its wealth and wisdom in Lithuania and White Russia [Belerus]. Peretz probably did not find happiness in his marriage and followed Potyomkin's advice and recommendations to move to Petersburg. In the capital, he acquired fame as a big contractor of shipbuilding, lessee of salt mines in Crimea, and other large businesses. He became famous among the government circles as a wise and educated man and he had personal relationships with high-ranking people at the topmost level of the regime.

Another Jew who penetrated the high society circles in Petersburg was Leib Nivokhovitz (Yehuda-Leib's son - Noakh, 1767-1831). He was an author and a journalist who gained fame with his book "Kol Shav'at Beit-Yehuda" [The Cry of the Jews]. Due to his friendship with Peretz and also because he was an author and intellectual, he was likable among high-ranking circles in the capital.

Peretz and Nivokhovitz were each preoccupied with their own affairs and were bothered to be involved in Jewish affairs. Probably they did not even have any connections with the few Jews that lived in the capital. However, when the government brought up the Jewish issue and established the "Committee to Remedy to the State of the Jews," and following the action by Notkin, the two started to cooperate in the fight. They participated in the consultations/discussions with the Jewish representatives who came to Petersburg and applied their connections with the members of the committee and other influential notables.

Eventually, after the cruel blow of the regulations by the committee (1804) against the Jews, when the liberal atmosphere evaporated some, and the treatment of the Jews continued to worsen, these two leaders felt uncomfortable belonging to the camp of the disadvantaged and converted their religion. As part of the Christian society, they achieved full rights and greater honor. However, during the period of operation of the committee, its inquiries, and discussions, the two, along with Notkin, were active in Jewish affairs.

It is appropriate to discuss Natan Notkin (Shklover) separately. He did not come close to the status of Avraham Peretz in terms of his wealth and the extent of his businesses. His education was not as extensive as that of Nivokhovitz's. However, in his fortitude and love for his people and particularly in his daring plan to make the Jewish peddlers, innkeepers, and sellers of alcoholic beverages productive citizens, he bested them both. He was a man of vision and feat. Peretz, Nivokhovitz, and the Jewish representatives who were invited to the capital struggled and fought to achieve equal rights for the Jews or at least expand their civil rights by as much as possible. On the other hand, while Notkin was also one of the people who acted in that direction, he was not satisfied with only achieving rights for the Jews. He aspired to change the ways of life of his people, mend their economy, and make them into a working nation.

A researcher of that period in the history of Russian Jews, the historian Julius Gessen, refers to this marvelous notable with great respect. He provided details that were kept in the memory of his family members. His grandchild or his great-grandchild, Dr. Neteh Sheptelovnitz described to him the nice attitude of the Czar and high-ranking notables towards his grandfather. A story was circulated about the gift that Notkin received from the Czar as an appreciation for his outstanding actions on behalf of the army. Another known story describes the visit by the Czar to Nitkin's home in Shklov while he was he was lying on his deathbed. These stories are a testimony to the accomplishment of the man

*[Page 29]*

in the fields of trade and economy of Russia in his days. However, in this chapter, we are interested in particularly emphasizing his actions on behalf of his people. As mentioned, he submitted, as early as 1797, the famous memorandum concerning the transfer of the Jews to work the land. In 1800, he lobbied again with Dyerzhavin by submitting to him a plan on that subject. On 9th December, Dyerzhavin turned to him on behalf of the "Committee to Amend the State of the Jews" and proposed to him to make himself available as the representative of the Jews and as an assistant to the committee in their inquiries on various issues.

There is no doubt that the circular sent by Interior Minister - Graf Kochubey - to the province ministers was because of Nitkin's influence. Notkin found the need to thank the interior minister for that act.

At the same time that the so-called "Jewish Committee" dealt with discussion about the Jewish issue, the authorities in Smolensk province decided to order an expulsion of Jews. Notkin contacted the authorities with a request to abort this expulsion. In his letter to Interior Minister Kochubey, in May 1803 he writes: "This negative event deepens the depression of the Jews and creates a most gloomy impression about their future fate. Your Excellency the Graf, have mercy on this miserable nation with all of your generosity - please strengthen and add courage to this oppressed nation's heart.

In the same -1803, Notkin submitted to the "Jewish Committee" a more detailed memorandum in writing.

*[Page 30] [blank] [Page 31]*

# B. The Settlement in Its Beginning

## First Attempts

The expulsion from the villages was to be implemented in certain provinces at the beginning of 1807 and in the rest of the provinces in 1808. In 1805, there was still no enthusiasm among the Jews to flock to the proposed settlement. In addition, many still wished for a miracle and hoped that the Czar's heart would be softened and the decree would be canceled. There was another reason for the Jews' reluctance: if the authorities had fulfilled the promises of the clause according to which the Jews were allowed to settle in the provinces of their current residence, there would have been, certainly, many who would have been ready to settle in their native region, close to the graves of their ancestors. However, attempts by Jews to do so ceased after some organized groups tried to negotiate with the government and were met with total refusal. For example, 125 families from the province of Minsk turned to the government with the request to settle in the province of their residence. The answer was negative, and the excuse was that there were no vacant lands.

In 1806, the fateful date was approaching. The Jewish lobbying effort to cancel the decree encountered a blank wall. Agile local police authorities started to implement the expulsion of a few Jews and when the fear of the expulsion became clear and near–the first pioneers for settlement in Novorossiya [modern Southern Ukraine], which was the only region where the government allowed the settlement, emerged. Two Jews – Israel Lenport and Nakhum Finkelstein from the Churikov [Cherikov] district of the Mohilev [or Mogilev] province, representing 36 families, contacted the government with the proposal to settle them in the Kherson prairies.

From this first case, we can learn how much this regulation about the settlement of Jews was like a tabula rasa with respect to the authorities. No real preparations were made in the areas of the settlement project. No lands were allocated, no economic plan was developed, and no budget needed for each settler was decided upon. Instructions were not even sent to the provincial and district authorities on how to act about the transport of the Jews to Kherson.

The two representatives, Finkelstein and Lenport, turned, according to customary protocol, to the district authorities, and they directed them to the provincial minister Bakunin.

*[Page 32]*

Bakunin did not have any idea where to direct the people who contacted him, and he turned to Interior Minister, Kochubey, and asked him for instructions and some allocation to transport the Jews. Kochubey, as the chair of the "Jewish Committee," was one of the supporters of the settlement plan in its general form, however, when he faced the need for a first act, his bureaucratic routine prevailed, and instead of providing instructions and the needed allocation, he asked Bakunin to provide more details about the nature of these Jews. What were their occupations? Have they paid their taxes to the government? What is the reason for their initiative? Were they knowledgeable about working the land? Was it reasonable to assume they would be diligent in doing physical work? Was there any guarantee they would pay off the loan provided by the government? Kochubey demanded that Jews who wanted to be farmers send representatives to Kherson to examine the area allocated to them so that they would not complain later on. Without these conditions, they will not get permission to be transferred.

Fearing that the official letter exchange between the minister and the provincial minister would last a long time and that without a verbal explanation, they would not be granted a positive answer, Nakhum Finkelstein went to Petersburg and was received by the minister. Finkelstein provided details about the people in his organization who were sellers of alcoholic beverages and peddlers of notions and personal items among the peasants. He stated that after the estate owners expelled them, they had to move to towns and cities, did not gain employment outside of their villages, and suffered deprivation and poverty. Finkelstein asked to know what would be the government's assistance to the settlers.

In the minister's office, he was again advised to travel to Novorossiya and contact the Guardian Bureau for the Settlers–the institution that handled the new settlers in the area.

A year and a half after 1804, and about half a year before the implementation of the expulsions, Interior Minister Kochubey, all of a sudden, remembered to discuss the matter with the authorities in Novorossiya. He turned to the provincial minister de Richelieu with the request to "please allocate some land plots, close to each other, for Jewish settlement, so that the Jews could settle in a concentrated area, for their benefit, religiously speaking of–course, and also so that. the authorities could easily supervise them."

De Richelieu allocated for the Jewish settlement 24 thousand *disiyatins* [about 65,000 acres] (a [Russian] measure of area, a bit larger than a hectare –109.25 acres) near the Ingulets [Inhulets] River. This was virgin land and was not considered to be very fertile. There was no drinking water there, and the closest cities (Beryslav, Kherson, and Nikolaiev) were 200–400 kilometers away.

Two months later, the Guardian Bureau for the Settlers notified Kochubey that the two emissaries, Finkelstein and Lieberman, had selected an area of 6,600 *disiyatins* [about 17,300 acres] on the left [Eastern] bank of the Ingulets River.

The rumor about Finkelstein's success spread quickly among the Jews. Spranchik[?], the representative of 52 families from the Mstislav District, contacted Minister Kochubey with a spirited request

*[Page 33]*

to accelerate the transport of the families of his organization to Kherson without prior investigations and without emissaries to search and check the areas, since his people were already expelled from the villages, their financial situation was very difficult, and they were wandering around from one place to another without food, and roof above their head.

Kochubey did not heed Spranchik's pleas. Instead, he wrote to the provincial minister, that he suggested that even the Mstislav's organization should send emissaries to examine the area first and that, in the meantime, the candidates should look for work as field workers in the villages. His reasons were that it would not be possible to prepare housing for the potential settlers before the winter and that the allocation of land for the Jews, without their preapproval, would open the door for future complaints in case of failures. In the meantime, another application was obtained from a group of 76 families from the province of Chernigov. They asked to settle them, according to clause 34 in the "Regulations to Remedy the State of the Jews" in Kavkaz. However, Kochubey told them that it would be better for them and it would satisfy the government's wish to settle the Jews in one concentrated area [in Novorossiya].

# The First Colonies

With the date set for the expulsion getting closer, the enthusiasm for settlement among the Jews was getting stronger. A more positive attitude toward settlement was created upon the return of Finkelstein and Lieberman from their mission. The Jews now believed that the government would not only allocate them land for their settlement but also build their houses, equip them with mules and oxen, as well as plows, seeds, and milk cows, and also transport them to Kherson, at its expense, and provide provisions for the road. They also believed they would receive an allocation to feed their families until the first harvest. These were attractive conditions. In 1806, 911 families, consisting of 4395 people, registered for settlement, according to de Richelieu. According to other government sources, 1436 families registered for settlement that year.

(de) Richelieu, the provincial minister of Novorossiya, was experienced in new settlements of German, Bulgarian, Greek, and Russian settlers. When he heard that the Jewish settlers were inexperienced in agriculture, he wanted to be cautious and suggested to Kochubey to limit the settlement to 200–300 Jewish families per year during the initial period. In addition, he demanded to receive, similar to the customary allotment for other settlers, a budget of 300 rubles per family (including 125 rubles for building a house, food for 8 months until the first harvest, and for acquiring oxen, tools, and seeds).

The first group to settle in Kherson were the people of the Finkelstein organization, consisting of 43 families, with some additional groups from Ukraine and Western Russia. For the travel period from their locations to Kherson, the government allocated five kopeks per day per person for provisions and food. Bakunin, the provincial minister of Mohilev, understood that it was impossible to live on five kopeks per day on the roads and turned to Jewish leaders with a spirited request that they would participate in the expenses of the journey.

*[Page 34]*

The community representatives allocated 6000 rubles for the settlers from monies that had accumulated over fifteen years from the sale of *etrogim* [citrons, a fruit needed during the festival of Sukkot–RM].

The year 1807 was the first year of the Jewish settlement in Kherson. Four colonies were established: Bobrovy-Kut, Izraelovka (also called by Its Hebrew name "Ya'azor" ["He will help"]), Sdeh Menukha [Field of Tranquility], and Dobroye. 294 families (1951 people) settled in these colonies. 248 settled with government assistance, and 46 by private means.

In 1806, the relationship between Napoleon, the Emperor of France, and Russia worsened, and a war was almost imminent. As the Russian authorities feared that the disgruntled Jews would help the French during a possible war, they did not enforce the first expulsion slated for the beginning of 1807. The overall attitude towards the Jews softened, and some optimistic people saw that as a sign of the abolition of the expulsion decree. However, in July 1807, a peace treaty was signed with Napoleon, and the authorities had a new wake-up call towards implementing the expulsions.

Despair and fear spread among the Jews who resided in the villages. The expulsions were executed rudely and cruelly with the help of the peasants and the military. The expelled were sent to towns and cities and were abandoned in the streets without a roof over their heads. The cruelty was particularly apparent in the villages of the Vitebsk province.

During these years (1808–1809), substantial pressure was exerted on the authorities of the provinces to transfer the Jews for settlement in the Kherson prairies. However, the government was not ready for the settlement of the masses. In Kherson itself, the settlement affairs were managed haphazardly and without coordination. No new areas were allocated for that purpose. The government considered the budgets requested for mass settlement as exaggerated. Inaction, incompetence, and confusion brought passivity. As usual, in cases of confusion and helplessness, the authorities were not strict on the formality details, and many Jews left on their journeys without passports and permits.

Kherson welcomed them with frowning faces. The provincial authorities received no instructions from the capital to ease the plight of the refugees and they wandered from one place to the other impoverished, hungry for a piece of bread, in tattered clothing, infested with lice, exhausted, and infected with diseases.

We do not have exact figures about the wanderers who burst towards Kherson. By some estimates, there were as many as 1900 families (10,000 people). Their final fate is unknown. Some expired, and out of the rest, many returned home and some scattered around in the cities of Kherson. It is logical to assume that a few people who had some money and showed initiative managed to join the colonies. In 1809, four more colonies were established: Inguletz, Kaminka, Nahar-Tov [Good River], and Yefeh Nahar [Beautiful River].

At the beginning of 1810, there were already eight Jewish colonies consisting of 800 families. This was a tiny achievement against the grandiose plan of transforming tens of thousands of Jews into people who work the land and thus modify their economic basis.

*[Page 35]*

## The Decline of the First Wave

When we come now, after 150 years, to investigate the first royal attempt to settle the Jews in agriculture, there are moments when we wonder about the decline and failures at the beginning of its road. After all, the regulations about the Jewish settlement were set by the state's higher echelons, seriously minded people, who issued the decree after lengthy inquiries and deliberations that lasted two years. Even the land issue was not an obstacle. The government-owned vast uninhabited areas throughout Russia, especially in Novorossiya, which had been conquered from the Turks a short while earlier. It was also easy to buy estates and whole villages from owners of large estates who became tangled with large debts due to debauchery and irresponsible spending. Even the allocations for settlement of 300-350 rubles per family did not constitute an overly hard burden on the state treasury. In addition, as far as the settlers themselves - we are talking about village Jews who were not pampered by luxuries and who were used to a life of poverty and hard labor; many of them were already close to working the land. They cultivated vegetable gardens or milked a cow. Their hands were used to working with a hoe, fork, or ax. The positive liberal atmosphere that prevailed among the high-ranking ministers and influential public figures at the beginning of the 19th century accompanied the whole enterprise. The results of this enterprise could have been entirely different, and at least a fifth of the 60,000 people who were banned and expelled could have been converted into people who worked the land. It was not impossible to establish a region consisting of a population of ten thousand families concentrated in a hundred Jewish colonies. However, the results of the first three years – 1807 - 1809 were quite pitiful. Altogether 7-8 colonies were established, consisting of eight hundred families in a catastrophic material situation; rickety houses, crowdedness and diseases, shortage of work-tools, and arduous hard labor conditions. It seemed that the settlement wagon sank into deep sand, and it was difficult to move it. To get rid of this misfortune, the government in Petersburg decided to end the settlement enterprise.

When we examine the affair in detail and add one event to another, the reasons for the failure become clearer and clearer. In fact, since the regulation that directed the government to prepare a detailed plan passed, the government did not lift a finger to plan the enterprise, and when faced with the pressure of the first pioneers, the bureaucratic machine was exposed to all of its faults.

The experience teaches us that the success of high-value ideas and enterprises often depends on finding somebody who is "obsessed" about implementing them. Many people think that if Neteh Notkin had lived a longer life and had represented the enterprise to the government, selected the candidates for the settlement more diligently, and perhaps conducted special fundraising among the wealthy Jews to better the settlement conditions, things would have looked entirely different. In our case, however, there was nobody around who was "obsessed" with this enterprise, and the obstacles kept piling up.

One critical factor that significantly impeded this enterprise was the cancelation of the explicit clause included in the regulations of 1804, which enabled Jews to settle in their own general area.

*[Page 36]*

Interior Minister Kochubey was the person who annulled that clause verbally after signing his name on it as the chair of the "Jewish Committee." On the other hand, the Jewish people, despite being accustomed to wandering, balked because of the distance to "somewhere on the prairies around the Black Sea," a destination to which wandering by foot was a matter of 90 to 100 days.

The settlement in Kherson could have been more successful if it had been guided and directed by experts and if the lands allocated for it would have been somewhat fertile. However, most of the areas allocated for the Jewish farmers consisted of poor soil with meager drinking water or lands with very hard soil, that required four oxen to plow it.

Another critical factor for the failure was the inexperience of the Jewish settlers in working the land, even though they originated from villages. If they had received guidance and direction similar to the one provided to the immigrants to Eretz Israel in our generation, even primitive guidance typical to those days, their acclimatization would have been easier and the new settler would have become a natural expert in holding the plow, within a year or two.

Moreover, the economic aspect should not be overlooked. The allocation by the government for construction and farm equipment was tiny, to begin with, and has dwindled even further because of the corruption by government officials and its inspectors. This is supported by the following fact - one of many: The interior ministry office in Petersburg demanded, quite a few times, to receive a detailed report about how the budgets allocated for the Jewish settlement had been spent. They received evasive answers. Only when the settlement was discontinued in 1810, and the ministry nominated the head Judge in Novorossiya - Kontenius, to investigate and review the activities of the Guardian Bureau, which implemented and managed the settlement, many appalling cases caused by the corruption of officials, were discovered.

In an un-named colony, the registration in the books stated that sums of money had been invested in building 127 houses. In actuality, only 96 houses were built. The head of another colony complained that he was forced, under the threat of imprisonment by the inspector, to sign a receipt for 1800 rubles, when he really did not receive even a penny. Four Jews were arrested for three weeks for disobedience. Incomplete houses were found in several colonies. They were incomplete because of a lack of money, and some settlers had to live in pits (Zmelianki [in Russian]). The Christian inspector of the Kaminki [Kaminka] colony, a person without any property who lived on his salary, built a luxurious house and a bathhouse in the city of

Kherson. The role of the bureau and its inspectors was to purchase oxen, carts, plows, rakes, and other farm tools. However, the investigating judge discovered that less than half of the equipment registered on the inspectors' documentation was actually purchased. It was also found that the seeds for sowing were handed over to the farmers late, in the middle of the season or at the end of it. The settlers also complained about cases of theft of oxen from their pasture that occurred during the night.

Judge Kontenius was shocked by the poverty, distress, and morbidity and submitted an objective report in which he detailed what he had seen with his own eyes. To counteract this report, comments and explanations

*[Page 37]*

were sent by the Guardian Bureau. The bureau claimed that the Jews were to blame for everything. They were not experienced in working the land, they were lazy by nature, and their diseases were caused by neglect and lack of cleanliness.

Two years after the visit by Judge Kontenius, another inspector submitted a review containing the following comment: "…The crowdedness in the settlers' homes is awful. 15–20 people live in a single house. Because of the lack of fresh air and uncleanness, the scurvy (*Tzinga* in Russian] disease takes hold. The sick dwelled together with the healthy, infecting them, and many died."

Either out of true concern or as a routine habit aimed at assisting the peasants who used to suffer from drought and other agricultural calamities, the government allocated an additional budget to improve the state of the Jewish settlers. Around the same time, Inspector Lipnov was sent to review the state of the settlers. Like his predecessors, he talked about the grave economic situation of the settlers and about corruption cases.

Here is a typical story:

The minister of Novorossiya, de Richelieu, who received an allocation from Petersburg to remedy the situation of the Jewish settlement, assigned a minister of the province in the Governorate of Yekaterinoslav - Kalgaoria, to purchase mules and oxen, as well as tools for the settlers. The minister boasted that he managed to purchase everything for a very low price. However, Inspector Lipnov found that the oxen were old, gaunt, and unfit for fieldwork, the wagons and the plows required repairs and everything he purchased was not worth even half of what was paid for it.

When discussing the factors that led to the failure, we cannot ignore the long, tortuous, and exhausting journey to Kherson. Along that route, the Jews wasted all of their savings, their bodies weakened, and they suffered from diseases. In this state of exhaustion, they could not find the energy to engage in strenuous work under harsh conditions.

In one of the documents sent by a group of Jewish farmers about their way to settlement, it was said: "…after a long journey that lasted four months, we finally arrived at Kremenchug. From there, we traveled on wagons rented on behalf of the government, and with a meager allocation of food, we arrived at the place of settlement. In front of us stretched a desolated prairie."

[They continue to describe their initial period:] "… Exhausted from the long journey, from the cold, the poor nutrition, and other mishaps, we had to begin building the houses. We were besieged by diseases. Our situation was desperate. We were not used to working the land and were located at a great distance from other settlements, which we could have learned from. We were forced to hire workers and pay them 15 rubles for the cultivation of one *disiyatina* [about 2.7 acres]. Instead of receiving the promised daily allocation of ten *kopeks* per day until the first harvest, we received only five. When we had to exchange our money with hard currency [to pay the foreign workers], we lost again. We had difficulties in acquiring seeds and flour on the prairie. There were many cases when we had to purchase grain but had nowhere to grind it. We were forced to mash the seeds by hand or bake them unprocessed. This was our situation during the initial period."

*[Page 38]*

farmers of Sdeh Menukha reported: "…as a result of the [contaminated] water, [difficulties in acclimating to] a new climate, lack of food and diseases, 200 of our people died during the first three years. Among them, were not just the elderly and babies but whole families. We are [only] 166 families today. There are orphans among us who lack clothing and food and widows without any support. We are all poor and miserable…"

In one of the documents, the farmers of the colony Nahar-Tov wrote:" …As a result of the change of climate and the [contaminated] water, half of our people are not able to cultivate the land."

From these stories, a bleak picture can be painted about the state of the settlers. Those thousands of people who burst towards the prairies of Kherson on their own, to receive salvation through settlement and were abandoned were not fortunate enough to receive even a memorial for their suffering and sorrow. There is no better evidence to describe their miserable fate than the state of the settlers. Dead from hunger, exhaustion, and diseases, their bones were scattered throughout their wanderings on the prairies of Kherson without a marker or a gravestone.

The failure did not please the people responsible, such as Interior Minister Kurakin and Novorossiya's Provincial Minister de Richelieu. They did not find the courage to admit their mistakes and to correct them to vindicate themselves. They chose to select a more convenient excuse. They blamed the settlers themselves and suggested that the Czar discontinued the settlement.

The Provincial Minister de Richelieu submitted a memorandum in which he wrote:

"As a result of the inexperience of the Jews in working the land and the lack of cleanliness in their colonies, the mortality rate grew substantially. It is therefore recommended to discontinue the settlement. Perhaps within two to three years, when they could prove that they can develop a better tendency for this way of life, we would be able to renew it."

Whereas Interior Minister Kurakin stated:

"As the finance committee for the reduction in government expenditure has not decided upon the next year's budget for the settlement of Jews, we must instruct the authorities of the provinces to discontinue the transport of Jews to settlement at the expense of the government. We also must instruct the Guardian Bureau for the settlers to take out the settlers who are unable or unwilling to persist in working the land, from their colonies, equip them with passports, and return them to their localities according to the law. We also must notify the remaining settlers that, if within a year it becomes clear that they are unsuitable to work the land and there is no hope for them to become farmers, the government would send them to work in textile factories until they pay off their debts to the government."

The Czar tended to accept de Richelieu's formulation better than the harsh recommendation offered by the interior minister, and he issued, on 6 April 1810, the following order:

"It is being ordered to discontinue the handling of new settlers and leave those who already settled at their current state in the colonies without changes."

The interior ministry's historian, responsible for the government records wrote in 1810:

The lack of cleanliness among the Jewish settlers resulted in diseases and high mortality. They did not succeed in agriculture, with which they were not experienced. These undesirable results led to the discontinuation of the [Jewish] settlement in Novorossiya."

That is how the first story of Jewish farming settlement in Czarist Russia has ended.

*[Page 39]*

## The Abolition of the Expulsion Decrees from the Villages

Even before the government's decision in 1810 to discontinue the settlement, the number of Jews who registered for it decreased. We can assume that the people who flocked to Kherson without licenses returned individually to their original localities and described the fearsome and horrible experiences of the refugees in their wandering. They obviously also described the gloomy state of the new settlers. Undoubtedly, this horrible news has damped the enthusiasm of even the neediest and the poorest.

In the meantime, the expulsion process continued. The expelled became a burden on their relatives in the cities, and when their savings were depleted they starved. They wandered from one place to another, and their state worsened by the day. Many of them contacted the authorities and asked to be transferred to Kherson despite the bleak news from there. However, even before the decision was made about the discontinuation, the Novorossiya authorities warned the province ministers against continuing the transports, as the ability to absorb new settlers was limited to 200 families per year, and in Kherson itself there were already candidates much above this number.

Some of the province ministers applied to Petersburg with messages saying that it was impossible to sustain the expulsion of the masses without totally destroying tens of thousands of families. With the execution of the expulsions, many estate owners discovered that they had suffered substantial losses because, besides the exaggerated leasing fees that they squeezed out of the Jewish lessees, the estate owners were also using the Jews as servants and as purchasing and selling agents. Without the help of "their" Jews, the *"paritzim"* [nobles in Yiddish] were helpless.

The desperate state of the expelled has certainly touched the hearts of some high-ranking notables. They applied pressure on the province ministers. The new attitude of many of the estate owners towards their [Jewish] lessees and, on the other hand, the failure of the Jewish settlement sector have embarrassed the government in Petersburg. This embarrassment led to the fact that in January 1809, a new committee was nominated on behalf of the Czar, with the task of finding ways to move the Jews from selling alcoholic beverages in the villages to other productive occupations. The following people were nominated to serve on the committee: The secret Advisor Popov (Chairman), Senator Alexeyev, Vice-Interior Minister Kozodavlev, and others. In the nomination documents, the difficulties in executing the expulsions were explained: "Because of their poverty, the Jews cannot acclimatize and find sustenance in their new locations after the expulsions. Because the government could not get them established in their locations, new ways must be found by which the Jews can make a living after being removed from selling alcoholic beverages in the inns and the villages."

*[Page 40]*

The committee was also ordered to review the opinion paper of the Jewish representatives, which had been previously submitted to the government.

The committee took almost three years to investigate the problem and submitted its conclusions to Czar Alexander the 1st in March 1812. This is what these conclusions said:

"The common view is that the Jews must be removed from serving alcohol because of the damage to the peasants. However, the source of the drunkenness is not with the people who sell the beverages but with the alcohol distilleries of the nobles, which are their principal source of income. Upon the expulsion of 60,000 Jewish families, 60,000 peasant lessees will replace them. These lessees would be people who were previously diligent farmers. However, the expelled Jews who were inexperienced and could not be converted into people who worked the land instantaneously, particularly because at this time the state treasure did not have the capability to resettle the Jews and turn them into farmers."

"The Jew is not getting rich from the wine trade. He is poor and hardly making a living. By the fact that the Jew buys the grain from the farmer, he releases the farmer from the need to waste time traveling to the city. The mediation by the Jew in buying and selling is required for both the estate owner and the farmer. It is not practical to convert the expelled Jews into industry workers, merchants, or craftsmen as most city Jews are also poor, and creating an artificial industrial plant is doomed to fail, particularly because the state treasury lacks the enormous amounts of money needed to establish a new industry."

"The expulsions lead to increased impoverishment of the Jews, as they are being dispossessed of the occupations they have been involved in for hundreds of years."

As far as the settlement is concerned:

1.  It was impossible to settle the Jews on lands located at their current localities because of the scarcity of available lands in the provinces transferred from Poland to Russia.
2.  As there is a shortage of needed financial means by the government, it is impossible to settle Jewish families in distant provinces (Kherson, Ekaterinoslav). Even if the budgets amounting to millions of Rubles could be found, it is difficult to find, in the desolate prairies, workers, mules and oxen, and equipment needed for the farms.
3.  To make the Jews become farmers required substantial training by counselors and inspectors.

As a result, the committee found it necessary to recommend the following:

"To put an end to the embarrassment, and leave the Jews in their places of residence, so that they would be able to make a living in occupations that were prohibited in clause 34. This recommendation comes because the committee recognizes the difficult situation of the people and the fear that if the persecution continues in the current political situation, it would anger the oppressed people."

The government gave up and approved the committee's recommendations. It is logical to assume that the bail-out did not come because of the humanitarian reasons stated by the committee but for what has been hinted by the words: "In the current political situation." The hint referred to Napoleon's army, which, in the meantime, had crossed the border and invaded

*[Page 41]*

Russia proper. There was a danger that the Jewish population, which was oppressed to the bone, would help the invaders.

The Jews, thus, continued to hold their "despicable" occupations, selling alcoholic beverages to the peasants, possessing inns located on the main roads, intermediation, and peddling. The storm that swept the Jews as a result of the regulations of 1804 has left hundreds, or perhaps thousands of graves scattered throughout the prairies of Kherson. Because of these regulations, eight colonies were established in which 800 families have settled, in distress and despicable poverty. However, from these wretched families grew the seed that developed, over the years, into a tribe of Jews who work the land.

## The Troubles of the Settlers During the Second Decade

Following the conclusions of the Popov Committee (1812), when the expulsions from the villages stopped, and many Jews were allowed to return home and old occupations, Kherson settlers considered themselves deprived because they couldn't return to their previous occupations. They would have willingly returned to their previous locations or looked for some of the common occupations in cities of the Kherson province. However, the regulations of 1804 did not encourage the transfer from the status of farmers to craftsmen. The debts of the farmers to the government aggravated the situation, as they could not receive passports and departure permits as long as they did not pay off the debts.

Because the colony inspectors, who served on behalf of the authorities, were absent most of the time and did not perform their roles towards the settlers or the government diligently, many farmers abandoned their land temporarily and wandered around to the nearby cities to find food for their families. Many farmers found employment in the occupations they held before the settlement or in occupations they had acquired after settling, such as glass installing, shoemaking, tailoring, cobbling, and wagon driving. Those who did not acquire a profession became peddlers or went into other occupations that promised profits and sustenance.

In 1815, the Kherson settlers sent emissaries to Lithuania and Belarus to collect handouts for the widows, orphans, and the poorest farmers. Another delegation traveled to the cities of Grodno and Slonim to consult with knowledgeable and wise Jews on how the farmers of Kherson could free themselves from working the land and return to their previous status. They placed their fortune and hope with rich lobbyers – Eliezer Delon and Zundil Zonenberg, who had good connections with the government.

Indeed, the situation of the settlers in the Kherson colonies was precarious. Some farmers managed to stabilize their farms and found sustenance in agriculture. However, these were just a few. The vast majority of the settlers from the first decade were casualties of natural disasters. Because of the corruption of the officials, many houses were roofless, and their walls were cracked.

*[Page 42]*

Two or three families had to crowd together in one house. Many came from areas where forests were plentiful, and where even the poorest people would have accumulated some firewood for the winter. However, the Kherson prairies were barren of trees. It was freezing cold in winter. Their winter clothing had worn out a long time ago, and new clothes were not purchased.

The crowdedness (15 people to a room), hard labor, meager nutrition, uncleanliness, and the freezing cold in winter – all of these causes played havoc on people's health. The mortality rate was very high. According to the statistics, half of the population perished during the first ten years, and they left behind widows and orphans without means of survival.

In one of the reviews that Lipnov sent to Petersburg in 1813, he wrote: " …The situation of the Jews is terrible. Weeping with tears, they are begging to be saved from extinction…They are weakened and degenerated in the prairie from the cold and the hunger."

The authorities in the capital city knew about the horrible situation of the Jewish farmers. It seemed that there was a real concern among the rulers about the state of the colonies. It is impossible to know whether this concern was caused by human sensibility toward an attempt that failed, by feeling of responsibility about the unsuccessful project, or perhaps, by chance, the people who headed the institutions that handled the colonies were people who regarded the state of the farmer with concern. The head of the interior ministry was Kozodavlev, the minister for religions and education was Graf Galitzin, a personal friend of Emperor Alexander, and the head of the office of religions and education ministry was Zonkovskii.

When Kozodavlev found out about the misery and the complaints of the Jews, he started to contact the Guardian Bureau of the Settlers, requesting details about the situation. The reports confirmed the grave state of the Jewish settlers but placed most of the blame on "the settlers who do not know and do not want to work." It was emphasized again that the high degree of illness among the settlers was caused by their lack of cleanliness. The Guardian Bureau and Richelieu did not place any blame on the local inspectors who were appointed by them and whose greed was not a small factor in the settlers' predicament.

Minister Kozodavlev was not satisfied with the reports that he received. As mentioned above, he nominated the primary judge in Novorossiya, Kontenius, to investigate the state of the settlers and later on sent Lenov for the second time. Each of them visited the colonies, and both submitted detailed reports and proposals. They also named the reasons for the failure, one by one: government budgets that were issued without coordination and order, meager personal allocation (the allocation every person received before the first harvest), consecutive years of drought, thefts, insufficiency of mules, oxen, and tools, which prevented timely cultivation of the land, epidemics in the various livestock, life in poverty and a high mortality rate. On the other hand, the two inspectors mentioned the "lack of passion of the settlers towards working the land" and "their wish to get rid of it." They noted that, even in their situation, if they had grown lambs and flax, they could have supplied themselves with clothing for the winter and the summer.

*[Page 43]*

Despite all of that, the reports by Kontenius and Lenov did not contain any pessimism toward the future. They emphasized that despite some sick and "good–for–nothing" people, the farmers showed signs of acclimatization to their new life and [had a chance of succeeding] if sufficient means were provided to fix their dilapidated houses and to purchase the needed mules, oxen, and tools. Lenov, whose review was more optimistic, found it necessary to emphasize that the Jewish farmers required more attention and a more sympathetic attitude from the government than the Germans, Bulgarian, or Russian settlers. The reason for that was that the latter, except for being farmers from birth, received from the government twice as many loans and equipment than the Jews. Their sound establishment may take longer, but if the government would allocate the required budgets for the Jews, in the end, they would be very good farmers.

Even the Czar understood that it would not be possible to make changes through the local officials who bore the blame for the failure and that there was a very good reason to nominate one or two officials from among the most talented and honest officials in Petersburg. Therefore, an inspector on the farm department of the interior ministry, Y. P. Lipnov, was nominated, and along with him, another official named Leshkrov. In reality, however, only Lipnov was active for several years. He was given the permission to dismiss officials and replace them, as well as establish new procedures as he saw fit, without relying on the "Guardian Bureau."

Lipnov was a talented person, smart, objective, and dedicated to his role. He dismissed some local inspectors who were absent from the colonies for long periods, purchased the required seeds himself, increased the flour allocation for bread, treated the farmers either severely or kindly [as needed], and inspired the farmers to [timely] start the plowing and sowing tasks.

His daring attitude towards the local authorities and the officialdom raised the people of the local authorities against him. Richelieu, the provincial minister of Novorossiya, was offended by the fact that an official from the capital acted independently of him. However, after the interior minister found a satisfactory formula for joint action, that obstacle was removed. However, the rest of the officials in the Guardian Bureau and the provincial finance department tried to disrupt Lipnov's actions and put obstacles in his way. The hostile attitude of the local officials, the frequent traveling, and the separation from his family who remained in Petersburg have prompted Lipnov to submit a request to be released from his appointment. However, the authorities recognized his effectiveness and talent, asked him to continue, and allocated a thousand rubles to transfer his wife and four children to his place of work.

After years of tribulations and suffering, a positive turn transpired in the colonies. The material situation improved. The disease and rate of mortality decreased. Obviously, the concern of the authorities and their dedicated emissary, Lipnov, were part of the reasons for this positive turn. Another reason was the end of the drought. Cultivation of the fields became more rational. While the farmers continued to work in profitable occupations in the cities during the dead seasons, the main reason for the turn, according to most opinions, was the process of acclimatization to fieldwork, particularly as the children grew up and started to incorporate themselves in the development of the farm sectors.

When the state of the farmers improved, a new worry popped up–tax and debt payments.

*[Page 44]*

One of the conditions of the settlement was the freeing of the farmers from various taxes and payments on their debts for ten years…and here, the tenth anniversary of the settlement was approaching. If the authorities insisted on the fulfillment of this cause, it would have been necessary to pay 100 rubles a year per farm towards taxes and debts starting the eleventh year. The farmers began to negotiate and asked to receive an extension of several years to I the taxes and debts.

Lipnov supported this demand and the managers of the Guardian Bureau recognized its validity seeing the positive turn that occurred in the colonies. With the support of Minister Kozodavlev and the Religions and Education Minister–Galitzin, a decision was obtained on 17 November 1817, by the Royal Council, and approved by Czar Alexander the 1st, which said: "It is decided to free the colonies from paying taxes for another five years and postpone payments on the debts for thirty years." The decision invigorated the farmers markedly.

The following statistics summarized the situation towards the year 1818:

The government had invested 300,000 rubles in establishing 8 colonies. The population in the colonies included 2003 males and 1654 females, a total of 3657 people. The land allocated for the Jewish settlement totaled 194 thousand *disiyatins*. Obviously, only a part of these areas has been cultivated, and the rest have been leased out.

According to the size of these areas, there was a workforce shortage, and that left room for new settlers. At the beginning of the 20th year, only 400 families remained in the colonies of Kherson because of desertion and mortality. It was felt that there was an urgent need to solve the problem of the diminishing population by additional settlement.

## A New Awakening and its Decline

The news about the improvement in the material status of the farmers reached the provinces of White Russia [Belarus], and many were aroused to the idea of abandoning their places of residence and getting a foothold into working the land. This time it seemed that better conditions had been created. Those who settle now would find established colonies and prepared institutions. The experience and knowledge acquired about the quality of the land areas and the mules and oxen would be available to them, and there would be people from whom they could learn about the work. It seemed that even within the management of the Guardian Bureau, a positive change took place. General Inzov and his assistant Padyiev were nominated to head the Guardian Bureau. Both men were people of action.

At the end of 1819, 40 families from Shklov applied through the Provincial Minister of Mogilev to settle in Kherson.

Religions and Education Minister Galitzin, whose ministry was responsible for handling the Jewish issue, treated their application favorably. However, when the issue of the budget allocation was raised, Yinzov, the head of the Guardian Bureau, was asked what allocation was required for a family of settlers he quoted

*[Page 45]*

an amount of 700–800 rubles per family. The finance minister announced that he did not see any possibility to allocate any budgets for that purpose. The negotiations lasted two years. The Shklov group had not moved from their localities. In the meantime, a severe drought hit White Russia in the years 1821-22, followed by hunger. The encouraging news from Kherson induced in many Jews the will to leave their localities, abandon their occupations, and move to settlement. Many applications flowed to the provincial minister of Mogilev, who contacted Petersburg. Despite the explicit order from 1810 to discontinue the settlement of Jews, the authorities did not find any wrong with adding settlers who settled at their own expense within the allocated areas. An instruction was sent to the provincial minister of Mogilev to oblige all candidates for settlement to sign, ahead of time, a statement by which they renounce any financial assistance from the government, either for the journey or for equipping the farm. The provincial minister of Mogilev notified

Petersburg that, based on the candidates' signatures, he issued transfer permits to 1490 families. At the same time, the Guardian Bureau announced that 197 families arrived in Kherson. In his announcement, Yinzov emphasized that these families are penniless. According to him, the people could not explain why they signed and did not pay attention to the content of the statement before they signed it.

It seemed that the heads of the [Jewish] communities, who wished to get rid of families who were dependent on them, encouraged the poor ones to sign the statement, hinting that the government would, most likely, settle them at its expense. In the meantime, many Jews continued to sign the waiver statement and receive permits to transfer to Kherson. Some of these people left immediately upon receiving the permit, and some remained to liquidate their businesses. According to the official announcements of the White Russia provincial bureaus, about 1780 families (8706 people) lest on the journey as of 7 December 1822.

In the meantime, a negative change in the government's attitude towards the Jews took place. Alexander the 1st who was liberal and tolerant during the first part of his reign, started to show an increased tendency for reactionary attitudes and anti-Semitism. One particular event intensified his grudge. On March 25th, 1817, an order was issued on behalf of the Czar aimed at establishing a "Christian-Jewish Society," which was basically a missionary institution, to be managed by Graf Gallitzin, the minister for religions and education. According to its regulations, converted Jews, members of the "Christian-Jewish Society," were entitled to receive government-owned lands for free, in the southern and northern provinces, as well as establish villages, towns, and cities that enjoy a self-governing autonomy and discounts on taxes. A special area was allocated for that purpose in the Ekaterinoslav province and a special inspector was nominated. A substantial propaganda and advertising campaign accompanied the establishment of the society; however, no real results were achieved. In 1824, Graf Gallitzin suggested abolishing the society and dispersing its supervisory board. The Czar with his religious fanaticism, refused to abort his idea, and the society, which had no members, continued to be included in the list of government institutions during the entire life of Alexander the 1st. It was closed only during the reign of his heir, Nikolai the 1st.

Upon the death of Interior Minister Kozodavlev, he was replaced by Kochubey, who served as

*[Page 46]*

chair of the Royal Committee that issued the "Jewish Regulations" in 1804, and later on served as the interior minister who helped establish the Jewish settlement in Kherson at the end of the [19th] century's first decade.

When he was re-appointed to head the interior ministry, he remembered the headaches of the first wave of settlement, combined with the [new Czar's] attitude towards the Jews, he was not in a hurry to burden himself with a new load.

Since forever, when a calamity was approaching, the arrows of the people's rage were directed towards the Jews. This time again, the drought and the hunger in the provinces of White Russia created a similar situation. To clear themselves from any blame, the estate owners pointed the finger at the Jewish barmen and innkeepers. When the heads of the nobility discussed a remedy for the state of the peasants, they decided to propose the expulsion of all the Jews from White Russia, or at least the expulsion of the liquor sellers, who "destroy the life of the farmers."

The slow bureaucratic machine showed miraculous agility this time and sent a high-ranking emissary to the provincial ministers of White Russia to ask for their opinions. The opinion provided was supportive [of that proposal]. The issue was discussed in Petersburg's "Committee for Remedying the State of the

Suffering Peasants in White Russia." It is not clear who established this committee; however, the expulsion proposal was approved very easily by it. From there, the proposal was moved to the Council of Ministers and was approved again. After all the approvals, the Czar agreed to approve it as well. On 11 April 1823, an order was sent on behalf of two provincial ministers of White Russia, which ordered "to prohibit the Jews from leasing and maintaining inns, taverns, hostels, and post offices in all the villages of Mogilev and Vitebsk and even to reside in the villages."

Immediately upon receiving the order, the authorities were quick to cruelly expel the Jews. The order went out in April. Based on the transportation conditions of those days, it arrived at the provinces of White Russia at the beginning of May. Until the end of the year (January 1824), 20,000 men and women were expelled from the villages during a six-month period. The expulsion continued during 1824 and the number of the expelled reached 40,000 people. They arrived at the towns and cities, and wandered on the street like stray dogs without a roof over their heads, with no clothing and no means of making a living. They slept in the synagogue, became sick with deceases, and many died.

Despite the explicit instructions in clause 34 of the "Jewish Regulation" of 1804, which allowed the expelled people from the villages to become farmers, the fact that the Kherson experiment proved that Jews were capable of being agriculturalists, the fact that there were vacant government lands for that purpose and the existence of settlement applications by the expelled, the authorities, headed by the Czar himself, were not willing to allow, even some of these miserable people, to transfer to agriculture.

Interior Minister Kochubey still found it necessary to issue a four-clauses proposal to the ministers' council:

*[Page 47]*

1.  The Jewish communities, freed from paying taxes for the people who left them to settle, must help every settling family with 400 rubles towards the establishment of their farm. The Jewish communities must transfer these payments directly to the Guardian Bureau of the Settlers in Novorossiya.
2.  The Jewish communities would also be notified that they must assist the Jews who were already in Kherson but had not managed to establish themselves as yet.
3.  Since many of those who moved to Novorossiya did not leave from their own goodwill but under the influence of the communities, the provincial ministers must make sure that no Jew would leave his residence unwillingly.
4.  As long as these conditions are not fulfilled, the transfer of Jews to Novorossiya must be stopped.

As the communities could not help the settlers with the amounts imposed on them, the flow of people to settlement in Kherson had stopped by itself. Many managed to leave their residence before the decree and wandered towards the colonies in Kherson. Only part of them arrived at their destination. Many died, and some returned.

## The Second Wave of Settlers

In 1822, 1780 families (8706 people) traveled from White Russia to Kherson. From them, only 1016 families (4431 people) reached Kherson. The rest of the 764 families disappeared without a trace. It can be assumed that some were scattered in the cities, some returned, and according to the testimonies of returnees, many died on the way.

Group after group wandered from the north southward to Kherson. Some had certain means, and some were penniless people who did not have anything to lose. Both groups relied on the kindness of the authorities and hoped that they would help them in the end.

The new refugees flooded the colonies, particularly Kaminka and Inguletz. Like their predecessors of 15 years ago, the second wave of settlers experienced their share of suffering, deprivation, and diseases. Cold, dysentery, and fever wreaked havoc and caused deaths among them. According to the physicians' diagnosis, the exhaustion was caused by the hardship of the long and tiring trip and the crowdedness and filth at their places of accommodation. During a very short time, 167 people died in Kaminka and Inguletz.

General Yinzov, the head of the Guardian Bureau of the Settlers (German, Bulgarian, Greek, Russian, and Jewish) instructed Padyiev to sort out the refugees and to determine who was interested in settlement and who was suited for it.

*[Page 48]*

The sorting process lasted for three months, and at its end the following numbers became clear:

443 families expressed their wishes to settle;
11 families wished to move to the city of Ekaterinoslav (the small number was a result of the fact that the city authorities refused to receive refugees);
511 families intended to return to the provinces of their previous residence;
51 families disappeared without passports, and their whereabouts were unknown;
Altogether 1106 families

Yinzov's attitude toward the settlement enterprise was thoughtful and objective, and his attitude toward the new refugees was humane. Padyiev, as the acting person, also showed a positive attitude towards the people. The head inspector over the Jewish colonies - Yiedamov, showed exemplary dedication. He ran around from one colony to the other, even during snow storms and freezing cold. During one of these trips, he fell sick and died (on 27 April 1825), leaving behind a poor family and many pleasant memories in the hearts of the Jewish settlers.

It can be assumed that following the personnel changes among the colonies' inspectors, made by Lipnov a change in attitude was apparent. This positive attitude, on the part of the people who headed the Guardian Bureau and Yiedamov explains the strange fact that, despite the explicit order to allow the settlement of poor Jews only if the Jewish communities would provide the required investment - Yinzov and Padyiev made preparations to settle 443 families.

Yinzov distributed the lands available for the Jewish colonies based on 40 *disiyatins* [about 108 acres] per family, both the old and the new settlers. After the distribution, an area of slightly more than 14 thousand *disiyatins* [about 38,000 acres] was identified as a reserve for new settlers if they arrived.

Because of the lack of technical, organizational, and financial abilities, Yinzov decided to limit the settlement to 200 families per year, assuming that those who were postponed for the next year would train themselves by working for the established farmers.

Knowing the negative attitude in Petersburg, Yinzov was modest with his budget requirements. He asked for 250 rubles per family or 50,000 rubles for the 200 settlers in the first year. Apparently, he relied on the self-participation of the settlers in establishing their farms because he knew that the settlers brought with them 2738 rubles in cash, 167 horses, and 159 wagons in which they traveled on their long trip.

Petersburg accepted his proposal, as they did not have any other choice, and allocated him 50,000 rubles. With this budget, 162 families settled on the land in 1824. Every family received two oxen, a plow, a harrow, seeds, and a house. The total investment for each family amounted

*[Page 49]*

to 307 rubles and 69 kopeks. Until 1828, 130 additional families have settled. Out of the total flow of refugees in the early 1820s, 292 families have settled. The total investment in establishing them amounted to 110,000 rubles; 62 families established a new colony called Yizluchistoye.

These were the results of the second wave. During the five years of that wave, close to 300 families have settled out of the 2000 families that traveled to Kherson.

## Once Again - a Drought and its Consequences

It would be reasonable to assume that after the hardships of the first years, the settlement enterprise in Kherson would march toward stabilization. The remaining farmers learned the work, the diseases stopped, and the children grew up and started to help. In the colonies, there were a few years of bountiful harvests. The attitude of the officialdom improved. New settlers joined the colonies, and even a new colony was established. 300 new houses were built. During the winter, when there was no work in the fields, the farmers would go to the city and work as craftsmen, artisans, and lessees of Jewish stores. This additional income was a valuable material support.

However, in 1824–25, a drought befell the region again. The meager harvest did not cover even half of the needed seeds. The days of distress, impoverishment, and hopelessness returned. The year 1824 was the first year of tax payments that had been previously postponed for five years. The first settlers had to pay 12,000 rubles that year and 25,000 rubles a year starting in 1825 and onwards. Hardly 600 rubles were collected from all the settlers. Yinzov explained to the government in Petersburg the situation of the settlers and noted that it was "a result of wandering habits, diseases, mortality, lack of knowledge about agricultural work," as well as drought, which hit every province in Kherson, during which even farmers who were born as such were destroyed by it. Of the 500 farmers in the Jewish colonies, only 120 farmers sowed their fields by their own independent means. Even the income from side employment lessened as the professionals could hardly find work, and those who lacked a profession could not find work at all. To save many from hunger it was necessary to help them by giving them seeds.

During this distressed situation, many people wander away to the cities, sometimes to far-away cities, to earn something doing work or by peddling. Even after the drought passed, its signs endured in the colonies. Many farmers preferred the pennies available from the pay for the work in the city to the physical effort and the financial investment in their fields where the harvest was not guaranteed. Some neglected the fields altogether, and some leased them to Christians without the knowledge of the officialdom. As a result, many farms were neglected, and the colony lost its agricultural character.

*[Page 50]*

The lack of persistence with farm work and the drift towards the city strengthened the opinion of the guardian officials that the Jews were lazy, wandering people and dodgers from physical work.

Like the Christian colonies, the Jewish colonies had a head of the colony elected by the farmers or the authorities. The head of the colony (named "*Schultza*" [or "*Schultz*" adapted from the German colonists]) was like the "*Mukhtar*" ["chosen"- in Arabic, head of a village], the intermediary between the farmers and the inspector. Only a farmer whose farm was sustainable and successful could have been elected a *Schultza*, and the Christian inspector had a say in this election. Even though it was forbidden for the Jewish farmers to leave the colony, they were allowed to leave temporarily and earn income in the city or other area villages during the winter months when there was no fieldwork. This was allowed, considering their tough time at the early stages of their settlement. The Jewish *Schultza* provided written licenses and permits for that. The *Schultzas*, who were forced, once in a while, to fulfill unpleasant orders towards their fellow farmers, were not always liked by the public. At elections, there were always people who supported a particular *Schultza* and those who opposed him. The elected *Schultza* was not objective and often favored his supporters and the people who elected him.

It would be fair to say that the Jewish colony had not yet acquired a rural character and had not yielded, as of yet, a true farmer figure. As mentioned, most of its residents worked in the cities during winter time. Some cheated the system, worked for most of the year, and neglected their farm. In contrast to them, some farmers cultivated their fields dedicatedly and also developed a livestock section- cattle and sheep. They were far from being wealthy; however, they did not suffer from scarcity of food and clothing. The farmers with the solid farms were liked by the officialdom, not only because they paid their taxes and their debts but also because they served as proof that Jews were capable of working the land if they were given the proper conditions and their ability to acclimatize nurtured.

## The Accusation

It is difficult to point at the reason for the change of attitude and the harsh accusations of Padyiev, General Yinzov's right hand. In earlier years, he was dedicated to his role and to the affairs of the settlers. Was it the influence of the hostile attitude towards the Jews that prevailed in the capital during the later days of Alexander the 1st and during the rise to the throne of Nikolai the 1st? The government officials were sensitive to the fluctuations of the barometer in Petersburg, to the side of either conservatism or liberalism. They were particularly sensitive about anything that was associated with Jewish affairs. Perhaps Padyiev, the diligent and practical administrator became disillusioned

*[Page 51]*

after seven years of activity, about the state of the colonies and the routine ways things were handled, and blamed the settlers for the failing.

To support his analysis and conclusions, he quoted some numbers. He prepared some detailed statistics about the sowed fields, inventories, population, etc., year-by-year for ten years - from 1814 to 1825. His statistics emphasize. in certain terms, the lack of progress and the instability of the colonies. He emphasized that out of a total of 714 families residing at that time in the colonies, only 411 were occupied with real farming. A decline in the milk section was also noted. Out of all of the vast areas, only a small percentage was cultivated.

The numbers brought up by Padyiev were correct and made a harsh impression in the offices and among the officials. If he had summarized his numbers at the beginning of 1824 instead of toward 1825, a more optimistic impression could have certainly been obtained. That is because 1824 was a harsh drought year, and, as mentioned before, one drought year can wipe out the fruits of prior bountiful years, like the story about the gaunt cows swallowing the fat cows as if nothing happened [Pharaoh's dream, Genesis 41]. It was also a very well-known fact that in a drought year, farmers, even those who were born as such, wander away from their farms to find work and earn an additional income in other places. The state of the colonies' Jews, who were not farmers from birth, was so harsh that they had to leave their families in wintertime and wander to faraway cities. Their lives in the cities were not easy either. The work was hard, the living conditions horrible, and they often saved their own food to send a few rubles to sustain their families.

Padyiev's statistics and his conclusions were accompanied by commentaries about the "wandering and lazy nature" of the Jews and their tendency to avoid paying taxes. At the conclusion of his review, Padyiev proposed to worsen the work regime, which would serve to tame and educate the Jews and force them to be diligent and persistent farmers.

Padyiev's proposal started with a list of clauses prohibiting leasing the land to others. Following these clauses, he listed some penalty clauses aimed at punishing "the lazy and wandering people." He fixed the penalty level as a typical jurist, from light to heavy, for negligence and wandering into the city. A penalty of several days of public work for the first infraction; after the second or third infraction, the criminal would be tied to a pole, and a black wooden sign would be hung above his head with his infraction written on it; if the criminal would offend again - he would get twenty-five floggings, and if all that would not correct him… he would be sent to Siberia.

One clause stated that it was forbidden to send the children to the city to study an urban profession. The heads of the villages would be prohibited from releasing the farmers from work except for holidays when work is prohibited by religion. It would be prohibited to be idle during the days of *Khol HaMoed* ["secular" days on weeklong Jewish holidays] (he called these days "half-holidays"). If an undesirable person was elected as the head of a village, the local inspector should notify his superiors and propose a more acceptable candidate. He also proposed to confiscate the silk clothing, adorned hats, furs, jewels, and pearls, as well as the use of gold and silver dinnerware owned by the farmers.

*[Page 52]*

He proposed that all these items be handed over to the Head Office to be sold at public auction and the money collected from the sale be used to pay off the owed taxes of the owners or to invest them in their farms.

Padyiev suggested prohibiting the Rabbis from arranging for a divorce requested by a woman or her parents for not fulfilling an obligation by the husband or his parents to bestow her with fine clothing and jewels (from this clause, one can get the impression that this was a common occurrence among the farmers. It was certainly not so - M.L.). He proposed to punish any Rabbi who would not observe this rule by imposing various penalties, starting with a fine and ending with expulsion to Siberia.

Another prohibition suggested by Padyiev was based on his intention to prevent or at least to make it difficult for farmers' daughters to marry grooms from the city.

Following a list of strict clauses dealing with the conditions under which it would be allowed to leave the village for the city for a short period, he required the heads of the villages to notify the officialdom, without any delay, about any unauthorized leaving, including the location of the criminal. All the punishments mentioned above are repeated and proposed for anybody who leaves the colony without a permit. These punishments were also in effect for those who did not return home on the date noted in the permit. The head of the village, who would not notify about a farmer leaving for the city, would also be liable. After the first offense, he would be fined. The authority would determine his punishment after the third offense according to its own view.

Padyiev also suggested that the authorities in certain cities (Kherson and Ekaterinoslav) would search for the people who come from the colonies without a permit and return them to their colony escorted by a police officer (*"Etafom"*- meaning guards who would change at every night stop).

As some of the farmers who were craftsmen were employed in their profession by estate owners, Padyiev suggested punishing these estate owners according to the clauses in the law that refer to people who hide army deserters.

To enact this strict regime, Padyiev proposed not to rely on local inspectors who might handle the settlers with a soft hand because of their weak heart or their relations with the farmers. He proposed to do it by adding administrative personnel, including a small platoon of policemen who would become available for the officialdom.

Padyiev submitted his analysis and conclusions to his superior, General Yinzov. It is impossible to comprehend what was the reason that drove Yinzov to approve that plan. It may have been due to the general atmosphere or his fear of his vice and assistant, who has acquired certain appreciation from the high authorities. In any case, the fact was that Yinzov approved Padyiev's plan, added some remarks himself, and passed it to the interior ministry in Petersburg.

In the interior ministry, they were not in a hurry to make a decision concerning Padyiev's plan. Two problems that required solutions complicated the issue - the collection of taxes from the farmers and the standing of people who neglected their farms, concerning the army recruitment duty. According to a 1794 law, the Jewish townspeople and merchants were obligated to pay double the taxes imposed on Christians of the same classes. The same law contained a clause

*[Page 53]*

that allowed Jews to free themselves from the recruitment duty in exchange for a cash- restitution of 500 rubles. The "Jewish Regulations" from 1804 contained no clauses regarding the recruitment of Jews to the army. That meant that the 1794 law was still valid.

In 1808, at the beginning of the Jewish settlement in Kherson, the provincial minister of Kiev asked about the rule concerning the Jewish farmers regarding army recruitment. His questions were passed over to the "Jewish Committee" (probably the one re-nominated in 1809, headed by Popov). Even the opinion of Alexander the 1st on this issue was not very consistent. The issue reached the Ministry of Religions, and there, along with the Ministry of Finance, a new proposal was developed, which stated that only those who default on their taxes would be recruited to the army. The proposal was submitted for discussion in the Council of Ministers, however, in the meantime, the office manager of the interior ministry, Lansky, submitted his own proposal. Instead of all the fines and penalties in Padyiev's version, Lansky proposed to punish those who neglected their farm with recruitment to the army.

Lansky expanded his plan to include a proposal for a law concerning the recruitment of Jewish farmers and townspeople in the three provinces of Novorossiya. He suggested that, because it was difficult for the Jews to serve in the regular army, given their laws and customs, labor battalions would be established, each consisting of 500 soldiers, who would be employed in public works, road maintenance, etc. Jews who volunteered to serve their own goodwill would be allowed to join these battalions, where the soldiers would not be discriminated against because of their religion. Furthermore, Lansky emphasized that, for those farmers who neglected their farms, recruitment would serve as a highly effective means of education.

*[Page 54] [blank] [Page 55]*

# C. The Period of Nikolai the First

## New Proposals

In the meantime, the Czar Nikolai the First ascended to the throne (1825). As the Czar's views were not known yet, Lansky did not dare propose an overall compulsory service of the entire Jewish population and was content with a general comment. In his comment, he stated that "it is recommended to enact in all provinces a compulsory enlistment of the Jews in military labor battalions, to fight against their tendency of wandering and their laziness, and to educate them towards the love of good order, honesty, and good citizenship."

The formulation was still cautious and flexible, and the lack of self-confidence was apparent. Lansky reiterated and emphasized that if the Council of Ministers would approve the plan, the battalion commanders should be instructed not to interfere with the Jews keeping their laws and customs. He added that it would be desirable to allocate incentives for outstanding performers.

The Council of Ministers also found it difficult to make a clear decision because they were unsure about the will of the new Czar. In the end, they passed a vague resolution that stated: "The problems of the compulsory service of the Jews are part of the "Jewish Issue," and it is recommended to enact new regulations on the matter" (28 July 1825). However, when the proposed assessment was brought to the attention of the new Czar, he immediately ordered the Council of Ministers to "produce a proposal of regulations about a military-through-labor service for Jews and to submit it to me as fast as possible" (1 December 1826).

The cautious approach has evaporated. Compared to the new proposals, Lansky's old proposal can be considered merciful, liberal, and humane. Nikolai did not rely on his ministers to formulate the new decrees and added his own harsh clauses as it was his will to author a law about compulsory army recruitment of the Jews that would be unique in the history of nations.

The rumor about the special set of laws concerning compulsory service leaked out, which caused substantial embarrassment in Jewish centers. Special fasting and prayer sessions were declared, and lobbyists were sent to Petersburg.

In the meantime, the world behaved as usual, and in the interim, the future victims worried about their day-to-day sustenance. Lives in the colonies, distanced from the Jewish centers, were conducted according to the regular routine. The head of the management team - Yinzov, continued to deal with the settlement of the second wave of refugees. The construction of the houses

*[Page 56]*

was completed, and the equipment was procured. Yinzov, indeed, approved Padyiev's plan concerning the enforcement of a semi-military regime in the colonies, however, he did not refrain from proceeding with any constructive step to advance the settlement project.

Lansky was influenced by Padyiev's review and, once in a while, bothered Yinzov with complaints about not collecting the taxes. He demanded to be provided with accurate details about the farmers who worked diligently on their farms and those who neglected theirs. Yinzov tried his best to soften and explain that following the drought of 1824 and the locust plague during the years 1825–6, the Jews were in a severe situation, and that it would be difficult to collect taxes from them. Lansky persisted in his demands for detailed numbers, meaning - how many of the second-wave refugees settled through the assistance of the government budget (amounting to about 100,000 rubles) provided by Petersburg? However, Yinzov's report left many of the details obscured. The new settlers became impoverished because of the drought, locusts, and the economic crisis, and they hardly had anything left to invest in their farms. Some of the 300 houses built through the government allocation [for the second wave of settlers], were handed over to the first settlers who were homeless. Also, some consolidations of families in a single farm took place as a result of marriage. Yinzov predicted that the turn of any second wave of settlers who have not settled yet would come in a year or two, with the help of additional allocation or other consolidations, and did not provide an accurate statistic. Padyiev, on the other hand, hinted that about half of the 443 settlers of the second wave had not settled yet.

On 27 March 1826, a Jewish seller of alcoholic beverages by the name of Yitzkhak Yafeh was killed in Sevastopol. It was discovered in the police investigation that he was one of the farmers of the Kherson colonies. That story reached the Czar, who wanted to know how a farmer from a colony became an alcoholic beverage seller in a distant city. Intra-office communication began about this topic. An investigation conducted by the Guardian Bureau found that 900 people from both the first and second waves disappeared without any trace and without any knowledge by the authorities. Yinzov was embarrassed. Out of fear of being made responsible, he hung his fate on Padyiev's conclusions and claimed that as long as the authorities do not enforce harsher means and punishments, which would deter the settlers from wandering around looking to make a living in the cities, it would be difficult to keep the order. He advised Lansky to approve Padyiev's plan. Thus, on 26 August 1827, Nikolai the First signed off on the cruel compulsory army service, which was later to be followed by additional decrees.

## Nikolai's Army Recruitment Decrees

Within the "the Law of Army Compulsory Service" of September 1794, there was a clause about the recruitment of the Jews, according to which, the Russian Jews, similar to Christian merchants, could free themselves from the army obligation by paying 500 rubles.

This law enabled Jews to free themselves from military duty for

*[Page 57]*

thirty–four years. Nikolai's law, from 26 August 1827, stated that every Jew from the age of 12 to age 25 is required to serve in the army for 25Irs. The younger boys are required to serve for six additional years of preparation and training. Only merchants and craftsmen registered in the merchants or craftsmen's guilds, supervisors operating machinery in factories, farmers, Rabbis, and graduates of Russian schools, respectively, can exempt themselves by paying a 1000–ruble ransom.

Jewish farmers were exempt from compulsory service for 50 years if they resided in large settlements or 25 years for individual settlers from the day of the regulation, or from the day of their settlement on the land. Those who abandoned farming were subject to compulsory service.

Based on the new regulation, Lansky requested that General Yinzov prepare a detailed list of the permanent and semi-permanent farmers and those who abandoned their farms. Lansky demanded the latter to receive the details about their debts and requested a proposal as to how could their debt be paid if these people lost their rights towards compulsory service.

In his response, Yinzov indicated that out of 1030 families (6484 people) in total, 800 families (5582 people), were entitled to exemption, and 150 families (902 people) were not. The total debt of those who abandoned the properties reached 36 thousand rubles. He stated that the authorities must discover where they reside, and collect the debts.

Lansky was also of the opinion that compulsory service should be enforced on the 902 deserters; however, due to the importance of the principle of that decision, he submitted the matter for a discussion for the Council of Ministers. As the final version of the clauses concerning the Jewish farmers and their rights were about to be formulated, information was obtained from Kherson about the return to the colonies of 1152 people (about 250 people more than in the official report).

With this new information, the proposal took an entirely new direction, and the Council of Ministers passed a resolution formulated according to the following clauses:

1.  During the years 1827–28–29, the Jewish farmers would be exempt from the compulsory service and from the cash ransom requirement.
2.  During the years 1828–9, all the farmers in the colonies would have to develop their farms dedicatedly and continually. Those who resided outside of their farms must return to them within 6 months.
3.  If the farmers could prove their dedication to farming through 1828–9, they would be exempt from compulsory service for 50 years.

Three additional details and conditions were set regarding the third clause above:

    a.  The farmers must be occupied in agriculture continually.
    b.  Farmers would be allowed to leave their colonies without licenses and passports, only for the neighboring villages

[Page 58]

    c.  To travel to farther locations and for periods longer than a month, they must obtain a license–passport from the authority representative and return on or before the date specified in the license.
    d.  The Bureau's representatives would be allowed to issue travel licenses for a certain duration only on the condition that there is a valid reason to support it based on the testimony of the heads of the colonies.
    e.  Those who do not obey the authority and its representatives and those who disturb the public peace would be recruited into the army.
    f.  Untalented people, those negligent in working the land, those who left without a license, or those who returned after the date stated in the license without a valid reason would be recruited into the army[1].

g.   The highest Supervisory Committee would be allowed to hand over farmers to the army even against the view of the heads of the colonies if, in its opinion, there are valid reasons to do so.

h.   If, after six months from the date of this regulation, the deserters would not return to their farms, they would be considered as wanderers.

The Council of Ministers asked the Supervisory Committee in Novorossiya for their view concerning the farmers' debts in cases of widowed or forsaken women who cannot pay off their debts to the government and whether it would be justified to burden the public with these dubious debts.

The Council also recommended, as a punishment, handing over the farms of those who would be recruited to the army to sons of married farmers or to homeless farmers without burdening them with the debts of their predecessors.

All these proposals were brought up for discussion and were approved by the "Committee for the Remedy of the State of the Jews." However, even before the clarification correspondence among the offices had been completed, a new review by Yinzov (probably responding to a request by Lansky) arrived, with numbers contradicting the previous reviews.

Yinzov divided the total number of the settlers–1030 families (6484 people) according to four types:

- Type A–those who work continuously in their farms – 1493 men.
- Type B–those who work on their farms but also outside –102 men
- Type C– those who work in the colonies in all sorts of occupations and sowed their farms for show – 917 men
- Type D–those who work outside of the colonies from the day they arrived – 493 people.

Correspondence between Novorossiya and Petersburg commenced again. In the end, the Council of Ministers passed the final legislation, which was named: "The Legislation Concerning the Compulsory Service of Jewish Farmers" and its clauses were as follows:

*[Page 59]*

A.   Those settlers who worked continuously [in their farms] until 1827, and their sons, were exempt from compulsory service for 50 years from the issuance of the legislation (1827). Those absent from the colonies, by their own action, or those who have prolonged their stay beyond the date stated in their licenses are invited to return to the colonies within a year. If they persisted in working the land for two years, they would be included among the exempt people.

B.   Those who were absent from their farms, or those who were unable to work the land, would be able to become townspeople, if, within a year, they could bring approval from the communities they had belonged to in the past that they agreed to pay for them their debts to the government.

Settlers of this type, who wanted to become members of the middle class as townspeople and were not recipients of government loans – must participate in paying off the debts of families in which all the members have died.

C.   Settlers absent from their colonies without a license and who did not return to their colony within a year, or settlers who would return to the colony but would not persist in agricultural work for two years, would be handed to the army if their health was good. Those who would not be able to serve in the army would be sent to Siberia.

(This clause was also meant to address settlers who were undisciplined, rambunctious, untalented workers, as well as heads of colonies and Rabbis who would not cooperate with the authority in exposing offenses by the farmers).

The colony will pay 500 rubles to the government as a payoff on the debt of every person punished by army recruitment or by a send–off to Siberia.

D.    Settlers who were licensed to work outside of the location of their residence for a limited time are prohibited from trading, pimping, or selling alcoholic beverages.

E.    The following kinds of settlers would receive a **silver medal** if their house and farm structures were sound. If they continued their practices for an additional 10-year period, they would be entitled to receive a **gold medal**: settlers who sowed their fields with crops or grew vegetables on an area not less than 10 *disiyatins* [about 27 acres] for five years; settlers who purchased oxen and plows to cultivate their fields ordinarily; those who grew flax and canvas plants; those who planted at least 50 trees around their houses; those who cultivated more than 20 heads of cattle and 100 sheep.
Medal recipients are exempt from corporal punishment (flogging) and when they reach the age of 50, they will be exempt from public works.

F.    Jewish townspeople would be allowed to become farmers following approval of the general assembly of the colony's farmers, to whom they submit their candidacy, as well as certification by the head of their community that they have sufficient financial means to sustain

*[Page 60]*

a farm without government assistance, and that they can work the land. These settlers would be exempt from paying taxes for several years according to the 1804 Regulations. They and their families would be exempt from compulsory army service for 50 years from the date of their settlement.

Based on the regulations from 20 July 1829, 30 families converted from the farmers class to the townspeople class and left the colonies. At the beginning of 1831, 996 families (6574 people) remained in the nine Kherson colonies.

General Yiznov, the head of the Supervisory Committee (of the Guardian Bureau) was not satisfied with the reports and accounts of the local inspectors and would visit the colonies from time to time, taking care of correcting anything that had to be corrected.

During the following five years, 1829–1834, the government was hardly bothered by problems in the colonies. The farmers adapted to working the land, the years were harvest years, and the relationships with the authorities were, more-or-less, orderly. Reports sent by the Guardian Bureau were routine, void of special significance. The reports' topics included matters such as the joining of a few families, cattle epidemics, a flooded barn, conflagration of the hay in one of the colonies, and similar matters.

During those years, Petersburg was busy dealing with more important matters. The war with Turkey, which broke in 1828, and the Polish revolt that broke and was suppressed in 1831. Only after quiet descended on the land, the interior ministry remembered the colonies, and the head of the Guardian Bureau was asked to provide a detailed review of the state of the settlers. Padyiev was nominated to fulfill this role again, and he visited the colonies wrote down some numbers, and authored a detailed report along the lines of his conclusion' of 1825.

Padyiev's visits took place after two years of drought in 1833–34. Because of the drought, the number of cattle heads decreased and the farmers were entangled in debts and were left without the means to sow the land for the following season. Following the economic crisis, a mood of despair and indifference prevailed again.

Like his previous review, Padyiev was not oblivious to the objective factors (years of drought, disease, poverty, and deprivation) when he reviewed the reasons for the pitiful state of the colonies. However, he did not forget to also list the factors associated with the "negative attributes" of the settlers. He repeated his claim that they hate work, deceive the government to extract allocations and demand discounts and exemptions from taxes without making an effort to improve their situation. He also indicated that their wives were not helping them, as if Jewish women always treated physical effort with disrespect and contempt.

The colonies spread over an area of 800 miles. Because of the distances between one colony to another (sometimes up to 100 miles), the inspectors could not supervise them efficiently enough. On the other hand, the proximity of the colonies to the cities–Kherson, Nikolaiev, and Odesa, was a contributing factor to the wandering and the flow of people looking after easy occupations… Padyiev

*[Page 61]*

proposed stopping any additional government assistance, establishing stricter supervision of the Jewish farmers' work, and punishing the "perverted" with all the severity of the law, according to the clauses of the regulation about the army's compulsory service.

The High Supervision Committee of the Guardian Bureau, headed by General Yinzov, signed off on all Padyiev's proposals. However, the committee found it necessary to add that despite the settlement movement's difficulties, "there is a benefit in continuing the enterprise and in the handling of it, and if the pioneers could not establish themselves, at least the next generations would be successful."

Padyiev's report was indeed sent to the correct address in the office of the [interior] ministry in Petersburg. However, this time, it was archived without being disc because, by that time, the view that the Jewish settlement should be expanded prevailed in the government. This view included the desire to allocate additional areas and to expand the rights of the Jewish farmers. A new proposal for a new settlement enterprise in the Siberian expanses, where the chances for natural disasters such as drought, locusts, and cattle diseases, were less frequent than in Kherson.

## Regulations for the Encouragement of Jewish Settlement

The government of Nikolai treated the Jews with certain liberalism in its early stages. It planned the expansion of education, started with granting rights to people who developed industries and trade, and discussed proposals to grant additional privileges to people who settled on the land. They did it for obvious reasons.

The objective of the decrees of the government of Nikolai the First was to "reduce the harmful influence of the Jews and to guide a people that is so wild in its wear, customs, and religious laws, towards assimilation and conversion through means of oppression." Following several years of compulsory army service, mass deportations, and steps to narrow religious freedom that were accompanied by the expansion of poverty, degeneration, and hunger–it was realized that despite the oppression, the tormented Jews are still defiant, and except for the *"Cantonists"* [the children who were kidnapped and forced to convert to Christianity], conversion to Christianity among the Jews was still very rare.

High–ranking officials who followed the practices of the governments in Prussia and Austria towards their Jewish subjects discovered that the road towards assimilation should not be through hostility and oppression but through education. Even some of the Jews haters adopted this liberal view. The view was that education would free the Jews from the darkness of zealotry, their ridiculous wear, and distasteful customs, and they would draw near the citizens of the land and adapt their way of life. They would assimilate, and from there–there is only a short step towards complete assimilation and conversion. Therefore, in 1840, a resolution was passed to enable the Jews to acquire education and grant the educated and the people who developed industries and trade additional privileges. As far as the beginning of the century, during the days of Alexander the First, the government tried to attract the Jews towards developing industries. During the second quarter of the century, some Jews reached substantial accomplishments. In 1828, the industrialist Yosef Bernstein owned 17 textile factories, and four years later,

*[Page 62]*

(in 1832), their number reached 20. According to the statistics, in 1832, 32% of the factories in the province of Podolia were in Jewish hands.

Even in foreign trade, the Jews began to play a major role. A substantial portion of the export and import trade was in Jewish hands. In the port city of Odesa, the commerce houses and the banks were concentrated in the hands of the Jews. During 1842, seven merchants of level A, nine of level B, and 187 of level C were registered as Jews with special privileges. The total capital of the [Jewish] merchants of all three levels reached 2 million Rubles. The liberal attitude towards Jews, who developed trade and industry, originated, therefore, from the economic interest of the state.

The awarding of special privileges to the Jewish settlers had two main reasons. The first was based on the need to settle vast areas in the Kherson prairies, which were conquered from the Turks, and in Siberia, which was sparsely populated. The second reason was the wish to free the cities from their poor Jewish residents, who competed with the Christian population in trade and craftsmanship through their fight for their very sustenance. Yet, we would allow ourselves to assume that in this wish to attract Jews towards a stabler economic channel, there was some humane thinking or something like a compensatory conscience. Many would view this assumption as strange and refuted, however, the truth is that there were some provincial ministers whose reports and reviews contained a humane concern about the horrible state of the Jewish population. Some assumed that even in this ruler's pity, there was a hidden intention to guide the Jewish masses–through working the land and rural way of life–toward the way of life of the Christian farmers and assimilation. May the factors and the reasons be where they may–the regulations for the Jewish settlement were formulated during that period in the most positive spirit.

On 13 April 1835, the emperor signed off on a new "Jewish Legislation" that included all the old Jewish laws, with the addition of new limitations. The map of the "Pale of Settlement" was reduced even further, and the residence of Jews within large cities in the Pale of Settlement was prohibited. However, within the system of prohibiting and limiting clauses, several positive clauses were found, particularly clause no. 23, which discussed Jewish farmers.

That clause stated that "the Jews are allowed to settle on government lands, or on lands they acquired permanently, as well as on leased lands throughout all provinces of the Pale of Settlement."

Government lands would be provided, for unlimited time, to any group of Jewish settlers if it included at least 25 men, the land is separated from Christian villages or estates, and the group would settle it within two years from the day of the approval. Jews could settle on lands outside of the "Pale of Settlement," with a pre-approval of the high authorities.

Land bought by Jews could be sold to either other Jews or Christians. Land leased from estate–owners, with the approval of the authorities, must be leased for a minimum of twelve years. The transition to settlement would be free, every person of his or her own will without compulsion.

*[Page 63]*

The settlers were exempt from paying personal taxes for 25 years. They would also be exempt from compulsory army service, as well as from *Zmestvo* taxes [taxes paid to the agricultural provincial institution] for ten years[2].

The settlers' debts to the government accrued before their settlement would be wiped out.

The settlers would be allowed to work as traders and craftsmen only within the colony. They would be prohibited from all commerce in the alcoholic beverage industry or from providing services to estate owners.

Every farmer would be allowed to distill beer or liquor for household consumption and for sale to the people in his village, if the village contains at least ten houses.

A Jew who employs at least 50 other Jews on his land would be granted the honorary title of "Honorary State Citizen." If he would employ at least 100 people on his estate–he would be granted a hereditary honorary title.

The Jewish colonies would be managed similarly to Christian villages by imposing local taxes. Through the income on the "meat tax," the colonies must support their sick, elderly and handicapped and employ the poorest.

The last and final clause–children of the settlers would be allowed to study in public schools, high schools, and universities. Another sign of charity was decided on April/24/1836, that the state agricultural school would accept several Jewish apprentices for advanced studies.

The regulations were publicized; however, no reaction was received from the Jews. The news about the [sorry] state of the settlers in Kherson did not attract many. The poorest who did not have anything to lose except their debts and the compulsory service, patiently waited to see how things would progress. The rich, attracted by the honorary titles from the government were also not rushing to invest money and burden themselves with acquiring or leasing land.

Perhaps the reluctance resulted simply from the fact that the Jews did not believe that the "evil royalty" could act to benefit the Jews and saw these considerate declarations – simply a deception and a gimmick. Among government circles, people wondered about the lack of response from the part of the Jews. Because they thought that the main reason for the rejection was the fear of settling in Kherson, a new proposal was raised by the Finance Minister, Graf Kankrin, to allocate land areas in Siberia for Jewish settlement.

*[Page 64]*

# The "Siberian Plan"

The proposal by Minister Kankrin was accepted by the Council of Ministers under the assumption that there were insufficient numbers of available lands in the western provinces ("Pale of Settlement"), and because of the refusal of the Jews to settle in the prairies of Kherson.

The proposal was approved with the signature by Czar Nikolai the First on 12 November 1835 and five areas of land were allocated for Jewish settlement in the provinces of Omsk and Tobolsk, totaling 15, 157 *disiyatins* [about 41,000 acres]. Groups of Jews organized and offered themselves for settlement in these areas. The applications came from all corners of Russia:

| | |
|---|---|
| From Ekaterinoslav province | 70 families |
| From Mitwa [Jelgeva, Courland] province | 80 families |
| From Vilna, Grodno and Minsk provinces | 286 families |
| From Liboh [?] | 37 families |
| From Vitebsk province | 40 families |
| From Mstislav province | 50 families |
| From Mohilev province | 247 families |
| The total number of families | 810 |

All applications and requests were transferred through the provincial ministers to Interior Minister Bludov. It is noted here the sympathetic attitude of some provincial ministers, whose goodwill and heartfelt humanistic sentiment were apparent in their wish to encourage the miserable people and ease their lives with this proposal.

The Provincial Minister from Minsk offered to assist the poor settlers-candidates by allocating the expenses associated with the journey to Siberia and the establishment of their farm. To attain efficiency in transportation, he proposed to transfer them in groups. He also suggested ordering the authorities on their way to provide guides for them and the authorities in the area of settlement to stand by them with advice and guide them on farming.

Jewish Farmers in Russia Fields

The Provincial Minister of Mogilev, General Diyakov, described, in his review, the horrible poverty of the Jews, which resulted from their expulsion [from the villages] and from the congestion in the cities. As an example, he indicated that there are 600 Jewish tailors in the city of Homel, while the city population could support just one percent of this number. In Diyakov's opinion, there was room for colonies within the "Pale of Settlement," where the Russian villages were separated by tens of miles. He stated that Jewish colonies could be established in the gaps between one village to another.

The General commanding the Gendarmes Corps, Darbush, also emphasized the impoverished state of the Jews and supported their settlement in Siberia and the material assistance to the settlers. He raised a painful problem: The leaders of the Jewish communities were usually from the wealthy class who did not encourage the poor community members to settle. They actually hinder [the idea of settlement], as much as they can. The leaders hid the royal declaration about the settlement from the public.

*[Page 65]*

Their adverse attitude came from the fact that the sons of the poor people served as an alternative for their own sons concerning the compulsory army service. General Darbush stated that the community councils were actually acting against the new legislation, as there was an explicit statement in it, which stated that the debts and taxes would be written off for those who settled. Therefore the community councils refused to issue approvals before the debts to the communities were paid off, just to make it more difficult for the candidates. To eliminate intraoffice red–tape and dependency on the community councils, General Darbush proposed to nominate, in every province, a special official, who would be independent of the provincial and district authorities and the community councils, who would be responsible for issuing the passports. This proposal had substantial significance in light of the bureaucracy and the corruption that prevailed in the government offices and the community councils.

The interior minister passed all of the abovementioned proposals to Finance Minister Kankrin because the implementation of the settlement project was associated with the allocation of substantial sums from the state treasury. Kankrin agreed to all the efficient proposals for the organization and allocation of the required budgets except Diyakov's proposal to settle Jews within areas of the "Pale of Settlement."

Based on the agreement of the finance minister, Interior Minister Bludov formulated a proposal for discussion in the Council of Ministers:

A. To nominate special officials who would handle all of the arrangements for transporting the settlers.
B. These officials would be equipped with all the governmental forms so that the candidates for settlement would not need to run around from one office to another office.
C. The details of the [government] assistance would be mentioned on the passports along with the arrangements for security and lodging, which would be imposed on the local authorities along all the stops on the way to Siberia.
D. The official responsible for the organization and implementation of the arrangements would need to provide the provincial authorities with the list of passports issued by him.
E. The transport of the candidates to Siberia would be implemented in organized groups and during the appropriate season of the year.
F. Throughout the entire journey, sufficient amounts of food would be allocated, except for alcoholic beverages.
G. The provincial ministers would need to provide the list of the candidates who left their provinces to the provincial minister of Omsk, sometime before the start of the journey. Omsk and Tobolsk authorities would have to issue a directive to construct houses for the settlers and complete them

before they arrive (the wood for the construction should be taken from the government's forests). The authorities should allocate 15 *disiyatins* [about 40.5 acres] for each male in the family and equip him through governmental funds with tools, oxen, mules, and needed houseware. They also must feed the candidates until the first harvest.

H. To annul the debts of the candidates for unpaid taxes and also not to collect these taxes from the community councils.

*[Page 66]*

The Council of Ministers accepted the entire proposal and Czar Nikolai the First approved them.

Operating under the assumption that the Jews would prefer to settle in Siberia, which was superior in its soil quality, amounts of precipitations, and healthy climate, compared to Kherson, and because they wished to achieve an immediate solution to the poor economic state of masses of Jews, by settling them in the vast areas of Siberia, the authorities publicized the new royal declaration about the Siberian settlements throughout all the large cities and the small towns. There was no city or town where applications were not received. The community councils issued certificates, and the provincial government offices, as well as the provincial offices and the special officials in them, sorted them up and added detail, although the authorities were not necessarily rigorous in approving the most suitable candidates.

The approved lists of candidates were passed to Petersburg. Even before 1836, 1134 families were registered and approved according to the regulations. According to the instructions, the authorities of the provinces of Omsk and Tobolsk had to prepare and construct the houses before the arrival of the settlers, however, due to the technical methods of construction during those days, houses were not built quickly. Even organizing the journey to Siberia was not an easy thing to do, and the candidates waited a long time before they set out. Many started to liquidate their business and even to pack their belongings and there were some people, who lost their patience and set out on the road on their own.

At the end of the fall, 17 families (71 people) arrived at Tambov and showed up at the office of the provincial minister and told him that they were traveling to the location allocated for settlement. The state of the travelers was miserable. They announced that they had spent their last savings on their way from Mogilev. They suffered from cold and hunger and were forced to panhandle. They stated that they did not have the energy to continue.

Because he pitied them, the provincial minister, with the help of philanthropists, placed the wanderers in houses for lodging and supplied them with clothing, shoes, food, and medical assistance. He contacted Interior Minister Bludov and asked what to do with them. With the approval of the finance minister, an allocation to cover their expenses was approved, and a directive was issued to allow them to travel forward towards the region of the settlement.

Considering the increased number of candidates for the settlement in Siberia, Minister of Finance, Kankrin, submitted a proposal to the Council of Ministers to add to the settlement authority an additional area of 13,363 *disiyatins* [about 36,080 acres], and the Council approved his proposal. However, when the resolution reached the Czar for his approval, he wrote on the protocol: "Stop transferring Jews to Siberia" (5th January 1837).

The ministers wandered about the change in the Czar's attitude, however, the reason for it was only discovered a long time after that – a confidential document that was submitted by Interior Minister Bludov and Police Minister, Backendorf, in which they argued about the need to stop the [Jewish] settlement in Siberia.

*[Page 67]*

## The "Retraction" from the Siberian

The decree [to stop the settlement in Siberia] surprised the public and even the state ministers, provincial ministers, and officials. A royal declaration appeared containing the reasons for the Czar's position. The official declaration was formulated by the interior minister in the spirit of the confidential document submitted to the Czar by himself and Backendorf. In this declaration, it was stated that the transfer of Jews to Siberia would involve many hassles. Siberia is a region populated mostly by people who were expelled there as a punishment for delinquencies and crimes and it would continue to be populated mostly by criminals. Because the Jews "are certainly not known for their moral and honest way of life, the Siberian atmosphere would ease their way for a life of wandering around and deception and allow for their destructive influence, and thus, the attributes of the Christian population would be destroyed." It would also be difficult to supervise them throughout Siberia, with the current conditions of the sparse population and lack of sufficient police force. In addition, the Jews would lose their meager property along their long journey and become a burden on the state treasury, which would need to provide them with assistance for a long time. There is also the danger that many Jews would drop out during the Journey, remain in the cities along the way, and spread in them their "aberrant and damaging ways." Based on these reasons, it must be determined that it is forbidden to hand over any land areas in Siberia for Jewish settlement. The areas that may have been already allocated for that purpose would be returned to the government. Against that, available government areas in the "Pale of Settlement" must be allocated for the purpose of Jewish settlement, according to the proposal of the Provincial Minister Diakov.

Jews would prefer to settle in areas close to their places of residence, which would acclimatize them faster, and it would be easier for the government to supervise them there.

Following the listing of the positive aspects of settlement in the provinces of the "Pale of Settlement," a recommendation for directing all the Jews who have submitted applications and have been approved for the settlement in Siberia, to settlement in available lands in Kherson was mentioned.

That is how the plan for the settlement in Siberia was annulled. However, the whole thing did not just end without consequences. As a result of the reasoning and explanation about the moral damage that the Jewish settlers may cause to the sparse population of Siberia, the Czar reached the conclusion that it would be logical to reduce "the bad influence" of the Jews who already resided in the cities of Siberia by reducing their numbers. He also decided to impose compulsory service on the children of the Jews who were sent there as criminals or as children of criminals who now enjoyed rights by being merchants. Thus, the Czar asked two of his loyal ministers, Bludov and Backendorf, to investigate the number of Jews in Siberia, their social class and occupations, and to draft legislation that would reduce their numbers.

The result of the investigation was quite pitiful. Within the three provinces of Tobolsk, Tomsk, and Yenisei–18 families, or 959 people altogether, were found to belong to the classes of merchants and townspeople (craftsmen, etc.). In the province of Omsk –13 Jewish families were found.

*[Page 68]*

There were no responses from other provinces, but it is reasonable to assume that the number of Jews there was not large there either. However, these numbers did not deter the ministers. They determined that Jews who belonged to the class of merchants or craftsmen were indeed exempt from compulsory service but that the children and grandchildren of Jews who were sent to Siberia as criminals had to be recruited, even if their fathers became merchants or craftsmen.

The problem of the few families who had already made their way somewhere in Siberia concerned the people who authored the new regulation. After all, it was not possible to treat them as an exception to the rule–lest they would multiply over decades and "infect" the population with negative attributes.

The following is the formulation of Bludov–Backendorf regulations:

1.  Means against the settlement of Jews in Siberia:

    A.  The Jewish settlement in Siberia must be stopped.
    B.  The areas allocated for the settlement in the provinces of Tobolsk and Omsk would be reassigned for other purposes.
    C.  According to the legislation of 13th April 1835, the settlement would take place in the provinces of Novorossiya, and, if possible, provided that available areas can be found in locations where the Jews currently resided in the Pale of Settlement.
    D.  The Jews, who are already on their way to Omsk, will be transported to the colonies in Kherson at government expense. They would enjoy all of the rights awarded in the Jewish Legislation of 1835, and according to the regulations from November 1836

        (The content of clauses E and F was not clear).

2.  Means for reducing the number of Jews residing in Siberia:

    A.  The Jews who resided in Siberia as people who were expelled by the government. They and their children born there would stay where they are. The rest of the Jews who penetrated Siberia's cities on their own or who joined families from the type mentioned above should leave Siberia and return to their previous locations or to any other location within the "Pale of Settlement."
    B.  Children of expelled people below the age of 18, including those who would be born from this day forward, are obliged to serve compulsory service according to the general recruitment laws.

This order was signed by the Czar Nikolai on 15 May 1837. It is noted here that after receiving the order about the termination of the [Jewish] settlement in Siberia, the provincial minister of Southern Siberia turned to Petersburg with the question of whether he would be allowed to settle the Jews who came from Mogilev "since they arrived here based on the previous legislation." Interior Minister Bludov passed the question to the Czar and his response was negative.

The new order placed many ministers and senior officials in an embarrassing position.

*[Page 69]*

The reason for the policy change would have remained a hidden secret for future generations, were it not for Graf Kisliyov (who was in charge of the Ministry of State Assets and had to get involved in the settlement matters). He turned to Bludov with the question about the reason for the sudden change in the preparation process for the Siberian settlement. Bludov gave him, confidentially, a copy of the review that he and Backendorf had handed over to the Czar, where they argued about stopping the settlement in Siberia. Indeed, Kisiliyov kept the document's confidentiality; however, he filed a copy of the review, absent-mindedly, in one of the files, which was transferred routinely to the departmental archives and was discovered years later.

This certificate demonstrates the hypocrisy of Minister Bludov, who officially handled, as the Interior Minister, the legislation of the Siberian settlement law and whom everybody viewed as the principal supporter of that law.

## The Return to the Settlement in Kherson

The new decree was fateful for those Jews who liquidated their business and sold their property at half its price and now their road to Siberia was blocked. Now they were willing to go to Kherson, despite its drawbacks, just to avoid idleness and inactivity. However, despite the clear declaration that they would be able to settle in Kherson instead, they still faced obstacles. Bludov was not in a hurry to implement that decision and preferred to first formulate new legislation for the settlement in Kherson.

According to Bludov's view, the success of the settlement depended on establishing a semi-military harsh regime. Based on that view, he formulated a new 19-clause plan in the spirit of Padiyev's proposals.

The plan determined, among other things, that the Jewish settlement enterprise must be taken from the supervision of the Guardian Bureau of Novorossiya's settlement (General Yinzov was viewed too soft by Bludov). He decided that a special manager should be nominated from among the ranks of retired military officers, who would be under the supervision of the provincial minister and for whom deputies and assistants would be nominated. He determined that the location of the management office would be the colony of Nahar-Tov ["Good River"], located in the center of the colony's region. The following clauses deal with the roles of the management and its officials; in addition, the document defined the clauses that concern the settlers, according to which a Jewish farmer would only be able to retire from his farm after 20 years of agricultural work, and only if he can provide proof that he excelled in it.

Bludov's plan stated the following:

From this day onward, it would be forbidden for non-farmers to reside in the colonies.

It would be prohibited to allow and to provide passports for leaving the colony for an extended period. Within the province of Kherson, it was allowed to issue passports for a limited duration, not longer than one month, and not more than twice a year.

The head manager of the colonies would be authorized to punish negligent workers. Punishments include an imprisonment of up

*[Page 70]*

to 3 days, and a penalty of up to 7 days of public labor. The head manager would be allowed to punish the undisciplined and the corrupted with physical punishment of up to 25 lashes.

That legislation was submitted to the Council of Ministers, was approved, and received the formal seal of approval on 4 November 1837. The Council of Ministers inserted a correction in one of the clauses, namely that the annual management expenses amounting to 8800 Rubles will be carried by the government during the first two years of operation and would be covered, starting from the third year and on, via an additional tax imposed on the settlers.

Bludov instructed the provincial ministers in Siberia to transfer to Kherson, escorted by a police guard, any Jew who settled in Siberia on his own. That decree led to a tragicomic episode. The provincial minister of Kostroma province, who naively did not understand what kind of Jews his superior meant in his instructions, notified Bludov that he arrested a group of 110 Jewish children, according to the instructions. This was a transport of Jewish children "recruited" to the *"Cantonists"* Battalion in Perm province. Bludov became furious because of that incident and sent a special courier to instruct the Kostrom provincial minister to immediately release the children, and as a punishment for this blunder, he imposed all expenses of imprisonment on the minister.

Some consequences of Bludov's instructions are known: The provincial minister of Somburg notified Petersburg that "a group of 17 families (70 people), who stopped to celebrate the Passover holiday in the province, was captured." The provincial minister of Chernigov announced - "due to the diligence shown by the police, 12 families were captured in three cities." One family of 7 people was captured in the Penza province. In Perm province, 3 families were arrested. In Vladimir province, 2 families and in Moscow, 5 people were arrested.

The bureaucratic machine was active and managed to discover, capture, and arrest the "criminals," many of whom were equipped with a government passport or approved certificates by the community councils.

People who did not commit any infraction in their journey to Siberia were sent to Kherson at the government's expense, and people who held authorized and approved certificates from the community councils – were considered illegal wanderers. They were sent to Kherson accompanied by police guards like criminals.

As a sign of charity, to avoid an unfavorable burden on the supervising authority in Kherson, Finance Minister Kankrin allocated 25 thousand rubles, with the Czar's approval, to settle 42 families captured throughout Siberia and sent to Kherson.

Meanwhile, the Siberian candidates abandoned in their localities showered the government and provincial ministers with letters. One letter reached the Czar himself. The letter author described his situation after liquidating his business and selling his property: "We are rolling in attics, cellars, and even beneath the open sky."

The provincial minister bothered Bludov with complaints and questions as well. He sent instructions to the provincial ministers to investigate the truth of the Jewish claims. He instructed them to select the people who were suffering the most and send them to Kherson accompanied by governmental representatives, in groups of 50 families (the intent was, as a first step, to send one group from each region. Tz. L). However, according to the law,

*[Page 71]*

transport of Jews to Kherson was not allowed without a mutual agreement between the sending authorities and Kherson's authorities, and even then, the number of people being sent should have been within the annual limited absorption capacity. According to that, the settlement process would have lasted for many years, even if the transport of the first groups of 50 people had been perfectly organized. In the meantime, the state of the "Siberians" worsened. Hunger and disease broke out among them. The provincial ministers started to bother Bludov again and demanded assistance for the sick and needy. A certain budget was allocated for that purpose, however, the number of people who turned to the authority for assistance grew, and many complaints were heard about the judgment of the officials about who was entitled to help.

People who saw themselves as deprived slandered their friends who managed to outsmart the authorities more than they did. The police intervened, and its investigations caused havoc among the needy but did not bring any positive results.

In the meantime, the office of the ministry responsible for the government assets (that included the government lands), reviewed the land reserves allocated for the settlers in Kherson and found that land suitable for agriculture would only suffice for 190 families, according to 40 *disiyatins* [about 108 acres] per family. That meant that only approximately 8,000 *disiyatins* [about 21,600 acres] out of the registered 14,000 [about 38,000 acres] were actually available for settlement.

One of the senior officials, Komarov, was sent to Kherson to clarify exactly what was the size of the area that could be settled. Komarov toured the colonies and the lands of Kherson and provoked anger among the officials of the local offices, even during his investigation.

Here is the summary of his survey about the available land:

| | |
|---|---|
| Within the Jewish colonies | 22,000 *disiyatins* [about 59,400 acres] |
| Within 11 specific government areas | 27,000 *disiyatins* [about 72,900 acres] |
| Within 6 additional areas | 24,000 *disiyatins* [about 64,800 acres] |

Total - 73,000 *disiyatins* [ about 197 thousand acres]

Bludov submitted the results of Komarov's survey and noted his opinion that if they distribute the land areas according to 30 *disiyatins* per family, it would be possible to settle 2434 families.

## Under the Mercies of Officials and Patrons

At one point, Bludov grew impatient with the whole Jewish settlement issue, which caused him only bothers and discontent. The ministers of the western provinces notified him one by one about the distress of the "Siberians," about disease, hunger, and discontent. They demanded that the settlers be transferred to Kherson as soon as possible. From Kherson, the authorities notified him that it was impossible to build housing on a grand scale because of the lack of forest trees and other construction materials, and because of the drought and the plagues, it was not possible to collect taxes from the established settlers as well. Moreover,

*[Page 72]*

every imprisonment of a Jew who set out to settle in one of the Siberian cities resulted in an annoying correspondence.

On 26 December 1837, a special ministry responsible for the state assets was founded, and Graf Kisliyov was nominated to head it. Bludov proved to the Czar that it would make sense to have the Ministry of the State Assets, which handled the government lands, manage the existing Jewish colonies and the continuation of the settlement with all of its problems. The Czar was convinced and transferred the nuisance of the Jews from Bludov to Kisliyov. However, even Kisliyov was not too happy to accept this role. That was the period close to the time of the peasants' emancipation, and the Ministry of the State Assets already handled 7,649,442 male farmers (besides the Jews).

The new ministry was headed by liberal people who looked for ways to emancipate the vassals without causing shockwaves in the stability of the state economy. The government-owned land areas were conquered from the Turks in Novorossiya, and many estates were confiscated due to the bankruptcies of the estate owners or due to the cruel treatment of their vassals. When the government took over the estates, the vassals were freed anyway. The ministry was loaded with work and tasks, including land measurements, divisions of large areas into farm units, and conducting censuses in the villages. Compared to the complicated problems faced by the Ministry of the State Assets, what was the significance of the problem of several impoverished Jewish families waiting for their transport to Kherson? However, from the day the task was transferred to that ministry, its management was bothered by the abundance of requests for transport, pleadings for help, complaints about journey provisions that were not supplied, and land that was not handed over, justifiably or due to lack of housing. The Guardian Bureau in Kherson also flooded them with questions, requests, clarification instructions, financial issues, and more.

The ministry management realized that handling the Jewish settlement consumed too much time. Kisliyov notified the Czar in writing that he had allocated eight land areas for the purpose of the settlement in Kherson, totaling 49,758 *disiyatins* [about 135,000 acres], enabling the settlement of 1244 new families; he indicated that according to the legislation of 4 November 1837, the Jewish colonies were under special management supervised by the provincial minister. He proposed that for the benefit of the important operation, the provincial minister should manage the settlement matters by himself because the dependency on Petersburg and the tiring letter exchanges impaired the efficiency of the operation. As per the decision of 4 November 1937, he proposed that the task be transferred to the sole supervision of the provincial minister who would be allocated a special supervisory manager. Nikolai agreed with Kisiliyov's proposal and signed it on 28 October 1938.

The provincial minister of Novorossiya, Vorontzov, was not very enthusiastic to receive the total responsibility for the Jewish settlement. He interpreted the instructions according to his own will and placed the whole responsibility on the shoulders of the head manager who resided in Nahar-Tov. For himself, he assigned the role of a superior consultant or an intermediary between the government and the head manager he would appoint. Based on that, Vorontzov nominated the deputy *polkovnik* [(administrative or) military rank, equivalent to a colonel] Demidov to be the head manager responsible for the existing colonies,

*[Page 73]*

as well as for the execution of the new settlement project. General Yinzov, the head of the Supervising Committee of the Guidance Bureau who acquired substantial experience with the problems of the settlement and was dedicated to it, was now replaced by Demidov, an inexperienced and corrupt person.

The officialdom began the execution of the separation [between the authorities] according to the new instructions, and the process took a whole year. In the meantime, the flow of candidates for the Kherson settlement grew in size, particularly with the urge of the provincial ministers who, for various reasons, were sending Jews to settle. They pressured Petersburg and Vorontsov, to allocate government-covered travel expenses and expenses to establish the farms, for their own candidates. Meanwhile, 65 families from Minsk and 70 families from Podolia arrived in Kherson and settled on their own. This served as a precedent, and it was decided to cover expenses for travel provisions and budgets only for the "Siberians." The rest of the candidates received permission to settle on government lands, only if they covered their own expenses

## Torturous Journeys

Baron Peln[?], the provicial minister of the Courland province, began to organize transports of (Siberian) Jews from the regions of Lapland, Eastland, and Courland. He made sure that the transports would leave on time, divided them into groups of 50 families, and allocated wagons for them. An official escort accompanied every transport, whose role was to distribute the daily food allowance, determine locations for night stops, and keep the order. In addition, three soldiers accompanied every group to guard the safety of the people and the food money held by the escort official.

Baron Peln [?] organized seven groups totaling 345 families (2552) people who set out, one after the other, starting at the end of August and September. The progress was slow. The autumn days were rainy, and the roads were muddy. The cold intensified during the night. Walking in the sloppy mud made the people tired. The wagons mainly served for transporting baggage and children. The autumn rains soaked the travelers. Four groups from Minsk and three from Bobruisk were sent to sail on the Dnieper to Kremenchug, through open and flat prairies to shorten the way. The river voyage on the crowded barges, in horrible sanitary conditions and with meager and dry food, weakened the people and caused diseases.

In Kremenchug, the wanderers paused for a month. The officialdom in Kherson was nominated to handle the food allocation in Kremenchug and from there to the settlement, and they were not in a hurry to release the money. In the meantime, the people were worn out, with foot injuries, and lacking proper clothing. Thus, moving on was very difficult for them physically.

The military physician Schindler notified the provincial minister of Kharkov [Kharkiv], Prince Dolgorukov (who was previously the provincial minister of Vilnius and was among the settlement supporters), that out of the 610 people who first arrived

*[Page 74]*

in Kremenchug, 173 people fell sick with dysentery, cold, and high fever. He added that these diseases were the result of poor nutrition during the long voyage and the crowdedness on the flat barges. Dolgorukov also notified the provincial minister of Poltava, Geseh, who was staying in Kremenchug at the time, and asked him to raise resources to ease, as much as possible, the life of the wandering Jews. Geseh found that 215 sick people were housed in a public building "under conditions of congestion, mold and stifling air were ill with infectious diseases, without medical treatment." Geseh immediately organized a few high-ranking people (such as the chairman of the regional nobility, the police commander, the mayor, and four physicians) and formed a public committee to mobilize the resources and the rapid assistance needed to improve the situation of these Jews. The committee, which Geseh chaired, mobilized the committee members who were physicians, to examine the sick, sort out the healthy and house them separately, move the sick to the "*Hekdesh*" (disabled and senior citizens house), sort the sick according to their diseases and heal them with the help of the institution's physician. They also took care of organizing a kitchen out of the government daily allowance of 25 *kopeks,* where meals ordered by the physicians would be prepared; they also took care of adding mattresses due to the lack of beds, changing the bedding as needed, providing the sick with appropriate medicines, and sending the sick, after they have recovered, to the settlement region in Kherson equipped with clothing and goods from contributions collected from Christians and Jews. They arranged to lodge the babies, who were separated from their sick parents, at a special care center for children and managed to find, among the Jews, governesses, and nursing women for the babies. The residents, Jews and Christians alike, responded to the call of the committee and contributed food, goods, and cash. About a thousand Rubles were collected. Many sick people were rescued thanks to the speedy action by the committee.

As the committee was taking care of the first convoys, a new convoy comprising 250 people arrived in Kremenchug. Its people also made their way on the Dnieper, on flat barges, and diseases caused havoc among them as well.

The provincial minister notified Kisliyov about the tortures experienced by the traveling Jews who stayed in Kremenchug. With the approval of the finance minister, Kisliyov instructed the provincial authorities to purchase warm clothing and shoes for the travelers at the government's expense, allocate budgets for provisions, and send the travelers to Kherson. In parallel, he instructed all provincial ministers to organize or send convoys of settlers to Kherson only during the spring months.

We learn about the extent of the suffering of Courland Jews from Backendorf's letter to Kisliyov, who received news from his agents as the police minister. The letter was written after the Jews arrived at the settlement location in Kherson, and its content was as follows:

"Courland's Jews suffered from the cruel treatment of their escorts and their officers. When they arrived in Kherson, they did not receive the bread they were promised, nor did they receive oxen and mules, sponsorship, or care by the local authority (meaning the colonies' management – Tz. L). Many lost their lives because of exhaustion from the long journey. They died from hunger and were busy every day burying their dead. This gloomy news cast fear, and spread resentment among Courland's Jews

*[Page 75]*

who stayed behind; it was doubtful whether many would be found in the future who would want to settle." To support his claims, Backendorf attached copies of letters sent by his agents and representatives.

Similar information has obviously also reached Vorontzov, the minister of Novorossiya's provinces. He received an order from Czar Nikolai to "investigate this matter rigorously." Following his investigation, he found it necessary to bring some proposals aimed at improving the efficiency of the transporting convoys. He suggested that one official should accompany the transport without any replacement throughout the entire journey. He proposed to instruct before the convoy's departure the municipal authorities in cities where the convoy was planned to pass through that they would need to help them with provisions, lodging, and medical treatment. He further suggested to plan the journey by choosing the shortest route. New instructions were issued based on these proposals, however, in the meantime, the state of the people arriving in Kherson after a long torturous journey was horrible.

Backendorf's letter had an effect. Kisliyov instructed Vorontzov to provide medical assistance and any other assistance to the newcomers who suffered from malnutrition, lack of clothing, and disease. Vorontzov established a new special committee headed by Demidov, the manager responsible for the settlement of the

Jews, and instructed him to take care of the new settlers. Through the intensive handling of the committee and the dedication of the physicians, the rampage of the disease weakened. The sick continued to recover, and the regime's conscience calmed down.

## Criticism and the Review of the Complaints

Ozshigov, the Police Chief in the Kherson province, dispatched a review of the state of the Jews in the province to Police Minister Backendorf. In his letter, after mentioning the sloppiness of the Jews in agricultural work, he moved to describe the state of the new settlers. "More than 500 families live in horrible crowdedness, in the small houses of the established farmers, about 20 people to a house, exhausted from the long journey, from insufficient nutrition and lack of warm clothing. Unaccustomed to the climate and the local drinking water, they were infected with diseases. Because of the negligence of responsible officials, the diseases gained epidemic proportions, threatening to spread among the neighboring population if not for the assertive action by the Committee established by Vorontzov. Due to the actions by that committee, the epidemic stopped spreading, the state of the sick improved, and they are recovering."

That description in itself was not a shocking discovery. However, in the remainder of the letter, Ozshigov describes the behavior of the management responsible for the settlement of the Jews and their mistakes. He mentions the delays in the construction of the houses and procurement of the equipment, even though the management had allocated funds. In his opinion, the responsibility for the transportation of the construction materials should not have been laid on the established Jewish farmers, who were busy with fieldwork from the beginning of spring through the end of fall. He also thought that a more rigorous supervision of the behavior of the colonies' inspectors should have been imposed. As an example, he noted that Inspector Krivesky was unfit for his role and was not trustworthy. The negligence of the officialdom has a negative effect

[Page 76]

on the settlers. For example, it was very well known that some of the wealthy colonists returned to their previous localities because of the bad attitude, disorder, and delays in the establishment of the colonies. "Wouldn't it be better to prepare everything needed before the arrival of the settlers?" asked Ozshigov.

This harsh criticism from the police authority was not sympathetically received by the authorities. After Backendorf's review was submitted to the Czar, the latter turned to Kisliyov with a demand to investigate the nature of the accusations. Kisliyov sent Vorontzov questions and instructions immediately.

All of these problems wore Kisliyov up so much that he decided to withdraw himself, if only temporarily, from the police criticism and from all the worries associated with the Jews. This time, he submitted a request to the Council of Ministers as well as to the Czar himself, to transfer all the settlement issues back to the interior minister, and his request was approved on 25 March 1841.

Vorontzov, as the person ultimately responsible for the actions of the special management overseeing the Jewish settlement, felt insulted by the harsh criticism and decided to withdraw, even only temporarily, from the responsibility that this role entailed. He demanded from the authorities in Petersburg to transfer this role to another institution, whichever it may be, and based his request on the claim that he himself and his staff are overloaded with work.

Kisliyov responded to this demand and wrote that he appreciated Vorontzov's feelings and understood him. However, with that, he asked him to continue temporarily in this role until things settled down. According to the Czar's demands and Kisliyov's instructions, Vorontzov initiated an extensive investigation into the torturous journeys. The Jews who were investigated stated that they were not equipped with wagons in sufficient numbers, so even the weak people were forced to walk. They claimed that they did not receive the daily allocation of food for the days added to the journey over the planned number of days allotted originally for the journey. During the four-day voyage on the Dnieper, they were beaten by the barges' workers with sticks and poles, and the escorts did not protect them. The officials who accompanied them treated them harshly as well and forced them to walk at night. This extra effort affected badly the health of pregnant women and babies. The escorting officials also raised their hands and hit people, causing severe injuries in some cases.

To investigate the officials who accompanied the convoy about the truth in these claims, Vorontzov turned to the provincial ministers where these escorts worked and resided with the request to conduct an investigation. The provincial ministers who handled the dispatching of the Jews' convoys to Kherson looked at this request as an insult, as if they themselves were blamed for not doing enough to ensure the success of the journeys of the convoys and responded in writing in length. Some provided proof that their arrangements were according to the instructions and that their actions were impeccable, others blamed the Jews for all the mishaps that happened to them. According to the ministers, the Jews sinned by disrespect towards the officials and by not obeying them. The Jews were to blame for prolonging the journey above the plan because they stopped in some places on their own, and for that reason, they were not entitled to the daily allocation of food for these extra days. The wagons that were provided to the Jews would have been sufficient if not for the unnecessary belongings the travelers carried with them,

*[Page 77]*

such as big copper pots, pales, and unnecessary wooden boxes. According to the responding ministers, there were strong and healthy people among the Jews who sat in the wagons because they were lazy, whereas, according to the regulations, every wagon was intended to carry 12 babies or 25 sick people. Regarding the voyage on the Dnieper, which caused much suffering for the travelers, the ministers explained that this voyage was unavoidable because the Jews themselves agreed to it and it eliminated the need for forcing the farmers in each area to make their wagons available for use by the travelers, as was the custom (It was the farmers' duty in each region, to provide the needed wagons for any official convoy such as transports of military, prisoners etc.). In addition, the officials at each stop were freed from handling the Jews during the voyage. Rest stops and other unnecessary stops caused by rains and mud on land were also prevented, and while on the river, Jews could not desert the convoy. It also prevented the possibility of unwelcomed wanderers, rovers, and criminals from among their faith joining them along the way. The local regimes were freed from the worry about lodging during night stops. Minsk Provincial Minister added the need to punish and bring to trial any person who was unruly during the journey, or who insulted the escort, complained, or lied.

Vorontzov decided to terminate the affair of complaints and blame by the Jews and explanations by the provincial ministers, and with that, the investigation ended.

## The Continuance of the Settlement

According to a compilation of lists (not very accurate ones), close to 2200 families were supposed to arrive in Kherson during the years 1840–41, of which the expenses of 730 were covered by the government (353 from Courland, 33 from Mogilev, 79 from Vitebsk, 102 from Minsk and 163 from Polden

[Ulyanovsk]). The rest of the families stated they would finance the settlement on their own. As mentioned above, 43 families were sent to Kherson from Siberia as early as 1838. 160 families sneaked into Kherson from various provinces.

The flaws in the organization of the settlement were never corrected. This time too, the responsible management, headed by Demidov, continued with its "tradition," and did not make the necessary preparations ahead of the arrival of the new settlers.

Even after the torturous journeys, the sufferings of the travelers continued in Kherson itself. Despite the specific instructions to construct the residential houses before the arrival of the settlers, this was not done. The new settlers were lodged in the houses of the established settlers, resulting in horrible crowding within the small farmers' houses. In addition to the house residents, who numbered 15 people on average, new people came in, some of them were sick with typhus and dysentery, skin diseases, and wounds that also infected the established healthy residents. There was a danger that the diseases would spread outside of

*[Page 78]*

the Jewish colonies. Five physicians had to be called from the larger cities with paramedics and medications. Only thanks to their effort, the epidemics subsided toward the summer. From 1 November 1840 until 1 May 1841, 256 people died from the new settlers and 292 from the established settlers. Altogether, 548 people died.

It was noted in the official bulletin – "This number was beyond the number of people who died on the way to Kherson."

Even after the new settlers recovered from their diseases, they did not receive sufficient nourishment, proper sanitary conditions, and comfortable housing to ensure complete recovery. In addition, despair and depression spread among them. Even the state of the established settlers was not very encouraging. They hardly made a living from agriculture. The ability to supplement their earning in the nearby cities was limited (according to the new regulations, the permits for going to the cities were limited to one or two months a year). The savings of people who settled on their own were exhausted, and no money left to establish and sustain a farm. Those who had any money left in their pockets ran away. Some new settlers returned to their native localities, and some wandered to the cities of Kherson province. It is difficult to determine how many remained out of the approximately 2000 families of the convoys. Even the authorities did not have accurate numbers because many Jews wandered back and forth between the cities and the colonies.

This tragic state woke the authorities in Petersburg and Kherson to hurry up and build the houses, allocate the areas, procure the equipment, and settle the remaining candidates. It is worthwhile to note that some farms were abandoned and remained ownerless. The abandoned houses constructed from clay crumbled and were ruined without their owners' care. The management built 138 new houses in the abandoned farms located in the established colonies. Four new colonies were established in which 493 houses were built: in Lvov [Lviv], 419 houses, in Berislav, 92, in Romanovka 132, and in Poltavska 150. Altogether, 631 houses were constructed. 684 families were placed in these houses and some additional houses remained undamaged on abandoned farms toward 1842.

Novorossiya's Minister - Vorontzov, who must have felt remorse about what happened as a result of the lack of preparations and disorder, demanded from the authorities in Petersburg to provide him with a higher budget - amounting to 600 Rubles per family. He also demanded a budget for those families who signed an explicit commitment to settle on their own. The government showed mercy and responded positively to his requests.

Toward 1842 it seemed that the authorities arrived at the state of tranquility. However, this was make-believe tranquility. Police Minister Backendorf became angry with them again. His agents provided him with detailed information about the corrupt accounts of Demidov, the manager responsible for the Jewish settlement:

a.  When Demidov purchased wheat seeds for sowing and supply, he debited the settlers 15 Rubles per a certain measure of the seeds instead of the 9 Rubles he paid for them.

*[Page 79]*

b.  A budget of 15 Rubles per wagon was allocated for procuring wagons, while the actual price paid for the wagons was 6-7 Rubles.
c.  In addition, Demidov imposed on the colonies a tax of 1000 Rubles per year for special expenses.

The difference between the sums that Demidov received for the needs of the settlement (205,000 Rubles) and the sums he actually spent (172,500 Rubles) amounted to about 32,500 Rubles, which he took for himself.

Backendorf ended his notice with a vigorous request for a thorough investigation by an honest and fair person, otherwise, all the goodwill on the part of the government would not achieve its purpose.

For the purpose of the review and investigation, a senior official by the name of Chirkovitz was nominated. The investigation, most probably, confirmed all the suspicions of embezzlement, as Demidov was fired from his job after the results of the investigation were submitted. He submitted an appeal in which he tried to prove that the complaints by the Jews were false accusations and that the Jews hated him because of the severe legal methods he used. He stated that he succeeded in settling about 700 families in Kherson and that the houses were built well. In this appeal, he asked to clear his name from any accusation and return to him the good name of an honorable officer.

Instead of fulfilling his request via an administrative routine procedure, his file was submitted to the court, which transferred it to the Penal Bureau and from there to the Senate. The case lasted for a few years, but we do not know whether or not he was punished.

## The Jewish Public and the Settlement

The return to working the land, the occupation of our ancestors in the old days, did not arouse excessive enthusiasm among the nation's masses and not even among the rising class of the "Jewish aristocracy" that started to capture important positions in the state as industrialists, military contractors, and people with free professions. Neither the learned rabbinical establishment nor the Hassidic movement with its *admors* ["admo"r" is the acronym of *"Adoneinu Morenu ve'Rabenu* [our Master, Teacher, and Rabbi," a Hassidic honorific title for a rabbinical leader] and preachers identified with the Jews who went to settle in the Kherson prairies. Diaspora life and the urban occupation as business intermediaries have uprooted from the Jewish heart the love for nature and agriculture. The pioneers who marched along the new road were only a few and were isolated. In fact, the first settlers, at the beginning of the century, were forced into this because of the expulsions from the villages after the destruction of their livelihood, and later on, during the days of Nikolai the First, because of the fear of assimilation of their sons who were in danger of being recruited to the army for 25 years.

There is no doubt that a few people were repulsed, sincerely and through clear intent, by the occupation of peddling or tavern ownership. However, without the assistance and charity of the nation's leaders and its spiritual principles,

*[Page 80]*

and before the days of the Enlightenment Movement and without a strong public and spiritual leadership in Russia, there was little attraction and debate, either verbal or in writing, on the benefits of working the land. One of the exceptions was Neta Notkin, who was both active himself and was driving others to the issue at the beginning of the century when his influence was felt among government notables and heads of communities. However, he was not fortunate to see the start of the settlement in Kherson. Even the preaching of the founder of the *Chabad* Movement, Rabbi Shneur Zalman [Schneersohn], about working the land and making *Aliyah* [immigration] to *Eretz* Israel - was an exceptional phenomenon in the Hasidic Movement. [His son] the *Admor* Rabbi Dov-Ber [Schneersohn], the "Middle *Rebbe*" of Chabad, also involved himself in encouraging settling among his followers, who were among the settlers who arrived in Kherson in the second wave. The same is true for [his son-in-law, the third "Chabad Rebbe"], Rabbi Menakhem-Medel [Schneersohn], also nicknamed *"Tzemach Tzedek"* ["a Plant of Justice"], some of whose followers established an agricultural colony in Shchedrin in 1842. However, these were few and scarce. Those who held power in the communities and the "respectable" people within the Jewish public looked at the Jewish farmer disdainfully. Most of the Jewish public leaders scorned those who turned to agriculture, who were mostly from among the poor, and who were exempt by law from paying taxes and serving in the army. The "beautiful souls" and the *"gvirim"* [Jewish landowners and rich business people] considered them as dodgers who escaped from sharing the burden imposed on the public...

Only upon the rise of the Enlightenment in Russia, the voice of the pioneers could be heard, praising the value of manual work and particularly the value of working the land.

The first among the *maskilim* [enlightened] who favored the return of the Jews to agriculture was Rabbi [Yitzkhak]-Ber Levinson (the RIBAL). As one of the first enlightened at the beginning of the 19th century, he did not win much sympathy among religious circles and among the class of homeowners who considered him as someone who defies tradition, an agitator, and an instigator. His book "Teuda be'Israel" ["Jewish Testimony"] was written in Hebrew and was published with a small number of prints, thus most of the Jewish masses did not know about it or read it. However, within the narrow circles of the enlightened, the views of the RIBAL had a tremendous effect. In the city of his residence, Kremenetz, where he was confined to his sickbed for many years, 34 families organized themselves and expressed their wishes to abandon their commerce businesses and transfer to become workers of the land. It is logical to assume that this awakening movement was a result of his influence.

As an author of fame, RIBAL represented this organization in negotiating with the government. He turned, in a long letter, to the interior minister, in which he emphasized the importance of the return of the Jews to working the land and asked the minister to allocate a land area for these families. Following this exchange of letters, questions, and clarifications about the duty for compulsory service, the interior minister suggested that the organization establish a colony, however, he stated that no budget allocation would be given for that purpose.

The plan probably did not materialize. It may be that some individuals from among that group turned to work the land in a later period when the permission to settle on lands within the "Pale of Settlement" was awarded.

Benyamin Mendelstam who was an author and a journalist, was also enthusiastic about Jewish settlement on the land and considered it a turning point on the way to economic and cultural recuperation of the nation.

*[Page 81]*

He was furious about the fact that the settlement did not make inroads and did not find encouragement among the Jewish public. Against it, he believed in the goodwill of the Russian government's goal of converting the Jews to become workers of the land.

In his book "Khazon la'Moed" ["Vision for the Future"], he expressed his anger and wrote:" It is only our fault for not encouraging the growth in the number of craftsmen, artisans and principally farmers...Didn't the charitable Czar announce in a fatherly manner: "Come and live among us?," and here we are not following other nations in advancing towards the enlightenment, art, and agriculture."

Mendelstam's book, like RIBAL's book, was not widely spread, and his preaching views hardly reached the masses. However, among the enlightened, his views made a strong impression. Under his influence, several youths, sons of rich merchants turned to Vorontzov, the Minister for Novorossiya, in 1840, with a proposal to establish an exemplary agricultural colony. They did not ask for government land, nor did they ask for financial assistance. They only asked for permission to purchase a land area in the province of Bessarabia with an area of 5000 *disiyatins* [about 13,500 acres]. Vorontzov replied that despite his approval of the idea, he was not able to find such a concentrated area available for sale, and the whole plan was subsequently canceled.

The news about the miserable state of the settlers in Kherson saddened Mendelstam, but he did not blame the government for that failure, but the lower-rank local officials who were given the responsibility for the implementation of the settlement. He poured his heart out in this spirit in a long letter to Minister Montefiori.

During the same years, a *maskil* [enlightened person], by the name Ya'akov Peres[?] authored a book by the name "Nachla Bli Meitzarim" ["Boundless Land"], in which he proved the advantages of working the land according to the Bible ("I am trying to prove, based on the holy writings and the national consciousness, that Jews must busy themselves in working the land...").

In 1842, 40 years after Notkin, H. Rosenthal, one of the *maskilim* among Vilna merchants, wrote a memorandum to the authorities in which he proposed the establishment of agricultural colonies and industrial development as solutions for the harsh economic state of the Jews. Minister Ovrov wrote on the margins of that memorandum a typical comment: "Rosenthal's view is a result of the Jewish deceit. Rosenthal does not understand the source of the problem. The Jewish issue would not be solved by the establishment of factories and agricultural colonies."

A different kind of awareness, with a unique character concerning the Jewish settlers, was found among the group of *maskilim* in Odesa. These enlightened people were natives of Galitzia and graduates of the Austro-German culture. This culture, its language and literature, notables, and manners were, in their eyes, the pinnacle of human achievements. Against that, the problem of the Jewish economy was not at the top of their worries. We could not find even a single document that could testify about their interest in the Jewish settlement process in Kherson, which was near Odesa, during its first three decades. However, when they heard that among the third wave of settlers arriving in Kherson, there were 450 families from Courland–they were awakened to help them. The province of Courland, which lies on the shores of the Baltic Sea,

*[Page 82]*

was, at one time, a long time ago, part of Germany. It was transferred to the hands of Poland in 1561. Even after the area came under Russian control, the German culture and language prevailed there.

Odesa's *maskilim*, who were natives of Galitzia, considered Courland Jews as "superior and more cultured human subjects. Even the letters the Courlan's Jews wrote to the Russian authorities were written in the German language. In their lifestyle, they were far removed from the zealot Jews of Lithuania and Podolia." According to the enlightened people of Odesa, it was not appropriate to settle the Courland Jews together with Jews from Lithuania, Podolia, and Vohlyn. One of the *maskilim*, a rich merchant, contributed 1000 Rubles for the establishment of Courland Jews in Kherson. Another *maskil* from the same group, Betzalel (Bezilius) Stern, who was a principal of a Jewish school in Odesa, and had connections with the authorities, turned to the government with a request to favor the Courland Jews. In his letter to the Novorossiya Minister, Vorontzov, he wrote:" Courland's Jews arriving in Kherson, differ from their brothers in the colonies, in their education, and by the fact that, unlike their fellow Jews, they do no hold ancient superstitions. They wish to become dedicated and diligent farmers, and therefore, justifiably, deserve special treatment from the government. They want to stay separate from the rest of the settlers to avoid potential unpleasant events that could erupt as a result of differences of opinion between them and the zealots. It is recommended, therefore, to settle them on lands that are more fertile and to aid them as much as possible. As they knew to read and write, they needed to have schools, which they asked to build in addition to a synagogue in every colony.

In the rest of his letter, Stern asked for an increased allocation for Courland Jews as compared to other settlers. He asked for 800 Rubles instead of the customary 600 Rubles.

Vorontzov agreed with the views expressed by "his Jewish *maskil*" and instructed to settle Courland Jews in separate colonies. However, since most of the more fertile lands were already occupied at that time, the fate of Courland Jews was to settle in worse areas, which lacked water, and they were forced to haul their water from far away in barrels or drill exceptionally deep wells. Towards the year 1841, the preparations were completed, and Courland Jews settled in four new colonies: Lvovo, Romanovka, Novo-Poltavka, and Novo-Beryslav.

## The New "Jewish Affairs Legislation"

At the beginning of the 1840s, it became clear to the authorities that the earlier "Jewish Legislations," although they were formulated carefully, needed review and updating. It seemed to the Czar and his advisors that those legislations, which aimed to speed up the assimilation of the Jews, had been unsuccessful because they were too generous and too "lenient." Therefore, the Czar nominated another special "Jewish Committee" assigned to coordinate and update the existing laws and add to them harshness and limitations.

*[Page 83]*

The new legislation was submitted for approval and was stamped with the royal seal of approval on 19 December 1844. That was when the last remnants of the Jewish community's autonomous powers were formally eliminated. The new order to "place the Jews in the cities and provinces under the authority of the general regime," eliminated the elected committees of the communities. However, the authorities were not interested in relieving any burdens such as those of the general and property taxes from the communities, as well as relieving them from the responsibility for the special army recruitment. Along with the order about the elimination of the communities' committees, a new law about a "meat tax" and a "candles tax," as well as other taxes, was published.

The "meat tax" had been collected by the communities' committees until the new law was issued and was used internally for the needs of the Jewish community but from that point forward, it was handed over to a leasing contractor who was called "*Ba'al Taxa*" [or loosely "the tax collector"]. The money from that tax was made available to the government via a special account. From this money, the government first covered anything owed from the quota of taxes on the Jewish communities. The rest was used as a resource for maintaining state schools for the Jews and for local charities. The "meat tax" also served as a resource for procuring equipment for the Jewish settlers, constructing their houses, purchasing oxen and mules, and agricultural tools. The people who leased the right to collect the "meat tax" (the "*taxa's*") were among the local wealthy people, and through their power, they ruled over the community in tyranny and exploited the poor.

Except for the meat tax every Jew would pay when buying meat, the "candles tax" was also introduced (on Shabbat candles). That tax was handed over to the education ministry for the financing of general education among the Jews.

In addition to the harsh regulations of the renewed legislation, the proposal about dividing all of the Russian Jews according to two types, or classes - "useful, and useless" was being considered. All the small shopkeepers and the poor belonged to the second type. The authors of the new legislation found it necessary to consult with and hear the opinion of the provincial ministers over this clause.

We do not know the answers provided by all of the provincial ministers; however, we do know about the response of Graf Vorontzov, the governor of Novorossiya, who came harshly against the proposal and called it "inhumane, impractical, and illogical from a national point-of-view." However, the proposal was not removed from the agenda. "The Jewish Committee" turned to it time and time again. However, because it was not desirable to implement all of the decrees, at the same time, it was decided to forward it again at a later time to the provincial ministers after a "rewrite."

Included in the new legislation was also a detailed framework of clauses dealing with the expansion of the Jewish settlement. Was it a human gesture, as it were, towards the Jews and towards the neighboring countries where liberal winds started to blow? Was it a consideration or a wish to thin out the Jewish populations in the cities, where cruel competition with the Christian merchants and craftsmen transpired? Or perhaps we can assume that there were a few, among the members of the "Jewish Committee," who genuinely wished to reach a rational solution for the problem out of a humane feeling. Undoubtedly,

*[Page 84]*

there were several factors, this time too that for different reasons and views have led to one positive solution - the expansion of the agricultural settlement of the Jews.

We do not know who the personalities were in that particular "Jewish Committee" and the extent of their hatred for the Jews. However, we can at least characterize one of them - General Kisliyov, who, as a person who was close to the Czar, was very influential in this committee, both as the Chairman and as the Minister of the State Assets that the Jewish settlement was within its responsibilities.

It is logical to assume that Kisliyov was not free of anti-Semitism; otherwise, he would not have been elected as Chair of that committee, as he was not one of the principal legislators of the Czar. Perhaps his negative attitude was not a result of racial hatred, but because he "only" hated the "unfavorable" attributes of the Jews who were "devious, and haters of physical labor and because of their occupations and ways of making a living that was harmful to the Christian population." He believed it was possible to purify their nature and ways of life and culture by having them work the land. During his service in the army, in the provinces of the "Pale of Settlement," he knew Jews very closely, and learned about their positive attributes: their diligence ("although mainly for their own business"), quick comprehension, sense of adaptation, and other positive traits. In his opinion, these attributes could make the "devious peddlers" into very diligent farmers, if not in the first generation, then at least in the second or third generation. This was probably where his positive attitude towards the expansion of the Jewish settlement found its expression in the clauses of the "New Legislation" that were formulated with greater tolerance and generosity.

The "New Legislation" provided every Jew, regardless of his previous occupation, the possibility to become an agriculturalist within all of the provinces where the Jews were allowed to reside. The government promised to allocate lands from its reserves in these provinces for the Jewish settlement.

As for the colonies in Kherson and the expansion of the [Jewish] settlement in Novorossiya, Kisliyov suggested to Nikolai the First to send there a high-ranking official from his office, whose role would be to study the state of the Jewish farmers and review the possibilities for additional settlement. That official would be required to submit a detailed review.

The Czar approved this proposal on January 25, 1845, and the Court Advisor Kartzev, a senior official for special roles, was nominated for that mission. We will not detail the written instructions that Kisliyov put in the authorization document for Kartzov's nomination. We also do not copy here the entire twenty - or thirty-page-long report. We will settle with only the details in which we have a specific interest.

Kartzev indicated that, towards the year 1845, about 1661 families (12,779 people) resided in 15 colonies; among them, 1495 owners of farms and 180 families who were waiting to settle and worked, in the meantime, in various jobs in the colonies or outside of them. Kartzev reviewed the religious and educational situation and stated that 19 synagogues and praying houses were built of stone. In the colony of Nahar-Tov, there was a school for teaching Russian. In all

*[Page 85]*

the colonies, private schools ("*Kheders*" [ Jewish elementary religious school for boys]) were founded, in which 533 students studied with 76 "Melameds" [Teachers of basic Jewish studies], mostly from among the local elderly. Almost all the Jews knew how to read and write in their own language, however, only 54 people knew how to read and write in Russian. He found 12 Rabbis in the colonies who exerted a substantial influence over the public.

Kartzev repeated the routine language about the fact that the Jews were greedy and that they would do anything for profit, cheating, fraud, and intrigues. Although he did not consider the Jews lazy, he stated that their activity "is not in the way of honesty," therefore, it is not a surprise that they do not adapt to the life of working the land. In addition, he stated that they have a "special tendency towards expressing grievances and complaining about everything."

Against all of that, Kartzev praised the Jews for their way of life within the patriarchal family's structure where Jewish children treat their parents respectfully and politely. He also stated that drunkenness is a rare occurrence among the Jews. He found one tavern in every colony (on average, about one tavern for every 913 people). He stated that the sales volumes in these taverns were much lower than in the Christian villages. During the year 1841, there were 44 criminals in all of the colonies.

We have a special interest in the list brought by Kartzev in his review, from which we can learn about the occupation of all the Jewish farmers before they settled. The list is as follows: sheet metal workers - 9, weavers - 2, tailors - 359, shoemakers - 144, hat makers - 35, painters - 24, blacksmiths - 11, stone masons - 75, copper artisans - 40, silver artisans - 11, scroll artisans -2, bookbinders -12, glaziers - 51, carpenters - 22, barrel craftsmen - 6 and other occupations - 37, altogether - 840 people. That means most of the settlers were not shopkeepers, peddlers, or bartenders, but artisans, who were laborers and people of toil.

Kartzev also tried to summarize the reasons for the failures in the agricultural settlement: The settlers were extremely poor in their native localities and suffered from a lack of energy and diligence. Their nutrition was meager, and their health was poor. They left their places of residence on their journey to Kherson in the fall. The winter descended on them during the journey, but they lacked warm clothing and shoes and did not have proper food. When they arrived at the place of settlement, they found a bare and arid prairie, where they were either housed temporarily, far from the final location of their settlement or forced to settle on their allotted land without proper housing for a long duration. The exhausted and despaired settlers were infected with infectious diseases that caused substantial mortality. It was only natural that they were attracted to commerce, which was the only feasible means of survival. It was an occupation they were knowledgeable about and familiar with. Some settlers sold the cattle they had received from the government and invested the money in their businesses.

*[Page 86]*

The houses built for the third wave of settlers during the years 1839 –1841 were also built about a year after the arrival of the people. The houses were built haphazardly, with insufficient amounts of construction materials. The overall manager, Demidov, also served as the housing construction contractor. Therefore, many houses looked like ruins. These factors have led, according to Kartzev, to the unavoidable result, and all the good intentions of the government did not materialize.

Khartzev found, that if the existing colonies would be satisfied with 9 *disiyatins* per male, there was a possibility of settling some several hundred families near them; he also indicated that there were government lands in the province of Tavria of about 33,000 *disiyatins* and an area of 28,000 *disiyatins* of black soil good for sowing in the province of Ekaterinoslav.

Contrary to the view that was customary until then, Kartzev proposed to establish colonies near Christian villages so that the Jews would be able to learn from them how to work the land. His opinion was that the Ukrainian farmers would not allow the Jews to cheat them, as they were witty themselves, not less than the Jews were and they treated the Jews with distrust.

Among the rest of his proposals was one that supported the expansion of the right to be absent from the colony for longer durations. The limitations on the exit licenses for a month or two did not allow the farmers to earn supplementary incomes, which were needed to sustain and improve their farms. However, he stated that it would be necessary to be strict about the farmers not being absent during the busy seasons.

## The settlement in Ekaterinoslav Province

Kislilov considered Kartzev's review an accurate analysis of the flaws of the settlement and the causes of the failures. He also liked Kartzev's improvement proposals. The budget proposed by Kartzev (175 rubles per family) was not too large, and the implementation of a new settlement effort could succeed if the construction, equipment, and organization were appropriately planned ahead of time. The government land in the province of Ekaterinoslav, mentioned by Kartzev in his review, consisted of black soil, which was good for wheat growing. That was how Kisliyov developed an interest in the establishment of some exemplary settlements during one year - the year 1846.

To guarantee the needed budget, Kisliyov turned to the interior ministry, which handled the "meat tax," which was collected from the Jews to support charity projects to finance the settlement. It was clearly emphasized in the "New Legislation," that the settlement needs would be financed from that Jewish tax. He investigated the financial possibilities for using the tax for the settlement during 1846. However, since the "meat tax" was just taken away from the communities and was reorganized (its collection was leased to "Ba'alei Taxa"), it was not clear whether the financial abilities were sufficiently secured. After some pressure, negotiations, and a positive hint from the Czar, a budget of 50 thousand rubles was allocated for the settlement in 1846. Through the negotiations, Kisliyov turned to the provincial

*[Page 87]*

ministers, requesting to find out whether there were candidates for settlement and how many were there. Here are the responses he received: From the Mohilev province - 83 families, from Vitebsk - 175, from Courland - 11, from Kovno - 41, from Kiev -14, altogether - 324 families. If the allocated budget of 50 thousand rubles was distributed according to 175 rubles per family, it would be possible to settle 285 families.

Kisliyov did not rely on issuing general instructions to a specific authority to implement the project and preferred to keep all the strings in his hands. He paid attention to every detail, consulted with experts, demanded rigor from the implementers, and instructed the head of Ekaterinoslav's Department of State Assets - Gladkii, to visit the colonies in Kherson and select the most beautiful design of the streets, parks, and public areas, as well as the best plan for houses. He also instructed to ensure a water supply on each parcel of land or to dig wells in areas not close to a stream or a lake.

He demanded from Gladkii immediately following his visit to Kherson to begin the construction of 285 houses that would be ready by the 1st of September 1846. He issued instructions to the provincial ministers to select the most suitable out of the registered candidates and gather them in the city of Mohilev no later than the 15th of May. That date was chosen so that the journey to Ekaterinoslav would take place during the summer months, and according to the plan, when the travelers arrived at their destination in September, they would be able to get into their new houses immediately upon arrival.

From his experience, he did not rely on the provincial officials, and selected one of his senior officials, Kulishov, a talented and experienced man, to manage this undertaking. He instructed Kulishov to divide the families into convoys (each convoy - 50 families) and select from among the Jews the most talented people to head the convoys. He instructed him to review the lists again, to select mainly families with at least 6 people, and to plan the journey route that bypassed the drought areas. He turned again to Gladkii to warn him that the houses must be ready on or ahead of the due date.

In the contract sent to Gladkii, Kisliyov emphasized the importance of the first experiment and asked him to send an agronomist to determine the cycle of seeds and find local reliable and diligent inspectors and guides from among the agriculturalists. It also hinted to Gladkii that his success would merit him the favor of the Czar. Kisliyov ended his note with these words: "I am sure you understand the importance of the activity you have been appointed for. I would be delighted with your success and would mention your good services to the Czar."

As mentioned above, the whole Jewish settlement sector was taken away from the Guardian Bureau of the settlers, headed by a Supervisory Committee. However, to ensure the success of the project, Kisliyov turned to Gaan, the head of the Supervisory Committee for all the German, Bulgarian, Greek, and Ukrainian settlers in Kherson and Ekaterinoslav and asked him to find from among the agriculturalists - preferably from among

*[Page 88]*

the Mennonites[3] - reliable and dedicated people who would agree to become inspectors over the Jewish settlers. Kisliyov promised that every local inspector would be allocated a parcel of land within the Jewish colony.

About a month later, Gaan submitted a memorandum to Kisliyov in which he expressed his views and proposals concerning the Jewish settlers. In his opinion, the Jews, who were detached from the land, did not receive proper treatment in the Kherson colonies. The Jewish farmer, unlike a Christian farmer, required a patient handling that would gradually endear working the land to him.

Gaan thought it would be beneficial to add to every Jewish colony a few German farmers who would serve as personal examples for the Jews and would teach the Jews rational cultivation methods. He believed that the Germans' influence would encourage the attraction of the Jews to farming.

In his memorandum, Gaan highly praised the Mennonites, particularly their countryman, Cornies, a talented and able man. He doubted that the Mennonites would agree to move to Jewish colonies as inspectors but promised to look into it. In his opinion, it would be good if Cornies could be appointed a head inspector of the Jewish colonies.

The construction of the houses did not progress at a suitable pace. Gladkii defended the delay by claiming that the wood he bought was located at 170 *parsas* [The author uses a Talmudic unit for a distance - about 487 miles. RM] away, and the transport was difficult because of the streams' flooding in the spring. He also claimed that due to a plague among the mules and oxen, it was difficult to find wagons for the transport. He also stated that he could not find a surveyor who could divide the plots where he had to construct the houses.

Kisliyov quickly provided Gladkii with a surveyor and agronomist who could determine how to divide the fields according to the cycle of the seeds. He demanded that Gladkii ask the civil engineer to cooperate in the construction of the houses. The instructions and demands by Kisliyov poured on Gladkii like rain, one after the other.

In the meantime, Kulishov began to organize the journey. According to the instructions, he was told to allocate 3.5 kopeks per person per day and an additional allocation for the poor. However, when he met the penniless crowd for the first time, he realized that he would need to provide everybody with the additional allocation. Based on his calculation, a sum of 11,670 rubles was needed to cover the additional allocation during the entire journey.

Except for the food, 20 wagons were needed for each convoy to haul the belongings and transport the babies, the sick, the elderly, and the exhausted. Kulishov leased 120 wagons

*[Page 89]*

for the duration of the journey for 3000 rubles. Altogether, he needed 14,653 rubles, while the budget was only 5000. He turned to Kisliyov and demanded an increase in the budget. He received an additional sum of 5000 rubles and was asked to get by with the money that had been provided.

The forests inspector, Tagaichinov, during one of the trips associated with his job, encountered a convoy of 11 families. He was surprised at the sight of the poor wanderers and wished to help them. In his note to Kisliyov, he wrote: being unaccustomed to walking long distances, many suffer from weakness in their legs. To transport 29 little children, two women with their babies and 6 pregnant women, they had only nine wagons, which were also loaded with belongings. Tagaichinov notified Kisliyov that he leased an additional three wagons to ease somewhat the suffering of the Jews in their hard journey.

Financial problems were also encountered during the construction of the houses. After an architect and engineer designed the houses, it turned out that it was impossible to build a house made of clay bricks for less than 125 rubles, while the allocation for the construction of a house was about 52.6 Rubles. Therefore, Kisliyov decided to provide Gladkii with 20 thousand rubles in addition to the 15 thousand he previously received.

Gladkii notified that together with the agronomist Gebel, he selected 16,500 *disiyatins* [about 45,550 acres] from areas in the Aleksandrov region for the purpose of Jewish settlement that would be divided among 8 settlements. He instructed a topographer to determine the suitable places for the colonies and the architect to choose the suitable places for the houses and the parks. In his notification, Gladkii was doubtful whether agricultural guides could be found among the Mennonites, who would have to agree to leave their estates and move to the Jewish colonies.

## Changes in Management – Yet Again

The convoys arrived at the settlement region in Ekaterinoslav one after the other. The construction of the houses has not been completed yet, therefore, the new arrivals were housed, in the meantime, in neighboring villages in various structures. Diseases that infected many of them during the journey have intensified and started to spread, and Gladkii expedited a physician and medicines for them. He went out to the settlement area himself, rented additional houses in the villages, and ordered to heat them up. However, the diseases spread and became an epidemic. The physicians determined that the diseases were the result of the grueling journey's hardships, the meager nutrition, shabby clothing, longing for their native lands, and change of climate and were principally caused by the cold that arrived early that year. As early as October, the number of sick reached 488 people, about a quarter of the new arrivals.

Despite the efforts by the authorities, 163 people out of the settlement's third wave became sick and died. Kisliyov was embarrassed and started to wonder whether Gladkii was the man who could implement that project and oversee it. He debated as to whether it wouldn't be

*[Page 90]*

logical to return the supervision over the Jewish settlement back to the Guardian Bureau headed by a Supervisory Committee with substantial experience in a settlement, led by a talented man such as Gaan, whose advice and guidance he decided to seek.

Gaan responded positively and submitted a list of suggestions. Among them, he emphasized that it would be desirable to add several German farmers to each of the Jewish colonies, such that they would serve as an example and model for the Jewish settlers, both in work as well as in establishing the farm and its organization.

As a manager for the Jewish colonies, he proposed Baron von Stempel, and until the settlers settled in their houses and fields, he proposed to spread them in the German colonies, where they would receive agricultural training and where the craftsmen among them could be occupied doing their crafts.

Kisliyov presented a detailed lecture for the Czar, in which he explained the need to place the Ekaterinoslav and Kherson colonies under the supervision of the Guardian Bureau as before. He hinted at the shortcomings in the current management of the colonies and repeated Gaan's proposals for improving the situation.

On the margin of Kisliyov's lecture, the Czar wrote one word: "implement" (5 November 1846). Based on that royal approval, Kisliyov turned to the Supervisory Committee with the announcement:

a. The Supervisory Committee must assume responsibility and supervision of the Kherson's Jewish colonies. The transfer from one authority to the other must be completed on January 1847.
b. A report about the state of these colonies must be submitted on the date mentioned above to Kisliyov and Provincial Minister Piodorov.
c. Starting 1st of January 1847, the colonies would be managed by the Supervisory Committee, whereas their annual balance would be prepared by the previous authority, namely the management headed by the provincial minister.
d. The Supervisory Committee must locate experienced and reliable German farmers who would agree to serve as agricultural supervisors and guides in the Jewish colonies.
e. The Supervisory Committee must talk to Gladkii, the head of the Ekaterinoslav's bureau of the state assets, and coordinate with him the date for the transfer of the affairs of the 285 settlers to the Supervisory Committee.

In the notification he sent to Piodorov, Kherson's Provincial Minister about the new arrangement, Kisliyov asked him to submit a detailed report about the shortcomings in the colonies and matters that require correction. Piodorov, actually wished to get rid of the troubles of handling the colonies but considered the notification an insult. Who else would be responsible for the shortcomings in the colonies besides the person who led the province? To clear himself, he responded at length and provided reasons on top of reasons explaining the current situation.

Gladkii also felt insulted by Kisliyov's notification and tried to hand over all the affairs to the Supervisory Committee as soon as possible. However, he was not in a hurry to hand over completed houses to the new authority. All the elements were interested in handing over the affairs

*[Page 91]*

of the Jewish settlement to the new authority. However, Gaan, the head of the Supervisory Committee, was not in a hurry to assume the responsibility for the new burden without thoroughly determining, upfront and in detail, the methods of operations, and before he could nominate inspectors and guides according to his own guidelines.

The change in authorities and the new arrangement resulted in tension in relationships between people of the various offices.

## Planning and Tight Supervision

Gaan, the head of the Supervisory Committee, burdened himself, for the time being, only with tasks that had not been started yet by others: cultivation of the land areas and sowing and other preparations concerning the equipment for the farms. He was wary of accepting the responsibility for continuing the construction of the houses that began under Gladkii's management.

In an investigation made by one of Gaan's people, it became clear that some of the houses were made of frozen timber, which was transported during a harsh freeze. When such timber is thawed within, the walls' material splits and crumbles the walls. Gaan also did not like the design of the houses. They were so low that tall people had to walk around the house bent over. They were also too narrow to provide sufficient air for the large Jewish families.

As mentioned above, the construction of the houses was not complete in the fall of 1846, as planned by Kisliyov. The houses were not completed even toward the winter of 1847. Only in 1848, the construction of 192 houses was completed by the previous authority, while the new authority completed the construction of 93 houses.

When 192 Gladkii's houses were completed, Gaan assembled an inspection committee out of the Mennonites he considered the most reliable to check the quality of the houses. The committee found that the houses were unstable, built too low, and provided insufficient breathing air. Gladkii apologized and proved that he only received 100 rubles per house and, therefore, adjusted the plan accordingly. He also stated that the delay was not his fault but a result of harsh conditions. There was no forest in the Ekaterinoslav area, and the trees for construction had to be brought over from a distance of 170 parsas and more. It was impossible to lease transport wagons during the summer months because the farmers were busy with the harvest, gathering, and threshing, and in the fall, when wagons became available, the cold came early, and by then, some of the imported woods were frozen. However, with all that, Gladkii stated that the houses were stable and would last.

Hearing about the dispute, Kisliyov sent one of the senior officials to investigate the quality of the houses. The official submitted a lukewarm review, stating that the houses are not so bad and that their stability would depend on the treatment they would receive from the future owners.

Baron Stempel, who was nominated as the manager of the Jewish colonies in Kherson and Ekaterinoslav, conducted a thorough investigation of the state of the colonies,

*[Page 92]*

he found that some tens of houses built by Demidov were crumbling and were not fit for residence. As it turned out, Manager Kondrentzov who followed Demidov, was also not an honest man. He also found that the current division of the fields makes cultivation more difficult. Some colonies were not built at the center of their fields but on the margins. The fields stretched along a narrow and long strip, as long as 45 kilometers. There was no hospital and even not a single clinic in all of the colonies. Gaan demanded that Kisliyov allocate a certain amount to fix the rickety houses and rebuild those that were completely destroyed. Following a long negotiation, a sum of 5000 rubles was approved for that purpose.

In consultation with the Mennonites, Gaan divided the land areas of the colonies in Kherson into sowed fields, pasture fields, and vegetable gardens. He set aside a quarter of the lands as a reserve. The colonies' farmers cultivated these fields, however, they were meant to serve, in the future, for special purposes. The advisors found that horses would be a better fit for the Jews, rather than oxen, even though the price of a horse was higher.

Gaan, who handled settlers from different nationalities and knew their attributes and nature, was great at learning about the character of the Jews. He understood well why their acclimation to this new occupation was more difficult, and why even when they were willing to take on working in the fields, they were always attracted to easier occupations, like butterflies to fire. He knew and understood that the main factors that drove them to settle, were the prior life of poverty and the compulsory service decree. Therefore, he thought that it was possible, using two methods, to educate the Jews to work the land and to make them like agriculture. First, it was necessary to provide them with good and comfortable conditions (a comfortable and spacious house, use of horses rather than oxen, sufficient equipment, division of fields according to the cycle of seeds, sufficient amounts of water, medical assistance, and minimal productivity to ensure elementary sustenance). However, with all of that, it was necessary, at least during the first few years, to implement a regime of harsh oversight, which meant prohibition on free movement in the neighboring cities and the duty to obey the guides and inspectors, using harsh punishment in cases of refusal and disobedience.

Gaan nominated farmers who excelled in agriculture from the German and Mennonite colonies as supervisors over the colonies. To bring in these guides, he asked for the help of Baron Stempel, who managed the colonies of all other nationalities and promised to award the guides, in addition to their salaries, with land plots, houses, etc.

In his instructions to the supervisors, he explained that the duty of every one of them was to train the [Jewish] farmers in all of the farm's categories, to conduct special lessons about agriculture, each in the colony assigned to him, to inspect every month the state of the inventories, and to submit a report about the work of each farmer. The punishments for farm offenses were listed in detail. For not executing the inspector's instruction, frivolous behavior towards property, or leaving the colony without a license - the offender would be punished with 30–40 floggings for the first offense.

*[Page 93]*

For the second offense - the punishment would be double the number of floggings. For the third offense - the punishment would be 3–6 months in jail. For a more severe offense, the offender would be handed over to the army, and if he was not physically able to serve in the army he would be sent to serve in a prisoner platoon for a period of 10–12 years.

To avoid arbitrary punishment, it was determined that the physical floggings for the first or second offenses would be imposed by the local official. However, only the highest authority would be able to impose jail time. Army recruitment or prisoner platoon punishments must be approved by the minister's office.

The harsh instructions instilled fear among the settlers. In official documents, it is mentioned that the Jews made exceptional efforts not to be punished. In one of the colonies, 15 of the 20 "negligent" farmers "were reformed" after the publication of the instructions and developed their flocks diligently.

At the end of 1848 and in 1849, the Jewish settlers settled on their land and entered their houses. In the province of Ekaterinoslav, 6 new colonies were founded: Novo-Zlatopol, Vesselaya, Krassnoselka, Mezhirich, Trudoliubovka, and Nechayevka.

***Author's Notes:***

1. The implementation of this clause would take place if the authority finds it necessary to do so and after the final approval by the highest Supervisory Committee–The Guardian Bureau.
2. Similar privileges were provided for people who lease lands, but the tax exemption was for five years rather than 25
3. The Mennonites were a Baptist [actually AnaBaptist or Re-Baptist] Christian sect founded in Zurich in 1523. Its members avoid taking an oath and therefore, refuse to serve in any public service. They avoid using a weapon and therefore, refuse to serve in the army. A similar sect was established in [Friesland, which is today in] Holland by the religion-reformer Mano Simons (1492–1559), after whom the sect is named. After his death, the sect expanded to several other countries, and its members were persecuted for their beliefs. Some immigrated to Russia, and several Mennonite colonies were established in Novorossiya.

[Page 95]

# D. The Settlement During the Reign of Alexander the Second

## Years of Calamities

Immediately after the colonies of Kherson and Ekaterinoslav were placed under the new authority of the Supervisory Committee, Gaan started to systematically concentrate on correcting some of the flaws to improve the situation in the settlement. The actual manager, Stempel, an experienced and dedicated administrator, consulted on all agricultural matters and farm management with the experts from among the Mennonites. He nominated some of them as inspectors in every colony, replacing the previous inspectors, who were mainly retired army people. Although the new inspectors were not completely untainted by anti-Semitism and rudeness, it was, nevertheless, a change for the better.

An improvement was felt in the state of the farms, which encouraged the settlers somewhat; however, following that, natural disasters occurred frequently, and according to official reports from those years, the colonies in Kherson suffered from human and farm animals' disease and epidemics. During 1848 alone, close to 6000 people fell sick with scurvy, fever, and other diseases, out of which about 1500 died. The hospital and the clinic that the settlers started to build, thanks to the generous contribution of the [Jewish] merchant Efrat from Odesa, were not yet completed during the epidemic season.

The drought year caused a sharp increase in the price of hay. It also resulted in a cattle plague, which almost destroyed the livestock sector. Most of the horses and the entire herd of sheep and goats died during the cattle plague. Only about a third of the cattle survived. The impoverishment in the colonies forced the government to instruct its officials to act mercifully and not to be strict about collecting taxes.

In addition to nature's perils, the regular failures occurred due to the errors and negligence of the officialdom. Stempel, who reviewed the state of the housing, determined that the chill and mold in the houses built during the days of Gladkii and were in the state of disintegration and collapse caused many of the diseases. He turned to the authorities with a request to fix the houses immediately or rebuild them. Kisliyov nominated again a new commissioner (senior official Strokov), to investigate and give his opinion. After the senior official confirmed Stempel's conclusions that the construction was

[Page 96]

negligent and faulty and improper materials were used. Another inspector, who was a civil road engineer, was sent to visit the colonies on the same issue. That engineer determined that the construction materials and their quality were not that bad, however, he stated that the fault was with the Jews who were not accustomed to maintaining their houses in order and cleanliness, and that was the reason for the disintegration of the houses…

However, at some point, the government was left without a choice, and it became clear that the houses had to be fixed. Kisliyov demanded that to save money in the construction and renovation budget, the farmers - the homeowners, would participate in the work.

Gaan insisted on the need to rebuild the houses constructed in the colonies during the days of Demidov; however, the matter was postponed due to the lack of hay needed for the firing of the clay bricks.

Among the people who arrived in Kherson three years prior, were several tens of families, natives of the province of Kovno. The Kovno Provincial Minister, who was responsible for the transport of the settlers to Kherson, demanded that the Supervisory Committee allocate land for them. The Supervisory Committee selected the 24 fittest families from among them and demanded an allocation from the government for their settlement. However, Kisliyov proposed to allocate the needed budget from the local revenues (leasing of the reserve areas, etc.) or to settle them gradually. In 1850, 26 houses were built in the colonies of Ekaterinoslav for the Kovno settlers, and they settled in their farms.

At the same time, two hundred families from Odesa requested to be allocated land. They claimed that they stopped in Odesa, on their way to settle in Kherson. Investigating the truth of their claim and finding the source location of each of these families required a substantial effort. However, as they committed to establishing the farms at their expense and were even ready to send 25 people to start the construction, and sowing, the Guardian Bureau tended to approve their request. However, due to the scurry disease, their arrival was delayed for some time.

## Islavin's Reports

A thorough description and more interesting information about the state of the settlements in those days were included in the letters and reviews of A. B Islavin, the personal secretary of Kisliyov. He described his impressions about his tour of the colonies. Upon his return following a tour that lasted a few months, he submitted a detailed report in which there were many repetitions of the reviews and proposals of his predecessors, but with some changes. He too, proposed tight oversight by the local inspectors and harsh punishments for the lazy and those who neglect their farms.

In his first letter to Kisliyov (from 13 June 1851), he elaborated ("without expanding due to the short visit") about the main reasons which led to the failures of the Jewish settlement. He listed the main reasons as follows: The indifference of the provincial authorities, from the most senior to the lowest in rank, procrastination in dealing with requests from people who turned to the bureaus, and in correspondence among the bureaus, the greediness of the officials, particularly among the lower ranked and the last of all, the poor quality of soil.

*[Page 97]*

This is what Islavin wrote:

"People who previously held a tailor's needle and mason chisel, who took on a plow, after dragging their feet from one office to another for four or five years waiting for government approval, exhausting their last pennies, got an allocation of 50 Rubles from the government and sometimes, did not receive even that. They were forced to settle on barren and poor soil, which, even after substantial efforts and the investments of a significant initial fortune, could not provide better harvests, even for an expert farmer. This was the source for the complaints of all settlers, some of whom abandoned their plots, and some left before receiving them. Now, there is only distrust and fear prevailing among the settlers.

Islavin proposed to allocate plots suitable for cultivation and to nominate guides and supervisors for the settlers and the candidates for settlement. He also issued proposals regarding the order and the regime within the colonies.

The criticism by Islavin about the provincial bureaus provoked resentment and responses from the bureaus. In addition to his general review, Islavin brought proof to support his criticism. He described the general phenomena of procrastination by the officials and the bureaus and pointed out many facts about the deprivation of the Jewish settlers even after they settled.

In mentioning the disorder in the construction of the housing, Islavin pointed out that, in most cases, the authorities did not lift a finger to perform a proper inspection. It was obvious that the faulty houses were also the result of the privation and poverty of the residents, however, the authorities could do something about it. As proof, he pointed to the actions of the head of the bureau in Bobruisk, Sologuv, who assisted in the construction of the houses and was very helpful and useful to the settlers. He hired the builders and inspected the quality of the work, offered wood at discounted prices, so each one of the 39 houses that he built, cost no more than 27 Rubles. Compared to the budget allocated for that purpose, it was a saving of 23 Rubles for each house. These savings could be used for procurement of other farm's needs.

The attitude of the neighbors, the Christian farmers, was depressing and unfavorable. The Jewish townspeople did not receive any guidance from them and only won laughter and mockery from their neighbors. These Christian neighbors blamed the Jews for receiving the land from the government and were sending their cattle to graze on Jewish fields. The local authorities never paid attention to the complaints by the Jews.

In colonies with a mixed population of Jews and Christians, tense relationships were formed. The Christians complained that the Jews were not careful in handling fires and about the fact that the Jews kept goats, which damaged the vegetable gardens.

Most of the Jewish colonies were fearful of visits by the regional police. The police would collect previously owed taxes from them, with the encouragement of the Jewish communities, and recruited their sons to the army even though, according to the legislation, they were exempt from both paying off previously owed taxes and from compulsory service from the day of their settlement. The authorities deliberately did not transfer them from the status of townspeople to the status of farmers.

*[Page 98]*

## The Problem of the Supervision in the Settlement

The main problem in the Jewish settlement was how to tie the Jews to working the land. This problem could have been solved, were the conditions appropriate for the settlers. However, despite all the goodwill by the settlers, things developed in such a way that the conditions could only make the Jews hate their new lives. The authorities wrongly thought that they could tie the Jews to the land by coercion and by a harsh regime, harsh regulations, inspection by officials, and ruthless punishments.

At the base of the government regulations about the Jewish settlement, there were three requirements, namely, that the Jewish farms be managed via dependence on self-labor; the settlers could be helped, at times of need, by hired labor, however, they could only hire help from among their people; the other requirement was that the settlers would be prohibited from working in commerce or in small craftsmanship for profit. The third requirement was that the settlers needed to develop a mixed farm, meaning not only cultivating crops but they should also rais cattle, growing vegetables, and planting orchards. These appropriate requirements, became, several decades later, the ideological base for the collective agricultural settlement in Israel. However, under the conditions of those days, these requirements were illogical and baseless, and the people who dictated these requirements upon the Jews were themselves owners of giant estates and masters of thousands of enslaved vassals. Even the liberals among them were far from holding views of social equality and respecting labor as a human value. The common Jews, who came to settle in Kherson and Ekaterinoslav lands looked for sources of sustenance and tranquility in their lives. They were not fortunate to find either, not at all. What power could have prevented the poor settlers from wandering back to town to earn some pennies so that they could buy some food for their children?

Indeed, even with the primitive cultivation methods practiced during those days, a diligent and organized farmer could have established a sound farm, paid his taxes, and lived a life without deprivation. The government hoped that the Jewish settlers would reach that level during the first six years after their settlement. However, many years passed, and most of the farms never progressed. The fields were sown or were somewhat cultivated, however, the cattle sector never developed, the vegetables were never grown, and fruit trees were never planted. The inspectors and visitors who were sent to inspect the situation as well as the local authorities, all indicated, even the most objective among them, that the conditions of the settlers were harsh but that the main factor was the human factor.

We cannot deny that there was a bit of truth in this criticism. Indeed, it was not easy for the Jews to free themselves from their old customs. Unlike the Christian settlers, who, in times of need and deprivation, could always look for work as agricultural laborers or in another physical labor type of work, the Jews only knew how to be occupied by doing "air business" such as peddling or salesmanship.

During the feudalist regime of those days, the officials "understood" that they needed to "uproot the Jewish characteristics" by establishing a harsh regime and strict supervision and by restricting the freedom of movement.

Gaan, as the head of the Supervisory Committee of the settlement in Novorossiya, was the first

[Page 99]

person who tried to manage the Jewish settlers by using constructive methods. Even though he, too, supported the government regulations, he nominated inspectors from among agriculturalists, and not administrative inspectors, to implement these instructions. The role of the inspectors was to guide the settlers in all of the farm categories, teach them order, help them procure tree seedlings, and guide them in handling the plants. He was diligent in seeing that the houses were constructed properly and they would be spacious and stylish in their appearance. He even took care of making sure to have ornamental gardens planted around them.

According to his proposal of 1858, 145 German farmers were settled within the Jewish colonies to serve as positive examples for the Jews.

As the years advanced, substantial progress occurred in some of the Jewish settlers' farms, particularly because of the effort of the second generation, which became accustomed to physical work. In every colony, some owners developed beautiful farms. Some farms developed the cattle sector, vegetables were grown, and trees were planted. However, some other farms were neglected, their owners suffered from deprivation, and they always tended to wander off to the cities where they could earn some income.

After visiting the settlement colonies himself, Islavin suggested dividing the settlers into four levels. He proposed awarding those who excel - rewards and benefits, thereby encouraging those whose situation was average, to rise and reach a higher level. For those who belonged to the lowest level, Islavin proposed to treat them harshly and escalate their punishments.

In the end, Islavin's original proposals, which were submitted to his patron and were also moved for discussion in other institutions (such as the "Jews' Committee" and the Council of Ministers), were not approved for some reason. However, they did generate interest. According to the proposals, the settlers who were considered as First Level farmers were those who owned established farms, and possessed all the required agricultural equipment, oxen, mules, or horses, and sufficient farm building. They cultivated their fields free of any pressure by the inspectors, their crops-growing fields covered at least 8 *disiyatin* [1 *disiyatin* = 2.7 acres], their vegetable garden was at least 1.5 *disiyatin* or larger, they were prepared for the winter by having sufficient amounts of hay and straw, their houses were in good repair and at least 15 trees were planted around them. Also, their behavior was good, they were obedient toward the local authority, they resided in the colony permanently, and when they left, they always returned on the date stated in their license and their taxes were paid off in an orderly manner. Second Level farmers were settlers whose farms were cultivated properly, but not to the extent and the range of those of the First Level farms. Their way of life and behavior were impeccable according to the criteria mentioned above. The Third Level included settlers who were honest in their behavior, obedient, and paying taxes, but their farms were not sufficiently developed; they cultivated less than half *disiyatin* of vegetables, did not own structures for their farm animals, and had no trees planted around their houses. The Fourth Level included people who did not own farm animals or agricultural equipment, their farms were neglected, their fields were cultivated neglectfully, and they lacked cleanliness and order. It also included people who were leaving the colony without permission or did not care to return on the stated date.

*[Page 100]*

Rude and insolent people who did not obey the local authority, or people who were late in paying their taxes and alike, were also included in their level.

According to Islavin's proposal, only farmers of the first two levels were allowed to be elected as the heads of a village or members of a village management team. People of the third level could only be elected to less important roles. On the other hand, people who belonged to the fourth level were not allowed to elect or be elected for any role. The first two levels were exempt from paying taxes on public pasturelands (first-degree farmers were exempt for 20 heads of cattle and 45 heads of sheep). The first and second-level farmers were allowed to hire paid (Jewish) laborers in times of need, something that was not allowed for the third-level farmers who had to cultivate their farms by themselves.

Theft, insolence, disobedience toward the authority officials, or leaving the colony and going to the city without a license, was punishable, on all levels, by jail, physical punishment, and reduction to a lower level. Fourth-level farmers were also punished for negligence in their work. For a first offense, the punishment was several days in the local jail or a physical punishment. On the third offense, if the farmer was late to return to the colony on the date stated in the license, his punishment was jail time for several months or enrolment into the army.

## About Rabbis and *Melameds*[1]

Islavin[2] thought that one basic reason for Jews' inability to acclimatize to agriculture was the zealous religious education that was being taught by the rabbis and the "m*elameds*." He thought that the religious leadership interpreted the Jewish laws after being exiled from their native land according to their convenience and usefulness to the leaders because of their greediness and desire for power. He was convinced that these interpretations were harmful, particularly towards the occupation of working the land. The holidays of Passover and Sukkot occur during the busy agricultural seasons. While in their native land, they would only celebrate four days of the holidays out of eight and would work during the "*Khol Hamoed*" [regular working days that fall during the 8-day holidays], and nowadays, they are idle even during *Khol Hamoed* days. Exactly during the season of preparing the fields for the winter crops, their holidays, including *Rosh Hashana*, *Yom Kippur*, and *Sukkot*, last for three weeks.

From that, Islavin concluded that the attitude of the Jews toward physical work and agriculture could be changed if the zealous rabbis were replaced by more generally educated rabbis who would educate their followers to love nature, work, and agriculture and would not confuse them with invalid and ancient superstitions. He thought that the children would benefit from replacing the zealous "*melameds*" with teachers with a general education who would educate the children in school using the state language and would widen the general curriculum.

*[Page 101]*

Islavin understood very well that his objective could not be achieved by an order from high up or by instituting a new regime by force. He understood that they should approach the solution of the problem carefully and with patience. The rabbis, with all of their bad influence, were very knowledgeable in the interpretations of the Torah and the Talmud, and the nation considered them as their spiritual leaders. Replacing them with young rabbis with general education could result in a negative response. Besides, there were insufficient numbers of rabbis among the graduates of the rabbinical and teacher colleges in Vilna and Zhytomyr[1]. There were also only a few generally educated youth who could serve as teachers in the schools.

Based on his belief in the power of change through education, Islavin proposed to award the rabbis with general education, graduates of the colleges in Zhytomyr and Vilna, land plots in addition to their salaries, where they could work in their free time, and also allow them to be helped by employing laborers form among the colony people. He also suggested exempting them from paying taxes for the first 10 years while their occupation in agriculture would serve as an example for the Jewish population, and in particular – the youth.

As mentioned above, Islavin did not wish to cause an immediate change through a revolution. He did not prohibit the *"melameds"* from continuing teaching using their old system. However, he did prohibit the studies in a *"kheder"* located at the house of the *"melameds."* He specifically emphasized that they needed to find a vacant house in each colony and dedicate it to teaching and education.

To establish uniformity in constructing schools and coordinate the supervision over them, Islavin suggested empowering the Supervisory Committee, which oversaw the settlement in Novorossiya, with that duty. However, to avoid misunderstanding between the supervising authority and the population, Islavin proposed nominating an enlightened and educated Jew for this purpose, who would serve as an advisor to the Supervisory Committee. The person who was proposed for that position was Herman-Bernard Gurovitz, the founder (in 1826) and the principal of the Jewish school in Odesa (He also founded a school in Uman in 1822).

Islavin objected to a "yeshiva" [Jewish religious high school] in the colony of Romanovka since it attracted Jewish youth from faraway cities. The existence of a "yeshiva" in an agricultural colony may, in his opinion, convert the agricultural village to a typical [Jewish] town in the "Pale of Settlement."

Islavin's proposals were submitted to the authorities in Petersburg for discussion and resolution.

During the spring of 1856, in his lecture in front of the new king - Alexander the Second, Graf Kisliyov emphasized that "various limitations prevent the assimilation of the Jews among the neighboring populate." Because of that lecture, the Czar[3] ordered (31 March 1856) to "review all the standing regulations concerning the Jews,

*[Page 102]*

to achieve the purpose of assimilation of this nation among the country settlements, as long as the moral state of the Jews makes them qualified for that purpose.

That view was the extension of the opinion that favored the assimilation and conversion of the Jews through the allocation of special rights and not through economic, physical, and spiritual servitude, as in the days of Nikolai the First.

The "Jewish Committee," which discussed the abovementioned proposals, concluded that most of the [Jewish] agricultural settlements in the western provinces – contained too few farmers. Every action in this area would encounter financial problems. Finding qualified teachers for the colonies was not a simple task, as the experience in establishing public schools for the Jewish population in the cities had shown. The "Jewish Committee" preferred to offer the Ministry of State Assets to consider, at least initially, to be content with establishing several schools in the colonies of Kherson and Ekaterinoslav, maintaining them through the "meat tax" account. As far as including religious studies as part of the curriculum or leaving this question up to the parents to decide, the "Jewish Committee" decided on the former, based on the experience acquired in public schools in the cities, which were not favored by the Jewish parents. The main reason for the failure of the state schools came from the fact that the Jews did not believe in foreign intervention in religious studies. That was why the local authorities decided to exclude religious studies from the general curriculum of public schools.

The Jewish Committee," also looked at the influence of the "*melameds*" as harmful but understood that as long as they do not have a replacement, they are necessary and that the termination of their work would be perceived as a prohibition of religious studies. Only after sufficient numbers of suitable rabbis and teachers were trained, it would be possible to proceed with removing the "*melameds*."

All of the conclusions by the "Jewish Committee" were approved by Alexander the Second on 4 May 1859.

***Author's Note:***

> \* During the 1840s, Education Minister Obarov established two seminars for rabbis and teachers in Vilnius and Zhytomyr. The supervisor of this school in Vilnius was von Gruber (a Christian) and the curriculum consultants were A.L. Mandelshtam and Prof. V. Levinsohn, a German subject. In Zhytomyr also, the management consisted of Jews and Christians, and the consultants were Jews.

***Translator's Notes:***

> 1. Religious Teachers
> 2. For consistency with prior changes.
> 3. For consistency with other articles.

When the settlement in the western provinces was discontinued by the Czar's decree towards the end of 1859, the attention was again directed towards the regions of the Jewish settlements in Kherson and Ekaterinoslav. About 80 thousand *disiyatins* were available for new settlers, where more than 2000 families could be settled. The areas were leased at the time, and the incomes from the lease were spent for the benefit of the existing settlement.

One of the first actions of [the new Minister of State Assets] Muravyov, like his predecessors, was to investigate the state of the existing colonies by sending a special envoy, Rudnitzki. This envoy also confirmed

*[Page 103]*

in his review, that "working the land may become a permanent occupation of the Jewish population, even though acclimatization with physical work and persistence with it required more effort than for people born as farmers. This was the result of customs that had been acquired for generations and the lack of character for fighting nature. The officials who handled the settlers, with all of their desire to fulfill their superiors' wishes, were not always vigilant or diligent in employing the means for doing their job."

"The Jews could not perform their agricultural work properly. Jewish farmers were perceived by their Christian neighbors with distrust, disdain, and ridicule. That weakened the self-confidence [of the Jewish settlers] and their ability to endure."

"The Jews who settled in proximity to cities (the intent here was the settlements in the western provinces), were placed in a continuous contest between the work requirements in their own farms and their customs and connections with their people. However, the people who settled in the prairie (Kherson), far from the cities, were in continuous fight with climate hardships, which were difficult to overcome even for people born to be farmers."

During 1858, a locust plague rampaged through most of the colonies, whereas in 1859, most of the pasture grass wilted from the lack of rain, and the cattle remained without food. The winter crop did not yield seeds and was harvested as straw. The spring sprouting was poor, making the economic situation of the settlers, who did not have sufficient seeds and savings from prior years, desperate.

"In places that lack ravines or streams, the farmers were forced to dig very deep wells, in some places up to 25 *sazhins* (about 50 meters), just to provide their needs of drinking water. Nobody talked about water for growing vegetables or planting trees."

"Many farmers leased and cultivated plots of their fellow villagers, in addition to their own land."

About one-third of Kherson's settlers, according to Rudnitzki, were owners of sound and established farms. About one-third were less established farms and the other third were poor, wandering, and miserable.

Rudnytsky also indicated that the appearance of some of the colonies (Sdeh Menukha HaGdola [Big Sdeh Menukha], Bobrovy-Kut, Novo-Berislav, and Novo-Kovna) was nicer than the Russian villages around them. He found there were ornamental gardens and trees around the houses there. However, some other colonies (Israelovka, Novo-Poltavka, and Lvov) made a poor impression: "The fields are laughable, as the cultivation work looked negligent. Only rarely were the adult settlers able to become dedicated farmers. However, those who came to the colonies as children or were born in the colonies worked diligently and smartly. Although they still did not rise to the level of the German farmers, they, however, were better than the Russian farmers.

*[Page 104]*

In Rudnitzki's opinion, it was advisable to continue with the settlement since the "Jews were able to be diligent farmers for their own sake and for the sake of the country. However, a suitable way for dividing the lands according to their types would be required. In addition, some additional privileges should be provided for the settlers."

The proposals were compiled and approved by Muravyov, with some additional comments and proposals by Gaan, who in the meantime, went up in rank and became a secret advisor and a member of the Council of the Ministry for the State Assets. The proposals dealt mostly with the implementation aspects. It was emphasized that the western provincial committees must be reminded they had to be mindful of the instructions concerning the dates of the departure, organization, and supply to the convoys transporting candidates to Kherson and Ekaterinoslav. They should also be reminded to be diligent when it comes to the selection of candidates.

He emphasized that the houses must be constructed and completed before the arrival of the settlers. It was proposed that discussions must be held with the interior ministry about increasing the allocation for housing from 100 to 150 rubles per house and constructing them according to the plans of the technical department.

The date by which the exemption from government taxes that Ekaterinoslav's farmers had enjoyed expired at the end of 1847. According to the personal tax tables, they had to pay 2872 rubles in 1857 and 4951 rubles in 1858, altogether 7823 rubles. The Supervisory Committee officials notified their superiors regarding the collection of the taxes that during the ten years of the exemption, the settlers experienced many hardships and were in a poor economic state, not better than at the start of their settlement. The officials indicated that the settlers would not be able to pay their taxes. They elaborated that 5 of the 10 years since settlement were years of drought and deprivation, and for 6 years, the settlers suffered from locusts. As a result, the harvest did not even return the seeds needed for the following year. During the year of 1848 730 heads of cattle died from a cattle plague, and during the years 1848, 1849, and 1853, 2584 people died from the rampage of the scurry and cholera diseases. They also stated that during the War of Crimea (1853–1855), the settlers fulfilled their civil duty and transported soldiers and military supplies in their wagons. The Supervisory Committee, therefore, requested to extend the tax exemption of the Jewish colonies of Ekaterinoslav for an additional period of five years.

Muravyov rejected the request of the Supervisory Committee and blamed the officials for their negligence in collecting the taxes since 1857 for two years. However, the Supervisory Committee insisted on its request and stated that it was possible to collect the taxes only by using coercion, meaning by selling some of the Jewish assets. There was no other way to do it. Muravyov brought the problem for discussion to the Council of Ministers, which decided to exempt the Jewish settlers from paying taxes until 1862. The resolution was approved by Alexander the Second on 26 January 1860.

[Page 105]

## Improvement and Stabilization

Rudnitzki divided the Jewish settlers into three types: One-third were established farmers, one-third were in a satisfactory condition and a third were in a failed condition. In considering the state of the Russian peasants, even 50 years later, we recall that they were retrograde, and most of the peasants had to sustain themselves by outside work in the cities. We can also recall similar situations, at the beginning of the 20th century in Romania, Poland, and Carpathian Ukraine. If we compare these situations to the state of the Jewish colonies, we find that two-thirds of the settlers were actually in a satisfactory situation, able to sustain themselves by cultivating the land. These Jews were doing this after only a single generation of working in the fields. This could be considered significant progress. It was also encouraging to see the fact that the second-generation youth were diligent and knowledgeable in the various farm categories.

It is worthwhile to note that during these years, after which the exemption from taxes ended, except for a few cases, the taxes were paid fully.

Four types of [annual] taxes that were imposed on the settlers:

a. Maintenance of roads, water, etc.…
    3.53 Rubles per person
b. Taxes for the needs of the Zemstvo [Elected regional government]
    60 kopecks per person and 1.5 kopecks for every *disiyatin*
c. Government debt payment
    1.42 Rubles per farm
d. Public needs of the village
    21 kopecks per person

These taxes amounted to about 30 Rubles per year for a family of six.

In the ten land areas where public forests were planted, about 11,693 forest trees and 25,530 olive trees were planted towards the year 1860,. There was also a vineyard, and 28,000 plants of forest trees, and berry trees in the nurseries. Overall, a total of about 30,000 fruit trees, berry trees, and ornament trees were planted in the gardens around the houses.

According to Gamm, the head of the Supervisory Committee in those days, "the colonies made a nice impression. The streets were straight and wide. There were quite nice houses on both sides, painted in white, and exceptionally clean. Farm buildings were located in the yards, including cowsheds, stables, barns, sheds for tools, and cellars. Some of the farmers excelled in the development of their farm, and some won prizes."

In Gamm's opinion, the Jewish settlers were influenced by the German farmers, particularly the Mennonites, who were placed in each colony to set an example for the Jews. The German farms were immersed in greenery, surrounded by vineyards and storage places full of food. These "exemplary farms" proved what could be done with diligence, knowledge, and goodwill.

The number of "exemplary German farms" reached 139 at the end of the 1850s

*[Page 106]*

among the Kherson colonies, and 60 "exemplary farms" among the Ekaterinoslav colonies, a total of 199 farms.

According to Gamm, some farmers were also involved with craft and commerce, however, their main occupation was agriculture. The farmers showed readiness to be introduced to more efficient cultivation methods and advanced tools.

Similar to the rest of the inspectors and the various visitors, Gamm was also of the opinion that "the Jews' morality was defective" and that they brought with them, from their previous locations and prior way of life, attributes of unruliness, stubbornness, cheating, gossip, and particularly the tendency for wandering around. However, on the other hand, he knew to pleasantly state that due to their transfer to the agricultural way of life, their morality improved. As a side comment, he continued to praise the honest way of life of the Jewish settlers and the fact that they avoided drinking and were not obsessed with sex and adultery.

Because of these attributes, Gamm expressed his confidence that the generation born in the colonies and the following generations would become natural farm workers, as long as "the "*melameds*" would not harm them with their invalid education."

We can learn, from some numbers provided in these reviews, about the way of life and the structure of the public management of the colonies in Kherson and Ekaterinoslav during the 1860s. It turned out that there were 83 orphans in the colonies and guardians nominated for them. The orphans' property (from their parents' farm) amounted to 7,745 Rubles. At that time, there were 176 disabled, mentally sick, and homeless people in the colonies for whose upkeep a special fund was established in 1854 via an internal tax that was imposed on every household. Towards 1860, there were six synagogues and 28 "*Batei Midrash*" [houses of learning and praying], where 14 rabbis served. In the Kherson colonies, 930 pupils studied in "*kheders*" taught by 94 *melameds*. Tuition costs the farmers about 7000 Rubles per year. In Ekaterinoslav colonies, 13 *melameds* taught, and 4 boys from the colonies studied in the agricultural school.

Besides the heads of the village called *Schultz's* [a word taken from the German settlers], 46 paid people worked on the internal management in various tasks.

Among the Jewish population in the colonies, which amounted to about 27 thousand people, 86 trials were held. Eight people were sentenced to serve time in jail, and 288 received administrative punishments for offenses such as negligence in farm work, disobedience, and leaving the colonies without a license:

| | |
|---|---|
| Cash fines | 181 people |
| Public work penalties | 49 people |
| Jail penalty for several days | 53 people |
| Flogging | 5 people |
| ------------------------------------------------------- | |
| **Total** | **288 people** |

[Page 107]

There were 14 taverns in the Kherson's colonies, one for every 654 people. In Ekaterinoslav, there were 13 taverns, or one for every 419 people.

The population towards 1861 was

| | | | |
|---|---|---|---|
| Kherson | 21 colonies | 1778 families | 16,932 people |
| Ekaterinoslav | 16 colonies | 864 families | 9,852 people |
| ---------------------------------------------------------------------------- | | | |
| **Total** | **37 colonies** | **2,642 families** | **26,784 people** |

Altogether, at the same time, there were 3829 horses and 9274 heads of cattle (including calves).

These seemingly dry facts and numbers give an idea about the way of life of this Jewish community of 27,000 people in 37 colonies cultivating close to a million and a quarter *dunam* [about 309,000 acres] of land. The community's internal life was managed by its elected people, its children were all studying Torah as well as reading and writing in Hebrew.

The settlers have not reached wealth as of yet. They were not even satisfying all of their needs. The drought and the locusts were still frequent guests. Some colonies suffered from a shortage of drinking water, and some failed farms could be found in every colony, not necessarily because of neglect. Over the years, several levels of material status have been formed among the settlers, resulting in some relationships of envy, hate,

Not every head of a colony ("*Schultz*") acted honestly, kindly, and with empathy towards his fellow farmers. There were, certainly some forceful *Schultze*s who encircled themselves with a group of yes-men, like in every other place in the world. The situation was far from ideal, however, it is clear that, at that point, the most difficult things were already behind the settlers.

## The Situation after the Peasants' Emancipation, during the 1860s

Upon the emancipation of the peasants in 1863, the Russian government turned to formulate regulations for an autonomous self-governing regime in the villages. Until then, all the land matters were included under the responsibility of the Ministry of the State Assets. From then onward, the handling of the improvement in the state of the farmers and modernization of their farms was transferred to the province's *Zemstvo* [local elected authority]. The local matters in every village would be managed by an elected village leader and the regional matters by an elected institution called *Volost*.

The writers of the regulations understood that they could not exclude the Jewish settlers from the new regime and its arrangements. The general regulations were approved only in 1866. In the meantime, as the regime was not strict about matters related to the internal management of the Russian farmers, they were also not strict about keeping the old regulations about the Jews (the prohibition of being involved in commerce or employing

*[Page 108]*

Christian workers, etc.) in the western provinces. However, that was not the case for the colonies of Kherson and Ekaterinoslav, which were under supervision since their establishment.

Based on the new order (from 22 October 1859) to discontinue the settlement in the western provinces and concentrate it in Kherson and Ekaterinoslav, the government turned to implement its decision in practice.

As mentioned earlier, 80 thousand *disiyatins* were available for the Jewish settlement in these two provinces. The Guidance Bureau was leasing these lands to the local farmers, and the incomes were used for the special needs of the Jewish colonies. These lands were big enough for the settling of about 200 families. The first candidates, some 200-300 families, arrived in Kherson and Ekaterinoslav several years prior, and they were spread, temporarily in the region while waiting to be settled. The officialdom did not know exactly where their places of residence were or whether they were still interested in settling. However, anybody who requested received a plot.

Based on their experience from prior years, the Guidance Bureau was strict about preventing the arrival of candidates before everything was ready to receive them, including housing, farm structures, etc. Because of a shortage of construction materials and workers, it was not possible to execute the settlement on a massive scale. The Guidance Bureau settled on settling 200–300 families per year.

From their experience, they also learned that tightening the fist on the allocation for the construction of houses and farm equipment caused the failures of the first settlers. Now everybody recognized that the allocation for the establishment of a new farm should not be less than 500 Rubles.

The budget for the Jewish settlement came from the "meat tax" account (that was collected from the Jews for Kosher slaughtering and was spent on the needs of Jews). These accounts were handled by the provincial authorities and were operating within the Jewish population of every province. Budget allocations from the "meat tax" for settlers were therefore available only for candidates from the same province. This arrangement caused problems because it required coordination with the provincial ministers where the settlers came from to confirm that it was possible to withdraw allocations from the "meat tax" account for the needs of the settlement.

The responses to these requests were sometimes elusive. Some officials responded that there was money available, but could not be withdrawn in large sums. Others responded that there were local needs and that all sums of money had already been budgeted for specific needs. Some provincial ministers doubted the whole issue of the settlement and hinted that in their view the failures were mostly because the Jews had no interest in agriculture.

Islavin, who, as mentioned earlier, had visited the colonies while serving as the secretary of Kisliyov in 1851, was asked again to visit the colonies, investigate and provide his opinion on the way by which the Jewish farmers should be incorporated under the new regulations. Islavin rose up in rank in the meantime. After serving

[Page 109]

for two years as the head of the Guidance Bureau, he became an advisor for the Ministry for the State Assets, and his opinion and proposals carried weight at that point.

During his visit current in 1865, about 15 years after his first visit, he was able to compare and determine the amount of progress and development. Islavin did find some progress, however, his impressions were mostly pessimistic. In one colony, he saw the same rickety houses he saw 15 years prior. Not everywhere, the planted trees took hold. Not in every colony, the taxes have been paid, and not all the gardens around the houses were attractive.

Rudintzki, as mentioned above, divided the settlers into three levels. Islavin agreed with him only regarding the settlers in Ekaterinoslav province. He stated that in Kherson, the number of failed farmers was about half of the settlers, rather than one-third. He blamed the lack of progress on the traditional education by the rabbis and "melameds." In this area, he did not find any change. The number of "melameds" increased, new "Batei Midrash" were built, and the "Yeshiva" in the colony of Romanovka was still operating and its influence seemed to him as harmful.

Islavin wanted to uproot the Jewish zealotry, which hinders progress." However, he did not believe this should be done by administrative means. He proposed again to mobilize some of the enlightened people from Odesa, particularly Gurevitz, who established there a Jewish school, had close relations with the authorities, and knew the colonies. He nominated him to formulate a suitable curriculum, select from among the "melameds," those who were qualified to fill the role of teachers, and then convert some of the Batei Midrash to general schools. He also asked him to find a way by which to convince the parents to send the girls to school.

Jewish Farmers in Russia Fields

After the new minister A.A. Zelenoi had read Islavin's review, he wrote on its margin: "…I believe that the whole enterprise was unsuccessful and faulty in its foundation. It could not be fixed administratively. It is doubtful if new Jewish colonies should be established and convert the Jews to become farmers through coercion. Only by continuous education and strict supervision, it would be possible to educate and improve their attributes and customs. However, because such supervision and tight handling are not possible, the only thing left to do is to develop the existing colonies and to hand them over, as well as all other villages, to the provincial authorities (the intent was probably to the *Zemstvo*. Tz. L). I would like to discuss this review in the special committee headed by the vice minister and to submit a recommendation."

According to Zelenoi's decision, a special committee was assembled to discuss this problem. The opinion of Minister Zelenoi, expressed in the margins of the review, reflects the change in the views and the mood at the beginning of Alexander the Second's reign. Liberalism was gradually evaporating, and conservatism showed its claws, especially concerning the Jews. The committee already operated under a restrictive atmosphere.

*[Page 110]*

The committee in which Islavin participated concluded and summarized that "the settlement enterprise was mainly external and formal (meaning that its existence did not come from the will of the Jews but from the government initiative). The weakening of the supervision in the western provinces made it easy for many settlers to fully or partially neglect agriculture.

The settlement in Kherson and Ekaterinoslav achieved, in the Committee's view, the desirable results, to a certain extent, because of the strict supervision imposed on them and the guidance by the Mennonites. A healthy core has developed, which could strengthen under comfortable conditions; however, this achievement paled in comparison with the substantial efforts and investments. The objective of easing the burden of the excess number of Jews within the Pale of Settlement has not been achieved.

The committee proposed to discontinue the settlement effort in the provinces of Kherson and Ekaterinoslav starting in 1867 and onward.

The committee proposed to take the following intermediate steps before the discontinuation:

a. Jews, who were taken out of their communities and had not yet arrived at their settlement locations, should stay where they were.

b. Concerning the Jews who arrived at the settlement location, had not settled, residing in the regional cities, and worked in various occupations, they would be given an extension to settle on their land until 1868. Otherwise, they would be returned to their previous locations.

c. Jews who were not approved for settlement and were residing temporarily in the colonies and working in agriculture would be approved to settle.

d. The opportunity provided to the settlers of the western provinces to leave the settlement before the expiration of the 25-year commitment would be extended to the farmers in the Kherson and Ekaterinoslav colonies.

e. The farmers who have abandoned their farms and reside outside of the colonies without the permission of the local authority – would be stripped of their status as farmers. Obviously, they would not be exempt from paying their taxes and debts to the government.

f. A colony would be permitted to expel any negligent, lazy, or disorderly settler and strip him of his rights to his land if the general assembly would decide to do so with a majority of two-thirds. The authorities should equip the expelled people with a passport for six months so that they can reregister in one of the communities. The vacated farm could be allocated to another candidate without awarding him with any special rights.

g.  The government-reserved land areas allocated for the Jewish settlement in Kherson and Ekaterinoslav have not been settled as of yet (the intent was to have the 80 thousand *disiyatins*) and would be returned to the government.

*[Page 111]*

We did not find anywhere in the archives any clear decision for the approval of the committee's proposal concerning the discontinuation of the settlement in Kherson and Ekaterinoslav. Perhaps such a proposal was approved without an accompanying publication. However, the fact was that the transfer of candidates from the western provinces to Kherson and Ekaterinoslav stopped, as every candidate required the allocation of 500 Rubles from the provincial "meat tax" accounts, and these amounts of money were not found in these accounts.

The Jewish settlement movement that started in Kherson at the beginning of the 19th century froze in 1866. Some supplement settlements were in farms vacant by the local residents or by the members of the second generation who married and inherited the estates of their parents. However, the settlement movement ceased. In the same year, there were 39 colonies in Kherson and Ekaterinoslav (see detailed statistics in Appendix C). Most of the farmers in these colonies were already acclimatized to the work in agriculture. The members of the second generation liked work. While some of the farmers were attracted to side occupations in craftsmanship or commerce, it did not take away from the agricultural character of the colonies, the fields of which were cultivated and contained herds of cattle, vegetable fields, and tree orchards. A village-characteristic atmosphere of physical work and simplicity was created in these colonies.

## Klaus's Report in 1870

Klaus was one of the senior officials in the Settlement Department in Novorossiya (Guardian Bureau). In 1870, he was nominated by the ministry to visit the colonies and submit a review to the authorities.

He noted that some of the settlers left the colonies temporarily – however, their number was not significant. He also emphasized that there was nothing wrong with the fact that a member of a large family, which diligently cultivates the farm, would go out and earn an additional income on the side. He too, like his predecessors, embraced the claim about "the bad influence" of the rabbis and the "*melameds*." However, his impressions were generally positive. The following are some statements from his review:

"…The Jewish farmers became convinced of the benefit that working the land brings, and they are working hard and diligently on the development of their farms."

"...Not only men are working in the fields, but also Jewish women, particularly members of the second generation."

In his opinion, one of the obstacles to the development of the villages was the shortage of water. "…Advanced settlement, even by expert farmers, depends on the abounded amount of water. Within the Jewish colonies, the shortage of water adversely affects the settlers. For example, the colony of Dobroye managed to receive water from a well dug by the members of the colony only as late as 1859. Even though pumping the water costs 1000 Rubles per year, the water is not always drinkable. In 1868, the colony dug a new well, however, its water was not good. The water shortage was amplified by the increase in population in the colony."

*[Page 112]*

"There are several wells in Novo-Poltavka, however, their water is bitter and salty and causes diseases. The issue of drinkable water became commercialized. The Christian farmers from the neighboring villages haul water to the colony before holidays and sell them in pales. There is good drinking water in nine of Ekaterinoslav's colonies. In the colony of Grafskoya, there was a well, however, its water was saturated with a bad mineral, and only the poor used it. However, the established farmers haul water in carts from the German colony Marienfeld."

"…In the colonies of Novo Zlatopol, Trudoliubovka, Nechayevka, there is no drinking water, and their farmers bring water from the neighboring Christian villages, from as far as 3–7 *parsas* [about 7.5–17.5 miles]."

"…in the colony of Vesselaya, the well water is good as long as it is fresh, however, it becomes bitter after standing in a barrel for some time."

"The colony of Krassnoselka uses two water reservoirs for watering the cattle, however, one of the reservoirs dries up in the summer."

Of all the inspectors who visited the colonies, Klaus was the first to thoroughly deal with this problem of water shortage and the first to propose some solutions.

While pointing at the factors for the lagging of the Jewish colonies, Klaus compared their conditions to the ones of the German and Bulgarian colonies: "The German and Bulgarian settlers are farmers from birth, and accustomed to agriculture. They received 50 or 60 *disiyatins* per family, regardless of the number of people in the family. Since they were expert farmers, they chose the best land areas for themselves. Only 30 *disiyatins* were allocated for the Jewish families. The bad land areas allocated to them were such that no other farmer would agree to cultivate them. The German and Bulgarian farmers were free to work in side jobs, in commerce or craftsmanship, while the Jews were prohibited from having any side occupation. The German and the Bulgarian farmers were able to receive additional land out of the land reserves. The Jews were prevented from doing that. The German and Bulgarian farmers were allowed to employ Christian farmers from neighboring villages, whereas the Jews were only allowed to employ Jewish workers, who were not usually occupied in fieldwork Jewish, and only during the busy season. Because of the regulation that stated that a family is suitable for settlement only if it contains three men who can work, two families were sometimes combined artificially to form a single-family unit, and they received only a single farm unit and a single residential house. This dual-family arrangement hindered the management of the farm, and the relationships between the Iilies were sometimes tense..."

Klaus also discovered that the population doubled in the German and Bulgarian colonies during a period of 25–30 years. However, in the Jewish colonies, the population had not only not increased but suffered a steep decrease.

*[Page 113]*

In 1870, there was no change in the number of settlers. The total number of families residing in the 39 Kherson and Ekaterinoslav colonies that year was 2788 families.

In his summary, Klaus noted that "the Jewish colonies consist of a community of real farmers. There are some farmers with quite established and advanced farms compared with many Russian farms."

The minister wrote on the margins of the review: " I thank Mr. Klaus for his successful completion of his task," and with that, the positive review was shelved in the archives…

In the years following Klaus's visit and review, many changes occurred in the life of the Russian villages and in Russian society as a whole. The government was forced to seriously discuss the regulations and the organization of its society according to the reality and the developments after the emancipation of the farmers. The new regulations were formulated initially according to a liberal spirit. A local self-management team was installed in every village. The farmers elected their own head of village. Every block of villages was included in a regional management named "Volost." An institution called "Zemstvo" was established in every judicial county, under the supervision of which all the agricultural and local matters of the villages were placed. The institution was responsible for issues such as roads, schools, hospitals, social institutions, and for some time also agricultural training and loaning banks. (For us not to consider that the Czarist regime allowed excess democracy, we need to note that the "Pristav" – the regional police commander"–had more influence and authority than the heads of the villages and that mostly estate owners were elected for the role of heads of the Zemstvos, at least during the initial period. Tz. L.).

There was a need to discuss the issue of handing over the government lands to the farmers for good and the whole legal system associated with that. As part of that discussion, the problem of how to integrate the Jewish colonies into this new system came about. Years passed since Klaus's review of 1870. Regulations were reworked. Ministers changed. Liberalism was diminishing and conservatism expanding, and with it, the hatred of the Jews. The Jewish settlement ceased to invoke the interest of highly ranked people in Petersburg, and based on the old regulations, many of the Jewish farmers were dislodged by the local officialdom because of "negligence," "laziness" and "unruliness." To integrate this creature called "Jewish Settlement" into the general regulation system, it was necessary to investigate its state and status. In 1880, Ivanschintzev was nominated for that role.

According to the numbers that were brought up in Ivanschintzev's review, only 1956 families were residing in all of the colonies, while according to Klaus's review, 10 years earlier, there were 2788 families in these colonies. We do not have any documents or records that explain the reasons for this reduction. However, we would probably be correct if we assume that during the 1870s when the reactionary forces strengthened and the attitude toward the Jewish settlement cooled down, the officialdom expanded the use of the "dislodging" provision toward owners of farms that seemed to them as falling behind.

[Page 114]

According to Ivanschintzev the occupations of the Jewish settlers were as follows:

| | |
|---|---|
| Agriculture (permanently) | 1450 families |
| Commerce | 49 families |
| Craftsmanship within the colonies | 160 families |
| Commerce and craftsmanship outside of the colonies | 147 families |
| Wanderers (probably occupied in incidental occupations) | 137 families |
| **Total** | **1943 families** |

Ivanschintzev too, like his predecessors, blamed the poor soil, lack of forests, shortage of water, frequent drought years, inconvenient climate, and calamities of nature such as locusts, field mice, and agricultural pests for the retardation of the Jewish colonies. He too, found fault in the regulation prohibiting the Jews from getting help by employing Christian workers, which caused tremendous loss during the busy season. He also noted that, despite all of that, the Jews vindicated the government's objective by their diligence and wishes to become good farmers. He emphasized that the acclimation of the Jews was proven by the appearance of their villages, most of which looked much nicer than the Russian villages. He viewed with kindness the Jews whose farms were taken away from because of their farming failure and who were forced to find sustenance in craftsmanship. He claimed that "they could have become good farmers after two to three years of good harvest."

***Author's Note:***

1.  During the 1840s, the education minister founded two Jewish rabbinical and teacher colleges in Vilna and Zhytomyr. The inspector in the college in Vilna was Von Gruber (a Christian), and the advisors concerning the curriculum were A. L. Mendelstam and Prof. V. Levison, a German subject. The management in Zhytomyr also included a Christian head and Jewish advisors.

*[Page 115]*

# E. Acclimatization and Struggles

## When the Hatred Waves Swelled

Upon the murder of Alexander the Second on March 1st, 1881, pogroms erupted all over Russia. The crowds rampaged and robbed Jewish property, destroyed houses, raped and murdered, and the authorities - the police and army forces, stood by idle. Only after three or four days, when the Jews were taught "a lesson worthy of its name," instructions were given to stop the massacre.

The pogroms erupted mainly in the large cities; however, small cities and towns were not spared. Even some colonies in the province of Ekaterinoslav had a taste of the pogroms. On May 6 - 8, 1881, the neighboring farmers attacked the colonies Nechayevka, Trudoliubovka, Grafskoya, and Mezhirich and conducted pogroms in them. The entire property of the settlers was robbed, and the cattle were scared away. The German settlers who lived in the colony among the Jews participated in the pogrom in the colony of Trudoliubovka. The Jews fled for their lives to the prairie, along with their elderly and the children. Some of them found a temporary shelter with one of the nobles in the estate of Stephanovka. The farmers in the German colony of Marienfeld, who initially gave shelter to some of the refugees from the nearby Jewish colony, regretted their generosity and expelled the refugees. The rioters surrounded the refugees who tried to escape from the German colony and robbed their belongings. The large estate of the Jew, G. Ostrovski, was robbed and destroyed. During the attack on the estate, the rioters shouted: "It is forbidden for a Jew to be the master of his own land."

Following the cruel and murderous carnages, a series of decrees began. The rights of the Jews were slashed. The "*Numerus Clausus*" law (limiting the percentage of Jews) was instituted in all government schools, including the universities. It became forbidden for Jews to privately purchase as little as a foot of land or even lease land for short periods. The existing settlement shrank regardless. The first steps aimed to shrink it came even during the reign of Alexander the Second, by discontinuing the settlement on government lands

*[Page 116]*

in the western provinces, as well as by reducing the settlement in the provinces of Kerson and Ekaterinoslav. The hateful attitude towards the colonies was already being felt as early as 1880 by the formulation of the regulations that followed the report submitted by Ivanschintzev. However, the discussion about the report started after the pogroms and the economic decrees. From the formulation of the decrees, it was evident that the Russian farmers in the regions of the colonies saw themselves as being discriminated against because large areas were given to the Jews and the farmers needed to pay full price for leasing them.

Concerning the general clause in the [Ivanschintzev's] formulation that stated that the government lands should be handed over to the farmers so that they can cultivate them as their own private property, a sarcastic note was attached stating: "The Jews, given their tendency to speculate, would probably lease the lands for profit rather than cultivate them."

Before the final formulation, the committee found it necessary to turn to Tikhayev, the provincial minister of Kherson-Bessarabia, and ask for his opinion. His response was filled with hatred and contempt for the entire Jewish settlement enterprise.

## Under the Signs of Awakening and Renewal

It is interesting to note that precisely after the lid was seemingly closing on the Jewish settlement and after Minister Yignatiev forbade the Jews from cultivating even leased lands, the recognition of the importance of working the land ripened among the masses of the Jewish nation. Prominent people idealists and people with pure aspirations woke up to preach for it verbally, in writing, and actions.

Nakhum Sokolov's plan and his call to establish "Jewish colonies to work the land" deserves a special mention (HaTzfira, 5th Year, No. 39, 12 Tishrei 5639 [9 October 1878]).

"About the Founding of Jewish Colonies for the Purpose of Working the Land[1].

A rumor was spread lately, and the news was also published in some periodicals in Hebrew, that the organization "Kol Israel Khaverim" [Alliance Israelite Universelle – or in short Alliance] gave its support to the realization of this exalted idea, that every Jew aspires for."

The rumor is not accurate because, for now, the proposal for this plan was submitted to the General Committee of the organization in Paris, and the committee has not decided to implement it as of yet. The proposed idea of establishing colonies for Jews that are residents of Russia and Romania was divided into two articles. One article presented the views of the idea itself, and the second included how the desirable objective could be achieved. The author of the (latter) proposal did not only disprove all the accusations placed on the Jewish nation by its own scholars and distinguished people that "the Jews are not capable, do not want to burden themselves with physical work,

*[Page 117]*

and therefore, should remain in their current position within the political society, namely, in their current occupations of merchants, speculators, moneylenders, shopkeepers, and peddlers," but also proved that this claim is based on national slander and is false. He would prove that the opposite is true that the Jews are longing to work the land - an occupation that sustains its holder in a much better way than the mediocre commerce occupation, which depresses body and soul. To popularize the idea among the masses, the author proposed establishing a committee representing all the nation's parties, which would be responsible for planting the idea in the people's hearts, using pamphlets, journal articles, and similar tools. In conclusion, the author urged the committee to recognize the fact that this exalted enterprise would bring much needed salvation to many.

In the second part of the proposal, which was formulated in good taste and knowledge, the author explained the path about the source of the money required for this project. To begin this enterprise, the first thing the organization would need to do is find a budget for 10,000 families of 5 people each. The organization must purchase 20 *disiyatins* and 400 Rubles in cash per family that were needed for procuring all the needs of the settlement. The cost of the 20 *disiyatins* along with the 400 Rubles totaled one thousand Rubles, which would be paid off over fifty years without interest. The payments would be divided in such a way that it would be easy for the farmers to pay them on time. During the first ten years, the colonists would be exempt from any payments. In the second decade, the family would pay 6 Rubles per year, in the third decade – 12 Rubles per year, in the fourth decade – 28 Rubles per year, and in the fifth decade – 54 Rubles per year; altogether, 1000 Rubles in fifty years.

As the source of money, the proposal's author suggested that the organization establish a tax on candles among the Jews in Russia[2] and Romania. The tax would amount to 50 kopecks per person per year. The tax would be instituted in the big cities by the leaders of the communities and in the small cities and towns by the rabbis. Two officials, one from the government and one from among the Jews, would be nominated to oversee the orderly collection of the tax and the money transfer to the committee. Since the number of Jews in Russia and Romania exceeded 3 million people, the tax should bring 1.5 million Rubles per year. Even after deducting 15% for expenses, wages of the collectors, and unpaid debts, 275,000 Rubles would be left. This sum could be used by the organization, as a base for budget expenses.

The Russian government demonstrated that it was ready to support and entice those Jews who wanted to adopt the idea of settlement. Therefore, there is no doubt that the committee would be able to purchase from the government an area of 200,000 *disiyatins* [about 540,000 acres], with fertile and rich soil in the northern and southern provinces for 20-30 Rubles on the condition that the debt would be paid off

*[Page 118]*

in payments over 25 years. The debt that the organization would owe the government would be paid off by one of the big banks abroad. Alternatively, the organization could sign a contract with one of the large banks and award it a quarter percent a year toward its involvement if the bank would agree to handle the government account for 25 years, guarantee the debt, and pay the promissory notes of the organization to the government amounting to 240,000 Rubles a year. The organization could also receive a license from the government to issue bonds (debentures stocks) over the debt for the 200,000 *disiyatins*, with the organization guarantee. There is no doubt that these notes would sell at a price higher than their nominal value because among their members were Europe's wealthiest people, such as Rothschild, Hirsch, and Bleichroeder. It is a commitment that any Jew who loves the nation would take on oneself to recruit people who would be willing to hold on to the tree of life of working the land and send them to the organization's office in Paris so that the organization would be prompted to assist in this big and admirable project. We are confident that if every Jew supports this proposal, it will be realized, and everybody with a heart will recognize the vast benefits this proposal offers.

Signed,

Nakhum Sokolov

This plan, directed towards the settlement in Russia, was published at the end of the 1870s. However, during those days, particularly after the murder of Czar Alexander the Second, it was like a voice calling in the wilderness.

In 1880, the ORT[3] organization was established in Petersburg. The organization's mission was to promote craftsmanship and agriculture among the Jews in Russia. Its range of activities included the following: assistance in the establishment and maintenance of workshops and agricultural farms, maintaining a fund for low–cost credit, and assistance in purchasing materials, equipment, and lands. This organization was very active in Russia, particularly in establishing workshops for educating youth and adults (after World War I, it continued to be active in Poland, the Baltic States, and Soviet Russia. After 1950, it expanded its activities in Israel).

At the beginning of the 1880s, several authors, such as L. Pinsker, Lilienblum, and others rose and laid down the foundation for the movement of *Khibat Tzion* [literally "The Love of Zion," the precursor of the Zionist movement]. With the establishment of the movement, several idealistic youths roused and created the movement of BILU [acronym in Hebrew, based on a verse from the Book of Isaiah (2:5)] – "*Beit Ya'akov Lekhu Venelkha*" ["House of Jacob, let us go to Eretz Israel"]). The movement's mission was to promote the idea of working the land, however, only in Eretz Israel.

At about the same time (1881), the nucleus for the movement "Am Olam" [literally in Hebrew "Eternal People"] formed in Odesa. Its founders saw in working the land a way to recuperate the nation's soul. Because of the turbid atmosphere prevailing in Russia during those days, the people of "Am Olam" concluded that their idea could only be achieved in free America, with its vast areas and big opportunities. Some of these people even dreamt about an independent Jewish state (in the US).

*[Page 119]*

The founder of that movement was a teacher by the name of Mania Bokal, who lived close to Ochakov near Odesa. Another teacher, Moshe Herder, a private teacher for boys from wealthy homes in Ochakov joined him later. Moshe Herder knew German, and he wrote poems in Yiddish and Hebrew. Shneor Ballia, a mathematics teacher at the Jewish high school in Odesa, where Lilienblum was teaching literature and the Bible, joined the other two founders. The basic idea of the three founders was to turn the Jewish masses into farmers.

After verbal and written propaganda, the idea spread throughout Odesa and many other towns. Merchan and students joined the movement. In 1882, they sailed to America in six groups; however, in America, the true reality hit them in the face. Although land was cheap in those days, settlements required substantial investments. The land was arid, partially forested, and required betterment and flattening. There were no houses, farm buildings, farm animals, or equipment. The money these people had, was mostly used for the trip's expenses, and almost nothing left for establishing the farms. The settlements, which were established with the assistance of philanthropists, struggled with extremely harsh conditions, and several years later, people started to abandon and escape to the city until the whole movement was liquidated.

In addition to the two movements mentioned above, another settlement enterprise was established by Baron Hirsch in Argentina, who invested many millions in it. He purchased vast land areas and provided farm buildings, equipment, and everything else needed. He also financed the costs associated with the immigration from Russia to Argentina. Had the ideological awakening of the 1880s occurred several decades earlier, thousands of Jewish villages could have been established with many hundreds of thousands of people working the land. However, it should be noted that this late awakening did help in encouraging and modernizing the existing settlement, which ceased to be isolated and began to be assisted by training and other means.

***Author's Notes:***

1. Copy from "The Israelite Archive"
2. The author of the proposal, from France, was not aware that, in Russia, there was already a candle tax imposed earlier.
3. ORT (Today called "World ORT") (Russian: *Obchestvo Remeslenogo Truda*, "Association for the Promotion of Skilled Trades") is a global Jewish organization that today promotes education and training in communities worldwide.

# The Settlement Movement at a Turning Point

Even before the pogroms of the 1880s reached their peak, hundreds of families were ousted from their farms in the 1870s as a punishment for their "negligence." Immediately after that came the pogroms in the four settlements. At that point, the authorities in Petersburg hesitated to bestow on the Jewish settlers the same benefits included in the clauses of the general regulation, according to which government land would be transferred over to the farmers and registered as their own private property. In connection with that matter, it is interesting to bring some of the views expressed by Provincial Minister Tikhayev:

"The experience acquired over decades of settlement proved that the Jew does not tend to earn his living by the hard work of farming."

*[Page 120]*

"More than 130 thousand *disiyatins* of land were wasted over decades without productivity and fruitfulness, and that is beside the huge investment provided to the needs of the Jews."

"Throughout Russia, there isn't even one village that was granted such generous assistance for food and even building of bath houses, like the assistance granted to the Jewish villages. These grants were not kept secret among the Christian farmers, and they give rise to unfavorable feelings towards the Jews…"

"…handing the lands to the Jews as their own private property would lead to a situation where every Jew would use its ownership over the land to lease the land and invest the money in a much more profitable business."

"The [Jewish] settlements should have been established based on fewer losses for the government and less provocation to the Christian farmers."

Tikhayev also proposed reducing the plot size given to every Jewish family. Instead of 30 *disiyatins*, he proposed to settle for just 20. He also suggested using regulation legislated 30 years earlier, that every farmer who did not reach a certain level within six years would be ousted from his land.

These views fitted the state of mind in Petersburg in the 1880s.

During those days, the Jewish settlement faced a turning point.

As a result of the prohibition on purchasing lands, the expulsion of "negligent" farmers from their farms, the pogroms, and, in addition, the calamities of nature, there was room to fear that the Jewish agricultural sector would degenerate until it would completely disappear. However, precisely during the years of decrees, agriculture started to gain currency and conquer the hearts of the Jewish public. The tavern lessees and the bartenders in villages, inn owners and small shopkeepers, peddlers, tailors, and shoemakers, all of whom were perceived by the country citizens as parasites and cheats, became a community of Jewish farmers, albeit scattered around in secluded colonies that were surrounded by hundreds of Russian villages or were isolated Jewish farmers in Christian villages, but they constituted a tribe, with a uniquely defined and distinguished way of life.

Undoubtedly, a principal and essential factor in strengthening the Jewish settlement was the economic despair, which prevailed in the cities within the "Pale of Settlement." However, we should note that the process occurred during the 1880s and the 1890s, decades after the expulsion from the villages and the regulation about compulsive recruitment. Following the negative turn in the attitude of the regime, it was not very difficult for the Jewish farmers to sell their belongings and move to the city. If instead of abandonments, we witnessed a determined strive for improvements and modernizations, it is because the settlers became farmers. The members of the second and third generations were already acclimated to fieldwork, and they liked life in the village. Thanks to them, the farm operated more efficiently and as a result, more profitably. The rickety house was fixed and enlarged, and the food basket was enriched. Even the hard work eased with the improvements in equipment and farm animals.

*[Page 121]*

The way of life in the colony was Jewish in the full sense of the word. Every colony had its rabbi, slaughterer, synagogue, public bath, Torah schools, and schools where they taught Russian and general studies. The youth had plenty of books in Russian and Yiddish. The control of the government's guardian authority has weakened. The farmers became more independent, and the life of the community was more autonomous. The heads of the villages were elected in general elections; even the external appearance of the colonies had improved.

The progress in the colonies of Kherson, Ekaterinoslav, Bessarabia, and the western provinces made its impression on the small shopkeeper who struggled to sustain himself and had to stand in his shop from dawn till very late in the evening and wait for a customer. It downed on him that Jews could sustain themselves by working the land and making a good living without being dependent on anybody.

It must be mentioned that, at about the same time, a railroad had already been constructed along the major lines, and a Lithuanian Jew did not have to wander for three months in the prairies to arrive at Kherson or Bessarabia. Many visited the colonies and witnessed, with their own eyes, the life of real Jewish farmers.

Not everybody who was fascinated by agriculture could purchase or lease land. However, Jews found ways to lease some *disiyatins* using the name of a Christian and to grow tobacco, a vegetable patch, or raise a cattle herd.

In years past, the wealthy Jewish house owners, who wore silk caftans, treated labor, craftsmanship, and physical laborers with disdain. A few classes existed in the Jewish towns: the Supremes, superiors, high, average, less than average, low, and lowest of the low.

On the ladder of society stood, from top to bottom, the rich, wealthy affluent landlords, small shopkeepers, peddlers, and obviously the servants, who were classified according to their occupations.

Following them were the goldsmith and the watchmaker, whose status was higher than that of the carpenter. In turn, he was more "distinguished" than the tailor, who was, in turn, on a higher status than the shoemaker. The blacksmith, who was shoeing the horses, and the cart driver stood almost on the lowest level. However, even they were higher than the porters and the daily hired laborers. There were nearly no farmers. The status of the Jewish farmer who lived in the village was measured by the size of the plot he owned and the size of his contribution to the synagogue. Their status would have been boosted if he or his wife had an uncle in their family who was a slaughterer, a "*Dayan*" [a rabbi serving as a religious judge], or perhaps a cousin who was a shopkeeper in the town's market.

Under that atmosphere, in the 1880s, prominent authors began to put physical labor and craftsmanship on the pedestal. They also began reminding everybody that our ancestors were shepherds, winegrowers, and yeomen. Students abandoned their studies and "made *Aliyah*" to Eretz Israel to work the land. Jews dissolved their businesses and registered in associations such as "Am Olam" to wander away to the far America and settle there as farmers.

Besides "Khibat Tzion," "Am Olam," and Baron Hirsch's organization, there were other prominent people and other leaders who sought

*[Page 122]*

to operate among the five million Russian Jews, develop craftsmanship skills among them, expand the number of farmers, and ease the economic struggle by providing constructive assistance. There were agronomists among them who understood that the Jewish farmer would only thrive and would be attached to his land and work if he would modernize his farm, establish a cycle of seeds, plant vines of fine breed, and introduce machinery. Agronomist instructors were needed for that, and therefore there was a need for research farms, farming schools, and cheap credit for the agriculturalists.

The Jewish Colonization Association (JCA) [established by Baron Hirsch in 1891] instituted a "Central Committee in Petersburg" that accepted the responsibility for developing productive occupation skills among Russian Jews and helping immigrants abroad.

## The Census of 1898–9

The JCA's "Petersburg's Committee" excelled, from the start, in exercising social awareness without being bureaucratic like the JCA's enterprises in Argentina and the officialdom acting on its behalf at the initial steps in establishing the colonies Eretz Israel.

In this committee and around it several notable people have been assembled, such as Baron A. Ginsburg, Dr. Y. L. Katznelson (the real name of the author "Buki ben Yogli"), L. Bramson, O. Gruzenberg, M. Winover and H. Sliozberg. An "Agricultural Society" attached to the committee was established. It organized a sort of "conference" of the Jewish agronomists. They numbered less than a *minyan* [10 people]; however, they were all devoted to the idea of spreading the agricultural vision among the Jews. Among them were: Akiva Ettinger (who became manager of the Settlement Department of the Jewish Agency after the First World War); B. D. Brutzkus, an agricultural economist who was one of the managers of JCA in Russia (and a professor of agricultural economics at the Hebrew University in Jerusalem from 1938); Z. Bertenzon, who held a high-ranking position in the [Russian] agricultural ministry; Y. Krasolshchik, who managed, on behalf of the Russian government, the fight against the phylloxera infection that spread in the vineries in Bessarabia; M. Weller, who worked in the *zemstvo* [elected provincial authority]; Sh. Lubarski and Z. Bronin, who also worked in the *zemstvo* and who were appointed later on to manage the improvement projects in the colonies and the agricultural school that was established by the agricultural ministry for the youth of the colonies in the colony of Novo-Poltavka as a result of Bertenzon's efforts.

The first step that the agronomists took was to conduct a census of the Jewish agricultural population. For that purpose, they traveled in horse-drawn wagons from one colony to the other and sat down, face to face, with the farmers in their location, filled out questionnaires, and talked to them. During these visits, the census-takers expressed their opinions and views about the cycle of the seeds, an advanced plow, fine varieties of fruit trees, and preservation methods. They also listened to the farmers about their problems, such as shortage of land, cattle disease, availability of loans based on the harvest, etc. This was the first contact between the JCA and the Jewish farmers.

*[Page 123]*

The census lasted for two years (1898–9). According to it, and based on other reliable sources about the agricultural sector, the following numbers were found:

| Location | Colonies | Families | People |
|---|---|---|---|
| Kherson province | 21 | 3,187 | 18,802 |
| Ekaterinoslav | 17 | 1,416 | 8,399 |
| Grodno, Mohilev | 62 | | 13,406 |
| Minsk, Kiev, Vohlyn, Podolia and Chernigov | 61 | | 12,184 |
| Vilna and Kovno | 23 | | 2,113 |
| Bessarabia | 6 | | 5,158 |
| | 26 | Tobacco colonies | 1,068 |
| | 8 | Winegrowing colonies | 1,068 |
| 10 provinces of Poland | | 2,509 | ~15,054 |
| **Total** | | | **78, 325** |

The total area cultivated by the Jews was close to 115 thousand *disiyatins* [about 310,500 acres].

During the general population census of 1897, 40,611 heads of household were registered as being occupied in agriculture, consisting of 192,721 people.

The difference between the two censuses is explained by the fact that city wagon drivers, forest wood cutter contractors, as well as their clerks and laborers, were registered as agriculturalists in the general census. Against that, about 2,000 city people who worked in one specific agriculture occupation in tiny areas, such as tobacco and vegetable growers, milkmen, winegrowers, and beekeepers, were registered as agriculturalists in the agronomists' census.

The following are the numbers about "agriculturalists of a single sector" who were counted by the "Petersburg's committee" of JCA with the help of agents in all the provinces:

| Sector | People occupied |
|---|---|
| Vegetables and fruits | 11,299 |
| Milk | 7,454 |
| Tobacco (including tobacco growers in Bessarabia) | 1,695 |
| Winegrowers (including winegrowers in Bessarabia) | 780 |
| Beekeepers | 200 |
| Other agricultural sectors | 93 |
| Total | 21,521 workers |

If we assume that for every worker in a family, two additional people were not workers (children, elderly), we have 64,656 people whose sustenance was dependent on agriculture.

*[Page 124]*

Besides all of these people, about 12,000 Jewish agricultural laborers were occupied by others, mainly in the beet fields, sugar plantations, and seasonal work. If we combine all these numbers, we arrive towards the end of the 19th century at about 150,000 Jewish people who were dependent on agriculture for their living.

The census of the "Agricultural Sector" performed by JCA divided the farmers according to the type of their work:

| Sector | People occupied |
|---|---|
| Sowing the fields and cultivation of field corps | 51,539 |
| Special agricultural sectors | 64,563 |

| | |
|---|---|
| Hired agricultural workers | 12,901 |

------------------------------------------------------------------

| | |
|---|---|
| **Total** | **148,933** |

According to the general census of 1897, the Jews who were occupied in agriculture amounted to 3.81% of the total Jewish population in Russia, and according to the statistics produced by the census takers of JCA, 3% of the total Jewish population were agriculturalists.

# Estate Owners and Lessees

Even before the "Jewish Regulations" of 1804, by which the Jews were permitted to settle on government land and were provided with loans to procure farm equipment, were enacted, Jews used to purchase land permanently or lease it.

The "Jewish Regulations" of 1804, and the rest of the regulations dealing with Jewish settlement during the entire 19th century, encouraged the purchasing and leasing of lands by Jews, except the regulations of 3 May 1882. That meant that the Jews could purchase estates, the farmers of which were practically enslaved by the estate owners.

Despite those rights, wealthy Jews were not in a rush to purchase estates. Industrial and commercial businesses were more profitable and ensured the right to reside in large cities, where Jews were otherwise not allowed to reside.

Under the effect of the decree enforcing a compulsory service for 25 years or longer, or perhaps also due to a certain awakening, middle-income Jews started to organize and purchase together an estate or a plot, divide the land among themselves, build houses, and establish an agricultural settlement.

In the early 1860s, many wealthy Jews began to acquire estates by purchasing them permanently or by leasing them for a long duration. Some were satisfied with cultivating the plots agriculturally, while others used the land for industrial and manufacturing development.

*[Page 125]*

In 1864, as mentioned, a law was passed forbidding the Jews from buying lands from farmers and estate owners in the nine most populated western provinces. Because the law was not in effect in the other provinces, Jews continued to purchase and lease estates in other provinces with more favorable conditions. From 1860, easements were given to the Jews in the ten provinces of Congressional Poland [established after the defeat of Napoleon in 1815, replacing the Duchy of Warsaw].

The laws of 3 May 1882 did not include the provinces of Congressional Poland. Only in 1891 purchasing land from farmers was restricted. However, purchasing estates from estate owners was not restricted.

Purchasing an estate involved in a financial investment that only the rich could afford. However, people who were not that rich could afford to lease. Thus, the number of leased estates was higher than those permanently purchased.

The laws of May 1882 erased that status quo. The purchased areas remained the property of those Jews who owned them. However, the prohibition led to a stoppage of purchasing or leasing of lands by Jews, neither owning a plot of a single *disiyatin* for growing tobacco nor leasing an estate of a few thousand *disiyatins*.

We do not have accurate numbers of the areas leased by Jews before the enactment of the law of 3 May 1882, but we do have numbers about the leased lands in the 12 provinces. As of that date, the total was 1,998,658 *disiyatins* (i.e., close to two million *disiyatins* [about 5,400,000 acres]). It is logical to assume that the land areas leased in the other provinces were also substantial.

After the passage of the law, Jews had to finesse the authorities to continue to lease lands, although on a limited basis. Leasing was done by naming a devout Christian on the lease, who agreed to do it in exchange for a "certain gain" out of the deal. The officialdom was obviously also bribed. Bypassing the laws was common during the regime of those days in Russia. It followed the old Russian proverb: "Nothing is impossible in Russia."

The amazing thing about this state of affairs was the fact that most of the estates that were leased to the Jews were owned by ministers, provincial ministers, and other prominent [Russian] notables. They were themselves, in most cases, Jew-haters but they considered "their own Jew" as an exception to the rule or their two or three "trusted Jews" as "nice." The noble would sell his estate's harvest through "his trusted Jew," at high prices and purchase everything needed for his estates and home at reasonable prices. All kinds of members of the nobility and other "*paritizim*" [wealthy estate owners] have also exploited their "trusted Jew" who was considered in their eyes as the most clever and wise among the Jews. This custom also continued during the reactionary years. When a member of the nobility wished to lease an estate, he would use "his Jew" or the "Jew of his friend" to achieve the most favorable conditions. The need to find a Christian, in the name of whom the contract was written, was not always necessary. The word of a prince or a Graf had more weight than the law.

*[Page 126]*

It is also self-explanatory that a Jewish lessee could manage the estate without any interference. The governor sitting in the provincial city, a Chief of Police sitting in the province capital, or the local officialdom all knew that the estate, which was leased by a Jew, was owned by a minister or by somebody who was once a minister and was, at the time, a candidate to be nominated to a higher position. Any harm brought upon the Jew would be considered as "harming his majesty." However, the sponsorship of the estate owner did not prevent the officials from requesting a higher bribe and gifts - left and right. When there was a will, or when the need came to shove, the law with all of its severity was not applied. However, all Russian laws were subordinated to the "law of life" that stated that "nothing is impossible in Russia."

"The law of life" was so prevalent in the regime that the areas leased by Jews were registered by the regime's official statistics and in the statistics published by the JCA during the last few years of the 19th century. These numbers were not very accurate because many lessees were hiding the facts about their lease for fear of harmful consequences; however, they were registered in the government registries, which were published without any fear.

## Under Signs of Wealth and Progress

At the beginning of the 20ᵗʰ century, the Jewish settlement in Russia experienced additional progress. The Jewish farmer felt he had been entrenched in the village way of life. His sons, too, grew, became rooted in the land, and began to assist him with the farm work. A new spirit of initiative and progress descended over the public of the Jewish farmers in the colonies.

Already in the last quarter of the 19ᵗʰ century, progress had begun in agricultural work in Russia, but only in the big estates, where machinery, new equipment, and modern methods were introduced, similar to those used in Western countries. The German settlers were already cultivating their land using more modern and convenient equipment and also utilizing more efficient farming methods. The Russian farmers continued to use the methods of their ancestors. The Jews, who initially considered the Russian farmer a symbol and model, imitated him. However, as mentioned above, the expenses of the Jewish farmer were one-third higher than the expenses of the Russian farmer, although their revenues were similar. Therefore, the Jew had to complement his income from external sources or modernize the farm sectors to substantially increase his profitability.

Already during the first meeting between the Jewish farmers and the agronomists, who conducted the JCA census in 1898-9, the visitors did not settle for just filling out the questionnaire and registering the numbers. The first Jewish agronomists were idealistic and enthusiastic and found it necessary to use every opportunity to explain the efficiency involved in using the cycle of seeds, the dangers hidden in blight diseases, and the pitfalls of the grape phylloxera disease They also emphasized the value of

*[Page 127]*

agricultural machinery that saves manpower, reduces expenses and produces higher yields.

To introduce an efficient cycle of seeds a general agreement of the entire colony was required to sow a specific type of crop in a specific area. To fertilize a specific field every year, the cattle sector had to have a minimum number of cattle. That meant additional cows had to be purchased when the money might not have been available. The investment was required to replace the sowing by hand with a sowing machine and the sickle with a harvesting machine. The problem with the farmer's cash cycle was also serious. The sale of the fields' crops occurred at the end of the summer, while for the rest of the year, the farmer was getting entangled in debts with the grocer, craftsmen, and moneylenders. The farmers also hesitated to get involved in new methods due to the shortage of guidance and guides. In general, by nature, a farmer was not inclined to drastic changes in his way of life.

The establishment of the JCA, which took action in the colonies, helped to turn matters around in the agricultural methods used by the Jews in those days. As mentioned in the prior section, one of these actions was establishing a farm school where hundreds of [Jewish] youngsters were trained in various branches of agriculture, both in the theory and practice of modern agricultural methods. Upon returning to their farms, these youngsters introduced improvements, and some graduates became guides in the Jewish colonies.

Because of the state of transportation in those days, the task of an agronomist was not easy. He had to visit colonies, the distances between which were quite substantial, and meet with farmers who were conservative and fearful of changes. However, the agronomists insisted on implementing the improvements, no matter what. Indeed, over time, due to the positive results, improvements, corrections, and changes were introduced, even on the farms of the most conservative farmers.

JCA established a "credit fund" in the colonies so that the farmers would not have to pay high interest on their loans. Any farmer who wished to take a loan received it with favorable conditions. Since the Russian "*Zemstvo*" operated along the direction of training, farm schools, introduction of machinery, and agricultural equipment in villages throughout Russia, a certain collaboration was established between the state's *Zemstvo* and the Jewish organization JCA.

Throughout the years of JCA operation in the Jewish colonies, from the beginning of the century until the revolution, the organization invested in development, training, and the rest of its operation, about two million francs.

Among the colonies of Kherson and Ekaterinoslav, wealth also spread because of the redistribution of the land. Out of the 40 *disiyatins* allocated to every family at the start of the settlement, 30 *disiyatins* were handed to each settler for cultivation, and 10 were kept as future reserves. That meant that 25% of the colonies' land areas (which were called in Russian "*Ubruchni uchastock*" ["restricted plots"] was outside of the direct control of the farmer. The Guardian Bureau leased them to anybody. The leasing income was spent to cover the expenses for the local officialdom, assistance, and welfare during drought years and other public expenses. The 30 *disiyatins* allocated to each family were divided among the heirs, members of the next

*[Page 128]*

first generation, and after them to the heirs of the second and third generations. If the heirs were just a few, the plots they inherited were relatively large. However, if the number of heirs was large, the plots were split into smaller plots. During the 3–4 generations, inequality in the plot areas developed. Some farmers, who came from families with a small number of children, owned plots of 10 *disiyatins* or larger, whereas others from large families owned plots as small as 2-3 *disiyatins* or even smaller.

In addition to the redistribution of the land, another successful action was redistributing the reserve areas. In the summer of 1902, every colony received a 25% increase in the area owned by every male.

During the same period, another positive change took place. The special governmental supervision of the colonies of Kherson and Ekaterinoslav in place for decades was removed. From that point onwards, the farmers were free to manage their farms as they wished and were also free to leave the colony and visit the cities without a special license. The farmers who specialized in certain craftsmanship could leave the colony during the winter months when the fieldwork ceased, and work in their craftsmanship in the neighboring villages or the big cities.

Every colony was managed by its own elected officials. As was the custom during those days, the head of the colony (the "*Schultz*"), was also the judge and the representative responsible towards the authorities. He was also responsible for implementing the authorities' instructions within the colony. In addition to the head of the village, two additional people were elected to manage each colony. The general assembly of the village would gather to make major decisions on important matters.

As mentioned, the settlement process lasted for quite a few years, and there was no shortage of errors and disappointments; however, as years passed more improvements were made in the state of the Jewish farmers. Even though they were scattered throughout Russia and were not organized among themselves, they constituted a unique tribe of Jewish farmers rooted on their land. This phenomenon of diligent Jews who were working the land proved to the Christians, again, that their view about the inability of the Jews to be acclimated to agriculture, was wrong.

# In the Days of the World War and the Russian Revolution

With the start of the World War, the best youth were recruited for the war effort. Like in other villages, the colonies were emptied of youth and their main workforce. The farmers were forced, from time to time, to transport military forces and equipment to the front. Horses were used for long-distance transport. Elderly men above the maximum recruitment age and young boys served as the wagon drivers. Both the elderly and the young boys became the

[Page 129]

main workers on the farm during the war years. Recruitment of these groups and their horses led to some neglect in various farm works.

We do not have numbers on the effects of the war on the Jewish settlement in the western provinces; however, we do know that the population in the colonies of Kherson and Ekaterinoslav, which totaled 42 thousand people just before the war, decreased by about a third during the war. Some of the houses were destroyed, and the animal inventory declined.

At the end of the war, when the soldiers returned home, the civil war between the Bolsheviks and the White Army began. Anarchy descended on the state affairs. Gangs of thugs were organized to murder Jews and rob them.

Pogroms erupted in thousands of cities, towns, and villages throughout the provinces of Ukraine and Belarus. Jews who survived in the villages abandoned their houses and everything they owned and ran away to the big cities. In some towns, most of the Jewish population was murdered. The Jewish population in the "Pale of Settlement" was defenseless against the robbers and thugs. Ten of thousands of Ukrainian Jews were murdered and their property robbed during 1918 –1920, the years of the civil war calamity.

The fate of the lone Jews who resided within Christian villages or in small settlements adjacent to the villages was similar to the fate of the rest of the village Jews. Those who survived abandoned their homes and properties and escaped to the cities. Some of the larger colonies, which were surrounded by tens of Christian villages, were destroyed. The Christian farmers collaborated with the gangs, robbed, murdered, raped, and destroyed everything that could be destroyed.

We do not have exact numbers that could reflect the extent of the destruction and devastation among the Jewish farmers, and we will, therefore, only bring some stories from the little we know about it.

In the colony of Kauzschitz, in the Pinsk Province, district of Bobruisk, all of the 500 residents were slaughtered.

The settlements in the province of Ekaterinoslav were located at the center of the activity of the gangs of the anarchist Batko Makhno. Almost all of Ekaterinoslav suffered from this gangs' attacks. All of the members of the settlements of Trudolyubovka and Nechayevka - 1000 people in total - were murdered. Their entire property was robbed, and no Jewish foot ever stepped on that land after that.

Jewish Farmers in Russia Fields

In most of the settlements of the province of Kherson, a self-defense force was established, which was very efficient and prevented many attacks and destruction. However, the self-defense force, could not defend against the torrent of thugs in some colonies. In the large colony of Novo-Poltavka, 132 people were murdered by the thugs of Makhno despite the heroic standing of the self-defense force. Many victims fell in the colony of Dobroye, and the residents were forced to abandon the colony for some time. The Jewish farmers in the provinces that have been cut off from Russia who joined

[Page 130]

the neighboring countries [after the World War] were saved from extinction. In the District of Bessarabia, which was attached to Romania, the winegrowers, tobacco growers, and the rest of the farmers continued their agricultural work.

Poland, which was reestablished as a state, conquered the 10 provinces in the areas of Congressional Poland and annexed the provinces of Vilna, Grodno, Pinsk, and Vohlyn.

In Northern Russia, the states of Lithuania and Latvia returned to life.

Out of the 200,000 Jewish farmers just before World War I, only 44,000 remained in the areas of Russia and Ukraine (including Kherson and Ekaterinoslav, and excluding the areas mentioned above) and 9000 in Belarus and other provinces, altogether 530,000 people.

At the end of the Civil War, the Soviet regime took hold throughout Russia; however, the hatred for the Jews still permeated the Christian villages. Many of the escapees did not return. The colonies that were saved from under the murderers' swords faced distraction, neglect, and economic distress.

The official statistical data reflects the state of the colonies and the Jewish farmers. Of a total population of 42,000 people at the beginning of World War I, only 28,000 people remained, according to the 1922 census. Only 3,000 workhorses remained in the colonies out of 14,000 before the war. The number of cows decreased from 16,000 before the war to 4,000, i.e. less than 31%. In Ekaterinoslav's colonies, only 630 cows remained out of the 4,000 before the war. That was less than 15%. Because of the shortage of workhorses and other inventory that deteriorated because it was standing idle or was otherwise sold during the years of distress, the sowed areas shrunk by 20% in Kherson's colonies and one-third in the colonies Ekaterinoslav.

During the same year, a severe drought hit again the regions of Ekaterinoslav, Kherson, and neighboring regions. While in Kherson, the farmers managed to save some of the crops, in Ekaterinoslav, not even one seed was harvested. The farmers sold whatever could still be sold for a piece of bread. Some ran away to the cities, and some died of hunger.

The farms and the houses were neglected, and shortage prevailed everywhere. There was a shortage of work animals, cows, and equipment. This was the beginning of the agony of the Jewish agriculture. It seemed that the community of Jewish agriculturalists was facing total decimation. However, economic and political factors helped again to create an environment favorable for the renewal of the Jewish hold on agriculture.

With the entrenchment of the Soviet regime in the years 1919-20, the authorities started to implement the Communist system consistently and systematically. A total prohibition over private commerce and industry was imposed. Private property was confiscated. The principal sufferers were the Jews, who lost their livelihood, as many of them were mainly involved in commerce. The Jewish population degenerated. Under the circumstances, barter commerce between the city Jews and the farmers began to flourish.

*[Page 131]*

A pod of potatoes could fetch an expensive holiday dress, a pod of flour - perhaps a coat or a fur. The city Jews unloaded their Shabbat clothing, silverware, and nice furniture. Hunger took hold among those who did not own luxury items or those who were robbed by robbers. Even the Christian population dealing in commerce or working in government jobs was gripped by economic distress. Among the Christians, many abandoned their homes in the city and moved temporarily to the neighboring villages, where food items could be purchased much below the exaggerated city prices. These people occupied themselves with fishing, hunting, and gathering forest berries. However, the Jews who previously resided in the villages did not return there. After all, the villages' farmers collaborated with the gangs in murdering the Jews in their villages and the neighboring towns.

In this state of shortage and real hunger, some people with initiative among the Jews looked for ways to get hold of a piece of land and make a living by cultivating it.

This phenomenon of the influx of Jews from the city to agriculture was encouraged by the Soviet government officials. Along with their hostile attitude toward small businesses and merchants, they were bothered by the question of how would millions of "unproductive" citizens find a way to sustain themselves. That was why the government perceived favorably the members of those classes who wanted to transfer to doing productive work.

The agrarian plan was not yet developed in detail, during the first few years after the revolution. If a decision was already made about enforcing collective agriculture, the time was not yet ripened for implementation. However, when the lands were handed over to Jewish settlers, it was hinted to them that the government would treat collectives more favorably. Presumably, a substantial part of the youth who were awakening to the idea of working the land looked at the issue of collective work, as a positive idea in itself. That was how the initiative to a collective organization, necessitated by distress and hunger, helped by the availability of lands, and fortified by the positive attitude of the government began to take root among the Jews. According to a hint from the high authorities, or perhaps due to a lack of capabilities, most of the collectives of that period consisted only of 10–15 families. During a very short period, about 300 collectives totaling about 4000 families (21 thousand people), for whom thousands of additional *disiyatins* were allocated, have been organized.

These collectives settled in the following regions:

| Region | Collectives | Families | Area (*disiyatins*) |
|---|---|---|---|
| Belarus (provinces of Homel and Smolensk) | 89 | 864 | 9,631 |
| Ukraine | 72 | 1331 | 4,126 |
| Odesa area (including Kherson) | 136 | 1750 | 20,211 |
| **Totals** | 297 | 3945 | 33,968 |

*[Page 132]*

In Belarus, where the civil war ended earlier, the Jews started to settle during the years 1918-19-20. In Odesa - they settled in 1921, and in Ukraine - as late as 1922.

As mentioned above, the government preferred the collective settlement. The Jewish Communists actually insisted on it. However, because no specific law forbade it, opportunities for individual settlement were also provided, although the parcels allocated for them were smaller.

The following are the numbers available to us:

| Region | Families | Total Area (*disiyatins*) |
|---|---|---|
| Belarus | 854 | The total area of 3384 (about 4 *disiyatins* / family) |
| Ukraine | 602 | The total area of 920 (about 1.5 disiyatins / family) |
| Odesa province | 744 | The total area of 4371 (about 6.9 *disiyatins* / family) |

According to these data, it turns out that during the initial few years of the fortification of the new regime, 6,142 families settled on an area of 42,643 *disiyatins*. As we do not have detailed numbers about the settling of individuals in Ukraine, we probably would be correct to round these numbers to 6,500 families on a total area of 45,000 *disiyatins.*

Although the Russian government allocated land for the new settlers, it did not assist them with any budgets or loans. Most of the plots were without housing and farm buildings. Even in estate areas, the houses were destroyed and the surrounding farmers robbed the farm inventory. New farm inventory (including live animals) was needed to cultivate the land, buy seeds for sowing, and cash to sustain people and farm animals until the first harvest. Some settlers, who sold their houses and remaining property, brought some money with them; however, most settlers were penniless.

The "Ort" organization, which was founded in Russia, as mentioned above, as early as 1890, came to the help of the new settlers. In Czarist Russia, the organization supported 82 learning institutions that taught craftsmanship to youth and adults. After the World War, during the revolution, the organization's management moved abroad. "Ort" supported the new settlers from donations it received from Jews from various countries. The organization helped the new settlers buy farm inventories, seeds, etc., by providing loans with favorable conditions. However, that assistance was insufficient to establish a sound farm.

The "Joint," a philanthropic association founded by American Jews, also provided substantial assistance to the distressed Russian Jews. Part of this assistance was provided to the new settlers as well. However, the state of the several thousand new settlers was very difficult. Due to the housing shortage, many families remained in the cities, and only the men worked on the farms. The new houses cabins were made of clay rather than real houses. The lack of expertise in building these houses affected the results.

*[Page 133]*

Initially, the collective work had some advantages. However, after a year or two, cracks began to appear in the collective way of life. In addition, the absence of a formal system and shortages in agricultural training and resources affected the settlers negatively. The first wave of settlers suffered from considerable abandonment. Only a few thousand families remained in agriculture.

The war and its calamities, the pogroms, and the revolution shook the established colonies to their foundation, too, and their population was reduced by a third. Most of the youth left the farms. Some made *Aliyah* to Eretz Israel, and some left for the US. Some joined the Communists and turned to building a new life in Russia. The farms were devastated, and the agricultural Jewish center was nearly destroyed.

Despite all that, the settlement in Kherson and Ekaterinoslav was not destroyed. It survived that crisis the way it survived other crises, mainly due to the farming nature of its people. They recovered quickly from the blows, which they absorbed during the pogrom years, and began to cultivate their fields again and restore their farms. They began to get accustomed to the new conditions and to market their products, which now fetched higher prices. The colonies' farmers foresaw favorable opportunities for rebuilding and expansion despite the difficult conditions. However, their main source of reinforcement came from the Jewish colonists who settled around them on the lands of the "*paritzim*" [estate owners]. The new farmers purchased the farms of those families who went abroad or the farms of the widows who could not cultivate their farms. By 1925, 800 new families joined the existing colonies, and tens of Jewish collectives settled around them.

This was a beneficial reciprocal relationship. The new settlers, who settled near the established colonies, acclimatized with the physical work and were absorbed faster than settlers in other areas because they settled among "their own people." They received agricultural training from the members of the established colonies, which they visited once in a while. Just as the new farmers benefited from the neighboring established colonies, the established settlement was invigorated by the sight of the hundreds of new settlers in the colonies. This was an important blood infusion, which helped in their survival. It encouraged them to introduce improvements and continue in their physical-work way of life.

***Author's Notes:***

1. Copied from the archive of the [Jewish Germen weekly] journal Der Israelit.
2. The French proposal's author did not realize that the candle tax was already implemented in Russia and was used to maintain various schools for the Jews.
3. "Ort" is an acronym in Russian that means: "The organization to promote physical or [and skill trades] among the Jews."

*[Page 134]*

# F.  Flourishing Ahead of the Holocaust

## The Settlement is Renewed with the Assistance of Jewish Organizations

The destruction of the Jews' livelihoods in the cities, the catastrophic state of the Jewish population, and the willingness of a substantial portion of that population to embrace agricultural work prompted the regime to direct that "unproductive" human sector more efficiently and on a larger scale towards settlement. Some high-ranking regime people realized that it would be beneficial to concentrate the settlement in certain areas and turn them into Jewish districts.

The government established a state committee in 1924 for dealing with the Jewish settlement by the name of "KOMZET" (an acronym in Russian for "Committee for the Settlement of Toiling Jews on the Land"). A government minister was nominated to head the committee. Its members included the Jewish community activists, M Litvinov, L. Karson, A Shinman, V. Larin, A. Merzhin, V. Golda, M. Frumkin, and others.

With the confiscation of the large estates and allocation of lands to individuals, big opportunities for purchasing lands became available. However, as discussed, it was impossible to settle on available land without housing, farm buildings, live and inanimate inventory, seeds, and the like. The Soviet government, in its first years, had very limited financial means and could not allocate the money required for that project. The government intended to allocate just a nominal budget for every settler and provide construction wood from its forests at reduced prices. The people in government assumed that the settlers would make the effort and invest their own money. However, it became apparent that most of the candidates for the settlements were people who lacked resources. The KOMZET, in 1925, established an association for collecting the needed financial resources and supporting the Jewish settlement by the name of "OZET" (in Yiddish, the association was named "GEZERD"). The OZET association recruited tens of thousands of members. During the same period, the KOMZET held negotiations with Jewish organizations abroad concerning their participation in financing the settlement. These organizations, which boosted their activities after the war, considered the Jewish settlement a constructive movement. The JOINT, which spent huge sums on its philanthropic social welfare programs, considered that project a leverage for the economic strengthening of thousands of families. An agreement for mutual cooperation between JOINT and the KOMZET was signed on 29 November 1925. The JOINT established a subsidiary named "JOINT-AGRO," which invested the largest sums of money in the settlement. According to the agreement, the JOINT was committed to investing no less than $400,000 in its first year of operation. The subsidiary was awarded special privileges. It was exempt from state and local government taxes, and its employees were assigned with privileges of government officials.

*[Page 135]*

Similar agreements were signed with the JCA and ORT organizations that were very active in Russia as early as during the Czarist period; JCA – in the area of agriculture and ORT - in the area of teaching craftsmanship skills among the Jews. After the revolution, both organizations transferred abroad, however, they never ceased to assist Russian Jewry.

To prevent frictions among the settlement organizations and duplication of effort was agreed, between them and the KOMZET to divide the operation according to the regions of the settlement and to allocate each organization a license to operate in certain areas. Crimea, for example, was divided into six settlement areas. AGRO-JOINT operated in five of them and OZET in the sixth one. In the provinces of Kherson and Ekaterinoslav, the settlement regions were divided between AGRO-JOINT and JCA. OZET operated in Belarus, and ORT in the Odesa and Balta districts.

From everything discussed above, it seems that three elements played a role in implementing the settlement, namely, the government, through KOMZET, which allocated the land areas, the settlers, and the Jewish organizations, who financed the settlement and provided equipment and agricultural training.

Every such organization had its own method of establishing the farms and the budget allocations. The OZET organization's objective was to ensure that the farms of the Jewish settlers would be similar to the farms of other farmers in the area. As the Christian farmers had small and simple houses and primitive equipment, the Jews had to have a similar arrangement. Every house built from clay bricks cost 400 Rubles, the stable - 150 Rubles, the life, and the inanimate inventory, seeds, and sustenance until the first harvest - 500 Rubles, and altogether - 1100 Rubles. The AGRO-JOINT and JCA organizations included in their plans a more spacious house, vineyard or fruit tree grove, and dairy shed. Their budget was 2000 Rubles or more.

As early as the first year of their operation (1925), 5,226 families were settled in an area of approximately 100,000 *disiyatins*. According to Z. Ostrovski in the Journal "Der Emes" [Yiddish for "The Truth"], the Jewish settlement enterprise required, in 1925, 3 million Rubles for its consolidation, and the organizations mentioned above took care of that investment. According to the same source, a collaborative conference of KOMZET and OZET and representatives of the settlers from Ukraine and Belarus took place on 23–25 October 1925.

In that conference, it was decided that upon settling, the settlers would invest certain sums in their farms according to three levels, 150, 300, and 500 Rubles. Obviously, people who were unable to invest were not prevented from settling, however, the organizations were committed to striving to have the settlers pay.

Until then, no attention was made to coordinate the human material in every collective due to the haste in securing land, allocations, and other resources. The collective farms were assembled haphazardly, combining wealthy and poor people, shopkeepers, and craftsmen. During the actual collaborative work, disputes erupted among the settlers who came from different backgrounds.

*[Page 136]*

It was therefore decided that every collective farm would be consolidated from people of common social background, meaning craftsmen with craftsmen, shopkeepers with shopkeepers, and learned people with learned people. It was decided that each cooperative would consist of no less than 7 and no more than 20 members. It was also decided that existing collective farms, where disputes have erupted, should be dismantled into smaller collective farms. It was also decided to be more diligent when selecting candidates for settlement. Every candidate had to fill out a detailed questionnaire, according to which it would be possible to determine the suitability of the candidate for settlement. A certain period was set as the registration - from 20 November 1925 to 15 January 1926. From that date forward, they started to approve the candidates and send them to the location of the settlement.

The original plan for 1926 was for settling 10,400 families in various provinces, on land areas totaling 250 thousand *disiyatins* [about 675,000 acres]. This mighty plan was supposed to cost about 18 million Rubles. This sum was too large for all of the organizations to assemble. Therefore, the settlement of the ten thousand settlers lasted two or three years. The plan was to settle 4,442 families during 1926, on a total area of 91 thousand *disiyatins*; however, either due to lack of financial resources or for other reasons, only 2815 were actually settled. During the three-year period 1925-1927, 12,483 families have settled on an approximate area of 300 thousand *disiyatins* [about 810,000 acres].

## The Settlement Enterprise at its Peak

When it was founded, the KOMZET had an impressive and visionary plan. The plan envisioned settling 100,000 families during a 10-year period, which meant 10 thousand families a year. Along with the established farmers from before the war, that would have resulted in about half a million farmers, or one-quarter of the entire Jewish population in Russia.

The government allocated about 300,000 *disiyatins* [810,000 acres], mainly in the provinces of Ukraine and Crimea, for settlement during the first few years. There were several proposals regarding other required areas, for example, the draining of swamp areas. Half of the initial land areas allocated for the settlement were located in the provinces of Ukraine, about a third in Crimea, and the rest in Belarus. The allocation for each family unit was determined based on the quality of the soil: 15 – 20 *disiyatins* in Ukraine, 20 in Crimea, and 25 in Belarus. The Jewish organizations also formulated their big plans for fundraising based on the KOMZET's plan. The settlement was accompanied by two aspirations. The first was the establishment of Jewish agricultural districts in which symbolic autonomy could be established, similar to the autonomy given to other nations in the Soviet Union; the other aim was collective agriculture. There was no explicit resolution regarding the autonomous districts. However, this was the state of mind of some of the regime notables and some of the Jewish communist officials who handled the Jewish settlement.

*[Page 137]*

At the OZET convention in November 1926, Kalinin, the president of the Soviet Union, gave a long welcoming speech in which he hinted at the intention that the Jewish settlement would gradually be transformed into autonomy and would perhaps reach a level enabling the establishment of a Jewish autonomous republic. The idea of a national self–rule regime for the Jews was a guiding light of the Soviet policy in those years. The heads of the settlement administration aimed at settling the Jews in concentrated areas to establish Jewish autonomous entities. These entities were called "districts" and named after prominent public notables. Such a center of Jewish settlement was established in the southern Kherson province between the Ingulets and Dnieper rivers. A total of 37 thousand *disiyatins* were allocated for the new settlers. This area linked the colonies of Bobrovy Kut and the two colonies of Sdeh Menukha with the colony of Lvovna on the bank of the Dnieper. The district, which stretched over an area of 70 thousand *disiyatins* and included 49 villages, was given the name of Kalinindorf; in this district, 39 villages were populated by Jews and 10 by Ukrainians and Germans. 11 rural councils were established in the district, eight of which were Jewish and the rest were Ukrainian and German.

A second center in Kherson was established in 1929 near Krivoy Rog. The center stretched over an area of 45 thousand *disiyatins*. The established [Jewish] colonies and the new settlements in the district totaled 37. 15 villages were Ukrainian, and 2 German. The area included 10 rural councils, among which 9 were Jewish and one was Ukrainian. This district was named Niozlatopol. The district's population, at the beginning of the 1930s, totaled 1,791 Jewish families, 665 Ukrainians and Russians, and 74 Germans.

The district of Stalindorf, established in 1930, stretched over 100,000 *disiyatins* with a population of 30 thousand people, half of whom were Jewish farmers and the rest were Ukrainians, Russians, and Germans. 23 rural councils were established in the district, 10 of which were Jewish, 2 Ukrainian, 2 German, and 9 were mixed.

The district of Freidorf in Crimea was established in 1931 and stretched over an area of close to 200 thousand *disiyatins*. It was divided among 31 rural councils, 15 of which were Jewish and 16 were mixed.

In 1935 an additional district, named Larindorf, was established.

(All the data about the Jewish districts mentioned above were taken from a pamphlet authored by M. Haft and published in Yiddish in 1936).

As mentioned earlier, the government preferred collective settlement. The people of the *Yevsektzia* [the Jewish section of the Soviet Communist Party], were particularly enthusiastic about that idea. However, the collective settlement was not mandatory. Many of the settlers tended to institute collective cultivation on the farm. However, as the years passed, it turned out that the collective cultivation caused disputes among the settlers. As a result, the collective plots were divided in many settlements into individual plots, and every settler cultivated his plot individually.

It is logical to assume that the [Jewish] associations from abroad, which financed the Jewish settlement,

*[Page 138]*

were not very enthusiastic about collective farming, as the people who headed these organizations did not favor Communism or Socialism. As partners for the settlement implementation, they, most likely, insisted on the freedom of choice by the settler. They preferred letting the settler decide whether to join a collective farm or cultivate the land individually. However, in the provinces where the settlement was established with the help of the communist OZET association, pressure was exerted on the settlers to move to the collective regime. This was probably the reason why most of the settlements in Belarus were collective in nature. In 1927, the settlement in this area numbered 1,211 families residing in 145 collectives, which meant, on average, about 8 settlers in each collective settlement.

In the province of Odesa, the collective farms received good land with sufficient fertile soil and allocations for construction and equipment. Most settlements managed to build housing and were furnished with all the needed farm equipment. The fields were cultivated more efficiently and yielded plenty of crops. In the settlements of the Kherson province, the new settlers benefited from the closeness of the established colonies. They learned from them efficient working techniques and farm management methods. The lands in Belarus were less fertile than the ones in Ukraine and southern Russia. However, the Jewish settlers, whose economic state was not very sound even before the war, were used to hardships and hard labor. They cultivated their fields methodically, with the help of the agronomists, and fertilized the fields according to the instructions of the agronomists. Instead of growing wheat and barley, crops that yielded poor harvests in these regions, they sowed other crops on their fields, which yielded more profitable harvests. Thanks to the methodical handling of the cows and proper feeding, the settlers also managed to greatly improve the milk sector.

In northern Ukraine, the Jews received plots with small fields. Had they sowed wheat and barley on them, like their neighbors, they would have doubtfully sustained themselves. Therefore, they grew corn, sunflowers, potatoes, and other field crops. To complement their incomes, the settlers leased land from the sugar factories and grew sugar beets. Following the destruction of the state economy, sugar crops were sold at high prices, ensuring decent profits for sugar beets.

After Bessarabia was annexed by Romania, there was an opportunity for growing tobacco in some areas suitable for this agricultural sector. The tobacco sector succeeded mainly around the bank of River Dnieper. In 1923, the Jews grew tobacco in the province of Podolia, on an area of 900 *disiyatins*. The tobacco sector sustained 1500 families. It is logical to assume that these numbers did not decrease and even increased in the following years.

Like before the war, the trend to specialize in a certain single agricultural sector was prominent. The Jews began to develop vegetable gardens, particularly near big cities such as Odesa, Minsk, Kiev, Kamenetz–Podolsk, and others.

The settlement in Crimea took a unique character. It started in 1923, even before the establishment of the KOMZET and its grand settling plan, when "pioneers," members of the labor Zionist movement, came to Crimea and established three communes colonies similar to the kibbutzim in Eretz

[Page 139]

Israel; these were the names of the communes: "Tel Khai" ["Hill of Life" in Hebrew, named after a village with a similar name in northern Israel where Yosef Trumpeldor was killed in 1920], "Mishmar" ["Guard" in Hebrew] and "Ma'ayan" ["Spring" in Hebrew]. The farm of "Tel Khai" stretched over an area of 1,900 *disiyatins*, and "Mishmar" – over an area of 750 *disiyatins*. The members of these communes intended to make *Aliyah* to Eretz Israel and establish these communes as places for training for themselves and for hundreds of other "*khalutzim*" [pioneers] who would follow them. The members of these communes were, like typical members of Eretz Israel's kibbutzim, idealistic youths, enthusiastic, diligent, and dedicated to their work. Their farms were cultivated intensively, and they enjoyed bountiful harvests.

As the first settlements in Crimea, where the human quality was superior, they exerted a significant influence over all the Jewish settlements that followed them. Of the 19 settlements that were founded in Crimea before 1925, eight were given Hebrew names: "Khaklai" [Agriculturalist], "Yetzira" [Creativity], "Avoda" [Work], "Hatikva" [The hope], "Akhdut" [Unity], "Ikar" [Farmer], "Kherut" [Freedom] and "Beit Lekhem" [Bethlehem, House of Bread]. Even though the first three settlements were established as pure communes, utilized advanced methods, and enjoyed bountiful harvests, they were not favored by the "*Yevskim*" [Jewish communists], who wished to establish themselves as partners of the Jewish settlement movement. Actually, the "*Yevskim*" were not allowed to set foot in the three communes. The atmosphere in the three communes was Hebrew–Zionist. Tensions prevailed between the members of these communes and the communists. As long as the "HeKhalutz" [Zionist] movement was still legal in Russia, no one could censure them. However, in 1927, when the latter movement was outlawed and many of its members were arrested, members of the communes who would not disavow the movement's ideals, faced the danger of imprisonment and punishment. They rushed to abandon their settlements and make *Aliyah* to Eretz Israel. The three colonies were handed over to other Jewish settlers.

According to the statistics from 1933–4, there were 84 [Jewish] settlements in Crimea, in an area close to 200,000 *disiyatins*. Their population totaled 25 thousand people.

The dominant language in all of the Jewish settlements was Yiddish. The books read by the settlers were in Yiddish and Russian. The management team in each settlement was elected by the settlement's residents elected. The settlers began to be acclimated to the work and village life.

In addition to the settlements established throughout the provinces of European Russia, the Soviet government decided in 1928 to establish a large–scale settlement enterprise in the province of Birobidzhan in Asia and to settle there a quarter of the Jewish population on an area of two million *disiyatins*. The intention was to turn Birobidzhan over time into a Jewish autonomous territory. However, the implementation of this colossal–scale and far-reaching plan did not progress as planned. Difficulties were encountered from the beginning and the large–scale was cut back substantially. Even with the reduced scope, the Birobidzhan plan constituted a tremendous opportunity for Russian Jewry during the 1930s. During the political purging at the end of the 1930s and later on during the years of the Second World War, the original plan, which was initiated during Kalinin's reign was archived and the Birobidzhan project was sunk and almost forgotten (see Appendices).

*[Page 140]*

According to the census of 1926, the Jewish agricultural population within the Soviet Union numbered 155,400 people. According to other official numbers, the Jewish agricultural population numbered as follows:

| Year | People |
|------|--------|
| 1927 | 165,000 |
| 1928 | 220,000 |
| 1931 | 255,000 |

These were the published numbers. However, according to statistical calculations by others (e.g. Ya'akov Leshchinski) who took into account the people that left, only 220,000 [Jewish] people were involved in agriculture in 1931. Some estimated the number to be even lower. These numbers did not correspond to the maximum plan the Soviet government decided upon in 1925–4. However, even if we use Leshchinski's numbers (according to which there were only 220,000 [Jewish] people in agriculture), and subtract the established farmers from before the war (about 60,000), we come up with about 160,000 [Jewish] people who settled in agriculture during the 1920s.

At the beginning of the 1930s, the ratio of the Jewish agriculturalists to the total Jewish population was 1:10, or 10%. This was the highest ratio of the Jewish agriculturalists in the history of the Russian Jewry, and the history of the Diaspora Jewry.

The total area of the Jewish settlement at the beginning of the 1930s was estimated to be 800,000 *disiyatins* (more than 8 million *dunams* [2,160,000 acres]). Although not all of the land areas were fully cultivated, they enabled the absorption of several additional few thousand families. These were the record years of the Jewish settlement in the Soviet Union. From then on, the decline started.

## The Decline and its Reasons; the Holocaust

According to the [Yiddish] journal "Emes" [The Truth], from the beginning of May 1938, there were 600 Jewish kolkhozes in the Soviet Union, accommodating 25 thousand families, whereas the [Yiddish] journal "Der Shtern" [The Star] reported in August 1939 that the number of the [Jewish] kolkhozes was 500 (based on the book by Y. Leshchinski about the Jews in the Soviet Union). This means the Jewish agricultural population declined in 1939 to about 150,000 people, or about 5% of the total Jewish population, which numbered 3,020,000 people in the same year.

What were the reasons for that decline? Based on the vast amount of material published about the Jewish population in Soviet Russia, we could establish the following factors:

*[Page 141]*

a. At the end of the 1920s, the first Five-year plan of the Soviet Union was announced. One of the plan's objectives was to accelerate the rate of industrialization in the country. Many industrial plants were built, which required an additional workforce. Employment in these plants was opened for the entire population, including the Jews, and without any discrimination. The work conditions in these plants were much more favorable than in the villages and ensured a higher standard of living. Working people started to flow from the villages to the industrial plants in the cities. The Jews captured a significant portion of these jobs. During the 1920s, the years of the economic shockwaves that followed the revolution, many of the proletarian craftsmen flocked to the villages. With the development of the industry, many of those craftsmen found better positions within the industry with better conditions.

b. The Jewish sections of the Communist Party placed great importance on converting the masses of Jews to proletarians in the full meaning of the word. During the conference of the Jewish communists in 1926, even before the Five-year industrialization plan was announced, some of the representatives expressed their view that it would be preferable to move the Jewish proletarians to key positions in the big industries rather than directing them toward agriculture. The view was strengthened after the announcement of the Five-year plan.

c. It is well established that manufacturing requires not just simple workers and artisans but also educated people and intelligentsia who would be able to specialize in delicate work in the laboratories. Many settlers had certainly acquired a high school education or knowledge of technical professions. Candidates of that kind were welcomed by the industry. Through their work, alongside experts, they also became professional workers of management rank. Therefore, the Five-year industrial development plan became a major factor in preventing many additional candidates from joining the settlement movement and even contributed to the decline in the existing settlement.

d. Another factor was the government announcement at the end of the 1920s concerning the imposition of the collectivist regime in Soviet agriculture. As described above, although there was a preference for collectivism over individual farms at the beginning of the settlement, the authorities did not insist then that the settlements be based on collectivism. Even settlers who originally settled on their land as a collective were allowed to disassemble and move to an individual settlement. We do not know how many continued to operate collectively and how many transferred to private farming. However, a certain number of collective farms were certainly disassembled, the fields were divided, and the farmers became independent. Like most farmers in Russia, who were not enthusiastic about the law of the kolkhozes, the attitude of the Jewish farmers towards the imposition of the collective regime was mostly negative. Anyone who was not pleased with the collectivization order and had the opportunity to find another occupation, abandoned farming.

At the end of the 1930s, the Jewish agricultural population still numbered 5% of the overall Jewish population in the Soviet Union.

Despite the decline in the scale of the new settlement, in the remaining 500 kolkhozes,

*[Page 142]*

the 25,000 Jewish families, or about 150,000 people who resided and worked there, constituted a direct continuation of the 130 years of Jewish settlement in Russia, a project that started at the beginning of the earlier century. We do not have any material about the relative success of the Jewish kolkhozes as compared to the Russian kolkhozes; however, the fact that they lasted for fifteen years supports the fact that they succeeded not worse than the others and proved their ability and skills in agriculture in the same way their ancestors did during Czarist Russia.

They flourished until the day when the torrents of destruction and annihilation descended upon them.

The German conquerors flooded the Russian Jewry and wiped out the kolkhozes, along with their Jewish settlers, from the face of the earth. The villages were robbed, burned, and destroyed by the conquering army and by the local Russians and Ukrainians. The fate of their residents, like the fate of the rest of the Jewish population in the conquered lands, was annihilation and obliteration.

A few Jewish agriculturists who survived the Holocaust may have returned after the war to their kolkhozes, where others have settled in the meantime. It is possible that somewhere in the Soviet Union, there were a few Jews who still worked the land. However, we do not know for certain. The families of Kherson and Ekaterinoslav settlers who reside in Israel told us that all of their relatives, who continued to work in agriculture before the war, were murdered and destroyed, and no trace was left of them.

This was how the [Nazi] ax put an end to the large group of people who worked the land and who sustained themselves on the farming villages in southern Russia for one hundred and thirty years.

*Note:* The bibliographic list for this section appears on page 428.

*[Page 143]*

# Folklore Chapters

*[Page 144]*

The steppe – with flowers adorned
Planted by G–d Himself
Spread far and goes further
Without a beginning, without an end.

**C. N. Bialik**
From his poems in Yiddish

**Translated by Yocheved Klausner**

*[Page 145]*

# Ba'Arva
## (On the Prairie)

## by David Tverdovsky[1]

*To my Parents - Nakhman and Khaya, of blessed memory*

## Translated from Hebrew to English by Moshe Kutten[2]

## Edited by Yocheved Klausner

## The Journey to the Fields

A custom common in this house from the days of my great-grandfather was to go out to the prairie at the onset of the harvest season to examine the crops. At the house, the children were already reminding each other, on the day prior, about the joyful news:

"Tomorrow we are going out to inspect how the winter crops have fared!"

"…and we will also visit the wheat and oat crops," said *Saba*
[grandfather in Hebrew.]

"…and you will eat breakfast near the Lake of Elimelekh," announced *Savta*
[grandmother in Hebrew.].

For the small children, this was a true holiday, and for R' Yehuda-Leib'ichka[3] [ichka is an endearment ending in Yiddish. MK], this traditional journey to the prairie was held, from the early times, like a holy ritual occurring every year, before the harvest season, with an exceptional festive spirit and reverence.

At the day's first light, the grandchildren, giddy and excited, were singing melodies of ditty songs, gathering in the yard and rolling, together with *Saba*, out from under its cover, the blackish polished carriage which, during all of its beautiful and usually easy life was only used for special and festive occasions. In this ornamented carriage, we used to travel during the period of *Shavuot* [the harvest holiday.], or even just on Shabbat to stay with the sons' families in *Sdeh-Ya'akov* [literally - "The Field of Ya'akov."], or to visit our relatives in *Nakhlat-Shefa Hagdola*[4] The carriage was also used to accompany a military recruit from the village to the train station or a groom to his wedding. On some rare occasions, the carriage also served to welcome a Gubernator [a governor], who had announced his intended visit in advance. However, this grandeur carriage was mainly used for trips, made from time to time, to the crop fields in the prairie.

Oh, how festive, worry-free, and pleasant were these journeys!

From early dawn, the carriage was already standing opposite the open gate, decorated, sparkling in its shiny blackness, and attracting the crowd of fiery grandchildren with its beautiful welcoming affability and springy softness.

*[Page 146]*

Those grandchildren were already climbing it up and down and cuddling on its black varnished wings, singing on its foot ramp from that side to the other and pulling R' Yehuda Leib'ichka's coat-wing every minute:

"*Saba, Nu* [a call of impatience in Yiddish]! When are we going, *Saba*?"

*Saba* was far from sitting idle. At that hour, he had already managed to return from the Morning Prayer, water the farm animals, bring the cows and the calves to the herd leaving for the meadow, and anoint the carriage's axels and wheels with resin. In fact, he had been busy during a good part of the morning with the preparations. At the crack of dawn, he had already sent his two gigantic youngest sons, Hirsch and Vevi, along with his eldest daughters on the green carriage loaded with tools, supplies, and a brimful barrel of water to the "fifth plot" which was the farthest away, to hoe the corn and sunflower tracts. After that, he saw to the shaking of the sleep out of the two slumberous girls, Dina'tshe *[tshe* – an ending of endearment in Yiddish] and Etly, and went with the girls down to the vineyard to give them instructions for the day's work. Later on, he took a pair of smooth and well-nurtured horses out of the stables - the two courageous and fiery horses brushed them thoroughly, trimmed slightly their rather long tails, and adorned them with a pair of splendid reins fitted with small bells, yellowish bronze shoeing, and twisted red fringes for decoration.

Even little Zelik[5], the oldest of the grandchildren, was not idle. He helped his grandfather with body movements that were meant to show sincerity and practicability. Above the hook of the rear axle, he hanged an empty pail for collecting corn cubs on the way back for cooking, and before climbing with the whip to sit on the bench, he hurried up to the doghouses to release the dogs.

Whereas the quiet and skinny Rachela managed, before climbing onto the carriage, to pump some rainwater and fill, for *Savta*, a tub from the concrete pool located near the new wide sheet-metal roofed house. She even managed to soak the laundry in the tub.

The two freed dogs, Vera and Pranaitis[a], participated in this hurried activity as well. They walked around under the legs of the household members, like two self-pleased in-laws, twisting their way among the children, waggling their tails with flattery. They licked, with appreciation, the faces of the smallest children causing them to fall from time to time. This was an additional and unnecessary annoyance for *Savta*, who was very busy anyway. The cries of the scared children made *Savta* restless, and she grumbled, from one minute to another, and moaned toward the opened door, full of outrage:

*[Page 147]*

"I am just asking you, Zelik! Didn't you have any other work before you had untied the dogs?  Look here, look, how the babies are being frightened!"

However, *Savta* did not have any spare time to worry about the babies at that moment. Everything was on fire now under her hands.

Just as the earliest reddish stains appeared in the brightening east, *Savta* Dvora Zisel[6] was already on her feet. She thought to herself that, on a festive day like today, anything she had to deal with had a taste of elation and childhood. Amazingly light and agile, she threw herself into the stove, below her waist, and moved the baking pans from here to there, taking some of them out as provisions for the trip. One of the pans was filled with poppy seeds cookies, and the other with fat dumplings filled with cheese. Besides the special boiled eggs, rolled thoroughly in ember, there were also dumplings filled with pumpkin and all sorts of other foods that she usually prepared for Lag BaOmer[1] - all of that was prepared to supply *Saba* and the grandchildren on their festive trip to the fields.

*Savta* had to pack these provisions with her own hands and secure every item in its place on the carriage to prevent any damage. She then also added a jar full of plum compote, which was left over from Sabbath, along with nicely cut and arranged honey-rye rusks for a meal-ending dessert. For the young crowd, who were always thirsty, she added a clay jug full of water, and for her old man, she stuck a bunch of sun-dried cheese triangles under the seat, along with a jug full of sour milk. To secure the jug and to prevent, G-d forbid, any turning over or spilling, she laid down some hay under and around it. She kept reminding the old man that a cocoa bottle was specially prepared for Rakhela - the little skinny and thin countess who was fussy with her food.

"…and just don't forget, Yehuda-Leib, that here, under the seat, I embedded the bottle."

In addition, just a short moment before they left for their trip, she reminded, and asked one more time, that - "he would not stay there too long and come back home as early as possible, and "for G-d's sake, don't make any of the children catch cold." At the same moment, she whispered to herself:

"It is on me and myself - whatever may happen to you!"

As the warm and impatient horses were already moving, she still stood there, with her hands hugging behind her apron and under her head shawl, which was tied under her chin for modesty, her luminous and wrinkled face peeked for a long while - a face by which one could never tell whether she was laughing or crying. This happy *Savta* exulting in gratitude, just stood there at the gate for a while longer, looking after the carriage exiting toward the street, following

*[Page 148]*

with her eyes, the carriage that carried her meager treasure, her cream of the crop, and just at the last moment, remembered to shout after the departing carriage:

"Please watch Yosa'le [le- endearing ending for Yosef], Yehuda Leib… yes, yes…Yosa'le! Pull his pants down in time before he goes, this little pig! …and watch Teiba'le. She has a runny nose…Teiba'le…. and as far as little Moshe-Khaim'ke [ke - endearing ending for Khaim], you should better move him near you on the bench… yes, yes…, otherwise he would pinch them all, this Mazik [endearing term which literally means a pest], and everybody would end up with blue bruises…"

However, nobody listened to her voice anyway any longer. The old man nodded his head, just as to fulfill one's duty, and hinted at the courageous and elegantly decorated horses to start their brisk galloping, but gradually he allowed them to return to their regular steady pace.

The carriage, with its quivering load, exited the lower street – also called the "Mem Tet Street" [Mem-Tet in Hebrew's Gematria - 39], crossed diagonally the six upper straighter streets, and soon left the colony. Swaying gently on its springs the carriage crossed under the Eruv [Sabbath range limit] and as if it was hovering and floating, sailed toward the flat, wide, and infinite prairie.

"Oh, how happy and beautiful were these outing trips!"

At first, the melon plots sprawled and extended - the plots with the bright green watermelons and the yellow melons, which were hiding among the intricate leaf blades. Only then, running and approaching from both sides of the narrow road, were the first wheat fields, quivering and shifting in the wind.

How widely and gracefully were the waves hitting - the waves of this huge sea of wheat stalks, heavy with the night dew-saturated grain and carrying within them the winter wheat!

How mystified and carrying a message of abundance was the heavy and somewhat yellowish rye bending over and whispering to the erect, unkempt-headed, and restless oat crops moving and gaudy in the wind!

The festive spirit was so plentiful here. The jubilant chanting of fast growth, the blessing of good luck and abundance, the melody of an approaching harvest, and the plentiful crop about to be collected to the barn were apparent everywhere.

Far, far away, in the bluish steamy horizon, the rising tall silhouette of the old monument named after "Ber'eh-Volf"[8] emerged and protruded more and more clearly. This was the old mount with the shape of a sharpened cone towering up. The sight of the old "monument" prompted R' Yehuda-Leib to begin his tale.

*[Page 149]*

## "The One who is Working His Land Will Always be Fed"

[Book of Proverbs 28:19]

"Look over there, children - near the monument of Ber'eh-Volf, your ancestors prayed their first prayer on their own land immediately upon arriving at Novo-Russia [Southern Ukraine], more than a hundred years ago. As you would soon learn, my beloved grandchildren, their journey was very long, extremely hard, life-threatening, and full of life dangers."

Upon hearing these words, the children quieted down and attentively observed the monument, which was still far away in the distance but protruding majestically on the horizon. From that point on, they settled into listening curiously and eagerly to *Saba*'s story.

R' Yehuda-Leib'ichka himself turned around, halfway toward his grandchildren, until they could see his profile and hung the loose reins on the broken handle that protruded above the carriage seat. The courageous-fiery horses were already running by themselves steadily at their own rhythm. With ease, they sailed through the prairie, which was divided by colorful stripes and bands.

"All of that happened in the days of Czar Alexander the First. He was just a very young man at the time and probably a good-natured king. However, his advisers incited him to stray away from his honest ways."

"With one hand, he signed an order to settle the Jews in the desert prairie of Novo-Russia around the Black Sea. These were the days when the prairie was new and wild land - a desert area conquered from the Turks. The young and ambitious king was therefore interested in settling this uninhabited area as soon as possible, and he promised your great-grandparents assistance during the initial settlement period - until they could stand on their own feet. He promised to give every family a pair of oxen, some seeds, and tools needed to establish a farm. He promised all of that, not as a gift, G-d forbid, but as a loan, on credit, until the new settlers would be able to pay their debt slowly, gradually, and incrementally. But in particular, the king promised the settlers to provide them with government-built houses. Not to loan them money for the houses but to build them, ahead of time, before they arrived at their new land."

This was, certainly, very kind and nice of him. However, counter to the first order, he signed, with his other hand, an order to expel all the Jews from their villages, namely to throw them out of their existing homes in their current settlements. You can imagine for yourself the situation, where thousands of families along with their elderly, children, and women - were driven away, one bright day, hurriedly and hastily, like prisoners under the guard of soldiers, leaving them without a roof over their heads. Just like a herd of sheep, they were expelled and pushed out from all villages to the provincial towns and cities and left abandoned and homeless on the city streets."

*[Page 150]*

That was the reason why many of the dislodged people, practically whole communities of Jews, who were uprooted of their places and left without means to support themselves - now grabbed onto the Czar's offer to settle as farmers in the prairies of this new land. Wild prairies, uncultivated for generations upon generations, waiting since the six days of creation, for owners to come, settle and work them.

This hasty race by the Jews to acquire land, started only after the expulsion from the villages, when the sword was already laid upon their necks. That was how this dashing toward settlement started. It became an even bigger panic, one generation later, as a result of another decree – the one associated with the abduction issue.

When R' Yehuda-Leib felt that his grandchildren did not understand what he was referring to, he proceeded to explain and provide more details:

"The abduction issue was about the Jewish children who were abducted to be turned into soldiers. They were abducted by their mother and father and were handed over, forcibly, to the military to become Czar Nicolai's soldiers. That is unlike the recruits of today who enlist when they reach the age of 21, serve two years and eight months, and then return home. No! These evil people were not satisfied with that. They forced little children – nine and ten-year-old, to become "*Cantonists*," meaning, servants of the Czar, for no more and no less than twenty-five whole years. That way, they would forcibly uproot them from their Jewish heritage. For example, take our old Michailo, namely, our gentile bath attendant, who is actually Jewish."

"Is he really? Our mute gentile-bath attendant is Jewish? asked the astonished children, raising wondering and amazed voices.

"Yes! Yes!" said *Saba*.

"He is a true Jew, and he is not mute at all. Tormented and pain-stricken he is. He forgot, for a long time now, how to speak Yiddish. His real name and place of birth escape his memory. Jewish customs are already alien to him. In his old age, he does not want to use *Fonye*'s language [*Fonye* – a derogatory name for a Russian, in general, and for the Czar, in particular], particularly among Jews. However, a Jewish spark was preserved in his soul. These Feldwebels [Sargent-Majors] could not uproot this spark out of him with their whips and lashes. And so - here he is, residing in the corridor of the public bath, and people in the colony invite him, from time to time, as a guest to stay with them on Sabbath."

The mood of the grandchildren became somber, because of this unexpected discovery, so the old man hurried to return the discussion to its main subject:

"This was the reason why, in my opinion, many new colonies were established later on. The reason was that the settlers were awarded a complete exclusion, during the first few years after settlement, from the threat of this horrible military duty. In any case, the first and the oldest colonies were established well before this panic migration."

*[Page 151]*

The actual founders of the first colonies, that is, the first who settled here more than a hundred years ago, were people who carried in their hearts, in most cases, the idea of walking on their own piece of land. They carried the idea for a long time, long before the Jews were expelled from their villages. These people dreamt about returning to working the land, to agriculture, to the life of farmers, like the life of our ancestors in ancient times who lived on their own land in our fatherland, sitting under their own vine [1 Kings 4:25 – a phrase used to describe peaceful life] – everyone as a homeowner and farm owner rooted in one's land.

Among the first settlers who came here, most of whom were storekeepers and craftsmen, were also quite a few learned people, young men of knowledge with modern views, who went out on the journey together with the commoners and devoted themselves, with all of their faith and warmth of their heart to the interest of the settlement. For these young faithful people, the land idea was the most important issue. They believed that the Jewish renewal would come from returning to their land.

For just a small piece of land, they were willing to go to the ends of the earth and even beyond the Sambation, just to break out of the narrow square cubit of the miserable Jewish domain and redeem themselves, once and for all, from the Jewish distress. They wished to rid themselves of the low-value bogus Jewish ways of making a living, escape and distance themselves, as far as possible, from the envy-hatred of the gentiles, and finally breathe freely the pure air of the spacious prairie, mixed with the smell of raw and fresh hay."

The old man encircled with his radiant glance everything the eye could capture around him all the way through the place where the waves of the wheat kissed the bluish heavens above, turned a bit more on his seat, and faced the rest of the young children.

The horses, which were left to run free, galloped by themselves very nicely and alertly along the lengthy field road, a route they knew thoroughly. While running along the familiar road, with their specially-made leather "glasses" that hid their view on the left and right, the horses nevertheless managed somehow to occasionally throw their gluttonous necks beyond the edge of the field, as if casually, tear off a bunch of barley spikes and grind them quickly between their teeth with the rein in their mouth.

And so, R' Yehuda-Leib'icka continued: "These learned people were those who, most of the time, served as the principal organizers of the pioneering groups in our original localities. They were the ones who convinced the rest of the people to come back to "mother earth" by using the phrase: "He who tills his land will have plenty of bread" [Proverbs 12:11], meaning - the Jewish salvation and sustenance would only be secured by working the land.

In addition, these young learned pioneers had to lead the first groups of settlers through the lengthy and dangerous journey; ...and when they arrived at the settlement locations, they had to shoulder the burden

*[Page 152]*

of all of the public matters.

Even dealing with *Fonye*'s authorities was not one of the easiest things to do - not at all! That was because they had to deal with Jew-haters and bribe-lovers. These thugs were the ones from whom they had to receive, those days, all the borrowed farm needs - horses and carriages, meager seeds, and needed tools. It was also necessary to watch the authority people closely so that they would not distort the bills and would not decrease or completely deny the support promised to the settlers. Besides all that, they had to deal with the headache associated with digging the wells equipped with ice cellars, "*Batei Midrash*" [Houses of learning and praying], and the "*Kheder's*" [religious classrooms for children], worry about finding a Rabbi and a medic, erecting a public bathhouse with a *mikveh* [ritual bath], and other thousands of concerns and matters associated with establishing a new settlement.

These young people were best fitted and able to deal with all these issues. They had not only devoted themselves to doing all of these tasks, but they were also knowledgeable and experienced with all the needed information. They were well-spoken in Russian so that they could relate their claims with the authorities appropriately and, in times of distress, they were able to serve as emissaries to the honorable Gubernator [governor] himself."

## About G-d's Grace

In the meantime, behind the horizon, the sun began to unfold and rise a little and, while still young and big, rolled and ascended above the Ber'eh-Volf monument, and from there, it shone all over the entire prairie and dazzled it to its edges. Only the far-far away margins retained their early morning fogs, which were still hanging in the air, painting the air silver.

From time to time, R' Yehuda-Leib'itckha sneaked in a brief glance at the horses and the two dogs that were running around uninterruptedly ahead of them. He enjoyed the crops that passed by on both sides of the narrow road above the vast sea of spikes, fluttering in the wind, and continued his story: "Our great-grandfathers originally gathered together into a small group containing about one hundred families and set out on this awfully frightening long journey. That was the reason, my dear children, that setting out on such a long and strenuous journey with one's family and all belongings required an abundance of courage in those days. It required plenty of patience and stubbornness to set out with wife and children, relying on G-d's grace and wander to the edges of the world, to start everything anew, from the beginning."

As said before, these were the days of Czar Alexander the First. There were still no railroads during those days, nor were there powerful and rested mail-horses provided in exchange for their tiring mules. Families were large and burdened by many little children,

*[Page 153]*

and the journey involved many months of traveling in canopy-covered wagons from Belarus, Lithuania, and Poland.

On my father's side, our family originated from a big metropolis called Vitebsk. However, your grandmother Dvora-Zisel claims that her parents' parents came from Courland [northern part of Latvia]. This in itself is not that important to our discussion. In fact, your grandmother is a native of Novo-Karslevka, [actually, Dvora-Gitel was one of the first-borns of the colony-settlement of Novo-Poltavka] - which is one of the later colonies or settlements in the Nikolayev [Mykolaiv] region. What we are talking about here – is the pioneering settlers who set out in those days in groups to travel on the harrowing wandering routes of Mother Russia and then scattered in all directions leading to the Black Sea on their way to the far, yearned for, south.

With the heavy oxen, they certainly did not advance very swiftly like a bow's arrow. They dragged themselves very slowly on all possible alternate desert roads of the desolated and remote Novo-Russia. In fact, they walked more than rode.

As they drove deeper and farther away, the tired and straggled groups lagged behind and scattered along the enormous stretches of the prairie, spreading over distances of hundreds of miles.

The meager coins and necessities that they took with them, were exhausted long ago. The five Kopecks per day provided by the authorities for food could not buy much – perhaps only some water for the porridge. Even that "poor man's loaf" was not always available to them in time. Many wagons had already deteriorated due to the hard and long journey, and the food for the oxen was also lacking.

The number of the sick increased from one day to another, and so did the number of the dead. Small children were the most vulnerable. Many pregnant women were lost on the way. There was hardly any family who was not struck by the bitter fate.

The groups dwindled and became impoverished. However, despite all the misfortunes, the settlers pressed on, and bravely broke their way south. Weary, hungry, and disheartened due to the frequent fatalities, they nevertheless pushed on, placing their fate in the hands of the Creator, and forced their way through, farther and deeper southward into Novo-Russia, and thus, filled with hope, paved the way for all of us."

While revealing his ancestors' tale, R' Yehuda Leib'ichka glanced delightfully at the group of young travelers on the carriage, for whom his father's fathers once paved here the new road. He took out a lighter from the pocket of his blazer, tamped his pipe, passed over the steel lighter with several swift motions, over the flint rock with the wick, and brought up the flame and the smoke.

"And so, my dear grandchildren, after several good months of wandering, the depleted group, originally containing more than one hundred families, the group that later on established our settlement of Nahar Gilovka [Literally Gilovka River][2] was by now shrunken and depressed from the unrelenting, day-and-night travel.

*[Page 154]*

This "little" journey was drawn out and entered slowly into the fifth month. Everything transformed into a wasteland. Even the strongest people weakened and withered.

Some of the wagons dried up from the weariness of the thousands of *verstas* [an old Russian measure of length – about 2/3 of a mile] fell apart and could not be used. Even the patient and formidable oxen could not always tolerate the hardship. Many of them kneeled under the heavy added load, and the lack of food just spread their hoofs and expired. Since families with broken wagons had to be moved from the damaged to the unbroken wagons together with the rest of the group, the crowding under the canopies became more and more unbearable. As a result, the numbers of the sick and the dying increased even more.

Our Novo-Russia settlers were never enormously wealthy people, to begin with. During the long journey that lasted months, the pockets of our group emptied until there wasn't even a penny left for any expense.

Despite the nice promises by the authorities given at their original localities that included a guarantee of a sufficient amount of food and wagons for the entire trip – the settlers became disappointed from the beginning. It had been agreed that they would be helped in the same way as the other non-Jewish settlers.

In reality, the German settlers, who could be assumed to be wealthier to begin with and who also received additional support from their government, received four times as much support from the Russian authorities, thus earning twenty Kopecks for every five promised to the Jewish settlers. Hence, the Jewish settlers realized, from their first step, that they had been lured into one big calamity. Their people were dropping, like flies, due to the meager amount of food. The farther they went on their way, the more victims the infinite wandering claimed. It got to the point that half of the original pioneers perished before they arrived at their destination.

Our ancestors left thousands of graves seeded along all the direct and by-ways of Mother Russia.

You may ask, why would the authorities do that, and for what purpose? After all, for the authorities, as agreed ahead of time, these were travel expenses given on loan, which were supposed to be paid back. The settlers agreed to eventually pay back their loan to the authorities to the last penny. They ended up paying all of their debts to the last penny, with interest and beyond - twice over. Even if any small portion of the debt was ever absolved, once in a blue moon, on the occasion of a Czar coronation or any other festive day, the government had never lost its share in that deal. On the contrary - the government grabbed and received a fat bone from us, when years later, it confiscated, with one swoop, the entire public fund, more than a million rubles that were accumulated in the colonies over decades.

*[Page 155]*

…But this really happened later. For the moment, the poor settlers had to undergo a new ordeal – namely, selling their own meager belongings for a slice of bread. Due to the scanty five Kopecks' food ration, which they did not always receive on time, a new series of selling everything they owned - commenced. People took the last shirt off their backs and their only pair of boots. They even bartered their Sabbath candlesticks, all of that for a loaf of bread, a pot of millet, or a jar of milk for the babies who were overcome by hunger."

R; Yehuda Leib'ichka adjusted his sitting on the bench and scolded Moshe-Khaim'ke, who went overboard with his mischievous behavior. He then continued his story: "Obviously, the settlers set out on their way at the beginning of the summer. However, in the meantime, the summer was already over, and the distance to the location of the new settlement with the promised new houses, somewhere in the remote prairie of Novo-Russia, was still very far. It was, literally, at the end of the world. The oxen seemed always to have spare time on their hand. Oxen are not horses. Unless it is particularly lazy, the horse is an agile creature. Just pour a bag of hay into its bowel and let it rest, it would then immediately continue to march ahead."

R' Yehuda Leibi'chka, glanced proudly over his two smooth and buoyant runners - swift and quick-moving horses and continued: "The horse swallows miles like an iron train, hurriedly and alertly. The ox, on the other hand – does not! They are like yesterday! You children never saw such heavy and sluggish beasts in your life. The ox is never in a hurry. It is an apathetic and easy-going creature - a bulk of indifference. This creature is like saying – "if I do not arrive today, there is always tomorrow." The ox, with its white and cold bile, was not interested in the fact that the tired convoy of exhausted wandering settlers had been tortured on this road for five months and that it was losing its last strength.

Indeed, the fall was already approaching, pursuing them on their heels but the way to rest and security of the Promised Land was still long and distanced.

Distant from the main road, cut off from the rest of the world, alone and forgotten, our muddled group wandered and strayed in the desolated prairie like a strange monster in the land of the last judgment, who was ordered to wander around until the end of time. Our poor wanderers were not sure anymore whether they would ever be granted the privilege of seeing the place they yearned for and the houses that were supposed to be built for them ahead of time as promised. The bright, clean, warm, and welcoming houses had certainly been waiting for them already for quite some time now. The authorities' delegates are also certainly standing and waiting for them, ready to welcome them cheerily:

"*Milusti prusim*" [welcome in Russian]. Kindly agree to accept these new houses, and settle down on your land. Good luck and all the best!"

…and the delegates would proceed to quickly light the fire in the stove, set a pot with hot stew on it, and hurriedly bake a rye bread, and before all of that, there would be a pot filled with cholent[10] to refresh one's soul.

…but, man thinks and G-d sits in Heaven [a Hebrew version of the Yiddish phrase which means – "the reality is always different from one's plans."]

It should have been, probably,

*[Page 156]*

expected from the start that all of their adventures would turn into nightmares. Outside, the fall could already be felt in all its strength. Our orphaned bunch, which was already reduced and dwindled enormously, perhaps about sixty or seventy families altogether, was drawn deeper and deeper into the heart of the open, cold, and infinite prairie.

Every morning, at dawn, dense and humidity-packed fogs descended, blinding the eyes and making the road more torturous - a road that was already challenging and unfamiliar. Many times, the fog caused the group to stray away from the proper route and proceed in an entirely wrong direction. When strong winds blew against the travelers, the heavy-moving oxen would carefully assess the situation, turn around, and pull in the opposite direction, like saying – "get me out of here." So now - with all of your wisdom, go and make them turn around and regain the lost few miles.

Yes, yes children, milk, and honey - your ancestors did not lick on this trip - not at all! In fact, as you can see, things turned out to be extremely misfortunate.

The fall came closer and closer and was already hanging over their heads every day, cloudy and furious, ready to unleash its wrath and its downpour. Torrent and cold winds blew their frozen breath over the torn, worn-out, and exposed wanderers' camp. At dusk, bitter cold and dense irritating rainfall chased after the travelers, penetrating the torn canopies and piercing through into the water–soaked wagons loaded with the frail. The rest of the camp - the exhausted walking travelers, would follow behind the wagon, dragging their swollen and bloody feet using the last remnants of their strength."

At that point, the old man quieted and encircled, with his penetrating eyes, the group of children who started to be raucous. The noise grew beyond his tolerable limit. He raised his long and threatening eyebrows toward the mischievous Moshe-Khaim'ke, as a precaution, until the child became frightened and quieted immediately like a scared kitten. On the other side, he turned toward tiny Yosa'le, who was just about ready to start crying, and cheered him up with a broad smile, playfully wiggling his eyes. He then took out a candy box.

"Who wants from these sweetie sweets?

"Me, me," yelled everybody in one voice, except the two older grandchildren Zelik and Rakhela. "I want a red one *Saba*! …and for me, *Saba*, a green one! …and a blue one for me."

*Saba* made sure to share the candy with everyone and thus calmed and quieted them all down. The slim and serious-minded Rakhela took Yosa'le and set him on her lap in an act of guardianship.

"This is good on your part, Rakhela. Watch over the little ones, and you – Moshe Khaim'ke – be quiet! I do not want to hear a noise or sound from you!"

*[Page 157]*

## "It is Good to Heap the Burning Coals when Somebody Else Does It"

"And so, my children - one evening, all sloppy and wet, the rain was drizzling slowly-slowly, not hastily, but uninterruptedly, soaking the tattered and torn canopies, penetrating to the bones. The whole prairie was dark and muddy, and the wagons were stuck in the mud above their wheels' axles. The worn-out oxen, slow and heavy to begin with, were dragging their hooves in the murky fog, crawling at an undeniable turtle pace. Any tiny advance or minute movement forward required an unbelievable effort; every mile forward seemed to be as difficult as the parting of the Red Sea.

The exhausted travelers were looking for a small flicker of light in the darkness. Perhaps a sign of a small village - a community of people, which might give hope for a sheltered night with a roof over their heads, and hopefully a little cholent to revive their soul and some hay or straw for the animals.

…But there was only darkness and pitch-blackness on the prairie - "a palpate complete darkness" [one of the ten plagues] …and the annoying misty rain continued non-stop to dampen the bones, sticking icy needles in one's back and freezing up the body.

The lone two guides, who were only slightly knowledgeable about the route, were still marching exhaustively in front of the group, trampling in the mud, scouting in the dark to find the flooded road. These were the two emissaries who were sent ahead of time to tour the place in Novo-Russia. They were your great-grandfather Ber'eh-Volf [actually Avraham-Ber Tverdovsky, *Saba* Moshe-Leib Tverdovsky's father] and his good friend Elimelekh Nevler - named after his native town – Nevel [Today a Russian city near the Belarus border]. These two public servants had some experience since they had already visited, by government initiative, the region near the Black Sea, which was offered to the settlers. As representatives of a large group of settlers, they were allowed to extensively tour the area ahead of time, select a nice piece of land, and decide upon the exact appropriate location for the first settlement. They had selected to establish it on the elevated bank of the Yeni-Gil River [actually the Ingulets River] – a name that means "the New River" in the tongue of the Turkish people.

G-d endowed these two vigorous people, both *Saba* Ber'eh-Volf and his friend Elimelekh Nevler, with wisdom and decisiveness. Both, thank G-d, were people without any faults. They were young, healthy, and well-learned people. Both had also carried in their heart for many years, the idea of establishing Jewish colonies.

The first, courageous *Saba* Ber'eh-Volf, was a fearless Jew who did not balk at any difficulty. Agile in his actions, cleanly dressed, opinionated, and decisive, he became the first "*Schultz*" – namely the first village elder [name adapted from the German settlers]. The second, Elimelekh Nevler, was not one of the frightened or the weaklings either. He was muscular and tall, with broad shoulders and a scary club that put fear

*[Page 158]*

in the heart of the prairie robbers of those days and all other kinds of wanderers with bad intentions. He generated respect and appreciation from anyone who met him because everybody realized that he could land a hard and "dry" blow at a time of need, which may cause any potential victim of his to expire on the spot with just a sigh. In fact, he was a good-hearted man by his character, a communicative person who liked to mingle with other people and was well-spoken even with the authorities. He was also an expert navigator. People said about him that he was some kind of an astrologer because he had a good sense of direction and could find the correct route even in complete darkness.

That was the reason why all of these brave and agile *Avrekhim* [Torah-ready youths] and their families converged around these two leaders. Even under these horrible conditions, the two were still treading ahead in the mud, groping and touching every step of the flooded road to avoid any pits, trenches, or dangerous sudden slopes.

Despite all the efforts, to their disappointment, they did not find any sign of a settlement or at least an inn on the side of the road. The prairie itself was one big expanse of darkness. The rain trickled and poured alternately, causing fear and terror under the torn canopies. Like a "*Hekdesh*" [a poorhouse] on wheels – a troubled and tormented congregation, crying out their heart to Heavens.

…But no, no. This was not just a "*Hekdesh*!" It was something much worse than that - a thousand times worse! Hell itself descended to earth, spreading over the entire prairie, penetrating the canopies accompanying our pioneering and courageous settlers in a horrific parade, traveling and marching to Novo-Russia.

People lay under the canopies in piles, cramped from pain, soaked, smelling of stench, and burning with fever. The most severe was the condition of the children. Sighing silently, almost every one of them was held by the claws of diseases. Every child was sick with diphtheria, scarlet fever, measles, or rubella, and some just with an intestine disease or malaria.

All those people laid down close together, unconscious and burning like a hot blaze. With scorched lips, they demanded a bit more from this world, numbing out of their fever, but no one was listening to them any longer, except the angel of death that followed them step after step. He was already standing guard under their headrests and spreading his commands openly and forcefully."

R' Yehuda Leib'ichka himself looked like he was reliving this old and remote time - in the gloomy past of sorrow, bravery, and suffering. Completely absorbed and excited, he clung passionately to his pipe and intensely pulled several suctions. He touched the reins as if just to do one's duty and continued cynically with deep bitterness - "It is good to heap the burning coals when somebody else does it"

Above the prairie, the air had already warmed up pretty nicely. The old man tossed

*[Page 159]*

his blazer off his shoulders and remained only in his shiny black vest. He took out his chained pocket watch and glanced over it. He asked Rakhel'le to serve as a temporary housewife and provide all the children with some snacks to keep their hunger in check until breakfast. He himself just blew a few smoke loops into his beard and continued his story.

"That was how, my dear grandchildren - they sent the Jews to settle - heartless, without a basic insight into the needs of the settler, particularly the Jewish settler, without any warm sentiment or some simple human compassion. That was how they sent our great-grandparents to Novo-Russia - without proper training, an expert guide, proper clothing, sufficient provisions and equipment, and anything else. Everybody was, by now, half-naked and exposed, torn and worn-out, and suffering from cold and starvation. Everybody had lost everything except the will to live and the faith in the Creator that He would lead them into a new and free life. They believed that He would stand by them during this second Exodus from Egypt, rescue them from this desert, and bring them finally, after all of these bitter and harsh encounters, to their settlement, yearned dwellings, and the place of their new lives.

…And this was just what happened and how the events really unfolded.

Silently, with a whispered and submissive prayer on their lips, our desperate and dispirited group poured its bitter heart toward G-d - compassionate and graceful G-d, and asked for His mercy:

"Our Father in Heavens, please observe our sick babies, our little and innocent chicks, lying there in the wet and cold canopied wagons. Please save them now before it is too late to do so!"

Their heart-rending prayer most likely did reach Heaven, and a miracle happened. Finally, the camp's scouts discovered a frightened and trembling flicker of light in the faraway distance. Tears filled *Saba-*Ber'eh-Volf's eyes – tears of joy. He quickly ordered some of the youths, who accompanied him in the scouting group, to return to the camp and apprise the people of this happy news and thus help cheer up somewhat the very depressed community.

## An Angel from Heaven

The intensifying flickering lights that were growing in numbers made it clear that they were approaching not just an abandoned hut or a tiny village but a large and well-populated settlement that had suddenly shown itself up in this desolate infinite and cruel prairie. Our heartened camp crawled forward with its last drops of energy and arrived, with G-d's help, to a large metropolis. As it turned out, that was a notable provincial city, which housed a Gubernator or a provincial governor, who was a gold-hearted person. Sokolov Voznesenski was

*[Page 160]*

his name. This was not just a person – he was an angel! I recall from my childhood days, that every time the settlers had mentioned his name, they could not stop praising him for his good heart.

This was a rare Jewish-loving person and a magnificent human being. Although it was a relatively late hour, definitely beyond his office hours, he welcomed the representatives of this pitiful group that arrived in his city without any delay.

These representatives had a few things to complain about. *Saba* Ber'eh-Volf told the Gubernator in minute detail about all the deep troubles the camp went through along the long journey - hunger and cold, death and suffering. He told him about those who died and about the many who lost their way and never came back. He told him about the broken wagons and the remaining oxen, which were also failing: "Enough, we do not have any more energy to continue in our way."

After *Saba* laid out all of his grievances, Elimelekh from Nevel did not scrimp and added some grievances of his own using some polished Russian phrases just to fortify his friend's tales.

While they were talking, the Gubernator glanced over these two strange fellows and thoroughly examined their thinning and shrunk faces and their sunken and feverish eyes and was moved by their circumstances. He tried to calm them down and asked them fatherly to come back at dawn when his office would be open and he would try to arrange for anything they may need to continue their trip.

*"Vasha Gubern'torskuya Visuchtavo,"* which means, "Your Honor the Gubernator"

*Saba* Ber'eh-Volf could not restrain himself again: "We thank you from the bottom of our hearts for your kind reception. However, if you want to help us, you must do it now - this minute! Our people are waiting for us outside in the rain, soaked to their bones. Hungry and frozen, they stand over there in the market square, trembling, and their teeth are shaking from the cold. We also have many sick people, some with dire conditions, we need a medic right away, a hospital, medications... especially for our children, our poor and tortured babies... and maybe also...but let's not open the door for Satan...G-d forbid...we need to check immediately under the canopies..."

...And with these words, our *Saba,* who was as strong as iron, could not control himself anymore. His heart broke inside, and he felt a vast weakness descending on him. Suddenly, he choked up and a wellspring of tears burst into his eyes. He started to cry like a little child against his strong will. That was when Elimelekh came to his aid: "Your Honor, dear enlightened Gubernator" - he said – "please have mercy and charity, come down with us for just a brief moment and see what is really happening there with your own eyes... Oy what is really happening there?"

Being an honest and good-hearted Christian, he did not need to let them beg any longer. He went with them down to the street that was occupied by

*[Page 161]*

wrecked wagons, loaded with strange figures, wrapped and bundled with all sorts of rugs, tattered garments, and sacks – torn, soaked, and rotten smelling from decay and dampness. The figures looked like terrifying scarecrows. Twisted from the chill and cuddled together, they stood there, leaning on the steaming oxen, exposed to the thorny wind, and shivered.

As soon as the Gubernator saw these frightening shadows, with their torn rags hanging and flapping on their exposed bodies and their swollen feet - as soon as he glanced over the torn canopies and the frozen load under them, he understood exactly what was shown in front of him and a huge sense of mercy was awakened in his heart.

Immediately, he gathered his deputies, sent messengers throughout the corners of the city, and sent orders to every appropriate place to summon help. First, he called for first aid and all the nurses in town along with any volunteers, most of whom were wealthy and high-ranking women, headed by the Gubernator's wife herself. All of these people started the rescue mission at once.

They immediately separated the healthy people who were still able to walk so that they would not need to witness the magnitude of their disaster and tragedy, while they were still exhausted and hungry. Then they turned their attention to the collapsed canopies, pulled and sorted out the frozen and sick travelers.

They sent the most fragile and sick people to the hospital. Those who were unconscious and frail were sent to poorhouses and other shelters. They separated the dead from all the wagons and kept them apart.

They sent the rest of the group to various inns throughout the city for the night. However, before they sent them away for the night, they brought them to city restaurants for a refreshing meal. This good-hearted Gubernator sent his delegates to every important inn and restaurant in town ahead of time to wake up their people in that late hour so that they could make a fire in the stove and prepare food for our wandering settlers, and ordered them to charge everything to him - the Gubernator's account.

First, they boiled some stew in the warmers to drive out the chill of the bones. Later on, they served a Kosher wholesome meal, everybody according to their preference. Ample hot and boiling tea followed, as much as could be consumed – without limits – according to each person's wish. The Gubernator would pay the bills later on.

Only the next morning, after they had a chance to rest and somewhat recover from the toil of the road, did our travelers realize how enormous the loss they suffered during last night's travel; Forty-nine people were dead, and close to two hundred sick, quite a few of them in a dire condition.

They were extremely fortunate that G-d dropped them into the hands of that Gubernator, who was a good-hearted and Jews-loving person. That governor, Sokolov Voznesenski, stood by them in their worst time and even comforted them in their big tragedy as if he were their own brother.

He kept calming them down and raising their hope for the coming days. The next day, he called the capital St. Petersburg, and spoke with the Honorable Czar Nikolai the First, himself. He lobbied with the Czar

*[Page 162]*

to provide them with an additional loan from the government. Only after he equipped them with new clothing, provisions, wagons, and hay for the animals, he made *Saba* Ber'eh-Volf duly and lawfully sign for all that and had him swear that he would continue his fight and progress toward the next province to the next city they would encounter on the way.

However, my dear grandchildren, good people - people who hold G-d in their hearts, like that provincial minister, our wandering travelers met only very seldom. More commonly, they met with Jew-haters and greedy people who competed with each other on who could better their colleague in soliciting a bribe. The entire route to the new land, which was destined for them, was a prolonged and torturous road – flooded with teary seas and seeded with countless graves.

## A Convoy of Mishaps

In the meantime, the carriage continued to carry them swiftly through the fields and sail into the prairie with a deep springy softness. The huge Ber'eh-Volf monument was approaching and rising up toward them and drew everybody's glances by its incredible enormity. R' Yehuda Leib'ichka was still sitting, half facing his grandchildren, talking to them as equals, continuing and adding to his story about that far, legendary, and sorrowful past.

Young Zelik, who mostly saw the good and beautiful in life, felt like he wanted to cheer up his grandfather somewhat, said:

"Against all that, everything advanced smoothly for them later on, didn't it *Saba*?"

"No Bears and no Forest!" [a phrase in Hebrew which means "nothing of the kind."]. All those troubles during the journey were a children's game compared to what was about to happen to our great grandparents later on, after arriving in Novo-Russia.

Like there is no end to the sea, there is no end to the troubles of the Jews. All of their real sufferings would only start from the time they arrived.

All the good promises they originally received were *Urva Parakh* – [literally translated as a "flown away raven," which means "a cock and bull story" or "a pie in the sky."], as if they never existed! They did not find any sign of housing, nor did they find horses, tools, or seeds. There was not even a single sack of flour to bake bread for the starved overdue guests. There was absolutely nothing!

They did not find anything except a cold and arid prairie, parched and wild, covered by thistles and wormwood plants as well as prickly burnets rooted deeply in the ground. The feather grass grew so tall that the people and wagons sunk in it as if they disappeared from G-d's earth."

"Only that thing," hinted *Saba,* pointing at the huge cone, protruding tall and enormous against the sky - the lone, erect, and elevated monument of Ber'eh-Volf stood there, waiting futilely for generations, that man would someday show up.

…And here, all of a sudden, just like that, so many unexpected guests,

*[Page 163]*

showing up with their wagons and even setting their encampment here for the first time. A heart-breaking Jewish prayer could be heard instantly. As I told you before – that was how your great-grandparents ascended onto their land for the first time – with prayer and tears in their eyes. From this high plateau, your great-grandparents saw for the first time the giddy fast-flowing river of Yeni-Gil [actually - Ingulets River.].

In his excitement of seeing this lively and refreshing river, he declared in *Lashon Kodesh* [the "Holy Language" (Hebrew)]: Nahar —Gil [meaning "River of Joy"], and we will settle it! The name for our colony - Nahar Gilovka was first mentioned here, and it remained as such from that day on, more than one hundred years later [as mentioned above the actual name of the colony was Yefeh-Nahar or "Beautiful River."].

Since they did not find any of the things that were promised to them, they temporarily raised tents around the monument. Later on, when the winter's bitter cold arrived, they did not have any other choice but to dig pits into the ground and spend the winter in these pits, which they covered with dirt. Under these conditions, they incurred additional losses. People died like flies from cold and crowding. Only forty-nine [in Hebrew – the letters Mem-Tet] families remained when the settlers finally moved into built huts, out of more than one hundred that started the journey. That was the reason why we called our lower street the Mem-Tet Street [49th St.] - in memory of the forty-nine-first huts. However, other people say that the street is named in memory of those forty- nine poor souls who were lost during that miserable night on the prairie.

"…And these old forty-nine huts, *Saba* - do they still stand?"

No Zelik'le! There is almost nothing left of these huts. They were built haphazardly, using anything available. The walls were built from crude bricks made of a mixture of straw and mud and were erected on trivial foundations. You can see for yourself - our settlement was completely rebuilt since, where most of the houses are now made of stone. Our old pantry - that patched-up structure, that stands between the pool and the storage room, is a reminder of these old "castles," built in the days of Czar Nikolai the First. However, our settlers had to yearn even for these scanty structures for a long time. Oh – truly, a very long time! They yearned for these structures while staying in their pits underground!

"If so, *Saba*, why did the settlers settle here first and didn't go to the place where the settlement is located now, in the first place?"

"Now - this is a very nice question!" answered the old man with a bitter smile.

"That was what the prophet has been weeping about!" Do you think the settlers received the parcel selected by their emissaries at the beginning? If you have said yes - you made a grim mistake! It never happened! As if all the effort exerted by two emissaries in their long trip to find a place to settle was nearly in vain."

"Take a look over there against the monument of Ber'eh-Volf, downwards on the left"

R' Yehuda Leib'ichka hinted to them by pointing the stick of his whip at the wide and green valley where the tall smoke chimney

*[Page 164]*

of Dubovits' wine brewery was proudly overlooking the valley with its reddish bricks.

"Here, just near the bank of Yen-Gil River was our settlement supposed to be established. There were even several groundbreaking houses built there. This was also where the first Nahar-Gilovka's [Yefeh-Nahar's] cemetery was located.

And so, go and do something about it! While for Fonya we were always like a bone stuck in his throat, then before we even started to do anything, the authorities came and reduced the promised settlement area; after that, they came and grabbed the prime part for themselves, and then, the Dubowits'es – a local family of distinguished *parits* [a Jewish term that means a rich man, nobleman or landowner] came to the area, and the authorities carved away for them several thousand additional *disiyats* [Russian old measure for an area] near the river, just as the settlers were ready to settle. That is just the way the world order always works - people treat each other by the old rule: "Scratch my back, and I will scratch yours." A parcel of the most fertile land on the other bank of the river was given to a retired old general, who once upon a time, according to the stories, fought the Turk; the other part of this fertile area was handed over to the neighboring Ukrainian village Kalinovka [Probably Plyushchivka]. You could see, therefore, that the authorities resented the fact that our ancestors would settle in such a fertile valley from the beginning. Therefore, the authorities did not have any intention of endowing this valley and promised land around it to the Jewish settlers to begin with. They asked them "politely" to leave and move far away to the plot where we are located today at the feet of the mountain.

Against all that, probably as a consolation, they allotted them parcels of land that were horribly distant. They shoved them into this long and narrow stretch of land. There was nothing we could do. As a result, the plots in the settlement were fragmented, dispersed, and spread, all the way to Nakhlat-Shefa, which is, as you well know, a distance of twenty *verstas* and more. These distances are really depleting us.

At the time of the harvest, when work is on high burners and every movement of the livestock counts, we can't bring more than one cart loaded with grain through that distance. In general, all of these frequent shuffling, going these distances for hours and hours, with food, water, tools, and sometimes with the children whose help is needed, was very tiring.

A distance of twenty *verstas* and more is not a child's game. How can one be a successful farmer with such distances?"

R' Yehuda-Leib'ichka asked, spreading his arms in amazement and resentment.

"But could we try to do something or change this situation when we were so dependent on others in everything, and we did not have control of our own affairs?"

The old man took out his oily velvet tobacco pouch, filled his pipe again, and passed the iron ignitor over the fluted flint with a skillful arm movement.

"Ay – my beloved! We could have had a pleasant and comfortable life here, a life similar to those of other nationalities. Unfortunately, we are not entirely independent. After settling, the settlers had to place their faith in the hands of strangers, and these people nominated

*[Page 165]*

foreign trustees - Germans or Russians, who could not and did not want to understand the settlers' plights. They clipped the wings of the settlers from the start.

The settlers were surrounded by hostile authorities, burdened by bands of parasites and charity bread eaters who did not let them lift their heads up. They were grabbed by the strong hands of the authorities who held them with strong arms and taught them how to work the land like the way recruits are tamed in the military - with threats and slaps, punishments, and jail. Only then, when they had arrived at their settlements, *Fonye* took the time to teach them the "Balak Torah Portion" [The seventh weekly Torah portion in the book of Numbers] with orders and commands…and here started a whole series of suffering and misery, epidemics and droughts, hunger and cold, thefts and bribes, false accounting, and just simple day-light embezzlements which lasted decades.

Whole bands of guardians, managers, rude retired officers, cruel administrators, countless cruel supervisors, and evil inspectors descended upon the settlement. If this was not enough, a new affair of the so-called "*Musterwirten*" – namely - "exemplary farmers"- was developed. These were scowling-faces German horsemen, with whips in their hands, who were ready to school the Jewish settler and instill in him some wisdom. Other uninvited "visitors" and human trash, had also gathered around to suck from the labor of the Jewish settler.

But, my dear beloved children- this is a story for another time…"

## Everybody is on Equal Footing with Mother Earth

Although *Saba's* sad story clouded the joy for a short while, it could not spoil the festive mood of the jubilant and happy youths, who relished the pleasure the trip itself brought upon them.

The fresh and pure morning air, the intoxicating smell of the flowering meadows, flying by on the left and right of the carriage, the joyful singing voices of the cuckoo birds, calling each other from their hiding places, and unwearied sniffing and poking by the two dogs, that were running around in front, helped to expunge the memory of the sad story and distant past.

R' Yehuda- Leib'ichka himself had already moved his thoughts from those distant times of his great-grandfather to the later years, when all of the land, which extended on the right-hand side, was severed from the land resources of the settlement and given away to those who were named the "Manchurians" [the veteran Russian soldiers who fought in the Japanese-Russian War].

His penetrating gaze could already recognize the first sparsely scattered ranches on the prairie's margins. The farther away they continued their progress, the more areas, familiar to him from the old days, were revealed – areas which once belonged to the settlement for several generations.

*[Page 166]*

He himself, the young Yehuda-Leib, invested many days and years of hard work around every step and every corner. So - the farther away they continued to go, the more reflective he became and the more pondering his glance over this familiar piece of land became. He and his friends nourished this piece of land, which lay just beyond the Shabbat boundary line. Not that many years ago, during his youth, this land was covered with an endless tangle of thorns and thistles. Not very easily - he and his friends converted this land, every yard of it, from virgin land to sown land. For decades, they had to pull out roots and straighten the area so that, at last, a considerable plowing-worthy fertile land could be added to the settlement.

Just as these desert lands were finally converted into fertile lands and started to yield bread plentifully, the authorities showed up again. Those were the days just after the Russian-Japanese War, so the authorities began to hand these parcels over as gifts to the discharged soldiers of the front in Manchuria.

"You see Zelik'le – you can see the Manchurians over there."

The old man finally interrupted his thoughts and hinted toward the small houses scattered like small islands in a green sea. And now, the old man started to pour his heart out toward his oldest grandchild:

"That was how they compensated the "courageous soldiers," of *Fonye*'s heroic war with Japan. They gave these parcels in abundance, as gifts, for their "courageous standing" in Port-Arthur[11] at our expense.

Our settlement, you can imagine, boiled over with anger. For some reason, the authorities could not find another piece of land throughout the entire Russian empire for the Russian settlers except in the area resources of Nahar-Gilovka settlement. Our settlers almost destroyed the building of the *Prikaz*[b] because of their anger. The *Schultz* – the village elder, tried to lobby their grievance matter at the district office – "for if this decree had to involve our land, why not give it to Jewish soldiers from the settlements in the region, who fought in the same war?" However, this is how the world always works. Your own shirt is closer to your body, meaning, your own needy, are closer to your heart. Very quickly, before we had the chance to turn around, they dug a ditch and it became the border, and everything beyond the border became the Manchurians' property.

And then there was also that matter of the "vacant" parcels. This injustice has been going on for many years. You must have heard about this issue before. Our area was decreasing from one generation to another. As the new generations grew up, their inherited plots started to diminish. The number of people, glory to our G-d, was growing, but no new area had been added to the colony. Jewish people were also forbidden to buy new land. On the contrary, they cut out our land from time to time, not only from the public parcels, as before, but also from the private-inherited land. There was no shortage of excuses for taking somebody's parcel became "vacant," that is – without heirs, as it happened once in a while, or if a craftsman who also owned a parcel neglected it

[Page 167]

and went to work in his trade somewhere else (e.g. the city of Kherson), the authorities came and confiscated the land, even–though we had many customers among us who would be interested in this parcel - large families who were rich in the number of people but poor in the amount of land. Those customers may have already leased the land. However, you can talk to the wall. They would listen to you the same way they would listen to the voice of the blowing wind on the prairie.

What did the Prophet Yeshayahu say, Zelik'el, in the chapter *"Nakhamu, Nakhamu Ami"* ["Comfort, Oh Comfort my people."]?

*"Kol Koreh BaMidbar* [literally translated to "a voice calls in the wilderness, Isaiah 40:2], said Rakhel unexpectedly, surprising both the grandfather and his grandson.

"Very true my little granddaughter. I see that you have listened well to what your brothers learned from the Rabbi, and you know already to mention both the verse and its location. You can continue to listen to my story."

When a parcel became "vacant," instead of allocating it fairly among land-poor people of the settlement, the authorities would capture it and divide it among the neighboring villages.

"It was, therefore, no wonder when your uncle Motia-Ber packed his belongings immediately after his wedding and left our house. You, Zelik'le, should still remember him.

Do you think that, perhaps, the house was too crowded for him? If that is what you think, you would be totally wrong. The new house was built broadly, "with no power to the evil eye," large enough for all my children, including their wives and children. Lack of land drove my son Motia-Ber all the way to Argentina. My other son, Naftali, whom you may not know at all, did a very smart thing as well. He left us while still in his youth and went to our old motherland, the land of Zion. Today, he is over there in a place called Metula. He writes that he is his own landlord who owns more than 100 *dunams* [an old Ottoman area measuring roughly a quarter of an acre] of black sown soil."

"Nevertheless, *Saba,* it is much better here now than it used to be, isn't it?"

The excited Zelik'le tried to cheer up his grandfather's heart. He encircled with his luminous eyes the impressive wheat fields, his beloved prairie - the prairie that fills his heart with fondness. He believed that he could reduce somewhat the weight of his grandfather's grievances."

"Look *Saba*, how tall the stalks are, how heavy their heads are packed with wheat seeds – they are much more bountiful than those *Goyim* [gentiles]. "That is what I think *Saba*. Today the state of the Jewish farmer is already good."

"Yes, it is so, now, thanks G-d. Our state is not bad at all.

There is no comparison with the state in those old days. We are already very proficient in our work. There is no denial. We know and recognize all of Mother Earth's secrets, and we are, generally speaking (without committing any sin against G-d), successful property owners with nice houses.

However…. what is the use of all of that, if even here, on this beautiful and free prairie, you are considered a stepson? After all, not every governor is Sokolov Voznesenski's kind of a governor, and not every *goy* in Kalinovka is like our honest friend Ofanas Ratonda. They managed to drag in the old hatred even here to the depth of the prairie. They keep reminding you often, with resentment, that even here, in your own homeland, bought by your ancestors with their soul and sweat,

*[Page 168]*

at the end of the day, you are but a foreigner - not more than a tenant or a guest who came to spend the night, and they would show you the way out of here at the first opportunity."

"…and you, *Saba*, are you afraid of the *Goyim*?

"Now, listen to this new invention! Now you are talking like a small child. We are not cowards here. We are not letting anybody do us any harm or dishonor us. Not every fight-seeker or bandit dares to face us in a fistfight. If the authorities would not intervene and would not secretly support the bullies, we could stand by ourselves and defend our soul and our honor."

However, what you said about the fact that our wheat is beautiful and more bountiful than the *goyims'* wheat – for that, we really need to thank Mother Earth," said R' Yehuda Leib'ichka, pointing his finger toward the expansive fields.

"She does not want to know about any trickery. She does not distinguish between a *goy* and a Jew. In her eyes, we all have the same notoriety, and she pays everyone back according to his faithfulness to her."

Following those words, R' Yehuda Leib'ichka turned back toward the horses, grabbed the reins just in time, and with his threatening-reverberating whip, stopped the horses who started to gallop because they could smell from the distance, the cool refreshing water of the approaching lake Elimelekh.

## The Grand Precious Sign in *Saba's* Hat

The festively decorated horses gulped the many *verstas* as easily as a game. The bells ringing in their curb bits announced with joy and knell, over large distances, the good news about the arrival of the new visitors. With this noisy and ringing message about the ripe crop waiting in the heat of the summer to be harvested into the barn, the carriage turned and climbed over the dam road of Elimelech's Lake.

Except on the side of the dam, where there was an access road for carriages and cattle, the long banks were surrounded by plot after plot of winter wheat and rye that spread from there and stirred waves far, far away to the horizon. From the top of the dam, the lake looked as if somebody dropped a silver tray over a huge bright-green velvety expanse, shimmering against the sun and persistently and tirelessly spraying its returning light rays to dazzle the eyes.

Following the last rainstorms, the willows that stood along the bank of the dam were dipped to their neck in water. Only the green crowns that covered their tops were visible, crammed with last year's grey birds' nests with black thrushes skipping around.

*[Page 169]*

On the flat bank on the other side, a frightened flock of wild geese uprooted itself from among the water lilies and crossed the air with noisy fluttering, and deafening chirping. Only the snipes continued courageously to hobble around with hastened steps on the dam's bank and rummage peacefully in the shallow water, seemingly unintentionally, with their long-sharpened beaks.

When they arrived at the lake of Elimelech, the day was already well established. The diligent storks were already hard-working here for a long time since dawn when they started on an empty stomach. They were now busying themselves in an intensive and studious hunt, although, it seemed that they were doing these things off-hand, standing on one leg, innocently as if they were immersed entirely in a dream of a summer morning. One remarkably industrious *Hasid* [a play on words – In Hebrew, it means a male stork and also a follower of a Hasidic movement], had completed his day's work in his innocence and was happily and cheerfully ready to turn and fly home to his mate, carrying a twitching eel for her for breakfast.

Everything here was already awake and fizzing. Everything was breathing young life. It was a young, fresh, and bright summer morning full of the smell of fresh soil.

When they traversed the dam road, the small and young children, who were the most sensitive to new sights, shifted themselves toward the edges of the moving carriage. Breathless, overflowed by glee, and with burning eyes, turning and twisting all around, they tried to swallow the beautiful sights around them. They listened to the musical trickle of the water that swayed ever slightly around them with a nearly unfelt ripple. They captured and sensed the songs of growth and ripening all around them. They felt as if they were being sucked into this big, green and whizzing world. As this big joy and excitement engulfed them, their hearts widened as if threatening to jump out from their young narrow chests.

Exuberant, with sharpened ears, the horses carefully strayed away, entered the water up above their knees, and quenched their thirst. And then, as they have been accustomed to do they turned on their own toward the hollow and shady willow tree, which stood there opposite R' Yehuda Leib'ichka's plot. Without untying the horses, the old man threw the reins around the tree's trunk and tied it. Just as he was fastening the saddlebag, which was full of oats, to the carriage's shaft for the horses, the dogs uprooted themselves with a bark, jumped into the tall grass, and viciously attacked a band of stray dogs that appeared unexpectedly. Suddenly, a bitter skirmish ensued. The experienced and cunning Pranaitis grasped the throat of the uninvited adversary as was his way. As Zelik hurried after the stray dogs with a whip, figures of unexpected guests appeared from behind the bushes. Ofanas Ratonda and his youngest daughter were coming to water their horses.

As this was an unexpected encounter with his good old friend, R' Yehuda Leib'ichka did not let them leave until after breakfast. Even the grandchildren troubled themselves around Ofanas, whom they all knew well, and took care of Ofanas's daughter cordially, and Rakhel'le offered the guests various refreshments packed for them by *Savta*.

*[Page170]*

After he filled half of a basket of berries for them into their flask, Ofanas said goodbye, and he and his daughter set off on their way back to Kalinovka. R' Yehuda Leb'ichka grabbed the whip in his hand and turned to walk into the first grassy access trail, which branched sideways.

Like a herd of young and frisky calves, the little ones ran cheerily, following *Saba's* long steps. Jubilantly jumping ahead of each other, the group members turned to the edge of the field, and there, along the sprout boundary band, some to pick a bouquet of red anemones, the others to gather a bunch of dark blue cornflowers.

*Saba* himself, now that he has reached the winter crops, his spirit lifted, tossing out his usual gray and solemn daily appearance, his face lit up, and he forgot all about everything and any matter that had anything to do with the daily grind and worry.

With his hands crossed behind his back, his chest projected forward - arrogant style, *Saba* strode forward near the waves of tall crops, experiencing pleasure at the sight of the straight-packed rows of the winter harvest. A long row of children marching in a shining parade decorated with colorful and fresh flowers followed him step by step. Unified through a soul-uplifting loud singing, the group now marched into the field with the song "The Prayer" by Frugg[12] on their lips:

> "God, bless this year with plentiful fruit
> Guard it against the harmful tempest
> Provide dew and rain onto our fields,
> Give us a jovial harvest."

Even he, this stern rationalistic Jew, was changed by this childish ceremony, and he became like a child among children, enthused and exhilarated like one of them. At the peak of his excitement, in the middle of the march, he removed his black vest and was left standing with only his white cotton shirt. He then turned to step deeper into the wheat field with buoyant and careful strides. The children stopped their joyful march and remained standing motionless in their position, not daring to follow *Saba*, G-d forbid, even one more step into the field among the wheat spikes. Only *Saba* had the "right" and the authority to do so.

As the children stood motionless at the edge of the field, waiting curiously but patiently with burning eyes, *Saba* took the poll of the whip and pierced the soil with it. He then scooped out a handful of soil and tested how deep the moisture managed to penetrate the surface. Only then was *Saba* ready to start performing his "Grand Precious Test," this old wondrous inspection that was customary in the family probably since the first generation of the settlers: One would take a hat and toss it over the spikes. Should the spikes stand tall and not yield like a "prayer kneeling" under the weight of the hat, then the rye spikes would pass the test, and the harvest would be indeed blessed. The harvest would then be considered as secure as being already in the barn.

*[Page 171]*

The children, who remained standing at the edge, started to ask anxiously:

"Well, *Saba*. Please tell us already. Is the rye a blessed one?"

"Thanks G-d – it is" – answered R' Yehuda Leib'ichka.

With a winning grin on his face, he stepped out of the field, projecting his chest forward again. Like a *kohen* [A descendant of the Great Kohen Aharon, according to the Jewish tradition, and whose role is to serve at the altar on holidays] during a holy service, he walked along the trail and stepped forward to the next plot. The cheerful parade of children followed him again, singing tirelessly. The process repeated. The parade stopped, again at the edge of the field, and again the children chanted their hearty childish prayer toward G-d:

> "A prayer for dew and a prayer for rain
> a prayer for green grass,
> a prayer for spikes weighted down by a heavy harvest
> endless wheat and rye."

How sacredly and how reverently *Saba* repeated his hat-tossing test! Like a seeder spreading a handful of seeds with an arc-like movement, was *Saba* tossing his hat, from time to time, over the winter crops, and with stretched-out arms, like a Kohen at the altar, would catch it and again toss it over the golden-greenish field, like a magician performing his act.

The children stared at *Saba*'s motions of the hat tossing with enthusiasm and much admiration. It looked to them like a combined magic act and G-d's miracle.

"*Nu Saba*, please tell us, is the crop successful."

"Successful, children; successful! We are going to have, G-d willing, plenty of braided challah loaves!" announced Saba joyfully.

Accompanied by cries of joy and wonder, he then proceeded to kiss every single grandchild. He whispered to himself, as he was leaving the field, something that sounded like a "thanks-giving" prayer. It was difficult to know, however, whether it was gratitude for the bountiful harvest or for G-d giving him such a wonderful and successful bunch of grandchildren.

Oh – these wondrous and happy trips and this traditional childish parade of growth and flowering, of abundance and shining joy!

[Page 172]

# After the Holocaust

When Ofanas Ratonda was still alive and already living with his youngest daughter - Nastia, he used to appear in this place once in a while. Just after the Holocaust brought on by the World War, or actually, even during the war, the old and silvered-hair Ofanas was the only man in the area who had the courage, acting against the will of the German, to visit this terrifying "Ravine of the Jews."

The earth in the ravine, which was soaked with the blood of the murdered Jews, was breathing with their last breath long after their death and made old Ofanas restless. As a result, the people in Kalinovka village considered him a mindless person or a bum. However, the old and honest farmer did not pay attention to what other people were saying about him. Every time he had the chance to pass through the place in his wagon, either on his way back from the hospital in Oostinovka [Probably Bashtanka, Myikolaivska's oblast] or with a load of squash back from his squash plot, he would stop and get off the wagon. The old man would then slowly lumber himself along the hillside slope, all the way down to that narrow ravine where the spirit of the murdered Jewish settlement was still hovering for a long time after the killing.

He was the only person in the entire big world who came here to honor their memory. He would just stand there; take off his cap, and pass a few crosses along his chest with his trembling hand, which was wrinkled like an old scroll. He would stand there for a long while, on the top of the fresh fluttering mound, and would wonder anew every time, this old man Ratonda:

"Why? Why, *Oh Yezus Christos*? Why did they kill them?"

That was how the old man was standing, reflecting, moving his bowed head from side to side, putting a small bunch of chamomile flowers on the big unmarked grave, crossing his chest several times, then tossing his hands in the air questioning G-d again:

"What is the reason *Hospodi* (King of the Universe in Russian) - why did they take an entire village full of hard-working Jewish farmers and bury them here alive?"

However, no answer to his innocent question was provided. Only one threatening echo could be heard rising from the narrow ravine, and then the silence would conquer it, once again, for a long time. The dead silence would return to the ravine in this remote corner of the thistles-grown prairie - the ravine named the "The Ravine of the Jews" since the day when the cruel German held his Jewish feast.

*

A few *verstas* away, diagonally toward the river, the lower neglected part of the mountain, where the colony of Nahar Gilovka once spread sumptuously along with its seven flowering streets overflowing with greenery, still watches over Kalinovka village with a stare full of grievance and importunity. The roads, trails, and cow trails, which led to that place for generations,

[Page 173]

do not exist anymore. Everything is covered with wild weeds and prickly thorns.

No roads or trails are leading there any longer. Only that single road from Kalinovka, which passes nearby, twisting forward toward the abandoned Nir-Gilovka's squash patch and grazing meadows, can be somewhat considered an access road.

One day, it would happen that a thin and tall woman in her forties would appear on this neglected weeded trail, here on the empty and deserted mountain slope, looking around in every direction like a stranger who came from afar.

She would come down here as if unintentionally or incidentally and would stop over during one of her infrequent trips from far-away Kazakhstan on a mission, as an agronomist, to the home office. Hence, when she comes here to visit her ancestors' graves, she does not have a choice but first to stop in Kalinovka by Nastia. Only then, she turns to come here, either on foot or by riding a horse – mostly alone, without Nastia's knowledge.

Dressed in her black-narrow dress, she walks slowly, immersed in her thoughts. She carves her way through the wild dense and acrimonious thorny weeds, glancing around as she goes, pausing often, looking around with her eyes, and trudging forward through the wilted shrubs.

Primarily, she is drawn toward "home" – the deserted and empty area of the seven streets, which were wiped out. Slowly and deliberately, she surveys around through her spectacles, examines the silent and desolate areas, and sucks into herself, passionately, the expanses that life was erased from, looking continuously for something specific in the empty space. From time to time, she bends down and rummages through the thistles, raising a broken piece of shard or a piece of broken glass and examining it, short-sighted, contemplating, then turns and throws it back. She thus continues forward with her long and peaceful stork-like steps, looking here for the yesterday that has passed.

However, there is nothing left of those seven streets that were once filled with motion and life. She is shaken by this disturbing idea that here, in this place or close to it, *Saba's* yard was once located.

In the past, a low fence was erected on the street side, swallowed somewhat by an abundance of flowers. Across the yard stood the house enveloped by the willow trees - that wide house with its painted roof, and in the corner was the cement pool that collected the rainwater from that tin roof. Behind them was the old kitchen, the barn and the cowsheds, and finally the wide hayloft hidden among the huge heaps of hay.

Farther down, deep in the yard, near the hayloft, leaning on the fence that was covered with manure stood, for generations, that colossal Mulberry tree spreading its wide boughs over the wild chicory and nettle plants underneath it. A laborious woodpecker was always nesting on it, and the little ones always played in its shadow, happy and worry-free.

*[Page 174]*

Now - there is not even a trace of that house and that lively yard, not a sign of that fence or the tree, not even a stump for a remembrance.

This destruction-thirsty and evil hand uprooted everything. It even dug out the foundations. The only survivors, peeking out here and there were the sun-scorched chamomile flowers.

Jewish Farmers in Russia Fields

She turns now and walks toward the old cemetery. At least over there, she could find some comfort, in her own way - in silence and thought in front of the old graves she knew well. However, even there, there was nothing left - nothing at all! There is no trace of the dead. Not even a pile of pebbles as a sign [A Jewish custom].

Thorns are clinging to her dress, and weeds are sticking to her socks. She leaves that place as well, soundlessly. She is distancing herself, with long and slow paces, from that desecrated place - a place that served her people for five generations. Her "home" is pulling her back again, like a magnet, to the bottom of the mountain, to the assumed location of the seven streets still etched in her heart.

She turns and starts to climb her way up the mountain. Deep in thought, confused in her spirit, she begins again to imagine:

"Over there! Just about there, at the edge of the grass meadow, on the hill, the windmill of Meir-Itzi once stood. The old mill, idle for a long time, is now crammed with grey birds' nests, entirely covered with dark green moss, used to embellish the landscape. Although it was unused and rickety, about to fall, it added a romantic aura to the scenery around it. The colony's courageous and tough young men used to bring their horses at night to graze on this grass meadow, spending beautiful hours around flickering bonfires. The smell of boiled corn and roasted brown potatoes spread around from that place during these blue-passion nights, along with the tea smell of the hay, alfalfa, and mint.

Across from the windmill, an unending rusty screech of the water pulley could be heard rising from the old well during those warm and choking nights. That was how the colony's youths used to water the horses, and from time to time, they, too, would swallow up gulps of water from the cool wooden bucket."

She paces, reflecting, and continuing to see with the "eyes of her memory."

Here is where, not so long ago, her school stood, in the shade of linden trees. Generations of mischievous children played and studied here. Across from here – stood this clean and nicely arranged library, where they used to borrow books from the very beautiful-looking librarian – Busia Krol. Little beyond that was the bank, the cheese factory, and Azriel's smithy. Farther down, beyond the alley, stood the hut of Sara Hinda and Moshe-Yosl. Storks used to nest on its roof in the summer. Day after day, they used to gargle and send their friendly welcome greetings all around the spacious seven streets of Nahar-Gilovka."

*[Page 175]*

She bent down to the ground and stuck her quivering fingers into the small dimple beside the bracket, digging, searching, and digging again, fixing her shortsighted eyes on that spot.

"Yes, yes, she almost recognized it. It looked to her that this was the location of the concrete water pool. Here is another projecting bracket."

The strange woman, with her binoculars, continued to dig and search through the fragments.

" …but look here… There is no doubt now."

Unexpectedly, she discovered a second sign. Her eyes captured the shining sparkle of a decorated glass adorned with all the colors. Yearningly, she grabbed it with trembling fingers and studied it with penetrating eyes.

" *Oy Ima'le* [Oy my mommy], I recognize this piece of broken glass."

She finally, positively, recognized the Pesakh [Passover]] cups of *Savta* Dvora-Zisl.

"Oy my G-d in Heavens, I see in front of me the shiny table, set for Passover, comprising of all the goodness! This was the tremendous *Saba's Seder* [Passover Meal]."

A drizzle of boiling and stinging tears was shed that hot summer day in *Saba's* yard, a place she hardly recognizes now.

"Then, is that the place where *Saba* lived? Is this the place that was once so teeming with life, faith, and vigor? There is nothing recognizable from all of that now. Everything was uprooted and disappeared. Everything was lifeless – silent and deserted, returning to its state in the old days when the ancestors arrived here one hundred and fifty years ago. There is one difference. This huge prairie, despite all the Jewish colonies that were established by sweat and blood of the settlers for generations - does not belong to the Jews anymore."

Bent and broken, lonely and orphaned, the wandering black-dressed woman turned and walked toward that last horrible unmarked place - "The Ravine of the Jews." Over there under the tall thorns, rises ever so slightly, the mass grave. The rains have gradually and slowly washed the soil above it a little. The soil itself settled down from time to time. Nobody, not even the people who inherited their place in the prairie, put a gravestone in their memory.

Lost and mournful, the woman turned under the scorching rays of the sun and walked over the prickly thorns until she finally arrived at this remote narrow ravine. Over there, on top of the flattened mound, she knelt and fell on her face.

She snuggled up for a long while on this flattened mound – the mound containing the remains of an entire colony. She absorbed into her, with all of her passion, the smell of the soil, which she knows so well.

With her eyes closed, she saw them all - her relatives, acquaintances, neighbors, and friends. She saw them all - from the little ones to the oldest - the entire colony.

Furthermore, she heard their voices very clearly, and above all, she heard *Saba's* lucid words:

*[Page 176]*

"The Jews never licked honey, anytime and anywhere, but even Satan himself could not have dreamt about such destruction."

\*

The long torturous day was almost over. The sun was setting slowly, and heavy oppressive shadows began to spread above the frightening ravine. At that time, a woman figure appeared above, leading two horses tied by their halters.

The woman called from the top of the hill: "Rakhil! Rakhil!" but there was no response to her call. Only a threatening echo could be heard moving, passing between the two ravine's inclines and getting lost in the deep canyon. However, the woman at the top of the hill did not give up. She walked down toward the deep ravine until she clearly saw her strange guest from Kazakhstan, whom she had been searching for a long while. Her guest was kneeling at the grave mount and seemed to be entirely taken away from the world. She touched her slightly, waking her up from her dream, and whispered to her, softly and secretly, like a sister to a sick sibling:

"Enough Rakhil enough! It is time to go home. The horses are waiting for us up on top."

"I do not have any place to go to, Nastin'ka. There isn't anymore any home for me anywhere."

"Still, Rakhil, please come! You must be awfully tired from being out here all day."

Without answering, worn-out and obedient, as if after a day of fasting, Rakhel followed Nastia. The two women mounted the horses and rode out of the dark "Ravine of the Jews."

With erect ears, the horses walked slowly, step after step, tapping with their hoofs, moving their long necks impatiently, blowing heavy breaths, and angrily expelling the gnats from their body.

A slight warm eastern breeze flew rapidly over the darkening and scotched prairie, bringing in its wing-uplifting, soul-refreshing good news.

Rakhel turns her head for one more look behind her. Above the frightening ravine, a pale blue moon appeared, new and young.

**Translated from Yiddish to Hebrew by Shimshon Meltzer**

### *Author's Notes:*

    a.   The dogs were named after Vera Cheberyak and the priest Justinas Pranaitis [the two prosecution "witnesses"] in the Beilis trial.

    b.   The official name of the local authority of the Jewish settlements until 1917.

### *Translator's Notes:*

1.   The story appeared in the book: "Jewish Farmers on the Russian Prairies," pp 146 – 176, Sifriat Hapoalim, The Kibbutz Haartzi Publishers, Merchavia, Israel, 1965. According to yleksikon.blogspot.com by Khayim Leyb Fuks, a short Yiddish version of the story was published in the American Yiddish newspaper "The Goldeneh Keit" (The Golden Chain) under the name of "Erev Pesakh" (Passover Eve) in (Tel Aviv, 1959]) and won the Bimco Prize from the World Jewish Congress, in 1961.

2.   Moshe Kutten is the son-in-law of the author - David Tverdovsky.

3.   Yehuda Leib was actually - Reb Moshe-Leib Tverdovsky, the author's grandfather. Moshe Tverdovsky was one of the firstborns in the colony of Yefeh-Nahar.

4.  *Nakhlat Shefa HaGdola* was the name of a nearby Jewish settlement, which in English literally means the Big Estate of Abundance, probably referring to the real village of *Sdeh Menukha HaGdola*, which literally means the "Big Resting Field." Another nearby village was called *Sdeh Menukha HaKtana* – the "Small Resting Field."

5.  Zelik – most likely refers to the author himself in this story.

6.  The name refers to Dvora-Gitel, nee Medem, Reb Moshe-Leib Tverdovsky's wife and the author's grandmother. She was one of the firstborns in the nearby colony of Nova-Poltavka.

7.  *Lag BaOmer* is the holiday celebrated on the 33rd day of the period between Passover and Shavuot.

8.  *Ber'eh Volf* – the great-grandfather of the author, one of the leaders of the settlers. His real name was Avraham-Ber Tverdovsky.

9.  Actually, the colony of Yefeh-Nahar, which means "Beautiful River" in Hebrew (pronounced Effingar in Russian). The colony was located on the bank of the Ingulets or Inhulets River.

10. The cholent (or chulnt as it is pronounced in Yiddish), is a slow-cooked Jewish stew that varies from one tradition to another. East Europeans typically prepare the dish with beans, sweet and regular potatoes, some meat, grits, and eggs.

11. Port Arthur – The battle of Port Arthur in Manchuria (February 8 – 9, 1904) marked the commencement of The Russian-Japanese war. The Russians suffered a shaming defeat in that battle.

12. Shimon Shmuel Frugg – a poet born in Bobrobi-Kut (one of the first Jewish colonies-settlements in Kherson province of Southern Ukraine).

Sdeh Menukha HaKtana – General view

Sdeh Menukha HaKtana – A farmer's yard

Sdeh Menukha HaKtana – The vegetable garden

*[Page 177]*

# Poems of Remembrance

## by Mordekhai Pitkin

**Translated by** Moshe Kutten

**Edited by** Rafael Manory

### 1. The village

Roofs made of straw and hay,
Toward the ground their margins dive,
Walls in white shining lime,
And tiny windows–like eyes.

And the huts–arranged in lines,
Pleasing a visitor's eyes,
And beyond them–a calm river
Stretching between its green banks.

## 2. Establishment of the colony

On wandering and sorrowful roads
Under the croaking sound of frogs,
Somewhere at the prairie's edge
A minyan of Jews has arrived.

One by one, the shovels were distributed
They ploughed furrows in virgin–land,
And wearing arm and head phylacteries
A couple of oxen they would follow.

Suddenly oy vey! The head phylactery
Fell down! Oh Merciful God
Spontaneously they call: "Pick it up" and plow
And so laughter is mixed with a tear.

Many paths lead to the heavenly throne.
They pleaded when the wet season come!
Give power to man and ox
And timely bring the rain!

The oxen listened to the chanting,
And with ease pulled their burden,
Behind them a furrow stretched,
Long lines of goodness and plenty.

The time for sowing has arrived,
The farmer in his wagon senses,
His feet are firmly on the ground,
His lips whisper the morning prayer

And the wagon is laden
With golden seeds to the brim.
The children spread around in its wideness
Gathering straw from end to end.

I do recall, at the field's edge
A baby is lying in his cradle,
And at his crying, a young mother
Is bending over him and singing.

And when the harvest's time arrives –
Reap, tie and hoist the sheaf…
Years of hard work are passing
Each conversing with the other.

[Page 178]

## 3. Grandma and Grandpa

Outside, the cold is stabbing-burning
Snow-mountains crown the village
Around the old man– the grandchildren gathered
at the flaming hearth.

One is wise, the other mischievous
and one is pleading "Please tell me a story!"
A heartfelt smile shines over them
and grandpa smoothes his snowy beard

He tells stories about the past
How they traveled southward to the end of the wilderness,
and with tremendous effort and hard work,
a colony of Jews established

How the village joined
with the neighboring city in the fairs.
Although the dwellers of our city were brothers,
Unfortunately,… their behavior was not right

And one day, misfortune happened
Accidentally he lost his wallet.
But these city dwellers, the clowns
teased and made fun of him—the fool.

When he tells that story—the old man blushes
as if this just happened yesterday,
and to sweeten his insult,
he brings a cup of liquor to his mouth

And grandma who was sitting in the corner
utters at him angrily while knitting:
"again a sip?…this is a deadly drink,
It's shortening his life".

But the kittens were playing with the spool,
a joyful game they played together.
Grandpa sees it and smiles:
"enough with the grumpiness, grandma".

In the hearth, the straw is burning happy,
smokeless the fire is burning.

Jewish Farmers in Russia Fields

A heifer is jumping—hop! hop! hop!
and suddenly is licking grandma.

Grandma the heifer softly caresses,
The fight is over, the grandchildren are pleased,
a true peace between them now prevails
Grandma and grandpa have reconciled.

## 4. The Village Boy

A tight worn-out fur,
a wide sash on his hips -
Went out marching with his donkey,
to water it in the evening.

At the well, it's bitter frost
Boys and girls, arduously engage in conversation,
Sound, and a white haze
The speaker's mouth would generate

*[Page 179]*

The cold intensifies, clap your hands,
Lift up your legs and dance, my child.
The hand pump squeaks,
And the rein's ring–rings.

Frozen eyebrows with a white curtain covered,
But the cheeks - burning fire,
In circles - circles they gather,
Noise, laughter and merriment.

Rows of teeth - lustrous whiteness
And the eyes' darkness - splendor and glamour.
The old man moans "oof!"
With filled hearts, the youth laugh.

## 5. On a Stormy Night

As the freeze intensifies, a storm
is rising, bursting and frightening.

In her flight towards the nest, a bird
freezes in the wind and down she falls.

Dark night, the woman is on her own,
She listens to the wind in silence.
The kids are sleeping, and the tree
bends over its broken branches.

The man is wandering far away,
Perhaps his knocking is in vain?
His teeth are shattering: "I'll die on the doorstep,"
If the door won't open for me.

Hush, do I hear a cry outside?
Perhaps an orphan just arrived at the gate?
She's holding a lantern in her hand,
The flame dies out…there's nobody there…just storm and thunder.

## 6. To the Uncle's Home – for Hanukkah's Pancakes

Evening time. snowy mountains in blue,
they change colors non-stop.
The street is by the moon illuminated,
invites us brothers - let's go out, this evening.

On the cart-sleigh crowded and packed,
We are riding together - to Uncle, to the pancakes.
A column of smoke is rising from the chimney,
the world is wrapped in a calm delight.

This is Hanukkah, we are trembling with joy
Candles wink from every window.
Aromas in the air,
Fill old and young hearts with delight.

Father would lash his whip, "Vyo!"
and we the children copy-emulate him.
The sleigh flows like the wind,
the horse is galloping as if it's got wings.

*[Page 180]*

## 7. The Youngest Uncle Is in the Foreign City

Grandpa reads his son's letter,
in Dnieper City his son chose to reside.

Jewish Farmers in Russia Fields

The old man looks at the picture again:
and sadness takes hold of his face.

Sad and gloomy is the letter,
The son must be missing his home.
He was still a boy when away he went,
my good child, so wise and knowledgeable.

He does not write much about his affairs,
he just wants to know every detail.
Whether any rain is falling, and how is the heifer doing,
and sends regards to those who know him.

How is he doing in foreign land,
not even a syllable, there is no mention.
But I feel from between the lines
longing and tears in the eye.

The time is passing, and one day
Uncle - the sailor, suddenly arrives,
humming songs of liberty,
an idea he swore allegiance to.

## 8. Jewish Theater in the Village

Alas, times–upheavals
grumbles the father–mother's camp,
sons deviate from heritage
going forward in the ways of the Amorites.

One day, a day of harsh freeze,
wanderers-visitors, to the village arrive,
dressed splendidly and strangely,
and speaking in language of wit.

The actors! …The show
is held in a warehouse. Trembling,
the crowd listens, open-mouthed and heart
Shulamit receives a pure oath,

an oath to a lover. The witnesses -
a hasty rat and a deep pit.
The crowd is probing: how would this end?
and laugh blushingly at each other.

The bitter end comes quick.
The group of the spectators moves with shame

The *Pristav*[1] :"*Gakh Nyelzia Pashol*!"[2]
meaning: "You are now divorced!"

Too bad! it is too late.
We still need to oil the wheel.
If you were not early to pay the bribe
Esau would act forcibly.

*[Page 181]*

## 9. Being Recruited to Serve Esau

The recruiting order for the age group has arrived,
The recruits' preparation is intensive.
They now rule the scene,
Who could resist them tonight?

 If you don't offer them a drink -
Your cellar is not safe.
They'll raid it with no mercy,
Better be nice to them and patient.

Passover wine would be served to the guests,
and the evening meal's leftovers.
Both sides would raise their cup -
"le'Khaim" - "To Life" to the sword bearers.

Here they sit in the wagon
together, and in a tight squeeze,
throwing a quick farewell look
at girl, mother, and farther.

Soon they will read letters -
A flushed-face maiden and father-mother.
Columns of words from the heart,
Written with care and respect:
I am praying here by myself
Holidays, Shabbat, and Rosh Chodesh,
In my mind - I can see the synagogue,
and in my heart - the Holy Ark.

## 10. Spring Evening

The southern breeze is tender,
The snows have darkened, only the ice remains,

## Jewish Farmers in Russia Fields

The windows were cleaned of any sign
of sketches of buttons or flowers.

Water drops trickle down from the roof and tinkle,
The frozen winds are fading.
At the wall, a group of toddlers
Warm up under the sun rays.

Near the hay, the cows are mooing,
And the calves are running around.
Spring has arrived. From the top of the dunghills,
The cocks are calling - it is here!

Water streams are escaping to the prairie
like prisoners from the jailhouse.
In the evening - listen to the commotion:
"Tomorrow, children, we'll witness the miracle!"

On the river - a sleigh,
Should we cross?   -she hesitates.
An old man's advice: "Better not,
It's better to be safe, than sorry."

Streams flow down from the highlands,
And find salvation in the valleys,
From day to day,
the hills get covered in joyful colors of blossom.

*[Page 182]*

A voice is calling: "Get out"
There is nothing wrong with knee-high mud,
and on Saturday on the river
we watch the last block of ice.

The rumor is saying: In the city
A "new spring" is making waves.
The enslaving iceberg smashed to pieces,
"Liberation" is marching on the streets with a flag.

And look: a soldier is standing,
Speaking to the crowd with no hesitation or recoil.
From the front's trenches
The truth is calling you.

The best of the youth fell in the battles,
What did they die for and why?
And who sent them to be slaughtered in vain?
the wild "*Samoderjetz*"[3]

The youths are singing, and the highland
Is carrying the echoes of the song,
People old and young applauding,
On both the speech and the song.

## 11. **What would Tomorrow Bring?**

The old man is looking up,
His eyes searching for the paths in the sky.
What would tomorrow bring? Would it be nice,
or perhaps it would rain shortly?

He smooths his splendid beard,
As if it was a precious jewel.
Would there be rain? Or maybe not?
His lips are asking his beard's mouth.

At twilight, during sunset,
people discuss the delicate puzzle:
If the sun sets in a cloud,
Then, this way the rain would come.

Beyond the river, the sun
is slowly setting between the highlands,
It would light the treetops,
and the huts are gleaming hot.

The breeze is light and delicate,
The trees in dialogue are rustling:
" No rain is brewing there,
It will be nice and dry tomorrow

## 13.  **Get Out to the Prairie**

"It's time to get out to the prairie" -
The people who seed the fields say.
We are going. The children are running on the side of
the wagon with the wild foal.

*[Page 183]*

From the distance, the prairie light,
Rules like a pure flow - it's shining.
Clear are the birds' chirpings,
Reaching the farmers' ears.

They sow a corner - then rest a bit,
they catch a nap, near the wagon.
Their clock is their hunger,
and the sun in the sky.

How pleasant is the horse's neighing
when its name is sounded:
a manly call of a young youth,
embarrassed, he blushes. He's annoyed!

Here, the farmer's son would hoist
the pale. He would drink from the water, first
and then give water to the horse,
and whistle a tune between his teeth.

## 13. Kiddies

Sweating, shoes in hands -
Who is coming to the prairie? The children!
Food for mid-day, in the basket,
Picking flowers on their way.

They would quickly return home,
Their thirst is burning – Give me water!
Their mouth clings to the nipple like with glue
It seems that they would never separate.

Later they share a bite,
"*Kezlech*"[4] they would not abandon.
Oh my God, their appetite is enormous,
Their mouths are drooling, and so are…their noses.

Their neighbor turns and smiles:
"Load up and fill up,
gobble up, without hesitating –
a bad eater - is a criminal."

Spontaneously he would pinch them,
A "tradition" familiar to any child.
It seems that something burned you so
Like an ember from hell's fire

Let's go, rascals, let's go now,
to learn a cart to drive.
The children jump with eagerness,
Still chewing their food.

Who would not want to learn the horses' conduct?
Learn more and more!

Jewish Farmers in Russia Fields

A tear appears in the child's eye
Due to a pinch or simply joy

*[Page 184]*

## [A poem about the colony Sdeh Menukha]

Images of an infinite number of shades of colors
Life-years from a distant past
Against my thoughtful glance
Come into my alert remembrance.

But, Sdeh Menukha, you yourself,
Fade like a dream, my heart is longing for you.
The memories of your past
Sprinkle salt on my wounds.

The few, have abandoned you,
And their homes were by others overtaken.
Their soul seeks consolation for you
With a song their generation is requesting.

### Author's Notes:

1. Head of Police
2. It is forbidden! Get out!
3. *"Samoderjetz"* Russian word for autocrat, i.e. the Czar
4. *"Kezlech"* Yiddish word for a type of cheese cake

*[Page 185]*

# **Memories**

*[Page 186] [blank] [Page 187]*

# Sdeh Menukha HaGdola

## by Menakhem Ben-Sadeh (Kfar Vitkin)

### Translated by Moshe Kutten

### Edited by Yocheved Klausner

*Sdeh Menukha HaGdola* [literally - the big Field of Tranquility] is the name of the colony I was born in. This is how the Jews who settled it, after a long wandering journey, named it when it was established about 160 years ago. We hardly had any connection with the neighboring Russian farmers. A market day was held twice a week. The neighbors brought produce for sale, and they also purchased produce. There were frequent brawls between the Jews and the Russians. The Jews always had the upper hand, and the [Russian] farmers had "respect" for the members of the Jewish colonies.

It was possible to borrow Russian books in the library, as well as Yiddish and Hebrew books. In addition, many amateur clubs operated in the colonies. From time to time, they presented shows by [Y. L.] Peretz and other authors. We did receive news about Eretz Israel. There were several Zionists among us, however, for them it was "a platonic" Zionism. There was not anybody who seriously planned to make *Aliyah* to Eretz Israel.

There was a Russian elementary school in the colony and several "*Kheders*," where children learned everything from the alphabet to the beginning of Mishna and Gemara studies. Some traveled to study Torah in "Yeshivot" as well as high schools. There were three synagogues in the colony, where "minyans" prayed throughout the week. However, on Shabbat, the synagogues were filled to capacity.

The community was well organized. It employed a rabbi and two "*Shuv's*" [slaughterers- examiners]. All the social and religious affairs of the colony were conducted according to the Jewish tradition. There was also a savings-and-loans bank, where the farmers received loans until the harvest, as well as charity loans, organized like mutual aid. That was how the colonies' affairs were conducted until the revolution.

Upon Kerensky's revolution (in Spring 1917), nationalistic organizations sprouted simultaneously, such as "Tzeirei Tzion" ["Youths of Zion"] and "HeKhalutz ["The Pioneer"]. Under the influence of Trumpeldor, who announced that Eretz Israel would only be built by communal groups, groups of agricultural youths began to organize to prepare themselves for communal life. We left our parents' farms and organized as a commune in the colony of Bobrovy-Kut. We received land, equipment, and farm animals with the help of the authorities, and everybody contributed to the communal fund based on their ability. We called our commune "Commune HeKhalutz" ["The Commune of the Pioneer"]. In the meantime, the regime in our region changed, and various gangs seized power. It was difficult to maintain a commune under these conditions, and we dispersed each person to his/her home.

Following the consolidation of the Bolshevist regime, the youth started reorganizing into sectors: Communist youth, non-affiliated agricultural youths, and Zionists-Pioneers. We were quite active, until

*[Page 188]*

we were snitched upon to the Soviet authorities. We had to disperse again, and everybody started to look for his/her own ways to make *Aliyah* to Eretz Israel.

When I last visited Russia, lately, as a tourist, to visit with any relatives that might have survived from my large family, I found out the details about the annihilation of our colonies.

I discovered that until 1938, most colonies became Jewish kolkhozes, which attained outstanding accomplishments and substantial harvests. However, some people could not adjust to the regime in a kolkhoz and had to settle elsewhere.

The only language that was taught in the schools was Yiddish. However, the Jews themselves asked to add studies in Russian as well. When the war broke out, the youths, both men and women, were recruited to the army or other military services. When the Germans progressed into Russia, and rumors reached the colonies about the murdering and annihilation of the Jews, the Jews in the colonies did not believe in that. When the Germans approached farther, and there was still a narrow path of escape beyond the Dnieper, some people still did not believe in the rumors. Many did not want to rely on miracles and loaded food and most needed items onto carts, intending to escape. However, the people who did not want to leave passed, during that night, from one yard to another and unscrewed the screws from the carts' wheels and thus forcing those people who intended to escape to remain at home. In the meantime, the German army blocked the escape route.

The Germans, with the help of the Ukrainians, gathered all of the Jews from Sdeh Menukha HaGdola and Sdeh Menukha HaKtana [the small Sdeh Menukha] into the kolkhoz's cowshed. They fed them a good meal made of beef and later transferred them all to an anti-tank ditch near the windmill. They ordered some of the locals to undress everybody and started to abuse the elderly and women. They finished with a massacre. They tied some women to the horses' tails and pulled them into the killing areas (these women were Bar-Cohen, Plushkin, and Lieberman). They organized the corpses in piles of 50 by 50 in a typical German order, head to feet and feet to head. They forced Hershel the *"Klezmer" to play with his clarinet the famed melody "Israel Cry," during the killing. Under the so*und of that tune, the farmers of Kherson's colonies were annihilated.

Today, kolkhozes are established in the colonies of Sdeh Menukha HaGdola and Sdeh Menukha HaKtana, however, their residents are mostly Russians. There are still 68 Jewish families among them: the minority among them consists of the old-timers who survived the war, and the rest are refugees who arrived after the war. The number of Jews is diminishing though. Most of the Jews are gradually leaving for the cities.

Nothing was left from the entire history of the Jewish colony except the large memorial erected on the top of the mass grave. The following inscription is written on the memorial: "Here, 1875 women, elderly and children were murdered by the German fascists with the help of the locals."

———————

*[Page 189]*

# *Sdeh Menukha HaKtana*

**by Tzvi Shadmi (Kiryat Khaim), Sara Shadmi, Leibel Kahanov (Kfar Yehoshua), Yehuda Menukhi (Nahalal), Ben–Tzion Komarov (Afikim), Shternah Ninberg, Mordekhai Simkhoni (Geva), Israel Ben Eliyahu (Ein Harod), Mordekhai Khalili (Mishmar HaEmek), Rakhel Pnini (Tel Adashim), Azriel Pnini (Tel Adashim)**

## Translated by Moshe Kutten

Our colony, Sdeh Menukha HaKtana [Literally the Small Field of Tranquility], was, as attested by its name, the smallest among the three colonies established along River Ingulets. The three colonies were - Sdeh Menukha HaGdola [the Big Field of Tranquility], Bobrovy-Kut, and Sdeh Menukha HaKtana. The distance between our colony and Sdeh Menukha HaGdola was about 1.5 kilometers and between us and Bobrovy-Kut – about 7 kilometers. From an economic perspective, our colony lagged behind the other two colonies, where some wealthy residents, including store owners, resided, whereas in our colony, most of the residents were people who worked the land and owners of small farms. Similar to other colonies, the people of Sdeh Menukha HaKtana suffered from a shortage of land; according to the Czarist laws, the Jews were prevented from purchasing land. The parcels that the first settlers received (300 *dunams* [about 74 Acres]) were divided, over time, among the sons. That resulted in a situation where many families owned parcels as small as 20 –30 *dunams* [5 – 7.5 Acres].

For many years, the farming was extensive. Only at the beginning of the 20th century, when the JCA organization began its operation in the colonies, agronomists visited us and trained the farmers to farm their land using modern methods. State schools existed in Sdeh Menukha HaHaGdola and Bobrovy-Kut. However, in our colony, there was no school, only some traditional *"kheders"* [Jewish religious schools for children].

My father was a native of our colony. He learned carpentry in his youth in the city of Kherson. He excelled in his general studies and attained the title of "rural teacher." He then left the carpentry occupation and began to teach lessons in Russian in several private homes, and a *"kheder."*

My father established the first school taught in the Russian language in our colony. With the help of his father, who was also a carpenter, he made the desks and the benches, a bench for every five-six pupil. He hung a sign in Russian on the school building, which he painted himself (he had very nice handwriting). The sign read – **A Private Jewish School**. There were three classes in the school, all in the same room. The curriculum spanned three years and included reading and writing in Russian, arithmetic, and grammar. Boys and girls studied together. Until the state school was established in 1911, most of the youths were my father's students, among them, some students studied one half-day in the *"kheder"* and the other half in the private Jewish school. A small library existed in the school, which my father received from the "Society for the Promotion of Culture among the Jews of Russia" [OPE organization]. I remember, until today, how they unloaded two wooden crates with books from a wagon' This was an unforgettable event in the colony – nobody had seen a Russian book or a newspaper in the colony before that. There was a library in Sdeh Menukha HaGdola,

[Page 190]

and my father was the only subscriber in our colony registered to receive books. For 10 Kopecks a month, one could borrow two books. Every week, I would walk to Sdeh Menukha HaGdola to exchange books. In our library, the students received books for free.

Upon the completion of their studies, the boys and the girls went to work since the farm needed their help. Only a few boys continued their studies in the agricultural high school established by the JCA organization in the colony of Novo-Poltavka, which was 80–90 kilometers away from our colony. The girls were not so fortunate, except for one girl who continued with her studies despite all obstacles. She received a high school diploma and became a teacher. While most of the colony natives who now reside in Israel were my father's students, many of the younger ones were the students of that teacher, about whom I want to tell.

During one of the winter days, one of the mothers brought a shy 10-year-old girl and asked my father to accept her to the school. This was in the middle of the school year, and the first class had already advanced somewhat. Because of that, my father assigned me the role of preparing her, so that she could continue to study with the class. I had already completed school and studied in the evenings in an advanced small class. Due to her outstanding talents (and not due to my pedagogic talents), the girl caught up with the class very quickly and became one of the most outstanding students. Over time, that girl played a major role in my own private life (she is my life partner), as well as in the life of the colony. She continued her studies after completing our school - a new thing in Sdeh Menukha HaKtana. Since we did not have a teacher in our colony, she would walk to Sdeh Menukha HaGdola, in the summer and winter, dressed in clothes that were not appropriate for the weather. She managed to complete four years of high school and later on taught in the state school that was later established in the colony. When she received the teacher certificate, some awakening took place in our colony. An amateur drama club was established, in which she was one of the most active, and a public library was established. The club presented several shows of which the entire revenues were dedicated to developing the library. Many other girls followed that girl and continued their studies after completing our school. During the war, she moved to the city of Kherson, where she worked as an educator in a private home and continued to study in the evenings until she received a state matriculation diploma.

While my father's home was the source of change in the social state of the colony, the home of that girl's parents was the source of national awakening. Her three brothers were among the pioneers to make *Aliyah* to *Eretz Israel*, through some devious roads.

In 1925, during the "NEP" [New Economic Policy of the Soviet government], several families with little children set out to leave our colony on their way to *Eretz Israel*. All the natives of Sdeh Menukha HaKtana in Israel belong to the Labor Movement. The majority are part of the "*Hityashvut HaOvedet*" [settlement movement aligned with the labor movement], in *kibbutzim* and *moshavim*, and the minority are workers residing in workers' residences [in the cities].

**Tzvi Shadmi** (Kiryat Khaim)

Jewish Farmers in Russia Fields

*[Page 191]*

When I come to put my memories from the distant past on paper – memories about the place where we were born and grew up and where we spent our childhood and youth, I see in my mind. our small colony – one long street and a row of houses on each side. At the northern edge, the street turned east around the mountain.

In my mind, I see very clearly the fruit trees orchard, which stretched on the bank of River Ingulets between our colony and the neighboring Russian village, Gradnovka.

In our old home, there was an entrance hall (more like a corridor – a *"hoiz"* in Yiddish), along the entire width of the house, which also served for grain storage when needed. Once, when my parents were filling up sacks of grain, two Jews from among the colony residents offered Father to register for planting fruit trees. My mother was skeptical about that idea, but my father proceeded to register. How much effort was invested in this orchard! Everything was done by self–work! Big holes were dug, and 120 trees were planted in an area of 3 *dunams* [0.74 acres]. Ten similar orchards were planted in contiguous areas. While these areas were located on the bank of the river, the beach was high above the water, and it took a long time until proper arrangements were made to water the trees directly from the river. In the meantime, they brought water from the other end of the colony, where the beach was low. Every tree received a barrel of water. This was hard labor [to fill up the barrels]. When the time came to eat from the fruits of our effort, there was a big celebration! Our own peaches, our cherries, and later on, our apples! (when we arrived in *Eretz Israel*, we brought with us a crate full of Red Shafran apples).

I remember well when our good mother was returning from the orchard with buckets full of fruit and distributing them left and right.

Many years passed since then. Mother passed away when she was only 35 years old. We were seven children, me the elder – a 15-year-old, and the little one, only 10 days old.

Fifteen years later, Father passed away as well, still in his prime at the age of 53, a victim of an incurable disease. He was not fortunate enough to fulfill his dream and make *Aliyah* with us to *Eretz Israel*. The orchard was sold for 300 Rubles. It was hard to say farewell to the orchard since every tree in it was like a live creature to me. When the ownership was passed to others, I could not go to that side of the colony.

The following is another chapter from our lives.

I was 13 or 14 years old when I completed elementary school. Besides the library in my father's house, there was no other reading book in the entire colony. My father subscribed, along with six other people,

*[Page 192]*

to the Yiddish journal "Der Fraynd" (The Friend). I recall one home, whose head of the family was completely ignorant, however, the woman had some affinity for books. She used to purchase small booklets. I do not remember what type of booklets these were, perhaps SHEME" R books [by Yiddish author Nakhum–Meir Sheikevitz]. The woman would allow us to borrow two booklets at a time for one user fee of a Kopeck. I spent every Kopeck that came to me incidentally for that purpose.

In Sdeh Menukha HaGdola there was a library worthy of its name, and one had to pay 10 Kopecks per month for the privilege of borrowing books. This was not a negligible sum those days. We lived a life of scarcity in the colony, and money was precious. However, in my thirst for books, I would press and request Mother to give me the ten Kopecks. Despite her understanding, she did not have the money.

Only after a long talk with Father, I would get the required amount. I was not satisfied with just reading. I wanted to study, and for that, I was willing to give up even on the most essential things. In the fall of 1908, I was already 16 years old. Father would go immediately after the holiday of *Sukkot* to the Russian villages to work in glazing. Mother would fatten geese and hoped the earn 15 Rubles by doing that, which were slated to buy a coat for me. I talked to her and convinced her that learning was much more important than a new coat. I would simply cover the patch on my old coat with the edge of the large shawl that I wore on my head. I spilled many tears until Mother took pity on me and agreed. "Ok," she said, "we will pay for the studies instead of a coat. However, what would Father say when he comes back?" My joy did not last long. I studied for two months with Mr. Lieberman in Sdeh Menukha HaGdola, and my good and dearest mother passed away. I (with the help of my mother's parents) shouldered the burden of maintaining the house and taking care of my little sister who was almost 5 years younger than I was.

One year passed. Father brought home a second wife [my aunt]. Before he did that, he turned to me and said: "You wanted to study; now you would have the chance to do so." However, the promise was not fulfilled. The family was so big (the aunt brought two daughters of her own) and I could not ask for money from her. I once was hosted in my aunt's house in Bobrovy-Kut. Our distant relative, who was a seamstress by the name of Rakhel Rozin, lived in my aunt's house. I was always sad; the desire for learning did not let me live in comfort. Rakhel asked me:" What is the reason for your depression?" I answered her that I wanted to study, otherwise, I would not have any purpose for my life, and then the thing that astonished me came. I did not believe what I was hearing: she offered to pay for my studies. A strange person offered to help me, while she herself was working hard to make a living. When would I be able to return the money? She calmed me down and reassured me that she was doing that on her own goodwill and that it would not be difficult for her to do it. She said that I would start to pay her back when I started to earn money on my own.

Six months later, I passed the tests for the four years high of school classes. I financed the continuation of my studies by myself, but first, I paid off the loan to Rakhel Rozin and started to teach children in our colony.

*[Page 193]*

I especially recall a large group of boys and girls, who passed a course of four classes of high school taught by me. The cultural character of our colony changed gradually and we established a public library so that people would not need to go to Sdeh Menukha HaGdola to borrow books. An amateur drama club was also established.

I remember the first show by the drama club, which was prepared with the help of an actor who visited the colony. I also was slated to take an active role in the show (this was during the time that Mother was still alive). However, Father did not agree to allow me to do so, and even words of persuasion by my mother did not help. The show was supposed to take place during the evening of *Hoshana-Raba* [the night of the seventh day of the Jewish holiday of *Sukkot*]. At the beginning of that evening, a local resident walked to the synagogue and announced along his way in a loud voice in Yiddish *"Yidden in schul un goyim in teater"* ("Jews to the synagogue and gentiles to the theater…"). After the praying session, a group of Jews came to interrupt the show and drive the actors away. I cried bitterly that night, not because I did not participate in the show but because Father participated in that group.

Jewish Farmers in Russia Fields

From his second marriage, Aba had two more sons and a daughter. When we made *Aliyah* to *Eretz Israel*, only these two brothers and the two daughters of my aunt stayed behind in Russia from the entire large family.

In the summer of 1961, when I visited Russia to see my brothers, I was not allowed to reach our colony, Sdeh Menukha HaKtana (The Soviets changed the name to Shterendorf). I was told that the colonies were now Russian villages and only a few Jewish families were residing in them.

**Sara Shadmi**

Sdeh Menukha HaKtana – The vegetable garden
(during the beginning of the 1920s)

Yefeh Nahar – The synagogue

I was born in 1891 and was a single son to my parents. My father wanted to train me to be a merchant and thus placed me as a shop assistant in a village, 60 kilometers away from our colony. However, I resented the store and returned home after three days. My father was angry but I asked: "Why don't we learn to also diligently work in our colony like the Christian farmers? It would be better if we purchase additional horses, and I would devote myself to agriculture." Indeed, thanks to my work and the work of my sisters on the farm, considerable progress occurred. We began to purchase agricultural machinery; we had 4 horses and about 40 heads of cattle.

In 1915, I was recruited to the army and participated in battles on the front. Close to the end of the war,

*[Page 194]*

I was admitted to a hospital. My mother *z"l* and my wife visited me, and I told them: "When the war is over, we are going to make *Aliyah* to *Eretz Israel*, no matter what." My wife was very enthusiastic. We started our preparation for *Aliyah*; however, the whole movement encountered many obstacles. Many colony bachelors who tried to steal the border had to experience the adventures of wandering from one edge of Russia to the other. Only after many months did they succeed in getting out. I, as the head of a family, could not put my small children in danger, and wander along the border towns. We continued to work on the farm and waited for an opportunity to make *Aliyah*.

The destruction of the Jewish occupations by the Soviet regime took away the source of their sustenance, and many Jews turned to farming. Since the estates were confiscated, it was possible to register and receive a piece of land. Groups of Jews from other provinces received land near us and began establishing new settlements. These merchants and shopkeepers were not accustomed to agriculture and required assistance from counselors. I was asked to become a counselor in a collective settlement that consisted of natives of Rokytna and I agreed. The new settlement was not very far from our colony, and I could visit my home frequently.

When Agro–Joint began to assist the settlement, I was asked by its agent to counsel seven collectives. That role of counseling Jews in agriculture gave me a lot of satisfaction. I was very pleased to see shopkeepers and merchants become farmers. During my job as a counselor, I started correspondence with the "HeKhalutz" organization's headquarters in Moscow. About eighty families from among the farmers of the Jewish colonies were organizing to make *Aliyah* to Eretz Israel to establish there a colony consisting of Kherson province's natives. The "HeKhalutz" organization wanted to assist us and nominated two emissaries, to travel to *Eretz Israel* to find work and land for the group members. The two that were elected were my friend Erev and I. The mission did not take place; however, with the help of "HeKhalutz," I got my license to make *Aliyah* to *Eretz Israel*. I made *Aliyah* in 1926 and was accepted as a member of the Moshav "Kfar Yehoshua."

### Leibel Kahanov (Kfar Yehoshua)

My parents arrived at Sdeh Menukha HaKtana from Nevel in the Vitebsk province. I really do not know how they traveled a road thousands of kilometers long on horses and wagons. However, I do know that the journey lasted two years, many children were born, and some people died on the way. When they arrived, they settled in the colony of Nahar-Tov [Good River], about a kilometer away from our colony, where the land was desolate. That area was conquered from the Crimea's Tatars, who had used the area for pasture rather than cultivating it. Our parents' parents did not reside in Nevel – they were "people of settlement." That meant that they resided in villages.

*[Page 195]*

During the reign of Alexander, the First, they were expelled just after the visit by the Russian poet–senator Derzhavin to their area.

The construction of the houses in the Jewish settlement was subcontracted to a contractor, and obviously, thefts were rampant. I saw a house that had just a frame filled with plaster clay. Even farm animals and plows were not delivered according to the plan. During the first few years, the people in the colonies were a source of mockery by their neighbors since they were not very knowledgeable in farming. Most of the people were visiting the Russian farmers in their villages, where they engaged in glazing, sold "*tulk*" sardines, or purchased leathers for trading.

About 60 years ago, they started to cultivate the land with the help of agronomists, using "modern" equipment, such as plows with three wings, which were called "*buker's*," harvesters that harvested the crops but did not transport it from the field, and threshing machines drawn by horses.

Thirty-five families settled in our colony, and all received plots of land. Over time, the families grew, and their land allocation decreased to as little as 10 *dunams* [about 2.5 acres]. Even though the soil was very fertile (Chernozem soil), it was not sufficient to sustain a family, since there was no source of water, and they had to rely on rains which were not frequent.

The area of the colony stretched over a plane, with no mountains or slopes, over thousands of kilometers, which bordered Tavria (in Crimea) in the east and the Province of Ekaterinoslav in the west. In my childhood, I was told stories about wolves, foxes, and hares that roamed the area. I saw only a small hare with my own eyes. The snakes were numerous, even in my days. There were also the "*susliki's*" – a type of field mouses, which was ruining the crops. To fight them, an order was issued to every farm that they needed to provide the village committee with a certain number of the "*susliki's*" feet every week.

The work in the fields lasted the whole week. We used to leave on Sunday and return on Friday. We bathed in the Ingulets River to wash the mud that accumulated on our bodies. There was also a deep well located at a distance of about 15 kilometers from the colony. A water drawer was sitting at the well permanently and in return he received a plot of land. The children studied in a school until the age of 13 and left school to work after that. There were several illiterates for whom the colony policeman, who was not a great scholar himself, used to sign.

*

The head of the colony was called "*Schultz*" and his two assistants were called "*Beisitzer*," names taken from the many neighboring German colonies. The "*Schultz*" and the "*Beisitzer*" were elected by a list of signatories and were not people who were nominated from above. The authorities were represented by the state policeman ("*strazhnik*" [a Guard in Russian]). People used to serve him liquor and herring with some black olives.

*[Page 196]*

During my days, we did not feel any hatred from the neighboring farmers towards the farmers of the colonies. On the contrary, there was some comradery. When the colony farmers went to the city, and there were no inns on the way, they used to stop by the homes of their acquaintances for the night and discuss matters of agriculture with them or matters of food and drinks. Some people exchanged recipes on how to pickle cucumbers and tomatoes.

The village committee was authorized to judge and impose fines of up to 25 Rubles or a month of imprisonment, which actually never materialized. When my late father was a "*Schultz*," and somebody was caught stealing a small amount of wheat from his friend's field, his friends would gather and punish him for a month in prison. The following day, my father would send Ya'akov, the policeman, to invite the man to our house (there wasn't obviously any jailhouse in the village, and "imprisonment "was supposed to take place in our house, which was, in most cases like a resort for the prisoner). Ya'akov the policeman would return and announce that the man did not have free time to sit in prison and would consider whether or not to come when he was done with his work. Obviously, that person never came, and the sides reconciled somehow.

The people who owned a big piece of land and, in addition, leased additional land from others, employed workers to help with the transporting and threshing work, particularly during the summer, during the harvest (people leased land because they owed taxes to the government – 12 Rubles per *disiyatin* annually – and did not have money to pay it). The price for 5 months of work was about 70 Rubles, depending on the quality of the work. Most of the workers were residents of the colonies who did not have much land. Sometimes a gentile would come to work; however, in most cases, he would spend all his earnings on liquor.

Jewish Farmers in Russia Fields

The closest town was Beryslav, which was located 45 kilometers away from the colony. That was where the wheat was transported, twice a year, before Passover and Rosh Hashanah, and that was also where they bought clothing for the summer and the winter. Just before the First World War, ships began to sail from the city of Kherson up the river all the way to the colonies, and Kherson became the main town for the entire area.

During the First World War, a general enlistment took place. Whoever was at the proper age, was recruited, trained, and sent to the war. Many youths were killed or wounded, and the enemy captured even more. Harsh poverty descended on the families whose main bread earner was enlisted. No government assistance was available to the families of the recruits, and honorable women would go around the homes with a red kerchief to collect cash contributions for these needy people. This state prevailed until the October Revolution when the Bolsheviks ruled, and the army started to fall apart and disperse and the captured soldiers returned home.

The overall situation changed for the worse. During the war, the government confiscated anything they needed, and many wealthy people lost their wealth. At the same time, pogroms began in Ukraine. While our colony did not suffer from the pogroms, many people from the surrounding area, who lost everything, escaped to our colony. When Hetman [Russian military and political title] Grigoriev [paramilitary Ukrainian militia and gang leader] came

*[Page 197]*

to our colony, he only demanded several pairs of boots. Some of our colony members joined his unit until he started pogroms, and they separated from him then.

The colony was Zionist, and our platoon of "HeKhalutz" was one of the best. Platoons of pioneers from nearby and distanced cities arrived in our colony and brought with them Hebrew books and news about what was going on in the world.

Seventeen members of HeKhalutz left the colonies [on our way to *Eretz Israel*] headed for the Romanian border, a distance of 400 kilometers, in two carts because we could not ride the train. There was no coal at the time, and locomotives were operated on wood, thistles, and straw. A passenger who was too cold would jump off the train and run in front of it, just to warm up.

**Yehuda Menukhi** (Nahalal)

During the First World War, all the young males were enlisted, and following them so did even the elderly and the very young males. The colonies almost emptied. Following the recruitment of people, the recruitment of horses and wagons for transporting soldiers and equipment to the front started.

We had two pairs of horses on our farm. It was customary that one pair would be recruited for the army's transportation, and the other would stay on the farm. The question was – who would be sent as the driver of the recruited wagon. I was the elder child in our home and started to work at the age of six. I had already plowed the fields and performed all other summer fieldwork when I was 9 years old. I went to school during the wintertime.

When the World War ended, the civil war started. Large forces of the "Whites" headed by Denikin were concentrated in Crimea, where they organized to fight the Bolsheviks. We, again, had to suffer another campaign of wagon recruitment, this time by the Bolsheviks, who transported recruits to the front. I was 17 years old then and all tasks were divided between my father and me. [During the civil war] he worked on the farm and I in the army transport.

The front was in Perekop, a distance of 300 kilometers from our colony, on the line between Beryslav and Simferopol. The tribulations of the journey were not easy. The journey lasted about five to six days. The military food was rough, dry, and monotonous. At the stops, we slept outside under the sky, and our ears were tired of hearing the roughness and the swearing of the soldiers.

We were relieved somewhat when we, the colonies' native Jewish wagon drivers, met occasionally for a short while during one of the stops. We brought our travelers –

*[Page 198]*

the soldiers and their officers to the front listened to the clatter of the shootings and returned with empty wagons home. Upon my entrance to the yard, joy descended over the family members, seeing the tan–faced boy and the horses coming back whole and healthy. I quickly threw off the dusty and sweaty clothes, which stuck to my body for twenty days, showered and wore clean clothes, and was served a tasty meal. Through the pleasure of stretching my bones, I lay down on my bed and fell into a deep sleep. In my absence, many tasks have been neglected. Thus, after a slumber of a night and a day, I shook myself out of my fatigue and assaulted the various works.

During one of the stops at night, when our passengers – the soldiers, were deep in their sleep, we took our horses out of the camp, as if to allow them to graze on nearby pasture, jumped on them, and raced towards home, abandoning the wagons behind.

The battles between the two armies were fierce and desperate. The consequences could be fatal for each of the two enemies, not only in that region but also in the entire area of southern Russia. A deep swamp stretched between Perekop and Simferopol. The Red Army managed to circle the White Army and push it into that swamp. Thousands of soldiers sank in the swamp and perished in it. The White Army suffered a defeat in that battle, and they escaped on ships that sailed on the Black Sea. The Red Army, intoxicated from its victory, entered the city of Simferopol with cheers and joy, and I, the Jewish boy among them.

Simferopol was known for its abundance of wines. The soldiers broke into the wine cellars and drank for a whole day. Many of the soldiers were lying on the side of the roads before the day was over. At night, the whole Red Army fell into a deep sleep.

During the same night, companies of Makhnovists entered the city and robbed the entire property and equipment of the Reds, and fled. The following day, the Red Army members were astonished at the "David and Saul" action by the Makhnovists and took means to fortify the city.

When I reached the age of 19, I said farewell to my family to make *Aliyah* to *Eretz Israel*. The story of my *Aliyah*, which lasted about a year, was rich with adventures, escapes, jails, dangers, and trials, which I all managed to survive. I arrived in *Eretz Israel* and I am a farmer in a Kibbutz.

**Ben–Tzion Komarov** (Afikim)

*[Page 199]*

A memorial candle in memory of my father Z"L Avraham Moshe Ninburg who stood heroically on guard to defend his home and village during the years of calamity and pogroms.

During those days, it was customary that any army unit, upon entering a place – confiscated the wagons and the horses. The Bolsheviks took wagons and four horses from us. We were left with only one horse. One evening, a company of soldiers passed, I think they were "Reds." Several soldiers entered our yard running and wanted to take the last horse. My father *z"l* locked the stable, hid the keys, and absolutely refused to hand them the last horse, claiming that an agricultural farm cannot manage without a horse and that he had already provided four horses. The commander pulled a handgun from his pocket, lifted it to my father's ear, and shouted: "Give me the key, or else I will shoot!" My mother fainted. My sister Shlomit and I (we were 11 and 13 respectively) began to shout. My sister Feiga grabbed the soldier and begged for mercy. However, the soldier kept insisting: "If he does not give me the key, I am going to shoot." But Father did not move, and continued to claim that he would not surrender the horse! The whole thing lasted perhaps three minutes, but for us, it seemed like an eternity. Finally, the soldier gave up and said: "If you – the Jewish farmer, are so strong, I will not take the horse," and walked out.

The *"shkutzim"* [a derogatory term for anti–Semite gentile children which literally means loathsome] from Gradnovka "liked" very much the apples and pears of the Jews and were stealing them at every opportunity. We – the youths served in the front line against the thieves and had to be on guard at all times. During usual times, a guard manned by one boy or a girl was sufficient. During the night, we employed a professional guard. However, during the civil war, the *"hutzpah"* of the *"shkutzim"* swelled. At that time, the Kantor brothers from Kremenchug hid by us, and they were guarding the orchard most of the time. However, one day toward the evening, a crowd of Gentiles assaulted the orchard and started to pick the fruits. The Kantor brothers escaped home since they were afraid to face the crowd by themselves. Father did not say anything, took a pitchfork, and started to head toward the orchard. My mother broke out crying and did not want to let him go by himself: "The whole orchard can go to hell," she yelled, "I would not let you go by yourself." However, father did not listen and he went out. Ashamed, the two Kantor brothers followed him. They also wanted to see what would happen – how would a single person fare by himself in such an uneven battle. A few hours later, the Kantor brothers came home with full admiration and told the story: "Father went quietly to the orchard, crawled to the stone fence, and suddenly called, in a stern and loud voice, as if he has a whole company behind him – one–two–three"!

The *"shkutzim"* panicked and left the orchard at once. Father came back home as if nothing had happened. In his opinion, this was normal – a farmer's duty was to defend his property.

*[Page 200]*

There is another case that was etched in my memory. During the period when *"Bandas"* (gangs) of murderers and rioters wandered around in our area, a Jewish horseman appeared one day, galloping on the main road of the colony yelling: "Jews, run away! The "Makhno" is approaching, coming from the hillside" During those days, the name "Makhno" was sufficient to make the blood freeze in the veins. Everybody began to harness the horses and load the family members and all sorts of belongings on the wagons to run away. My mother, big sister Doba, mother of five children, and we, the children, wanted to run away because we were scared. However, Father and my sister Feiga announced that they would not abandon the house. Father claimed that if everybody would run away to one side and gather in the field, the danger would be greater. However, after my mother and Doba pleaded with him repeatedly, he harnessed a wagon and seated Mother, the grandchildren, me, and my sister Shlomit, and we escaped with everybody. My father and my sister, Feiga, remained at home and began to prepare weapons for defense – pitchforks and a gun without a butt and were prepared to defend their honor, home, and life. To our contentment, this was a false rumor. If the Makhno gang had actually come – the gang could have annihilated everybody with several hand grenades. When everybody returned home, my father and sister came to welcome us and proved to us again that "one does not run from one's death, nor from one's home. One needs to defend one's life and should not flee."

## Shternah Ninberg

I was born in the colony of Sdeh Menukha HaKtana, a third generation of farmers. There were forty households in Sdeh Menukha HaKtana when it was established. Its settlers arrived at the location after Sdeh Menukha HaGdola already had existed for 30 years. During my days, there were 120 farms in our colony.

It is logical to assume that the settlers of Sdeh Menukha HaKtana were more fortunate than those one generation earlier. Despite all that, the experiences of the journey to the South and the encounter with the new reality were etched so deeply in the memory of the settlers' first generation that their story affected us as if we took part in the actual events.

The settlers of Sdeh Menukha HaKtana originated from the city of Nevel in the province of Vitebsk in Belarus. They traveled thousands of kilometers with wagons loaded with women and children, food supplies, tools, and housewares. The wagons were equipped with wooden shafts. A bucket full of tar was hung on the wagons to anoint the shafts, once in a while to prevent a fire due to friction with the wheels.

*[Page 201]*

The settlers traveled for many weeks on rickety roads and off-roads in forests. My maternal grandfather was a baby in diapers then. One day, the travelers realized that the baby was not in the wagon and not around it either – he just disappeared and was lost. They stopped the journey and back-tracked along the wheel tracks until they found him lying down on the ground sleeping. Apparently, he rolled and fell off the wagon during one of the wagon's bounces. Since he was wrapped in many covers and blankets and was not pulled out of his diapers, he was not hurt. This story about my grandfather was known among all of the colony's members, and they would mention it as a miracle from the heavens.

My paternal grandmother still remembered the arrival of the settlers to the colony. She used to tell us about the fear the fields caused among them since they seemed to be infinite with no end to them. There were no borders to separate one plot from the other. In the winter, gangs of hungry wolves used to roam and attack the oxen, which were tied to the shed. Once, a young cow was caught by the wolves. In those days, the farmers went to the field with the entire family and children since they were afraid to leave them home alone. To scare the wolves and prevent them from approaching the wagons' camp, they used to hang iron rods and make them chime in turns, during all hours of the day and night. During my time I did not run into wolves; however, their terrifying nightmare was still hanging in the air. Everybody who happened to stay alone in the field would envision these animals in their mind.

Poverty reigned in my home. My father inherited half the plot from his father (about 160 *dunams* [about 40 acres]). We sustained ourselves by growing field crops, which we used primitive methods to cultivate, and just one pair of horses. We had only two cows in the cowshed. We had a few chickens that lived in the attic. The colonists did not grow vegetables in the colony and had not yet planted fruit trees.

Jewish Farmers in Russia Fields

The family was large, and the children were small. My father was burdened by the need to sustain his wife and children, his widowed mother, and elder sisters who lived in our house until they got married. Father worked above his abilities. During the working season, he would leave on Sunday, very early in the morning, to the distanced fields – about 20 kilometers from the house, and return on Friday afternoon. During the days that he did not have to work on the farm, he would make himself available to a Christian estate owner, earning some meager pennies and cutting wheat with a scythe from dark to dark.

During the beginning of the [20th] century, substantial progress occurred in the Jewish colonies. The JCA organization assisted the settlers in purchasing advanced agricultural equipment and made agronomists available to them. The agronomists trained them and introduced many improvements in the seed cycle and land cultivation methods' A credit union was established where the farmers of the three colonies (Sdeh Menukha [HaGdola], Bobrovy Kut, and Sdeh Menukha HaKtana) could borrow money at a favorable interest. During that period, fruit orchards were planted, the harvests grew, and the cattle sector improved. We experienced substantial progress on our farm as well, particularly when we, [the children], began to work on the farm, first me, then my elder sister, and after her the rest of the brothers. Instead of the pair of horses, we had already four workhorses, and their number multiplied over time. Instead of sowing

*[Page 202]*

the fields by hand, we used a sowing machine. Instead of harvesting with a scythe or sickle, we harvested with a harvesting machine. The number of heads of cattle grew. We enlarged the house and our life conditions, including food and clothing, improved. With all of that, it was still a hard life under the primitive conditions of the Czarist Russia. We felt fortunate with the material improvement and enjoyed it. However, when I look back at the years of my early childhood when we lived in poverty, I think that we did not suffer by being poor. Even though candies, sweets, or toys were considered luxuries, which we could not even dream about, the children's lives were full and lively. We were part of everything that happened on the farm and in the large family. I knew how to gallop a horse as early as at the age of four. We were playing with the small carts as much as one play with the best toys. With sleeved-up pants, we danced in the sparkling puddles after the rain. I was happy when I sat at the top of the ladder wagon, which was moving slowly, filled with crops, on the three–hour journey from the field to the house. Even the Ingulets River itself gave us many hours of joy and freshness. There was hardly any kid, who did not know how to swim. These were the sources of life–happiness for the colony's children, who grew up within nature, free and confident.

Our mother did a lot to take out the pain associated with the stinging–poverty from our life and to deepen the feeling of a warm home during my early childhood years. She passed away when I was fourteen years old, and did not leave behind even a single picture since she never posed for a picture. However, her image stands in front of my eyes, until today, clear and shining. I believe that Mother was a wonderful woman, diligent and blessed with good hands. We were seven children, and our births were adjacent to each other. Besides taking care of the young children, my mother baked bread, cooked, did the laundry, sewed the clothes for the entire family, smeared clay on the floors every Shabbat eve, and plastered the house on the outside every year. During the threshing, she used to stand at the top of the heap, receive the straw pitchforks from Father, and arrange the piles neatly in the yard. She built, with her own hands, together with Father, the baking oven in the yard. Together, they built the fence around our house. She took care to make sure that the children would be dressed in clean and mended clothes. If we were fortunate enough and received a new garment – Mother sewed it according to the details of the latest "fashion."

Unlike Father, who was reticent, our mother was open to communicating with us. Nice looking, welcoming, and full of laughter, the house was not too narrow for her, and she willingly shared our meager food with her mother–in–law and her sisters–in–law' During Shabbat evenings, our house was open and served as a meeting place for my father's sisters. Mother always found something to serve for them, and she was like a friend to them. As long as Mother was alive, our home was the center for our numerous relatives, and she ensured that my father's connections with his own family would not be loosened. Not only had our family benefited from her work, but also other girls in the colony. A girl who was about to get married and needed to be trained how to cut and sew,

*[Page 203]*

found support with Mother. She treated Father with love and respect and planted the same attitude toward him in our hearts.

The life–year in the colony was based around the work seasons and around the holidays.

*

The month of Elul was under the seal of its gloom. The field emptied after the harvest from men and the piles of crops. The corn and sunflowers were picked up. Also gathered were the watermelons, melons, and cucumbers. We were picking the apples in the orchard and transporting them to the attic, which filled up with their intoxicating smell. The women's hands were busy making food for the long winter when all crops stopped breathing and growing until the spring. We were now heading for the plowing and sowing work. Only a small part of the fields would be sowed with rye and winter wheat. These fields needed to sprout and strengthen before the cold was coming when a snow cover would fall on this germination and wrap it. When spring came, the snow would melt, and the winter wheat would rise again, grow quickly, and be the first to be harvested.

The fall plowing of the fields and advanced cultivation methods were introduced under the influence of the agronomists. Before that, they were sowing on the top of the fields of stubble. Only after receiving the guidance, they tried to plow the fields before the winter ahead of time to let them rest and absorb the wetness. That way, the spring harvest was also increased. Later on, they allowed the fields to rest from growing grains for more than one season, and they managed to obtain larger harvests. Ukrainian fields did not need to receive fertilizers.

Many of my memories are associated with the fall plowing. I was only 14 years old when I went out together with a hired boy, to plow the fields by myself using a "*sok*" plow. We two used to work from dark to dark, at a distance of 15 kilometers from home. We would rest the horses twice a day only to feed them, otherwise, we continued to work continuously to complete the plowing before the rains came. We marched about 40 kilometers in one day of work while one of us held the plow and the other drove the horses. At night, we tied the horses to the wagon, where their food was loaded, and we slept near the wagon. One night, one of the horses collapsed and fell on top of us. We managed to pull it off and release our bodies from under the load of its body only after a substantial effort. Even if we wanted to yell for help there was nobody who could hear us, as we were far from the colony, and there was nobody around.

Every house lived through the preparations for the "*Yamim Nora'im*" [Days of High Holidays– "Days of Awe"]. During the small hours of the night, the synagogue beadle would go around the town and knock on every window of every house, calling the farmers to say "*Slikhot*" [communal prayers for the Divine's forgiveness, recited during the High Holidays or on Jewish fast days]. My father served as a cantor on Shabbat and holidays. He knew the meaning of every word; he had a good hearing and a pleasant voice. He had melodies of his own, and they liked his style of praying in the colony.

[Page 204]

At the beginning of *Yom Kippur* [Day of Atonement], he would pray the "*Kol Nidrei*" [recited at the opening service of *Yom Kippur*] and the next day he would serve as cantor during most of the day and finish with the "*Ne'ila*" [closing] prayer.

Upon the approach of the "Days of Awe," Father would start humming the prayers, prepare the tools for plowing and the sacks of seeds, check the wagon to ensure that it is fully equipped, and practice the prayers.

During the holidays, the settlers would lengthen the prayers and follow the commandments to their last details. On the day before *Yom Kippur*, they went out to the cemetery to visit the graves of their loved ones and then gathered in the synagogue for the night and the following day. During the holiday of *Sukkot*, they would build a Sukkah near every house and decorate it according to the best of their ability and imagination. For the children, this was a source of Joy and happiness. During days of the *Khol HaMoed* ["intermediate days" of a long Jewish holiday], relatives would travel outside of the colonies for mutual visits.

The peak of the joy prevailed in the colony during the day of *Simkhat Torah* [Jewish holiday of the Rejoicing of the Torah at the end of the holiday of *Sukkot*]. During that holiday, our father and the adults became like children and we the members of the young generation, participated with them joyfully and with amazement. They behaved as if they had forgotten all of their worries. The attention was distracted from the worry about the approaching winter days and their tough problems. The disputes and conflicts between neighbors were forgotten, and the partitions were removed. Everybody was united in the joy of the holiday. Bearded and wrinkled-faced Jews, wearing long capotes, jumped and hopped with the Torah scroll, made braids of their beards, danced on the table, and carried the *gabbai* [synagogue administrator/ manager] on their joined hands. In this joyful tumult, they circled the colony's yards, opened ovens, went down to the cellars, and brought up the tasty foods. They did it without asking for the permission of the homemaker, on the contrary, the more the family was known to be stingy, the more powerfully they would storm the dishes in the oven and the more zealots they would be in raiding the cellar. The colony's young recruits, whose recruitment took place during that season, participated in this *Simkhat Torah* tumult. Although the young recruits' level of disintegration and rampage never reached the level of the youth from the gentile villages, the Jewish boys would "lose control of themselves." This rampage was considered as "allowed" for those who were slated to leave their home for military service for a few years far away from home.

Weddings were celebrated throughout the entire year during times allowed for marriage. However, most of them concentrated during the period between *Yom Kippur* and *Sukkot* and on "*Shabbat Bereshit*" [the first Saturday after *Simkhat Torah* – the Shabbat when the reading of the first chapter of the Torah takes place]. For the agriculturalists, this was the most appropriate time, since it did not interfere with the burning harvest season. A wedding was a big joyful event in the colony, and its customs reflected the agricultural character of the place.

As early as the morning hours, a band of "*klezmer*" [musicians] was passing among the relatives and the in-laws to rejoice and to remind them of the event that was about to take place that evening. If the groom was an outsider, they would go out to welcome him with wagons decorated with ribbons and flowers. The "*klezmer*" played, and the people on the wagons would serve the groom drinks and pastries. On the way back to the colony, the joyful wagon drivers would accelerate the horses, competing with each other, passing each other in fast galloping.

*[Page 205]*

The groom would walk through the streets of the colony, accompanied by the relatives and the guests to the bride's house "to cover her face" [with the veil, a Jewish custom before the wedding]. After that, the groom and the bride would walk, separately, through the colony, the groom led by men and the bride by women until they arrived at the synagogue, where the *Khupah* [wedding ceremony] took place. Everything moved in the solid path of tradition, and even the orchestra melodies were fixed for every stage of the ceremony. The wedding feast lasted until the following morning, and later, they celebrated the wedding's gift-giving at noon.

In the poem "Khatunata Shel Elka" ["The Wedding of Elka"] Shaul Tchernikhovski described the details of a wedding in our area. However, the one thing that was not discussed was how heavy the financial burden that such a wedding imposed on the poor Jews was. My father had to arrange two weddings for my two sisters and provide them with the same dowry since who would dare to discriminate between the daughters and between them and their friends and deviate from the customary tradition? There was a difference of eight years between the weddings of the sisters. When the date of the wedding of the younger sister arrived, my father was still paying off debts from the wedding of the elder sister.

The holiday season and all the celebrations associated with it were like a crossroads in the year for the agricultural colony. Beyond it, the winter was already knocking on the door with all its problems and the meager earnings. The work on the farm was slight. We used to pluck straw from the big heap in the yard and take it bundle after bundle for heating the house and feeding the animals. We also worked on fixing the harnesses and carried water for the home needs and the livestock. The winter was also the season when people were leaving for outside jobs. The farmers rented themselves along with their horses and wagons to transport loads into and from the city. Some went to the towns and gentile villages to repair windows and trade in leathers, dry fish, or iron. Father was absent from home for long durations on these trips, and Mother would gather us all into her bed, to ease the feeling of loneliness. On Friday nights, Father's chair at the head of the table would stand empty. We were looking at Mother, who was saying the blessing over the Shabbat candles and paused for a long time with her hands on her eyes. We knew that Mother was praying for the well–being of Father, who was traveling on the roads and hiding her tears from us.

When the farms expanded and the cattle sector developed, they started to produce hard cheese and butter for sale. Winter employment was more readily available; however, that was still a period of respite when one could recharge and make oneself available to do other things, such as social activities.

\*

When the spring approached, the farmers started to prepare for the sowing. During the winter, they tried to save on the horses' food, while before the spring, they would feed them diligently to fatten them up and be able to withstand the harsh work. They would pass the grain through a winnowing machine and select the best seeds for sowing. They prepared the tools and equipment

*[Page 206]*

required for the field. The sowing period was short – about two to three weeks and the effort associated with it was substantial since the fields were far away and there was always the fear that the rains would begin and disrupt the work.

To waste time on back-and-forth trips they would stay in the field for the entire week. They would build a camp and sleep clothed in a canopied wagon. They would leave for the field at dawn. When the time for praying arrived, my father would cover himself with the tallit and whisper his prayers while riding in the wagon. When we arrived at the field, Father would cook breakfast and pray while kneading the dough and mixing the big pot hung on the plow's shaft.

At the young age of ten, I had already started to ride horses. We were marching the whole day, without any rest, on the earthclods – while Father was holding the plow and I was driving the horses. While we were plowing, Father would pray aloud the *Minkha* [afternoon prayer]. He would only stop for a short moment when he reached the "*Shmoneh Esreh*" part of the prayer.

When the sowing period happened to fall during Pesakh, it would cause a lot of trouble. They could not postpone the sowing for fear that the rains would come before they had a chance to put the seeds in the ground. However, it was forbidden to handle the seeds because of the rule of *Khametz* [leavened food]. The farmers would bypass the rule by "selling" the seeds, the horses, and the equipment to a *goy* [gentile], usually the colony's shepherd as if they were not sowing the seeds for themselves. This enabled them to continue with the work. There were cases, however, where the gentile exploited his status as a buyer, as was written and signed in the agreement, and insisted on executing the sale according to the agreement. They had then to explore ways by which they could appease him.

When they finished the sowing, they waited for the rains. Between Pesakh and Shavuot, they would cultivate the fruit tree orchard and sow the summer crops – corn and sunflowers, watermelon, melons, pumpkins, and cucumbers. Soon, whole families, along with the children, would go to thin out the sowed fields. Suddenly, the sky would darken, lightning and thunder came, and a fierce summer–rain pounded the ground. Young and old would roll up their clothes and start running. Beards swung, *tzitziot* swayed, while everybody was dashing panicky to find shelter under the wagons.

The harvest season was the season of tremendous effort. It was short, but its results determined whether the farmers were able to enjoy the bounty given to them by nature. Every hour was valuable. Although we would exchange the horses. once in a while, to let them rest, the harvester did not stop for a minute. This was quite a primitive harvester compared to the stacking and bundling machines we are familiar with today in our country.

The work with the harvester required two people

*[Page 207]*

and a substantial physical effort. After the harvest, we needed to pile up the grain and transport it immediately from the field. Every family tried to mobilize as much work power as possible. They would even take out the children from the "*kheder*" to help the adults. I transported grain from the field by myself when I was 15 years old. The transport involved substantial efforts. They tried to pile as much grain as possible on the wagon. For that purpose, the arrangement of the ladder wagon would have to be done properly since The road was lengthy. We would leave our yard at two o'clock at night and complete the day's work only at eight o'clock in the evening.

With the 18-hour work a day, we could transport from the field only three times. The ambiance during the harvest season was different from the one of the sowing seasons. Many people of many ages were in the field during the harvest. The field–camps were humming with many families. They would keep a cow in the field to get a fresh supply of milk. They hauled barrels of water and cooked meals of two dishes. In the evenings, after a hard day's work, the laughter and singing voices of youths would echo through the place. Black from the sun and the dust, sweaty and dirty we would return at the end of the week to the colony and, holding a clean change of clothes, would rush directly to the river, which absorbed our sweat, washed and refreshed our bodies from the grueling work.

We would thresh the grain using a method similar to the one used by Arabs in Israel. However, instead of their threshing sled, we used a heavy hexagon-shaped stone that was perforated by slits. This stone roller was harnessed to a pair of horses, circling with it around and around and pressing on the scattered layer of straw containing the seeds. From time to time, we would turn the layer of straw with pitchforks to enable the stone to penetrate it and separate the seeds. Then, we would pass the seeds through a winnowing machine. That was also hard work since we needed to rotate the winnowing machine's wheel, by hand. With all that, one cannot compare work in the barn, near the house, to work in the field. With the winnowing machine, we used to work mainly at night and change often the people who rotated the wheel.

The threshing season was the favorite season for the children, and the yards were buzzing from all the activity. The children would drive the horses, which pulled the threshing stone and gallop in the rounded barn, rake the golden seeds coming out of the thresher, and jump on top of the wheat sacks that were piled in the yard. For the farm animals and the poultry that was the season of plentiful food. It was also the favorite season for people because the watermelons and melons ripened.

The agricultural work season was complete then. Finally, we could load the wagons with the filled and flawlessly sewed sacks and transport them for sale to Beryslav, located about 60 kilometers away from the colony. There were years when the revenues from the sale of the wheat were spent entirely on paying off debts, which accumulated during the year. However, when our situation improved, we could purchase clothing and footwear for the family members after the harvest and even bring a bundle of Rubles home.

*[Page 208]*

The society in the colony was based on a crisscross of relations – family relations, neighbors' relations, and age relations. Every family who settled in the colony sprouted additional families. When sons and daughters got married, the in-laws with their families joined the circle of the family's relatives. On top of the initial family connections, grandchildren and great-grandchildren were added. The closeness of the family was preserved since it was fed by the continuous contact between people in a small place where everybody knew everybody else.

The neighbors' relations played a special role in the colony's life. The families resided in a house near a house and a yard near a yard. This closeness resulted in relations where the neighbors were active participants in both the joys and sorrows of the family, they were the first to know what was going on and the first to provide help.

The age relations were also natural and deep among the relatives, neighbors, and the entire population. The fathers shouldered the burden of taking care of the farm. managed the public life, and represented the colony to the authorities. The colony farmers did not rely on the judicial system. They solved any dispute among them according to the judgment of an agreed-upon mediator. They needed to ensure the existence of all the needed community services by themselves – synagogue, "*kheder*" for the children, cemetery, and "*Khevra Kadisha*" [Burial Society]. Along with the common affairs stemming from the agricultural work, the above services served as the background for the relations among the elderly. The youth were rooted in the colony, and only a few left it. After the study in the "*kheder*," the youth joined the adults in shouldering the burden of working the farm and ensuring sustenance. They worked hard, and the portion of idle time for social pastime was small. It concentrated around the holidays, Shabbats, and sometimes during the winter season. The youth were organized in groups, which met in its members' houses or while walking on the main road on Shabbat, cracking sunflower seeds. We sang a lot, repeating the melodies we heard from the *klezmer* at the weddings or other songs that somebody got from somewhere else. Work experience, horses, and colony events captured a central part of our conversations. Later on, when the library was founded, we read books together or argued about a book, read at home.

Relations between the male and female youths were established through the social pastime with the group, and new families were added to the colony. When a young man approached the age of marriage, the family would make sure that he would have a coat and a city-style suit, although these things were not very useful for our way of life and were just purchased to express his status as "a member of the society," and to signify the status of the family.

Like the rest of the youth in the colony, my wife and I considered the development of the farm as our goal.

*[Page 209]*

We realized that it was possible to increase the farm's revenues and earn a decent living by introducing improvements in the cultivation methods and in the diversity of the farm sectors.

Indeed, the farms of the Jewish farmers began to surpass the farms of the gentile farmers in our area. However, the events that followed each other after the revolution in 1917 changed the course of things, and life was directed to another path.

\*

One day, a young man by the name of Khaim Bebilov – the son of the Rabbi of Sdeh Menukha HaGdola, arrived in our colony after staying with his family in the cities of big Russia during the days of the World War. He brought a wealth of news, which we drank thirstily. He told us about the Zionist movement and the pioneers of BILU [The Zionist movement whose goal was the agricultural settlement of the Land of Israel. The name is an acronym based on a verse from the Book of Isaiah – "House of Jacob, let us go"], who made *Aliyah* to *Eretz Israel* decades ago and began to settle it. He told us about the Jewish colonies in *Eretz Israel*, the pioneering Jewish workers and Jewish guards, and the awakening of the Hebrew language. He said that youths are organizing themselves throughout Russia, as nuclei of the "HeKhalutz" Zionist movement to fulfill the dream of making *Aliyah* to *Eretz Israel* and settling its arid land. During those days, after the revolution, the youths were confused. Some were ensnared by the leftist atmosphere and declared themselves communists. Against them, some others felt as if they were standing at a crossroads, asking themselves: "Where are we going now?"

The Zionist message fell on fertile soil and fascinated us. A new world was unveiled – a world that connected with our own lives. We can continue to be farmers. We will develop exemplary farms, not where we were, but in our own land. We were not only going to develop farms but also build a new just society. We would establish exemplary villages, which would serve as models and educate Jewish workers who would continue to build chains of these villages.

From that day, when this new message took root in our hearts, a new life began. Although we continued to plow, sow, harvest, and thresh, the work itself was not the main purpose of our life. The goal of attaining stability and continuity in our life in the colony diminished since all eyes were now focused on making *Aliyah.*

I, who until the appearance of Khaim Bebilov, did not know anything about Zionism, was completely taken by the idea. I was active in the movement during all of my free time. We organized as the local chapter of "Tzeirie Tzion" [Literally – "Youth of Zion" – the youth organization of the HeKhalutz"], started to collect contributions to KKL–JNF organization and spread Zionist propaganda in the colony. In 1918, members of the HeKhalutz movement, who came from various cities, arrived at the colony to receive agricultural training. Those guests introduced a breath of fresh air among the colony's youth. We gathered, every week, to listen to news about what was going on in *Eretz Israel*, which was disseminated from the HeKhalutz movement's center. We spent whole nights on stormy debates about the future of *Eretz Israel* and about ways of building it up. Somebody stepped forward and started to teach Hebrew. However, the center of our aspiration was making *Aliyah*, for which we devoted the best parts of our discussions – when and how would we be able to make *Aliyah*? The time when our aspiration would be fulfilled indeed came.

*[Page 210]*

We left on our way to make *Aliyah* to *Eretz Israel*. We said farewell to the colonies established by the grueling work of several generations and served as the root of our lives.

The horrible Holocaust descended on the colonies upon the Nazi occupation and wiped the Jewish settlements from the face of the earth. We, who continue the agricultural tradition of the Jewish farmers here in Israel, guarded in our hearts their light, which was lost and gone forever.

**Mordekhai Simkhoni** (Geva)[1]

The following memories are dedicated to my acquaintances, friends, brothers, sisters, and parents, to those who passed away in old age, and to the many who were annihilated by the animals during the Holocaust, gathered like cattle, to ease the annihilation work. Among them were my three brothers, Shimon, Zalman, and Peretz, who hugged each other when the Nazi troops pumped the bullets into them with their killing machines and thus fell together, blending their blood – all those who once were and who are not anymore.

Our colony, Sdeh Menucha Haktana, was located on a slope. Our fields (15 kilometers long but only one kilometer wide, on average) stretched a bit east of it, on a flat plane beyond the high plateau. The Ingulets River, which spills onto the Dnieper, meandered west of the colony. The neighboring colony of Sdeh Menukha HaGdola was located south of it, about a kilometer away. Five kilometers farther south, the colony of Bobrovy-Kut was located where the poet Sh. Sh. Frug was born.

According to estimates, our colony was established in 1840, among dozens of other colonies established dispersedly over an area of hundreds of kilometers in the province of Kherson, in southern Russia [southern Ukraine]. Most of its residents were natives of the city of Nevel in the province of Vitebsk – Jewish farmers, people who liked to work and lived according to the verse [Genesis 3:19]: "By the sweat of your brow you will eat." They raised and educated their children, each according to the best of their ability. They were familiar with the phrase: " If the children would know how to work, pray, and after we reach 120 they say *"Kadish – "da'yenu [enough for us]* ." They were simple people. They were simple in their manners and views: honest, decent, trustworthy, and liked by anybody who had contact with them.

*[Page 211]*

Most of those people sustained themselves by the labor of their hands in the various sectors of farm work. They all knew each other, more or less, and were influenced by each other, just like in a family. Their education (except for a very few), did not go beyond an elementary school, including studies in the "*kheder*" for the boys. That fact probably contributed, in a small part, to the setting and the characteristic image of these people, who were very similar in their positive attributes.

They lived well and had a beautiful life. They never aspired for luxuries and simplicity ruled everywhere. They lived as workers and farmers, or as they were defined by Jews from the cities – like "*goyim*" [gentiles]. Despite that, the Jewish attributes remained in them – the gentleness and the Jewish wisdom, the mixture of joy and sadness.

They walked and worked erect and with confidence and without arrogance. They did not surrender to the "*goyim*" when these tried, once in a while, to raise their hand on them.

I remember the long winter evenings at the elongated fireplace, used as a partition between rooms and heated by burning straw, radiating pleasant heat. On one of its sides, along its entire length, a one-meter-high step-like structure was built, and its width was just sufficient to allow one adult person to lie on it. Its name in Russian was "*lazhanka.*" The family's father used to lie down on that step, taking a nap and resting after a long day of work. A smooth wall was located on the other side of the fireplace around which the other family members, neighbors, and relatives – colony residents or guests who came from afar, would gather and listen to the stories told by mothers and grandmothers about people whom we, the children, were not fortunate enough to know.

We listened intently, G-d forbid not to miss any details about those people, their qualities, anecdotes, and phrases. From our father, uncles, and the colony elders we would hear stories about glazing and trading in cattle, leather, and geese (which was the main occupation during the dead season – in the winter). From them, we would hear stories about travels to near and far away villages, episodes, and adventures on the roads or on pathways in places where there were no roads, during days and nights, in a world full of snow. They told us about the roads, so badly obscured or broken that one could not continue the journey, especially at night when the snow fell – stories of "thousand and one nights." … They told us about mishaps on the roads, a broken wagon–axle, a horse that fell and did not get up, and a wagon that got stuck in a ditch could not be seen due to darkness or snow. They also told us stories about good "*goyim*," who helped them to get out of difficult situations and about meeting with *goyim* with tainted intents about property or money that belonged to others… The children's attention rose from one moment to the other, and their pride soared when they heard about how they fought against those bad "gentiles" with anything handy. Obviously, the storytellers always won at the end.

While we are talking about winter–nights, I remember one particular night during the year, the night of

*[Page 212]*

the gentiles' New Year (Silvester, or Novigod in Russian), which was, most of the time – a freezing night with a lot of snow. We, the small and the older children, were laying in bed, dreaming dreams, some children daydreaming and some – night dreaming. The adults were immersed in their worries about the family's livelihood and daughters who reached marriage–age, or tuition for schooling. All of a sudden, at midnight, there was a knock on the door, and several "*shkutzim*" [derogatory term for gentile children, which literally means pests] from the neighboring village in their winter outfits, full of snow, wearing felt boots ["valenki's"] and fur hats on their heads entered the house and the cold broke suddenly into the warm house. The children woke up and surrounded the strange guests, half welcome and half not. The guests were taking a handful of barley seeds from their bags, which were hung on their left and, while spreading the seeds like people who were sowing, they recited a blessing for the coming New Year in Russian. At the end of the blessing ceremony, they received some coins from the head of the family and a loaf of bread from the woman of the house. They thanked the family with a bow and got out, continuing their visit with the rest of the colony houses.

When the long winter–nights approached their end, darkness still prevailed. Mother woke up to prepare all needs for the new day – preparing the dough and baking the bread. While working, she threw a glance over the sleeping children to check whether they were covered properly, G-d forbid they catch a cold, and she put a kettle on the fire. Father woke up for G-d's' work, and just before the dawn prayer, he hummed some Psalms verses with a soft tune soaked with sad melodies. The children woke up, opened their, eyes, and listened to the happenings around them, lying covered well in their warm beds. Sounds could be heard from the yard: the rooster's crow, the dog's barking, the ringing of the chains by which the horses were tied to their stalls, and the mooing of a cow. The humming of the kettle or the samovar could now be heard throughout the house – a whole symphony.

Sometimes, the mooing of a cow was not just a regular mooing but could also be a mooing that announces the calving pains (and it was very well recognized in the house). Father was forced to interrupt the humming of the psalms and go out to the cowshed. A short while later, he returned, brought the newborn, still wet, into the house, and put it down near the stove on the floor, on top of the scattered straw. Very often, another calf, born a few days earlier, was already there, and the children's joy on such occasions was indescribably great. Father, who knew about the children's excitement, would approach their bed and hurry them up with playful fatherly mischief: "Nu children. Get up and look how the calf is doing." One slight jump and we were already there and saw two instead of one, and the joy was multiplied.

The mother who took care of the children – shouldered the entire burden of the home, starting from preparing the dishes (and what dishes!), the delicacies, the bread, and the rest of the pastries for a family

[Page 213]

of 8 – 10 people on the average, including milking the cows. I remember the special taste of the milk Mother milked directly from the cow's udder into the cup I drank on the spot, without leaving any trace, only the fresh taste of the milk in my mouth.

The cleaning of the house and the yard and the handling of the children and clothing required a lot of attention, particularly the house, since the colony's houses, in those days, were very simple, much different from the houses we reside in today in our agricultural settlements in Israel. The floor was usually a dirt floor, which the house stood on. The floor was leveled and straightened as much as possible, and to give it a pleasant look, they spread a layer made of fresh cow manure and yellow clay and a thin layer of golden sand on top. They repeated that process every Friday. Do not let anybody tell you that the smell of that mixture did not result in a good Shabbat feeling! On the contrary, the closer they would integrate this work with Friday's sunset, the blessing over the Shabbat candles by Mother, and the "Kabalat Shabbat" service by Father upon his return from the synagogue, the more special the atmosphere the house would attain toward the Shabbat.

Only at the end of the Shabbat the atmosphere of the holy day and rest would dissipate. The new week would begin when the homemaker would approach the somewhat sweaty window glasses, rub her hands, and whisper: "*Got fun Avraham Yitzkahk and Ya'akov…Der liber Shabbat Kodesh geit avek*" … ["G-d of Avraham, Yitzkhak and Ya'akov…Our beloved holy Shabbat is leaving"…].

A new week would begin with its regular worries – the kids were growing, and with them, the needs. One must fit the clothing passed over from an elder child who "grew them out" to the little ones, who were still not big enough for them. One needed to buy fabric for new garments and sew according to the sizes of the family members. I remember the picture: Mother sitting under the light of the kerosene lamp and patching the garments of the family members. Father, too, took a seat by her and fixed the harness's yoke, since the tear in it began to injure the horse at the base of its neck.

The homemaker took care of the poultry – –geese, ducks, chickens (we also had pigeons in some yards, but not in all of the farms. However, they were more like the "boys' hobby" and their handling was done by the boys). The children had a warm heart for all the birds. I remember the days when we waited impatiently until the eggs would hatch and the chicks would start to chirp. When the eggs would finally hatch and the chicks came out, it was a big joy for the children! Several days later, some chicks would be brought out to the yard, where the sun would warm them and the children were supposed to keep watching over them to avoid any harm to the chicks by the other animals roaming in the yard – a cat, dog, horse, foal or a calf, which could harm them unintentionally. They were also supposed to watch the birds in the sky (e.g. a crow) that could intentionally and with cold blood swoop up these soft creatures and harm them or cruelly devour them. We played that role with reverence. However, a crow would often succeed in swiftly assaulting the chicks from high in the sky and devouring one.

*[Page 214]*

Oh – how deep was the sorrow about the beloved soft creature taken away, whose chirping was ripping one's heart! Most of all it was horrible to see the sorrow of the hen that raised a croaker that reached heaven.

A special experience was a Jewish wedding in the village. There was certainly some difference between a regular Jewish wedding and a wedding in a Jewish agricultural colony. It is doubtful whether one could see the following picture at any other wedding – the "*klezmer*" playing the joyful melodies ("*Freilekhs*" [cheerful]) and Uncle Zalman entering the dancers' circle carrying a heifer on his shoulder, which he would, later on, hand over to the young couple as a sermon–gift ["*Droshe Geshank*"]. Who can recall a wedding in our colony or other colonies in the same area, and not see, in one's mind, the band of the "*klezmer*" from Romanovka, who were the family of Bar-Cohen, headed by Hershel the "*klezmer*" with his clarinet?

While they were leading the bride to the *Khupah*, Hershel would play the melody "The Cry of Israel" ("*platch Izrailia*"), and he would charm the listeners with his penetrating tunes. The clarinet did not play but talked to every heart. Women used to say that when Hershel played, stones could melt. Sorrow and joy were mixed together in these melodies. Even today, I can see Hershel's big eyes rolling up when he played the tunes on the clarinet turned upwards as if he was uplifting his listeners to the heights of his tunes. In the days that followed the wedding, these tunes would still echo and reach you, no matter where you turned.

(A native of Sdeh Menukha HaGdola returned from a recent trip to Russia not long ago, where he visited survivor members of his family and some acquaintances from those colonies. He heard from them how 1875 women, men, and children, natives of the colonies were annihilated, while Hershel was forced to play the melody of "Israel's Cry" on his clarinet during the massacre, the same tune that was heard during every wedding in the area).

*

With some hesitation, I will describe an area in which my expertise is limited. I remember how I felt as a boy when adults would express their opinions about the quality of some tool, its advantages, and disadvantages. I, who was not very knowledgeable about that, could not participate in the conversation. The only person who came to the rescue was Yoelik – the slaughterer (*dem shokhet*) since his expertise in these things was even less the mine (cold comfort). Likewise, was my knowledge in preparing the soil for the sowing and the sowing work itself, harvesting, gathering the crops, bringing it to the yard, and threshing, as well as everything else associated with this work.

That is why I would only touch, very little, on that part. I meant here the description of

[Page 215]

the season, which was named – "the working season." The season started with the harvest of the crop using a harvester tied to three horses. A boy sits on a seat fastened to the front edge of the harvester and drives the horses. An adult sits on a seat located in the backside of the harvester. Between the two seats, along the width of the surface, there is a knife consisting of two triangular blades, well sharpened, as well as four rotating wings, which feed the harvested grain toward the surface between the teeth. The knife is rotating at a very high speed and the grain falls down on the surface. The adult collects the grain from the surface with a fitted pitchfork and throws it pile after pile on the harvested field. Girls, and sometimes boys, would pile the grain in round and big piles (called "*kapitza*").

Then they would come with long wagons equipped with ladders hanging instead of a box. Two of the ladders were situated on the side of the wagon and the other two were built like wings and rocked on polls fastened by long screws in the front and the backside of the wagon along its width on the fixed ladders. When the wagon was empty, they would lower the ladders and raise them up via fitted hooks as the grain was piled up. In this way, they would transfer the grain from the fields to the colony, everybody to his own yard. There, they would unload the grain from the wagon and arrange it in extended piles, sloped on both sides, shaped like a roof, as a protection against the rain.

When the transport of the grain from the field was done they started the threshing. The threshing stone was rotated by two horses harnessed to it, running in a circular motion over the grain, which was scattered over a wide circle. The weight of the stone and the teeth, which pounded on the grain continuously, separated between the straw, the seeds, and the stubble. They used a special threshing sled to reduce the straw into chaff (a machine made with a wide board on the bottom side on which flints or sharp steel plates were attached). This tool was also moved with the help of harnessed horses driven mostly by boys.

The children would play around by jumping over the threshing sled while it was moving fast. They jumped up and down, accompanying it by screaming, laughing, and fooling around. It seemed that there could not be any more fun than that.

They worked on the threshing from the morning to dark with no interruptions. They would gather the stubble, seeds, and chaff with special tools into the center of the barn and create a big rounded pile shaped like a pyramid. Every Saturday night, a winnower would be placed at the pile, through which they would pass the harvest using a wooden five teeth–pitchfork ("*pitrik*") or "*fineferik*" [pentacle], as the gentile Dunika Tatianes, who was fond of the Yiddish language, used to call it. The person holding the pitchfork would lift the mixture and feed it into the winnower's muzzle. The winnower was operated via a rotating handle. The winnower's wing would fly the chaff forward, and the nets fixed in the winnower separated the seeds and the wastage, which fell down separately near the winnower or beneath it. They would continue to work on that from the beginning of the evening until the morning. The winnowers' noise could be heard throughout the entire night,

*[Page 216]*

the only monotonous noise in the colony: the noises combined like a single tone from all the yards of the colony.

I left home in 1921, along with some friends, natives of the colony, and wandered around throughout big Russia during the post-revolution years. During the first years of the new regime, the wandering from one place to another was as hard as the parting of the Red Sea. We wandered through huge train stations among crowds of fate–stricken and sick people. Some of us fell sick with typhus, and our dear friend, Tuvia Ninburg *z"l*, was buried in the cemetery in Minsk, Belarus. After wandering for a year and a half, we arrived in *Eretz Israel*, at the end of 1922. Along the way, we called ourselves "the group from Sdeh Menukha." When we arrived in *Eretz Israel* (some of us were delayed in Russia and succeeded in joining us only in 1932), we were welcomed by the colony natives Mordekhai Simkhoni (then Vesilnitzki) and Yehuda Menukhi (Ninburg). They had two farms in Nahalal, and we built a hut in the yard in which we resided and began our first steps in *Eretz Israel*. A rumor was spread in Nahalal that 12 Mordekhai brothers arrived, and they called us the "tribe."

We are now scattered all over Israel, some in *kibbutzim*, some in *moshavim* and a very few outside of the *Hityashvut* [agricultural settlements], all of us are members of the *Histadrut Haovdim* [Israel's Workers' Union].

All of us, the "Sdeh-Menukha people," remained strongly connected and we used to meet often at parties and festivities, remember the songs we used to sing and repeat them here, bringing back the memories of home and of the various people – the funny and the serious ones – the synagogues, the "*kheder*," the "*melamds*," the weddings, the "*brit milah*" celebrations, the holidays, the Shabbat, as well as the weekdays, the view, the river, and the fields.

In 1925, I joined my mate, Rivka, our son Shaike, and some of my friends who came before me as members of the kibbutz Ein Kharod (Ein Kharod was located then near the spring). During Passover of that year, after my first "*Seder*" there, a wonderful feeling descended when many guests and the boys filled the dining room. We were crowded in there but it was infinitely pleasant, standing close together, reassured. After the "*Seder*" and festive meal, we continued to drink and party. As I returned to my tent where I lived at the time, at the small hours of the morning, I was thinking about my home, where I was born, where I spent the best years of my youth, and where people close to my heart still remained. While deep in thinking, I sailed in my mind to places far away (probably also with the help of the wine still in my stomach). And here I am, in my colony, on the plot of land where my father's home stands. It is evening; the darkness keeps taking over the universe. I am almost at the entrance. A faint light can be seen through the windows. The doors are open, and I enter but I do not find anybody. The time is the milking hour. I go out of the house toward the stable also used as the cowshed. A faint light is also coming from there. And here I am already standing at the entrance. My late mother is sitting down and milking a cow. My father stands by her holding a calf, otherwise, the cow would stop giving its milk… Everything is as it was in those days. Nothing changed …

*[Page 217]*

40 years passed since then, and nothing has been left from all of that.

These pictures and others keep coming and rising, sometimes in my dreams and other times while I am awake. They do not let go, even for a single day… Here is the house you were born in and grew up in, and the colony in which you played, were educated, entertained, loved, wished, got disappointed, stuck to new dreams and ideals, and those brought you over here. Thanks to these dreams and ideals, it became possible, even only in a limited way, to bring the memories to writing. Everybody did their best to immortalize the healthy, simple, and beautiful life of the Jewish farmers in the diaspora; it was so rare and remained unknown to most of our people even to this day.

### Israel Ben Eliyahu (Ein Harod)

We had a spacious farmhouse. In the front of the house, paved with a red wooden floor, were a big room and a bedroom. In the other part of the house, there was the kitchen, with a big stove in it, a dining room, another two rooms, and a room that served as a parlor.

Our yard was sloped. Behind the house, there was an entrance to the stable and the cowshed, and on the other side, the storage place, a large and deep cellar, sheds for the young cattle, a large barn, a threshing barn, and big piles of hay and straw. We had a large agricultural farm. Although our land consisted only of half of a plot – 15 *disiyatins* [about 40.5 acres] (according to the number of males in the family, we received an additional area of 3 *disiyatins*, altogether 17.5 *disiyatins*), we cultivated three times as much, and sometimes even more by leasing additional lands. We had some 10 horses, 15 cows, and some fruit trees. During the work seasons, we were helped by hired work, and we employed an almost permanent worker, during the entire year.

In my childhood, I was running around in that yard, which was full of animals, chickens, geese, turkeys, and ducks. Only the turkeys and the male geese used to attack me and the Russian worker; then one of the aunts would run to help me when hearing my yelling. In the summer, *Savta* used to sit on a low chair in the shade, knitting or fixing some things while watching over me. I was always in her company. In the spring, when the fresh weeds were poking out of the ground, *Savta* would go out to take the geese to graze, and I trailed behind her. We would sit on the hill and oversee the small creatures. Sometimes, the turkeys along with their chicks joined us.

Because of frugality and poverty, we would pass the garments from the elder kids to the small ones toward the winter.

*[Page 218]*

As the eldest in the family, I always wore new garments, and they were usually big for my size so they would also fit me the following year. I had to diligently watch not to get caught in the coat's wing and not to play in the mud, frozen ground, or snow. Sometimes, when I fell, the shiny brass buttons, which I was very proud of, would be plucked out. I wore a *"Bashlik"* [a triangular-shaped head shawl with two stripes on its sides] on my head that wrapped the head and protected the ears and the face. The changes in nature that brought with them the winter heightened my desire to romp around the snow and the cold and to run to the frozen river. In the winter, people would drill a hole in the ice, pump the water, and water the animals from a small trough. I would venture out to slide on the ice until they chased me out. Sometimes, they would slap me a few times on my face, to calm me down. Oh, how much I loved to breathe that frozen and fresh air!

During the long winter days, the entire family life was concentrated around the stove built to heat up the house. It was built as a long double wall, in the middle of which a place for the firewood was available, and above it, a chimney was constructed. *Savta* was knitting, *Ima* [mother] was mending garments, *Saba* [grandfather] was studying Torah or calculating bills on his abacus and *Aba* [father] was reading a newspaper that happened to be available, or he would put me on his knees and play with me. Neighbors, particularly female neighbors, would join our company.

An emissary would always come to *Savta*, and she would take her to another room, where she received information about the needy people in the colony who required assistance and support. This family did not have food in their house, that person was sick and did not have money to pay for the physician, this family did not have money for firewood, or that maiden reached the age of marriage and her parents did not have money for a dowry… *Savta* would secretly leave the house, with some money from her hidden sock and a basket of food with two loaves of bread… *Aba* [father] and *Ima* [mother] would exchange glances about *Savta's* mischiefs. *Saba* would be furious but swallowed his anger until he went to sleep. He would straighten the account with *Savta* over there – in their room.

The winter persisted, and with it, the suffering of the poor. Looking for work in the villages was associated with much suffering. The Russian farmers were stingy with food goods, the currency by which they paid for haberdashery items or even for repairing windows. After wanderings for many weeks, the farmers would return home frozen, swollen from the winds, red-faced, with cracked hands, and the profits were too meager to sustain their families. Everybody was yearning for the summer. I too, wished for the change in the weather, the awakening of nature, and the period when ice and snow were melting.

The river was beautiful especially, when the ice broke, and the journey of the ice blocks began in earnest. The river would widen then, and the water would reach the row of the houses closest to it. The movement of the ice blocks and the tree fragments proceeded noisily, and natural forces captivated me to the point of losing consciousness. More than once Mother would run around looking for me,

*[Page 219]*

and would drag me back home by pulling on my ears and offering a stern warning. With time, the river would free itself entirely from the load of the ice blocks, which made their way for hundreds of kilometers from the river's source in the "Black Forest" to the Dnieper, about 75 kilometers away from my colony.

Before the sowing season, they would fatten the horses and prepare the harrows, sacks of seeds, and a long ladder wagon, on which a tarp stretched over an arched frame. That wagon was used for storing the seeds and carrying supplies for man and horse and as a cover for people who stayed in the field for a week.

When I was four years old, I was placed in a "*kheder.*" Children were studying, chanting, and making noise. The rabbi was sniffing tobacco and sometimes taking a nap on his throne, resting his head on the table. On those occasions, the children would increase their noise, somebody would be plotting a plot, like smearing glue on the desk near the rabbi's beard, and when the rabbi would move his head, the beard would get stuck to the glue. When the laughter and the noise would intensify, the rabbi would wake up, lift his head, and his beard was stuck to the desk. The rabbi would become furious, and he would grab his regular authority tool - the scourge that was called "*kantchik,*" – and would start hitting the children right and left. Then, the idea of destroying the scourge using "chemical means" came about. One child told us that leather would crack instantly if we smeared it with garlic and would break on the first lash. We smeared the *kantchik* with garlic, and when the rabbi lashed it on his desk to quiet the children, a piece of it was indeed ripped apart. There was no end to our joy. We buried the fragments deep in the ground. At the end of the school year, before *Rosh HaShannah* [Jewish New Year], I already knew how to read and write. I strengthened myself in preparation for the next season. The break took place during the threshing season, the burning season at the end of the summer, when the crops needed to be brought from the fields in a hurry, and threshed before the approaching autumn.

The feeling of freedom instilled a new spirit and much vigor in me. The opportunities to spend that vigor were numerous – jumping on the piles of straw and rolling down, running on the threshing floor after the horses that pulled behind them a heavy and sharply grooved stone, which threshed the seeds, and other activities. I ran after the threshing board that rotated speedily above the threshing floor, and it was the ultimate pleasure when I managed to jump over on top of the board and rotate with it. One needs to know the threshing work very well – spreading the crop, threshing with the stone, and removing the first layer of the straw, while leaving the seeds in the lower layer. The work with the wooden pitchforks was a unique art. After the upper layer was removed, a compacted layer was left behind filled with the seeds and one had to turn it so that it would remain well spread and fluffy. Following that, one had to thresh that layer again with the threshing board, which converted everything to chaff and stubble along with the seeds. In the end, they threshed the mixture with a diagonally slanted board pulled by a horse.

*[Page 220]*

Following the threshing, they collected the chaff and seeds into a pile preparing it for winnowing. The winnowing work also required agility and a special sensitivity for the pitchfork and trowel. Anybody who was not trained could throw away half of the seeds into the straw. Many people were required for that work – the entire family and some hired workers. Therefore – this was a "lively" work. People worked many hours during a 24-hour period, in a race against time and nature, since the rains, which often occurred early during the threshing work, caused damages.

They would work with the winnower during the night, after a long day of regular work. One person would hand the straw and the seeds over to a container using a wide wooden pitchfork with five teeth. Another rotated the winnower with a handle. Yet another person would receive the seeds in sacks or piles and separate the waste and the chaff. There was a feeling of joy of creativity during the night winnowing work, which often lasted until dawn, and the continuous buzz of the winnower was accompanied by enormous singing. The scene in the background of the threshing building was etched in my young brain – the beautifully arranged piles, the wagon loaded with crops, and the workers scattered around the crops with all the noise and the commotion around.

The Organization for the Jewish Settlement (JCA) established an agricultural school in the neighboring colony of Novo-Poltavka. Under the advisement of the agronomists who came from there, it was decided to plant fruit tree orchards. About ten farmers planted the orchards along the river with a tall stonewall surrounding them. The orchards consisted of trees of several varieties of apples as well as cherries and pears. The orchard was closer to the Russian village than our colony. During the fruit season, it required continuous guarding. Despite the guarding, most of the fruit harvest was stolen. It was particularly difficult to guard the apples of the variety that ripened late, with the first frost, which had an exceptional taste. Due to the thefts, we needed to pick up the fruit before it was ripened and store it. In our yard, we had a storage shed, the attic of which served as the ripening place. They would spread straw on the floor and spread the apples on it. The apples ripened there for the enjoyment of the residents, and sometimes the enjoyment of many friends.

Several research studies on the state of the colonies were taken on behalf of the JCA. Two young men, wearing black shirts tied with a string and black pants, appeared once in the colony, went from one yard to the other, asked questions, and wrote down the answers. This happened before the 1905 revolution, and the farmers feared them. I heard the farmers saying that these young men "were certainly socialists." I did not know the meaning of the word but I thought that it must have been something "terrible."

Uprisings and revolts broke out later. Punishment missions visited the villages, and the incitement against the Jews began. We received rumors that bands of peasants were going to assault us. Self–defense groups began to organize. All sorts of sharp and blunt tools were made in the smithy so that they could be used as weapons in a time of need. My father owned a gun, although totally rusted since it was always buried away. It was a gun, nevertheless.

*[Page 221]*

A long spear, headed by a pointed, sharp, and bent hook, stood in the corner of the house. Many times, the alarm sounded at night. Father would grab his weapon, and Mother would dress him in warm clothes. She would cover and lift my little sister into her arms and give me her arm. We would go out and wait – if there was an assault, we would run away and hide. With fearful eyes, I would look out at our street. Sometimes, a few drunk gentiles who happened to pass through, screamed, or a singing sound arriving from far distances with the wind, causing panic in the colony. Those nights were also etched deep in my memory – people running around and several young men riding horses and galloping around the colony to warn about the approaching danger.

The Gentiles who rioted when drunk did not escape without harm. In an area far from a city and from any authority, the character of the Jewish farmer hardened, and his national pride intensified. One could not very easily subdue a Jew from the colonies with threats or beatings. I traveled once, with my father, on a narrow road at the foot of the mountain. It was customary when two wagons met that the wagon, which was less loaded, yield to the more loaded wagon. However, if a Ukrainian farmer approached my father, he would never yield. He would say to me; "You should not show a gentile that you are yielding, regardless of how loaded his wagon is. He needs to learn to respect a Jew."

They transported most of the grain to the nearby city of Beryslav, located on the Dnieper. The wagon owners were Ukrainians, who were strong and dressed coquettishly and their beautiful horses were harnessed to a big painted wagon. They had a long-braided whip that had a piece of lead at its end. The second leash of the whip was interwoven with horse's hair, which whistled while the whip was snipped. They would not make way for a Jew, even if his wagon was loaded. They would just snip at the horses that came toward them and would not spare the horses' owner either. Fights developed once in a while since the Jews did not give up their right to travel on the paved roads. Legends circulated around about brave Jews who stood their ground against convoys of Gentiles. Indeed, Jews conquered an honored status for themselves among the neighboring gentiles.

A story was told about a Jewish farmer who traveled on a wagon loaded with grain and encountered a convoy of grain transporters who traveled with empty wagons but did not want to make way for him. He jumped down from his wagon, took out the shaft, and advanced toward them. Despite the lashings by the hooligans' whips, he hit them right and left with the shaft without mercy. The hooligans' horses went haywire and cleared the road. The Jew came out of that only with a few marks of lashings.

The village committee's house was located not far from our house. A wagon covered with a canvas tent once approached the house, and a Russian man who probably came from one of the estates in the area, jumped down from it. He had the rank of Feldwebel [noncommissioned officer] in the Czar's army. He cursed and vilified the Jews, stuck his hand in his wagon, took out a big hunting rifle, and started to wave it

*[Page 222]*

toward the committee's house and yelled: "I will annihilate all the Jews." I shrank from fear and squeezed myself against the fence. However, my father *z"l* did not stay idle. He jumped quickly onto the anti–Semitic "hero" and, with a sound slap in the face, dropped the gun out of the man's hand. The policemen who arrived in the village by chance released the agitator and submitted a complaint against my father to the court. They called my father to trial for eight years, but the gentile was ashamed to show up. The complaint was eventually annulled, only when the First World War began since the authorities had more important worries to deal with.

The rural Jews were not usually people who strived for a quarrel or a fight, but working people, peaceful and modest. However, the bitter fate of a farmer in a foreign land, surrounded by people-beasts, led to the need to develop the ability to defend himself against any calamity. The village youths knew how to work, ride horses, swim, and fight their enemies. When Russian youths would meet a Jewish youth, they would invite him to a wrestling match. If the Jewish boy could not defeat his rival, he would face a bad and bitter end. Most of our boys were trained in all sorts of fighting techniques and managed to stand their ground with honor. The need to be always strong and brave taught the youth to be ready for any trouble. When they assembled the young recruits, they would gather many youths from the villages, among them boys from the colonies. The attitude of the authorities was not very polite; they put them all in one big hall and ordered them to strip naked. They would spend several hours being naked. The "*shkutzim*" always tried to abuse a Jewish boy by sitting and riding on him. A native of my colony, a tall and sturdy youth, approached the leader of the hooligans and invited him to ride on himself. The hooligan immediately agreed, and when he climbed on top of him, the Jewish boy held him with his hand like a plier and hit his body on the wall forcibly until the victim began to whine and beg to take him down. However, the Jewish boy did not abandon his victim. It is interesting to note that nobody in the crowd dared to intervene. Only after he punished his rival, as he deserved, he threw him down to the floor.

There were fights among the Jews, more than once, due to trespassing, however, only rarely did that lead to physical fighting. In most cases, they would turn to the village elders for arbitration.

The Jewish farmers learned to love their land and cultivate it with joy and warm relations with the livestock, particularly the horses. They would take out the horses at the beginning of the spring and lead them to graze along ditches, creeks, and border areas between the fields. If the horse penetrated a field of crops, fights would erupt. Groups of youths and children would watch their horses along roads or abandoned fields, they would tie the horses' front legs together, leave them to look for food, and sit down on the side of the road to tell stories or play games.

That was how they would spend the day, particularly on Shabbat. They would return home galloping on their horses in the evening upon the emergence of the stars.

*[Page 223]*

A special folklore was created during that collective pasture. The common subject of discussions was the wondrous attributes of the horses and stories associated with cases that occurred on the road, work or just riding the horses. The colony's natives knew all of the hundreds of horses in the village by name and the names of their owners. When we were waiting for Father to come home from the field or from a faraway trip, we would recognize the owner of the wagon by the sound of the wheels.

After the failed revolution of 1905 and the following wave of pogroms, the spirits calmed down. In our corner, too, quiet was felt; it lasted until the First World War broke out. The [Jewish] farmers became soundly established. They modernized their farms, and as a result, the standard of living was improved. The image of the village and its unique character, including its celebrations and holidays, was stabilized as if we felt that those years were the last time given to us where we could live according to our will and ability.

At that stage, the war came, and with it the end of that idyll. Since then, the Jewish village has not seen even one bright light ray. The enlistment of the youth and adults separated families and left them without the means to sustain themselves, with no manpower for the work on an agricultural farm. The women and their daughters mobilized themselves to carry the burden of the work on the farm. The dream of many to continue their studies in the agricultural school was shattered to pieces. My father was also recruited to the army, and then, it was I, the young one, who was tasked with carrying the burden of the farm. I had to continue my studies through private lessons; however, I learned more from life itself, than from schooling. The big country of Russia experienced a dark period with numerous victims during the war that made no sense or had no goal.

Life in the village became unbearable. Father managed to free himself from the army and returned home. He was elected to be the head of the village. The attention of the authorities was directed toward the villages, both because of the recruitment of people as well as the recruitment of farm animals and transportation. Quite a few youths did not see any sense in fighting the war and chose to defect from the army. Every time the regional policemen appeared in the village, my father sent me, secretly, to warn the hiding defectors. I knew almost all of the pits and holes where they were hiding. Although I despised them in my heart, I did understand that there was nothing, that could motivate them to fight for the "defense of the motherland," as they used to call it then. The expression on the faces of the defectors was frightening. Fear was in their eyes, the hair on their heads and their beards grew wild, and their faces were pale since they hid away from the sun's rays for many months. In their long loneliness, they yearned to talk to somebody, and they talked much about the approaching revolution and about life in paradise on earth when their dream would be fulfilled.

Indeed, the dream of those poor souls and the masses of people who were fed up with the old and rotten regime was fulfilled in the end. The revolution broke out in February 1917.

*[Page 224]*

Joy engulfed everybody - men, women, and children, old and young, who danced and kissed in the streets. Beautiful slogans were hung in a variety of hues. Above all, stood the slogan – "Peace, Bread and Land." It seemed that all of the heart's wishes would be fulfilled. Anybody who was not in Russia during those days did not witness a celebration of happiness and joy in one's life.

However, the radical reorganization began. The soldiers who defected from the front with their weapons expressed their requests, threats, and vigorous demands. The deprived and the oppressed became haughty. Although we did not have excessively rich people in our villages, and most of the public belonged to the deprived class, there were some, even among the Jewish colonies, who came up with sufficient reasons to try to stick wedges between close people and strive for the realization of the terms of the class wars.

The commotion among the political parties towards the election for the constitutional assembly began. It was mainly concentrated inside the synagogue. Kerenski's temporary government was not in a rush to take revolutionary actions and only promised that the constitutional assembly would gather, pass resolutions, and make decisions. In the meantime, the election campaign, in which some Zionist parties participated, developed into a full-swing battle. Speechgivers and representatives of all parties came, particularly representatives of soldier assemblies from various streams.

That situation did not constitute a blessing for the agricultural farm. The Russian peasants in the area were impatient to wait for the happiness and wealth to be bestowed upon them by the revolution and began to rob the estates. They took anything they could get their hands on (we need to mention that some Jewish farmers – albeit not in large numbers – did not stay idle either).

The security situation in the area deteriorated. All those soldiers, who abandoned the front and returned to their villages with their weapons presented a substantial threat. It was necessary to boost the protection and to acquire weapons. The discontent in the villages increased even more after the October Revolution. The ideology of the peasants was anarchy and resistance against everything – against the Communists and against the "Whites."

The Germans took advantage of the disorder, penetrated Ukraine, and conquered all of its rich areas without firing a single shot. They managed to empty all of the grain barns and transfer the content to Germany. In the beginning, they treated the residents with silk gloves, however, in actuality robbed everything and aroused the rage of the peasants, who began to organize a war with them as well. In our area, some villages consisted of tens of thousands of people. Every village had its own armed militia. The Jewish villages were vulnerable to those gangs, and it was difficult to distinguish who were the real rulers of the country.

Around the same time, the first members of the "HeKhalutz" Zionist movement started to appear, bringing the message of salvation to the colony. The best of our youth began to join its ranks. The decision was not very easy. The revolution blinded many, with its abundance of light and promises, and these Zionists were talking about a far–away and unknown land. It was difficult

Jewish Farmers in Russia Fields

Sdeh Menukha HaKtana – Drawing water

The well in the colony's fields

Jewish Farmers in Russia Fields

*[Page 225]*

to contrast one path against the other. However, after I listened, one evening, to the speech of a Ukrainian soldier who came back from the front, my path became clear to me, and I registered as a candidate for He'Khaluz." Many others joined our ranks later on. We felt that there was a new substance for our lives, and we began to dedicate ourselves, with a youthful fervor, to action within the movement. We also did not abandon the cultural life of the village. We organized various clubs, among them a drama club, which prepared and presented shows whose income was dedicated to the library's expansion and other cultural needs. Our pioneering–Zionist activities, in studies, discussions, and singing, acquired a unique charm.

The authorities did not notice us at the beginning. The distance from the city–centers played in our favor. However, a short time later, they started to send *Yevsekis* [Jewish Communists] propagandists to us to limit our activities. In the meantime, the reactionary forces recovered, and the armies of generals Wrangel and Denikin barricaded themselves in the Crimea peninsula, with the help of the allied forces, and took control of the area all the way to the Dnieper. All the battles on the Dnieper took place in geographical areas close to our colonies. We became unwillingly, essential participants on this front. The Red Army would recruit wagons and waggoners from us to supply military equipment and food to their warriors. We would spend many months on the front, and our farmers had to travel all the way to the first fire–line. Only a few farmers abandoned their horses and wagons since the bond with the farm animals was an essential part of the farmer's life, and they would not abandon them easily. They would often seize me, for transportation service and later on seized Father as well. It happened once that a Whites' gang captured Father and loaded on his wagon the looting they had plundered and immediately after that, the Red Army came and enlisted me. We were then serving two opposite warring armies; I was with the people from the Red Army and Father with a band of the Whites who were chased by the Reds.

During those days of "in between the regimes," our entire wide area became a "no–man's– land" and an ample space for the activities of gangs of rioters of all kinds – the gang of Makhno, the militias of Petliura and the armies of Denikin. The lives of the Jews, especially in the villages, were in danger, and their state was desperate. They kept the horses harnessed at all times and the wagons ready so that they could escape at any moment. I recall one case vividly on the evening of the Shavuot holiday. After we completed the last preparation for the holiday, a Russian girl from a neighboring village, about 30 – 40 kilometers from us, came and told us that a gang who planned to attack the Jewish colonies was in her village. (I will never forget that dear friend, who endangered her life during those days of lawlessness and anarchy and came to warn us about the danger). I immediately jumped on a horse and rode to the top of the hill where it was possible to observe far distances and watch whether anything was occurring on the vast prairie plane. The three colonies organized and sent out many horse riders to strengthen the guard and prevent the gang from surprising us. In the following days, several horse riders went out to tour the area, and they encountered the gang's horsemen. The gang succeeded in capturing one of the youths and tortured him to death. The rest managed to escape.

*[Page 226]*

However, the colonies were saved from a surprise attack. The captured youth was one of the best of our youths, a member of the "HeKhalutz." Before he died, he warned the hooligans not to attack the colonies since a large well-armed corps defended them.

That period lasted for a long time until the Red Army pushed Wrangel to the shores of the Black Sea. Only after that, the Soviet authorities turned to clear the country from the hooligan gangs, and the doleful and suffering country started to heal its wounds. The entire agricultural sector was neglected and abandoned but the authorities sent whole battalions to squeeze the last grain of seed and the last cow out of the farmers.

The Zionist movement had to go underground but that did not weaken our activity. The members actually increased their activity in all areas with added vigor. We also began taking practical steps to prepare people for making *Aliyah* to *Eretz Israel* in all possible ways. The first group of "HeKhalutz" left, and the second group started to prepare and waited for the signal. Transportation was almost non-existent, with only one train per week left from our area of Southern Ukraine.

During one of the autumn days of 1921, we received a rumor that one of the members succeeded in reaching Belarus. Based on that rumor, we decided that our group would leave as well, however, we decided to divide it into two parts so that it would not stand out.

We went to our parents that night, woke them up, and notified them about our plan. It is difficult to forget that picture. Aba *z"l* became pale, and Ima broke up crying and asked – "how would you do it? There is no transportation in the country, and in this situation where the country is not yet peaceful, where would you go?" We asked them not to raise their voice since our exit had to be kept secret, and we only had one day to prepare. Ima baked cakes and pastries (which became soaked with her tears). I went through the entire colony to say farewell to everybody, to every corner of the village, every tree, stream, or rock. I also said farewell to the fields.

We left at night after midnight – a group of boys and girls climbed the mountain to go around the colonies. We were horrified to see that despite the secrecy, the entire village came out to accompany us, and they dragged their feet, following us weeping silently. When we climbed the mountain and set down in a wagon, the entire crowd kept running after us.

That was the way we said farewell, forever, to the village we were born in, to my widespread family, and to all the Jewish farmers and their children who worked their land in faith.

## Mordekhai Khalili (Mishmar HaEmek)

*[Page 227]*

Sdeh Menukha HaKtana – its name suits it. It was small and Jewish. All of its residents, except the cattle herd shepherd, and the women who milked the cows on Shabbats (they and their children spoke Yiddish), were Jewish – natives of the city of Nevel in the province of Vitebsk [then in Belarus, today in Russia, close to Belarus border].

The Inguletz River, mountains, hills, and streams – added a unique beauty to the colony and the entire landscape. For the young generation, these places served as locations for playing and recreation. We loved the colony, its people, and its work. Father and Mother, boys and girls, we all worked in plowing, sowing, harvesting, threshing, and gathering the seasonal crops. The women, in addition to being in charge of the yard farm, took care of the children, prepared the food for the entire family, fitted and maintained the clothing, everybody according to their size, cleaned the house and the yard during regular days, evenings of Shabbats, holidays and celebrations, and did all of that with taste and pleasantness.

The people in my colony observed the Jewish tradition. The Shabbat was felt everywhere. They helped others because of their inner feeling, without an organization or a decree of authority; it was the normal thing to do. If a person needed help – the help had to be provided. There was no differentiation between one needy person to another – a distant or a close relative, a neighbor, a friend, or just an acquaintance. The girls also carried the burden of the work at home or on the farm during their free time or school breaks. They also participated in the fieldwork, particularly during the burning season. With all of that, studies were never neglected, even if there was a need to walk a kilometer and more to the nearest colony – Sdeh Menukha HaGdola. We walked to school, day after day, in the heat and cold, when it rained or snowed. We often went without our parents' permission. They claimed that schooling led to getting married late, or according to the concepts of those days – could also result in remaining an "old maid" which was the worst. Those who were given the opportunity continued their studies in the high schools in Kherson, which was located 70 kilometers away from our colony.

In June 1962, I traveled to the Soviet Union for a visit to see the remaining family members who miraculously survived. They live, until today, in the city of Simferopol in Crimea, where they arrived after wandering to Kazakhstan as refugees during World War II. My mother *z"l* passed away in Kazakhstan in 1941. I managed to meet with my relatives residing in Odesa, Yalta, Simferopol, and Moscow after 38 years during which we did not see each other. I will not be able to describe in words our mutual excitement.

*[Page 228]*

In Simferopol, I found my father, who was already bedridden on his deathbed at the age of 86, just before he passed away to join his people.

Among my relatives, some were members of the Communist Party, from as early as the days before I left the colony. I realized that in their heart, there was always the Jewish feeling that could never be extinguished.

On that occasion, I heard details about the extermination of the colony members. I heard these stories while sitting on benches in the city's parks, due to the fear from uninvited ears... I was told about the plan to run away when they felt that the Germans were approaching, and about other members of the colonies who remained in the colonies under the illusion that the Germans would not hurt people who worked the land. In any case, most of them began to prepare, some by harnessing the horses to the wagons and some by packing the necessary belongings and food items. When the Germans approached, they ran away toward the Dnieper, trying to cross it before the cruel hand would get hold of them. When they arrived at the river, an abyss opened in front of them. The bridge was blown–up.

There was no escape, and the murderer's hand caught up with them. Some did not want to fall into the hands of the murderers and threw themselves into the Dnieper and thus avoided the horrible suffering experienced by those who were transported back to the colony. These people were transported back like a herd of cattle by three brothers – members of our colony, whom the Nazi sadists forced to gather and hurry the returnees by riding on horses accompanied by armed troops.

In the colony – the hunt for the people who were hiding, went rampant. The same three brothers executed it. They were forced to discover the hideouts and to promise them that they faced no danger and that the reason for concentrating the people was that they were needed to perform urgent tasks.

The neighboring Ukrainians took part in all of the murderous acts and in the concentration of the Jews from the two sister colonies and of those who were brought back from the Dnieper. Everybody was gathered, and the preparations for the annihilation began. According to an ordered plan typical to the "exemplary Germans," they first separated the children from their parents, and after conducting a count, the exact number was determined in the two separate camps. They brought the children to the top of a hill and operated their machine guns on them. According to the typical order by the Germans, it was imperative to make sure that the number of the murdered was equal to the number of the counted live ones. One of the mothers, a member of the colony was tasked with counting the bodies. The poor mother collapsed and lost her mind. She was relieved from her misery along with the rest of the adults by the bullets of the murderers.

A ditch that previously served as a canon position for the Soviet army became a mass grave.

I was told about a 12-year-old boy who miraculously avoided being hit by the murderers' bullets who laid down among the murdered, managed to free himself from the pile of bodies that weighted down on his tiny body, and by crawling on the ground, distanced himself from the horrible killing field.

At a certain distance, he stood up and turned to the nearby village.

*[Page 229]*

He encountered a German guard on his way, but thinking that he was Christian, the guard let him continue on his way. He arrived at a farmer's house of one of his father's friends, exhausted. They welcomed him with pity "like nice Christians," fed him, watered him, laid him down to sleep, and... notified about him to the Germans. The boy was executed on the same day.

The cruel murder spree lasted for thirty days, from 16 August until 16 September 1942. Jews from other districts were brought to the same mass grave between the two "Sdeh Menukha," altogether 1875 people, old and young, women. and children were buried there.

On these same benches in the city park, I heard about other known colonies, some near–by and some further away from my colony. I heard about the Bobrovy-Kut colony, whose residents were murdered with the same cruelty. Their bodies were not thrown into dugouts or ditches, but into water wells, as deep as 60 meters – the same water wells that served the Jewish farmers to quench the thirst of man and animal for more than 100 years.

The entire Jewish population scattered along the vastness of Ukraine was annihilated. Without any mercy, they abused the people with horrible cruelty, which cannot be comprehended by a human mind.

In 1960, my sister Nekhama and one of our cousins came down to witness with their own eyes what was left from this corner of the beauty of our childhood and they were horrified. The truth of the rumors was validated in all of its brutality. There is no comparison between hearing about it and seeing it in one's own eyes. There was nothing left of everything that existed there. They found perhaps just a sign of a house of a relative, friend, or acquaintance, here and there – but all the rest, just piles of ruins.

Horrified, they ran away from there and left behind them the dear views they remembered from their wonderful childhood: the fields, the hills, the streams, and the river. They ran away, afraid to look back.

When they ran away, the memories of those days and those honest and innocent Jews accompanied them – the memories of old and young who are buried in the mass grave between the two sister–colonies of Sdeh Menukha. These memories and the horrible scenes followed them, racing and screaming, demanding and ordering them:

**Never forget – to the end of time.**

**Rakhel Pnini** (Tel Adashim)

*[Page 230]*

From all the stories that I heard during my childhood about the colony and its history, the stories of my parents, Khaim and Zisle *Z"L*, about how they built, with their own hands, their home and the smithy of my father, are preserved in my heart the most.

My father became a blacksmith when he was only 16 years old. He specialized in it during his service in the military. When he returned home after five years of military service, he married my mother, without a dowry, against the custom of those days. He received a plot and, with the help of my mother, built their house with his own hands, using simple stones, clay, and mud. Half of the building served as a residential home and the other for the smithy.

The entrance to the house was through the smithy. Therefore, my father used to cease work on Thursdays to allow Mother to prepare the smithy for Shabbat. She smeared the floor with clay and spread reddish sand for decoration. She would cover the anvil with a white embroidered and ironed tablecloth. When she lit the candles, an atmosphere of Shabbat would descend in all the corners of the house, including the smithy.

My mother gave birth to six children in that house without the need for a hospital or physician. She was only helped by the village midwife ("*babeh*"). They would call for Doctor Burschuk from Sdeh Menukah HaGdola only in most urgent cases. I recall only one such case when my father was wounded on his job from a hit by a hammer – his right hand broke. The physician called by one of the neighbors, took Father to a hospital in Kherson where he stayed for several weeks.

I recall the smithy as it was during the days of the pogroms when it was decided by the village management to prepare weapons for defense. They would anneal the needed weapons during the night in Father's smithy.

My parents were evicted from their home and property during the collectivism as a punishment for their "sin" of being connected with their sons in *Eretz Israel*. Only after years of hardships, expulsion, and wandering they were fortunate enough to make *Aliyah* and live in kibbutz Tel Adashim during their old age. From their work and the entire village's way of life, only memories were left for them and us.

I kept these memories in my heart during all the events that I experienced in my life – first as a soldier in the First World War, on my way to *Eretz Israel* during the [Russian] Civil War, and here in my home in Israel. I saw in my mind – our yard, the fields and the garden, the cowshed and the stable, and especially the smithy. I saw it in my dream, but I did not have any tangible memory until a friend, a native of our colony, who visited the Soviet Union that year, brought me a picture of our yard and the house where I was born. Indeed, the house is still standing, and so is the smithy, however, there are no Jews there. A Russian blacksmith works where my father once worked.

### Author's Note:

1. Mordekhai Simkhoni – one of the founders of Moshav Nahalal in Israel, is the father of Asaf Simkhoni, a Major General of IDF, who was the commander of the Israeli campaign in Sinai during the 1956 Suez Crisis. Asaf perished in a plane crash on the night the 1956 war ended.

**Azriel Pnini** (Tel Adashim)

*[Page 231]*

# Sehaidak

## by Khaim Cohen, Tzipora Kaminker, Avraham Toren & Israel Zeltzer

**Translated by** Moshe Kutten

**Edited by** Yocheved Klausner

I moved with my family to live in the colony of Sehaidak, when my father *z"l* was nominated as the Rabbi there. I encountered a Jewish settlement whose residents were farmers, people who worked the land, there were no Christian residents and the administration was held by Jews. Instead of the [Russian] "*Politzai*" [police], there was the Jewish "*Stutzki*" who reported to the "*Schultz*" [elected head of the village], which was recognized as such by the authorities. All work ceased on Shabbat. I studied in "*Kheder Metukan*" [literally Corrected *Kheder* - a modified *Kheder* in which general studies were incorporated along with traditional Torah studies]. During vacations, in the summer, I was lucky to receive, along with friends of the same age, a wagon harnessed to two horses, and transport bundles of crops or wheat from the field to the threshing machine in the farmer's yard. In the spring, I helped one of the farmers to tune the sowing machine ("*Dril*") or to drive horses that pulled the plow (*Buker*). Sometimes I even received a horse for an outing pleasure ride or a ride for a competition.

One of the colony's elders told me that in the year 5608 [1847/8], Jews came there from the province of Kiev [Kyiv], with the encouragement of the authorities and settled on the bank of a ravine, which flows south to the River Bug, and the name of the valley was Sehaidak. They found a fertile and rich soil there that was growing a man-tall wild grass and began immediately with the construction of the clay houses. They kneaded the clay with chaff and made bricks in wooden molds which they dried in the sun. They quickly built small houses, plastered the houses from the inside and outside, and covered the roof with straw. Over time, they built other, more modern houses from fired bricks and roofs made of tin or wood.

During the 1870s-80s, the government built the Kharkov [Kharkiv]-Nikolayev [Mykolaiv] railroad. According to the plan, the railroad was supposed to pass near the colony; however, the farmers asked the government to build it farther away for fear that the noise would scare the poultry. The government accepted their request and placed the railway about 3-4 kilometers away from the colony. The members of the second generation regretted that decision since the closest train station was located 10-20 kilometers away, all the way to Dolinsk station, which became a train hub over time. Without a train station, the progress of the colony was slowed down.

Every settler was allocated land of 30 *disiyatins* [one *disiyatin* = 2.7 acres] – about 300 *dunams* and some additional government land via leasing. With the growth in the number of descendants, the size of the family plots diminished, until a problem of land-poor farmers developed at the beginning of the 20th century.

The main crops were grains in the winter, and corn, sunflowers, and watermelons in the summer. Another important sector was the cattle sector, which was based on natural pasturing in the summer and, which was harvested hay in the winter

[Page 232]

from fallow fields in the summer with the addition of bran. Due to the long distances to the city markets and lack of transportation, the milk was used to produce butter, marketed to the nearby cities.

During the First World War, refugees who arrived from Lithuania who were experts in the production of Swiss and Dutch cheeses developed a modern dairy plant where they produced hard cheeses and butter. As a result, winter performance was based on hay, and the profits of the farmers, who marketed the milk to the dairy plant, grew.

A tall dam, which accumulated the rainwater, was constructed in the valley, producing a large reservoir, which served as an important source of water for the cattle in the summer and winter. Fish, named "koors," proliferated in that lake. They would fish them out of the lake using a long net tied with ropes pulled by people from the two opposite banks.

When the water froze in the wintertime, the youth used to skate on the ice using iron skates. They used to cut blocks of ice from the lake, for use even in the summertime. At the end of the winter, they used to announce mandatory recruitment of all the men to cut the ice in the lake and to transport the blocks to a big storage cellar fitted for that purpose. Ice was provided to everybody, free of charge, and it lasted the whole summer for food preservation and for ice packs for the sick.

As mentioned above, the management of the colony was in the hands of the "*Schultz*" (the head of the colony), who was elected by the residents every several years (using confidential ballots). When the election day for "*Schultz*" approached, the number of people who criticized the incumbent increased, and the unrest against him intensified. Despite that, the "*Schultz*" – the old Hershel-Aba Milman, of a shining face and clever eyes, was elected again every time and served as a "*Schultz*," if I am not mistaken, until the day he died.

Like in every other Jewish community, a rabbi, a *shu"v* (slaughterer and Kosher inspector] and a healer (*feldsher*) served in the colony. Craftsmen who made a living by working for the colony's farmers and the farmers of the neighboring villages resided in the colony. They provided all the needed services to the farmers in the colony and the needs of the entire rural area.

In the colony they had a "*kheder metukan*" [a traditional *kheder* with the addition of general studies] where they taught both Hebrew and Russian as well as a regular "*kheder*" with a Melamed for Gemara studies.

My father, Rabbi Israel-Dov Cohen *Z"L*, always insisted on ensuring the existence of a high-level *Kheder Metukan*. He employed excellent teachers, graduates of the Yeshiva in Odesa, and graduates of the seminar for Hebrew teachers in Grodno. The synagogue served not only for praying and studying Mishnah and "Ein Ya'akov" [A book by Ya'akov ben Khaviv and son, containing commentary and legends from the Jerusalem and Babylonian Talmuds] but also as the colony's house for the community committee and a hall for lectures and gatherings. It was always full of activities. Welfare organizations such as "Khevrat Talmud Torah" [literally – "The organization of Torah Study"], "Lekhem Evionim" [literally – "Bread for the Poor"], "Hakhnasat Kallah" [literally – "The Bridal Canopy"] and more were always present. Those who collected contributions for the welfare organizations were the school youths, who were going around the colony's homes once a week holding notebooks with stickers.

Until the February Revolution broke and the prohibition of Zionism in Russia was introduced, the colony was mostly Zionist. Even after the Revolution, the Zionist Shekel [membership fee in a Zionist movement] was still being sold,

*[Page 233]*

and the activities of the JNF [Keren Kayement Le'Israel in Hebrew - the Jewish National Fund] took place. The JNF was very popular among the Jewish public, and large sums of money were collected on holiday evenings, during marriage celebrations and parties of *Briths* and *Bar Mitzvahs*.

After the February Revolution, the Zionist party "Tzeirei Tzion" [literally-"Youths of Zion"] was active in the colony and included many members. The party organized gatherings and celebrations that attracted the entire public. Branches of the [Zionist movements] "HeKhalutz" and "Maccabi" were also organized. An association by the name of "Geulat Akhim" [literally - Brothers' Salvation], which included about one hundred members, was established. The members intended to make *Aliyah* to Eretz Israel and work as farmers there, but their objective could not be realized because the Bolsheviks forbade the existence of the organization and the *Aliyah* to Eretz Israel. Only some of the youths of the "HeKhalutz" and "Tzeirei Tzion" [movements] managed to illegally break through the border with Poland and, from there, make *Aliyah* to Eretz Israel. Part of them settled in Kfar Vitkin.

Following the October Revolution when the regime was transferred to the Bolsheviks, the number of gangs in the provincial cities whose commanders declared themselves as leaders proliferated. Their sustenance was mainly achieved by robbing and looting Jewish colonies. An exceptional guard with weapons was organized in the colony. In 1918, a train full of people from Hetman Grigoriev's gang stopped on the railroad near the colony, and the gang members started to march toward the colony and shoot at its houses. Panic descended, and the colony people escaped to the fields and hid amid corn and wheat stalks. Thanks to this mass escape, there were no victims only property was stolen. However, that incident urged the colony youth to organize a proper self-defense force and every youth was recruited to weapon practices and guarding during the day and night. A common command center with the neighboring colony Ya'azor was established. The command center was responsible for organizing assistance and self-defense for the two colonies at times of need. Peace prevailed in the colony since then: the neighboring gentile villages spread the news about the establishment of a strong self-defense force. In 1919, when the Red Army retreated from the Dinkin corps [the Whites], which passed through the colony for three full days, a small cavalry company was seen returning from the same direction as the retreating army. The guard commander thought that they were a gang who came to loot the colony and ordered them to stop the riders and shoot whoever approached the colony. However, these were a forward company of commander Budyonny of the Red Army. The vast army that followed the forward company surrounded the colony and conquered it through shooting by guns and machine guns. The guard commander and seven of his assistants were killed during that day, trying to defend themselves against the soldiers. Twelve additional people were killed by the shooting of the soldiers. When the neighboring villagers heard about it, they flocked to the colony in droves, robbed and looted everything they found in the houses while Budyonny's soldiers stood by.

It is appropriate to mention and memorize the brave guard commander – Eliezer Zeltzer. His young wife – Shoshana, refused to be consoled and was the first in the colony who made *Aliyah* to Eretz Israel as a pioneer. In Israel, she became a nurse in Kupat Kholim [an Israeli workers' HMO] and was devoted to her work with her soul and heart.

The colony of Yaazer was several folds more populated than Sehaidak. It was founded before Sehaidak with the help of the Russian government, who sent to it agricultural counselors of German origin. Several farms that stood at the edge of the colony and which were owned by German Christians,

*[Page 234]*

the descendants of these counselors attested to that. What was the source of the Hebrew name "Ya'azor"? Rabbi Drabkin from Ya'azor gave me the answer. The colony was given the Russian name of a Pravoslavic church; however, the Jewish settlers wanted to change the name to a Hebrew one. They investigated and found out that according to the Onkelus translation of the Bible, the name Komrin is a translation of the Hebrew word *Ya'azor* in the *Torah* book of "BaMidbar" (Numbers 32:3), so they converted the name to Ya'azor. Over time, the Russian government called the village by the name of "Izraelovka"; however, the Jews and the Christian neighbors called the village by the name "Ya'azor."

Ya'azor's farmers grew, besides winter and summer field crops, fruit trees, and particularly grape vines. Since the colony was managed by regional management ("*Volost*" in Russian), the management team of the credit union, common to the two colonies, was also located in Ya'azor.

**Khaim Cohen** (Kfar Vitkin)

When I recall the fields, the folklore, the lively youth, the Hebrew school, the colony people – my entire heart is roused. Was all of that really wiped out from the face of the earth?

We had one hundred families of diligent farmers, simple in their way of life but courageous in their spirit. Unlike other colonies, the farmers in our colony worked mainly in agriculture. To have wedding clothing tailored and shoes made, they had to travel to the city, as we did not have a tailor or a shoemaker in our colony. For many years, we did not have a barber in the colony either until one day, farmer Zeidel announced himself as a barber. Zeidel was a very established and wealthy farmer who had hands of gold. He probably learned that profession by cutting the heads of his children. On holiday eves his house was crowded from end to end, some people were sitting and some standing, and the people who waited in line argued about everything – about the Beilis Trial or an anti-Semitic article in the "Novoye Vremya" newspaper. It sometimes happened that one of the farmers, who knew how to play and sing, would begin to sing a Hasidic song or a chapter from the praying book and everybody would join in. Even Zeidel would stop his work then and would conduct the singing crowd.

These simple and hearty Jews did not excel in general knowledge or in the Torah. They sent their children to study in the "kheders" by "melameds" [Jewish teachers] who were brought from the outside and were not all very knowledgeable in the Torah, the same way they studied during their own childhood while helping their fathers on the farm than studying.

However, during my youth, a fundamental turn in the area of education and study took place. This turn occurred

[Page 235]

thanks to two or three people who instilled a new spirit into the colony. One of them was Rabbi Israel Cohen, who was accepted after his predecessor was fired due to his love for the bottle. Rabbi Cohen was a Lithuanian Jew, a great scholar with nice attributes and Zionist views. He created an atmosphere of love of Torah and culture in the colony. His sons and daughters, who were educated by him, all made *Aliyah* to Eretz Israel and became farmers. He himself made *Aliyah* several years later and served as a Rabbi in Mount Carmel in Haifa, Israel.

The other person, who was a native of the colony, was Eliezer Popkin. From his early childhood, he excelled in the study of the *Talmud*. When he was *Bar Mitzva* he studied in the Yeshiva of Kremenchug and stood out with his talents and persistence. From there he transferred to Lubavitz, the center of the *Khabad Hasidism*, to study the "Revealed" [traditional Jewish *Halakha* interpretation] and the "Concealed" [*Kabalistic* Jewish Hasidic interpretation of the Jewish scriptures]. During his Torah and Talmud studies, he was exposed to general books. He left Hasidism and began to study in the Yeshiva in Odesa where Kh. N. Bialik [greatest Jewish and Israeli Yiddish and Hebrew poet], Dr. Y. Klausner [famed Jewish historian and professor of Hebrew literature], and the "Rav Tzair" ["Young Rabbi" – the literary name of famed author, teacher, and Rabbi - Khaim Chernovitz] were teachers. Popkin was the one who founded a modern Hebrew school, whose students spoke modern Hebrew, read Hebrew books, and wished to make *Aliyah* to Eretz Israel.

A partner in the educational activity of Popkin was Shmuel Dashkovitz. He was among the graduates of the Yeshiva of Odesa who married one of the colony natives. He settled in the colony and served as a teacher in the Hebrew school. When Popkin was nominated as the principal of the Hebrew school in Samara and joined the agricultural university, Dashkovitz continued his educational activity. Many of the youths of our colony made *Aliyah* to Eretz Israel and became diligent farmers in the workers' *moshavim*.

During those days, revolutionaries who acted underground were suspected by the police, and those who were about to be arrested escaped to far corners. Our colony served as a convenient hideout for Jewish suspects from the nearby cities since the police considered the colonies as consisting of simple farmers "clean" of the revolutionary virus. These refugees, most of them educated people, were bored in the colony from being idle. Therefore, they found an interest in connecting with the local youths and spreading, among them, revolutionary ideas. Among them, there were Zionists who preached Zionism and Socialism. Due to their resistance to the Czarist rule, many of them refused to enlist in the army during the war. For these people, and for those who enlisted and deserted, our colony served as a safe shelter. We called them "hares." Under their influence, there were local youths who refused to enlist. The "hares" could not be seen in the streets during the days, due to fear that a farmer from the neighboring villages, who knew all the locals, would see the strangers and notify the police. A special committee ensured that the "hares" would not be seen outside, particularly during the days of the "fair." Upon Kerensky's-Revolution, the colony was emptied entirely of these guests.

The awakening of the Jews following the revolution in Russia did not pass over Sehaidak. The percentage of Hebrew-knowing people in our colony was the highest among the Jewish farmers in Southern Russia.

*[Page 236]*

The youth used to organize Purim and Hanukkah celebrations, present shows, and call for gatherings to discuss the state of the Jews in Russia but mainly about Zionism and making *Aliyah* to Eretz Israel. In our Zionist activity, we were helped by Zionist leaders such as Zeev Tiomkin, Dr. Stein, and especially one of the leaders of "Tzeirei Tzion" – Nakhum Verlinsky. He was a brilliant speaker and very active among the youth circles. Like in other Kherson colonies, youths from the nearby cities came to Sehaidak to receive agricultural training before they made *Aliyah* to Eretz Israel.

When the Bolsheviks took control, and the borders closed, our Zionist activity became more difficult from one day to the other. The roads for making *Aliyah* were blocked. Some colony natives joined the Komsomol, which hindered our activities and there was also the fear of imprisonment. To escape the control of the authorities we organized in small groups and secretly left the colony. We made our way at night. We moved to the city of Berdichev, where we lived as a commune for a year and a half. From there we went through Poland and Romania, experienced adventures, and faced life dangers. Under difficult conditions, including under-nourishment and exposure to infectious diseases, we finally arrived in Eretz Israel.

Thanks to our agricultural past and life of work, which we grew up on, and our Zionist-Hebrew background, most of us continue to work in agriculture and other work-related occupations in Israel. About forty years passed since we left. Children and grandchildren were born to us. As a state we were granted independence; however, when the memories of the colonies are brought up, our hearts are wrenching. The colony with its hearty, good, and simple farmers who excelled in working the land and in working with their hands; this unique and wondrous Jewish folklore – where is it? Except for those who made *Aliyah* to Eretz Israel and the few who escaped to other countries, everybody else was murdered by the preying animals, and the land of Sehaidak, which was plowed and cultivated by Jews for more than a hundred years, was cleared entirely from the Jewish effort and work, from any Jewish foothold.

May these lines serve as a memorial for the pure and innocent victims!

**Tzipora Kaminker** (Haifa)

Since the beginning of the century, the farmers in our colony established themselves substantially, thanks to the help of counselors, the cultivation using modern tools, proper organization of the local institutions, and most of all, thanks to the youths and the local children who got used to the work and learned to love it. Unlike other colonies, the fields of Sehaidak were close to the colony. That eased their cultivation. Besides the field crops, many expanded the cattle growing sector. Some of the farmers established themselves to the point of being wealthy. Those farmers, whose farms were not as developed, worked in transporting the grain to the city.

*[Page 237]*

This became a secondary sector of agriculture, even by most Christian farmers in the neighboring villages.

Our teacher, Popkin, established a school where they taught "Hebrew in Hebrew." Under his initiative, a Zionist club of young farmers and youths was established. During the war, Popkin instructed a youth club belonging to the politically right section of the "Tzeirei Tzion" ["Youths of Zion"] movement. We established a public library, which contained many books in Hebrew, Yiddish, and Russian. Thanks to our Hebrew and Zionist education, our colony contributed a substantial number of pioneers, most of whom continue in Israel as farmers. Unlike in our colony, only a third as many made *Aliyah* to Eretz Israel from our big neighboring colony Izraelovka (Ya'azor).

During the war, our colony experienced all of the calamities experienced by the other colonies – enlistment of the youths to the army, recruitment of horses for transportation, and confiscation of food products. Our colony also experienced a shocking murderous event. Gangs who murdered hundreds of thousands of Jews throughout Ukraine and destroyed entire communities did not dare to break into our colony due to the self-defense force, organized and armed by the colony native Zeltzer *z"l*, a young brave man who served in the artillery corps during the war.

Fate would have it that the mass murder was rather executed by a company of the Red Army. The event happened due to a critical misunderstanding. When the army company passed near the colony, it unarmed two of our defenders. To Zeltzer, this company was suspected of being one of the murderous gangs, and he ordered to shoot at it to prevent it from entering the colony. These shootings raised the anger of the company's commander. Even though nobody was hurt by the shooting, he ordered them to break into the colony and take revenge. During the next few hours, they managed to murder close to forty people, among them the self-defense force commander. They also did not shun robbing and destroying the colony during their stay.

If before, it was only the wish of the Zionists and "Tzeirei Tzion" to make *Aliyah* to Eretz Israel, then after the bloody event and the taking over by the Bolsheviks, everybody wished to make *Aliyah*. One initiative man by the name of Dr. Stein from Yelisovetgrad organized the colony's farmers and some additional members from the city into a cooperative, which aimed at making *Aliyah* and settling in Eretz Israel. A committee was selected, by-laws were established, and a plan to send a delegation to Eretz Israel, to guarantee an area for the settlement was formed. However, in the meantime, the borders were closed and it became impossible to implement a mass exodus. The bachelors and the bachelorettes took some provisions for the road and some belongings and set out towards the borders. All those who managed to steal the borders arrived in Eretz Israel and settled in it. The others, particularly those with families, waited for an opportunity and missed the opportunity. During the late 1920s, the colony was announced as a kolkhoz. During the Holocaust, a cruel end came to the colony and its Jewish residents.

**Avraham Toren** (Kfar Vitkin)

[Page 238]

The name of my native colony was different from the names of other colonies in the province of Kherson, which all had Hebrew names such as "Sdeh Menukha" and "Ya'azor." Our colony was named after a Ukrainian national hero – Sehaidak. Sehaidak and Ya'azor, located six kilometers away, were established farther away from the rest of the colonies of the Kherson province and farther away from the provincial cities and the rivers flowing into the Black Sea as if they were simply thrown into the fertile prairie.

There were two elongated streets and one hundred households in the colony. The houses were covered with straw or wooden roof tiles and were not different from the other farmhouses in the area, except for some large houses and small business houses and groceries, which were crowded with shoppers during the market days, when the gentiles from the area came to sell vegetables and fruit and buy kerosene, fabric, etc. During the market days, we caused worries to the "*melameds*" [Torah teachers], who taught us the Torah and fear of G-d. Instead of studying the Torah portion of the week, a *Mishnah* chapter, or the *Baba Metziah Tractate*, we ran around the market stalls and were late to the lesson, bringing back with us all sorts of "bargains" – blueberries, plums, or sunflower seeds. We hid these "bargains" well inside our pockets for fear of our "*Melamed*" who would harshly punish those who were caught. The temptation was strong, despite the potential punishment, perhaps because they did not grow fruit trees and vegetables in our colony. Only one settler in our village owned a big orchard with all sorts of fruit. He also owned a beehive. He was a watchmaker, and his name was Alter "der Ligner" ["The Liar"]. Why would they stick a title like that to him? Probably because he had no difficulty bragging about his fruit harvest and exaggerating about his inventions with new fruit strains. We – the youths, "helped to reduce" the size of his harvest. We knew about all sorts of breaches and openings through which we entered the orchard to taste his first fruits, and also put some in our bags.

The main sectors in our colony were the cultivation of field crops, cattle, and the production of Dutch cheese. The yards were large and had fences made of cattle manure. The soil was fertile and it was not profitable to fertilize the fields. The manure piles would break apart and fall into the lake that was stretched along the colony and would feed the fat tilapia fishes. Every holiday eve, the *gabbai* [synagogue administrator] would bring fishermen to the lake who spread the net from one edge of the lake to the other. The entire village

[Page 239]

would go out to pull the net's ropes. The fishery was abundant, and the sale revenues paid for the expenses of the synagogue, the public bath, and the rest of the public needs and it was even possible to hire a cantor for the "Days of Awe." The peak in the agricultural work was the threshing, which ended by putting the grain in the barn. Young and old worked in the threshing. Ladder wagons loaded with sheaf would unload the crops into machines. The uproar of the threshing machines, the dust clouds, and the flying straw were common scenes in all of the yards.

We the children, were educated initially by a "melamed" and later on by the village's native, Eliezer Popkin, who graduated from a teachers' school in Zhytomyr. He taught us Hebrew poetry and literature. He was also the person who established a club of the Zionist movement "Tzeirei Tzion," which was actually a branch common to the two colonies.

I lived peacefully until the age of seventeen. I was seventeen years old when the revolution broke. "Freedom harbingers" ran around on the roads and fields chasing after the "*bandas*" [gangs] of Petliura and

Makhno [Ukrainian leaders that fought for Ukraine's independence during and after the revolution]. Several retreats and assaults by the various camps passed through the village. We were horrified by the frequent mad trampling of foreign people and vehicles. The *"bandas"* did not hurt people, only imposed taxes and demanded a supply of food for their soldiers. Our self-defense was aimed not toward them but toward the gentile villagers who boasted that they would attack the Jews for the purpose of rioting and robbing them.

My uncle, Eliezer Zeltzer, organized the self-defense force. He was a sergeant in Czar Nikolai's army. He organized about 40 youths, natives of the colony, and acquired weapons and ammunition. He placed guards at the entrance to the village, and every convoy that passed through the village on the way to Dolinsk (the train station) was checked thoroughly and its weapons confiscated. Indeed, there were no attempts to attack the colony. We would have probably been able to pass through the regime change unscathed, except for the case when battalions of the Red Army passed through the colony. One of the battalions, which returned for some reason to the colony, was mistakenly thought to be one of the gangs that wanted to loot, rob, and murder. My uncle ordered them to resist forcibly and not to let them enter the colony. The rest of the battalions, which also returned following that battalion, encircled the colony and started to shower it with fierce firepower. As a result, most of the defenders were killed, among them my uncle Eliezer, the commander of the self-defense force, as well as some elderly who were killed by stray bullets. Since then, we felt we were not residing on our own land. The colony was vulnerable to rioters and robbers since we did not have the means to resist them. Most of the residents left the colony and traveled to the cities and to relatives in other places. About 10 youths arrived in Eretz Israel, and most settled in Kfar Vitkin.

*[Page 240]*

From letters we received from relatives, we found out that the remnants that stayed in the colony experienced years of hunger. Most died in 1921, and the rest scattered throughout all corners of big Russia which was so cruel toward people who worked the land, whom the state professed to help.

**Israel Zeltzer** (Kfar Vitkin)

Jewish Farmers in Russia Fields

Water drawers in the field

Cooperative work group (Artel) in the 1920's

Lvovo (on the bank of the Dnieper) – in the colony's vineyard

*[Page 241]*

# Netchayevka

## (Nechayevka, Ukraine)

**47°30' 36°46'**

**Translated by** Moshe Kutten

**Edited by** Yocheved Klausner

My colony, like all the other colonies in the provinces of Yekaterinoslav and Kherson, does not exist anymore; however, it is etched very deep in my heart since it was where I was born where I spent my first childhood years and where I made friendships among my age group. These were my first years of teaching – years full of amazement and wonder and also fighting and overcoming routine. These were the years of my dreams, which were in tune with the dreams of the generation about the salvation of human society along with the salvation of the Jewish people. Some of the dreams were fulfilled in a much deeper and broader scope than what the imagination dared to dream during those days, and some were found to be false in a way much more extreme than even the most pessimists and cynical could ever think about…

My colony was not related to those dreams. It did not take any part in all of the social and political events that happened in Russia and to its nations, the Jewish nation among them, during the days that I resided in it, except for two or three of its youths who were ignited by the fire of the idealism. However, it received a major part of the troubles and suffering during the stormy fights between the various freedom fighters and all sorts of demons, which erupted out of the opened bottle, and of the bitter disappointment that followed the awakening from the far-flung illusions. How tragic and cruel was its end! How big and horrible was the price it paid for a sin it never sinned in dreaming vain dreams, which captured a few of its best sons, who took part in the events that occurred in the "big world." It paid in its heart and blood for the flame of their muddled social struggles, stormy discussions, fervent songs, glamourous dreams, and sleepless nights. It paid with its actual existence. It is no more. When I write these lines, my heart is crying without consolation…

# A

Netchayevka was one of the Jewish colonies in the province of Yekaterinoslav, and not the biggest one. There were only fifty-plus courtyards in it, arranged on both sides of one street. The houses were spacious single-floor clay houses with roofs made of straw, which grayed out from the years that passed. The yards were spacious – about half of a *disiyatin* (about 5

[Page 242]

*dunams* [1.35 acres]). Every one of them was narrow and long, stretching towards the fields, which encircled the colony. Except for the residential house itself (sometimes two houses facing each other beyond the entrance – if the family was large), one could also find, in the front side of the yard, a cowshed (most of the time not more than one cow), a stable (not more than two horses), a small chicken–coop serving the house needs, and a shed for the wagon, plow, harrow, scythes, threshing stone, oil press and other primitive tools they used for agriculture in those days.

In some yards, one or two trees were planted near the house (mostly fruit trees, a blackberry tree by us) and some small and meager vegetable beds, serving only the family. The rest of the yard area was used for the cultivation of grain crops and sometimes corn and watermelons.

Besides the few trees in the yards, there were no other fruit or ornament trees in the colony. The street was quite wide, relative to the rural standard in Russia during those days. It was covered with a thin layer of dirt in the summer and, in the winter, with thick waterlogged mud, which could not be passed through without tall boots. Along the street, near the houses, there were narrow walks covered, here and there, with wood boards to walk on during the rainy days.

I do not recall having a well in our yard. We might have drawn water from a well in a neighboring house. It goes without saying that we did not have toilets in the house, and certainly no bathtubs. One would do his business outside, at the edge of the yard, under the open sky in a ditch that separated the yard from the fields. Only Aharon Noodle, the old bachelor, who did not get married and never established a family due to a disappointed love, built for himself, in his old age, a "modern" toilet close to his home. Jokers in the colony who were book readers used to say about him that "he is not rich after all, since the toilet is near his home but not near his table…" [a phrase by Rabbi Yosef in the book Ein Ya'akov].

They would take a bath (only during summer days) in a small and shallow pool with a muddy bottom located beyond the yard. They would also bring the horses to be washed there. The big children would take a bath with the horses while riding on them. During the months of Tammuz–Av [roughly July – August], the water in the pool would evaporate, leaving only some mud puddles and broken tools and rugs that the small children would throw into the pool when it was full and overflowing, to see the stirred rattling ripples moving in expanding circles, fading away and disappearing.

A synagogue, not quite large, built from dark–red fired bricks, stood in the center of the colony within a small yard. The arcs above its entrance and windows and the reddish tiles on the roof looked like a wondrous puzzle to me during my early childhood. Facing the synagogue stood a new building, which was built when I was a youth, 15–16-year-old, while I was away from the colony. This was the large building of the state school, also built from fired bricks and a tile roof, however, with no arcs above its entrance or windows. I saw it for the first time when I was 19 years old when I returned to my native colony as a state teacher.

*[Page 243]*

That building had a large yard of about 1 *disiyatin* (about 10 *dunams* [2.7 acres]), which was slated for the cultivation of vegetables and fruit trees by the students under the teachers' guidance. In actuality, people from the colony were supposed to take turns cultivating it, as a "tax" to the government for the benefit of the teachers, in addition to the salary paid by the government. In our colony, like in many other colonies, this "garden" was mostly unkept. When the state inspector over the schools came, he would categorize this neglected area as a nature.

From my early childhood and later, from my four to five years of serving as a teacher in Netchayevka, the colony is pictured in my mind as one gray lump, in which only in the spring and summer, several green spots would sprout, here and there. This is how I saw it when I returned to it for a trip, riding on a primitive wagon, most of the time sitting on a bench with no springs, a distance of 20–25 kilometers from the nearby train station in Tsarikonstantinovka. The wagon would swing around on an unpaved dirt road, which stretched through the wild prairie bushes that filled its desert wilderness in all directions to the horizon.

# B

Like the rest of the colonies in our area, Netchayevka was a real agricultural colony. All the family members who resided in the colony (more than fifty families), worked the land with their own hands. The name along with the title – "*Yevrei zemliedieliyetz*" ("a Jew who works the land") was written on their passport. This must be understood literally – not "agriculturalist" or farmer but a person who "works the land." This was also what was written on Hebrew documents. During the first decade of the 20th century, some youths left for the city to acquire a general education, settle in the city, and work in one of the "free" professions, among them some who were ashamed of the title. However, these were the minority, if there were any. At the end of the day, we were all proud of that title, especially when we became Zionists. The members of the "Bund" [an East European socialist party – by the name of the General Jewish Worker Alliance], the Social Democrats party, and the Social Revolutionary Party among us, actually bragged about their "pure" proletarian background. There was nobody in the colony who did not work his land by himself – him, his wife, sons, and daughters. Everybody worked – even the only shopkeeper. A native of the colony was also the *Sh"uv* [slaughterer and Kosher inspector], as well as Yanke (Ya'akov) Cohen – the "melamed" [Torah teacher] (partially, at least, during the burning season), and obviously also the "*starosta*" – the colony elder, the owner of the wealthiest farm. Everybody worked the land except for the Rabbi and the teachers in the state school, who were mostly not natives of the colony. Even among them, I do not recall anybody who considered working the land as a disrespectful occupation. If there were people who did not themselves work the land, it was not because they were ashamed of that work but because they did not find it important from a national or general human point of view. I do not recall

[Page 244]

having more than a *minyan* [10] Zionists among all the seventeen colonies in the province of Yekaterinoslav.

The colony members performed their work in the fields, mainly plowing and sowing, by themselves. However, they hired workers from the neighboring villages for the harvesting and threshing tasks. During that season, the colony was bustling with male and female "*Shkutzim*" [derogatory term for gentile youths] from the neighboring villages Heichur. In the evenings, they filled the streets with singing, games, and laughter. We were amazed at their "gentile" energy which was ample enough for games after a hard and long day of work, from before sunrise to after sunset, although our youths were not weak either. These workers were hired in return for half of the harvest. That was the reason why they were called *Polovinchik* (*Polovina* in Russian means "half"). Almost every farmer in our colony had permanent workers who came to work with him every year during the harvest season and would work along with their "masters" and their families during the same hours of the day.

It happened, albeit rarely, that the youth of both sides hung out together. It also happened that an initiative "*Shiksah*" [a gentile girl] would drag behind her a husky Jewish youth, who was captured by her scorching gazes and would connect with him in one of the yard's hideaways. The following day the youth would get plenty of calls of contempt and booing from his male friends, and the Jewish girls would evade meeting with him or would act as if they were avoiding. However, I did not hear, during my many years in the colony, about any serious attachment resulting from such unions…

One of the colony residents was a German Christian family. Like in other colonies, it remained in it from the period of the initial settlement. The second generation of these Germans, and certainly the third and the fourth, spoke fluent Yiddish. Their agricultural expertise diminished somewhat, and they were like the Jews in all aspects except for religious matters. By the way, none of the second generation's members was orthodox in piousness, and many boasted about being non–believers. The German family did not excel in their piousness either, and they did not have a place for praying in the colony. One sign of their uniqueness was the fact that they did not circumcise their sons, nor did they get married to Jews. They served as the "gentile of Shabbat" in the houses of the elderly and the synagogues. On Passover's Eve, they would buy the entire leavened food in the colony from the Rabbi.

The cultivation of grain crops was done in an extensive style, and it was nearly the only agricultural sector. It included mainly wheat and barley, a bit of corn, and sometimes millet and oats. They virtually did not cultivate orchards, at least not in my colony. Even the ornamental trees were very few – perhaps one or two in some yards. Only in the middle of the first decade of the 20th century, the JCA organization [Jewish Colonization Association] which began to take interest in the state of our colonies (established a credit union and introduced modern agricultural machines), tried to plant fruit trees and vineyards. However, as far as I know, that development bypassed Netchayevka, at least until 1909 when I left the colony.

We also did not grow sheep or goats nor did we raise bees. Only at the beginning

[Page 245]

of the activity of the JCA organization, one could see a beehive here and there. However, one could find, in every yard, something like a chicken coop, in the corner of the cowshed, or in a small clay structure attached to the cowshed.

I do not recall seeing a dog anywhere in the colony during my early childhood and not even when I returned years later as a teacher in the state school. I resided in the colony and in the neighboring colony Merapeskaya for more than four years. I did not see any dogs in these two colonies or perhaps its residents fulfilled the statement in Exodus [11:7]:" But against any of the children of Israel shall not a dog move his tongue, against man or beast…," so well that I did not hear them, and therefore the fact about their existence was wiped out from my memory? Against that, I do remember the many cats very well. Cats of all sizes and colors, who received a tolerant treatment, were also allowed in the rooms of the house as they were the only solution for the plague of the many mice.

# C

The ancestors of our colony people, the people who established and built it, came from the province of Kovno, Lithuania, most of them from the city of Shavli, where they were shopkeepers and craftsmen. The colony elders, who were children during the days of the foot and wagon wandering from Shavli to the southern prairies, used to tell stories they heard from their parents about the hardships they encountered on the long road and during the first years after they settled. They described the hard and grueling labor in building the first clay houses and digging the water wells and their introduction to the primitive agricultural methods under the guidance of the arrogant German farmers, who treated them like the treatment the Children of Israel received from the oppressors of Pharaoh. They experienced many troubles until they learned the hard labor. They even managed to succeed in it, particularly during the days of the second and third generations, if not for the calamities from the heavens such as drought, diseases, mice, and the like.

The fathers described how they drove away, with the handles of the shovels and rakes and with sticks, the young hooligans from the neighboring villages who attacked them in droves during the pogroms of the 1880s. Throughout the pogroms of 1905, during the days of Czar Nikolai the 2ⁿᵈ, the colonies were not harmed at all and the elders explained that their fathers learned the lesson during the first pogroms. Indeed the Christian population learned to treat the Jewish farmers with a certain amount of respect, or at least with some care.

The entire colony knew reading and writing in Yiddish, and the Torah portion of the week,

*[Page 246]*

mostly with Rashi's commentary. Some people had a taste of the book "Ein Ya'akov" and knew how to write a short letter in Hebrew. Obviously, the traditional Jewish way of life was accepted by everybody, and in times of need, many knew to read the shortened "Shulkhan Arukh." Some had knowledge of the Mishnah tractates and knew some Gemara [Talmud]. There were even some "enlightened" who read some of the Enlightenment literature. A few knew to read and write in Russian and even express several sentences, in a marred language, which was half–Ukrainian and half–Russian. The people of the colony did not need to use the state language except for some exceptional cases such as for giving instructions to the farmers from the nearby village, who worked in the colony during the harvest season, and when selling the grain in the nearby city, a business that was done using city Jewish brokers. When somebody wished to write a letter, once in a blue moon, or read a document that was received from the authorities and had to be responded to, or other such cases, the elementary knowledge of the few learned people was usually sufficient. In a time of need, they could turn to the colony clerk, who resided in the colony where the official management of several neighboring colonies was concentrated.

Upon the establishment of the elementary state school, whose main objective was to spread the knowledge of arithmetic and reading and writing of the state language, as well as a shortened version of

Russia's history, the elementary knowledge of the Russian language, both verbally and written form, increased, particularly among the young generation. During the first few years after the establishment of the school, a few older boys and girls, 15–16 years old, were among its students. During my first year as a teacher in the Netchayevka school, three big girls studied there and one of them left the school in the middle of the academic year, to get married with good luck and all the best. I would not prolong the description of the school and my work in it, except to add that the state schools in the Russian villages were three years long. In the German colonies, the Greek villages in the south, and the Jewish colonies, they added a fourth year, to add the study of the state language to the existing curriculum.

The teachers who worked in the state schools in our colonies were all (except those who only taught Jewish studies) certified teachers who passed special state examinations. Only a few were among the graduates of the "Hebrew Pedagogical Courses in Grodno," and those were considered elite in the colony as opposed to the "*melameds*" and "private" teachers. Most of these graduates did not boast about their "European" education or about their position as state teachers and were involved with the public. The few observants among them, used to come to the synagogue during the Shabbat and holidays.

With the awakening of the freedom movement in Russia in 1905 and the following years, some of the teachers discussed the social revolutionary trend in libraries, discussion groups, and lectures. I, in Netchayevka, organized a youth club to discuss "current social matters" and the subjects were socialism, Zionism (sometimes), general culture matters, literature (mainly in Yiddish), and more. We sometimes gathered in the large classroom of the school, particularly during the long winter nights, and included adults, especially the "educated" homeowners, and their wives in the lecture.

*[Page 247]*

L.M. Shapira, the school principal, would lecture on one of the subjects in a popular style in Russian while translating the hard words and terms into Yiddish. I would read to a larger crowd from the stories of Shalom Aleikhem, Peretz, Pinski, and others.

Some of the colony elders would sometimes come to Shapira's private flat, which was located inside the school, for a cup of tea, to discuss general political topics. Shapira was a man of an extensive education, an intelligent and clever man, from among the leaders of the Social Democrats party from the county seat Yekaterinoslav. He was sent to our remote colony, to serve as the principal of the small state school, as a punishment for his revolutionary views. Twelve to thirteen years later, when the punishment system of the Soviet government (and not only during Stalin's days) was introduced, what could a "deviant" like him, particularly a Jewish person, who undercuts the government foundations expect to receive?

**Moshe Avigal (Beigel)** (Tel Aviv)

[Page 248]

# Novo-Vitebsk

## (Novo-Vitebsk, Ukraine)

## 47°58' 33°54'

## (Nehora, Lakhish District)

## Translated by Moshe Kutten

## Edited by Yocheved Klausner

To Gideon Hausner:

"We need to mention the Jewish kolkhozes as a unique phenomenon. Between Krivoy Rog and Dniepropetrovsk there were Jewish kolkhozes, which consisted not only of Jewish managers but their entire manpower was Jewish"

…Unit no. 6 operation command decided not to kill these Jews, but allow them to continue their work, and only annihilated the Jewish leadership and replaced it with a Ukrainian one."

> / Report no. 81 of the operation- command (from the opening speech of Israel's Attorney General in the trial against Eichman)

Lucky is he whose work is done by others!

Hitler's hordes were "lucky" since they did not have "to kill by shooting" the Jews who worked the Ukrainian land with their sweat for five generations. The Ukrainiań "management" did that for them. With its own hands, it annihilated tens of agricultural colonies with a Jewish population who enjoyed autonomy like no other Jewish communities did: the local authority, the police, and the state education were handled by Jews. These were the Jews who were revered by the hero of the book by Hazaz – "Daltot Nekhoshet" [Copper Doors], who asked, at the time of the collapse of Jewish life in Russia at the beginning of the revolution: "Where would the Jews find salvation in their fight? Who would lead them and who would help them?" The hero turned to "the Jewish colonies in the south where I would find the youth I am looking for, wholesome and healthy workers of the land, who are like the sons of the Gentiles."

These colonies, in which established Jewish folklore existed for generations, were named after the native cities of the settlers, who came from Lithuania – Novo Vitebsk, Novo Kovno, Novo Podolsk, etc. In the same way, the people who sailed in the ship Mayflower named their new settlements with their origin names - Plymouth, Boston, New Bedford, New London, etc.

There were also some other names, which looked strange written in Latin letters and heard in gentile pronunciation. These were the Hebrew names – "Sdeh Menukha," "Nahar-Tov," etc., a testimony to the yearnings of the settlers towards the land "where the spring lasts forever" [Bialik – "El Hatzipor"].

These colonies, whose population was tiny compared to the enormous population

[Page 249]

of the Ukrainian farmers kept the tradition diligently; however, new terms and unique holidays were added – "*Kosovitze*" – the harvest time, "*Dreshtzeit*"– the threshing period, "*Noye Broit*" [literally "new bread"] – the new harvest, which is also the time for paying off debts and laying down plans for next year. This is how an old settler of the Jewish settlement in Israel recalls her childhood in the fields of Ukraine:

"I am a native of a Jewish colony in southern Russia. My parents had only girls, and from an early age, we had to shoulder the burden of every hard work done by boys. When I was only six years old, I would drive out the Gentile's pigs and chickens, which penetrated our plot from all directions. During the harvest and wheat transportation, my father would wake me up at 2 a.m., when I was only 10 years old, to travel to the field, -located 20 *verstas* (25 kilometers) from the village. Wrapped in my sleep, I would curl on the stiff wagon while all my bones ached from the jolting. When we arrived at the field, my father would hand me over the sheaves, and I stood on the wagon and arranged them so they would not fall out on the road back. How pleasant was it, on the way back, to cuddle on the sheaves and allow the tired body some rest? Soon, the sun rose slowly, and her golden rays danced pleasantly and graciously."

"Our father was proud of our agility when we met some Jews on our way back who were late going out to their work. My father and mother were probably anguished about waking us at midnight to work, however, it was a real necessity, and it was my sacrifice to the life on the land, the flora and fauna that roused in me the strong desire to excel in the work on the farm just like the gentiles. Indeed, our farm in the Jewish colony was exemplary. We were attached to the farm with all of our heart, and many (including gentiles), would come to ask for Father's advice" – (from an article by Leah Lev, Collection of sayings by female members – "Beit Moshav").

The Jews, who knew how to work, knew also how to celebrate. Shaul Tchernikhovski describes a wedding in "Khatunata shel Elka" ["Elka's Wedding"] as if it was told by a settler, similar to what I remember from my childhood days. The traditional celebration, which was planned and organized to its last detail, lasted a week, and all of the colony residents and many outside guests, took part in it.

The boys studied in a "*kheder*" and Lithuania provided most of the *melameds* [Torah teachers]. However, in parallel to the many "*kheders*," there was a four-year state school, and in the big colonies, a six-year state school whose teachers were Jewish. Among the exceptional teachers was the famous poet Shimon Frug. He served as a teacher in my native colony for many years. My teacher, Moshe Izaackchik z"l, who arrived in our colony from Riga when he was young, resided in the colony until his last day. He taught in the "zemstvo" [district] school and was its principal for 42 years. I was fortunate to be a teacher under his management in the same school where I studied in my childhood, and found in one of the cabinets a report card of my father when he was a student, signed by Moshe Izaackchik.

[Page 250]

That teacher was a man of culture. He founded several public enterprises in the colony, such as a public library, a credit union, and more.

In the neighboring colony of Novo Kovno, they had another wondrous teacher – Arie Nekhemkin, who possessed a broad agricultural education, and he guided the farm owners with his advice. He also introduced new agricultural sectors, such as beekeeping and fruit tree cultivation.

Only a few natives of the Jewish colonies left the colonies to the city to continue their studies since working the land required the participation of all members of the family, and the studies in high school and beyond required substantial financial means beyond the ability of the farmers. However, several boys graduated a university. For girls, leaving the house was even more difficult; however, with the new times, some girls left to study in the city. In my colony, I was the first girl who left to study in the big city. I still recall the warning of my grandfather to my father: "She will finish high school and would want to be a doctor. Potential grooms would demand a dowry of 10,000 rubles from you. Where would you take it from? She would stay single in her old age."

However, in actuality, those who studied outside were the cream of the crop in the small colony. They brought a flow of fresh life, ideas, and new thoughts. They brought the news about the political movements and organized clubs of the Bund [the General Jewish Labor Federation in Lithuania, Poland, and Russia] and Zionist movements. In our colony, we organized an amateur theater group. In one of the shows, the role of the suitor for the daughter of the "rich man" in the colony was given to a timid youth. The poor "lover" would have never dared to approach the pompous girl even in his dream, and the names and nicknames given to both of them stuck with them for the rest of their lives.

The idol of our youths in that period was a young student, a native of the colony, who graduated from his medicine studies in Switzerland. He was the first in our area who receive higher education. When he would appear in his native village, once every two years, and pass in the street tall and good-looking in his blue uniform and a student's hat, the village elders would welcome him with affection and respect. The girls would stop breathing when he passed in front of them…

When he returned home as a "doctor with a diploma," a cholera epidemic raged throughout southern Russia, which could not be restrained due to a lack of medical manpower, and the horrible backwardness of the Russian population. People got sick in our colony as well, and there were several death cases. I recall the strange sight when I woke up one Shabbat morning and saw smoke rising from the chimney of one of the houses. In the winter, the "Shabbat gentile" would go around and light the furnaces. However, that happened in the summer. I was told that a woman got sick with cholera in that house and that they ordered her to take warm baths.

In the nearby Christian village, with a population of thousands, the epidemic raged without any restraint. The melon and cucumber season was approaching and with no medical help,

[Page 251]

the peasants used quack medications. The angel of death took victims without any pity. The young [Jewish] physician, who had just arrived from Switzerland, volunteered to fight the epidemic that spread in the neighboring village. One can just imagine what happened next. The rumors about the revolts against the physicians, known to have erupted that year, must have reached that backward village. Perhaps just the fact that the physician was the son of "Zhids" from the nearby colony, known to them well, angered the Gentiles. One Sunday, some people gathered near the tavern, and from there they went to conduct a "pogrom" in the "zemstvo" [district] clinic claiming that the "Zhid" was poisoning the sick. I recall well the event when they brought him back home. I learned since then, how dangerous was the situation of one enlightened person among a crowd of ignorant people, and that a person in such a responsible position should not be left alone in such circumstances.

Generally, life in the colony was not very stormy. There was joy in the peaceful life at the colony. Honest working people, whose lives stretched in front of them, lived in the colony. There were people with some original characters among them, who entertained and amused the public with their jokes and their witty inventions. There were also welfare organizations such as "Hakhnasat Kalah" [literally "Marrying a Bride"] or "Ma'ot Khitin" [literally "Pennies for Wheat"] and others. However, one could not find in the colony, which was poor to begin with, local beggars and panhandlers. Very rarely, Jewish beggars from the outside would arrive in the small remote colony and their appearance would become an "event" in the colony.

I recall a story that was told by our neighbor in Novo Vitebsk, a mother of many children whose husband was a "unique character" in that he was endowed with a pleasant voice and a tendency to cantor singing… During the "Days of Awe," he would be invited by small communities, who did not have a cantor of their own, to pray and stand in front of the synagogue's "bimah" [podium where the Torah is read from]. When the summer would reach its end, and the "Days of Awe" were approaching his "artistic yearnings" would overpower him, and he used to neglect the field work during "the burning season" and visit his friends' houses to sing "pirkei khazanut" [cantor songs].

The harvest was completed but not yet piled up. Signs of the approaching rain would be seen, while the mind of that "singing lover" would be completely distracted from the harvest, which could rot in the field if it got wet. All of a sudden, two strangers knocked on the door and asked for a handout. The woman saw that these two beggars were young with undiminished vigor, and offered them to go with her husband to pile up the harvest. There was not much work, and they could complete it in only two hours. She promised to pay them nicely for their work.

The beggars consulted with each other. Was it worthwhile to change from their "clean" work of collecting aims to gathering the harvest, and which occupation would be more profitable? In the end, they relented and all three of them went.

They were late to come back, and the woman started to sense trouble. She went out to see for herself how the work was progressing. When she arrived at the field, she was horrified. The guests were lying down comfortably on a fragrant pile of hay, and her husband was standing in front of them, curling his voice with songs of the "Days of Awe." He acquired listeners and the hay was left scattered in the field.

The smart woman did not say anything and called them back home for dinner.

*[Page 252]*

At home, the guests had a serious talk with her and offered to take her husband with them to collect alms. Why should he soil his hands in gentile's work? A person with such a voice! People would throw gold at him if he would become a beggar…

When I said that the Jewish colonies were only populated by Jews – I was not accurate. In fact, there were some colonies, among them my native colony of Novo Vitebsk, where tens of German families resided from the start. They belonged to the Anabaptist denomination and were persecuted, at the time, in Russia. When Alexander the First tried to settle the Jews on the land of the infinite and entirely desolate prairies of Novo-Russia [Southern Ukraine] he decided to attach ten German families to every colony to teach the Jews agriculture. As agriculturalists, the Germans were much superior to their Jewish neighbors, and their farms were beautifully developed. The family structure, the unlimited authority of the head of the family, and their innate discipline enabled them to build exemplary farms. They did not mix with the Jews. In our colony, there was the "Germans' Street" with straight fences, nicely painted, with spacious houses, which hid behind huge trees, with large families of tall blond residents. They did not usually leave their confine. We knew that they celebrated Christmas and they brought a beautifully decorated fir tree to their houses. We also knew they would gather every Sunday to pray and sing in a chorus, whose members knew to play various musical instruments. However, all of that was and remained foreign to the colony's Jewish residents during the period of more than one hundred years of their existence as neighbors.

The First World War fell on the agricultural population of Russia and the Jewish colonies like a hard blow. While it was like a disaster for a family when a son enlisted in the Czar's army during peacetime, during the war, the sons and the husband were taken together, and the farm remained in the hands of the women. My father *z"l*, also served three years, during his youth, in the regular Russian army and was called to the reserve corps during the Russia-Japan war. In 1905, he arrived in the swamps of Manchuria. He was recruited again in August 1914 and participated in the battles of Lvov [Lviv] and the siege of Pshemishel.

After three years of poverty and suffering during the war, the March 1917 Revolution ["February Revolution"] took place, which displaced the regime of the Czars. A few months later, the "October Revolution" followed, and following it, the Civil War. The state of the general Jewish population during those days is described faithfully in "Sipurei HaMa'hapekha" ["Stories of the Revolution"] by Hazaz. However, the destruction of the Jewish colonies has yet to be expressed in our literature. Every new regime tried first to take revenge against the Jewish population, which served as a "scapegoat." During a very short period, the colonies dwindled markedly, and the robbing and looting did not cease even for one day. The regime passed from one hand to another many times.

*[Page 253]*

On top of that, the plague of the "*bandas*" [gangs] made things worse. These were gangs of Kosaks, partisans, or members of the neighboring villages whose aim was robbing and taking revenge against the Jews, whom they considered the "enemies of the Russian people."

I remember well the day of Yom Kippur 1919 when the army of "Father" Makhno retreated through our colony. They cleaned our houses from any item and then set them on fire. Early in the morning, we were told about the dreadful event: Makhno's people killed the head of the village - Meir Gilbof, after horrible tortures. People who dared to approach the place, hearing the cries of the house members, were shocked. As they stood there, a new wagon, shining in its fresh paint and pulled by two healthy horses, passed. These were the residents of the "Germans Street" who went to their daily work upon sunrise as if nothing had happened. The murderers treated the Germans favorably and entirely passed over their houses.

When they heard the cries, they stopped the wagons, and one of them came down, looked at the body lying in a puddle of blood, and said in German (they never talked in any other language): "You wanted a revolution? It's all yours – enjoy it!"

I spent the rest of that Yom Kippur, which I will never forget, with another dozen young girls in the attic of the synagogue. The Makhno gang left the colony by noontime, and in the rear, a few additional groups of bandits roamed. They delayed their departure with the malice intention to look after girls. This fear forced the youths to search for hideouts in places that they could not think about. When we were lying in the attic, we heard shouting and shooting beneath us inside the synagogue. We did not believe anybody remained alive in the entire colony. When the sunset, the street quieted and emptied of the horse riders. We dared to go down from the attic to the women's section of the synagogue to listen to the closing prayers of the day.

The bandits had rioted during the whole day in the synagogue, hit and drove away the people who prayed. Only some very old men, less than a *minyan*, stayed behind fulfilling the commandment of "*Kiddush Hashem*" [martyrdom], their clothes and praying shawls were taken away. The girls' cries seeing the elders in that condition, were heartbreaking.

The years that followed were years of oppression, poverty, and hunger. We forgot what the sight of a human garment looked like. Even young girls wore sacks. During that period, I was studying in the city, and my father came to visit me, dressed in garments made of rough sacks. The woman of the house, who opened the door for him and saw him standing at the entrance, mistook him for a beggar and gave him a piece of bread as a handout. A long time following that incident, she could not calm down and was asking for our forgiveness, saying that at times like that, she could not recognize people by their clothing.

In the summer of 1920, I walked in the field with my boyfriend, whom I married later, at the end of the year. Walking outside the colony was dangerous, and Jews did not go out of the colony alone, even when they went out to the field. When we approached the colony, we saw a strange sight. An old man, who had a long white bird, was standing near a wall,

[Page 254]

fully naked as in the day he was born. Our sudden and unexpected appearance surprised him and he fell flat on the ground.

I was horrified since I recognized him as one of the village's old men. There were rumors that his family, which had many children, was penniless, and that they were left with only one pair of pants in the house, which was shared by all members of the family. The person who would leave the house wore it. Rumors said that they all slept on one mattress filled with feathers covered with sacks since the linen had worn out a long time ago. The old man, who was always locked at home without clothes, probably wanted to breathe some fresh air and warm himself in the sun, at a time when everybody was immersed in their Saturday afternoon nap and did not expect that a couple of impudent people would suddenly frighten him.

Many people participated in my wedding that year. I am sorry that I do not have any photographs left from the event since the attire of the distinguished guests was very strange. The people in the colony would buy their clothing from the city folks who would travel huge distances to exchange their "luxury" items for essential commodities, such as bread and potatoes. It was no wonder, therefore, that a woman appeared at my wedding wearing a fancy gown, fashioned in the style of one hundred years ago, with wooden slippers on her feet. One of my uncles wore an open lace shirt under his old *kapoteh*[long coat], with his wide beard covering his bare chest. Nobody mocked or even noticed that attire, since there were many other things to worry about. There was a horrible tragedy associated with my wedding as well. My cousin, an 18 old youth, who wanted to get me a wedding gift, found out that in Krivoy Rog he could find a pair of used towels (a very rare product during those days). He insisted on traveling there despite the warnings and pleadings and was murdered along with another six of the colony youths immediately upon leaving the colony.

Upon the establishment of the stable Soviet regime, we were initially happy and many of the people in Jewish colonies tended to support the Communists. The hope was that the new regime would fight anti-Semitism since everybody was considered equal in the country of the Communists and everybody had the right of self-determination. However, these hopes were soon proven false. The "*Yevsektzia*" people arrived at the colony and their first action was to close the *"kheders"* where Torah was taught and to convert the state school into a Yiddish school. Even though Yiddish was the spoken language in every home, the new arrangement was not liked by the residents.

When I came to visit the colony, the parents of the students complained to me that the children were learning nonsense instead of Torah and Rashi and that the teachers were telling the children not to obey their parents.

After I made *Aliyah* to Eretz Israel, the colonies became kolkhozes. They wrote to me from home that they "nationalized" the house of the wealthy farmer, the same wealthy farmer whose daughter was forced to hug a "proletarian," even though just in a show… This was an amazingly diligent and organized family, whose sons and daughters managed to acquire education and at times of trouble scattered all around.

*[Page 255]*

The Soviet authority began to incite hatred among the population to the *"kolak's"* [the wealthy]. As it turned out, the fear of the wealthy people was justified. When they announced the conversion of our colony to a kolkhoz, only two old people were left in the house of the wealthy man.

People wrote to me that they were not allowed to take with them any property. They had to return all the property they "stole" from the public during all of their life. They were driven away from their home in the evening, and they did not know where to turn. Nobody dared to offer them a place to sleep, for fear that they would invoke the suspicion of the authorities. The only one that dared to do it was the old *melamed* since he himself was left without sustenance and protection and was not afraid to take a risk. As they wrote to me, early in the morning the two "wealthy people" went out on foot to the train station, which was twenty kilometers away from the colony. The same *melamed* did them another favor and gave them a small wooden stool so that the old woman could rest along the way. To satisfy the censor, the person who wrote the letter to me ended his description with the words: "That was how they got what they deserved!"…

There is no chance or hope that I could find the cemetery where my parents and grandparents are buried. Only a few natives from the colony survived. I do not know whether there is anybody from our colony who currently lives outside Russia, except for the Yiddish poet - Ya'akov Glantz, who became a citizen of Mexico and was involved in Zionist activity. The small group among us, who were brought up under the ideas of the Zionist movement, made *Aliyah* to Eretz Israel and integrated into its existence. Among us, some well-known public figures serve in important roles in the country. However, most of the colony natives took root in our country, in the Izre'el Valley, Jordan Valley, and settlements in southern Israel. The devotion to the land and the love of work, which they brought with them to our ancestors' land from the Jewish fields in Ukraine, they bequeathed to their descendants here in our motherland.

**Rivka Guber**[1]

*Translator's Note:*

1. Rivka Guber was a famous social activist and educator in Israel. She was known as the "mother of the sons" after losing two sons in the War of Independence. She was a recipient of the Israel Prize for her life activity in the education and absorption of new immigrants.

[Page 256]

# Ruzhany

## [Nehora, Lakhish District]

**Translated by** Moshe Kutten

**Edited by** Yocheved Klausner

I studied in the Yeshiva of the city Ruzhany and on Shabbat, we would sometimes tour the Jewish colonies which were close to the city.

I was captivated by the life of the Jewish farmers and their peace of mind compared to those of the townspeople whose occupation was mainly in shopkeeping and craftsmanship.

During one of the Shabbats, when I entered the colony's synagogue. During the opening of the Ark, for taking out the Torah scroll, one of the residents came up to the Ark and stated that he was delaying the reading of the Torah. It was customary that any person who felt deprived by somebody in the crowd was allowed to delay the reading and force the public to intervene and correct the wrong. So that person announced that he was delaying the reading since he was deprived by his neighbor. He claimed that this neighbor collected the dung droppings from half of the street near his house after the herd passed there. The crowd considered that action a public scandal and decided to impose a fine on the neighbor who collected the dung droppings on the side of the street, which was not located near his house.

During that time, as a yeshiva student, I saw that behavior by the village residents as a desecration of the sanctity. Can a dispute about dung be brought to the podium where the Torah reading takes place? However, when I grew up, I realized that the village atmosphere, which I absorbed in the Jewish colonies during my childhood, was much stronger than my distaste for the desecration of the sanctity and that those experiences from my childhood were the ones that led me to the settlement in Eretz Israel. Only then I understood the sanctity of that delay in reading the Torah, because of the robbery of the dung in the half of the street near the house of that farmer.

**Mordekhai Guber**[1]

*Translator's note:*

1. Mordekhai Guber, a famous public figure, was one of the people who established Kfar Tuvia and Kfar Warburg, new immigrant settlements in the Lakhish District. He was the husband of Rivka Guber (see article page 248) and a father who lost two sons in the Israel War of Independence.

*[Page 257]*

# Kil'yanovka

## (Ukraine)

### 49°7' 28°00'

### Translated by Moshe Kutten

### Edited by Ingrid Rockberger

Kil'yanovka was located in the province of Podolia, near the town of Lityn, which was considered by the residents of Kil'yanovka as a noteworthy city. They considered the closest city to Lityn, Vinnytsia, a real metropolis. The residents of the rest of the world did not consider Vinnytsia a big city. In fact, when it was conquered by the Germans, they did not even bother to boast about taking it.

There was a single street and twenty houses in Kil'yanovka; however, despite its minuteness, it was the whole world for its residents. I was 12 years old when I left it with the rest of its residents.

It was founded during the period of the "snatchers." A group of Jews who served a substantial time in the Czar's army settled it under the promise that their children would not be conscripted into the army because they were land owners.

My mother, Feiga Adler, may peace be upon her, was a third generation in the colony. Her sisters were married and moved to other settlements, so my grandfather's plot was divided between her and her brother. My father, Meir Astitas, came to the colony from Berdichev. He learned agriculture from my grandfather, whose daughter he married, and settled there. My parents had a plot of 250 *disiyatins* [675 acres], 50 of which was swampland, and the rest was good agricultural soil. Our house was surrounded by orchards of fruit trees, a vegetable garden, and a plot for the cultivation of field crops. We had a cowshed housing 12 cows, and a geese and chicken coop. We also grew sugar beets, which we supplied to a factory in the city of Luginy. Compared to the neighboring villages of Bahrynivtsi, Meidan, Novoselytsya, and Lysohirka, Kil'yanovka was a prosperous colony.

The above-mentioned villages supplied us with hired workers during the burning season and collecting the sugar beets. The shepherd also came from one of the neighboring villages. We sent the milk to Lityn, and merchants, who came from Odesa and Kiev [Kyiv], bought our milk products (butter and cheese). Apart from oil and salt, we didn't need anything. The farm supplied all of our food needs – grains, wheat, vegetables, fruits, milk, and even meat. We pickled any excess from what we grew in barrels located in the cellar to use all year round. During the long winter days, we sat at home, fattening geese and preparing groats and chopped food for the cows. In the evenings, we gathered in one of the residents' houses. The hosts would bring up, from the cellar, a bucket–full of *"kvasnitzes"* to serve to their guests. The women baked potatoes served with sour cabbage or a pastry stuffed with cabbage. The children sat next to the adults and did their homework. All the children were taught by the *"melamed"* to read and write, as well as Torah and arithmetic (in Yiddish). The *"Kheder"* and the *"melamed"* moved,

*[Page 258]*

in turn, from one house to another. Every resident hosted them for about 4–6 weeks (one of our *melameds*, old man Shlomo Kutin, resides today in Haifa). The children were between 3 to 18, sat on long benches, and studied together. The unique thing about our "*kheder*" was that boys and girls studied together.

Those of us who were thirsty for knowledge continued their studies in the elementary school in the village of Meidan and later on, moved to Lityn or even Odesa. One of the boys, from the Shternges family, studied medicine in Kiev and immigrated to America at the end of his studies.

Except for studying, the kids were burdened with duties on the farm: feeding the animals, picking fruit, hoeing, and mainly drawing water from the valley and hauling it up to the village, located on the mountain.

On Sabbaths and festivals, the residents changed from their working clothes, dressed in their satin capotes, and gathered in the synagogue, which stood in the center of the street. The synagogue contained a holy ark covered with a gold–embroidered red velvet curtain and a decorated Torah scroll. The residents were pious in their religion and were very strict about keeping the commandments.

A Jewish person with a blue box [JNF donation collection box] would visit us once in a while. Under his influence, my father planned to sell his estate and make *Aliyah* to Eretz Israel. However, in the meantime, the First World War broke out. All the people who were obligated to be enlisted – were forced to enlist. My brother Shmuel served for two years on the front and returned to the village when the revolution started. Upon his return, he organized a group for self–defense…

The pogroms could have been seen coming on the horizon. One evening, the neighboring villagers attacked the colony. They gathered all the residents in one house and locked them up. One of the children sneaked out through a window and fetched the defenders. They only had three guns among them, however, their shooting drove away the rioters. Three days later, eight of the gang members came to the colony and demanded the weapons. Intimidated by their threats, the colony surrendered its weapons. We were attacked a few days later. The attack occurred in the evening; some residents escaped to the forests. We witnessed them looting our house until the morning. They seated us on a bench in one of the rooms after my father refused the demand of the rioters to go down to the cellar as they intended to throw a hand grenade and bomb the entire family. My father recognized the rioters and said to them: "I cannot believe that you, our people, would do something like that to us." The rioters drew back and claimed: "We are foreigners here; we just came from Kiev." The rioters killed my father and my two elder brothers, may G–d avenge their blood, in the morning. During that night, the rioters murdered 10 of the village residents. The adult men escaped to the forests, and only women and children remained in the village.

During the following three months, the rioters robbed the property of the entire community. The harvest, animals, and seeds for sowing were transferred to the neighboring villages. We wandered around in the forests. When we returned home for a short while to pick fruits from our fruit trees, the gang members came and drove us back into the forests.

All of us fell sick, but we could not lie down even for one day and did not receive any medical treatment.

*[Page 259]*

When we recovered, we dressed like peasants and were hired to work in the fields of the nearby villages. Some short while later, we moved to the city. When the regime changed and the "Reds" took over, my father's murderer was arrested. My mother was requested to testify in his trial. The court messenger came to us on Shabbat, and my mother, who feared testifying, did not want to desecrate Shabbat. However, the Rabbi of the town of Lityn demanded that she should gather her courage, and he allowed her to travel on Shabbat. The murderer was executed by shooting in the courtyard following her testimony.

Many gentiles tried to benefit from our ruin. A policeman (*gorrodovoy*) in Lityn offered us to come and live with him. He offered his help in bringing the Passover dishes from our attic. When Mother arrived at the house, several rioters, "showed up by chance," and tried to injure her. She was saved because one of the rioter's horses went wild. Several days later, the *gorodovoy* brought Mother several pictures he happened to "find" in our house when he went to take our property, as if with our permission.

My sister and I decided to leave that country. I joined a group organized in Lityn, which planned to make *Aliyah* to Eretz Israel. This was the "Sixth Group" of the HeKhalutz from Ukraine. Many years later, I found out that one of my sisters returned and resettled in Kil'yanovka, which turned into a Soviet "kolkhoz." She resided there until the Nazis annihilated Ukrainian Jewry.

**Breina Likhtman** (Jerusalem)

*[Page 260]*

# Novo-Poltavka

## (Novopoltavka, Ukraine)

### 47°33' 32°30'

### Yehoshua Medem (Binyamina), Rakhel Yehudai (Nahalal)

**Translated by** Moshe Kutten

**Edited by** Yocheved Klausner

My native colony, Novo-Poltavka, was set apart by its fertile soil. The agriculture in it was homogenous, and the main crops were grains of various types. During the First World War, a few vineyards were planted, which prospered and became a very profitable sector. Growing cows for milk played an important role in the colony's economy. It did not require too much work since during most of the days of the year the cows would pasture in the colony's fields. However, the main sector was the cultivation of field crops, which provided the main source of sustenance for the farmer family, albeit scarcely.

In 1921, a drought prevailed throughout Ukraine and hit many families among us as well. It was a usual scene to see people swollen from hunger or corpses on the ground in the train station, public places, or the street. I get the chills, even today when I recall the horrific scenes during that period of hunger. It is difficult to believe that we used to pass apathetically near the corpse of a person. I do recall a scene I saw once when children played over a dead body, and a short distance away, the parents of those children sat waiting for the train and did not even notice. The robbery and the looting during the period of the Civil War resulted in the neglect the agriculture. The movements of the various armies and all sorts of gangs were enabled by the enlistment or kidnapping of the farmers along with their carts and horses, who were forced to transport soldiers without any consideration of the working seasons or any other factors. Those who did not own horses were happy.

On one of the Shabbats, the "White" armies raided the colony and collected wagons for transporting their people southward as part of their retreat. Due to the sanctity of the Shabbat, my father could not go, and I went instead. I was just a 14-year-old boy. For some reason, the journey did not take place that day, however, the cart drivers were not released and we were forced to spend the night with the army in every house or warehouse they happened to find. Upon the end of Shabbat, my father came to replace me and sent me home. During the night, the retreating White Army captured four scouts of the Red Army, and my father was tasked to transport the captives with a guard of riding soldiers behind him. The moment the convoy left the colony, the guards decided to kill the captured while they were still sitting on the wagon with my father. Only by a miracle, my father was not hurt along with the prisoners. The wagon was filled with blood. One of the murderers jumped on the wagon, threw out the bodies, and sent my father home, still stained with blood and pieces of bones and flesh stuck in his beard. We lived under the impression of that nightmare for a long time.

*[Page 261]*

A large library containing Yiddish, Hebrew, and Russian books was located in the colony. There was also a drama club. From time to time, they would organize literature debates on various subjects. The cultural activities were mainly organized by the youth, who were mostly Zionist. During the years following the Revolution, the youth split. One part joined the Communist camp, convinced that the *Yevsektzia* [Jewish communist section] would solve the Jewish problem. Another part remained in the Socialist Zionism movement (S" Z) and went underground.

The Komsomol people began to follow us, and there were imprisonments from time to time. The Communist youths began to seize positions of authority in the colony. However, with their anti-religion propaganda, they provoked hatred among the entire population. Our life became harder and harder. Due to the control by the authorities, we were forced to meet in hideouts, sometimes as though strolling in the street. Members were arrested and the Zionist activity was strangled.

During the Civil War, death was lurking at every step and turn, not necessarily from the warring armies but at the hands of all sorts of robbers and murderers. The Ukrainians in the area took advantage of every opportunity to rob and loot from the Jewish farmers. The youth of the colony organized itself for self–defense. We would go around in the streets to guard the properties, and we managed to prevent several robbery attempts. In the fall of 1919, when robbers appeared in the colony robbing and raping, the youth, who were outnumbered, came out with weapons in their hands to drive the rioters away. That was when the big disaster occurred: the robbers, members of the Makhno gang, called for enforcement. During the following several hours, 132 of the colony residents were murdered, and the gang continued to riot for an additional week, and without any hindrance, robbed, raped, and destroyed everything they got hold of. The villagers of the neighboring villages also did not sit idle, and many of them came to the colony to join the looting. The victims were not just among the warring youths. The rioters also killed the elderly and women. They simply extracted people from their hideouts and killed them for their enjoyment. They positioned people standing with their faces to a wall in a long row and killed them one after the other.

When things calmed down a bit, the rioters gathered some of the colony elders and forced them to collect the bodies and bury them in pits at the edge of the colony. My father was among the gravediggers. It was horrible to hear from him the shocking descriptions of the scenes the gravediggers encountered. Bodies were discovered in hideouts, and killed in sadistic ways. The most horrible story was about a man who was found alive among the row of people killed at the wall. It turned out that the bullet did not pierce his heart and the youth just fell down wounded. However, he did not show any sign of life, otherwise, they would have not spared him. That was how he lay down until the gravediggers came to collect the body. The gravediggers did not inform the gang about the person who was found alive among the dead, for fear of the murderers who followed and urged them to hurry up.

They loaded the youth on the wagon above the rest of the bodies. At the grave, they laid him

*[Page 262]*

down on the side and after they unloaded the rest of the dead off the wagon, they used the opportunity when the murderers went to drink water, loaded him up back onto the wagon, and covered him with straw. When they went back to load up the wagon again, they managed to leave him in one of the nearby houses. The youth survived, and the miracle of his survival was later a subject of discussion in the colony.

The colony was destroyed and robbed. People looked after their relatives to find out who survived. Workers who came to gather the harvest, several weeks after the pogrom, found the last of the murdered people in a cornfield.

These events changed the face of the colony. Agriculture was neglected, and people held onto every type of occupation to sustain themselves. During the following years, people sold their estates and inventory and moved to the city and the colony began to lose its Jewish character.

**Yehoshua Medem** (Binyamina)

# A memorial candle for my mother *z"l*

When I come to recall memories of my colony Novo-Poltavka, I cannot detach myself from my dearest memory – the image of my late mother.

My mother, Khana Yankelevitz, was a native of a colony in southern Ukraine, second generation to Jewish agriculturalists. I was proud of my mother who excelled in singing and doing every type of work at home and in the field. I did wonder about the fact that she was drawn to Zionist preachers in the synagogue. I considered them to be total bums, and it was strange for me to see her lodging and taking care of them. My grandfather who was somewhat pious, was a lover of Zion and agreed to teach his daughter in a *"kheder"* along with the boys. That was where she received her initial knowledge of the Torah, and she worked all of her life to expand that knowledge at every opportunity. She would improve her knowledge of Hebrew during the days after birth. When she lay in bed, she occupied herself with learning Hebrew grammar. She also copied writings from books.

A few years before the break of the First War, the officials of the JCA [Jewish Colonization Organization] tried to convince the farmers of Novo-Poltavka (near which the agricultural school that was founded by the JCA was located) to plant

[Page 263]

vineyards under the guidance of their experts. A stormy argument commenced between my parents: My father supported the planting, but Mother claimed that Jews do not plant vineyards in the diaspora.

In 1915, her elder son was recruited into the army, and my father passed away two years later. My mother was left alone with seven children at the relatively young age of 40.

We had six horses in the stable ready for work, but there was nobody who could climb the sowing machine and go out to the field. My mother did not hesitate and went out to the field to sow, an act that was considered extraordinary. In 1918, my brother was released from the army, and my mother's situation improved. She kept smiling to herself and quietly enjoyed seeing him taking the heavy load of the farm on his shoulder.

She then decided to liquidate the farm and make *Aliyah* to Eretz Israel. The news about the Balfour Declaration reached our corner, and the handful of the Zionists in our colony dreamt and sailed on the wings of their imagination. However, the Bolshevist Revolution and the Civil War, which flooded Russia with blood and horror, reached us as well.

It was the latest part of the summer of 1919. We were busy transporting the harvest from the field and piling the heaps in the yards when a company of riders entered the village at dusk and demanded animal feed and money. Worries ensued. The galloping of horses could be heard from the street in the center of the village. We stood with Mother at the gate, alert and tense. Her face was calm, but she wore a decisive expression. In the morning, rumors started to spread about raping girls and looting property. Groups of people stood in the street, pale and confused from the night's lack of sleep. My mother approached them suddenly, with an awful expression on her face: "I am ashamed!" she yelled: "They are raping our Jewish girls, and you keep silent! There are some guns in the village, take the weapons and drive away the scoundrels." She quickly went to the barn, brought my brother's weapon (every soldier returning from the army brought his gun with him), and put the bullet belt on him with her own hands: "You go my son, and may G–d of Zion be with you." The horsemen retreated from the village. leaving two dead men behind them. In the meantime, it was found out that in the nearby town, thousands of armed Makhno gang members were staying and our young defenders had only 18 guns and a limited amount of ammunition.

At noon on that day, the colony was flooded by blood-thirsty rioters. 150 of the village residents were killed, small children among them also. Mother found out, in the evening, that they murdered her father (they found him working near the sowing machine) and my younger brother. I never saw my brother again, but my heart was beating between hope and desperation.

I went along with my mother to fetch *Savta*. We found her at the body of my murdered grandfather with half of her body paralyzed. My mother did not cry, even during the next day, when she found her son in the pile of the murdered, who were brought to a ditch near the river where they were buried. She kissed his eyes, took his short coat from him, and walked slowly home. During the same night, my mother left the smaller children and *Savta* with me, took a basket of bread and a jug of water, and sneaked out of the house. She walked around the harvest heaps, during the entire night, under which

[Page 264]

the surviving men hid. She would kneel, hand them water and a piece of bread, and continue to the next heap, trying to sneak in the heaps' shadows.

In the streets, the rioters galloped with drawn swords, looking for more victims. During one of the nights, we sat down on the floor in the house corridor, along with girls aged 14-15 years, who became orphans just yesterday and were staying with us. A small lamp flickered on the floor while Mother stood alert at the window. Steps approached, and she went out to the nearby storage room and came back with an ax. Without looking at her, I knew of her intention. "If there are not many of them, we will finish them here," she whispered. Her frozen face expressed a total determination. "Let me die with the Philistines!" [Judges 16:30], she said repeatedly stroking her youngest son's head.

Two years later, I planned to make illegal *Aliyah*, which involved risks. I was afraid of the moment I would have to tell Mother about it. My family members seemed to me so lonely and abandoned, facing hunger and pogroms along with the rest of the villagers. I was surprised when my mother answered me that "one must make *Aliyah* in any way possible and the risk of dying exists at home too."

Only five years after I left, I was able to bring Mother and my three younger brothers to Eretz Israel (my elder brother and sister made *Aliyah* as pioneers before me). She sold her vineyard and farm for pennies.

Her life-long dream and wish to be in the chosen–land was finally fulfilled. She looked at Mount Carmel and Jezreel Valley with childish enthusiasm. She knew these places well from the holy scripts and the Weekly Torah Portion.

Our village – Nahalal, was in its initial phase of construction. The size of the farm, the methods of cultivation, and the farm equipment were primitive compared to what we had in Novo-Poltavka, however, in her eyes, the fields of Nahalal were superior to the wide crop fields of her native village. "And the climate – this is really a gift from G–d," she said. "It is not required to bury the vines in the winter and uncover them in the spring. It is also not required to turn over the piles of crops in the field and dry them up after the rain."

Life was not kind to Mother when she lived in Israel, either. She encountered a difficult crisis, which depressed her greatly, upon the death of her 24-year-old son. She moved to live near her two other sons in Rekhovot, where they both had found a job. From there, she used to write us letters filled with tenderness and love, written in oratorical Hebrew, imbued with the smells of the Bible, without paying attention to the grammar rules.

When she found out that we were paid a certain fee for hosting a girl from the Youth *Aliyah* [the organization that rescued Jewish children during and after the Holocaust] she wrote to us: "Shame on you for getting paid for that. I am asking you stop doing it, and with that (doing what she was asking us to do) you would fulfill two commandments at once: The commandment of "honoring one's mother and father," and the commandment of "Love the weak and the foreigner." When we notified her that the committee that dealt with that matter on behalf of the Jewish Agency

*[Page 265]*

objected to hosting youths for free, she responded: "If you are forced to receive a fee, you ought to deposit it in a bank under the girl's name, and you should not receive money for sustaining a Jewish girl who came from the diaspora."

With these words, I have lit a candle in memory of my mother. How meager and pale this light is compared to the lights that illuminated her soul!

Today, from a distance of time and place, my colony seems to me as if illuminated by bright lights, like any memory connected to one's childhood and youth, although I did not think about it that way at the time. It is fair to say that my heart was not too attached to it then, since from a very young age I looked at my residency there as temporary. Now, that nothing survived it, the colony and its way of life were illuminated by another light – calm and sad.

The colony of Novo-Poltavka was located on a wide and infinite plain. The colony was big (300 families) and bustling with life. Sturdy and self–assured Jews worked and lived there, grew sons and daughters, and celebrated Shabbats and holidays tastefully and gracefully. They talked about the Messiah as if he was already standing behind their wall. Most of them were occupied in agriculture, but some added craftsmanship or trade in grain. The number of houses for each family depended on the ability of the head of the household; however, the yards, which were all slated for the threshing and for arranging the straw and the hay, in preparation for the winter, did not differ from each other.

During the summer and the winter, we used to water the horses and the cows from the lake that crossed the colony, while we would haul home the drinking water by barrels from the well located near the JCA school farm, about 6 *verstas* [about 4 miles] from the village.

Acacia and cherry trees, and here and there some roses grew near the houses. One summer day is rising clearly in my memory. My mother wakes me up at the appearance of the first light ray. The yard is already bustling. The horses are harnessed to a wagon loaded with water, food for the people, and work tools. We are leaving for the whole week. The fields are far and it does not pay to waste time traveling home every day just to sleep.

The harvester was named "*Lobo–Greika*" (forehead warmer) because of the hard work in unloading the harvested crop from it with a pitchfork. They would harness one pair of horses to that harvester, and one of the brothers would leave with it first. They would tie a cow to the wagon to ensure that there would be enough milk for the dinner's millet. We would leave on Sunday and return on Friday at noon – being at the young age of 13 years then, I was already considered a full-fledged member of the girl team who would pile the crop in the field.

Following a trip of close to one hour (we would travel slowly because of the water barrel and the cow which was tied behind), we would arrive at the field. Father would assign the workers the various tasks without raising his voice. Everybody obeyed him. I recall a burning hot mid-day hour when the harvester was humming, and the urging calls to the horses to hurry them up could be heard coming, especially from the edge of the furrow. My father's calls from the distance could be heard:

[Page 266]

"Don't leave any unplowed corners, I recall working while half running, out of my wish to challenge the Ukrainian worker, leaving her often behind. Until today, I feel something glittering in me when I remember that competition.

During the same summer, something happened that could have ended very badly. At the end of one scorching day, my father decided to send somebody home to fetch some food products we ran out of. Since they took pity on the horses who worked the whole day, they harnessed a pair of two-year-old foals who were exempt from the harvester due to their age. I accepted the mission gladly, as I was looking forward to traveling and sleeping at home, receiving ripe cherries from Mother, and returning the next morning with the food that Mother had generously provided. Sunset time was approaching when I mounted the wagon

(Father warned me not to race the horses). Everything went well at the beginning but when I approached and had to cross the railroad tracks, the horses suddenly got scared and started to gallop madly. I pulled on the reins with all my might since I knew the train was approaching. I was engulfed with despair until a thought came to my head (until today, I really do not know how I came to that idea), and with a sudden pull, I turned the wagon towards a field of tall rye sheaves. The horses' gallop was stopped when their legs were snarled with the roping tangle. When I went down to check the rein, I realized that the bridle had fallen off one of the horses' mouths.

Most of the youths, except a few who went out to study in the city, did not develop an exceptional career. They continued to work on the farm and occupied themselves with taming and racing horses. Some were singing in the chorus during the summer nights.

Upon the break of the Revolution, the subsequent Civil War, the pogroms in the Jewish communities, and all of the despair that accompanied that dark period, I made the decision to make *Aliyah* to Eretz Israel. I made that decision even though my heart hurt for leaving that Valley of Tears and immigrating to a land that seemed from afar wrapped in splendor and magic.

I know that my colony and the adjacent agricultural school are worthy of my lengthy descriptions. Hundreds of youths, natives of the southern Russian colonies, studied in the school founded by the JCA. Most of its principals had an affinity to Zionism. That school brought visits of notables from Israel, for whom the revival of the Hebrew language and working the land were the whole life substance.

I recall the visit by comrade Tzvi Yehuda [Rabbi Tzvi Yehuda Kook, leader of Religious Zionism] to our house. He adorned a beard and was dressed with peasants' fur. I listened to his talk with Mother, telling her about Eretz Israel. His words inspired me and nourished my imagination for many days. I have already nurtured the idea of making *Aliyah* by then. I also recall the visit of the author Ya'akov Rabinowitz *z"l*, who later visited our house in Nahalal. In that later visit, he innocently told me a story about his visit to Novo-Poltavlka when, on one of the mornings, he strolled in the village and turned to the vineyard where… and I just continued his story: "I met a girl, about 12 years old whom I talked Hebrew with…"

Here I told my memories about the colony where I spent my childhood and where three generations preceded me.

**Rakhel Yehudai** (Nahalal)

*[Page 267]*

# Nahar-Tov HaGdola [Greater Nahar-Tov]

## (Nagartava, Ukraine)

### 47°18' 32°51'

## by Israel Betzer, Yehudit Guzman, Nesya Avidov, Khaia Berkin, Atara and Nakhman Parag, Yehoshua Dukhin, A. Gurevitz, Leah Palkov-Lev, Itah Hurvitz, Moshe Yevzori-Yevzorikhin, Yehudit Simkhoni and Yehuda Yevzori

### Translated by Moshe Kutten

### Edited by Yocheved Klausner

In a narrow valley, about 300-400 meters from a bald, rocky, and steep mountain, which served as a source for building stones, a small spring gushes its water into the Wysun River. In the winter, the water is rising up to a width of 15-20 meters and then freezes. In the spring, during the days of the snowmelt, the river flows rowdily and sweeps everything in its way.

The authorities brought Jewish settlers, the founders of the colony, to the southern bank of the river. A large Christian village, by the name of Pasad Brezneguvate, was located on the opposite side of the river. Another Christian village, located near the river, was called Dobro, named after the spring, and the Jewish colony was called Nahar Tov HaGdola [The Greater Nahar Tov, literally The Greater Good River].

The spring was located southwest of the colony, within its land, and only the members of the colony drew water from it. Further away from that, on the stream's edge, behind the main street of the colony, opposite the large synagogue, another stream whose water was good for drinking and laundry, ran; however, its banks were very steep, and it was not possible to approach it with a wagon. Therefore, only the members of the families who lived on the street close to the spring and who could not travel with a wagon to the big spring drew water from it in pails, which they carried on their shoulders, with a yoke.

During the 1890s, the days of the colony's third generation, all the farmers' yards had wells, which the farmers had dug for themselves, with a depth of 6-8 meters. The water in these wells was not good for drinking, therefore all of the farmers continued to haul water for drinking and laundry from the spring, and the water from the wells was only used for the needs of the farm — watering the horses and the cows, washing the dishes and similar uses.

At the end of 1904, when I left the colony, the farmers still hauled drinking water from the big spring and with a yoke on their shoulders from the other spring.

A hundred families founded the colony; each received 40 *disiyatins* of land (one *disiyatin* – 12 *dunams* [or 2.7 acres]). The settlers were not farmers by birth, and many did not even wish to become farmers. The Czar's government was the one that wanted to make them and other Jews into a productive element of society. The compulsory army service and the expulsion from the cities drove these Jews away from their cities and towns to the remote and desolate southern prairies, where the Czar's government provided them with large plots and supported them with some meager sums. On the other hand, the government forbade them from engaging in trade or other occupations and allowed them only to work in occupations related to agriculture, such as construction, carpentry, or blacksmithing. The adaptation of the settlers to the

*[Page 268]*

life of working the land was taxing, and their economic state was dreadful. They were not able to cultivate all of the areas allocated to them and therefore did not have enough sustenance to pay even the minimal taxes for the land. The land was leased to them and their descendants permanently, without allowing them the right to sell or bestow it to anybody, including relatives whose surname was different from theirs. A farmer who had only daughters could bequeath the land to one of his sons-in-law with the government's permission.

During the first generation of settlers, a quarter of the colony's area, which was the farthest from the colony, was dedicated as an "area available for leasing" (*ovruchnoy uchastok*). That area was leased, by public auction according to the law, to the big estate owners for a period of five years, which enabled the settlers-farmers to pay the land taxes on the leased land and on the land they cultivated by themselves. During the first 25 years, ten families left Nahar-Tov, returned to the city, and found sustenance there, some in trade and some in tailoring or similar crafts. The government did not expropriate the ten units (300 *disiyatins*) but left it as public land, which was leased for two or three years in a public auction, with a full right of the families who had left, or their sons, to return, receive back the land and cultivate it.

I recall that one day during the year 1900-1901, a young man about 25-28 years old, appeared in Nahar-Tov. He was the grandson of one of the farmers who left the colony. The young man came from Odesa or Nikolayev [Mykolaiv] and demanded his grandfather's *ochastok* (land unit). The process of transferring the land to him did not take long and three to four months later, the young man brought his family and started cultivating the land. He was absorbed nicely into the colony. In another case, a Jewish person, about 45 years old, has married a good homemaker and had two daughters, one of whom was at marriage age, and another was a mature girl, both working as seamstresses in the city. The family was very pleasant and wished to return to their ancestors' land. They rented a temporary apartment in Nahar-Tov and started the formal process of getting the land. However, the process took too long, and in the end, they did not achieve what they wished for and, heartbroken, they had to return to the city.

During the days of the second generation, some of the settlers rose to a level where they could compete in the public auction and win a leased area for five years. After leasing a plot, the area was never taken away from them and their descendants, according to a new arrangement of dividing the colony's land, which we called an "agrarian reform."

At the end of the 19th century and the beginning of the 20th century, a young workforce was added to the colony – the members of the third generation who were already adapted to working the land. At that time, some farmers managed to consolidate their farms, particularly those who had families with many children who added many available working hands to the farm. The problem was that some of these families did not have sufficient land. At the same time, many settlers still did not adapt to the life of working the land,

*[Page 269]*

and lived in poverty and privation. Among them were those whose father was the only son who received the whole unit of land (30 *disiyatins*) from his father, and they were also the only sons to their father who owned the whole unit. These people did not establish a farm and owned only a wagon and a pair of wretched horses, and they worked in all sorts of jobs related to wagon hauling. They leased their fields to a Jewish or gentile farmer from a neighboring village for a portion of the harvest (1/3 or 2/5 of the harvest). Because of that situation, Jews haters criticized the settlers and demanded that the authorities confiscate the land from any Jewish settler who did not cultivate his field and hand it over to landless Pravoslav Christian farmers. I recall that in the winter of 1890-91, a delegation consisting of two officials nominated on behalf of the authorities came to inspect the farmers' yards. They passed from one yard to the other to inspect the agricultural tools. They found organized farms, with more agricultural tools than in many of the farms of the neighboring Christian village. Although they did find some poor farms, the colony passed the inspection. During the time the delegation passed from one yard to another to inspect the agricultural tools and look at the structure of the farms, a diligent group of youths was active behind the yards and supplied the needed tools to yards that lacked them.

The inspection awoke some gloomy thoughts and fears among the farmers who worried about the fate of the colony and its future. It was decided by the general assembly of the colony, that even farmers who lacked means should make the effort to cultivate their land by themselves and those who could not do it would only be allowed to lease their fields to members of the colony. That decision raised the anger of the Christian farmers from the neighboring village, who already cultivated many land areas in Nahar-Tov. One of them said: "If I meet the head of the colony's committee in the fields, I would take out his intestines with a pitchfork." The word got out to the head of the colony's committee, and he did not wait for long and showed up at that man's field while the man was piling his harvested crop. He entered into a friendly discussion with him, as a long-time friend and acquaintance, and said: "I heard that you are angry about our decision concerning the leasing of land in Nahar Tov, and I would like to talk to you about it, perhaps you would change your mind. You are, after all, a farmer who sustains himself by working the land. If you do not have land, you can lease land by paying for it. There are landless people among us as well. However, as Jews, the law forbids us from leasing land outside of our colony. We are not allowed to lease from the public land of other Jewish colonies, such as Sdeh-Menukha, Bobrovy-Kut, or Yefeh-Nahar either. You are allowed the lease lands there, but we are forbidden from doing that. What is your opinion about that? Who should have a priority on leasing available land in Nahar-Tov, you or us?" The gentile was persuaded and he kept it in his heart. During May-June of 1889, when pogroms erupted against the Jews, that gentile came to the head of the committee and told him: "They would not touch your house. I would come to keep guard."

During the first week of June 1889, rumors were spread that pogroms would take place against the Jews in Pasad Berzneguvate where Jewish merchants competed with Christian ones.

*[Page 270]*

The Christian merchants openly incited the villagers to pogroms against the Jewish merchants in Berezneguvate and Nahar-Tov. As usual, there was nobody around to turn to for help. The police minister (*pristav*) disappeared. During Friday, the market day in Berzeneguvate, when the farmers from the neighboring villages passed through the main street of the colony in wagons and on foot on their way to the market, they gazed into the houses and yards as if saying: "We will visit you today." As early as before noon, groups of 4-5 farmers from the neighboring village started to barge into the colony through the bridge, pretending to be drunk and asked to give them liquor. The head of the colony's committee sent them back, every time, by convincing and preaching to them to behave like good neighbors.

During the afternoon, crowds of the village people began to cover the steep mountain across the river opposite the colony. They were dressed in holiday clothing like on Sunday. From the mountain, one could see everything happening in the street and yards of the colony like on the observer's palm of the hand. The colony members realized that they would not be able to resist the rowdy crowd without the assistance of the authority. They decided to act according to the phrase: "…and ye shall watch yourselves…" [Deuteronomy 4:15]. The entire colony flocked to the yard of the "popuchislestvo" (the administrative office of the colonies) near the fruit trees orchard, where they found shelter. The colony emptied before dusk. The families of Rebosnikov and Samuelov escaped to a farm about 12 kilometers away from the colony. They found a shelter in a hut and hid there through Friday night and Shabbat. Only the head of the colony's committee remained in the colony to guard the street from his yard. Upon sunset, the crowd began to glide down the mountain and storm into the colony like ants. The head of the committee came down to the edge of his plot and fired a shot at the crowd, which was only armed with primitive hacking tools. When the crowd heard the shot, they retreated to their village. As the head of the committee was coming out to the street from his yard, the priest just happened to show up in front of him, riding on a carriage, and asked excitedly: "Who fired a shot? This angers the crowd." However, the head of the committee was not obliged to confess to the priest… They each returned to their place, the priest to his crowd of believers and the head of the committee to his community.

Upon dark, a pogrom started against the Jewish products and grocery stores in the Christian village. The rioters broke the steel doors and the windows, looted products and grocery items, and loaded sacks and packages of goods on wagons. Whatever they did not take, they trampled with their feet and burned inside the shops and in the streets. They hid the looted goods in hideouts in the village, neighboring quarry, and neighboring villages. The noise of the crowd and the movement of the wagons in the village could be heard from far away until a very late hour of the night. Later on, they broke through to the colony. They did it carefully and not noisily but executed their pogrom faithfully. They broke windows and doors in all of the houses, tore pillows and feather covers, and robbed things that they were interested in. However, they did not take out much property from the farmers' houses and did not even break one window at the house of the head of the committee.

At midnight, when quiet descended, several Jewish farmers came out to visit the yards and houses.

*[Page 271]*

The farmers from the neighboring villages gathered on Shabbat morning, intoxicated by their success from the night before. When they saw that the authorities did not intervene, they attempted to attack the colony of Romanovka, which was located about 15 kilometers away from Nahar-Tov, and being surrounded by Christian villages was isolated. After a week of fear, the Jews in Romanovka gathered all in the synagogue, ready for any calamity. When they sensed that the crowd was approaching, they all went outside of the colony, including the children and the elderly, to face the arriving rioters. They did not fear desecrating the Shabbat, basing their action on the verse [Psalms (119:126):" It is time to work for the Lord, for your law has been broken" [It is time to act when the wicked are breaking the commandments]. They came out with sticks, pitchforks, firefighting equipment, and other tools that could cause harm, and taught the gentiles a lesson. Ashamed, the villagers retreated from the "*Zhids*" and returned to their village empty-handed, with broken legs, injured heads, and bloody faces, injuries which the Jews of Romanovka managed to inflict. After that Shabbat, the government woke up and began to investigate what the villagers caused to the area's Jews. The officials went from one village to the other, gathered public assemblies, and lectured to the rioters. The police wrote some reports, and with that, they closed the book.

Following the pogroms, the Jewish merchants from Berzneguvate and members of Nahar-Tov organized and hired two of the most famous Jewish lawyers in Russia (one of them was the famous lawyer Gruzenberg [who appeared in the Beilis trial) and sued the rioters and the Christian merchants, who incited to riots. The trial was held in Nikolayev [Mykolaiv]and its echoes reached the Jewish and Russian newspapers. Eachinciter was sentenced to 20 months in jail with hard work. The Jews were fortunate to see them jailed and head-shaven. The rioters were sentenced to one-year imprisonment and hard work.

The colony had a committee elected by the general assembly, and its office was officially called the "*prikaz*" [command in Russian]. The colony's secretary and the committee janitor were located there. The janitor was available to perform all sorts of errands: sending messages, announcements, or warnings to the farmers, calling for a gathering, performing any public work, and the like. The "*Schultz*" (the head of the committee), was also sitting in his office every day, if he was not busy doing other public work. During the general assembly, the committee members would bring up and explain issues and sometimes would bring forward a proposal. Every discussion in the general assembly was followed by a vote (done by raising hands), the secretary would read the minutes and the results of the vote and the assembly had to approve the proposal with a signature by everyone, without any exception, even those who voted against it. The "*Schultz*" would approve the resolution with his signature and so would the members of the committee.

The central management of all the colonies nominated regional officials, one official for each of the 4-5 colonies. Their role was similar to the role of a social counselor. The official responsible for our region was a man by the name of Kessler, a tall man of about forty years of age, with a dignified appearance and everybody respected him. His permanent residence was

*[Page 272]*

in the colony of Yefeh-Nahar. He appeared in every colony in the region under his responsibility several times a year to see if things were conducted properly, check the minutes of the committee meetings and those of the general assembly, and investigate whether the resolutions had been carried out.

\*

At the end of the 19th century, the JCA organization [Jewish Colonization Association] started to take interest in the Jewish colonies in Kherson and Yekaterinolsav and provided loans with low interest for two or three years to people who lacked the means. Agronomists and officials began to visit the colonies on behalf of JCA. I remember the names of Halperin, Mirkin, and Loversky (who later became the principal of the agricultural school established in the colony of Novo-Poltavka). Under JCA's initiative and help, trial fields for new crops were allocated, such as soy and corn for seeds. The fields produced good harvests, and the farmers began to sow the seeds in their own fields. JCA also introduced fruit-tree orchards and vineyards. However, the fundamental problem of lack of land remained unsolved.

After many discussions in local gatherings within the colonies and in regional conferences, the colonies decided to demand from the government, that all of the "lands for lease" and public lands, which were considered temporary "leased lands" be returned to the colonies. They requested that the ownership of farmers who cultivated their land (three generations) be revoked and the land be reallocated among the farmers according to the number of males in each family. The colony people turned to the central management of the colonies situated in Nahar-Tov and to General Simov, who was the patron of the colonies on behalf of the government and who guarded their interests (in the colonies, he was named "the loyal devoted father of the colonies"). According to the law, the colonies belonged to the Interior Ministry. General Simov recommended to the ministry to accept a delegation from the colonies, which would request to change the allocation of the land among the farmers. The positive response from the interior ministry was swift, and a three-member delegation, two of whom were residents of Nahar-Tov and one from the colony of Novo-Poltavka, was elected.

The delegation traveled to St. Petersburg and stayed there for 8-10 days. They found a sympathetic audience in the interior ministry and returned home with the good news that the ministry approved the entire plan. A group of 9-11 members headed by a surveyor went out to all the colonies, as early as the same summer (1902) and completed the entire division (parceling) in 10-12 days, according to maps prepared in advance. I was fortunate to be a member

[Page 273]

of the group in Nahar-Tov. As an 18-year-old, I was the youngest in the group, the rest of the members were all 30-35 years old. This was a pioneering group, which ushered in a new period in the life of the colony. Following that group, another committee, consisting of people from among the community elders was elected. These elders knew very well every inch of the land. That committee conducted many meetings. It toured and substantially checked the new parcels (plots) and adjusted the allocation based on quality, topographic location, distance from the house, the roads that lead to the fields, and similar factors.

The colony breathed a sigh of relief when, as part of this plan, it received an additional allocation of 25% of its land. Every male son (even as young as one day old), was allocated a private plot of 3 ¼ - 3 ½ *disiyatin* as a permanent lease to him and his descendants.

Not in every colony, the allocation was equal since the ratio between the male population and the available area was different. Many farms, particularly of those families that had many sons, developed nicely after the parceling, and their owners were satisfied. However, that solution was not a radical solution for those families who lacked sufficient land. Many farmers had to look for a side income. Despite that, there was no mass influx from the villages to the city. People knew that those people who had left the colonies during the 60-70 years since they were founded, found neither happiness nor wealth in the city. Most of them were forgotten, except two, whom the second and the third generations knew very well, although they did not have the chance to see them face to face. These two were the poets Shimon Frugg from the colony of Bobrovy-Kut and M. Tz. Maneh from Nahar-Tov HaGdola who wrote the following poem at the time:

> "Where are you, where are you - the holy land
> My spirit is yearning for you
> If only you and me together
> Come to life again."

\*

At the end of 1904, when the Russia-Japan war broke out, and all of the young men were recruited to the front at Port Arthur, Jewish immigration to Argentina began. According to the agreement with JCA, the Russian government allowed Jewish families to immigrate to Argentina and settle on JCA's land there. They even allowed families whose sons were of the age of enlistment to leave, provided they notified the authorities about their wish to immigrate during May of that year, half a year before the date of enlistment. They were allowed to leave Russia with their families, forfeiting their right to ever return. During that year, several families left the colonies of Nahar-Tov, Romanovka, Dubrovna, and Novo-Poltavka to settle in

Argentina on JCA land. That was just the first group. In later years (1905-1907) many additional families from the colonies left to settle in Argentina.

*[Page 274]*

During 1953 – 1954, I visited Argentina to see my relatives and the members of the colonies who immigrated there 48-49 years before. I found that only a few elderly people were still alive. Their children and grandchildren left the settlements and moved to cities and towns, where they worked in trade, craftsmanship, textile factories and printing houses, construction materials, and various other professions. The Zionist activists were mostly descendants of members of the JCA colonies. Many of the grandchildren of the first Argentina settlers are now in Israel - in the labor movement's settlements, border settlements, and IDF.

Not a long time after that, chaos took hold of Russia – the Revolution, Civil War, robbery and murder by Denikin and Petliura ["Whites" leaders], and later on, the new arrangement, which was introduced by the new authorities. In the Jewish colonies, a new regime was introduced, and a new division between the more affluent farmers (kulaks) and those who were unsettled. The management of the affairs in the colonies was handed over to the poor farmers. The destruction of the colonies began then; the Second World War and Hitler annihilated them entirely. Some of the colonies were not destroyed and only their Jewish residents were murdered.

Recently, I received news from people who immigrated to Israel from Russia who were once residents (not farmers) in the colony of Bobrovy-Kut. When the Nazis conducted the killing of the Jews, they managed to escape from the colony and went through the "Seven Departments of Hell" in greater Russia. They said that they visited Bobrovy-Kut three years before and saw that the colony was settled by Christians. There were there only a few Jewish survivors, who had returned to the colony. They said that they did not know anything about the rest of the colonies and their Jews.

### Israel Betzer (Nahalal)

*[Page 275]*

Like most of the Jewish colonies in Lesser Russia [Ukraine], my native colony, Nahar-Tov, was actually like a chain of colonies – the Old Nahar-Tov, Nahar-Tov HaGdola [Greater Nahar-Tov], and the New Nahar-Tov and they were all called by a single name. This is unlike Sdeh Menukha, which also consisted of a chain of colonies but with different names. Outside the colony, like an extension of the chain, was the Russian village of Berzneguvate, whose population was mixed but was mostly Russian. There were other Russian villages a short distance away, around the Wysun River. There was a positive aspect to the closeness to the Russian rural population – the government built an organized regional hospital opposite the center of Nahar-Tov, which served the entire region population. Large fairs took place three or four times a year, and big markets were held three times a week. There were also several big shops of all kinds in the neighboring Russian village. However, there was also a disadvantage to this closeness, since anti-Semitism erupted from it following every change in the country's atmosphere. I felt that well, almost from my days in the cradle. In 1905, rioters gathered to start a pogrom but were scattered away before they managed to rob much.

The relatives and acquaintances from the neighboring colonies who came to the fairs, the hospital, or big shops were our guests. From discussions we had with them, I knew about the confiscating of leased land from wealthy Jews, murders, barn arsons, and thefts. The topic of self-defense was a major subject of the discussions. A guard would walk around the colony, every night. He would announce his alertness by knocking with a hammer. People in the colony took turns serving as guards.

I recall evenings when friends of my elder brothers and sisters would gather, and one of them would read in Yiddish from the writings of Shalom Aleikhem or Mendeleh Mokher Sfarim. All of the children, young and old listened to the readings with pleasure, open-mouthed, until midnight.

People exchanged whispers about revolutionaries. I recall a young youth, the same age as my brother, who worked as an apprentice for a tailor in the city and whom people were pointing at as a revolutionist. The police, who came to look for him, encircled the house of one of the colony people, a poor and stuttering man, also a tailor, who was far from any revolution affairs. He was imprisoned and was sentenced to four years of hard labor. In the meantime, the suspect himself escaped, leaving no traces.

There was a four-year elementary school in the colony. The students and the teachers were all Jewish and the language of study was Russian. Teaching Torah to the children and youths

*[Page 276]*

took a higher priority over general education. Most of the children in the colony studied in a "*kheder*." In the neighboring village, there was also a four-year municipal school, where most of the children were Russians. In a later period, an evening high school was also established there. When I studied there, I felt the neighborhood's hostility. Young children threw rocks at me and accompanied me with the calls – "*Zhidovka.*" When the Revolution erupted, the activity of the Zionist movement strengthened and I joined it.

The main agricultural sector in our colony was grain crops. Some of the grain was allocated for house needs during the entire year and for farm animal feed. The rest was sold to merchants at the train station. Side sectors were growing farm horses, cattle, geese, and chickens. The work tools were plows, a sowing machine, and harrows, considered sophisticated during those days. They used horses to move the machines. Sowing of the summer crops started just after Purim. Only men worked in plowing and sowing in the distanced fields; however, there also was plenty of work left for those who remained on the farm. They were busy preparing firewood, repairing structures, re-plastering, and whitewashing the house. In the spring, we sowed summer wheat, rye, oat, corn, flax, and sunflowers, and at the end of the sowing season – watermelons, melons, and cucumbers. Before gathering the summer or the winter crops, we would take out the dried firewood from the barn, clean it, and prepare it for the threshing. The most difficult season was the harvest season when we required many working hands. Everybody went out to the fields, including young hired workers from the neighboring villages.

We had two harvesters on our farm, each harnessed to horses. Two people worked with each harvester, one drove the horses, and the other gathered the harvested crop in small piles. Three or four people followed the harvester and piled the harvested crop into big piles according to the height of the crop stalks. We would leave for the field every week and come back home for Shabbat. One person, riding a wagon with a pair of horses, would bring a barrel of water from the spring and food for the workers every day. We slept in our clothes, on the harvested straw around the wagon, while a primitive tent served as a roof on our heads. We would start the harvest before sunrise and finish after sunset. We cooked dinner inside a big pot and hung on the edge of a wagon's plow shaft. Sometimes, the wind disrupted the cooking and it lasted longer. On these occasions, I would be tired and fall asleep without eating.

The harvest lasted for three weeks. At the end of the harvest, we would immediately assemble the large wagons and begin transporting and threshing the crops. They would wake us up at half past two or three o'clock at night to transport the crop. The field was far away and we had to return with a loaded wagon before breakfast, for the work to progress at a quick pace. The most difficult part of the threshing was separating the grains from the chaff. The wheel of the winnowing machine was operated by hand

*[Page 277]*

and the dust generated was substantial. When the threshing was completed, the fields had to be prepared again for the autumn sowing.

This cycle of the agriculture seasons continued uninterruptedly until the break of the First World War. The men were recruited to the army, and the workload and the grief of the separation weighed down on us. The farm deteriorated continually. Upon the outbreak of the Revolution, the gangs or the government confiscated all of the harvests. I began to think about making *Aliyah* to Eretz Israel by then. My first attempts did not succeed and I was arrested twice. I worked in agricultural Kibbutz training camps in Tel-Khai in Crimea and in Leningrad, before I finally made *Aliyah* in 1929.

We were four sisters who made *Aliyah*, however, not in the same way or at the same time. In Israel, we all turned to the labor settlements, either a kibbutz or a moshav. I participated in the Haganah [Jewish defense paramilitary force during the British mandate in Eretz Israel]. I established a home and a small family. My son is a graduate of the agricultural department at Rekhovot [University]. My four brothers, who stayed in Russia, perished during the war and in the Holocaust.

**Yehudit Guzman (Kfar Avikhail)**

A lot can be written about my native colony – Nahar-Tov in the Kherson Province. However, it is my wish to point to one of the contributions of my native colony to the state of Israel. My large family – father, mother, and nine sons and daughters, was uprooted from its native land, cultivated and loved by four generations, and replanted anew in our motherland. We are proud of the fact that all of us continue the tradition of working the land, in Israel – in Nahalal, Kfar Yehoshua, Kfar Vitkin, and Ein Kharod. We do not have even one city dweller among us. The entire new generation also resides in *moshavim* and *kibbutzim*. The nine sons and daughters of my father's home produced 31 grandchildren and 36 great-grandchildren, and all of them together number as many as the house of Jacob, who went to Egypt.

At the beginning of the 20th century, during my distanced childhood, our situation, like in all other farmers in the Jewish colonies, was very difficult. However, with time, along with the progress of agriculture in general and with the maturing of the family members, the farm developed progressively. We had eight milking cows in the cowshed, and we owned four horses for the field cultivation work. During the winter months – the dead season in the fields – my father and elder brothers went out to work outside the colony. We enlarged the house as the family grew; however, it always remained a village house. Its roof was covered with straw and the floor with clay. Once a week, on the eve of Shabbat, we covered and plastered it with a sticky material.

During the summertime, work was on fire – harvesting and piling, hauling and threshing, separating

*[Page 278]*

between the seeds and the chaff and dust with the winnower, filling up the sacks, hauling them to the nearby city for sale, and grinding the flour. Father and the sons were the main workers in the field; however, we - the girls – helped as well, piling the crops into piles and rotating the winnower. My parents used to pamper me – the elder daughter. When I was a young girl, I liked this pampering, however, when I grew up, I participated in all of the tasks.

The days of the summer were characterized by waking up, eating in a hurry, moving around in the yard, neighing horses when they were leaving, or coming into the yard, dust, and sweat. The winter season brought respite, peace of mind, long and deep sleep, the pleasure of being able to read a book in bed, a gathering of girls and boys on the verge of adolescence while being entertained by jokes and laughter and stories and sometimes. by having one of the group's members read a book aloud. That does not mean that we did not work in the winter. In the wintertime, we still had to feed and milk the cows, bake, do laundry, fix clothing, sew, and do various other works, performed during the cold and the snow. However, the days were shorter and the nights – longer, which allowed for more sleep and rest, reading a book and entertaining together. Sometimes, we used to go out to freshen ourselves in the shining snow, which was creaking under our feet, and play pleasurably.

Our basic education was based on a four-year elementary school. We did possess a strong desire for additional knowledge, to study and widen our horizons. However, the gates to the high schools were closed for us, due to the "numerus clausus" – the law limiting the number of Jewish students. Only the sons and daughters of wealthy people managed somehow, to get into the high schools. The colonies' youths who wished to obtain a high school education had to study as externs. Only when the Revolution started, in 1917, the limitations were removed and many of the youths in the colonies made plans to enroll in the various schools and I wished to study medicine. However, the events that took place disrupted many plans, mine included. The Revolution's storm, which raved with enormous forces, wiped out everything that existed to build a new world.

A group of inspiring youths, organized to make *Aliyah* to Eretz Israel and build there a new life, came to us to receive agricultural training. They lived with the farmers and accompanied them or their sons, who trained them how to plow, sow, and harvest. These young men brought with them a new spirit into the colony. Some of them spoke Hebrew and taught us the language, as well as songs in Hebrew. They infected us with their enthusiasm, and many youths began to feel their place was in Eretz Israel. Being agriculturists from birth it would be easier for us to continue working the land and living a village life in Eretz Israel. We dreamt about being able to build and establish a new Jewish life there.

The girls in the colonies were not engaged in enhancing their appearance. I did not own any ornament or jewelry. My Shabbat shoes were not high-heeled or sharp-nosed and were not made of good leather either. My dress was made from simple material –

*[Page 279]*

with red flowers on a blue background. I was very proud of my shirt, which I embroidered with my own hands during the winter nights.

One day in the summer, I was working in piling up hay, and one of the young pioneers, who came to us for training, worked with me. The sun was hot, and my tanned face was dripping with sweat. I wrapped my hair with a kerchief. My dress – a fading work dress, had a big patch and another small one on the left sleeve. I wore open sandals on my feet. The young man worked vigorously. All of a sudden, he stuck his pitchfork in the hay pile, sipped water from the jar, wiped his sweat with his sleeve, and stood in front of me, reviewing me with a big smile and muttered admirably toward me: "*A sheineh shikseh*" [a nice gentile girl. "*Shikseh*" - a term usually used in a derogatory way, but sometimes with affectionate intent]. My heart was beating with excitement. I was touched by that compliment. My self-confidence about my looks was strengthened.

I deviated from the main story, but this is a typical older woman's weakness – to recall with pleasure and pride any compliment they had heard during their youth.

I will end the way I began – our family lived and worked in the Kherson colony for four or five generations. All of my brothers and sisters continue with the village way of life and work the land here in Israel. I am proud of the fact that my elder son is a member of *Moshav* Nahalal. My younger son is in *Moshav* Nir Banim and my daughter is in Moshav Ganei Yehuda.

**Nesya Avidov** [Nahalal]

I was born in an agricultural colony in Southern Russia, which carried the Hebrew name - "Nahar-Tov." I absorbed the quiet Jewish village way of life from my childhood. However, at the beginning of my youth, I left my village and moved to Kherson, the nearby city. I did not adapt easily to the bustling life in the city. I longed for the village wished to breathe the smell of the fields, and always dreamt of returning to the village life.

When I returned to the village, I met there the lively youths who worked in their farms during the day, and devoted their evenings to activities in the Zionist movement and organized an evening class in Hebrew. Together, we devoted ourselves to producing shows in the new theater, and the revenues were contributed to the JNF (Keren Kayemet Le'Israel). We arranged balls where we sold books from the "Kopecko Bibliotec" [A library for pennies], and JNF stamps. We also sold Zionist Shekels [Zionist organization's membership tax]. We transferred all of our revenues to Dr. Bodenheimer [A prominent Zionist leader, an assistant to Dr. Herzl, and founder of the JNF] in Cologne. The box [The JNF blue collection box] was not absent even from weddings. They would build a big tent in the bride's yard

*[Page 280]*

where the "*klezmers*" [Yiddish for musicians] of Rabbi Yehuda-Leib and his sons, each with his own instrument, along with "Motl *der klezmer*" [Motl the musician] with his fiddle would entertain the crowd. JNF box was the main attraction in the tent.

In July 1914, our family's dream was fulfilled – we made *Aliyah* to Eretz Israel. Only part of the youth in the colonies dared to make *Aliyah*. Many lingered since nobody expected that a world war would break out and put an end to all the dreams.

Who knows what was left today from the colony, which was so dear to all of us.

**Khaya Berkin** (Tel Aviv)

Our first experience in the colony, connected with Eretz Israel occurred when we were 7-8 old. While we were in the classroom, two wagons loaded with belongings, people, and children were observed traveling towards the train station. We were told that the Berkin family was making *Aliyah* to Eretz Israel. The Zionist activity in those days of the beginning of Zionism was concentrated on selling [Zionist] Shekels and stocks of the Colonial Bank [Later Israel's Bank Leumi] and procuring Zionist literature and journals. However, in the spring of 1917 and with the national awakening, part of the youth and some additional older adults organized themselves into an association called "HaTkhia" [The Revival]. During that same year, pioneers from the Ukrainian cities of Kremenchug and greater Kiev, as well as from other places, came to us for the first time to receive agricultural training. They, along with the local Zionists, constituted the nucleus for the local branch of [the Zionist movement of] "HeKhalutz" [The Pioneer]. Among them was the activist - Mikhael Kafri *z"l* who handled the new arrivals and distributed them among the farmers. Not all of the farmers were excited about taking in a "Khalutznik" ["pioneer"], a young man who came directly from a school bench and did not know what work was. Tender girls who had just completed high school or just started their studies at a university also came to us. They tried diligently to become hard workers as well. They all used to gather in the evenings, sing songs about Zion, and weave their dream together about building and settling Eretz Israel.

Families would go out together to thin the corn or weed out the sunflowers. Children excelled in these tasks due to their agility. The youth were also involved in tasks associated with the harvest performed by mechanical harvesters harnessed to three horses. Workers from the gentile village would compliment us: "How nicely these young Jews are working as if they are ours." During the harvest, we would rattle ourselves on wagons to the distanced field, still half asleep. We would catch a bit more of a nap under the rattling of the wheels and the jolting wagons' ladders until we arrived

*[Page 281]*

at the location of the harvest piles. The sun would rise then, and dawn would open our sleepy eyelashes, and the work began. An adult would load the crop and a boy or a girl would arrange it on the top of the wagon. We would leave for the field for the entire week and return home only to bring additional food and water in barrels for the people who stayed in the field. We would all return home only for Shabbat to recover and prepare for another week of work.

The harvest lasted several weeks. During the summer of 1919 or 1920, when gangs were roaming around our area, I would be sent home to bring food for my father and brothers, who were harvesting in the field, located 10 kilometers away from home. I was only a 13 or 14 years old girl at the time. One evening, when the harvesters stopped their chattering noise, we sat by the wagons, and my father *z" \l* went back to fetch something from home and had not returned yet. The meat, which was being stewed for dinner, was hanging above a small fire on a wagon's shaft. My brother Khaim handled the cooking, and we helped him. All of a sudden, we heard shouts, and shots pierced the air. Robbers attacked us. We quickly spilled the soup over the fire and my brother commanded us to hide in the piles of crops, which were scattered around. We did not have any weapons, and my brother Mar'el understood immediately that the robbers intended to rob his beautiful thoroughbred horse. He jumped on the horse, broke his way through, and disappeared towards the colony to call for help. My brother succeeded in tying the legs of the rest of the horses to prevent their theft by the bandits, and we all scattered around the crop piles. Many people from the colony, the police, and my parents who were fearful for our fate, arrived at midnight. They did not find us easily since despite the fear and the excitement, we all fell asleep, exhausted, inside the piles of crops, while lizards and bugs were crawling on our bodies.

During the year of 1922, the persecution of the Zionist movement began, which forced it to go underground. Until then, large groups of pioneers arrived in the colony for agricultural training, and the local Zionist youths organized themselves in a branch of "HeKhalutz." The first group of pioneers left on their way to steal the border and make *Aliyah*. In 1917, during the short period of freedom, the Zionists organized a bonfire for the Lag BaOmer holiday celebration in the colony. This was a beautiful celebration. The schoolchildren chorus, the entire youth, and the colony adults, all waving the national flags, went out on foot and wagons, singing songs of Zion, all the way to the fields. At the artificial lake, about 2 kilometers from the colony, a picnic was arranged. The holiday symbolized embracing the nation's past, longing for a future of national independence, and fulfillment of the Zionist dream. This short period of freedom illuminated the later years when the Zionist movement had to operate underground, along with the suffering and heroism associated with an underground operation – wandering on the roads, stealing borders, imprisonments, and expulsion.

Following the departure of the first generation of pioneers, the second generation's branches of the "HeKhalutz" movement and the "Social Zionists" were established by the brothers and sisters of those who left. Many who joined the Komsomol [communist youths] followed the youths suspected of being Zionist with apprehension and watched our every step.

*[Page 282]*

It happened during the year of 1925. We were collecting contributions among the movement's supporters for prisoners and exiled Zionists. I found out that my imprisonment was nearing and traveled to another colony for some time to avoid arrest. I returned at one point and stayed at home to hide. During one of the evenings, my younger sister, who went to one of the Zionist branch's activities, did not return home. We were informed that the entire group of members who participated in that activity were arrested, and there was a fear of impending searches in their homes. I escaped to the neighboring village through a desolate road as if to visit the home of a farmer – a Ukrainian family friend. I could not stay there for long and I came back through the same road but did not enter the house. I stayed in the yard and sat down in the barn. My father was at the fields, as that was the period of plowing and sowing of the corn and the sunflowers. The son of my father's partner came from the field to take a barrel of water to the field. I laid down in the wagon by the barrel and covered myself with the tarp that covered the barrel. I was soaked with water from the barrel, from time to time. That was how I traveled to the location of the plowing.

I participated in the plowing work that day. That was the last time I plowed the soil of the foreign land. My father brought me a few items from home, and after sleeping under the Ukrainian sky for the night, my father brought me to the nearest train station. From there, I traveled to the large city on the coast [of the Black Sea, Possibly Odesa] where I waited for a few months until the papers were arranged. In the meantime, I continued to be active in the underground Zionist movement. In the fall of that year, I boarded the ship "Lekhon," which transported 500 passengers to Eretz Israel, and two weeks later, I began to plow the fields of Ein Kharod in the Jezreel Valley.

**Atara and Nakhman Parag** (Ein Kharod)

*[Page 283]*

I was told by the colony elders that the colony was founded 100 years before I was born. During those days, the prairie was covered by tall weeds above the height of a person, and packs of wolves, which would attack people, used to roam the wild area. People did not dare to enter the tall grass for fear of wolves. The life conditions were very hard, and people lived in poverty. The bread was made of rye and they would make it very seldom. By the time it was eaten, it would be hardened and become stale. No knife could cut it, so they would break it with an ax and dip the crumbs in water to be able to eat it. The first settlers performed their work in the field using primitive tools, and their horses were fed naturally in the weed forest. The settlers would stay awake at night to guard their horses, but that was hardly helpful as theft was rampant.

In the summer, they all walked barefoot; however, in the wintertime, when they had to wear shoes to get out of the house, only one person from each family could be outside since the entire family owned only a single pair of shoes. The houses were rickety and uncomfortable. In the winter, the entire family gathered in the kitchen, which was the only heated place in the house. The kitchens were very crowded in the winter since the families had many children.

During our time, our colony was already very well organized. There was a dairy plant in the colony, where the cheese industry flourished and sent cheese products to the big cities. They would buy cheap work tools and supplies for the money they received. There was no more fallow land available, and land was actually very expensive. There was really a shortage of land.

It is worthwhile to note that even during the most difficult days in the life of the colony, the children continued to study in *"kheders"* and yeshivas. We had many scholars in our colony. When I asked where they received their broad education, they told me that during the early days

*[Page 284]*

people used to get married at the young ages of 13-14. Obviously, since the young husbands and wives were still children, they could not get along with each other. If the husband was talented, he would run away from home to study in Vilna, the city with many Yeshivas. He would sit and study for 10-15 years until emissaries would be sent to bring him back home to make sure that the wife would not remain *agunah* [according to Jewish Law - a woman bound in marriage by a husband who is missing]. There was also an opposite phenomenon when people from Lithuania fled to the colony.

When I reached the army age, I was recruited. That was during the First World War. The Czar's army retreated tens of kilometers a day, and the head of the army issued an order to leave behind scorched land. A company of Cossacks' commando was assigned to fulfill the order. The Cossacks would coat the wooden beams of the houses with kerosene and ignite entire villages and towns. The residents would flee in all directions and the Cossacks would use the tumult to rob and murder.

Two and half years later, I came home. The Revolution erupted then, and I did not return to the front. A decree was issued by the government to reallocate the land according to the number of people in the family. The owners of the large parcels did not agree to do so, and disputes and rifts ensued. In the meantime, the Revolution strengthened, and the wars between the Whites and the Bolsheviks continued as well. The regime changed hands continuously, and large areas went from one side to the other. In the area of the colony, the Ukrainians, who wished to achieve independence and freedom from Russian rule, were active. The Ukrainian battalions constituted a regular army that was busy performing robbery in addition to fighting in the war. Following a few defeats, the Ukrainians stopped fighting and shifted to organized robbery in the entire area.

Due to the rifts and disputes in the colony, no self-defense was organized. The attackers constituted a regular army with modern weaponry relative to the period while the colony members owned only meager and cold arms. At one time, the robbers entered the colony, took ten hostages, and announced that if they did not receive 65,000 Rubles by 11 o'clock the next morning they would execute the ten hostages and destroy the colony to its foundation. Messengers were dispatched, and they succeeded in securing loans from many places but managed to collect only 40,000 Rubles. That amount was less than what was required. The two gang's soldiers, who came to take the messengers to their command, announced that the amount collected would suffice. On the way to their camp, the escorts robbed the money from the carriers and ran away. The messengers returned to the colony and announced that everybody should take shelter since the gang would surely appear shortly. People just managed to hide when the soldiers appeared. The property in the colony was looted, and the people who were found were murdered. Many houses were destroyed to their foundations. The rioters raged for three straight days and finally left the colony. After the gang left the colony, several youths, including me, went out towards the fields where members of the colony hid, to notify them that the rioters had left. However, our calls were not responded to, due to an event that had occurred previously in the neighboring colony of Nahar-Tov HaGdola. Messengers went out on horses to announce that the gang had left, however, the colony people thought that the announcers

[Page 285]

who rode on horses, were the rioters, raised their feet, and ran away. The flight also stirred the people of Nahar-Tov HaKtana to run away. Only when everybody returned to the colony the mistake became clear.

After the gang of rioters left the colony, a battalion of the Bolshevik's regular army, which was known from the horrible pogroms it executed in Poland, arrived at the colony. A heavy fear filled the hearts of the residents. The soldiers became insolent hour by hour, and everybody fearfully waited for a pogrom to begin. However, things changed entirely by chance. About an hour away from the colony, a conference of the Revolution's leaders took place, where Kamenev, who was at the time one of the prominent Bolshevik leaders, participated. Kamenev gave a speech at the conference, and following his speech, the public was allowed to ask questions. Some colony members infiltrated the conference and I remember it in detail. Kamenev announced that it was possible to ask questions in writing. Among the written questions the following question was included: "What should we do with the *Zhids*?" The question was pushed all the way to the end. When it was presented, the communist leader rose up and announced firmly that whoever would dare to cause harm to a Jewish person – would be held responsible, even if he was an officer. The following morning, the attitude of the gang's members changed from one extreme to the other. They became polite and friendly and did not take anything when they left the colony.

**Yehoshua Dokhin** (Afikim)

As far as I know, none of the Nahar-Tov's farmers knew precisely when the settlement in the colonies began. I could learn only a little from the colony elders, who also received their information from their elders. I was told that the whole area was desolated. Some people told stories about meeting wolves and bears, who took their toll on the sheep herds.

A few Germans settled in every colony along with the Jewish settlers. They told us that the authorities settled them among our ancestors so that they would train them and also prevent them from forming villages consisting only of Jews (The colonies were called "settlements of Jews and Germans"). However, as far as I can recall, in our time, our people surpassed the Germans in their diligence and definitely surpassed the Russian farmers. The Jews excelled in introducing methods to make the work more efficient, and they acquired every modern agricultural machine. While the Russian farmers still harvested using sickle and scythe the Jewish farmers used harvesting machines. There was almost no cultural life except a single public library for the entire colony, where only a few visited. During the revolutionary years, a person visiting the library was suspected of being a revolutionist. The attitude of the farmers toward anybody who was against the monarchy was hostile. Some of the farmers were also hostile towards the Zionists.

*[Page 286]*

During my time, there was no Zionist movement in my colony, and as far as I know, not in any other colony. Only a year before the war, a small Zionist club was organized in Nahar-Tov, however, the entire Zionist activity was expressed by a gathering of our group to read about Eretz Israel and dream about it. Only during my last Yom Kippur, I dared to place a bowl in the synagogue for contributions to the JNF [Jewish National Fund]. I did that under the patronage of my uncle, who was a "*gabbai*" [synagogue administrator] in the synagogue. Not many dared to think about a journey to Eretz Israel. The youth were so attached to the farm and their family that even thinking about leaving seemed like an impossible task. Only a few among the colony members came to Eretz Israel during the years of the Second *Aliyah* [Jewish immigration to Eretz Israel 1904 – 1914].

In 1913, I visited an adjacent colony to say farewell to my relatives before my journey to Eretz Israel. I met with the youths there and tried to discuss Zionism with them, but nobody showed any interest. Only during the Revolution years, when everything began to fall apart, branches of the Zionist movement were created in all the colonies, and part of the youth arrived in Eretz Israel.

### A. Gurevitz (Kfar Mal"al)

*A memorial to my father, Alter Palkov, who was murdered for sanctifying his Jewishness and the Shabbat and did not receive a Jewish burial.*

One of my roles during my distanced childhood was to greet the returning herd. When the sun was setting, I would hurry up, along with the other children of my age group – 6-8-year-old, to the edge of the colony, to greet the cows' herd. I would fetch a thick piece of rye bread, covered with spicy garlic spread and salt, game rocks (*Tzekhin*), and a long stick. We would sit down on the side of the road, and while chewing the bread with a great appetite – we would play with the game rocks. All of a sudden, a dust cloud would rise - the herd! We would jump on our feet and burst into the dust.

Usually, every cow knew where the stall in the yard of her owner was and would confidently turn towards the yard by herself upon approaching it. However, just as it is with people, some extraordinary cows would do things just to get somebody angry. We had a cow like that in our cowshed. Her sisters had been obedient, more or less, and would make their way to the yard with some directing and guidance on my part. However, that rebellious cow was not satisfied with the pasture and the straw and bran portion waiting for her in the yard, and when the herd would approach the colony, she would burst aside and gallop straight into the vegetable gardens of the neighboring Russian village.

*[Page 287]*

More than she managed to gorge with her mouth it was her feet that did the damage - crashed, trampled, and destroyed. My role was to prevent her from doing that bad feat. I would jump into the herd; my eyes would search for her in the dense dust cloud, and with my long stick and my hoarse shouts, I would fight with her like a matador in the bullfighting arena. She would turn right – I went in front of her, hitting her with my stick and yelling: "Despicable, stubborn, and imbecile!" Like a creature experienced in planning ploys, she would then turn left, but I was agile and would immediately jump in front of her and hit her in the face. The rest of the cows would progress and go farther, but I would continue to jump right and left with my last drops of energy. Usually, I had the upper hand, and after I managed to direct her towards the colony street, she would walk, innocently and scrupulously while I dragged myself behind her with my stick, reminding her, once and a while, that there was law and order and a judge and that she needs to be obedient. When she would enter the inner yard, I would close the gate and would breathe a sigh of relief. It is a pity that I do not have a picture of my face and my appearance in such moments. I looked like coming from a long journey in the desert. Barefooted, with my fading dress, my face doused with a layer of dust and sweat, but my heart jumped for joy. Who else was as victory-happy as I was?

However, there were times when I lost, despite my agility, long stick, and desperate shouts. The rebel would use a cunning ploy, twist here and there to surprise me, raise her legs, run away, gallop, and burst straight into the vegetable garden where juicy cabbage grew. I would hurry after her with my last drop of strength. When I would arrive in the garden, my eyes would grow dim seeing the destruction she managed to cause. I would look fearfully at the Russian farmer running towards her, trying to drive her away by cruelly hitting her with his pitchfork while his mouth spitting curses towards the cow and the Jews. The following day, the farmer would receive three rubles from my father as compensation for the damage. The humiliated and defeated cow would march head-down, in the street, and I would follow, breathing heavily. I would be filled with bitterness because of the farmer's curses, humiliated, wretched, and covered with a layer of dust and sweat would drag my feet, heavy like wooden logs, my eyes in tears, with a darkness, as deep as the darkness that descended on the colony, in my heart. When the cow would enter the yard, I would slump down on the stone at the gate, groaning and breathing heavily. My tears would be dried out by then but there was still a bitter dryness in my mouth and heart.

Years passed, and childhood experiences were covered with dust; however, when I saw a herd of cows returning from the pasture, my heart began to quiver. Is that because of the shining childhood memory of the experiences of greeting the herd, eating a piece of bread smeared with garlic spread, playing the game of stones on the side of the road, and crying from joy when we jumped into the dust-covered herd? Or perhaps this is a result of touching again the scar that rebellious cow left in my soul?

Our family was not blessed with boys. My sisters and I engaged in many tasks. As the youngest daughter, I was assigned trivial tasks – greeting the herd, driving away,

*[Page 288]*

several times a day, the pigs from the neighboring Russian village were enchanted by our piles of straw or the potato patch. From time to time, I would hear the calls of Mother or one of my sisters:

"Leah, hurry up, the pigs are already burrowing! Run!"

"Leah, the pigs had already destroyed the garden! How did that happen? "

Several tens of chickens laid their eggs in one of the corners of the pen; however, just like that rebellious cow, a few chickens that sought solitude laid their eggs in the attic. One could only climb there through a narrow hatch, at the roof edge, and only my small body could pass through it. Once every day or two, my job was to climb up there, reach the hatch, slide in, and fetch the eggs. Besides these roles, they would assign me errands to go to the store or to the neighbors. I wanted to play, but I was busy with all sorts of tasks throughout most of the hours of the day.

We had a shoemaker as our neighbor. He was also blessed only with daughters like in our family. One of them was my age. I envied her and her sisters being the daughters of a craftsman, who were not tasked with the duties of a farm and were free to roam around and play. Their clothing was always clean, and their hair combed. But sometimes, my friend envied me, such as when we would climb on the thresher (a device similar to the Arab thresher. It was made of wood and equipped with flint rocks on the bottom. A pair of horses were harnessed to it and they rotated it over the straw to chop, crush, and soften it until it was ready for the teeth of the farm animals). We, the children, would pleasurably sit on the thresher, sometimes, just to add weight to it, as the thresher was more efficient, the heavier it was. I am not sure whether the children who ride on top of wooden horses or on wagons and trains in an amusement park today enjoy their rides more than I did then. The horses would loop around – gallop like mad over the straw in a circle. Clouds of dense dust, and thin chaff would envelop me, penetrating my eyes, ears, and nose and I would melt with happiness. I felt it all over my body – I was really a princess. My friend, the shoemaker's daughter, would stand on the side, at that time, her face expressing her envy and her eyes begging me to put her too on the board. How sweet a reparation was that for my envy! …and my joy would surge. Nevertheless, after I had received full satisfaction, my sense of generosity would suddenly awaken, and I would allow her to come up to my seat. Both of us holding and embracing each other would fly, rejoice, shout from joy, and sing.

It would seemingly be possible to claim that my childhood was depressing. There was no kindergarten, no toys, and no flowery dresses. Even a red ribbon for the hair was considered a big event. There was certainly no chocolate or fine candy, and in addition to all that – there were those duties – greeting the herd, chasing away the pigs, collecting the eggs, and going on errands. However, that claim would be erroneous. Wasn't I happy when I whirled on the thresher? Didn't I enjoy the rye bread smeared with garlic like a kid who enjoys chocolate? Wasn't I feeling joyful and filled with a sense of triumph when I succeeded in forcing the rebellious cow into the yard without a mishap?

Father would leave on Sunday for the distant field

*[Page 289]*

and return on Friday. Sometimes, my mother would cook Father's favorite dishes, comb her hair, and wear a clean dress. Holding a basket in one hand and my hand in the other, we would leave for that distanced field. The field was more than 10 kilometers away, and it took us two hours to reach it. On the way, we would pass the rainwater reservoir, which served for watering the herds. I remember the beautiful sight of the stalks of grain on both sides and the cemetery surrounded by a tall and mysterious fence. When Father would see us from afar, he would wave to us with his arms, and turn his horses towards the wagon. When he would reach us, he would put some hay for the horses, and the three of us would sit down in the shade of the wagon. Father would eat heartily the Borscht and the dumplings and throw some compliments to Mother. She would tell him, with charm and a smile, about this and that. I would be running around like a jumpy goat, here and there, and my heart would be filled with happiness and joy of life.

During the harvest season, when I was ten years old, my father used to wake me up at two o'clock at night to travel with him to a distanced field located 15-20 kilometers away from the village. Still wrapped in my sleep, I would curl up in the stiff wagon, all the bones in my body aching from the jolting. The sun would rise slowly, and I would take out my books from my bag and immerse myself in reading. Father was priding himself on our nimbleness when we met some Jewish farmers who were late leaving for work. When we would arrive in the field, my father would hand me the bundles of crops, and I would stand on the wagon and arrange them. On the way back, it was comforting to cuddle over the bundles of crops.

Jewish Farmers in Russia Fields

When the crops were ripening, Father would harness the horses, and we would go out to examine the fields. I would sit on the wagon's springy bench, between Father and Mother. The crop stalks would be nice and tall and my parents would be happy. When my father would cut the hay, I would roam around in the field to pick red pea and blue star-thistle flowers.

Years passed and I was already a grown girl, carrying the burden of farm work. My elder sisters were married and it was the harvest season. Working with a pitchfork is a task that is hard even for a man. The sun was burning, the sweat dripping, the back hurt, and the feet stepped over the chopped stubble. The eyes rose up continuously - is the sun still far from the western horizon? At last, the sun tired as well, and she crawled down and disappeared. Father released the horses from the harness and tied their legs. They walked on the chopped stable, their mouth looking for a forgotten uncut stalk. I hung the pot over the wagon shaft to cook the groats soup in it and arranged the fire underneath it. At a certain distance from the wagon, under the cover of the evening dimness, I poured a bucket of water on my dusty and sweaty body, put on a clean robe, and made my hair.

Father and I sat on the ground and had a hearty meal of green cucumbers, onions, eggs, and groats soup. Father then spread himself on a pile of crops, close to the wagon, and fell immediately into a deep sleep. I stretched over the soft straw inside the wagon. I was, too, tired from the day's work. My eyes were half closed, but my senses were awake though. I fixed my eyes on the heavenly stars. Silence descended over the world, and I felt light like a speck of dust

[Page 290]

in the infinite space. My eyes closed, and I was hovering in dreams of an adolescent girl yearning for the future.

It was a late hour. The entire universe was in deep sleep, even the horses. A few stars, older and less romantic, withdrew from the sky décor. All of a sudden, a song of an outpouring of soul burst out of me. My eyes were closing, and the sweetness of sleep engulfed me, and I was sinking into a world of oblivion. Suddenly, a burning sensation in my eyes: a ray of a young sun was tickling my eyebrows. My eyes opened lazily. A new day with a new fiery sun, pitchfork, sweat, and exhaustion arrived. The horses were already harnessed to the harvester. Father's face was sweaty. Morning tiny flies gathered around the remains of the meal from last night. I quickly jumped off the wagon, joined the other working women, and grabbed a pitchfork. It is not good to lose time in the morning when working is done at a relative comfort. I worked vigorously, enjoying my agile progress. The sun was still soft and caressing, and the work in that hour was still pleasant. While lifting the pitchfork, a soft and caressing smile would pass through the edges of my lips when I recalled one of the dreams, which fascinated me during the night.

About fifty years passed since then. I was fortunate to become an agriculturalist in Israel; however, how large is the distance between the past agriculture, difficult, primitive, and stingy, and the ample life of the agriculturists today? Today, a cow, even the most rebellious, would not run away from the herd. The chickens would not recluse themselves to lay their eggs in the attic. Farmers do not go out to the field or the orchard for two weeks at a time and not even for a whole day. People rest at home during noontime. They have nice furniture, an electrical refrigerator, an electric washing machine and, an electric or gas stove in the house. At that time, we did not even use firewood for heating, cooking, and baking since our area was not blessed with many trees. During those days, the fire was lit using bricks made of cow dung. The time difference between that period and today when gas stoves are used, is only one generation.

During the Russian Revolution, tens of young men, "members of the HeKhalutz," arrived at the colony for agricultural training and ushered in a Zionist atmosphere. Our youth joined the movement as well. We studied Hebrew and listened to discussions until the arrests came. They sentenced us to exile in Siberia. We walked for days and months throughout Russia – Kharkov [Kharkiv], Samara, Chelyabinsk all the way to Tomsk and Semipalatinsk [Semey]. We waited for assistance from our friends in Eretz Israel. That assistance came after a year, from the Authority for Prisoners of Zion [Prisoner of Zion is a detainee arrested and jailed due to Zionist activity forbidden in their country]. I returned from Siberia on a train. The happy group of people who would make *Aliyah* gathered in Odesa. The joy of the people was bitter-sweet due to the sadness of the separation from friends. There was no way for us to know when we would see each other again. On the ship, I was assigned to hide the certificates, which could be used as proof of our illegal activity and our struggle for the subsistence of the "HeKhalutz" organization. I hid the certificates well in the belt of my dress. All of a sudden, policemen boarded the ship and separated me from my travel companions. A thorough examination commenced from head to toe. My heart pounded from fear, but my treasure was not discovered. With a restrained joy, I joined my friends…

We finally reached the day when we disembarked on the shore of our motherland.

**Leah Palkov-Lev** (Kfar Bilu)

*[Page 291]*

My father inherited his farm from his parents. It was a property of 25 *disiyatins* [67.5 acres] of high-quality cropland. During my childhood, we owned very primitive tools for land cultivation; we resided in a shack that protruded from the ground. One had to go several stairs down to enter it. It just had two windows towards the street and two toward the yard. The shack had a door with a wooden handle, and a rope tied to it that had to be pulled to open and close it. The roof was covered with straw. About sixty families of farmers resided in the colony. The shape of the houses was uniform, and so was the way of life. The borders of the colony were: In the east - the Wysun River and a large and beautiful grove, in the south and north - the cultivated and pasture fields in the west, and gentile villages.

We had a beautiful synagogue in Nahar-Tov, located opposite our house, with a large hall for weddings. I loved that corner of the colony. Our elementary school and the teachers were Jewish, but the Russian authorities supervised it. Russian teachers participated in our matriculation examinations, and the curriculum was taught in Russian. The school was dear to my heart, and I loved it deeply. The education in the school was tuition-free since we were legitimate citizens who paid taxes to the state like all other Russian citizens who worked the land.

Young men from the colonies served in the army from the age of twenty to twenty-three. I got to see my colony constructed in a new style – nice houses with sophisticated tools for cultivation, large herds of milking cows, and herds for meat. We owned two pairs of horses for work and leisure, a wagon for transporting the crops from the field, and a snow wagon. We received a loan from the JCA under favorable payments to establish our farm.

In 1917, pioneering youths arrived at our colony from throughout Russia to receive agricultural training. I loved my colony, and my mate was also a native of Nahar-Tov. We built a new farm for ourselves and worked on it together. We were filled with the joy of creation.

However, our idyll vanished very quickly after that. During the years of the Revolution following the First World War, our colony was destroyed, and the entire Jewish folklore was destroyed with it. I, by then, without my mate, with three young children, left Russia and made *Aliyah* to Eretz Israel. This was in 1925.

**Itah Hurvitz** (Mikhmoret)

*[Page 292]*

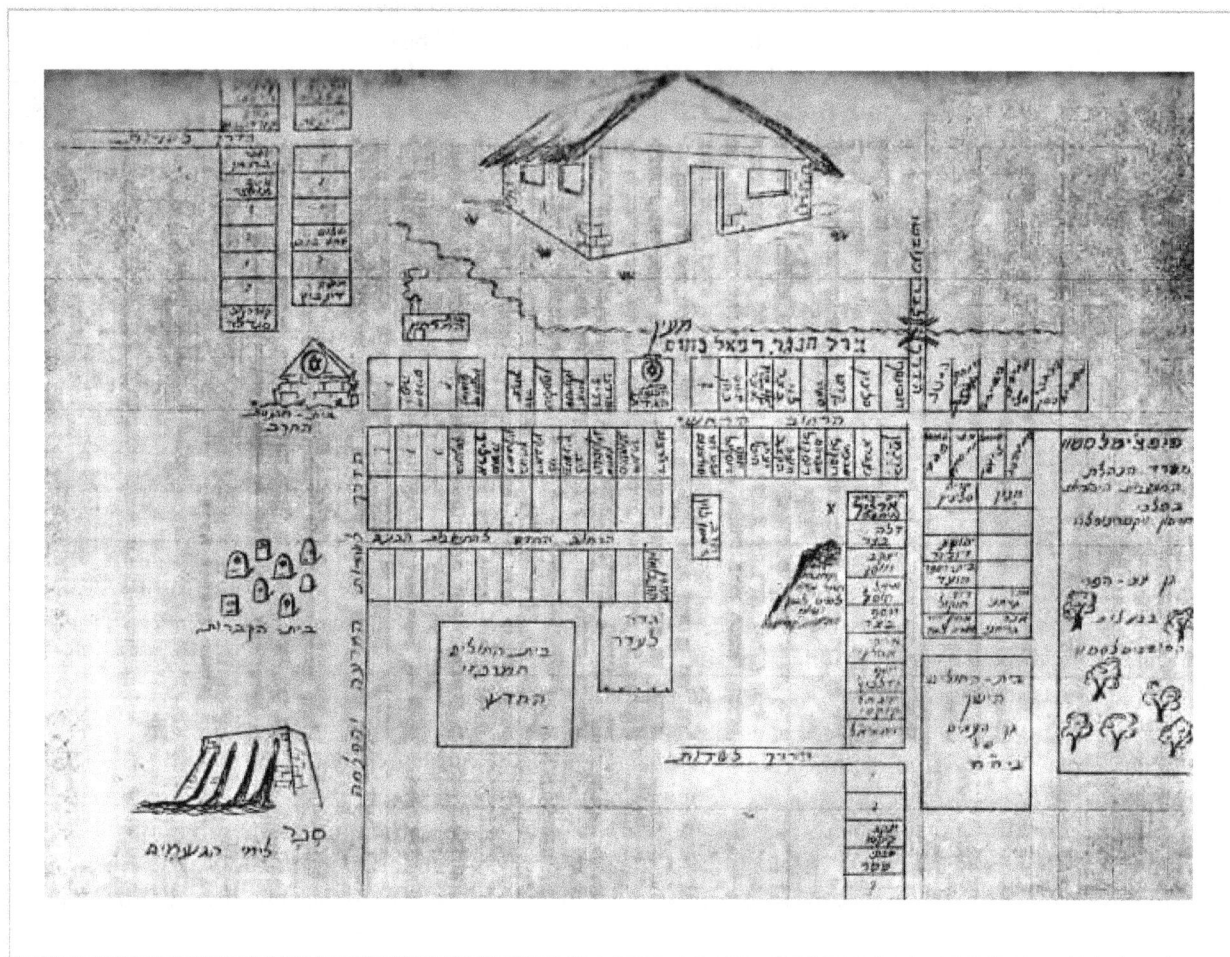

The colony of Nahar-Tov
(drawn from memory by Israel Betzer)

*[Page 293]*

The city of Nikolayev [Mykolaiv] – a bustling and wealthy city, had a large shipyard and big factories with tens of thousands of permanent workers. The streets and the markets were always filled with people. Among the city's rich, there were many Jews as well as many Karaites[1] I think that all of the big commerce was in the hands of Jews. There were several synagogues in the city. I even discovered a "Khabad" synagogue with a beautiful sign; however, there was only a meager content in it beyond the sign. I did not like Nikolayev. I did not feel any Jewish life in it since the Jews constituted an insignificant minority in the city. The workers used to receive the weekly wages and would go shopping and pay debts on Saturdays. That was the reason why only the big wholesalers among the Jews could afford to close their shops on Shabbat; however, almost all of the Jewish shops were open on Shabbat. The vegetable market was full of Jewish women, and the same goes for Jewish horse traders in the horse market. The horse market was as noisy and crowded on Shabbat as on a weekday.

I visited various synagogues and other places to meet Jews. At one time, I would enter into a conversation with an old man and another time with a young one. I also knew teachers and "*melameds*" [Jewish religious teachers]. I once met an elderly Jew with a beard who wore a "*casquette*" hat (a cap with a visor). I assumed he was not a Jewish city dweller and started to interrogate him about who he was and where he was from until he said he was from "Dobrinkeh" [Dobroye].

"And where is this Dubrinkeh?" I asked.

"This is a Jewish colony, about fifty *verstas* [about 33 miles] from Nikolayev."

"Are you a farmer?"

"And what do you think I am doing? Scribing Teffilin?" he answered with a question.

"I am just asking" – I said. "I have never seen a Jew who really works the land."

"Then you should come to us and see many Jews who are working the land" – he challenged me.

I told Mr. Schwartz that I saw a Jew from a Jewish colony who told me about Jews who worked the land there, just like the Gentiles. I got this encounter into my head and my heart. I had to go there.

"What kind of discovery did you make?" asked Mr. Schwartz. I see these Jews every day. They bring grain for sale and serve as waggoneers for the local merchants.

*[Page 294]*

"What is there to see? You had better travel to Odesa or Kherson. There you would see something!"

"Obviously, there is more to see in the city of Odesa than in the colony" – I answered, "but I want to see how Jews work the land."

I was free during the entire month of Tishrei, so I traveled; I visited Kherson, Voznesensk, Ochatkov, and Odesa. These cities were more Jewish than Nikolayev. I particularly liked Kherson, which was the administrative center of the province. I met many colony natives there, people from Romanovka, Nahar-Tov, Sdeh-Menukha, Bobrovy-Kut, and others. I found them in an inn with a big yard that served for parking the horses and the wagons. Almost all of them complained about being poor. One could easily see from their faces that they were workers. They were tanned and muscular. You shake their hand and feel that it is coarse and calloused. I felt much love for these Jews in my heart.

I decided to terminate my "time" with the children of Mr. Schwartz and leave for a Jewish colony. When I disclosed my intention to Mr. Schwartz, he and his acquaintants laughed at me and said that I was imitating the people from the "Narodiya Volya" [A 19th-century revolutionary political organization in

Russia that advocated indigenous socialism] – the people who left the city and moved to the village. "It is all right," I said. "I wish that the children of the wealthy Jews would imitate some of the children of the gentile estate owners and the gentile intelligentsia. Both here and in Ryasna, I saw Jews who were dependent on the Gentiles. If the gentile was rich – so were the Jews who worked for him; I wanted to see Jews who were not dependent on a gentile. Jews who do the work of the gentiles by themselves: sow, harvest, and eat the fruit of their work.

I chose to go to the colony of Nahar-Tov, which was also called Berezneguvate, due to its proximity to the *pasad*, which carried the same name. The title "*pasad*" was given in Russia to a settlement that was no longer a village but was not quite a city as of yet. Due to its proximity to the "*pasad*," Nahar-Tov was considered more developed, and I hoped to find work there.

I traveled a distance of about thirty kilometers from the train station and arrived at the colony. A wide street, with houses, not quite big, standing on both sides. All were stone-built and covered with red shingles. The colony looked more beautiful than a farmer village in Belarus. I asked the waggoner to bring me to the inn.

"There is no inn in the colony" – he answered – "but I will bring you to a good home." He stopped the horses at a gateless yard and called with a loud voice:" Sara, I brought you a guest."

A woman about thirty-five years old came out towards us and led me into the house.

*[Page 295]*

I immediately smelled a strong odor of animal dung. "What is it here, a cowshed?" I thought. Since there was dirt rather than the floor in the house, they covered it with a mixture of clay, plaster, and dung. I recalled seeing this type of floor in my native area.

The woman brought me to a hall – a spacious room – that had the same smell as they prepared the whole house for Passover. In the room, there was a large table with three chairs around it and a wretched sofa with three legs. A small wooden box served as its fourth leg. "This furniture was familiar to me from my childhood" – I said to myself – "This is your true place, Moshe. You were like an alien in that house of the wealthy, over there in Nikolayev."

The woman was standing in front of me as a defendant in court. From my clothing, she assumed that I was an important official or something similar to that. She began to justify herself: "I am not sure why they brought you to us. There are better homes in the colony." I calmed her down: "I am a Hebrew teacher, and I would like to see the colony." I told her that her house was quite suitable for me. In the meantime, the man of the house arrived, also a young man, sporting a yellow beard. He stood there as if he was ashamed. He greeted me and wanted immediately to know where I was from, and what brought me to the colony. The children also arrived. Three were studying in a "*kheder*," there was one in diapers and a little three-year-old girl, all wearing tatters.

I have a sense of poverty. I understood that they do not have anything to host me with, and they do not get food on credit in the store. I convinced them to accept a down payment from me since it was my intention to lodge with them for Passover. Sara vanished from the house immediately and went out to the store with five Rubles in her hand.

Jewish Farmers in Russia Fields

During the evening, I found out more details about the situation of the Samuelov family. The head of the family did not hide his family's poverty but was very ashamed about it. The house and the structures in the yard – a cowshed, barn, and cellar – showed that he did not come from a poor home. He had inherited them from his father, a farmer and a merchant who was considered a wealthy person within the colony. However, in his latest years, he fell sick often. In addition, he also experienced a drought. After the father passed away, the horses were stolen from them. Since then, Samuelov has not managed to recover. He owned ten *disiyatins* [about 27 acres] of land, but due to the lack of horses, he was unable to cultivate it and he leased it to others and received only part of the harvest. His elderly mother was a midwife in the colony. She gave birth to 17 children herself, but only two survived – a son and a daughter. Thanks to G-d, there were plenty of births in the colony, so the elderly woman was the one who brought some food and money to the family.

I liked these people with their humility and candor. I interrogated them about the colony and found out that Nahar-Tov consisted of three colonies: the Old Nahar-Tov, the New Nahar-Tov, and the regular Nahar-Tov [the Greater Nahar-Tov or Nahar-Tov HaGdola]. I lodged in the Nahar-Tov HaGdola. The big synagogue, the only one in Nahar-Tov HaGdola, was standing across from the house I was staying in. Most of the farmers were considered to be Hassids of the "Khabad" Hassidic movement.

*[Page 296]*

An emissary of the Rabbi visited the colony every year. He collected contributions and made sure that the children were not licentious. In every colony, there were about ten wealthy farmers, however, the rest of the farmers were very poor. A state elementary school existed, where they taught only in the Russian language. The school closed for a summer vacation in the summer. It also closed for the dead of the winter because the school was cold and the children did not have proper clothing and therefore, could not get out of the house.

There was no library; what was it needed for, as a matter of fact?

I went to the Synagogue at eight o'clock to pray. These were the days of the spring and the farmers were all in the fields. I found only a few people in the large hall, most were "religious ministrants" who were exempt from working in the fields: The Rabbi, slaughterers, and "*melamed's*" – all donning a beard and *pe'ah's* [side-locks], looking at me, the shaved young man with a hostile foreignness. I said to myself – "from everything I heard and saw, the conclusion is that I would not be able to be employed here." They would not trust me and would refuse to hand over their children to me. On the other hand, perhaps I am mistaken. Perhaps I could do a lot here, but I still did not know how. How should one approach that task? That required some thought.

A few days later, I went sightseeing to the *pasad*, located about 300 meters from the colony with a river separating them. This is the same river after which the colony was named - Nahar-Tov [in Hebrew - Good River]. During that season, the river looked more like an irrigation ditch. It dried out in the summer. I thought I would find roads or, at least, some sidewalks for pedestrians, but none existed. A footpath served as the sidewalk. Instead of a paved road, unhewn stones were scattered in the middle of the street as if they were thrown haphazardly into the mud. It was impossible to walk on top of the stones or ride a wagon over them. I realized that that settlement was still a village rather than a town.

I arrived at the market square, a wide square filled with garbage and animal dung, which reminded me of the market plaza in my native town of Ryasna. A large-sized Christian church, with a tall roof shining under the sunlight, welcomes the arrivers. I remember that well, as our house in Ryasna, stood exactly opposite a church. Around the square – big shops in stone buildings, while wooden huts housed the small shops. That was not a market day, but the shops were filled with buyers since it was the period before Passover for the Jews and the Christians. Among the Jews who lived in the *pasad*, were merchants and craftsmen. Not many of them were wealthy but they encouraged the Gentiles' hatred by their behavior. The Jews owned good horses and lived in nice houses. Their wives had the habit of dressing up and tended to stand out and ignore the envy and hatred that this behavior invoked among the Gentiles. I was familiar with that phenomenon [from my own native town]. I recognized some of the visitors in the synagogue who were not religion-fanatical, who could afford to keep a teacher

*[Page 297]*

and pay his wages. The fact that I served as a teacher at the home of wealthy Mr. Schwartz in Nikolayev, reached one of the merchants and he was willing to employ me as a teacher for his children. Although that was not what brought me over to the colony, I needed a source of income and felt better here than in the big city.

*

My first Passover Eve at the colony has arrived. The synagogue was filled with light and people. Most of the farmers were dressed quite nicely. I saw long black capotes: the "religious ministrants" wore these, but I also saw many others with brimmed hats. The young and middle-aged people wore short jackets. The cantor was young. He prayed with a clear voice. The humming was loud, but these were praying Jews. They did not just stand there as if they did not understand the language of the prayers. There was nothing to be ashamed of about our farmers. I came out of the synagogue, very pleased. I saw healthy Jews who stood tall. I saw joyful youths – natural without any agendas, perhaps less learned and less witted than the youths in my native town, but healthier in their body and more assured of their future. Just give him a piece of land, a plow, and a pair of horses to harness them to the plow. He would know how to do the rest. I hadn't yet learned at that time about the life calamities that hit the farmers and the mishaps suffered by the colony, however, what I saw – I liked and it made me happy.

------------ I continued to wander around the colony to explore it closely. The colony's poor, the ones who lacked land, tools, and workforce lived, as customary, on the side streets. The farmers were working very hard, but their economic situation was pitiful. The main farm sector was the cultivation of field crops. Some of the farmers owned a cow or two. The farmers' situation, who remained without workhorses, was grave. During that period, no governmental or public assistance existed. If the farmer failed, he had to rely on people who, in addition to being merchants or farmers, lend money at an exorbitant interest. The lender would confiscate the land for a year or two if the farmer was unable to pay off his debt. A farmer who needed a flour sack or grain for his animals before the threshing season must acquire them from a merchant in the *pasad*. He paid up to two rubles in interest, while the price of a flour sack cost no more than six or seven Rubles. Whoever leased his field to others got only a small part of the harvest.

I found out all of that from Samuelov. He was ruined because of his inability to purchase horses. He was leasing his land, and in the middle of the spring, during the burning sowing season, he sat idle at home. His son, who could help him with the work, also did not have a future on the farm. I could see how numerous their needs were. How can I win their trust, and how can I help? I am only one person and so foreign to them.

*[Page 298]*

------------I secured a position for myself as a private teacher of Hebrew and general studies at the home of a wealthy family in the *pasad*. I had a small group of children that did well in their studies, my wage was respectable and my lodging and food were not worse than what I had at Mr. Schwartz's home. I made a friend by the name of Davidovski, who taught at the state school. I was also teaching him Hebrew. We both felt the poorness of our spiritual life and decided to do something about it. We decided that I would subscribe to the [Jewish newspaper] "HaTzfira" and he would sign up for the Jewish weekly magazine in the Russian language – "Voskhod" [Russian – "Sunrise"].

We tried to distribute news from the Jewish world in the colony. We were helped in that by a farmer whose name was Yoel Brekhman. I have never seen a short and thick person like him. He looked to me like a monster with his beard and thick eyebrows. However, as time passed, we developed deep friendly relations and his appearance did not bother me at all. He was the richest farmer in the colony. He leased tens of thousands of *dunam*s [1,000 square meters (11,000 sq ft)), which is 1/10 hectare] of land, and employed many gentile workers whose supervisor was Jewish. He had a long wooden beam in his yard, on which he used to sit, surrounded by a circle of young and old, and tell news from the world, or just stories. That man liked to listen, and even more - to talk. Brekhman served as our mouth. We would tell him the news that we read in the evening, and the following morning he would begin to tell them to every passer-by, because everybody knew that Brekhman would not just tell them stories, but "the truth" obtained from the world's respectable newspapers. That summer, Czar Nikolai the 2$^{nd}$, the latest of Russia's kings, was crowned. The Jews pinned their hopes on this Czar. I did not know the basis for these hopes, but they were universal. Excitement and expectation ensued – and the circle around Brekhman grew, the people were alert and had a desire to listen. "We are not staying in the dark anymore" – Brekhman told me once – "The colony changed…"

------------I had an idea. Why wouldn't I loan money to Samuelov? They seemed to be good and honest people, and only because they lacked a small amount of money to buy horses, they were unable to improve their pitiful situation – and I still had my savings from Nikolayev and my wage now was good. I thought about it and acted. In the beginning, they did not understand me, and could not believe what they were hearing. However, when I laid down the money bills on the table in front of Samuelov – he understood that my intention was serious. He knew that he would have to prove that he would be able to use the opportunity given to him. Only a short time passed, and the change in that family was apparent. Samuelov bought a pair of young horses, almost foals, and took care of them during the summer. He put them to work a little and they grew and became beautiful horses. That year was a blessed year. He received his portion of the harvest, made a thresher in the yard, and threshed the grain with a six-wing stone.

*[Page 299]*

I had not seen a stone like that until then, since in the Mogilev Province [where I came from], the threshing floor was located in a special building and the grain was threshed during the entire winter. Here in the colony, the grain was threshed outside, under the sky, and in a very short time. The yard was filled with piles of grain and the house was filled with joy. I compared that with the situation that I found here about half a year ago, and I could not believe what my eyes were seeing. The difference between their situations was like the difference between day and night, and all of that blessing, that was begotten upon them, happened because they had the means to work the land.

The colony elders told me that they learned from their elders that one hundred years ago, the Jews could if they really wanted to, settle the entire province of Kherson, which was totally empty and desolate. Jews were given all sorts of incentives, but they did not want to become farmers. Now, there are more than four million residents in the province of Kherson, and it is considered one of the richest in Russia. The land here did not require fertilization, just provide rain and there was no limit to its ability to absorb water. It absorbed and reciprocated. With time, I came to know the attributes of that soil and loved it tremendously. Now, it was forbidden for Jews to become farmers, and a Jew who was not a farmer, could not lease land from a Jewish farmer. The prohibition on buying and leasing land was issued in the 1880s along with the Ignatyev decrees, as well as the prohibition on the settlement of Jews in the villages for those who were not already residing in the village. These decrees yielded many troubles for the Jews and quite a few of them lost their life because of the decrees.

*

------------The holiday of Sukkot, obtained its true meaning in the colony – the harvest holiday. They have already finished threshing and gathering the grain, some into the barn and some into the house. Most of the farmers sold their grain directly from the barn. They lived the entire year on the account of the next harvest. There was brisk traffic in the colony: The grain merchants would run around from yard to yard, buying, weighing, and sending it to Nikolayev. Usually, the prices were depressed immediately after the threshing, and brave farmers would keep the harvest and sell it later on. The farmer was usually the waggoner and he would earn the additional fees for transporting the grain to the city. That was a time when money filled the pockets, and every colonist celebrated Sukkot with a joyful spirit. There was a *sukkah* in every yard, but where would they take tree branches for the *skhakh* [*sukkah's* roof]? After all, there was no forest in the area. But the One "who calls the generations from the beginning" [Isaia 31:4] also secured tree branches for the roof of the *sukkah*. The authority that managed all of the colonies in the province of Kherson, was located in Nahar-Tov. They came up with the idea of planting a grove in the colony. Every farmer who sinned against the authority was punished to work several days in the grove. That was how a grove of more than 100 *dunams* came to be several years ago, and thus tree branches to cover the *sukkah's* roof became available. I remember the holiday of Sukkot in [my native] cold Ryasna. Over there we could not enjoy the *sukkah,* even for a single day. The intermediate days of Sukkot's holiday were also the season of matchmaking. Young men and women wandered around to, ostensibly, visit with uncles and aunts, but

*[Page 300]*

their real intention was to see and be seen. The aunts and uncles were assisting, and the "matchmaking" was done, and not just one or two.

------------ This was an epic period in Russia, and our Jewish world was in upheaval because of Hertzl's [book] "Medinat HaYehudim" [The State of the Jewish People]. Neither in the colony nor in the *pasad* people knew or heard about the important matters in the Jewish world. Only we, the young teachers, spread the name of Hertzl among people and told them about his book, ideas, and plans.

It cannot be said that we found a listening audience. People looked at us as tellers of untruths and dreamers of hallucinations. It also cannot be said that we, ourselves, comprehended the immensity of the Zionist political idea. However, it did capture our hearts and imagination. We were angry at any article in the "HaTzfira" or HaShiloakh," which criticized Hertzl's book. We decided to subscribe to HaMelitz," which was more pro- Eretz Israel, instead of "HaTzfira," however, we could not give up on the "HaShiloakh" from the point of view of "Wounds of a lover are faithful" [Proverbs 27:6].

Yoel Brekhman did cooperate with us. Whatever he heard from us, was passed over quickly to anybody eager for "news." Things got to the point that on Shabbat evenings, a big crowd would gather in front of Yoel Brekhman's house, a crowd bigger than the one who came to the synagogue for reading of the Psalms. Many just listened to the Zionist idea and some became believers and fans. Brekhman told me that he believed in my stories like a *Hassid* who believed his rabbi. He only knew how to read a simple Russian, but that was not that important. I would tell him in simple words in Yiddish the content of every good article in the Jewish newspapers, and that way, he would know and understand all the affairs.

In 1897 our group of young teachers from the colony and the *pasad* reached ten. As we reached a "*Minyan*," we decided to contribute ten Rubles each so that we could subscribe to newspapers and magazines in Russian, Hebrew, and Yiddish. One hundred Rubles was a large sum those days. All of a sudden, our remote place was connected to the big world – the world of capitals, journalists, authors, and philosophers. Everybody interested and able to read could borrow reading material, and everybody read according to his or her ability and understanding.

*

---------- In the winter of 1898 – 1899, I stayed in the city of Odesa. I wanted to progress in my general studies. I had means through savings I accumulated from my work and could afford to immerse myself in acquiring additional knowledge. The best spiritual powers of Russian Jewry – "political Zionists" and "spiritual Zionists" gathered in Odesa. Fiery speeches were given in the synagogue "Yavneh." How could one avoid being swept away by the whirlpool? I fought hard with myself so that I could continue with my plan

*[Page 301]*

and avoid submitting entirely to Zionist activism. I knew I had to prepare for life in Eretz Israel, and it was beneficial to have an occupation that could contribute to building a new life there.

During the same time, I have experienced a wave of new thoughts. I wanted to be a good teacher to the Jewish children. People were talking about reviving the Hebrew language among the children. There was already a school or a "Zionist *kheder*" and there were already some teachers who had experimented with new methods, looking for new ways to stimulate the toddlers to talk. The new teaching method was called "Hebrew in Hebrew." I got in touch with teachers, visited the school of Sh. Ben Tzion, and attended the class during the lessons. I have decided to return to the *pasad* and the colony, where I would open a school and teach the children Hebrew in Hebrew.

When I came to the colony, I obviously turned to visit Samuelov, who was already one of the wealthy farmers in the colony. I could not describe the way the family welcomed me.

A rumor was spread that the teacher Yevzrikhin arrived and that he wanted to teach the children Hebrew in Hebrew. People did not exactly know what that meant. However, they knew that it was something new. Besides, I had already made a name for myself in that place, and people knew that the children loved to study with me. I began to prepare myself for the opening of the school. With the help of friends, two rooms were allocated in a new building to serve as classes, and appropriate furniture was furnished. Students became available even before I opened the school. I did not have to search for them. Fathers came and offered me to accept their sons. I accepted ten students from the *pasad* and eight from the colony, among them, six beginners and twelve students who had already studied for a year. I did not want to accept older children who had already acquired different ways of learning from others. I wanted to start with the new method.

All the beginnings are hard, and speaking Hebrew to children who never heard the language was obviously not very easy. What was the essence of the studies? Movements, hints, repeated and re-repeated talks. The elder ones caught faster and the little ones followed. For a month and a half, I did all the talking and the children acquired numerous words. I bought the book by David Yelin and started to teach them how to read and write. We also had a board, and we wrote every word we learned on it. The parents came every day to see how I was teaching and hear their children talking Hebrew. In their homes, the children did not have anybody who understood the language, and this hindered their learning. Upon returning home, the children would forget their teacher's order to talk only Hebrew at home. Who would they talk to? In any case, the children progressed nicely, and I realized that the method was effective. Those who criticized it at the beginning quieted down. They realized that the children knew how to read and write, so there was no harm if they also learned a bit about how to talk. My school grew, and with the growth of the number of students, another teacher joined me. There were some excellent children among the students and the school became a corner of light and friendship.

*[Page 302]*

---------- A representative of [Vladimir Ze'ev] Tiomkin visited the colony and the *pasad* and delivered Zionist sermons. He excited his Jewish listeners, and they purchased [Zionist] Shekels; that showed that we had Zionists in our colony. If there were Zionists, we also needed a Zionist association. We decided to establish an association and called it "A'havat Tzion" ["Love of Zion"]. A few farmers from the colony, some of the residents of the *pasad*, and several youths I was previously connected with, joined the association. We elected a chairperson of the association – Yoel Brekhman, and I was forced to accept the role of secretary. We began to assemble every Saturday night. The gatherings were "non-Kosher" in the eyes of the authorities as Zionism was not yet allowed in Russia and Zionist gatherings in particular. We gathered every time in a different house, and most of all – in my school. Besides the permanent members, other farmers who wanted to listen to what the Zionists had to say, came. The colony's youth who were attracted to every spoken word, came as well.

I became a speaker and propagandist, which I actually hated. I did, however, like to read for them. I read from the newspaper, as people were thirsty for news and knowledge. I decided that we needed to establish a library. We opened a reading room at the library so that anybody who wanted could come and read the newspapers for free.

We obtained a sample of bylaws and edited it according to the local situation. We determined that there would be two types of members in the library association – honorary members who would pay 5 Rubles annually, and regular members, who would only pay one Ruble and would be able to borrow books as they wished. We easily gathered ten honorary members, all of them from the *pasad*, who paid the required fee. We managed to secure a nice location for the library. Yoel Brekhman gave us, free, a large hall, which occupied almost half of his spacious house. We also obtained a license from the provincial minister to open a library.

We, therefore, sat down to prepare the list of books we wanted to purchase. It was a big joy to add one book after another to the list, from among the best books available in literature, in three languages – Russian, Yiddish, and Hebrew. I paid special attention to the children's Hebrew literature that began to appear as small pamphlets. We also subscribed to a children's newspaper called "Olam Katan" ["Small World"].

With the money available to us – 120 Rubles – we made a good beginning. In addition to the Jewish readers – adults, youth, and children, non-Jewish subscribers joined from the intelligentsia of the *pasad* and from among the staff in the state regional hospital, which was located near the colony. We held a literature ball, twice a year the revenues of which were allocated entirely to the library. The library became an important element of the local social life. Youths were reading a book; argued about it, and followed new literature compositions published as sequels in the important journals of the time.

\*

---------- We were now in 1900. About twenty-five people, elderly and young, participated in our gatherings on Saturday nights. They considered themselves

*[Page 303]*

as members of the Zionist movement. They purchased Shekels, gave contributions, and even purchased stocks of the "Jewish Colonial Bank." I hoped that this Zionist nucleus would grow with time, but that was not the case. As mentioned above, the colony's farmers were Hassid's of the Rabbi from Lubavitz. The Rabbi himself did not visit his followers, but his emissary would arrive, once in a while, to collect a fee of up to three hundred Rubles per year. At one point, one of the colony farmers traveled to the Rabbi to ask for his advice and receive his blessing. Through a discussion about what was going on at the colony, the farmer told the Rabbi about the Zionist gatherings, which took place every Saturday night, about the [Zionist] Shekels and the [Jewish Colonial] bank stocks purchased by the Jews. It is easy to assume how shocked the Hassidic Rabbi was about that news. He immediately dispatched a letter to his followers in Nahar-Tov, to warn them against Zionism and notify them that Zionism was improper for any pious Jew and that they were not allowed to establish any contact with that secular and harmful movement. This letter frightened the people, and some of the participants in our gatherings ceased any contact with us. That retreat saddened me greatly; however, in actuality, not everyone abandoned me. Several loyal colony farmers and a larger number of the *pasad's* Jews remained. A few among the youths, who were proficient in the Hebrew language and knew the Zionist songs, stuck with the Zionist idea. They would gather on Shabbat and hold debates. Some brought up plans to make *Aliyah* to Eretz Israel to settle in it. Others wished to continue studying general studies. The zealousness did not have any control over them since, by then, it had already been breached.

\*

------------ At the same time, an improvement in the material condition of the farmers took place. The JCA association began to introduce improvements and advances on the farms and that activity bore fruit very quickly. A regional agricultural school for the farmers' children, where they taught advanced methods of farm management, as well as general studies, was established. A cooperative association for savings and loans was also established. Through that association, the farmers were relieved from the burden of the exaggerated interest rates. In 1901, a cooperative shop for flour and animal supply was established. From that point on, if the farmer needed flour for his family or food for the stable and cowshed, he could receive them on credit, with a low-interest rate, until the following threshing period. The cooperative institutions required management, and nobody was available to guide the farmers in managing their affairs. The authorities just gave them the license for the associations. The farmers would gather to elect management and would raise an indescribable commotion. The number of proposals was the same as the number of participants in the gathering. Everybody talked at the same time and in loud voices, in Yiddish spiced with many Russian expressions. Their shouts were blended and lost as if without any purpose.

Since I was a bystander and since I did not derive any personal benefits from their institutions.

*[Page 304]*

I was considered as impartial, and they listened to my opinion. Although my heart was not with public service, I was forced to participate in public life.

I could see how things changed during the few years since I came to the colony. Yoel Brekhman was right when he said "This is not the same colony." My standing also changed, and these Jewish farmers were now trusting me.

### Moshe Yevzori-Yevzrikhin (Mishmar HaEmek)[2]

From the northeastern outskirts of the colony of Nahar–Tov, the expanse of a wide-open field could be viewed. On that side of the colony, houses and yards of new farmers were popping out once in a while. That was where the regional state hospital, which seemed like a settlement of its own, was located. The hospital contained many structures – all covered by green tin roofs and surrounded by colorful flower gardens and shady groves. These structures included houses where the patients were hospitalized, residential houses for the entire working staff, and clinics for outpatients who came to ask for the advice of the physicians and receive medications. During reception days, the hospital area bustled like during the days of a fair.

The open field on the side of the colony winked with its expanses and the swales of its furrows. In the spring, we would go out to explore the new growth. In the summer, we searched for the various flowers. We even dared to peek into the desolate colony cemetery. Its desolation seemed to have vanished under the bountiful sun. In the fall, the fields and the bayous sent whistling gusts, knocking on the quivering windows of the cramped houses. During the winter, the field expanses seemed even wider under the snow–cover.

On the southern side of the colony, a shallow river meandered – the Wysun River. The name of the colony, the wide river bed, and the massive bridge testified to the fact that upon the arrival of the settlers, the Wysun was a river with abundant water. However, I knew it as a meager river, and the bridge looked like a tall hat worn by a shriveled body. The river would fill its river bed only in the winter. Large blocks of ice were carried by the power of its stormy waters during the thaw, and the sounds of their collisions could be heard throughout the night. We were then thankful for the wide river beds and the tall and stable bridge, which imbued a sense of security against the forces of nature. That bridge connected the colony of Nahar-Tov with the large town of Berzneguvat.

My parents were not from among the farmers in the colony. My father arrived at the colony during the 1890s.

R' Zalman-Leib VesInitzki, the patriarch of the large Simkhoni family in Israel – under his cherry tree in his farm in Sdeh-Menukha Ha'Gdola

The educator, R' Moshe – Yevzory
– Yevzrikhin, the grandfather of
Asaf Simkhoni on his mother side

The grandson – Major General Asaf Simkhoni,
the commander of the 1956 Sinai campaign
who was killed [on the last day of] the war

*[Page 305]*

In the beginning, he made a living as a teacher, but he became a merchant later on. My family resided alternately in the colony and the village, and I crossed the bridge thousands of times during my childhood. I was attached to both places. I had friends whose houses I would visit often in both places. The scale balance of these connections used to go up and down. At times, it would move toward the colony, and other times it would tilt toward the gentile village until it finally moved and attached itself to the colony due to the force of love.

My family also finally moved and settled among the colony's farmers, but that had happened during the days of the Revolution after I made *Aliyah* to Eretz Israel.

Farmers resided on both banks of the Wysun River – on one side were the Jews and on the other – the Gentiles. The seasons talked to either side in the same language: sowing, harvesting, and gathering the crops and the fruits. People and animals prepared for the long winter. Farmers traveled on both sides of the river on wagons loaded with barrels to draw water from the springs near the river. Women washed laundry on both banks of the river and the sound of their banging on the laundry mixed with the singing voices and the shouts of the children. During the winter, smoke rose up from the houses' chimneys – some were clay shacks covered by straw roofs, and some were stone houses equipped with tin roofs or cheerful shingles.

When the river was covered with stable ice, boys from both sides of the river skated on it and met each other in a commotion. Shops were concentrated in the village and that was also the location of the officials. The colony residents passed over the bridge, on wagons or on foot, during the market days and flocked to the village during the fairs. The bridge connected the colony and the village but also separated between them. The lifestyles on the two sides were different, and the human landscape was also dissimilar. Crossing the bridge was like passing to another world, different and intimidating. A narrow alley led from the bridge to the village, ending with a sharp turn. One would never know what was waiting around the corner. Courtyards of gentile farmers were located on one side of the alley and the estate of a wealthy Jew on the other. The wealthy Jew, a land owner and lumber merchant, owned a citadel–like a house with tall ceilings and employed many servants and workers. Flower beds grew around the house and trees shaded its windows. A huge yard surrounded it, containing the estate owner's barn, stable, and warehouses of lumber, organized in an amazing precision.

To protect his immense property, the man erected a tall stone wall that stretched along the entire alley. Glass shreds were placed on top of it. The sealed wall added a mysterious aura to the narrow alley, associated with many legends. Somebody saw a ghost-like figure walking on top of the wall, on the glass shreds, during a moon-illuminated night. Somebody else remembered a story about robbers who staged an ambush for passersby in the shadows of the wall... During the years of the Revolution, when the gangs rampaged, the wealthy house was robbed and its Jewish residents murdered. The house was isolated and nobody came to their help. After the killing, the feeling of fear that the alley imposed deepened, and it remained forged in my memory as a distinct experience.

*[Page 306]*

A tall hill, which served as a place for meetings and entertainment for the youths, protruded beyond the alley, on the left side of the road. A loud singing sound could be heard coming from the hill – the sound of Ukrainian songs in a melancholic harmony, soaked in folklore and tenderness but also power; great power. When the hill was covered with snow – people would climb to the top with sleds. The sleds sped down from the top with their passengers hugging each other, screaming of fear and joy, competing with each other, and turning over. The hill was the Gentiles' territory. When we passed by we feared to be hit by a hurled stone, a derogatory word thrown at us, or even a badgering arm hugging and inviting us to join the good time.

The silent alley and the rowdy hill located between the colony and the village were a physical symbol for the two different worlds that were located on both sides of the river in such close proximity. We passed through them on our daily route and absorbed the difference deep in our souls.

Jewish Farmers in Russia Fields

The existence of Jewish farmers in the heart of Southern Russia's prairies, their working of the land, and their connection to the land – did not arouse any wonder in my heart. I was born and grew up among them, and the agricultural lifestyle became my second nature. Their Jewish uniqueness – that was forged in my memory. It was as if Judaism was stretched over all the hours and the days of the colony, and it was popping out everywhere, despite the similarity between the life of the Jewish and the gentile farmers, and perhaps precisely because of the geographic proximity of the colony and the village, and because of the fact that the colony farmers were simple people, with no knowledge or education.

The life in the colony was an earthly life. The colony was populated by laborers. They and their clothing emitted a pungent smell of sweat. They had big families, and they were continuously worried about making a living and fighting against nature's powers. Joyous times were the breeding and procreation at the cowshed and the stable. The men would harness the animals before dawn and go out to work and the women hurried up to milk the cows in time to beat the shepherd who would pass through the colony with a loud whiplash, with the herd, on his way to the pasture. The women took part in every task in the yard, and if they had any time left, they even went out to the field during the busy season. They lighted the heaters using dried loaves made from a mixture of manure and straw. They cooked and baked, pickled cucumbers, tomatoes, cabbage, and watermelons for the winter, plastered the houses, and sewed and patched clothing for the adults and children. During the long nights of the winter, they sat together and plucked the feathers of the slaughtered poultry, made pillows and down comforters for the family, and as dowry for their daughters. The women were busy farmers; their faces were wrinkled from hard work, their hands coarse, their heads covered with a kerchief tied under their chin, and an apron tied to their hips, usually with a child in tow. Jewish mothers were not stingy with their effort when it was time to keep tradition; a special atmosphere, dish, and taste were reserved for every holiday, as if the colony farmers were determined not to disassociate themselves from the collective lifestyle, which unified all of the Jewish homes throughout Eastern Europe.

*[Page 307]*

Miraculously, the "greater Jewish soul" was preserved within the earthly life of the Jewish farmers. Most of the colony natives were *Hassids*. Revealed and concealed threads connected them to the courts of renowned Hassidic *Rebbes*. Once in a while, when a "*maggid*" [Jewish preacher], a famed Jewish scholar, or somebody who knew to how "sing a *nigun* [a Jewish religious folklore melody]" happened to stop by – the colony residents were deeply thankful for the hour of exaltation he had granted to them.

We, the children, peeked curiously and fearfully, into the window of Reb Itche'le, a Hassidic Jew who spent his days and nights studying the Torah, and who removed himself from earthly life. The man was very strange and frightening with his waxy ascetic face. However, he was esteemed and admired, as if the materialistic public said: "Who knows, perhaps he discovered the secret of happiness."

On Shabbat, the colony rested. People drank chicory with milk which formed a thick golden crust after it was boiled in a sealed stove for many hours. They walked in measured steps to the synagogue, scrolling in the afternoon, along the main street amongst the row of wealthy people's houses and the big state park; colony notables, male and female youths, walked leisurely while children ran around mingling with the dust clouds raised by the herd, returning from the pasture. This was a single big family, who departed, at dusk, from the Shabbat, the kingdom of respite.

*

The yards in the colony were different from each other – some organized and well–established, others meager and unkept. In comparison, the yards of the wealthy Russian farmers were more nurtured than those of the wealthy Jewish farmers. They were more organized and the gentiles also grew ornament plants that did not bring any other real benefits. However, there was something else about the Jews – their lifestyle customs that protected a person's life. The kosher rules, which dictated the rules of keeping the food and use of the cooking and eating tools, contributed to that protection. The holiness of the Shabbat and holidays, that forced even the poor to purify themselves thoroughly, bathing in the public bath and changing their shirt and clothing, contributed to that as well. Ignorance, which makes life easier, but degrades the rules of cleanliness and health, did not exist in the colony. The results of that approach were evident during the hard times of the epidemics, particularly during the days of the cholera epidemic in Southern Russia. The poor Jewish farmers with their meager food and scanty housing fared better than the wealthy gentiles.

In the [gentile] village, people used to get drunk. Around the tall fence and along the alley leading to the state liquor store ("Kazionka"), the drunk rolled on the ground like corpses. The Jewish farmers did have a taste for the "bitter drink." They did have a drink to warm themselves during the long winter nights or during a trip at the end of a purchase or sale deal. They licked their lips during an obligatory drink of

*[Page 308]*

wine in a "*Kiddush*," "*Simkhat Torah*," wedding, or *Bar Mitzva*; some more than others – however, everybody thought that drinking to the point of losing one's control and honor was not a way of a Jewish person. Maybe because of that view, a horrific story was engraved in my memory about the drunkenness of the old Rabbi's wife. She was the only daughter of a wealthy colony resident and was a weak baby whose parents were worried about her health. The parents were enticed to accept the advice of the peasants to wash the baby in liquor baths to strengthen her. That was how, according to the people in the colony, they accustomed her body to alcohol. When the time came, they married her, lavishly, to a young scholar, who was later hired as the colony's Rabbi. The couple built a house and bore children, but the Rabbi's wife was never cured of the drinking disease. Despite all the efforts to hide the drink from her, she somehow managed to get it. The story that circulated among the children said that the rabbi ruled for her to receive a public punishment to atone for the shame she had brought to the community. According to the story, they tied her to a tree near the synagogue and flogged her. I could not tell today what the end of that poor woman was, and whether there was any truth to the story. However, the fear in which the story about the Rabbi's wife was told, from mouth to mouth, and the deep aversion to the sin of drinking were forged in my memory.

\*

Although the colony's farmers were not big scholars, they adhered to religion and tradition. The colony notables zealously guarded against the penetration of any heretic views into the colony; guarded but did not succeed. The spirit of the time penetrated from the edges of the camp, which had contact with the intelligentsia in the village and the hospital, or from contacts with relatives and acquaintances in the cities and towns throughout Russia. Among the causes of the change was the library, which my parents were among the people who conceived and founded it. The library was located in the house of one of the colony's wealthy farmers. It was clean and well-heated in the winter and attracted the youth by its cabinets that contained the best of the Russian as well as original and translated Hebrew literature. A good selection of the newspapers and journals, published in the cities of Russia, was spread out on a wide and elongated table. The library unified the small intelligentsia of the colony and the young generation that was thirsty for contact with the intellectual world. There was a large barn in the yard of that [wealthy] farmer where theater shows were performed by local amateurs and traveling troupes, and readings and singing balls were held. It is logical to assume that the level of the shows was low, however, the impression that they generated on the thirsty souls was deep. We prepared for every assembly, lecture, or play as for a big event and we continued to talk about them for a long time after the show. In actuality, the books, newspapers, discussions, and lectures were all within the law, as the sharp eye of the guards of the czarist regime was always watching over them; however, below the surface, they represented the discontent and the longing for something new – something that was a mixture of the enlightenment spirit that spread among the youth, national salvation, and deep social discontent. The air was soaked with unrest and the youth was searching for

*[Page 309]*

wider expanses. I recall boys from among my father's students who left the colony, but the change was more apparent among the girls. Our house served as the meeting place for these youths, and I recall several girls, some whom I knew personally, or others from my parents' stories, who went out to study in midwife-medic courses, or in teaching courses. They resided in gentile cities in which the residency of Jews was forbidden. I also remember a case when a girl was wedded in a fictitious marriage to free herself from her parents' authority. Another particular girl was forged in my memory: she studied abroad and became an opera singer. I saw her on the stage in a concert she performed on the occasion of her coming to visit her family. She was beautiful, tall, and sturdy (fitting a soprano), luxuriously dressed and adorned with shiny Jewels. She brought with her the sheen of the big city. The kiss that the *"Pristav"* [head of the police] gave her on her hand at the end of the concert served as a symbol of her rise and success. …But from all of those girls, I best remember the daughter of a wealthy Jew, owner of many assets, whose family's house was a mansion in every respect. His daughter studied in the high school in the provincial city and came home to her parents during the vacation. I adored her tremendously. She was beautiful and gracious. I still remember the reddish color of her face and her bountiful and wavy brown hair, which she used to tie to the back of her neck with an urban grace. I remember the impression that her virginal room – its curtains, the bed's awning, the table at which she arranged her hair and her dress left on me – everything was covered with a transparent fabric with an azure background soaked in spring-like air. She looked to me like a princess.

Later, I found out that she connected with a youth from the village, who was one of the visitors to the library. The youth was good-looking and wore an orange tie. He was the son of an old farmer widow. People whispered behind his back that he belonged to the Ukrainian revolutionary circles. The begging of her poor parents did not help. Her father's ploy to send her over to her sister in the big city, to erase her love from her heart, did not help either. She left her azure room and moved with the youth in the village. I do not know, until today, whether she had converted to Christianity or married him in a civil marriage, since, in the meantime, the Russian Revolution began, and the rules about marriage and religion were pushed aside. She invited me once to her new home. The house was located in a community near the river, which was known for its brazen and anti–Semitic residents. It was a wealthy and nurtured Christian home, with closed shutters, dark pictures of the saints hanging on the walls, an oil lamp lighted in front of the Christ icon, the smell of frankincense dispersed from a bowl, and an old gentile woman walking around quietly and slipping away without any sound. We did not talk long. When we parted, she whispered her question slowly: "How are they doing over there?"

During the horrific nights that descended upon the Jews later on, when the bandits rioted everywhere, I thought about and remembered her. A delicate Jewish flower, a bird jailed in a cage filled with holy pictures – what has happened to her? How could she carry her self-esteem in that Christian home when her colony – her origin – held its breath trembling with suffering and fear?

*[Page 310]*

The revolutionary youth who was inflamed with the Ukrainian national revival spirit was not alone. The ideas about the Ukrainian revival were seeded in the hearts of the youths who went to the city to acquire education. When they returned to the village they spread these ideas. They used to copy, on pieces of paper, the song "The Will" by the Ukrainian poet Shevchenko, and pass it from one to another. In that song, the poet glorified his native land – Ukraine and called his people to rise after his death and conduct a bloody revolt against the oppressing Czarist regime. We knew the song by heart and used to sing it enthusiastically.

At the start of the Revolution in 1917, the national Ukrainian discontent boiled over from the depths of the underground onto the surface. The call for an independent Ukraine was heard and the azure–yellow flag was raised. People began to honor the national dance, dress, and song. Among the Ukrainian nationals, some people envisioned the national freedom of their country to be in line with the aspirations of the Big Revolution. They thought that achieving freedom, justice, and equality meant also achieving a national revival of the people. However, some people looked at the Revolution as an opportunity to sever the ties between Ukraine and the big body whom they hated and return to the days of the Cossacks and the Hetmans.

For those of us who lived near the youth in the village, that national awakening became a source of inspiration. We witnessed how a movement grew and how a national unity, unheard of previously, was formed. However, that movement provided not only an inspiration but also a warning about a new type of diaspora. The physical signs of that warning did not lag behind. They came in the form of the national bandit gangs of Petliura and other Hetmans.

From the songs of Bialik and Frugg (in Russian), which we used to read at our balls, from the well–known pictures of Herzl and Nordau, from the dim memories of the few boys who dared and made *Aliyah* to Eretz Israel and from the blurry news about the Balfour declaration, a new and unified being began to realize. We learned then that we are people of a nation waiting for its salvation and that the time has come for the Jewish youths to act on their own behalf. During the stormy days of the Revolution and the national shock we had experienced, the Jewish colonies were illuminated with a new light for their visible and concealed contents. We looked at the people of the colony – people laboring in grueling work people who worked the land in a country that placed the worker and the farmer on a pedestal. It seemed then that they could face their future without the fear that the social revolution would destroy their livelihood. With their own existence, they served as proof that Jews were capable of working the land, loving it, nurturing it, and raising its productivity. A simple and deeply graceful Jewish folklore spirit bubbled in them. We clung to it, looking for ways to connect with our nation again. For us, the colony served as an artisan's workshop and an anvil that could be used to forge a natural Jewish power. It also proved that the Jewish farmers, with their national identity, had not been and would never be accepted by their neighbors as equals and as people who had the right to settle and work the land.

Not many days passed, and the colonies bustled with youths (among them only a few girls),

*[Page 311]*

congregated in groups of pioneers, from the expanses of stormy Russia. They heard about the Jewish colonies in the south and risked their lives to reach the colony during a period when a trip through Russia, for a Jewish person, was dangerous. They hoped that with the help of the colonies – Jewish farmers with their farms, experience, fields, and gardens – they could receive proper agricultural training. Many colony farmers doubted whether those urban youths would become accustomed to work. On the other hand, some said that there was no risk in accepting such an enthusiastic and cheap labor force. There were also some

Zionists who connected with the pioneers and tried their best to help them. Everyone had their own reason, but the fact was that doors were opened for the urban students, and the Jewish farmers taught them how to work, trained them to be farmers, and adopted them as family members. New singing could be heard in the colony – Hebrew speech.

New centers for amalgamation were formed. We became a unified group – those for whom the colony was our home and those who came to warm themselves in its light. Together, we established the "HeKhalutz in the Colonies" and weaved our dreams about fulfillment in Eretz Israel.

Still, only tens of the colony natives arrived at their destination and integrated themselves into the effort to build the homeland. Most of the others – who were attached to their native land – remained. They remained and were lost.

**Yehudit Simkhoni (Geva)**[3]


*[Page 311]*

I had a peaceful childhood in a remote corner of the giant Russia in a wealthy house whose atmosphere was characterized by the phrase "man does not live on bread alone" [Deuteronomy (8:3)]. People who came over – adults and youths, either from the Jewish colony [Nahar-Tov HaGdola] or from the [nearby] village [Berzneguvate], used to discuss together the happenings in the world and the events in Eretz Israel. A large picture of Dr. Herzl hung on the wall as if he was casting a spiritual shadow over everything discussed regarding the Jewish question and anything else.

How pleasant was it to mix with the adults and listen to their talk, some of which was clear and some obscure! Everything was so peaceful and secure that even the news about the start of the war [WW I] did not cause any shock.

…And the war continued.

Horrible news arrived to grieving families from the front; the authorities had already begun to recruit people of more advanced ages. The first signs of discontent appeared. People read the critical speeches of Kerensky and others in the "duma" (the Russian parliament in the days of the Czar) - fiery speeches against the rotten regime. Things were also being published in the newspapers, hinting openly that "the current situation cannot continue as is"… There were those who even dared to define the Czar as "worthless," and stories were being whispered secretly, mouth to mouth, about Rasputin's mischiefs and the Czarina who was being suspected of treason…Holy symbols

*[Page 312]*

were losing their brightness, and even the overgrown mustache, the colorful laces, and the heavy sword of the head of the local police force did not frighten the children any longer.

February 1917…

The Revolution has broken out. The end of Czarism has come, bringing freedom, equality, and brotherhood. People were kissing in the streets. Revolutionary pamphlets and songbooks were taken out of the stashes. Huge assemblies and parades, some common to the village and the colony, were also taking place, the blue and white flags being hoisted along with the red ones and the azure and yellow flags of the Ukrainians. Father [Moshe Yevzori-Yevzrikhin], was among the speakers everywhere. The spring has arrived. The Zionist activity was flourishing. Fancy balls benefiting the Keren Kayment Le'Israel [JNF] were held in the village theater (the only big hall). Informative assemblies and amateur plays and shows based on the sorrowful and longing songs of Frugg and other Zionists were held in the colony's synagogue. Emissaries were coming from the big cities. We, the children, heard and saw everything. Students who studied in the city were coming home during the summer break, and they, too, were filled with impressions and stories about the big new tide in Jewish life there, in the big cities.

Elections for the first national constitutional assembly of the republic were going to be held. The various parties competed over the votes – utilizing assemblies, posters, and proclamations; proclamations of all kinds – the Bolsheviks through the pro-monarchies. The Jewish and Zionist parties were, of course, among the parties. We, the children, were everywhere. It looked as if the adults were playing a new game, which they were not used to playing "hazard" until their last breath. We imitated them in our games, trying to give speeches from above fences, benches, or a big rock, repeating the various slogans, totally confusing them.

In the meantime, the goods shortage has grown more and more severe. The money has lost its value since it could not be used to purchase anything. The situation in the front has deteriorated and the interim authorities demanded an additional effort for the war at a time when the masses were already tired of the war. The rich were still rich, and the estate owners were still holding on to their land. There was no news about an agrarian reform… It is no wonder, therefore, that radical views about immediate peace, the distribution of lands to the peasants, and a regime of the workers found more and more attentive listeners. Nervousness and insecurity prevailed.

A new custom was introduced. An alarm bell was installed near the village's big church for cases such as fire and other emergencies when help was needed. The bell had a robust and dreary sound that could be heard for great distances. Everybody recognized the sound. They used it, once in a while, even when a fire broke out in the Jewish colony. And they began to use the alarm bell to call people for political assemblies. Every emissary of a party or a movement – and there were quite a few of them going around – operated the bell. Its horrific sounds would fill up the space, announcing a disaster, and people in masses would drop everything, leave the work they were doing in the village or the colony, and run toward the village's central square to hear what had happened. Now, it has become almost a daily occurrence. Sometimes it seemed to me, even today, that I could hear the bell's wailing.

Anti-Semitism began to sprout in the speeches:

*[Page 313]*

1"The Jews are selling out our homeland." Jews began to behave more cautiously – retreating farther. [The colony's] residents stopped going to meetings in the village. However, we lived in the village, and as children, we did not give up on any attraction. That was how we found out about the October Revolution.

The bell rallied, and the masses flocked. An armored vehicle (the first one I have ever seen ), stood in the center of the square, and armed riders surrounded it. A speaker announced from the top of the vehicle that, from now on, the power is held by the toiling workers and farmers who would elect their representative to manage their locality. The speakers asked: "Are there any bourgeois here?" A woman's voice was heard from among the big crowd: "Yes there is – he is the flour mill's owner who exploits the people. Here he is!" "Take him away" ordered the speaker. Two riders crossed the crowd, took the man (a Russian with progressive views), and led him outside of the crowd. Nobody understood what was happening. We, the children, including the man's two sons, who were our acquaintances, ran after them. All of a sudden they shot him. Horror struck us. The man has been smiling until now. He did not understand what they wanted from him. Now he was lying on the side of the road in a puddle of blood. We took his sons and accompanied them home. A murder of a person – the first murder I have witnessed in our neighborhood, which has been peaceful for so many years. How accustomed to murder we became in the coming years!

At that time, we learned about the Balfour Declaration. A section of a newspaper arrived from Odesa containing the full version of the declaration. Many people gathered in our house, and the declaration was read aloud anew. People cried with joy; there were calls for England's victory, thereby advancing peace and enabling our people to join the builders of the national home. Father has already promised that we will study at Jaffa's high school. We continued to weave the dream.

The lack of any connection with other Jewish centers was astounding. There was also no connection with other Jewish colonies. Rumors and intuition fed the Zionist activity. There was substantial progress in the big cities, which we did not know about. One bright day, about twenty boys and girls arrived from Kremenchug. That was the first time we heard about "the pioneer who walks before the army" [Deuteronomy 3:18, reference to "HeKhalutz" (The Pioneer) - Jewish Zionist Youth movement]. They came to train themselves for agricultural work in Eretz Israel. When they arrived from the train station in a rented wagon, the waggoneer dropped them at the only public building of the colony – the library. When we were notified at home about their arrival, we first collected all the food supplies we had at home and took them to them. Later on, Father and some of the sworn Zionists mobilized to convince the wealthy farm owners from among the colony farmers to accept them one by one and hire them for farm work. It was not easy to do. Except for a few families, who were close to the Zionist idea and who willingly accepted that burden, the rest were apprehensive about the fact that "*beleruchki*" (those who have "white hands" [in Russian]) would not be able to earn their worth, as they were not required to provide more than a shelter and food for those youths for their work.

You could probably still find one of these pioneers who would be able to tell you what they have experienced

*[Page 314]*

during these months of *hakhshara* [literally – training, or preparation before making *Aliyah*]. There was a big gap separating their lifestyles from the reality of the farmers' lives in the colony. When one of the pioneers was not employed he would lodge with us. During Shabbat, everybody would gather – and through stormy debates, they would "devour" any food product in the house or the cellar. During those days, Zrubavel and Yehudit [the author's elder siblings] stayed home for the summer break. They and some of the colony's Zionist youths united with the newcomers to form a single group. Who among these elder youths would pay attention to a child going around among them to listen? But I listened and listened: Trumpeldor – what a fascinating name! Sacrificing three years of one's life for the benefit of one's nation, in Zion, to work and guard – [what a captivating idea]! I learned about "Gvurat HaShomrim" [literally - the Heroism of the Guards] – the memorial book of the "HaShomer" [The Guard – the Jewish self-defense organization]. They kept reading from it. ...and the singing! What a singing! "*In Eretz Israel tzu Unzere Brider*" [from Yiddish – To our brothers in the land of Israel], "*Loz di Zun unz Brenen Braten*" [from Yiddish - Let the sun shine on us and burn us], "*Sham Be'Eretz Khemdat Avot*" [from Hebrew – There, in the beloved land of our ancestors and many more…

Among the pioneers from Kremenchug, there was one who had been already in Eretz Israel, and was expelled by the Turks as a Russian subject. He was the oldest in the group. His stories about Eretz Israel and the hardships faced by the pioneers only helped to enthuse everybody, and when he sang the song "*Yad Anuga*" ["Tender Hand" by Zalman Shneor], or other songs from Eretz Israel, including some Arabic songs, – the heart would skip a beat.

There was one very prized asset in Nahar-Tov – it was called "The Park of the Authority." The offices of the Guardian Bureau of the Jewish settlement in Southern Russia were located in Nahar-Tov. During the days that the bureau inspectors were allowed to impose punishments on the settlers, among them forced labor, forced laborers planted a beautiful botanic garden on an area of 100 *disiyatin* (about 1000 *dunams* [about 270 acres]).

During our time, the garden became a magnificent park, stretching along the river, opened for people to relax or stroll by, particularly on Shabbat. I think the park had never experienced such joy and singing as during the time when the pioneers stayed in the colony, joined by the colony's Zionist youths. Some debates ensued. It turned out that pioneers from various cities arrived at other colonies and they attracted youths from the best in the colonies. The issue in those debates was whether the colonies' natives required "*hakhshara,*" since there was no need to promote the alignment of the Jewish nation with more productive work and to raise the value of manual labor vs. the traditional Jewish ways of making a living in the colonies. The need to consult arose. People from other neighboring colonies – Sdeh Menukha, Romanovka, Dobroye, and Yefeh-Nahar, began to arrive in our house; our house was open to all, but that time they did not come to see Father [Moshe Yevzori-Yevzrikhin]. They came to see Zrubavel and Yehudit [Moshe Yevzori's elder children]. They discussed the subject of the "Colonial Pioneer" – the "HeKhalutz" of the colonies' natives. They discussed and established the movement "HeKhalutz in the Colonies." Zrubavel and Yehudit felt that they were different from the colonies' regular natives since they were not farmers, and they decided to train themselves. It was not possible to do it in Nahar-Tov; who would be the farmer who would agree to employ, in such grueling work, a child of R' Moshe Yevzrikhin? So, they left, Zrubavel to Sdeh Menukha HaKtana and Yehudit to

[Page 315]

Romanovka. The road was clear. The seed that had been sowed previously produced its fruits. The two summer seasons during which pioneers arrived from the city for *hakhshara* in the colonies resulted in the establishment of a new Zionism – Zionism of aspiration for fulfillment and of searching for ways to make *Aliyah*. They also established the connection between the colonies. Venerable people were discovered, from among the colonies' natives, whose most important property was their moral and mental wholeness and a steadfast belief in the righteousness of their way and lofty purpose, for which one must be ready to make any effort and sacrifice. The storms of that time could not extinguish that flame after it was ignited. Although there were times when the flame diminished – it was never extinguished, and indeed, there was no shortage of storms and tremors.

Numerous authors described what Southern Russia experienced during those years, from the beginning of the Revolution until the consolidation of the Soviet regime in 1919. The horrific Holocaust brought by the Hitler regime upon the European Jewry during the Second World War pushed out of memory whatever was experienced by the Ukrainian Jewry during the Civil War in Russia. We were part of that Jewry; probably the part that suffered somewhat less, due to its lifestyle, which was different from the lifestyle in the Jewish *Shtetl*. There was another factor: the colonies located farther away from the railroad and main roads suffered less than those located on crossroads. Those colonies experienced the calamity fully.

Following the fleeing of the Austrians and the Germans after their defeats in the West and the revolutions in their countries, the country remained without a rule. Hundreds of thousands of soldiers returned from the front with their weapons and tens of [Ukrainian] Hetmans rose, each one with their own *"banda"* [gang] and the aspiration to become the ruler, if only for a single day. They roamed throughout the vast prairie and made a living by robbing and looting. In the Jewish settlements, they also raped and murdered. The common denominator of all of them, including the biggest ones – Makhno, Grigoriev, Petliura, and toward the end, also Denikin, was the hatred of Jews. Thanks to the self-defense in the colony – a load carried by the returning soldiers and mainly the Zionists who joined them – the colony of Nahar-Tov did not suffer that much except for one case, which I am going to talk about later. The situation of the Jewish families in the village was much worse. The huge village, which was also the center of the provincial authorities, attracted the various gangs, and it contained more than a few dubious armed elements, which were going out at night to "prowl for prey." Shots reverberated at night for months and months. Shots were fired by attackers, by people who wanted to scare those with bad intentions, or just as celebratory gunfire.

The word *"nalyot"* (raid in Russian) was born. At dawn, the people at the colony didn't know who had been the ruler that day, who was alive and who had been murdered, and how many Jewish families in the village had been annihilated. In one case, only two small children who witnessed the murder of their parents and siblings survived. Some gentile acquaintances came to us often and offered us to sleep at their house at night – but my mother did not approve. She said that if our fate was to be killed,

*[Page 316]*

we should die at home as proud Jews. Her calm stand inspired a sense of security in everybody who heard about it: the Jews in our close neighborhood started to believe that our house was safe and gathered at our house at night; about 20-30 people used to sleep in our house every night. It was not clear to me, until today, why the village Jews would not move and stay in the colony. It is interesting to note that all of the [Jewish] shops were broken into and robbed at that time, except Father's shop. I will never forget the "escape Shabbat." It was a quiet Shabbat. My brother and I went out to scroll in the colony. There were many people in the street. All of a sudden, we saw three horse riders approaching and turning to a Jew who was walking innocently from the village toward the colony. They killed him and continued on their way to the colony. When they entered the colony, people in the streets attacked them, trying to catch them. Two of them managed to sneak out, but one was captured and beaten until he fainted; however, he was later released and allowed to continue on his way. We found out later that these riders served as a reconnaissance group for a gang of the size of a battalion. When they returned, they summoned the gang, which camped in a neighboring village for a revenge attack on the colony.

When the colony residents saw the approaching dark group of riders – fear descended upon all, and minutes later, everybody who owned horses and a wagon loaded their family and left, galloping toward the colony of Dobroye (a distance of about 30 kilometers). A wagon of our acquaintances stopped by us. They urged us to climb over quickly and we went with them. At home, the rest of the family did not have any idea where we had disappeared. Later on, we found out that the gang caught up with a part of the escaping convoy and brought the people back to the colony, which was almost deserted. They killed 12 Jews, robbed the contents of the houses, and imposed a substantial monetary fine which was paid with the help of the village Jews. Those who reached Dobroye, which was located near the railroad, almost doubled its population. A Soviet administration was located in the city of Nikolayev, which contained a large population of working-class people and carried a revolutionary tradition. A "Red Guards" battalion equipped with a cannon battery roamed on a train along the railroad line, particularly to collect wheat for the hungry city. The train parked at the local train station, a few days after we arrived at Dobroye. A delegation of Nahar-Tov refugees presented itself in front of the battalion commander to request his help in restoring order in the colony and the return of the refugees. The commander agreed to do so. Wagons belonging to Nahar-Tov refugees and Dobroye residents were mobilized, the battalion and its cannons were disassembled from the train, and we went on our way with the gunners. Between Dobroye and Nahar-Tov, about 12 kilometers from Dobroye, a big Russian village by the name of Yavkino, was located. There was no hostile activity by the village residents towards Nahar-Tov refugees when we had passed through it previously. This time, heavy machine gun fire was directed toward the convoy. The gunners spread for action immediately. However, they managed to fire just a few shells (as a result, the head of a church steeple was cut off) before the whole battalion began to retreat, including the gunners with their cannons. The village residents harnessed their wagons and began to chase after the escapees. They barely managed to place the cannons on the train – under fire from the pursuers. Some of the infantry did not manage to reach the train, threw their rifles to the man-made lake in the colony and

*[Page 317]*

mixed with the crowd. Bullets whistled above the colony. Again, the residents of Dobroye and the Nahar-Tov refugees boarded the wagons within a few minutes and went out on their way to Yefeh-Nahar (about 15 kilometers away). Dobroye remained empty.

Yefeh-Nahar wasn't a large colony at all, even during regular days, and the unexpected addition of such a large population resulted in a situation in which almost all of us were left without food. We starved. We would go out with the horses to pasture in the meadows by the river and try to eat grass too. Sorties to Dobroye, made by a few people, found that the colony was ransacked, but empty of enemies. They managed to bring some dried bread left in the ovens at the moment of abandonment. Dobroye residents began to return, but the road to Nahar-Tov remained blocked.

The hunger pushed us to find a solution. In the end, via an indirect route passing near more peaceful villages, we returned to Nahar-Tov. At home, they welcomed us as if we were resurrected from the dead. I assume that we looked like people who returned from the "afterlife." Our exile had lasted three weeks. During that time, we starved and did not have changes of clothing, or a blanket to cover ourselves. Our experiences were certainly evident on our faces. We did not learn our lessons from that adventure. We continued to curiously wander around in the streets to investigate the nature of any gathering and lend an ear to any rumor. There was no rule nor any legal institution. The concept of "*Samosud*" (crowd Justice) was established. People had to helplessly accept the confiscations of property and horses by the various armed forces; however, they did not treat horse thieves, robbers, and murderers mercifully, if they managed to catch them. Actually, if a *Samosud* by the crowd took place, it meant a killing, through cruel abuse, mostly with a cold weapon and particularly for horse theft. (For the farmers, the horses were the source of life, since a farmer without a horse was condemned to extinction. That was the reason why the punishment for horse thieves was so severe if they were caught. In that sense, the Jewish colony farmers were no different from their fellow Russians).

During all of those years, there was a family in Nahar-Tov that was suspected of theft. People said that their grandmother used to say: "Kids, there is a lovely darkness outside and you are sitting home!" They encountered bad luck and two brothers of that family were caught stealing horses. A crowd of farmers gathered around, harnessed them in horse bridles, and led them through the colony's streets hitting, bruising, and mocking them, and in the end, killed them with iron and wooden rods.

How could we witness and hear about all the horrors of that dreadful period without getting our souls damaged forever? A solution to that riddle can only be attributed to the character of the human race. The atmosphere at home remained unchanged. Our economic condition was good (I could not even explain how and why). The house continued to be the center of Zionist gathering. Visits by people of the neighboring colonies continued, and we all hoped for better days. Hetman Grigoriev aspired to strengthen his rule for a longer period and declared a general recruitment.

*[Page 318]*

Zrubavel's turn to be recruited arrived. Usually, Jews avoided recruitment to military service during the Czarist regime and even more so during that period of insecurity. The inequality, abuse, and life-threatening conditions – resulted in a situation in which people who had to be recruited either hid somewhere or used the old method of self-mutilation, so that they would not be fit for the service. However, Mother did not agree to any of those methods. In her opinion, a Jew must withstand all the hardships and fulfill his duty for his own honor, and the honor of the nation. Zrubavel proffered and was recruited. However, by the time the train with the recruits arrived at the city of Kherson – the regime of Grigoriev fell apart, and the recruits returned home, some on foot and some by other means.

In the meantime, the Red Army continued to overpower all of its enemies. Southern Russia was conquered as well. With the consolidation of the Soviet Regime, calm arrived specifically the security for the Jews. However, the destruction was substantive. The trade was dying. There was nothing left from the estates and their owners. The city could not offer any industrial products in exchange for food, and it starved. The farmers who could not purchase anything for their money did not sell food, except for bartering for products and houseware. They dressed with clothing made of self-produced fabric and remaining sacks. They wore clogs and self-made moccasins and lighted their house with smoking oil lamps. However, they hid their crops. Farmers did not lack food. Many bought all sorts of belongings from the city dwellers for a meager amount of wheat. With a substantial effort, confiscations, and enforcement of quotas (Rezviorstka), the authorities managed to distribute a meager amount of bread in the cities.

During that period, the members of the "HeKhalutz" movement began to search for ways to make *Aliyah*.

*

In Crimea – at a distance not far away from us, the regime of the White General [Piotr] Wrangel still prevailed. Red Armies often camped in Sdeh-Menukha, like in other locations. They were divided among the farmers' yards and we, the children, used to frequently wash their horses in the river. The relations with them were good, even though the colony children did not speak the Russian language nor did the adults in the colony. During a certain period, Makhno's forces, who washed their hands in Jewish blood, joined the Red Army to fight the forces of General Wrangel. They joined the units of [General Semyon Mikhailovich] Budyonny that camped at the time in the area of Sdeh-Menukha. The Makhno's did not hide their affiliation. Sdeh-Menukha was full of them.

I was hosted by the family of my brother-in-law Mordekhai [Veslintzki-Simkhoni] and the days were the days of crop gathering and threshing. All of a sudden, heavy rain clouds appeared in the sky. Frantic work ensued. It was necessary to arrange the heaps of wheat, which had not been threshed yet, to prevent penetration of the rain, and gather the spread on the threshing floor for threshing; it was also needed to finish the winnowing of the threshed wheat.

*[Page 319]*

Everybody who could hold a pitchfork was mobilized – from the little ones to the adults. We worked like mad people. Two riders, armed from head to toe, sporting the unique forelock of Makhno people, entered the yard. They stood there and observed, and I heard one of them yelling to the other: "Hay, have you ever seen such *Zhid's*?" The other answered, in all seriousness: "These are not *Zhid's*, these are Jews!" I could hear the respect in his words and understood then what had been my mother's intent when she explained to us that we could live and behave in such a way that nobody would dare to mock us in our faces. It was no wonder that, with such feelings, [my brother-in-law] Mordekhai [Veslintzki-Simkhoni], who embodied Zionism and manual labor, totally believing in both and in their liberating character, became one of the figures who affected me the most during my years in Russia and later on in Eretz Israel.

Rumors about opportunities to cross the border to Romania and from there to Eretz Israel spread at that time. Khaim Bavli was sent to find out what was the way to reach the border and what were the necessary certificates to guarantee minimal security on the road. Upon his return, we began swift preparations. It was decided to travel the few hundred kilometers to the border on wagons. Several members took a horse from their farm. Father bought three horses and a wagon to account for the share of Zrubavel and Yehudit. He also arranged for the necessary certificates for the entire group through an acquaintance – the head of the local Soviet. The group concentrated in Sdeh-Menukha. We left at night to avoid generating attention in the colony. The first stop was Nahar-Tov. Several last arrangements needed to be made there. As I was staying in Sdeh-Menukha at the time, the plan was also to use the opportunity to bring me back home and leave me there. I felt like an orphan because of their leaving and did not really want to stay behind. The wagons left without their passengers to a substantial distance from the colony. People still feared that a person of authority would wake up and ruin the whole plan. The members left in small groups, marching under the light of a scant moon, in the silence of the night without making noise. I accompanied them [for a short while]. That was how they said goodbye to the place of their childhood and youth, going towards a foggy and uncertain but also promising future.

We have not received any news from the immigrants for a long time. The mail was almost nonoperational. My brother Benyamin returned suddenly with a sad story. They arrived at the border town safely, however, they did not manage to cross the border for two months, and they suffered from food and supply shortages. Zrubavel's wife became sick and he had to move with her to the nearest city. The members decided to send the younger ones home – that included Yeshayahu Simkhoni and himself - a bitter fate! It turned out that, a short while after the departure of the youths, the rest of the members managed to cross the border. Zrubavel, his wife, and the two youths remained behind.

Upon the return of Benyamin, we purchased a pair of horses and a wagon and began to cultivate a piece of land in collaboration with a farmer who owned all of the required tools and a pair of horses (by the way, we also owned a cow or two for our own needs as well as for producing milk products). Farmers were forced to form such partnerships due to the shortage of horses created after the war and the Civil War. There was no shortage of land. There were two estates, close to the colony's lands

*[Page 320]*

which were destroyed and their lands were not cultivated. There were also pasture areas of virgin land, which were allowed to be cultivated. We managed to cultivate our share of 25 *dunams* of virgin land during that same spring. We sowed oats, according to the advice of the farmers, as well as 20 *dunams* of sunflowers.

*

In 1920, rumors circulated that in the Tavria province and in Crimea, which was conquered from Wrangel, the wheat had not been confiscated yet and that the farmers exchanged it cheaply with any products. We decided to try our luck too. For some reason, it was decided that Benyamin would stay with Mother and I would go out with Father as a waggoner. We took some haberdashery products, joined a wagon convoy organized in the colony for that purpose, and went out our way. Until that journey, I had not traveled farther than Dobroye and Yefeh-Nahar on one side (about 45 kilometers away), and Sdeh-Menukha on the other (about 25 kilometers away). We traveled in a convoy over an infinite prairie. There were no clear roads or highways, only simple field roads, which required a good sense of orientation and direction to avoid going around in circles. There were people in the convoy who knew the roads very well, and we just followed them. I felt as if we were sailing into a vast ocean, and who knew when we would reach its end. We crossed the huge Dnieper on a floating bridge near Kakhovka. The river attained a width of more than one kilometer at that point. The Dnieper astounded me with its size and beauty; it was beyond my imagination, from things I knew from reading about it. Beyond the Dnieper, we dove into the center of Tavria. There were only a few large villages there. The rest of the settlements were isolated ranches spread over the plain surrounded by their lands. The Tavria plain was very arid. Centrally located deep wells with a horse walking around in a circle drawing water buckets to quench the thirst of humans and animals supplied water to several ranches around them. Each rancher would bring water to their house in barrels. We camped at these wells and often had to beg to allow us to water our horses. I would sleep on the ground under the wagon, and Father tended to feed the horses at night. We would continue on our way at dawn. However, in every settlement we reached, we were told that nothing was left to trade.

There was no sense in pushing forward as a convoy, and we parted ways, each trying their own luck. We began to wander around on the vast plain by ourselves. Each time I saw a settlement on the horizon, we would approach it, but the answer was negative everywhere. "Have mercy on your child and go back home," Father was told several times by Gentiles. I may have made a very poor impression with my pitiable appearance. One day, a windstorm erupted on the prairie. I have never seen a storm like that in our area. The wind uprooted prairie plants and whipped our faces and the faces of the horses with them and lumps of dirt. The wind howled in thousands of voices. We couldn't see beyond a few steps in front of us and the horses couldn't walk

Jewish Farmers in Russia Fields

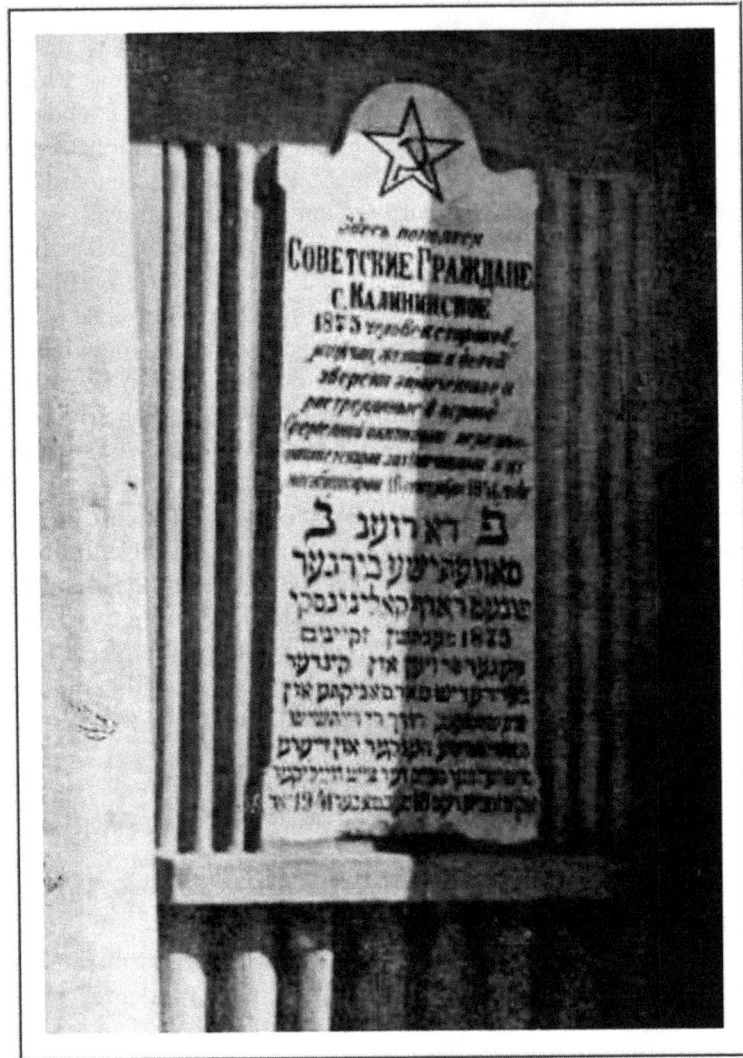

The memorial to the colonies' martyrs

Built by the Holocaust survivors from Sdeh-Menukha
The inscription on the memorial, in Russian and Yiddish, says:
"Here lie buried Soviet citizens from the village of Klininsk (Sdeh-Menukha), 1875
people, elderly, men, women, and children, who were tortured and murdered by
the fascist executioners and the collaborators during the temporary occupation,
on the 16 of September 1941"

At the victims' mass grave on the memorial day for the colonies' martyrs

*[Page 321]*

against the wind. We felt lost. "We are returning home," said Father. The concept of home seemed to me nonexistent. "Let's try to look for cover," I said to him. I turned to the wind direction and continued to drive in the dark at high noon. All of a sudden, some buildings appeared in front of us. It was a ranch with the Red Flag flying on top of the house, probably a seat of the authorities. However, we did not have any choice. We knocked on the door, and they welcomed us warmly. It turned out to be simply a large and wealthy ranch. The flag was probably there as a camouflage. The farmer helped me to untie the horses and lead them to the stable to feed them. They welcomed us as worthy guests and fed us the best of food. It became clear immediately that they were willing to barter wheat with anything we had as if they were eager to get rid of their wheat. Indeed, we saw a barn full of several tens and perhaps hundreds of tons of wheat. The farmer loaded a ton of wheat for us in exchange for several sawing threads and other negligible items and added a sack full of crashed barley as food for the horses for the road. The storm subsided at night, and we went on our way in the morning. I am not sure exactly how, but I did not find it difficult to find the way back home. Certain signs that were forged in my memory previously appeared, from time to time, as proof that I was going in the right direction. I saw the Dnieper in front of me again with great joy. Only a two-day trip back home from there. Another night lodging stop with our in-laws in Sdeh Menukha, and we brought the treasure home. That trip lasted eight days of non-stop travel while I was only eleven and a half years old.

We harvested a bountiful harvest that year. The virgin soil yielded about 500 kilograms per *dunam*. The sunflower crop – the source of cooking oil, yielded plentifully too and our apartment became a barn with rooms full of wheat. We prepared a fallow field [third field in a three-field crop cycle] for fall seeding and sowed it. We worked hard – obviously, mainly Benyamin and me. We held on, but one of the horses was exhausted. We simply let it go and had to purchase a new one. A catastrophe arose in the following winter, experienced by the whole country of Ukraine. In the fall, the fields sprouted and developed nicely, and then the rains began and continued endlessly. Following the rain, without any break, and before the snow fell, the intense freeze came.

The saturated and flooded soil became one big icy surface. People could skate everywhere, like on frozen rivers and lakes. It turned out, when the spring came, that only islands of wheat survived on the slopes and soil lumps. The summer crops were only a small percentage of the overall amount of crops. Taking into account that the seeded areas were substantially reduced because of the Civil War and the shortage of work animals, and the fact that the entire inventory emptied out due to the confiscations to supply the cities and to help the people in the Volga Region, where hunger spread during 1920 – it would be obvious why signs of hunger appeared after the harvest season of 1921. [Luckily] our supply was sufficient to last for two years, but we understood how big the risk was. Nobody could be blamed for calamities; life dictated its own demands.

Zrubavel and his wife arrived home with a new plan to travel to Crimea and from there, in fishing boats, to try to reach Romania or Turkey on their way to Eretz Israel.

*[Page 322]*

Another group of friends organized to implement that plan, among them another resident of Nahar-Tov by the name of Yehoshua Dukhin (now in Kibbutz Afikim). Money had to be collected, Father achieved that and the group left.

We couldn't continue to reside in a rented apartment in the village and work in the colony without the minimal assortment of tools. If we wanted to work the land we had to become farmers. We bought a house in the colony, although it would only become available in the spring of 1922. We bought a *buker* (a plow), a sowing and piling machine, an accessorized crate for the wagon, and ladders for a ladder wagon for transporting the crops from the field. In addition, we had to replace the horse that died during a trip I made with Father to the city of Kherson (a distance of 80 kilometers) with a wagon loaded with crops for sale. We hardly made it back with one horse and the cart after many adventures. That was how our savings from being merchants dwindled.

In addition to hunger, a typhus fever epidemic hit the country. Millions of people took to the road, looking for ways to feed their families. People would travel crammed on the few trains. Many traveled riding on the roofs risking their life. The poor and tortured Russian people, after lying on dirt on the front during the World War and the Civil War, without a change of clothing and without minimal sanitary conditions, were infested with lice, and the typhus traveled with the lice. The peddlers we called them *Meshotzniki* (bagmen), from the villages, would go out to the cities with a bit of flour to barter for merchandise or items available for sale. They got infected at the market, spread the epidemic, and brought it home to their families. Malnutrition and poor sanitary conditions reduced the ability of the people to withstand the epidemic, which took a horrible toll.

Four of us got sick – Benyamin, I, Leah, and David [Moshe Yevzori-was Yevzrikhin's younger children]. We were sick for a month and a half. How Mother managed to save us all is unclear. It is also unclear how Father managed to secure the minimum for our survival without selling the horses, the cow, or the machinery previously purchased. As a side note, there was no price for that property back then. We did not have food for the horses anymore, and the cows stopped giving milk. I am not sure whether our parents ate – but they fed us. There was insufficient heating to warm up the apartment – Mother warmed us out alternately. How did she avoid becoming sick herself? We all recuperated. I recovered first. The spring showed its first signs, the snow melted; the ice moved on the rivers; the soil thawed and became mud, and the first sprouts poked out.

\*

To save the horses and the cow it was decided to take them out to the fields, where they could find food in the stubble of last year and the sprouting weeds. I was the only one that could be considered for that task. I harnessed the horses, tied the cow to the wagon, loaded a barrel of water, and went on my way, with Father walking behind to hurry the cow. The horses stopped walking from time to time, as they did not have the energy to pull the wagon through the mud. I walked by them like a drunk, swaying from weakness.

*[Page 323]*

I still remember the fact that my legs never hit the spot I chose for them on the ground in the mud. It took almost a full day to drag ourselves to that fallow field, about 5 kilometers from home, where we decided to camp. We were not alone. Several other farmers from the colony did as we did, and a whole camp of wagons, horses, and cows gathered there. My father returned home, and I remained in the field with the others.

The colony farmers had a lot of experience in camping in the field. The custom was to leave for the fieldwork on Sunday morning and return at dusk on Friday, albeit people were not doing it so early in the spring. Actually, the time has not come for any field work. However, there was no choice at that time; we needed to act as if it was already warm and dry. For cover, we used the wagon's accessorized crate, which did not leak when it was turned on the side with the wagon against the wind, and its upper side served as a narrow roof. A few youths helped me to turn the wagon and I settled myself for the night. Like the others, I gathered some straw and thorns for fire and cooked myself a meal: "You hang a pail at the edge of the shaft and heat it underneath." That's the whole theory. I boiled the water, added a handful of flour, and a bit of salt, and that was the "meal." We were not accustomed to more than that back then.

The night silence was very strange. Only once in a while, the mooing of a cow or the sound of a horse jumping on its front legs, tore through it. But the animals had food there. The objective was achieved. I was tasked with guarding our pricy property. Light rain began to fall the following day. We sat under the wagon, and stories were told endlessly. The people were happy that they did not have to water the animals. I could hardly cook a single meal for myself throughout that whole day. Several farmers decided to go back home; obviously without the animals; just "to visit" they said, and asked to keep an eye on their animals. The rain intensified and fell throughout the night. Even the animals felt uncomfortable, and they gathered around the wagons and the people. I was happy the see light in the morning, but the joy did not last long: the rain continued to fall. One after the other, the people decided to return home. Obviously, they could not take their animals back home with them because there was nothing they could feed them there. They simply abandoned them. They offered me to join them, but I could not. Something prevented me from doing so. It was like the eyes of my family were looking at me critically: "You did not pass the test. You have abandoned the animals!" I refused. One adult farmer, our future neighbor in the colony, tried to pull me with him forcibly – I circumvented him and stayed by myself – with the entire camp of wagons and animals. The rain continued. I added some hay sacks taken from somebody else's wagon for my berth and some additional covers, but everything was soaked with wetness, and there wasn't any dry corner. The plain was gloomy, grey, and desolate; and as if just to add to that misery, ruins of destroyed estate buildings, covered with secret and mystery, stood nearby. I lay on my berth, bundled with layers of covers, trying to warm up my body in this horrible humidity, without any will to move away from that position. The hours stretched endlessly. It was impossible to cook under those conditions. I gathered my strength, kneaded some dough, swallowed it as is, and returned to my berth. With water-soaked soil, one could hear every step for far distances. I did not know who the walking person was: a human

*[Page 324]*

or an animal. After all, it wasn't long ago since we experienced the horrible nightmares. I covered myself above my head; I did not want to think, neither did I want to listen.

I wanted to fall asleep – I did not care what would happen. Indeed, I fell asleep and woke up at night by the sound of breathing close to me. My blood froze in my veins until I realized that it was the horses. They stood by my berth and stretched their necks towards me while pushing each other. They smelled me by their breathing and blew warm vapor over me. All of a sudden, my fear evaporated, as if I was not alone anymore in the center of the vast fields, far from any settlement, and defenseless against anybody who would want to hurt me. I actually talked to the horses, and later I fell asleep again under the guard of the horses and slept deeply until the morning. The following nights, I wasn't afraid anymore, as I got used to the company of the horses. The rain continued to fall, but I got used to my wet clothes and berth. During the breaks in the rain, I wandered around among the animals and warmed myself in the sun. Suddenly, I came up with the idea of trying to milk a cow. To my surprise, there were several drops of milk in her udders. I milked her directly into my mouth. I went from one cow to the other and milked as much as I could. Most of the cows stayed calm as if they were waiting for just that. I was guaranteed not to be hungry again, which, by the way, stopped bothering me by then.

The rains and the heat resulted in the tremendous growth of the weeds. The animals simply continued to recover from one day to another. However, a sea of mud separated me from my home. Of those who had abandoned their animals, none came to investigate what the situation was. One day, I saw a figure approaching from the direction of home. It was·Mother who came! I could not look at her face and see the tears trickling down from her eyes despite her efforts to avoid them. She was not sure whether she would find me alive. She told me that Benyamin was still very weak and that they were about to move to our new home in the colony. She brought some food for me but asked that perhaps I would join her and we would go home together…I felt a pinch in my heart that there was nobody who could take over from me, and decided to stay. I tried to calm her down. I described how beautiful my life was there. I pretended to have self-confidence and proved to her that my situation was better than that of the rest of the family. I stood there for a long time, watching how difficult it was for her to drag her legs through the deep mud until she disappeared.

I continued with my Robinsonian life. I cooked my meals with milk rather than water. The horses obeyed my calls, but the rain continued to fall. One time I was brought food by… Zrubavel. I heard from him that the Crimean plan failed. They did not succeed in getting out, ate whatever they had with them, and could not find other means to sustain themselves. Swollen from hunger, each found the way home, with great difficulties, on his or her own. Zrubavel said he intended to leave to work for the movement [in Russia]. By the way, he found the family residing in our new home in the colony. Zrubavel left, and I stayed behind. The days passed and I lost count. At times I thought that I was in the fields for eons. One day, that same farmer neighbor came to take his horses back home. "It is time to prepare for the spring's sowing," he said. He offered me to join him. We harnessed four horses and a wagon and went home.

*[Page 325]*

The settlement and everything else looked very strange to me. I was a guest in my own home. It was the first time after twenty and some odd days that I took off my clothes and my shoes, and washed up. It would be easy to guess what my shape was after rolling around in the mud and taking care of the animals during all of those days. They fed me, of course, from the best food in the house, but I threw everything out. I probably managed to shrink my stomach pretty well. It did not bother me. I was at home, washed up, and lying in my bed. I missed the silence of the field though. Sounds echoed in my ears with a homey resonance – the resonance of a roof above one's head, after long days and nights of rainy and cold outdoors. I felt pity for myself, all of a sudden, and burst into tears. Mother sat by me without saying a word, as if she understood what was going on in my heart, her hand caressing my head, and that was how I fell asleep.

*

From that point on, we were anchored with all of our bodies and souls in the life of the colony and only the colony. I could fill many pages with the description of the desperate struggle to make a living that the family got itself into during the first two years of our lives in the colony. As a memory of our distinguished status in the past, only the personal respect that the colony residents felt towards my parents remained and even deepened; perhaps respect toward all of us in light of our steadfastness against all the hardships that had befallen us. From a political point of view, my father was disqualified, as a Zionist, to be elected to the Soviet. However, in economic matters and internal affairs of the colony, and in representing the colony at the Jewish welfare organization, his advice was listened to, and often accepted. Many colony residents needed immediate assistance with food and seeds for sowing the land; otherwise, there was no chance for satiation even in the future. The [Jewish] American welfare union – the "War Relief" organization, which was allowed to operate in Russia on the condition that it would also provide assistance to a certain percentage of non-Jews, agreed to operate in the colony on the condition that my father would be their representative. That brought some income to the family. My mother did not shy away from any type of work that she happened to find. She worked as a cook in a soup kitchen for the needy – established by the "War Relief" and baked bread for distribution for a meager wage, and that was how we made a living until the harvest of 1922. We obtained seeds and sowed about 30 *dunams* [about 81 acres], even with difficulty, since the horses were not able to work hard without feeding on prepared food. The Ppasture was not enough. However, the worst was already behind us. After a break of nine months, we ate bread, real bread!

We did not experience hunger again, but plenty of quandaries hit us. Somebody emptied our laundry ropes, sheets, and underwear after washing at a time when clothing was precious. We were left with nothing. We needed to get used to that, too. Zrubavel was on the road then, on behalf of the [Zionist] movement. Being one of its founders under the new conditions, he was arrested and put in jail in Kherson.

We were not accustomed to arrests then. My father traveled to Kherson to try to handle his release

*[Page 326]*

and bring some food for him and for his friends. He had to stay there for a while. The policy towards the Zionists was probably not very clear then; indeed, the jailed members were released after approximately one month. Zrubavel, his wife, and their daughter, who was born in the meantime, stayed with us. She became used to all of the farm work, and he returned to work for the movement in various regions of Russia, often without us knowing where he was.

In the meantime, Benyamin decided to leave home. Several *hakhshara* [training] farms of the HeKhalutz movement were established in several places in Russia. The chances of receiving a certificate to make *Aliyah* to Eretz Israel were slim, so he went to join one of those farms. Father tried to convince him not to leave us during such a distressed economic condition but Benyamin was firm in his opinion that the only solution was to make *Aliyah* not [stay] in Russia. I supported his view with the promise that I would take charge of all the work on the farm. That summer was, for me, one of the most difficult tests in my life. All the family members worked as hard as possible. Everybody worked in hoeing the summer crops (sunflowers and corn), but my main helper was my brother David, who was only eight years old. That kid knew how to harness horses when he was only 6-year-old. He would drape the straps over the horses by standing on top of the manger, or the wagon, since he did not reach the horses' necks by standing on the ground. I doubt there was any other kid in the colony who knew to work like him, particularly in tasks associated with the horses.

The harvest season of that year was a nightmare. Whoever knows the name of the Russian piling machine, knows that its name - *lobo grika* (meaning "warming the forehead) fits what it really does - instead of the piling machine lever placing the harvested crop directly on its own floor – a person had to sit in the back of the machine, and gather, with a chopped teethed pitchfork, one pile after the other and place them down in a single row behind the piles from the previous runs. That was grueling work because one had to be careful not to put the pitchfork between the moving blades, particularly when the green and heavy hay was harvested. I was like a baby compared to my partner in the harvest, a strong man with muscles. Despite that, he did not cede anything to me – he did two rounds and expected two rounds to be done by me. I did that with the last of my strength, sometimes by standing since I did not have the strength to do it sitting down. On top of the hard work, I was infected with dysentery and could not get rid of it for many days. I had to stop and run aside frequently, to the sound of the urging calls that accompanied me. There was plenty to harvest that year. I held on and surprised myself. We did not have much choice in selecting our partners. That particular partner eroded my faith in humans; he broke all of our agreements, relying on his strength and our lack of choice. He would harvest his share out of turn. I once noticed that the turn of harvesting our wheat came, and was about to be abandoned while he was turning the machine to his field, I could not hold myself back and attacked him with my fists. Obviously, since the forces were unequal, I was the one that absorbed most of the blows, but our wheat was harvested.

The partnership continued. One week we were transporting and threshing, and the other week – our partner. There was no guarantee that the good weather would last to allow us to collect everything. Obviously, we tried our best. I almost did not have a chance to lie down, before I had

*[Page 327]*

to wake up my sleepy brother David. I would lie him down on the ladder wagon and go out for the transport, while he continued to sleep on the way to the field. After I had loaded the wagon (we had a large wagon, 6 meters long with an upper tall ladder) he would receive and compress the wheat, and drive the wagon home while I slept. Very often, we were returning from the field with a loaded wagon, while others were just going out with their wagons to the field. Father's role would be to feed the horses any time we had a break from work, during the day and night. Mother, in addition to all of the housework and handling of the cows, would help in every task during the threshing. Father and Mother rotated in turning the winnower.

How envious was I of those who had a pair of horses and more, and could perform all of the field work without worries and special efforts. Many of those people did not perform their work well, as if they did not like their fate as workers of the land; they continued without innovations, like their ancestors in days past, they did not bother to study crop rotation, seed selection, or introduction of new crops. We learned to work enthusiastically and do the work well. For me, it was like a mission of honor. We strove to cultivate all the lands allocated to us, but could not. It made no sense to terminate our milk sector to be able to buy another horse, because what justified field work at all was making wheat and hay cultivation more profitable. Wheat itself had a very low official price. Except for securing bread for family and animals, vast quantities of surpluses were required to sustain us.

The desire to accomplish as much as possible was beyond the strength of our new horse, and it reached the point of total exhaustion. We were lucky that we managed to exchange the horse for a new one by adding one fattened pig.

This was an outstanding horse, one of the few owned by the colony's Jews, which was also awarded a red card (grade A for military service when needed). There was no limit to its workability. It set us back on our feet and brought back our honor. We could then become more selective when the time came to look for a partnership. It is easy to guess how happy I was when we could afford to purchase another horse after the harvest of 1924. At last, we could attack the work as we wanted, without feelings of inferiority and helplessness. It can be said that we have not experienced poverty since.

*

These were the days of the new economic policy (NAP). The easing of the ownership of production resources in industry and agriculture, brought a quick recovery of the market, following the Civil War and the militant communism. The establishment of the uniform agricultural tax, which allowed every farmer to know in advance how much he would need to pay that year while keeping the rest for himself and his own benefit, brought a rapid development of agriculture. The import of the first tractors and various agricultural machines commenced. Groups of 10 – 12 farmers organized into "artels" [agricultural cooperative associations] –

[Page 328]

and thereby received priority in purchasing a tractor (Fordson) and other machines. Artels organized in our colony too, but we did not join. We did not want to commit ourselves, as our aim was to make *Aliyah*.

I could not tell why we procrastinated in deciding. I was so busy with the work and, in parallel, in the [Zionist] movement that I did not pay attention to it. One of the main reasons was certainly the fact that my elder brothers were still in Russia. The liquidation of our property would have been likely sufficient for the road expenses, but the fear that we arrive in Eretz Israel penniless with a family consisting of a manpower imbalance, probably deterred my parents.

Zrubavel, who was a member of the "HeKhalutz" center, which was "nearly legal" at the beginning and later on legal (and also issued a newspaper, which Zrubavel was mentioned as its editor) - spent a considerable amount of time in dense Jewish centers where the movement was operating underground. Chance greetings and occasional letters allowed us, barely, to track him down. Odesa, Kharkov, Homel [Gomel], and Minsk were some of the stops in his work. He happened to stop by for two days at home, at the beginning of 1924. These were two nights that became festive in our local branch, which was thirsty for information and guidance. My parents tried to convince him to leave Russia when it was not too late but to no avail. He saw himself as standing in the front's first line, and leaving it could be considered a desertion. His words were blunt and clear: "There is a very limited active Zionist leadership, meager resources, and only a few certificates [for making *Aliyah*]. On the other hand, the foundations for the existence of the Jewish *shtetl* were destroyed and therefore *productivization* [abandonment of traditional

Jewish occupations in favor of more productive and "white collar" professions] is the order of the hour. There are opportunities for a vast Jewish agricultural settlement in Ukraine and Crimea. We must direct those circles of supporters towards settlement with clear national character, to create, until the rage subsides, centers which could provide, when the time comes, candidates for *Aliyah* – candidates who are skilled in manual labor, in large numbers, much larger than those that exist in the "HeKhalutz" *hakhshara* farms. The settlements would serve as a passageway for prepared candidates supplementing the existing scant *Aliyah*. The Jewish street should absolutely never be abandoned to fall into the hands of the *Yevsektzia* [Jewish Communist sector]. We need to encourage ourselves – even if the opportunities don't exist and the forces are unequal. The masses of the Jews must be organized in the localities and given social-Zionist content and hope. There is a need for people to carry the flag."

Zrubavel left. That was the last time I was fortunate to see him, and also the last time the rest of the family saw him, except Mother who traveled in the winter of 1926-1927 to visit him in Verkhneuralsk in Siberia where he was jailed in isolation as a political prisoner. The last news from him, which also arrived from Siberia, was heard in 1935. Since then, we lost any trace of him forever.

Benyamin's turn to make *Aliyah* had also not come, and he continued to work in *hakhshara* camps of "HeKhalutz." He was transferred from one place to another, according to the needs, even though he had a family already. As the [Zionist] activity widened, and the imprisonments increased, he was recruited to headquarter-related activities and his chances for making *Aliyah* became more remote.

*

*[Page 329]*

We had quite a few arguments at home about the underground activities of the [Zionist] movement. We formed two camps; on one side – Father, and the other, Mother and I. Father, with his typical realistic sense, did not see the logic in a dynamic clandestine Zionist activity against an iron regime that uses loathsome means to justify its actions against those, according to the regime's own view, who did not act according to the (regime's) rules, even if the activity was not against the regime itself. Even though he was loyal to his Zionist views, without any exceptions, and he announced them in public on many occasions, he did not participate in the clandestine movement's formal activities, although he did not inhibit our undertakings. He also did not prevent, except for some grumbling, the lodging in our home of emissaries from one of the headquarters or other colonies, who came to visit me. It became clear that we would encounter a bitter end. We would sacrifice ourselves without being able to erect a wall good enough to withstand the *Yevsektzia*'s rule in the Jewish street, which was helped by all the devices of the regime and was inciting and informing about the Zionist movement to the heads of the regime and the [Communist] party (incidentally, we could find a sympathetic ear among many of the party's heads, during a certain period). It cannot be said that we did not foresee the lurking dangers. The fact was that, among other things, every member was prepared to withstand the hardships of imprisonment and investigation. However, our conscience was clear – we were not among the people who acted against the Soviet regime. The opposite was true. We thought that the solution to the large-scale Jewish anomaly could only be found under that regime. Trumpeldor's "Pioneering Manifesto" and our adapted "Borokhov's Platform" served as our bible. It was necessary to fight for the self-determination of the Jews and their national language.

My situation was very peculiar at that time. I was still very young, not yet 15, in 1923. The elder Zionists, whom almost all of us knew, left the colony, most of them to the *hakhshara* farms and others to the cities to study; there was no formal frame for the Zionist youth. I participated in the cultural activities organized by the Komsomol. Everybody knew about my views (I even insisted on singing a Hebrew song – KeShaon

Ra'am BaShama'im" ["Like the Sound of a Thunder in the Sky," by Naftali Tzvi Imber]," at an amateur ball in the public hall).

Yet these activities attracted me more and more, and there was the danger that I would be swept by the current. I was not the only one in that situation, and the end would have been entirely different if not for a fortunate event.

The envoy who came and presented a direct request that I would help establish a local branch of the Z" S *Yugent*" ("Zionist-Socialists Youth") in the colony. To my question about what prompted him to trust me, and whether I was even close to that ideology, he responded that Zrubavel vouched for me. He was an older adult, a member of the Z" S party headquarters. We discussed the request the whole night, and I decided to help. He took me the following day

*[Page 330]*

to meet representatives of existing branches in other colonies, and to learn how it was possible to begin. I shall provide here some of the details about our organization there.

The base for our recruiting activities was those few older members who stayed behind in the colony and did not leave for *hakhshara* and their younger brothers and sisters. Later on, to create additional cells, every new member had to provide recommendations from two people. Every club held two meetings weekly. We renewed the movement of "HeKhalutz," which was an apolitical Eretz Israel union and could absorb elder youths regardless of their social views. The only common ideology was the aspiration to make *Aliyah*. I, despite my young age, also worked among them. In the end, when a cell of the Z" S party was established, I was also allowed to join the party (outside of the regulations). I became a member, and so was my mother, who, unlike Father, did not believe in a passive approach and gave her hand to any activity. In our conditions, it was a great organizational and intellectual effort. There was insufficient printed material, a lack of tight connections with Eretz Israel, and a terrifying shortage of locally educated leaders. In addition, the leaders who had to prepare for every meeting based on the available material took upon themselves an additional load. We issued an internal (handwritten) monthly newspaper, and I was its editor. That required quite a few additional night hours. We tried, several times, to bring permanent counselors from the centers in the cities; however, under the conditions of a small settlement, every foreigner stood out; particularly, his association with people, whose ideological identity was very well known, would point to his occupation. None of these foreigners managed to hold on for more than a month. Luckily, we succeeded in getting them all out in time, except one who, indeed, was arrested. We reached a point when 50 – 60 people were registered and organized in three bodies in our colony, we considered that a significant achievement.

I was fortunate to be nominated as a representative of the entire Southern Russia in the Congress of the "Z" S Youths" as well as a representative of the Z" S of Southern Russia in a congress that was called off before it ended due to a wave of mass arrests of the party's members and its youths, which suddenly erupted and actually constituted the destruction of the physical existence of the party. I myself was lucky. After all, local regime officials knew about me, and my views and the title "disloyal from a public point of view" were attached to me all the time. Despite all of that I had good relations [with these officials]. For example, there was a civil defense organization in the colony. The Soviet official responsible for the armory and the guarding schedule, who knew about my devotion to the Jewish defense affairs, would often hand me over his responsibilities of supervising the guarding schedule and its execution and I had, most of the time, a rifle and ammunition from the Soviet armory in my house. There was no sense in pretending to be innocent. I never denied my views. The problem was not to be caught during an actual "clandestine" activity, which we tried our best not to do.

Jewish Farmers in Russia Fields

Yehuda Kopelevitz (Almog) arrived at our colony in 1924. He came to Russia with [David] Ben-Gurion, using the opportunity of a Russian agricultural exhibition, to try to mediate between the rightist and the leftist factions of the HeKhalutz movement.

Yehuda extended his visit and received a license to visit the [Jewish] communes that still existed,

*[Page 331]*

here and there throughout Russia. Obviously, he visited many of the HeKhalutz branches, and he also arrived by us. It is hard to describe our excitement to host somebody who could provide regards directly from Eretz Israel, tell us about what was going on there and about the chances for the future, as well as regards from relatives and acquaintances. Due to the short time for preparations, we did something we usually did not do – gather all of the people from the various cells into one assembly because we could not deprive anybody of obtaining the information from the source, things about which these people were willing to sacrifice their own life. Tens of people crowded in one house sat in the dark, and listened throughout almost the entire night. I could not afford that pleasure for myself. I made rounds around the house and the adjacent streets to prevent a complete surprise from occurring. The Komsomol people probably sensed that the gathering was taking place and went out to sniff in the streets. I had to spend a long hour with some of them who approached the place too close, in a joyful bash, singing, and telling dubious jokes. The principal objective was to make sure that the gathering went well. In the meantime, it turned out that Yehuda's license was about to expire in a couple of days. We came out with a daring idea to exploit the lack of experience of our provincial authorities in contact with foreign visitors. I went with Yehuda to the Soviet office, residing in the neighboring village, and presented him to the head of the administrative office as a member of a commune in Eretz Israel who is visiting communes and villages in Russia. We presented Yehuda's certificate and requested an extension. The astounded official was sweeter than honey; He stamped the required seals with hands shaking with excitement and even accompanied us to the door. Following that authorization, Yehuda was free to go around in the colony. I also took him to the Komsomol club to meet the colony youth. They surrounded him with many questions and even wanted him to have a discussion with them; however, the Komsomol's secretary stopped the contact and isolated us. In the following evening, already not in secret but seated along long set tables under bright light, Yehuda continued with his stories in front of the adult crowd, mainly from families who were known as Zionists, so that the risk of getting informed upon was minimized. In our conditions then, his visit was like a big bright light shining in the darkness. We need to note that there was a big gap between those people who were fans of Zion, and close to the idea of the Return to Zion or were relatives of people who had made *Aliyah* to Eretz Israel and the people who were active in the underground movement. These members paid the membership dues and took on themselves the full risk, knowing well the suffering they could expect to be inflicted by the regime, whose attitude and means were very clear. The members who were organized in the various branches of the movement rarely had the chance to gather and see each other in a general assembly. The meetings were held in small cells while the members did not know how many cells there were in the colony. Even if they would gather, once or twice, in an assembly, they really did not know whether it was a general or partial assembly. As a result, no social life was developed in the movement. Songs were taught mouth to mouth; friendship relations were developed within the groups. If we allowed ourselves to unwind, it was only done during friendly meetings on Shabbat or in the evenings,

*[Page 332]*

but never during meetings – when we needed to keep silence and humility. It is logical to assume that a similar situation prevailed in other colonies where an organized movement was established.

We did not rely only on our own innovation skills. There was a central directing hand – by the central management team of Southern Russia. Study material and information duplicated by a typing machine or by a hectograph were transferred to various places by messengers or by loyal members who happened to travel to neighboring cities, and who had received in advance an address for handing over the material. That was also where the reports about the local activities, applications of new members, and membership fees were handed over.

We received from the center names and addresses of members from other settlements whom we could trust and could turn to, in time of need. Without authorization from the center, we had to treat everybody with caution (for example, Yona Kosoi-Keseh [native of Dobroye, later on, a member in five sessions of Israel's Knesset], visited his relatives in the colony, who were also members of the movement. Knowing that he was a Zionist they directed him to me. However, according to the rules – I could welcome him warmly, and talk to him about rocks and trees, but absolutely never bring him together with the members of the movement, or tell him about our activities).

Due to the limiting and trying clandestine conditions, we had to instruct our members, despite the risk involved, to participate in all of the cultural and general educational activities of the Komsomol, which were held in public. We even coordinated our activities to leave some evenings available for that, as we did not have the means to provide for the needs of people who wanted to learn and had no means to do so.

At the inception of the Soviet regime, the slogan "The children and the youth are our future" was emphasized and the activity of organizing the youth was initiated – very innocent at the beginning - the "Kramsomol" ("Krestianski Soyuz Molodivzhi" – "The Agricultural Youth Union"). No constraints were imposed on becoming a member, neither of views nor of class. For the first time, organized systematic actions were developed to elevate the cultural level of the peasant youths. The primary counselors came from the part of the intelligentsia that was studying in the cities and had joined the Communist Party enthusiastically, or those who were already underground members during the Whites' regime. Other manpower for these activities came from local advanced and educated people, without considering their political views. Of course, not all the youths participated in these activities, which, by the way, were always public and open to anybody. The peasant population always contained circles that were not interested in anything beyond satisfying their immediate but limited needs.

These activities were very diverse. We need to recall that no radio existed at the time and only a limited number of newspapers was available. An overall review of what was happening on the international front was provided. A newspaper was read aloud to disseminate news about Russia.

*[Page 333]*

Evenings devoted to questions and answers were also held, at least weekly, as the principal means for deepening the youth's knowledge. An opportunity was available to ask anonymous questions for those who, for various reasons, avoided asking questions in public. The people who provided answers could be anybody who had volunteered to do so after the question was read. That resulted in cases where a discussion about a topic was initiated. If there were questions to which nobody, including the counselor, could respond, a response was prepared for another session. Obviously, the youths who were inclined to support Zionism, participated in these activities, alertly and diligently. They could be identified clearly, during the sessions devoted to questions and answers, by their approach to the various general questions and particularly to questions related to the Jewish nation. In addition to these activities, a chorus, drama club, and literature club were also organized. Various members were given the responsibility, from time to time, to prepare lectures and reviews of defined subjects. That was a welcomed activity.

Tens of the elder youths began to leave the colony to study in various institutions in the cities, in departments for workers, and in technical schools of an appropriate level. These students were equipped with certificates that granted them the right to scholarships, dormitories, and other benefits. Many students who were leaning toward Zionism were included in these programs. However, that freedom did not last long. A decree was issued, even before a year had passed, about the abolition of the "Kramsomol" and the establishment of the "Komsomol" ("The Communist Youth Union"). Constraints were imposed on membership in that organization. First of all, the doors were closed for youths who came from a "suspicious" class (e.g. wealthy farmers, merchants), sons of those who were not eligible to vote, and those whose views were not compatible with those of the regime. All of these were recognized from the time of the "Kramsomol" activity. Not many knocked on the doors of the new organization. Members of the "*Kombed*'s" ["Committees of Poor Peasants"] pressured their sons to join the organization. One could get a "*Komandirovka* (A certificate for sending somebody to study) only through the "Komsomol," and this was a major enticement. Incidentally, the "Komsomol" accepted members in the age range of 14 – 24. If somebody, who was suspected because of his views or his class origin, wanted to join the "Komsomol" he would have had to denounce his connections to his past, prove in practice his loyalty through a long candidacy period, and obtain affirmation of two "Komsomol" members. That was before the Zionist movement organized itself in the underground, and before it forged its ideological and physical resilience against the enticements and risks it faced. During that period, many youths who had joined Zionism before were swept away by the current and became integrated with the Soviet regime operation, some exploiting it for their own benefits and others as loyal converts. These youths caused many troubles, later on, in the Zionist movement. In many localities throughout the Soviet Union, the Komsomol branch whose head was usually nominated from above, and mostly not from among the local people, conducted clandestine operations, part of which, in addition to other tasks, involved actual surveillance. However, as mentioned above, cultural and educational activities continued, in which we were forced to participate for the benefit of our members. With the consolidation of the regime, and the establishment of the methods associated with its economic policies – the nationalization

[Page 334]

of the means of production, dissolution of private plants (even of those of artisans), dissolving of the private trade, and putting an emphasis on the social origin in any matter associated with opportunities for studying and making a living, the situation of the Jews in their big centers within the "Pale of Settlement" got worse and in many towns and cities, their sustenance and existence were completely destroyed. The Z" S party, which in parallel to its Zionist activity engraved on its flag the slogan of taking care of the situation of the masses of Jews, their livelihood, and their future wherever they resided, started a full swing for the "*productization*" [direct the Jews to more productive types of work]: the organization of Jewish *artels* (cooperative associations) of artisans, the establishment of organizations for agricultural settlements and the abolition of limitations associated with the social origin of Jews, whose social origin was considered deficient due to historical reasons. As a result of that activity of the Z" S, the central forces of the movement dwindled, as members were forced to appear with their full name in various assemblies and congresses, knowing very well that they would be arrested immediately following their participation. Although the government implemented many of the demands of the Z" S, under the pressure of the [deteriorating] situation of the Jews, it also increased the operation against the Zionist movement, and the number of arrests continued to increase (more about this topic - see the book "Sefer Z" S," published by "Am Oved" [editor Yehuda Erez, 1963, Israel]).

That misfortune had not reached us as of yet. We were an agricultural settlement, and our problems were different. We were occupied with the absorption of new settlers who arrived from the Podolia region; many of them were our [movement's] members. The same is true for all other settlements in the Kherson province and the new settlements in Crimea (by the way, the new settlement movement that took place in 1923-24, which was called the Crimea Settlement, took place in the Kherson province). Even though we did not incur arrests, we knew all about the new methods employed by the [Z" S] party and the "Z" S *Yugend*." We knew about the sacrifices made to reach the masses of Jews with our message. We knew about the general assemblies of the party's centers and branch management teams that disappeared and the establishment of new centers that replaced them according to arrangements made ahead of time. We also took emergency measures and determined who would replace whom – in case a person would be arrested. We formed a narrow regional commission consisting of one member from each of the colonies of Sdeh-Menukha HaKtana, Sdeh-Menukha HaGdola, and Nahar-Tov to ensure consolidation and coordination of activities, in case we lose our connection with the center. We also decided to make our voice heard during pertinent opportunities, but we tried to prevent the immediate arrest of the speaker by having the speaker come from another settlement and by organizing a self-defense group, also consisted of residents of another colony and who would smuggle out the speaker, immediately following the speech, using the element of surprise.

Before such an appearance had been organized in Nahar-Tov, I participated in a festive rally that took place on 7 November 1924, celebrating the October Revolution. The only planned speaker was the secretary of the Communist party, but I could not restrain myself and asked to speak, something which was very uncommon on those occasions. I spoke Russian since I did not know Yiddish well enough. I spoke in my name and not in the name of the Zionist-Socialist movement. I noted all of the issues that the movement is fighting for. I emphasized the achievements of the

*[Page 335]*

October Revolution in the Soviet Union, but noted, in parallel, the lack of understanding towards the Jewish anomaly, the lack of action to correct the situation, and the sin of not recognizing the aspiration of the Zionists-Socialists to build a nation in its old homeland using new ideas. I received applause. The [Communist] Party's secretary was forced to stand up and angrily attacked the traitors who shoved sticks into the wheels of the enormous development of the country. Obviously, people stopped cheering me. I was not arrested, perhaps because I was only 16 years old, or because I spoke on behalf of myself.

It was decided in the regional office that we would not be satisfied with that appearance, particularly since I spoke Russian and not on behalf of the movement. We prepared our appearance at a rally on the 9th of January 1925, commemorating the 1905 revolution. A traveling speaker, who worked in the colonies and who knew Yiddish well, was selected as the speaker. Ten "[Z" S] Yugend" youths from the colony of Dobroye, located near the train station, about 30 kilometers from Yefeh-Nahar, served as the self-defense group. The youths arrived at dusk, in two wagons, and everything worked according to the plan. They tried not to let him speak, but calls from the crowd could be heard "Let him talk"! The speaker was requested to climb over on the stage – but he continued from his seat. A total silence fell in the crowd when the words "on behalf of the Zionists-Socialists Party" were sounded. Movement among the "Komsomol" people toward the speaker could be seen even during the speech. However, the hall was crowded, and they couldn't do so too openly. A total silence fell in the hall when the speaker finished his speech.

The movement members in the hall, who were concentrated around the speaker, began to sing. The crowd stood up and did not fully comprehend what was really going on. The shouts by the chairman could not be heard and the passageways were clogged up. In the meantime, the self-defense group along with the speaker left through the nearest door, followed by many of the local movement's members and others. They turned toward the yard where the wagons stood with the horses harnessed and ready to go. The "Komsomol" secretary with several other members ran around the entire marching group with notebooks in their hands writing the names of the people that left the hall whom they recognized. The youths from Dobroye left peacefully and arrived safely. Nobody was arrested. Everybody talked about that event for a long time, and as a result, we acquired several new members for our branch.

\*

In April 1925, we suffered our first failure. Before that, we hosted and successfully hid an emissary counselor. During one of the evenings, the branch management gathered with the counselor in the house of two of our members to prepare a plan for the following summer's activity of all the clubs. We prepared a detailed plan. We held two meetings per week, every meeting with scheduled subjects and their outlines, etc. The pages piled up on the table, and the small hours of the night approached. All of a sudden, we were frightened by loud knocks and an order to open the doors. We took our time so that we could burn all of the documents. However, shouts could be heard

[Page 336]

from the outside at the windows – "they are burning papers." We also heard sounds of attempts to break the door. I collected all of the papers, put them in my pocket, and we opened the door. It turned out that these were the members of the "Komsomol" who surrounded the house. Since they did not represent any official authority, we did not let them come in. However, as it turned out, they anticipated what they would encounter in the house they sent over people to summon the lawful authority – the criminal investigation bureau (since there was no local representative of the G. P. O [the Soviet Union's secret police 1922-23]). In the meantime, they kept guard around the house so that we would not be able to sneak out. Around 4 AM an officer and several militiamen arrived and conducted a thorough search. The officer sat at the table, and they brought him every suspicious book or

item for examination. They moved the men, one by one, to an adjacent room and searched their clothes and bodies. The women had to pass their hands on their bodies to prove they did not carry anything. My turn approached, and I had the incriminating pile of papers in my pocket. When I was called to be searched, without thinking about it beforehand, I took the pile of papers and quickly put them at the edge of the officer's table. Obviously, nothing was found during the search. When I left the room, I saw that the papers were still resting in the same place on the table where I put them. I grabbed them and put them back in my pocket in the same way I had taken them out before. I have never separated from them again.

All eight of us were arrested along with our hosts, the owners of the house. After staying for two days at the provincial police, it was decided to transfer us to the offices of the G.P.O in the city of Kherson via the customary way (on foot). The authority of one village would transfer us to the authority of the next village, and so on. A transfer in that way, over a distance of 80 kilometers could last two weeks. We requested to hire a wagon, at our expense, and our request was approved. We related that to our relative, so my father arrived at the designated hour with his wagon to take us with the armed guard to Kherson. Our setting off was a thrilling event. The militiamen stood guard along the staircase with a crowd of curious onlookers behind them. Our horse was harnessed to the wagon, which was standing some distance away. When I went out and saw the wagon, I called the name of my beloved horse that I had not seen for the last two days. The horse responded with a joyful neighing, and suddenly, dragging the other horse and the wagon broke through the crowd and the line of the policemen, running toward me at the head of the stairs. The crowd consisted mostly of Gentiles, who did not fully appreciate the ability of the Jews to befriend animals, was delighted, and many tapped me on my shoulder.

We decided to transform our setting into a type of demonstration. We walked through the streets of the village and the colony, guarded, from two sides, by armed guards with bayoneted rifles, the wagon behind

Jewish Farmers in Russia Fields

us, and we were singing the whole time. We repeated the same type of demonstration in the streets of Kherson, a city with a large Jewish population. At the G.O.P. we were scattered among various cells, but we managed to decide, along the way, about how to behave during our interrogation.

The inspector for Zionist affairs was on vacation, and his temporary replacement did not know what to do with us. We denied membership in any organization and claimed that we gathered for a birthday party… After a series of interrogations that lasted for about a month and which did not lead to anything, the main investigator by the name of Oschuk, returned and expressed his outrage about our arrest and released us (apparently, our incidental arrest was contrary to their plan). We returned home and continued to operate during the entire summer according

Sdeh-Menukha HaGdola – the fruit tree orchard

The harvest in the field (during the 1920s)

Sdeh-Menukha HaGdola – in the orchard

*[Page 337]*

to the same plan which we had prepared before the arrest, and which was with me during the entire month at the G.P.O. jail. During that month we managed to meet with several people who were later executed – remnants of the heads of gangs, Jewish murderers, and "white" officers. We also met with some of the first Trotsky people who were arrested in Southern Russia. I shared a cell with one of them – a Russian who was a member of the Social Democratic party since 1903. While he promised not to share his information with the interrogators, he described to me the role of every one of us at our branch. He found out all of that information only based on his acquaintances, during our daily circular walk, so extensive was his experience from his years in the underground.

Obviously, my absence was very much felt on our farm. Luckily, we completed the spring sowing before my arrest and I came back just in time for the summer harvest and cultivations. We were not disturbed during the harvest and the threshing and I even managed to complete the fall sowing. My father used to complain: "How can you not sleep during the night and work endlessly – you will kill yourself if you continue like that." Indeed, sometimes I felt like falling off my feet without the ability to go on. However, we had to go on. Dreadful news about additional arrests of activists arrived once in a while from throughout the movement; however, quiet prevailed in the colonies. The summer of 1925 – was a summer of fruitful activity. Making *Aliyah* to Eretz Israel was still allowed to whoever possessed a certificate and money. A ship sailed from Odesa every two weeks bound for Jaffa, and passports were supplied almost to everyone. However, the news from Eretz Israel was not encouraging, signs of a crisis appeared, and some people came back. We sent some of our members to the "*hakhshara*" camps of the "He'Khalutz" in Crimea as candidates for *Aliyah* and as counselors for agricultural work. Some families who had relatives in Eretz Israel had received certificates, liquidated their farms, and made *Aliyah*. The rest continued to hope that the happy day would arrive for them too someday.

During that summer, a traveling Jewish theatrical troupe appeared in the Jewish colonies, which showed Jewish plays on a high level and even with a national overtone.

This happened in parallel to the establishment of the autonomous district in Kalinindorf (they changed the name of Sdeh-Menukha HaGdola after the name of the president of the Soviet Union, Kalinin, a person who undoubtedly tried to act for the benefit of the Jews). Jewish schools were added in the colonies, and they even talked about Jewish courts. It seemed that the Jewish life was deepening, something we were fighting for. Around the theatrical troupe that consisted of pleasant and intelligent people who symbolized the revival of the Jewish culture, concentrated those from among our people who were interested in that revival without suspecting anything.

\*

During one of the nights in September 1925, a secretary-friend and I sat down in our house, working on editing the local internal newspaper, which we issued monthly. We worked till 3 AM when we reached exhaustion. Although I had a hideaway,

*[Page 338]*

I did not hide the material left it on the top of the closet, and went to accompany my friend to her home in the neighboring village. On my way back from the village, I saw a group of about 50 people marching toward the colony, and despite that, I did not perceive any trouble and went to sleep without getting undressed as I needed to wake up a short while later to go to work.

My mother used to wake up early for her work. She woke up and went out to bring some materials for the fireplace from the yard, leaving the door open. That was how I found myself being shaken up and ordered to stand up while the entire family was already standing, not being allowed to approach me. Obviously, the newspapers included all the various writings found during the search, and I could not deny anything. Tens of members were arrested in our colony that night. For 24 hours, they were busy sorting through them. Some were released; the rest were transported to the train station, where a special train waited for us and where we met with hordes of arrested people from the rest of the colonies. It turned out that the arrests were executed at the same time throughout the entire Southern Russia. Although we pretended not to know each other, the people of the G. O. P. told us in advance that we would see many of our acquaintances on the train and indeed, our movement absorbed a huge blow. At that time, not only the movement's principal activists were affected but also the masses of members.

We were transferred to Kherson, initially to the G. O. P. and later on to the old jail where people sentenced to hard labor were imprisoned. They put us in separate cells, and the interrogation affair began. We were astonished to see one of the principal players of the theatrical troupe, Pivniak, as a G.O. P. interrogator, who knew most of us and called us by our first name. He threw us a question: "I didn't play so badly, did I?" Pivniak was an expert in internal Jewish affairs and in Zionist movements in Southern Russia. There was another interrogator, perhaps senior to Pivniak, by the name of Gusak (whom we could not verify whether he was Jewish or not), who was a person with a broad education and knowledge of many foreign languages. His area of expertise was different. He was an expert in international Judaism and Zionism, ideological contention, and betrayal coaxing. On his table, he always had big packages of Jewish newspapers from all over Europe. I saw, for the first time, titles that we heard about so much, such as the" Yiddishe Rundschau," the "Jewish Chronicle," and others.

Luckily, it was still a period of lawful treatment of prisoners and complete separation between political and criminal prisoners, without the use of physical punishments or tortures during interrogations. There were also fears of the "Procurator" who served as the state attorney and comptroller who audited the legality of the interrogation organizations and courts. We took advantage of that situation to the best of our ability.

My situation was advantageous. According to the customary rule of the movement, a member caught with compelling evidence that prevented them from denying being a movement member had to keep quiet during the interrogation, and that was what I did. The interrogations were all held at night. The interrogator's rooms were located in the management building. To go there,

*[Page 339]*

one had to pass through six yards of the giant jail with heavy gates separating them. The echo of the steps of sentries and prisoners and the call of the guards: "Who is there?" disturbed the night silence. Sometimes, I was happy for that opportunity to breathe fresh air since we were only allowed 15 minutes daily to walk outside in a circle, and I had a strong longing for fresh air.

I had to go through 28 interrogations, among them, 20 in the first two months. I had to sit through long hours of speeches by the interrogators about the Jewish plutocracy throughout the world, about the people who were the servants of imperialism, the people who robbed the lands from the Arabs, the interventionists, and the agreement with Petliura – and I was sitting, keeping my silence. I read my speech from the rally on November 7th, word by word, and things I said during parts of various cultural activities of the Komsomol and just during discussions. I discovered that a spider web was woven around me the whole time. Nothing was hidden from them. I kept my silence. They described to me my demise somewhere in "nowhere," if I would not cooperate with them. Against that, they described a bright future for the Soviet Union and the international revolution, the need to concentrate all the powers towards building the economy where a solution for the Jewish National issue could be found. I was offered to study in the best educational institutions, and piles of money bills were placed on the table accompanied by tempting offers: "After all, you are a smart person, and a bright future is waiting for you with us." I kept my silence. One time, the interrogator Gusak, could not hold himself, and he threw a juicy Russian curse at me. I answered him, a few seconds later in the same style (I was an expert in that area). "Oh, I only intended to say it in a third person," said the interrogator. "So did I" I replied.

That was the only [improper] incident during my arrest. They treated us as political prisoners. Criminal prisoners served us, doing everything for us – cleaned the cells and took out the excrement pail. We tied strong ties with them. The criminal prisoners were allowed to roam around their building and yard throughout the day and were only locked up in their cells at night, following a count. Among them, there were many analphabets, so I became their expert writer of letters. The prison guard on duty did not object them to approaching my cell's door, one at a time, and provided me with their details. I often saw, in front of me, tough murderers, robbers, and thieves shedding tears hearing the sentimental letters that I wrote to their wives, girlfriends, or parents. After I hid a pack of cards and other forbidden games, before a search they had projected to take place, I earned their trust totally. They became our messengers along the entire corridor of our isolated cells.

The indictment was finally submitted to us after two months. Using the help of the criminal prisoners, we began a hunger strike to request the submission of the indictment. It was submitted after two days of hunger, which became known throughout the jail (the criminal prisoners passed the news about it to the city when they went out for various works there) and during the visit by the Procurator. The indictment contained just a few lines. We were accused of being members of an illegal association,

*[Page 340]*

which endangered the public safety. If it could have been proven, we would have faced a jail time of 3 to 4 years and expulsion to far provinces of the Union. That was all. We continued to be jailed. I used the time of my arrest extraordinarily, for my own benefit. The jail contained a huge library, which was confiscated from a famed rich person. Since we were not allowed to go to the library itself, we were allocated a dedicated librarian who fulfilled our requests by bringing the books to our cells. The librarian was an artist with an academic education who was sentenced to 15 years for drawing an engraving to forfeit money bills. He did his best to provide books, and often also explained matters in literature, arts, and sciences. I painfully lacked education and I jumped upon that opportunity, taking advantage of the fact that the lights were on during the night. We did not suffer from food shortage as we received packages from relatives and the welfare fund. We were also allowed to smoke at our own expense, as much as we wanted. I therefore could devote myself to reading and learning. During my entire life, before my arrest and even after that, I did not do as much for myself as I did during my six-month arrest. That jail period provided me, a peasant youth who lacked education, the opportunity to find his ways in matters associated with a developed social life, perhaps as an amateur but not as an ignorant. Except for a bit of exercise, dance for the preservation of one's physical fitness, and the daily walk, the rest of the uninterrupted time was devoted to reading and studying.

*

The days became weeks, the interrogation had ended for quite some time, and we began to demand a sentence. However, we were not promptly responded to. We decided to announce a second hunger strike. We refused food and water for 4 days, despite all the persuasions, while our friends from among the criminal prisoners served as messengers since we were scattered among isolated cells. Only after the procurator visited us and promised to fulfill our request, we stopped the strike. Several days later, they led us, one by one, to the interrogator's office, and read us the administrative sentence.

Knowing that a certificate was reserved for me, I requested, immediately after my sentence was read, to change the sentence (three years deportation to central Asia) to a permit to leave the Soviet Union forever. For some reason, I did that without receiving explicit approval from the movement's institutions, which, at that time, did not encourage deserting our campaign that way. However, I sensed the need to make that fateful decision. In my request, I mentioned September 1926 as the date of my departure, however, I asked to be released immediately for me to be able to gather the harvest and perform the fall sowing on my family farm, where I was the only adult worker. Several weeks later, I was surprised to receive an order to get out with my belongings.

That took place at the end of March 1926. I dove into the ocean of work waiting for me at home. The summer and fall came immediately after the spring cultivation work. I felt a strong obligation to ensure the livelihood of the family until the time when we would be able to bring them too to Eretz Israel.

*[Page 341]*

In the meantime, I tried to do as much as possible to patch the tears in the movement's colony branch to ensure the continuation of the activity. I was also busy handling the papers for the trip. I did not encounter any difficulties in securing a travel passport but was invited, during that summer, to appear about three times at the G. O. P. office in Kherson, where I was warned not to continue with the Zionist activity, otherwise, my permit to leave the Soviet Union would be canceled and the expulsion sentence would be executed. That threat was not executed and I sailed from Odesa on October 20th in a ship containing only 18 passengers, all of them people just like me, who were making *Aliyah* after they had exchanged their expulsion order with a permit to leave the county permanently.

I arrived at Jaffa on 2nd November 1926, which was my 18th birthday, however, it seemed to me that I was much older and rich in life experiences. I felt older as I carried behind me the memory of the hardships during the World War, the bloody Civil War, and the years of hunger during the militant Communism and later on during the days of the new economic policy – the "NAP." In parallel, we had lived the lives of the Jews of the colony, along with their hopes and fears, and experienced the non-ending fight to make a living as well as the rises and falls of the Zionist flame until the final abolition of the Zionist underground during the years 1926 – 27.

I began my new life in our homeland, keeping in my heart those bright childhood and youth days and the fight days in Nahar-Tov and its environs.

**Yehuda Yevzory** (Mishmar HaEmek)

---

### Translator's Footnotes:

1. Karait Judaism is a Jewish religious movement that considers the Jewish Bible alone as its supreme authority in Halakha (Jewish religious law) and theology, as opposed to mainstream Rabbinic Judaism, which considers also the Oral Torah to be an authoritative interpretation of the Bible.
2. Moshe Yevzory-Yevzrikhin, the patriarch of the Yivzori-Simkhoni family, made *Aliyah* in 1927 from Nahar-Tov with his family and settled in Nahalal. After losing his first wife he married again and moved to Kibbutz

Geva. After losing his second wife, he moved back to live near his son in Mishmar Haemek. His daughter, Yehudit Simkhoni (nee Yevzory), was a member of the first Knesset representing the MAPA"I party. Her son, Major General Asaf Simkhoni, the commander of the 1956 Sinai campaign was killed in a plane crash at the end of the Sinai War. Her grandson, Avner Simkhoni, was killed in 1968 when a mine exploded in the Gulf of Suez during the military operations in the War of Attrition.

3. Yehudit Simkhoni, the daughter of Moshe Yevzory–Yevzrikhin, was a member of the Israeli Knesset and an activist in the Israeli labor movement. She was also the mother of Asaf Simkhoni – the commander of the Sini campaign who was killed on the last day of the campaign (See note about her father, Moshe Yevzory–Yevzrhikhin, the patriarch of the Yevzory–Simkhoni family and the author of the article pages 293 – 304).

*[Page 341]*

# Yefeh-Nahar and Dobroye
*[No longer exists]* **(Dobre, Ukraine)**
47°24', 32°19'    **47°19' 32°27'**

## Yehoshua Bar–Dromah and Tzipora Bar–Droma–Gallili

**Translated by** Moshe Kutten

**Edited by** Yocheved Klausner

I was born in the colony of Yefeh-Nahar [Beautiful River]. In 1908, my parents moved to the colony of Dobroye and lived there until the October Revolution.

The colony Dobroye was divided into two parts, with three lakes separating them. The small part was called the "Polish part" (probably because its residents were natives of Poland), while the larger part was called the "Lithuanian part," whose residents were natives of Lithuania. The two parts were connected via dirt embankments. The Lithuanian part was more developed, perhaps because of its proximity to the Yavkino train station (the station was named after a large gentile village located rather far from the station).

A grove was planted between the colony and the nearby train station. The colony's cemetery was located near the grove. The colony of Dobroye

*[Page 342]*

was different from the colony of Yefeh-Nahar in its heavy soil, sticky swampy mud, and the poor quality of its water. It was known that the water in Dobroye was not tasty, and whoever settled in it would cover the roof of his house with sheet metal and dig a whitewashed pit by the house to collect rainwater.

During the last year of the First World War, members of the "HeKhalutz" ["The Pioneer"] movement came to work in the colony under the influence of my sister, Tziporah Bar-Droma-Gallili, who studied in the agricultural department of Kharkiv [Kharkov] University and was also a member of the center of the "HeKhalutz" movement. My mother *z"l* convinced the farmers in the colony to accept these pioneers to work on their farms. The pioneers worked in the field, vegetable garden, cowshed, and stable.

There were vegetable gardens in all of the yards, even by residents who were not farmers. There were cows in almost all of the yards. Some had only a single cow, and others had more than one. The excess milk and milk products were sold to people who did not have cows. Several housewives took care of chickens and grew chicks for self–consumption; however, there were no chicken coops. Every farmer owned farm animals, namely horses. Some had a single pair, and others had several; some farmers owned riding horses. When the district minister visited the colony, the colony youths would perform horse riding maneuvers as a reception along the main street called the "Train Station Street" since people were coming and going to and from the train station through it.

Vineyards were introduced to the colony under the influence of the JCA agricultural school in Novo-Poltavka. Farmers began to plant vineyards, replacing the vegetable gardens.

During the dead season in the winter, some farmers worked as waggoneers. They would harness a pair of horses and go to the train station to welcome guests who came to the colony and bring them to the hotel or their hosts' houses. Some of them worked in transporting goods to and from the city of Nikolayev [Mykolaiv]located about 60 kilometers from the colony.

The awakening of public life in the colony was felt particularly with the break of the First World War when the regime started to expel Jews from areas adjacent to the battlefields between Russia and Germany. The heads of the committee, who handled the expelled refugees, came to the colony to persuade the residents to accept the refugees courteously and handle their arrangements and lodging. A big crowd would gather in the big synagogue of the colony, old and young, to listen to the visiting public official. When the refugees arrived, the colony residents accepted them courteously and helped them settle locally. A Hebrew school was established for their children by the "Tarbut" ["Culture"] organization and the teacher taught his students using the "Hebrew in Hebrew" method.

In the spring days of the Russian Revolution, namely during the days of Kerensky's government, a substantial flurry of preparations for the constitutional assembly took place. The Russian Jewry psyched–up for national autonomy: "A personal autonomous national rule" – was the term coined specifically for the Jews since they had no homeland. It meant giving the Jews in Russia national civil rights and recognizing the Jewish public as a unit, the same way an individual was recognized as a civilian who enjoys civil rights if he pays his civil taxes and fulfills his duties appropriately, even if they were not owners of land. Based on that

*[Page 343]*

idea, an autonomous territory for the Russian Jewry was not considered an acceptable concept. The Jewish parties sent propagandists to all of the Jewish communities and did not skip over our colonies. One of the leaders of the "Bund" organization – Merzhin himself (a relative of a local owner of a private pharmacy), arrived for a debate. The local Zionists called the Zionists in Nikolayev for help in debating such a "lion."

**Yehoshua Bar–Dromah** (Tel Aviv)

The accounts from the failed 1905 Revolution arrived at our colony of Yefeh-Nahar too.

We heard about the pogroms in Nikolayev, Kherson, and other places. Rumors also arrived that the farmers of the neighboring village of Privolnoye intended to cross the Ingulets River at night and conduct a pogrom in our colony. All the men organized themselves quickly for self–defense. My grandfather, R'

Ya'akov–Leib Barinski *z"l*, dressed himself in a coat, girded on a black silk sash, which he used to wear during a prayer, stuck a "Kliuchka" (an elongated and sharp hook used to pluck straw from the heap for heating) and an ax, and left with the defenders in the darkness. They brought us – the children and the women, from the streets adjacent to *Saba*'s [grandfather] house over to the elementary school of the colony, a large and beautiful red–tile roof building built of stones. They packed all the belongings from the houses and expensive garments and brought them to the school attic. Other children and women gathered in the synagogue (also a large and the most beautiful building of the colony). The men went out of the colony to "meet" with the rioters at the river. The courage of the Jews frightened the gentile farmers, and they ran away.

During the years 1905 – 1906, many young males and females Social Revolutionists (S" R's) and Social Democrats (S" D's) came from Nikolayev, Kherson, Yekaterinoslav, and other places to hide in our colony. The colony was distanced from the railroad tracks, and visits by the officials of the authorities were infrequent.

*Saba* had several daughters, and they had girlfriends. His house was considered a house of the educated, and everybody was treated courteously. Therefore, all the "hiding youths" gathered at the house on Shabbats for joint book-reading sessions ("*Tchitki*" in Russian). I was a small girl, an eight-year-old at the time, and I was tasked to play at the gate, stand on guard, and warn against any surprise visit by the police officials.

During those days, a Social–Revolutionary (S" R) underground was active among the peasants in the colony surroundings. The result of that "activity" was apparent every evening when we witnessed fires in large estates. The people who lighted the fires were the peasants. One single estate, which was leased by a Jew named Levinstein (from Novo-Poltavka and Nikolayev), was the only estate not burned by the Russian peasants.

After graduating from the studies in the elementary school, many of the girls in the colony studied with female teachers privately. Twice a year, in May and August, they traveled to the cities of Nikolyaev, Kherson, and Voznesensk,

*[Page 344]*

to take the high school (external) examinations. The boys traveled to "Yeshivas." There were only two girls who studied in high school in those days. I recall one episode: My aunt, who was a very successful teacher, taught many girls and prepared them for the external examinations. She also taught boys, among them the son of the colony's Rabbi who said: "It is allowed to study arithmetic and Russian with the daughter of R' Ya'akov–Leib." That aunt taught a girl whose father did not allow her to take the external test, for fear that she would be writing on Shabbat. The aunt went to him while he was sick and lying on his deathbed. She was asked to give him a "handshake" [solemn promise] that his daughter would not write on Shabbat during the examinations. The teacher agreed. Sometime later, she had to run around the high schools in Nikolayev and Kherson, during the examinations, and find a high school where the examinations were not held on Shabbat. In the end, the girl graduated from medical school. She was a Zionist and served as a physician in the Siberian exile. She made *Aliyah* to Eretz Israel and served as a physician there too. She died there at a young age. She was the famous – Dr. Bilha Poliastro *z"l*.

Many of the natives of the colonies were involved in self-studies and continuing education and participated in joint readings. When the Revolution broke out in 1917, the stream of youths (called "emigration") from the colonies to the big cities began when the gates for high education were opened for them.

\*

The first physician serving in the colony was Dr. Gitl – daughter of Moshe (Ekaterina Moiseievna) Dorfman. My father *z"l* was the secretary of the colony assembly at the time (seated in the "House of Offices" [the administration building]). He interviewed her in his office while she was still a 25-year-old youngster, right after she graduated from her medical studies in Switzerland. She handed him over a letter from the "Zemstvo" [Provincial Authority], which sent her over to become a physician in the colony.

The members of the assembly management team were dumbfounded and asked each other: "How could we manage with a female physician in a colony where the Rabbi is a sick man, suffering from a severe medical crisis, and requiring the frequent help of a physician?" They intended to summon the colony honorees for consultation; however, they first turned to my grandfather, R' Ya'akov–Leib Barinski *z"l*, requesting to hear his opinion as he was considered a smart man and was respected by them. *Saba* talked to the physician. He was positively impressed with her and went to Rabbi Ya'akov Tokarvitz to talk to him. The Rabbi agreed with *Saba's* assessment that medicine does not distinguish between a man and a woman and that every physician is G–d's messenger. Dr. Dorfman was accepted as a physician and served in the colony for three years. When she came to *Saba* to meet him, she handed him her hand (she was unaware of the custom among religious Jews who avoid shaking hands with a woman). *Saba* handed her his hand. The affair of the "hand-shaking of a woman's hand" became quickly known in the colony, and many came to him with a question: "How could you?" *Saba* explained that it was a greater sin to insult another person by not responding.

The colony of Yefeh-Nahar stood on a beautiful hill that descended down on an inclining slope towards the Ingulets River. Beyond the colony, there were the vineyards and a large grove. The streets were wide

*[Page 345]*

and were designed to crisscross each other. A yard of about one *disiyatin* (about 12 *dunams* – [about 3 acres]) surrounded each house. A street of German settlers was located at the edge of the colony (descendants of the German settlers who served as counselors during the first years and who established sample farms for the benefit of the Jewish settlers).

Upon the approach of the holiday of Shavuot [a harvest holiday and a celebration of the giving of the Torah], the children of the colony would go out to the hills located outside of the colony, with sacks in their hands to gather fragrant weeds and honey flowers to spread them in the rooms on the floors. They brought them also to the synagogue. The smell of the fields and the white acacia, the milk dishes, and the tale about the sky opening during the evening of the holiday excited me all of those years, wherever I was during the days of Shavuot. I remember that, as children, we refused to go to sleep before midnight. We wanted to discover the "concealed" which was supposed to uncover itself after midnight. We sat down outside and waited. Obviously, as my grandfather used to say, we fell asleep just before the "concealed revelation."

\*

I came to know Dobroye in 1908 when my family moved from Yefeh-Nahar to live there. My father *z"l* was transferred to serve as the secretary of the "House of Offices" ("*Prikaz*" in Russian). The work of a secretary then, was not the same as the work today. He would start his work at 7 o'clock in the morning and finish at 7 – 8 o'clock in the evening, and would also bring with him home, "thick books" to work in the evenings, until very late hours of the night. The concepts of an annual vacation, accumulated recreation days, or social conditions did not exist then. The secretary handled all of the settlers' affairs: development of the budget ("Smita"), organization of the general gathering of the settlers, writing of settlers' applications to the government, performing inquiries and managing courts (courts were held by elected judges once a month), approving the birth certificates issued by the colony Rabbi who was a government official, assistant to the Chief Rabbi – which was also named the "Rabbi acting on behalf of the authorities" (Rabbiner). The colony's Rabbi was responsible for handling the records of births and marriages and issuing birth certificates approved by the colony's secretary. In cases when the Rabbi did not know Russian, he would be content with signing his name, and the whole certificate would be generated by the colony's secretary. When a male was born to a colony farmer, he was entitled to the addition of farmland (*disiyatins*) from the land reserves of the colony. The secretary was responsible for marking the location of the additional land plot allocated to the farmer. As government officials, the secretary and the "*Schultz*" [village elected leader] were responsible towards their superiors: the Police Commissioner (the "*Pristav*"), and the villages' commissioner. The District Officer and the "*Zemstvo's*" representative would also visit the colony often. The responsibilities of the secretary and the "*Schultz*" increased at the beginning of the First World War. The authorities took an oath of loyalty to the state from all the secretaries and the "*Schultzes*" of the colonies and the villages and announced that if they found a deserter within a colony, the secretary and the *Schultz* would be sentenced to three years of exile in Siberia.

*[Page 346]*

Despite that, we had "dodgers" staying in the colony and not just a few. Whenever the authorities came to look for them (mostly on Fridays), we – my mother *z"l*, myself, and our gentile domestic helper – wandered around in the colony's streets to notify the "deserters" – after all, they were all Jews. On the other hand, there were quite a few youths from among the colony natives who served in the army and went to the front.

During those days, they did not distribute the letters to the houses according to the address on the envelope. People would gather at 11 o'clock in the morning and 4 o'clock in the afternoon in front of the "House of Offices," and the names of the addressees were read right there – outside of the building. Many people cried when they received letters from the front. There were also letters received from far–away America, from people who managed to get away during the war. A letter like that would "travel" for almost three months.

During the days of the First World War, Jewish refugees from the border areas between Russia and Germany and from Lithuania and Poland arrived at the colonies located near the railroad, such as Dobroye, Novo-Poltavka, and more. The colony adults and youths organized to provide economic, social, and cultural assistance. A committee was nominated to handle every type of assistance. A school in Yiddish for the refugees' children was established by the OPE organization – "Khevrat Mefitzei Haskala" ["Organization for the Dissemination of Education]. We accepted their youths among our youths and joined their elder youths in our Zionist clubs.

People from the Central Committee for the Assistance to Jewish Refugees came from time to time, to investigate the state of the refugees in the colony and provide financial assistance.

During the years of the Russian Civil–War (1917 – 1920), "Grigorovich" gangs (named after the Ukrainian leader – Hetman Grigorov who conducted a war against the Bolsheviks) and the gangs of the "Greens" (*Zliyonevs* in Russian named after their commander Zliyoni) assaulted our colony. The colony's residents became refugees, and along with the refugees from Lithuania, escaped over to the nearby colony of Yefeh-Nahar to distance themselves from the railroad.

314

Jewish Farmers in Russia Fields

The White Army too, on its retreat from the Bolsheviks, was shooting at the colony from the train cars, and would also conduct surprise attacks. Our youths who went out to the train station to defend the colony were murdered by them with cold weapons, and then the rioters entered the colony (since the murder was executed with cold weapons, other people did not get warned). The colony residents had again to move to Yefeh-Nahar which was located farther away from the railroad. A few days later, the Red Army caught up with Grigorov's gangs in Nikolayev, where a battle with the conquering Germans was taking place, by the White's [Ukrainian leader] Skoropadsky's forces. We then returned to our colony.

The colony of Dobroye, like the rest of the colonies, played a major role in training "pioneers" for Eretz Israel. As early as the years 1915 –1916, when I was studying in Kharkov, I was a member of the Eretz–Israel committee of the "He'Khaver" [The "Comrade"] (the Students' Zionist Union), and later a member of the "Tzeirei Tzion" [Zionist Youth] organization. Even before the establishment of the "HeKhalutz," I suggested to begin training members of Zionist organizations in our colonies. When I presented the idea, all the members of the Eretz–Israeli committee were

*[Page 347]*

astonished to hear about the existence of the Jewish colonies. The general question was: "Who do these colonies belong to?"

In 1916, the first groups slated for agricultural training were organized in the cities of Kharkov and Poltava and arrived in Dobroye to work. During the holiday of Passover, when I came home for vacation, I began to organize the farmers to accept young female and male students to work on their farms. My mother helped with that task substantially. It was not that easy to gain the acceptance of the farmers. They cringed at the idea of accepting a Jewish student to do hard work. They would say – "has anybody ever heard about anything like that before?" However, in the summer, when the students-"pioneers" came to work, the farmers woke them up at 3 – 4 o'clock in the morning, each saying to his pioneer: "Wake up pioneer. Over there, in Eretz Israel, you would have to wake up even earlier." The pioneers had accepted that burden with love and joy. Following the "HeKhalutz" conference in Kharkov, a year later, the movement's center managed to assign many "pioneers" to the colonies for training.

During the years 1918 and 1919, following the October Revolution, an agricultural cooperative consisting of "HeKhalutz" members who were staying in the colony for training (natives of Kharkov, Poltava, Minsk, and Yekaterinoslav) was established in Dobroye. They owned several beehives and a vegetable garden, and some of them worked as temporary workers for the colony farmers. The members of the cooperative participated in the defense effort when the hooligans of the Grigorian "Greens" gangs and their collaborators – the farmers from Yavkino village – rioted in our colony. The local defense force was not sizable, and we did not own any firearms. Some of the pioneers were killed during the riots, and one was lost along unsafe roads on his way back home to Poltava. However, some of the cooperative members were fortunate to have found their way to Eretz Israel.

During the initial days of the Revolution, messengers came from Nikolayev, to train the colony elected officials how to establish a farmers' and workers' council. The general gathering of the colony residents took place in the big synagogue. The new constitution allowed those who were not farmers to organize themselves in trade organizations, and these organizations were obligated to send a representative to the elected assembly. During the general assembly meeting, one of the honorable farmers – Berl Kosoi (a relative of Yona Keseh, Israeli Knesset member) stood up, knocked forcibly on the stage, and shouted:" Blood would be spilled before we allowed people who were not farmers to vote. There is a danger in allowing them to do so. People would realize that there are people who are not farmers here, and will convert the agricultural colony – "the *Kolonia*" to a town – "*Mestetchka*."

As a Zionist, I was proud of his worry about the agricultural character of the colony. It is a pity that in our own country today, that feeling does not exist, and every agricultural settlement in it aspires to become a large city in Israel.

**Tzipora Bar-Droma-Gallili** (Tel Aviv)

*[Page 348]*

# Pavlova and Konstantinova

**Translated by** Moshe Kutten

**Edited by** Yocheved Klausner

During the days of Czar Nikolai I, some Jews were allowed to settle on land only in a few locations in Russia. The city of Ruzhinoi [today Ružany in Belarus] was privileged to have had two such [Jewish] agricultural colonies established near it: Pavlova and Konstantinova. This was what [a settler] Yosef Storevelsky wrote about them in the [Russian – Hebrew newspaper] "Ha'Melitz," 1882 (242):

"The colony was founded by thirty families who settled in it in 1850 and another fifteen families in 1851. The settlers came to the colony from Yashinovka, Piesk, Liskova, and Volkovisk. In the beginning, we experienced some bad years. Our land did not yield crops, the costs escalated, and without the work in the factory for wool clothing established by the Pinnes sons in Ruzhinoi, we would have died from hunger. Gradually we held on. The land was enriched by fertilizers, which we bought with our hard-earned money in Ruzhinoi. Our farm animals increased in numbers, and we made an honest living from the crops of our land and the milk from our cows. We now have 25 field plots, the same as the number of families. The number of people is 120 males and 124 females. Of the thirty families originally settled here, five returned to their native towns during the first five years, as they were not fit for working the land. Their land was taken away from them by the government. Every one of the plots is of the size of 25 *disiyatins* [about 68 acres]. Three of the plots are meadows, one plot is for buildings and gardens, and sixteen plots for sowing of all sorts of crops. The craftsmen among us include nine house constructors, seven industrial factory workers, three tailors, four leather craftsmen, three wall builders, one pottery maker, one carpenter, two blacksmiths, and two cooks (butchers). Some of us were also serving as waggoneers in the city.

Eleven families settled in the Konstantinova colony, on the other side of Ruzhinoi."

The Jewish farmers were diligent, working their land most of the hours of the day. However, they set aside time for both work and Torah. This is what Yosef Storevelski tells about that in the "HaMelitz" (second year 1862 – 11,13):

"Twelve years ago, thirty families arrived in Pavlova. We lived in hunger and scantiness for seven years. Despite that, we built our own Beit Midrash [Jewish Synagogue and learning house], during the first five years, without relying on anybody, not even the wealthy man – the late Arye–Leib Pinnes. We accomplished everything on our own. For five years now we have been hosting a scholar Rabbi, and teacher. We give him crops for the sustenance of his family and a place to stay. We also give him firewood, candles, and even a Ruble – every week. He teaches "Khayei Adam" ["Life of Man" – Jewish law book by Rabbi Avraham Danzig (1748–1820)] and the bible every day. During Shabbat, he teaches the weekly Torah Portion, and morals every "Shabbat Mevarkhim" [Shabbat before the beginning of every Jewish month].

*[Page 349]*

From the eve of the [Jewish] month of Kheshvan until the spring, we study the bible and Mishnah vigorously. Some people study Gemara. The allocated time for studying is between Minkha [Jewish afternoon service] and Maariv [Jewish evening service]. Some people remain beyond that allocated time to study further. The children's *"Kheder"* is in the "women's section." It contains three levels (grades), employing three teachers. Their salaries are paid by the parents. The Russian language is also being taught there."

**Arye Rozhenski** (Kfar Bitzaron)

*[Page 350]*

# Inguletz

## (Inhulets, Ukraine)

## 47°44' 33°15'

### Translated by Moshe Kutten

### Edited by Yocheved Klausner

I arrived in Inguletz in 1920, after marrying my husband Shmuel Simongauz, the grandson of R' Avraham Simongauz, who was one of the colony founders. These were the days of the Civil War. Trying times had befallen the whole of Russia and did not skip over the Jewish colonies. The colony's ways of life sanctified by tradition, began to disintegrate. The majority of the colony residents did not work in agriculture any longer. Indeed, some flourishing farms were cultivated diligently by their owners – the first pioneers who intended to make *Aliyah* to Eretz Israel and came for training. Some other colonists cultivated vineyards planted during the days of the First World War, under the influence of the agronomist Zusman; however, most of the residents abandoned agriculture. Even during the early years of the colony, many colonists found it difficult to sustain themselves by working the land, and they leased their land to the Gentiles for a certain portion of the harvest. The revenues from the unirrigated cultivation with all of its crops – barley, wheat, rye, or oatmeal, were scanty. They marketed the harvest in one of the neighboring cities, a distance of a two-week round trip journey, using a wagon harnessed to oxen. It happened that after the harvest of a whole season, either from the fall crops or the summer crops, the farmer would come back home carrying just a sack of salt.

In 1920, there were still some flourishing farms whose owners succeeded in becoming wealthy. The fact that they were wealthy was apparent in their houses, among other things. Their houses were made of fired bricks and the roofs were made of sheet metal, as opposed to the rest of the houses of the colony, made of bricks of clay mixed with straw the roof was a straw roof, and the floors were made of clay as well. They did not have the sanitary infrastructure and arrangements we are accustomed to having today. The water was drawn out of a well and carried home on the shoulder in pails hung on a yoke. In wealthy homes, gutters collected rainwater for laundry; however, in most houses, laundry was washed with well–drawn water. There was no rainwater sewer infrastructure, roads, or sidewalks. During the rainy days and the days of the snow melt, the roads in the colony became puddles and swamps. The main material for heating was the straw they bought at the end of the harvest, piled in heaps, in their yards. In the wintertime, the heaps were covered with a layer of ice that protected the straw beneath.

*[Page 351]*

They plucked the straw for heating from the straw heaps using a special instrument (a handle with a rounded hook at the top, called "Klosha"). Only the wealthy heated their home using firewood.

The main public buildings were the synagogue, the public bath, and the state school where they taught Russian (four school years), some grocery shops, and one shop for textile products. These buildings served the basic needs of existence. For all the rest, the colony residents had to travel to the city. There was also a "kiosk" in the colony where they sold soda drinks ("*Zeltzer Vasser*" in Yiddish). On Shabbat, after eating the fish and the cholent [a traditional Jewish stew brought to boil on Friday and kept warm on a hotplate to conform to the Jewish law prohibiting cooking on Shabbat], the colony residents who wanted to quench their thirst would gather there. Since it was prohibited to receive money on Shabbat, the owner of the "kiosk" invented a special arrangement. She built a special board with numerous matchboxes stuck on it – a box for each customer. When a customer would come to drink, she would drop a piece of paper through the hole into the box. The following day – Sunday, she would run around to collect the debt from the women of her kiosk's customers.

The organization of the social and municipal affairs was not very different, in its essence, from what was customary in the rest of the Jewish communities. The colony committee and the head of the committee, who were elected by the residents, were subordinated to the government authority. An inspector on behalf of the authorities would arrive from time to time from Kherson to inspect whether affairs were handled properly. In fact, the social life took place mainly around the synagogue. The building was built by the grandfather of my husband – R' Avraham Simongauz, who was also the gabbai [synagogue administrator] for forty years. The impact of that man was very apparent in the life of the colony. He established and headed charity organizations, as was customary in the Jewish communities during those days – "Lekhem Evionim" ["Bread for the Poor"], "Bikur Kholim" ["Visiting the Sick"], and "Talmud Torah" [literally "Study of the Torah" – children's school]. The origin of that grandfather was the city of Propoisk in the Mohilev province [today – Slavgorod, Belarus]. When he heard, in 1820, about the king's decree allowing the settlement of the Jews, he sold his property, bought a wagon and a pair of oxen, and left on his way with his wife Khana-Stesya and their baby. They wandered around on the roads for about half a year, until they arrived along with several other young people like themselves, at the beautiful valley on the bank of the Ingulets River, and established the location for the colony.

Many stories were going around about R' Avraham Simongauz, and his wondrous image was memorialized in a book by his grandson Moshe Simongauz. He was a tall and sturdy man who was privileged to reach the ripe age of one hundred and three. In his hundredth year, he still carried a yolk and pails from the well, and in his free hand, he held another water pail for balance… He was from among the Lubavitz's Hassidim and his grandchildren knew to tell about him that during the Celebration of 19 of Kislev [Festival of the liberation of the first [Lubavitz] *Rebbe* – Rabbi Shneur Zalman who was charged with treason for sending money to the poor in Russia's enemy – Ottoman's Eretz Israel], he danced the whole night on the table while he was in his nineties. His wife, Khana-Stesya, who was the godmother to hundreds of the colony's children, became blind at the age of seventy, however, she regained her eyesight at the age of eighty after she was operated on by a physician who happened to stop by. After her death, her dress was torn down to small pieces that were snapped up by the women in the colony, as a remedy for long life. Their son, my father–in–law, Aharon Hirsh, was a medic

*[Page 352]*

(*Feldsher*), in his trade. He learned it while serving in the army and continued to work in the state hospitals in the area.

R' Avraham Simongauz was the main rival of the colony's wealthy, notoriously rich man – Schwalbin. The dispute between them was about the position of the Rabbi. When the position became vacant, R' Avraham went to consult with famous Rabbis, and under their recommendations, he brought to the colony Rabbi Novkovsky, an enlightened man and moderate in his views. The rich man Schwalbin wanted to nominate, to that position, one of his relatives. The discord between the rival camps was so intense, that things resulted in a quarrel. As it turned out, the Rabbi's sons were not observant. His daughters studied in a high school in Moscow. One day, during the Khol Ha'Moed days of Passover, when they made their way home on the train, residents of the colony saw them eating *Khametz* [any food that is made out of grain that has been allowed to rise (ferment) and it is not allowed in Passover] ... It was no wonder that the colony was in turmoil. A son of that Rabbi, Yehuda Novkovsky, a multi-talented youth, joined the Communist Party in his youth, became noticeable among its ranks, and later on, as an author and a publicist at the beginning of the Soviet regime, climbed to an elevated position in the party's hierarchy. (My late husband was telling with a hint of pleasure, about him being sent, during his youth, by his father to the Rabbi's home, to sell the *Khametz* [the Rabbi arranged for the Jewish *Khametz* to sell to a non–Jew before Passover and buy it back after Passover]. The Rabbi was sick and his son Yehuda sold the *Khametz* instead. As told, the son took the ruble which was meant to support the Rabbi. Yehuda even offered my husband to "pull on the kerchief" as a symbolic act for "receiving the asset," according to the law and tradition as it was customary during those days [a Jewish custom that demonstrates one of the required actions at the time of sale (the two required conditions – the intent to sell and the act of sale itself)]. My husband used to tell that story when Yehuda Novkovsky reached prominence in the Communist Party, to the displeasure of the communist youth in the colony because they resented somebody talking badly about a Bolshevik...).

The social upheaval that had befallen Russia brought with it a change of values among the classes in the colony. As an example, the grandson of that wealthy man Schwalbin married the daughter of the poor shoemaker. The old rich man said bitterly: "I would have invited my in–law to the Kiddush [Literally "sanctification," the Jewish blessing recited over wine or grape juice to sanctify the Shabbat and Jewish holidays], but I am afraid that he would steal the cup..." The Schwalbins ended up dying from hunger during the revolution.

When I came to the colony in 1920, I was asked by my husband, who headed the local Zionist activity, to teach the Hebrew language. The lessons, which took place in the women's section of the synagogue, did not last long. One day, a representative of the *Yevsektzia* [the Jewish section of the Soviet Communist Party] prohibited conducting them.

The local intelligentsia: the physician, the school teacher, and the Zionists made attempts to organize modest cultural life in the colony. A drama club in which I participated was established. We showed a play in Yiddish by Shalom Aleikhem:" Tzuzeit un Tzushpreit" ["Scattered and Dispersed"] as well as shows by Ya'akov Gordin and others. The revenues were always allocated to charity. An interesting episode occurred during one of the premiere shows, one of the colony's bullies (yes –there were also some of those), took over all the seats in the first row. He laid down his boots on one seat, his hat on the second, He stretched out his coat

*[Page 353]*

on the rest of the seats, and did not clear out of the place until he received "his portion" from the revenues.

Our entire sustenance came from the vineyard. This was an exemplary plantation. At the time, when the agronomist Zusman arrived at the colony, my husband came to his help and went around with him from one house to another to convince the doubters to plant vineyards. Some of the farmers who were stubborn in their resistance claimed: "Grapes would grow in Inguletz when hair would grow on the palm of the hand." Nevertheless, the persuasion activity convinced many to plant, and they did not regret their decision. My husband nurtured his vineyard with love and dedication, and the vineyard yielded excellent fruits, which was the source of his pride all of the years.

Our stay in Inguletz did not last long. Life in that place became hopeless with no prospects for the future. The youth wandered to the cities. **We practically witnessed the last days of the colony.**

R' Avraham Simongauz
One of the first settlers of Inguletz
(one hundred years old)

Dovora–Gitle Tverdovsky (nee Medem)
One of the first girls born in NovoPoltavka
(85 years old)

**Malka A'haroni** (Tel Aviv)

*[Page 354]*

# Memories about the Colonies
# After the Revolution

# The Colonies during the Days of Calamities

**Translated by** Moshe Kutten

In 1905 after the new constitution was issued by the Russian Czar [Nikolai the 2nd], the authorities reconsidered and regretted the liberal policies they had promoted in a moment of weakness. They decided to go back and oppress any symptom of the revolution, and as far as the Jews were concerned – "they were always suspect of starting revolutions – and they needed to be taught a real lesson." It was hinted to the local authorities that a free hand should be given to the haters of the Jews. A wave of pogroms soared against the Jews under the slogan "Hit the Jews and save Russia."

These were the days of autumn. The threshing in the barn had been already completed, and we started to prepare for the winter. Horrible news began to arrive about pogroms in cities and towns throughout Russia. News began to circle around, by word of mouth, about dead and wounded people in various places, about robbery of property, rape of women, destruction and devastation. The atmosphere was filled with fear and became more dense and gloomier by the day. News arrived that in the neighboring Christian villages, the peasants were preparing to follow the commandment of revenge against the Jews, with the expectation of enjoying the loot from the robbery of their property. It was believed that they would break into the colony at any moment and conduct a pogrom in it.

With torment and fear in their heart, the women labored to hide clothing, silverware, dinnerware, and pillows in hideouts and prepared hideouts for their families while the men prepared to stand up for their lives and property.

Except for a single handgun rusted from lack of use (a property of one of the farmers), there was no other firearm. Since there was no available weapon, the men turned to making knives in the smithy from iron. These were pointed knives with long blades – a weapon that was very difficult to define. It was unclear whether it was a knife or a spear, but in any case, it was more effective than a regular stick. Every suitable piece of iron was quickly brought from the yards to the smithy and converted into this "weapon." Not more than two or three days later, every man in the colony possessed this primitive defensive weapon. The peasants in the area, who sensed the preparations for self–defense in the colony, changed their minds and, in the end, did not dare to attack. That was how our colony [Sdeh-Menukha HaKtana], and the neighboring two colonies [Sdeh-Menukha HaGdola and Bobrovy-Kut] were spared from the pogroms of 1905 (as a side note, twenty-four years later, during the 1929 riots [in Eretz Israel], while I was a member of *Moshav* Nahalal, we faced again a severe shortage of weapons. I remembered the knives of Sdeh-Menukha, and we produced similar knives for the men in Nahalal who lacked firearms).

Concerning the single handgun in the colony – his owner tried to shoot it several times and failed, probably because of the rust that accumulated in it over the years while

*[Page 355]*

it was not used. Angry and disappointed at his Shlumielic [Jewish nickname for somebody who just does not have it together – a slang for useless] weapon, the farmer went into his house, and, while holding the gun in his hand, he complained to his wife about the unresponsive and stubborn tool. Just to prove that he was right, he lifted the gun and squeezed the trigger. Precisely then, the tool rejuvenated and, with a loud sound, released a bullet that whistled very close to the head of the farmer's sister, who had just happened to enter the room. The frightened wife grabbed the handgun, quickly ran to the river, and threw it into the water.

At the end of the First World War, the Czar was forced to abdicate his throne, the army fell apart, and the soldiers abandoned the front in masses and wandered on the roads back home. They were shocked and disappointed at the military failures and defeats and placed their trust in the gun, bayonet, and machine gun, which they carried with them when they ran away from their crumbling units.

In Russia, the Civil War raged between the "Reds" who strived to enact the Revolution, and the "White" generals who fought to save the country and its former rulers from the claws of the revolution. The regime passed from one hand to another, chaos prevailed, and might was right. Within this disarray, the hatred for the Jews intensified. Petliura's militias who fought for the independence of Ukraine, and the militias of General Denikin who fought to protect the regime of the Czar – more than they invested efforts to achieve their declared goals, they directed their strength and energy to conduct cruel pogroms among the Jews. In addition to these "formal" armies, other gangs raged. Despicable people, thirsty for murder and robbery, joined these gangs, which were named after their leaders. The gangs wandered throughout the vast Ukraine and brought devastation and destruction to the Jewish population. Any time a rumor spread about an approach of such a gang to a Jewish settlement, the peasants from the neighboring villages prepared to join them. The Christian residents of the towns were also eager to receive the benefits from the robbery of [Jewish] shops and homes. All of the Jewish settlements in the Kherson province experienced a Holocaust. Horrible news began to arrive at our colonies about the murder of Jews who resided in Christian villages and about the destruction of [Jewish] communities in various towns.

In general, there was a difference between the farmers in the colonies and the people who resided in towns. Among the people who worked the land, many broad-shouldered and muscular farmers were accustomed to holding a pitchfork or an ax, and in a fight with a gentile in the market or in a fair, they would not run away but would grab a pitchfork or a wagon's shaft and hit their rivals with them. Even if they were hit they would not surrender. The days of 1905 were still fresh in the colony's memory, due to the keenness to protect life and property against attacks. Now with the new eruption of the annihilation lava that threatened Jewish settlements, self–confidence weakened. We doubted that any individual colony could defend itself against gangs armed with firearms, joined by hundreds or thousands of the neighboring farmers, armed with axes and hatchets. After consultations, it was decided to elect a defense committee common to the three colonies – Sdeh-Menukha HaKtana, Sdeh Menukha HaGdola

*[Page 356]*

and Bobrovy-Kut. Two of the members elected to the committee, had been sentenced to a long confinement period during the days of the Czar because of their socialistic views and were released from jail during the revolution. The third member was the author of this article. We prepared a complete plan of organization, however, we knew that its value would be limited if we did not acquire firearms.

We traveled to the provincial city of Kherson and appeared before the authorities. We explained the dangers that the three colonies were facing. We presented our application for a permit for self–defense and the purchase of firearms. Indeed, the license was granted and we were then faced with the problem of securing funds for the purchase of the firearms. My friends returned to the colonies to try to raise the required money and I stayed behind in the city to look for sources where the weapon could be purchased. The farmers in the colonies did not agree to contribute money for the purchase of firearms. They claimed that the risks involved in self–defense based on firearms were greater than the risks without them. A

323

Jewish Farmers in Russia Fields

handgun held by a warm–headed young man could result in an accidental discharge of a bullet even during a private fight, and then the entire colony would have to defend itself against the revenge attack by the Gentiles. The colony's youths were furious about the refusal of their fathers to acquire firearms – a refusal for which the real reason, according to our opinion, was stinginess and the unwillingness to spend money on anything that was not needed for the farm. Since we did not have a choice, we worked on organizing and equipping ourselves with cold weapons. By the way, the license that we had succeeded in obtaining was not in vain. It was used to acquire firearms for the self–defense of the Jews in the city of Kherson.

The agitation in the region intensified. Horrible news arrived about the murder of one hundred and thirty people in the colony of Novopoltavka. In the colony of Dobroye, thirty people were murdered. The atmosphere was electrifying and it seemed that they [the gangs] would attack us as well. We decided that the time had come to demonstrate our force. Every day, about five hundred youths rode and galloped their horses through the fields guarding the surrounding areas. The act impressed the area villagers and the gangs in the area did not dare to attack us with inadequate forces. They probably assumed that we were armed with firearms and they made preparations to strengthen their forces. Although our weapons were sticks and farm tools, we saved the colonies from an attack by a good organization and demonstration of force.

The threat passed but the fear was renewed. A battalion of [General] Grigoriev established a stronghold in the train station at Sneigirovka, some 20 kilometers away. His soldiers were in army uniforms. They were well-armed and maintained an orderly military regime. Was that battalion associated with Petliura, who was notoriously known for his hateful attitude toward Jews? From our bitter experience, we knew that if this was a formal military battalion – its soldiers would not deny themselves the opportunity to rob, rape, hit, and even murder. Our fears strengthened when the battalion's soldiers captured two youths from the colony that they encountered near the train station. They threw one of the youths into a 60-meter-deep well, and the other was found later after he went through cruel torture. He was unconscious for a whole month and he did not talk since.

*[Page 357]*

Fear descended on the colonies. What was the worth of self-defense based on sticks against murderers armed with firearms? The farmers began to pack their belongings and hide in their yards and fields. Some planned an escape to the nearby cities, where many Jews resided. As my family was in the midst of their hurried preparations for an escape, I decided to check the situation in Sdeh-Menukha HaGdola and Bobrovy-Kut, which were closer to the Sneigirovka train station than our colony. I mounted one of our best horses and set out toward these two colonies.

Another young rider joined me in Sdeh-Menukha HaGdola, and we turned to Bobrovy-Kut. We entered the main road and were astonished. There was not a soul in the yards. It looked as if everybody was dead. Against this emptiness, the airspace was shuddered by the mooing of the cows in the cowsheds. It was a mooing full of horror and supplication for the owners to relieve their udders from the pressure of the accumulated milk. Our hearts broke seeing the flight of the farmers and their families even before the appearance of a single thug in the street. We understood that if the colony people who were hiding in cellars and attics heard the sound of our horses' hoofs beating the ground they would think that the thugs had arrived, and their fear would intensify. We stood in the middle of the street and began to shout in a loud voice, in Yiddish: "Fellow Jews, where are you, show yourself... we are Jews...there are no thugs here..."

One after the other, trembling pale figures with wrinkled clothes began to show up. When they saw us, their fear lessened somewhat. They hurried to the cowsheds to milk the cows. Some of them returned to their houses.

The night passed, then one day, and another. The people calmed down somewhat. While everything was ready for an escape, they took care of the farm and cooked. Life became "a life of the fleeting moment." Observers were placed to watch for any approach of the enemy so that the people could abandon everything and flee to the hideouts.

Indeed, the signal has been received. A company of the battalion, headed by its officers, entered Bobrovy-Kut. The soldiers did not murder or rape anybody but engaged themselves in looting. From there, they moved and entered Sdeh Menukha HaGdola, and there they loaded their wagons with looted food products – flour, poultry, preserves, and anything else they got hold of.

The colonies' residents quickly decided to confront the officers with a proposal: It would be better if the farmers would provide the battalion with produce according to an agreement, rather than the soldiers taking whatever they got hold of without any order and coordination. Following some negotiations and some bargaining, an agreement was reached about the quantities of food that had to be provided, as well as the ransom money in cash. Upon signing the agreement, the commanders ordered their soldiers to stop the looting. As fate would have it, a messenger from the battalion commander Grigoriev arrived with an order for the company to return to the train station at once, even before the produce quota, promised by the farmers, could be collected. Perhaps they received news about the approach of the Red Army.

We got out safe and sound from the pogroms that engulfed the Russian Jews, which resulted in

*[Page 358]*

about 200,000 victims. The brave spirit of the people and the independent life in the colonies played a major role in that. If there were some signs of fear, escape, and hiding, it would be difficult to blame the people, who lacked appropriate defense, of weakness. They knew that the well-armed soldiers strived to rob and loot, rape Jewish women, or stick a knife or a bullet in the heart of a Jew who they just happened to meet on their way.

**Mordekhai Simkhoni** (Geva)[1]

***Translator's Note:***

1. Mordekhai Simkhoni was the husband of Yehudit Simkhoni, a native of Nahar-Tov. Their son – IDF Major General Asaf Simkhoni was the commander of the 1956 Sinai campaign. He was killed on the last night of the campaign in a plane crash. Asaf's son Avner was killed in Sinai in 1968.

*[Page 359]*

# In the Hakhshara [Pioneer Training] in the Colonies

**Translated by** Moshe Kutten

**Edited by** Yocheved Klausner

With the start of the 3rd *Aliyah* [third wave of Zionist immigration to Palestine from Europe 1919–1923] and the establishment of the "HeKhalutz," the need arose for agricultural training for the youth preparing to make *Aliyah* to Eretz Israel. The Jewish settlement in southern Russia began attracting the youth from the cities and the towns in the area. For the first time, we met people whose ties to the land were natural, like among the gentiles.

We – the urban youths, went to work with vigor and tried our best to be like the farmers and absorb their spirit since we saw in them the symbol of the Jewish farmers in Eretz Israel whom we yearned to join. I would mention one detail as an example: The farmers and their sons usually worked barefoot during the spring and summer. We suffered tremendously when we walked barefoot in the stubble in the fields that was called "*Strinia*" [In Russian]. Our feet became bloody and infected. We suffered but tried to hide our suffering from the farmers to hide the shame of our "urbanization." We also tried to get accustomed to that habit. How else would we be able to live in Eretz Israel? After all, that was why we were in the Hakhshara. We did not put any bandages on our wounds. Some of us overcame somehow, but the rest had to return to the city shamed because they could not stand on their feet. Some returned to the colonies two or three weeks later, and some gave up entirely and never returned after that bitter experience in the life of farmers.

Another detail: Upon the arrival of the spring, the colonists used to plaster the outside walls of the house or repair the floor inside. They prepared a special plaster mixture for that purpose: They gathered on a single surface a pile of horse dung, a pile of suitable clay. and a pile of straw. They would mix all of that and with the addition of water would knead the mixture with their feet. That was the job of the women. They would lift their dress a bit (or more than a bit), and with bare feet, they would knead the mixture until it became uniform and solid. The straw contained splinters and the clay – small stones, which injured the women's feet. Our female members, who did not wish to lag behind the colony's women, joined in that chore with their white and delicate feet. They worked like that until they bled – but continued.

Rumors about these details arrived at our families in the city, and they started to shower us with letters demanding that we return home. They asked: "Was it worthwhile to graduate from high school with a gold medal to knead dung for strangers?" In their eyes, the work was not only hard but despicable.

However, we – the pioneers, had totally accepted our new status. Although we experienced quite a few failures and humiliations, they were forgotten quite quickly because our work was in preparation for making *Aliyah* to Eretz Israel, which gave us satisfaction and purpose.

The hard work lasted from dark to dark. In the evenings we were so tired that we fell asleep right after dinner. Only Shabbat was devoted to meetings, gatherings,

*[Page 360]*

hikes, bathing in the rivers, and other activities. The flow of the ebullient youth that suddenly penetrated the conservative colonies had a major influence on the farmers and especially their sons. These colony youths welcomed us with open arms and tried their best to ease our difficulties in adapting to the work. Many of them joined us and became members of the "HeKhalutz" [The Pioneer] movement and even made *Aliyah* with us to Eretz Israel.

Except for a few cases, the pioneers were accepted to work for the farmers only during the busy seasons, in the spring, and especially during the summer crop harvest season. The fields stretched on distances of tens of kilometers away from the colony. To manage two harvested crop transports from the field to the threshing floor, it was required to wake up at two o'clock in the morning and work until nine o'clock at night. We could sleep quite a bit during the transports since the trip on the double ladder wagon, lasted for two hours, or even three. There was no need to direct the horses as they knew the road to the field and back home very well. There was also no danger of rolling over either since the fields and the roads were flat and smooth.

I have seen, many times, a wagon loaded with sheaves entering the colony, turning into the yard, and standing at the threshing circle near the harvested heap. The wagon would stand there for a long time until the farmer's wife would go out by chance, look at the scene, and start to yell, wake up, and curse at her slumping husband sleeping on the loaded wagon. Another scene was common: The narrow field roads were enveloped on both sides by the tall and ripe stalks of the crop. A fully loaded wagon laden with crop sheaves, standing, and opposite it, another empty wagon directed toward the field was standing. The waggoneers in both wagons were sleeping. The two pairs of horses would face each other and fall asleep standing. Everything was sleeping – the air, the crops, the waggoners, and the animals. Only when a third wagon would appear, and the farmer driving it would start yelling, waking the others up, and cursing, everybody would wake up. They would turn left and right and the whole entanglement would dissipate.

I was very proud when my farmer–employer turned to me once at noon and told me: "I am busy this afternoon. You go to the field to transport the sheaves. Take your girlfriend with you, and she will help you load." Two people were always involved in transporting the crops. One person would lift the sheaves and the piles with the pitchfork and throw them into the tall wagon, and the second person (usually a female) would arrange the crop on the wagon. I was very pleased by the farmer's trust, however, to my shame, I discovered that I did not know how to locate our plot. The whole area, as far as hundreds of kilometers, was one vast plain, without a hill or a mountain, with no bush or tree, a rock, or even a single stone on the road. All of the plots were seeded with the same crop, according to the uniform colony cycle of seeds, and all of the colonies were alike. One would travel in the fields like sailing in an ocean without a compass, surrounded by the stalks and the sky. I was embarrassed. The farmer laughed at me and said: "Don't worry, just rely on the mares. After all, they were there in the morning. They know the way. Just don't distract them. Tie the reins to the wagon and don't worry. You will find the blue teapot we left in the plot and bring it home."

Worried, we left on our trip to the field. I knew that the trip would last about two and a half hours.

*[Page 361]*

We traveled and traveled some more, and it seemed to me that the time had passed already, and we did not reach our destination; perhaps we passed the place and entered the fields of the Ukrainian village? I was ready to turn the wagon back and return, embarrassed, home. Nevertheless, I continued to progress, and all of a sudden, the horses turned left, progressed for several hundreds of meters, and stopped by the blue teapot. We loaded the wagon and returned happily to the colony at dusk.

The work in the colony, for three years, served me, and many others like me, like a corridor leading us to the agricultural work in our homeland. I will remember the kindness of the farmers forever.

**Zeev Dor Sinai** (Ein Harod)

[Page 362]

# The "Volga Guard" Group

**Translated by** Moshe Kutten

**Edited by** Yocheved Klausner

After many days of exploring the big labyrinth of the Soviet government's offices and institutions, the members arrived at the offices of the Ziemotdiel (Department of Agriculture). The negotiations were successful, and we got a job as a commune in a large vegetable and fruit farm called "Babkova." We named the place the "Volga Guard" because it overlooked the Volga River, which flowed 3–4 kilometers east of it. That farm (located 8 kilometers from the city [Saratov]) once belonged to one of the most prominent estate owners. The farm grew mainly irrigated and unirrigated vegetables. Some varieties were grown in greenhouses. There were two fruit tree orchards at the western edge of the farm. One orchard was an apples and pears orchard, and the other cherries and plums. A vineyard, which was equipped with defense means against the winter frost was located near the orchards. The apartment houses allocated for our residence, nice wooden houses, were located inside the first orchard in the area bordering the river. A silent water pool, hidden from the world, situated on a stream that ferried its water calmly, was located behind the orchard in a square plot of thick and ornamental trees. The pool provided us with drinking water and water for the rest of our needs. However, mainly the swimming in it, which was very pleasurable, was etched in my memory. We used to dip ourselves in it when we woke up, upon returning from work, and even during our afternoon rest. A magnificent wide and colorful view could be seen from the veranda of the outer house. The greenish river flowed on the horizon edge, silvery and bluish. Between it and the horizon, a narrow field band spread, green in the spring, golden in the summer, and orange in the fall. The river vegetation could be seen from the river ribbon inward. Anything that was sown and grown in the province was located along the river and westward: all sorts of grains, hays, and legumes, all the way to a strip of land close to us covered by all kinds of vegetables. Groves were located on the southwest and northeast. One of the groves was large and dominant, and the other - small and diminishing due to cutting. Lone farmhouses, situated on their plots, most of which existed in the shadow of the vegetable farm, were scattered around. Only on the southern edge, a few villages sparkled. The place was filled with tranquility. The changes and tremors that took place throughout Russia were not evident within that blessed view, although they were substantially apparent on the farm itself.

Our work on that farm was based on a contract between us – "The Commune of Agricultural Workers" – and the "Municipal Department of Agriculture" ("Gorziemotdiel"). Among the usual contract clauses, there were two other unique clauses: Complete autonomy in the internal division of the work, and a statement about days of rest during the Jewish Shabbat and holidays rather than the Christian ones.

*[Page 363]*

(However, we had to notify the farm management, two days in advance, about every holiday and day of rest). These two clauses allowed our group to form an independent Jewish corner within the Russian sea.

The "Ziemotdiel's" officials took an interest in our group. They inquired about our human resources qualities and probed about the motives that brought us to agricultural work. We explained to them the big issue of shifting the Jewish masses to productive work. We told them about the yearning and throbbing heart of the Jewish youth – towards agriculture and working in nature's bosom.

We were asked again whether there was already such an established movement among the Jews or whether we were the first pioneers since the Communist Movement did not find any sign of it. We told them about the Jewish settlement attempts in various countries, the enterprise in Eretz Israel, and its pioneering manifestations. We talked about the conditions under which we wished to work on the government farm and about the fact that we have submitted a request to be approved under the name "The Agricultural Workers Commune of "HeKhalutz" ["The Pioneer" was an agriculture training movement founded by the labor Zionist movement – "Tzeirei Tzion" – "Youths of Zion"]. When we explained to the "Ziemotdiel" officials the meaning of the name and its translation to Russian, they gave us a sample of a commune's by-laws, so we used it as a guideline when we prepared our own by-laws. We used the sample by-laws and added our usual clause about our general objective, and the specific objective of the "HeKhalutz" commune: "The purpose of the 'HeKhalutz' commune is to shift the Jewish nation towards productive work, particularly agricultural work, based on the principles of a commune, and to prepare it to the establishment of a Jewish center of labor in Eretz Israel." We added a special paragraph to the clauses that dealt with the commune's activity: "The HeKhalutz" commune prepares its members to work in all sections of agriculture. It prepares a group of people to act among the Jewish masses aiming at transferring them to productive work, in general, and specifically to agricultural work in communes."

The second clause was received willingly and enthusiastically by the "Ziemotdiel." Not so – the first clause. About that clause, they told us: "What is it with you – idealistic youths who believe in the commune idea, and Palestine, which is under the control of the world's reactionary forces – the British Imperialism?" We discussed again our movement and tried to explain the value of Eretz Israel in the context of the Jewish revival and redemption enterprise. They still could not grasp the essence of that idea and tried to convince us to abandon the romantics and devote all of our efforts to the benefit of Soviet Russia, the only place where the conditions existed to accomplish our aspirations – the revival of the Jewish life and the shift to agriculture based on communal foundations. They emphasized that proceeding in that way would secure full support for our activity throughout the entire country, by the Soviet authorities. The argument did not yield any results; however, the "Ziemotdiel" people did not withhold the required permit from us. The preparation for our departure from the city to the farm began on the day after Passover 5680 (1920) after receiving the approval of our by-laws and the "HeKhalutz" commune and signing the contract between us and the "Gorzimotdiel."

When we arrived at the place, we found neglect, dirt, and filth – an inheritance from the military,

*[Page 364]*

who previously camped in the houses and yard. Our first action was to clean the yard, and then we proceeded to the apartments. We worked for two days – Thursday and Friday, and rested on Saturday. We left for work on the farm on Sunday.

Jewish Farmers in Russia Fields

The tasks that we performed initially were very simple and did not require more than just a physical effort. One of the tasks was deep hoeing in the greenhouses using shovels. Farmers and their sons worked before and alongside us. Their work progressed lazily and with substantial indifference. When somebody from the farm management reprimanded them, they responded: "We work according to the wages we receive."

We came yearning to work the land. That was the road we talked about and dreamt about for a long time. That was the fulfillment of a dream, the absence of which was like a curse to our people. And there we were, being tested. If we were successful – we would become pioneers worthy of the name. When our efforts did bear fruit, we were so proud. All the longwinded debates about Zionism and Socialism, about the contradiction between them and possible bridges, seemed dull and detached. At once, we felt we were above the storm that prevailed in the Jewish community of thirty thousand in Saratov, with all of its parties, classes, and currents...

We slowly moved on to various other tasks on the vegetable farm: planting, irrigation, hoeing, and weeding. Some of us were fortunate to follow a plow, which for us – the natives of the ghetto – was the symbol of redemption. The village natives who saw us working wondered: "*Zhids*, sons of Satan, perhaps the murderers of G-d – and here there are, people of labor, honest and calm like regular people." Our effort and dedication to the work became a parable by the farm management. We were asked once: "Are you working under a scope contract?"

Our farm manager – Ivan Vladimirovitz, a whimsy and educated villager, was amazed by our work. In the beginning, he tried to explain our diligence by our devotion to communism. However, when he realized that that was not the reason, he tried to obtain information about us from the people at the "*Ziemotdiel*" whom we also talked to, and directly from our representatives whom he talked to while the work schedule was handed out.

Slowly, the talk about us spread around from mouth to mouth. Stories reached the neighboring villages. One day, we heard the villages' youths pointing at us: "These are the communists from Jerusalem." There was a certain amount of wonder, suspicion, and respect in these sayings. There were a few who treated us entirely friendly, recognizing the good in our lives. One of them was the vice farm manager – Nikita who was a member of the Communist Party.

As we had expected, there were various other tasks at the house besides the farm work: Food preparation, laundry, carrying food products from the city and the neighboring villages, and keeping the yard and the houses clean. All of these tasks, except the laundry, were partly done by the single person on duty who remained in the house and worked the whole day and night, with a break of only 3–4 hours for sleeping. The other part was done by all the members either before work or after it. An exceptional effort was needed

*[Page 365]*

to maintain a commune life, not for the sake of "Babkova," but to do it without accumulating deficits – the curse of all the communes during those days, according to Zionist officials. When we needed to bring bread from Saratov, the person on duty would wake up one or two of the members at three o'clock at night so that they could travel to the city and carry the bread on their backs before they went to work. When we needed to bring potatoes from the nearby villages, we would go there after the work–day and come back very late at night.

Life in the bosom of nature, making do with little and nonstop effort, cultivated our self-confidence, and sense of daring. The efforts invested in the work and the adaptation to it, replaced the academic dispute about the Realization of Zionism[1], the abstract theories about the merging of Zionism and Socialism, and the futile discussions about the policies of the "Consensus States " [Unofficial name give to the countries who fought against the "Central Powers" in World War I] regarding Eretz Israel.

Almost all of the members who went to "Babkova" knew Hebrew, and some knew it well. However, [before coming to the farm], members used the language only in clubs and in matters not related to the day–to–day life. We tried to use the language during our work on the agricultural farm and found that the language we used was lacking. Among the members, some used their knowledge from what they recalled reading in the books that were the buds of the agrarian literature in Eretz Israel, and were willing to search for the missing expressions and words in these books. The Hebrew that we spoke, initially with stutter and dryness, was renewed and invigorated from the scent of the land and the graciousness of the view until it became fluent among our small crowd. It is difficult to describe the efforts required to form a Jewish island within a Russian sea, with a limited number of Hebrew books and a lack of any Hebrew press. We overcame all that, and during our wandering, we awed people, who knew and talked the language with our Hebrew talk.

Speaking Hebrew strengthened the ties between us and the Hebrew book, which was read during our free time. Our will to create a Hebrew way of life that would draw from the Jewish vitality of the past but also face the future – the life of working the land in the Kibbutzim, was reinforced. We imagined that the group in Eretz Israel had already achieved that dream, and we imitated that group in our imagination. During the general assembly on Friday evenings, we began by discussing our own minor affairs and moved on to the affairs of the movement, nation, work in the Kibbutz, and relations among the members. The assembly was an important cultural venture in itself, although we did not know at the time to appreciate it. The communal singing after the assembly, which could be heard for long distances, was filled with Hassidic melodies and saturated with longing and yearning.

During the holidays, our corner looked completely different in everything: in food and drink, clothing, illumination of the rooms, as well as in the official and unofficial cultural activities that took place in them. At times, crowded balls took place in which youthful joy would erupt. To organize Shabbats and holidays in our corner members were forbidden from leaving "Babkova" on Saturdays without a special permit from the group's secretariat. However, our regular weekdays were not grey either. The strenuous work

*[Page 366]*

was accompanied by times of rest, with discussions about world affairs faced by the pioneers' movement.

The relations among the members were simple and not sentimental: internal relations of respect through the elevated stature of the "HeKhalutz" flag, accompanied by mutual criticism and demands to behave appropriately as a group and as individuals. From time to time, we gathered around a dull lamp for a mutual report on everything we had accomplished and read.

Our first celebration of Lag BaOmer [the 33rd day of the counting between Passover and the Harvest holiday of Shavuot] ended in a gathering to which many guests from all movements and associations of the Zionist movement came. We heard many praises of the "HeKhalutz" movement; also, from people who, until then, treated it dismissively. The news about us spread in all corners of Jewish Saratov. Even people who woke up early to pray and the people of the "Bund" [The International Jewish Labor Bund] talked about us respectfully. The news reached the "*Yevsektzia*" [The Jewish section of the Communist Party] who feared that the new force within the Zionist movement would shame them among the Jewish circles, and they started to undermine us. A hostile article was published in the local newspaper, but it did not make any impression. The "*Yevsektzia*" did not succeed in breaking up the good relations between us and the authorities. Our influence on the Jewish masses strengthened and the youth began to dream about work in "HeKhalutz."

When our activity became known to the "HeKhalutz" center in Russia, they asked us about our affairs. We answered all the questions but did not want to participate in conferences and conventions before we passed the test.

The calm did not last. During the [Hebrew] month of Tamuz, news about the areas taken by the Poles in the provinces of Western Russia and about the following wave of pogroms throughout the Jewish "Pale of Settlement" reached us. The Soviet Union issued a decree concerning the recruitment of Jewish volunteers to the war with the Poles. A volunteering movement among the leftist Jewish parties, from the "*Yevsektzia*" through "Poalei Tzion Left" [Marxist Zionist leftist splint which separated from the main Jewish Labor Party "Poalei Tzion" – "Workers of Zion"]. The propaganda in favor of volunteering aimed at preventing pogroms among the Jews. Doubts aroused: "Can we, at this time, continue calmly with our work on the banks of the Volga? Isn't it a disregard for the blood of our brothers?" The question was discussed in the general assembly during one of the evenings. Deep sorrow was weighted on our conscience and our hearts. It felt like we had been disconnected forcibly from the camp of Eretz Israel's workers, which we had joined in our imagination, and returned to the Jewish Diaspora's "Valley of Tears" [Psalm 84:6]. We arrived at the following conclusions following our discussion:

"Participation in a foreign army is not like self–defense, which is a duty that takes precedence over other duties. No action of helping the Jewish masses in the diaspora is more valuable than the activities of pioneering training, which harbors the only hope for the nation's survival. As a result, the single answer to all the disasters and calamities that take place is – strengthening the pioneering activity, deepening it, and spreading it throughout the nation."

Several weeks later another trouble appeared: a heavy army of Denikin [leading general in the "White" Army] camped afore the city and the whole area around the Volga was covered with troops preparing for battle. They did not skip our Babkova ("The Volga Guard").

*[Page 367]*

One bright morning, a military company took over our residences, and we were forced to leave with our belongings on our backs. In haste, we moved to the farm of "Gusiolka" where a group of students worked. We found work there for several days, but then the work ended. We began again to negotiate with the "*Ziemotdiel*" about a place of work for us. Although it was during the harvest period, and it was not difficult to find work, the conditions we placed on our residence and our unique demands about the work conditions on the farm weighed on the search (our demands included rest on Shabbats and Jewish holidays in return for working on Sundays and Christian holidays as well as the demand for internal autonomy in the division of work).

We spent several weeks of forced idleness in Gusiolka, experiencing a difficult economic situation and a dark mood. In the meantime, Denikin was defeated, and we received harvesting work on the farm "Gornaya Poliana" according to our conditions.

Loaded with bundles, packages, and tools we traversed the distance of eight kilometers and arrived at the place. A day later, we started with piling the crops, loading the wagons, and unloading them on the threshing and treading floor. We were pleased since that was the first time we were exposed to real farming of field crops and were able to learn about the big threshing machine and the tasks associated with it. The work was tiring; however, the work hours were not longer than eight per day. In the beginning, the commune people did not trust us, but several days, later the attitude improved.

That place did not resemble "Babkova" in the splendor of its view. It was not a place where first dreams about the group operation were weaved. Therefore, it was not etched in our memory as an Eretz Israel settlement on the Volga prairies. A Jewish family, whom we found working on the farm, as well as the "Sobbotniks" [Russian sects of Judaizers of Christian origin] from the neighboring area, who treated us respectfully, called us "Israelis" and demanded that we fulfilled all of the required 613 commandments, were etched in our memory.

On the eve of Rosh Hashana [the Jewish New Year], we left "Gornaya Poliana" and returned to the city, pleased with anything we had accomplished and wondering about our future. During the first few weeks, we made plans to make *Aliyah*. We devoted the money left in our savings–box to the *Aliyah* fund. However, when it became clear that there was no hope for making *Aliyah* in the near future, we had to separate to make a living.

The activity in the branch of the "HeKhalutz" union replaced the "HeKhalutz" commune. We devoted our time in Russia to training for our new role. The professional aspect was clear to us, and we progressed in that direction to the best of our ability. Against that, the question about the character of the social–spiritual training came to light. At the "HeKhalutz" union they did not treat that question as a priority. They were satisfied with learning Hebrew and adapting to life with social interactions. However, we could not be satisfied with that. We wanted training not just for the Jewish masses but among them. Not as preachers and official counselors, but as friends at work and as people who give direction in action. We decided to establish an agricultural corner, in the next season, whose gates would be open to every Jew who wanted to train in agricultural work for Eretz Israel and in which pioneers would

*[Page 368]*

be the living spirit. We decided not to stand out as a separate group and not to do anything that could be interpreted as an act of imposition against the general will. With all of that, every member of "HeKhalutz" had to remember, without assemblies or special meetings of the branch, his or her honor oath, and that all of his or her behavior and actions at home and in the field should be following the spirit of pioneering, so much so that that spirit would be dominant in the entire camp.

. About three hundred Jews expressed their wish to join us. Among them, there were people from all circles: starting from Zionist youth and ending with heads of families struggling to make a living; some were craftsmen and some were occupied in useless occupations [in Yiddish – Luft–Geshsheft – "business of air"]. Some were learned people, alumni of "Beit HaMidrash" and others were of "Istra Balagina" type [an expression in Aramaic that translates as "a coin in a jag" or "much ado about nothing"]. Some pioneers of inner Russia craved agricultural training and pioneering surroundings. After a process of selection, eighty people were fortunate to get to work on the farm and seventy completed the season.

We yielded to the general assembly of the people who were going for the Hakhshara (which we called for by posting advertisements in the streets and publishing advertisements in the local newspapers) the authority to decide on the format of the Hakhshara. It was decided that the format would be a commune, a format which was desirable for us. We did not impose any special attitude towards the Hebrew language on the people who joined us. However, every one of them wished to become knowledgeable in it. Everyone began, after a short period, to look at Eretz Israel and agricultural work as the only way for Jewish life and at the end of the summer submitted applications to become members of the "HeKhalutz" union.

The negotiation with the authorities brought us back to Babkova which we missed. A group of members went out there for preparations. The work was in full force after Passover. Our work in the previous year awarded us with certificates of praise from the province authorities. The attitude toward us was friendly, despite all the verbal and written slandering by the *Yevsektzia*. Generally, the people acclimated to the work and the pioneering spirit we were so worried about. The hope for Zion opening her gates for the masses strengthened. The belief in the opportunity for the nation's salvation and the society's revival was reinforced and with it our confidence and willpower. Opposite the views of the shallow "Marxism" that was spreading in the markets and streets, which rejected human willpower as a driving force of history, our recognition of the value of willpower was paramount.

During the second summer, we adapted to additional agricultural tasks: working with animals, furrowing, plowing, and chopping. We were determined to continue the pioneering activity in that place. The idea that not all the members should make *Aliyah* at once was raised, and thereby the need to split the camp into an *Aliyah* group and "the remaining" group which would continue the activity.

During the [Hebrew] month Elul, we announced the opportunity to submit applications to the "HeKhalutz" union, and almost everybody in the commune submitted applications. We began to review the applications during the "HeKhalutz" gathering, which took place on Tishrei 5681 [September 1920] in one of the rooms under the weak light of a small oil–lamp, which we called "the smoke riser." Every person submitting an application had to justify their wish to join the "He'Khlautz" movement and the applications were discussed in the gathering. Twenty-five members were accepted, in addition to pioneers from other branches who also joined

*[Page 369]*

our branch. All the members of the *Aliyah* group were later elected by the branch and also among themselves. Almost everybody who joined the commune earlier became members of the *Aliyah* group, and the rookies were given the task of continuing [the pioneering effort].

The *Aliyah* to Eretz Israel was planned to take place through the Caucasus region. Entering the region was not that easy to begin with, not to mention exiting from it. We decided to use the opportunity of a "legal" permit, which we happened to receive. Hebrew teachers were transferred to Caucasus under the permit of the Education Ministry. Since we had some Hebrew teachers and people who were knowledgeable in Hebrew, our group was included among the people sent to Caucasia. The story about our *Aliyah* through the Caucasus spread in the Jewish community. "Mi She'Berakh" prayer ["He who Blesses" – a public prayer or blessing for an individual or group] was chanted in the synagogue for the people who would make the *Aliyah*, and the faces of the Jews filled with tears… A farewell ball was also organized by "Tzeirei Tzion."

The trip from Saratov to Petrovsk and to the Caspian Sea was usually taking place on the Volga River. However, during our trip, the sea froze and we had to return and travel by train. On the way, the whole group fell sick with Typhus, a disease that repeats itself. Whoever took care of a sick person the day before would become sick a day later. The disease, with all of its recurrences and strains, tortured the group until the arrival in Petrovsk. In the city, the group could finally find rest, aid, and treatment in the Moradov house until most members recovered and went to work.

The work in the vineyards and wineries was very hard, in poor conditions. The members would drink too much wine, which was readily available, instead of eating bread, which was not available. The struggle for sustenance, and the lack of prospect for a near future *Aliyah*, had an impact. The members' spirits dimmed, and the relations among the members soured. Three of the members left, among them the founders of the group. Contrary to that, the group acquired experience and a realistic view of life. We mocked the amusing childhood dreams in the "Volga Guard," and the aspirations and plans which were based on faith and will only. Due to a lack of prospects for a quick *Aliyah*, people despaired. There was no use in staying in Caucasia. When the members got the news that there were some prospects of arranging *Aliyah* through Moscow, they left for the city. They began to work in construction on a house with a name that attested to its size – "*Volikan*" (Giant in Russian) – one of the biggest buildings in Moscow.

The members who stayed behind on the banks of the Volga River did not go idle and tried to justify the expectations placed on them by the people who left. During the winter, they embarked on a vigorous cultural activity in studying literature, Eretz Israel, geography, and history, as well as involving themselves in discussions about the issues of the time. The group that remained inherited the joy of pioneering that prevailed in the "Volga Guard."

We were a camp of 60–70 people, many of whom were commune members who saw themselves as candidates for the "HeKhalutz" and some were members of the "HeKhalutz" from other branches. We received a farm that we called "Naveh Sheket" ["Tranquil Oasis"]. That farm was more suitable for us, as a place for pioneering training than Babkova. It consisted of several hundred *disiyatins* [1 *disiyatin* =2.702 acres] of crop fields, a big fruit orchard, and a vegetable garden. The new members were able to learn from the experience acquired in the previous years. The prospects for economic success were favorable at the beginning of the season, since besides the earnings from the work, we expected some income from the vegetable plots, which we cultivated in the evenings on our own time and account. During those same years, the fields on the Volga Rivers were marred by an arduous draught. Not every seed sprouted, and whatever sprouted did not grow, but yellowed out

*[Page 370]*

and withered before it could be harvested. As a result, hunger descended on the entire province. The commune members who were not pampered with satiated and nutritious food for years and for whom high-quality food was essential due to the hard work in long days (usually 12 hours long) in the government farm and the "additional" vegetable gardens – weakened. Their loud singing – which could be heard throughout the surroundings – quieted. The public and private debates ceased. The members' vigor diminished and the question of wandering around was raised…

In our *Aliyah* camp, a rumor was spread, which was based on unfounded good news: The place to go was Caucasia. We packed our belongings before the end of the season, abandoned the fruits of our work, and followed our members who went to Caucasia. In Petrovsk we received a contract work in an abandoned vineyard. The ground was hard as a rock due to the lack of rain and neglect. The conditions of the contract were bad and we had to work from dawn to dusk. Some members were meticulous and they fixed their "pick-axes" (this is what we called the Russian "*mutigai's*" – hoes) during the afternoon break and before the night sleep time.

Several weeks later, the economic situation in Caucasia worsened, and the prospects of finding work diminished. One of the reasons for this was the fact that Russian masses flooded the area when they heard that they could find a piece of bread there. Our work was about to be ended. Foreign and alien, uprooted and isolated, we resided in a cracked–roof stable near Petrovsk. Despite our efforts, we were not successful in finding work. The way to Eretz Israel was also blocked. It became clear that we needed to go back – but where? Our situation was desperate. Only under the roof of the Moradov family in Petrovsk, we found some encouragement.

At about the same time we received good news in a letter from the "*Aliyah* group's" members who stayed behind in Moscow. They told us about their good arrangement with work and invited us to join them.

The "HeKhalutz" center also advised us to go there, so that the groups could be unified, and also because the prospects for making *Aliyah* seemed to them as being more promising from there. We had to go through the weariness of the road again but we have not regretted it. The "exceptional" work conditions of the members made a great impression on us. They had a sufficient amount of bread. After all, that was our goal even in the "Volga Guard," the fruits of which we cherished later on during our days in Caucasia…

During the first Shabbat after our arrival it was decided in the general assembly to unify the groups and a "Unification Ball" took place with the participation of the members of the "HeKhalutz" center and close friends in Moscow.

**Israel Heller**

*Translator's Note:*

1. The dispute between the modern Zionists and traditionalists who believed that redemption would only come with the Messiah and claimed that attempts to immigrate to Eretz Israel were hastening redemption.

*[Page 371]*

# A Stack of Letters from the Colonies

**Translated by** Moshe Kutten

**Edited by** Yocheved Klausner

### Sdeh-Menukha HaKtana, 7 September 1930

…As to the question about the old settlements, I won't be long. There is nothing new to report about the last half a year. As an example, I would bring the colony of Sdeh-Menukha HaKtana, which I passed through not long ago. The farmers hoped that with Stalin's new agrarian policies, they would see the end of the hardships they had experienced as a result of the collectivization. However, the situation has not improved, even by a bit. Although, formally, they were allowed to leave the collective, the number of farmers who dared to do it is small because they are afraid of the consequences…

The farmers, who handed over their entire lives and inanimate inventory and are working hard in the collective, are getting a daily wage until their account is settled. An experienced farmer receives one ruble and 25 kopeks per day; however, usually, a member receives 75 kopeks per day and 15 *poods* [1 *pood* 16.4 kg = 36 lb] of bread per year.

The colony of Freiland is located 25 kilometers from the colony of Effingar (Yefeh-Nahar) and 1.5 kilometers from the colony of Novopoltavka. Freiland is a daughter colony of Yefeh-Nahar since it was founded by its farmers.

In 1921, during the redistribution of land in the province of Kherson, the officials of the anti–Semitic "Zimautdil" (The Department of Lands) confiscated some of the Yefeh-Nahar lands in favor of the Ukrainian villages adjacent to it, and instead they "awarded" the colony an area located 25 kilometers away as if they were mocking the poor for their misery. This strange exchange caused many difficulties in the cultivation of the remote land. In 1923, 30 families left Yefeh-Nahar and established a new colony in the place, calling it Freiland. The settling of these families on the land was not easy. They did not receive any real assistance from anybody and had to live in huts or clay houses. Only during the years 1925 – 1926, brick houses were built in the colony with the help of the "Joint" ["JDC" – "American Jewish Joint Distribution Committee"] and "J.C.A" ["Jewish Charitable Association"]. The main agricultural sector in the colony was crops; however, vineyards were also planted, a very successful sector. In 1928 – 1929, the farmers' situation improved, and they planned to expand their farms and introduce new sectors.

During the last two years, the situation of the colony deteriorated substantially. Heavy taxes and the violent means by which the regime accomplished the collectivization in the area resulted in migration out of the colony. Farmers began to wander around and look for work, some in the nearby city and some in Donbas (a [Western Ukrainian] province of coal mines around the Donets River basin).

*[Page 372]*

Only three families remained in the colony today. The houses are crumbling and are being sold by the regime's officials as construction material. The destruction and neglect raise gloomy thoughts about the enormous Jewish property and the immense efforts that were invested and are now going to waste. There is no guarantee that the three remaining families will not leave the place soon.

Pale and worried, the people run from their houses to the Villages' Council and from there to the "RIK" (Russian acronym of the "*Rayoni Komitat*" – the District [Executive] Committee) and back to their houses…

I met an acquaintance, a young man of 25 years, whom I knew as early as 1925, during my work among the settlers. When I asked him about what happened in the colony, he told me:

"I, my brother, my sisters, and the entire family joined as members of the kolkhoz. We gave them everything, and they demanded more wheat as taxes, better–quality wheat for seeding, and more money. They imposed anew, a tax of 100 *poods* of wheat (besides the wheat they took from me a while ago). I began to look for sources for these 100 *poods*. After leaving some wheat for seeding, barely enough, I brought over 20 *poods* of wheat. However, all of my evidence and pleas proved to be futile. They began to threaten me that they would throw me out of the kolkhoz, and then what would I do? I hurried to my grandfather and my uncles and managed to gather another 19 *poods* of wheat. I was sure that, with that, I fulfilled my duty, but I made a big mistake. Only a few days passed (these were the days of the hastened collectivizing), and a panic ensued in the colony. Armed riders arrived, and following them, about 200 farmers–prisoners from our neighboring Ukrainian villages. Some people said that these prisoners were thugs; others said that these were contra-revolutionaries who were sent to [the gulag of] Solovki Islands.

However, we immediately understood the reason for their arrival. Fear and fright fell on all of us. Everyone decided: we would take our last shirt off our back, only not to meet the same bitter fate of those poor farmers. I forgot to note that besides the wheat, I also paid a tax of 20 rubles. A day later, they called me to the "RIK" [the Regional Committee] and suggested that I should bring the wheat I still owed – 61 *poods*; otherwise, my fate would be the same as the fate of the prisoners that passed through our colony the day before. I pleaded, swore, and appealed that we do not have bread to feed the people of our household, but all of my pleas were in vain. They offered me a pair of horses and a wagon to go and gather the rest of the wheat.

What could I do? I did not want to go to Solovki or any other remote places. I harnessed the horses to the wagon, loaded all the pillows and eiderdowns, and other belongings, and traveled to the colonies of Lvovo and Bobrovy–Kut where the harvest was better that year than in our colony. In short, after I pawned everything we owned, I brought an additional 40 *poods*. I thought that the authorities would be satisfied with that but I was wrong. When I returned home, I found an invitation to bring an additional sum of 120 rubles. I brought the money to the "RIK" and told them: "Now you can send me to Solovki because I do not have anything left."

*[Page 373]*

A few days later, I visited Sdeh Menukha HaGdola again and happened to read the issue of the "Pravda" newspaper with Stalin's article "Dizziness from all the Triumphs." My acquaintance smiled but his smile was bitter: "Our communists are the leftists of the leftists. Despite the article and all the pamphlets, they continue with their action, although it is evident that they are giving up." A women's gathering took place yesterday in Sdeh Menukha HaKtana. They insistently demanded to get their poultry and cows back and dissolve the collective farm. They continued with their revolt until 4 o'clock in the morning. The local residents claimed that there hadn't been such a noisy and rebellious gathering in Sdeh-Menukha HaKtana since the establishment of the Soviet regime. A policeman arrived from the "RIK" and demanded that the women should disperse otherwise he would arrest 40 of them.

## Sdeh-Menukha, May 1930

…There is no strength to endure anymore. Many are leaving the farm and the colony and going to Donbas [coal mining area] and other places. Perhaps they could find work there. After we sold the entire content of our house to pay the taxes, they came one bright day and forcibly took our horses and cows. Deep grief fell on the colony. They took the most important source of our sustenance. They started to distribute milk. A family of five with small children received 3 – 4 cups of milk a day. The cows are losing weight day by day. The horses are not recognizable anymore. There is no will left to go to the field to work…and in the midst of that, a women's demonstration was organized to try to get the cows back – an uprising. Several women took their cows out of the council's yard and brought them back home. A general assembly takes place in the evening – noise and commotion. One of the farmers stands up and announces: "We should not miss the opportunity. Stalin's article forbids the communists from doing what their [predecessors] have done to us." All the farmers broke out of the gathering and everyone took their cows. The people of power – the Jewish communists, feared more serious consequences, and kept silent about that "revolt."

## Sdeh Menukha HaGdola, January 25, 1931

The situation in the colony is very tense. They began to coerce the farmers to join the collective. Is there any other choice? We must join – otherwise, the authorities would impose such high taxes that we could not afford.

We haven't joined as of yet, but there was nothing that could help us to stay independent. We will soon need to submit an application to join the collective and believe us, we really do not want to do it, the same as we do not want to die…

During the same time, a decree was issued for us to supply beef. They take our two cows away. This would be an indescribable blow. The cows are our major source

*[Page 374]*

of sustenance. Without milk, we would not be able to acquire sugar, salt, kerosene, and other things.

There is no solution to this situation!

## Znamenka, May 1931

I had to spend a whole day in Znamenka during my travels. Znamenka was one of the central stations in Ukraine. I met there eight Jewish families who were returning from Crimea. They attracted my attention with their faces and especially with the sight of their children's faces: hungry, with torn clothes, they trolled around the station: On my questions as to why they were leaving their place of settlement, they replied that their endurance was over. They could not tolerate the living conditions of the Jewish colonies in Crimea, which were under the supervision of the "Komzet" (The Government Committee for Assisting Jewish Agriculture).

I inquired about details: Some of these families were originally from the Mohilev area and some from the Berdichev area. They were sent by the "OZET" organization [Society for Settling Toiling Jews] in 1930 to settle in Crimea. "We decided to start new lives there, although we knew how hard these were." In Crimea, they sent us to one of the new kolkhozes. They had us do hard and grueling work. The sanitary conditions in the Kolkhoz were dreadful. We received only 300 grams of bread a day. Family members who did not work, except the children, did not receive anything. I remarked that it was not possible for people who do hard physical work to get only 300 grams of bread a day. They replied that in the new Kolkhozes, there is no supply of food like the one available in the cities. Every new *kolkhoz'nik* receives 300 grams of bread a day and various other foods. Only after the season is over, the *kolkhoz'nik* gets what's owed to him in bread and money.

Except for the 300 grams of bread (black, not baked properly, similar to a bun made of un-sieved flour), the kolkhoz member receives only tea in the morning, soup (groats in water), and porridge at noon and again tea with a piece of sugar and soup in the evening. There was no way anybody could do hard work and survive with these foods.

The settlers who came to Crimea 4 – 5 years ago and sustained themselves, albeit with substantial difficulty, until the last year, are leaving their farms and returning to their native towns since they do not have the strength to continue with their work in poverty and half hunger.

## Horostaipoli, Kiev [Kyiv] Province

A Jewish collective has existed near that town for three years now. Its area, about 600 acres, was provided by the "Zimautodil" (The Department of Agriculture") from the land reserves. Fifty families joined the collective when it was established.

*[Page 375]*

Many necessary tools are missing, and the authorities are not providing them to the settlers despite many requests. The authorities do not provide any assistance for the farm development either. The collective has been requesting a tractor for two years now. A tractor has been promised, not once, but until today, they have not received it.

The representatives of the farm were called to come to Kharkov in the winter of 1931. The members of the collective were happy. They hoped that the authorities would finally give them the promised tractor. The collective sent a delegation to Kahrkov. However, they were astounded when the representatives of the *Ukrainian Agricultural Komissarion* suggested they turn to natives of Horostaipoli in the USA with a request to send them a tractor as a gift. The delegation went back home frustrated.

Not once, decisions were made in the general assembly to ask the authorities for assistance with tools and needed foods; however, the authorities supplied the collective only with promises for the future, but until today, they have not provided the farm with anything valuable.

In the meantime, the collective members are weakening from one year to another from hard work and unsuitable sustenance. The collective members spend most of the winter nights in the dark for lack of kerosene. The social and cultural situation is not encouraging. The excessive exploitation of the members at work and the frequent friction with the farm management resulted in a depressed mood.

There is no cultural activity worth its name taking place. There are "preachers" who come to lecture about the "political situation," once in a while. People ask them, sometimes, "Why are the residents dying from hunger? Why do we need to sit in the dark at night without kerosene, and this is after the kerosene quota was fulfilled 100% according to the Five Years Plan?" and other questions. The lecturers had only one answer to these questions: "The people who are guilty are the Contra–Revolutionists who hinder the Soviet government in accomplishing its wonderful plans to benefit the workers and the farmers"....

**Submitted to Print by Yehuda Erez** (Tel Aviv)

*[Page 376]*

# The Colonies after the Revolution

**Translated by** Moshe Kutten

**Edited by** Yocheved Klausner

As part of my role from 1917 and on, I visited many Jewish settlements, among them some colonies in Kherson. I am putting in writing my memories and impressions about the colonies in which I visited and worked.

In the colonies, like in the rest of Russia, and especially throughout the Jewish "Pale of Settlement," the effect of the Revolution was enormous. New forces, mostly young, that had risen out of all of the nation's classes and particularly out of the intelligentsia began to change the colonies' way of life. The youth became more active in the political parties, established by the elder farmers, most of whom did not distinguish between the S.R. [Social Revolutionary Party], and the S.D. [Social Democratic Party]. In that respect, there were several curiosities – like the political propagandist who was sometimes registered with the Social Revolutionists and the Social Democrats in the same province. There were almost no revolts in the colonies against estate owners for a simple reason – there weren't any estate owners among them. Only in one colony – Yefeh-Nahar, several farmers took part in a robbery organized by the neighboring village against a liquor factory. Only when the Soviet regime was established, after several years of regime changes and attacks by gangs (Makhno, Grigorov, and others), "*Komentsmod's*" (Committees of land–poor farmers) were established with the leadership of the district and provincial authorities and a sort of a "class–war" with the few local wealthy commenced.

The February Revolution manifested itself in the colonies as a state without authority and management. The "*Uriadnik*" ([district] police commander) disappeared, and nobody had replaced him. However, it should be noted that people of the underworld did not emerge in any of the colonies, and the thefts or fights have not intensified like in the neighboring villages. The village leadership was elected in personal elections in almost every colony and without a regular political system. People with organizational skills emerged as the heads of districts. When the regime was finally ready to operate orderly and handle the organization of the villages and the colonies, the center's envoy for colony affairs would find there a regime structured democratically, with organized departments of agriculture, education, and other departments. The J.C.A. [Jewish Charitable Association] organization played a major role in structuring the local organization. The J.C.A was centered in the colony of Novopoltavka, where it had a farm and an agricultural school (in particular, the agronomist Leizer Aharonovitz-Shteinberg was active in public life. It turned out later that he was an assimilated Social Democrat, and when the movement of "Tzeirei Tzion" ["Youths of Zion"] strengthened in the colonies, we worked very hard until we succeeded in removing him from public activity).

*[Page 377]*

The colonies experienced a lot until the year 1924 and the labor Eretz Israel movement, which included the "HeKhalutz" ["The Pioneer"], "Tzeirei Tzion" ["Youths of Zion"], and especially the Z" S ["Zionist–Socialists"], was very active. We were not successful in introducing Hebrew as the teaching language in school. The conflict between "Tzeirei Tzion" and the "Zionists–Socialists" contributed to that failure to a certain extent; however, the main factor was the shortage of teachers knowledgeable in the Hebrew language. We were successful though, in introducing studying of the Bible and the Hebrew language and its literature as compulsory subjects (in some colonies the practice lasted for two or three more years after the rule passed to the hands of the communists). [Branches of the] Zionist parties and the "HeKhalutz" movement were formed in all of the colonies, and during the years that [the Zionist] movement became illegal, also some assistance and supportive groups were established.

# Novopoltavka

Novopoltavka stretched over rather a wide area near the railroad line of Nikolayev [Mykolaiv]– Kharkov and therefore was the home of many crops–merchants and expeditors, agricultural machines repair workshops, where many employees worked (non–Jewish among them), several big merchants and white color professionals, such as pharmacists, medics, nurses and clerks and even a music school. Many youths traveled every day to their high school in Nikolayev. Some students studied in Kiev or Odesa. However, most residents were farmers (there were 2520 residents and about 200 farms in Novopoltavka in 1917). Due to the proximity to the railroad, the colony experienced two dreadful years. None of the gangs skipped over it. Some gangs stayed in the colony for several weeks. They destroyed the farms, conducted pogroms, and left behind tens of murdered people.

There was a member of the Nikolayev branch of the "Zionists–Socialists" party whose name was Tzelik Sakhanovski. He was an expert metalworker who worked in a shipbuilding factory – "Nevel." He looked like a Ukrainian and spoke fluent Ukrainian. In 1918 – 1919, when the factory closed, Tzelik went to Novopoltavka and found work with an agricultural machines repair workshop. When the Makhno gang attacked and stayed in the colony for a long time, Tzelik introduced himself as a Ukrainian, befriended the Makhno gang members, and learned how to drink without getting drunk. He knew how to sing Ukrainian songs, and was liked by the gang members. Secretly, he hid several young women in his apartment and often acted to protect the people, and property of the residents, most of whom ran away from the colony. When the members of the Makhno gang left the Nikolayev area, a committee for assisting the refugees and people who suffered from the pogroms was established. Tzelik appeared before them and handed over a great number of watches, rings, diamonds, and a large amount of cash, which he managed to take away from the Makhno's gang when they were drunk. That contribution became the basis for the committee's assistance fund. When the communist regime was established, somebody talked about Tzelik that he was one of the Makhno gang's members. He was arrested by the Cheka (the Soviet secret service). We barely managed to free him by providing the Cheka the list of members of the "Zionists–Socialists" party from the years 1918 – 1919 that contained the name of Tzelik (to Tzelik's claims

*[Page 378]*

how could a Jew be a bandit, the Cheka investigator replied: "You are an anarchist aren't you?").

# Sdeh-Menukha HaKtana [The Small Field of Tranquility] (Nevel)

The riots in the city and the regime changes hardly ever arrived at Sdeh-Menukha. It was a small Ukrainian village whose lifestyle was very different from life in Christian villages, Jewish towns, and even from life in other Jewish colonies. Silence and tranquility prevailed in the streets of the colony, in the farmers' homes, and in their hearts. Although the elders mostly wore "kapotes," it was difficult to find anything in them that was different from the *Mozhiks* [Russian peasants]. The Jews of Sdeh-Menukha were different from the town Jews. They were sturdy, tall, and healthy with quiet eyes, assured body movements, and without nervousness.

When I first met with them, they impressed me as being some sort of an evangelistic religious cult. I was amazed when I later realized that the longings in the eyes of the farmers were longings for Zion – for their own homeland. Most of them were religious and observant. At dawn, before leaving for the field, they would pray in public, and even in the field, they made an effort to pray the Minkha prayer [afternoon prayer] with a "minyan" [a quorum of 10 men above the age of 13, required for a Jewish public prayer]. They were tolerant of the youths, who, following the revolution, disassociated themselves from their parents' lifestyle. It seems that the reason for that tolerance was the fact that the youth inherited their longings for Zion.

The look of the houses and the yards, the low fences, the small brick benches near the brightly shined yards, as if attested to their rooted and secured existence on their land. The front of the residence apartment was typically covered with a tin or tile roof with big and clean windows. In the yard on the left, the solid cowshed building was located. In the depth of the yard stood a barn, a crop storage warehouse, and a covered stable and deeper yet the threshing structure with the primitive threshing machines. At the door of every entrance, a big "mezuzah" was prominent. There were three or four rooms in every apartment, a big kitchen, and a spacious corridor, which separated between the rooms and the kitchen. The furniture was semi-urban. In the kitchen stood a table covered by a tablecloth, embroidered by one of the girls or the housewife, with chairs and a buffet with embroidered towels. Hanged on the walls were pictures of the Rabbi from Liadi [Rabbi Zalman Shneur – founder of the Chabad Hasidic movement], the Gaon from Vilna [Rabbi Eliyahu ben Shlomo Zalman] and Dr. Herzl. There was absolute cleanliness in the apartment throughout most hours of the day and night. The dedicated handling by the girls or the housewife was apparent. Every yard was surrounded by a low stone–fence, which served as a barrier for the livestock in the yard. The residents of the colony worked only in agriculture. During my stay in Sdeh-Menukha, I did not see even a single store in the colony. When I asked about it, I was told that only two people worked as shopkeepers and that their stores were in their houses. I did not find anybody in the colony who smoked. When I wanted cigarettes, a friend had to send his son to ride to the nearby colony (Sdeh-Menukha HaGdola [the large Sdeh-Menukha] also named Tatarka), to get them. During the winter months, the farmers of Sdeh-Menukha were busy preparing for the seeding season and repairing the machines, wagons, and farm structures. Some had a side occupation, working as glaziers

[Page 379]

in the colony and neighboring villages, or transporting freights to and from Kherson, the neighboring colony, and nearby villages. Some transported their summer harvest to the city markets in the winter.

The influence of the local intelligentsia was not felt in the colony's public life. The "Schultz" [The head of the village] was one of the farmers, the village clerk was an owner of a farm, and the teachers were also owners of auxiliary farms. Nevertheless, there were people with a high school education among the youths and the young adults (particularly among the females). There were also some Yeshiva students (particularly the Yeshiva established by the Lubavitz–Hasidim). These people became active on the farms of their parents. In 1917, during the Kerensky's Revolution, and in 1923, during the Soviet rule, I knew only one political movement in the colony – the Zionist movement, particularly the Zionist–Socialist Party and the "HeKhalutz." When the Yevsektsia people [Jewish Communists] gained control of the colony, the colony was forced to give up its local rule.

In the fall of 1923, when the Zionist movement, with all its factions, was already illegal, I had to organize a list of "supporters" who wished to make Aliyah to Eretz Israel. An opportunity to secure a limited number of "certificates" became available. I knew that the people of Sdeh-Menukha were ready to make Aliyah at any moment, especially those who had a part of the family already in Eretz Israel. [At that time] it was [already] dangerous [for a Zionist activist] to travel to Sdeh-Menukha and every foreigner would attract attention. It was therefore agreed between me and the representative of Sdeh-Menukha (the member Leibl Kahanov, [later] a resident of Kfar Yehoshua), to meet at another colony – a larger one, where we also had members. Moshe Ninburg, *z"l* as well as Leibl Kahanov and Ya'akov Erev, may they live long, came to the meeting. We met at a friend's house, whose main entrance was on the side of the colony, and the back entrance was on the side of the village that was unified with the colony. We placed a guard outside. The owner of the apartment looked out the window and noticed that a foreign person, who was not from the colony, was watching the house. I left by the back entrance toward the village and turned to a trustworthy friend in the village (the home of Yehudit Simkhoni's parents). As they feared that people who may have followed me would reach their house, they transferred me to the house of their friend, a woman who was not suspected of being a supporter of Zionism. In the meantime, the local people went out through the front entrance and turned to the inn where they left their wagon and the horses. The foreigner watchman, who was probably waiting for me, stayed put and did not move from his position. In the meantime, Ninburg harnessed the horses and went out to the field on the road to Kherson. We arrived at his wagon, everyone in a different way, and Ninburg proceeded to gallop the horses. Ya'akov, who sat facing backward, said that he saw two riders from afar. The crops stood erect in the fields, at their full height. Ninburg did not think twice and turned the horses into the crops. We passed through the field, on its entire width, and entered a Ukrainian village. Ninburg turned to a farmer's house, owned by a good acquaintance of his. He whispered to him, and the farmer welcomed me into his house, placed me above the fireplace, and covered me with all sorts of things. The farmers and my host went out to the yard to drink orange juice and wait for the chasers. About half an hour passed, and the chasers did not show up. The Ukrainian farmer went out to the field, riding his horse, to investigate where the chasers were. When he came back, he said that he saw them from afar on the way

*[Page 380]*

leading to Nevel (Sdeh-Menukha). Ninburg harnessed the horses again, and despite his tiredness and the tiredness of his horses, he brought me to Kherson – a distance of 80 kilometers.

## Yefeh-Nahar (Effingar in Russian)

Yefeh-Nahar was the only colony in the Nikolayev [Mykolaiv] district that was distanced from the railroad. As such, it dodged the visits by the gangs and served as shelter for the refugees from other colonies, when the gangs were active in the area. The colony was called Yefeh-Nahar, probably because of its proximity to the Ingulets River, which ran nearby through a wide and amazingly beautiful valley. The colony did not have muddy soil because it was built on a mountain, which had sandy soil. The two neighboring colonies were drowning in the autumn mud. The houses in the colony were built in straight lines. Three streets climbed up from the slope to the peak of the mountain. The German quarter was located at the main entrance to the colony. The houses were whitewashed and their stone fences were also whitewashed. Fruit trees and flowers were planted near every house. The Jewish houses did not have that uniformity. Houses and yards looked neglected, along with some of the houses, here and there, that were neat. There were no trees or vegetation by the Jewish houses.

During my first visit, in the summer of 1917, during the days of Kerensky's, there were about 2000 residents in the colony, with only 150 – 160 farms. Many of the local residents were working in trade as merchants, small manufacturers, haberdashery traders, shoemakers, and wheat traders (of the local farmers and of the neighboring Ukrainian villages). Others were occupied in the industry – flour mills, a seed oil factory, a soda water factory, and in crafts – tailoring, shoe repairing, blacksmithing, and carpentry. The intelligentsia occupied an important place in that colony. It included a physician, a medic, a midwife, pharmacy owners, and teachers as well as religion officials (a rabbi, slaughterers, cantors, synagogue administrators, and "melameds" [religion teachers]). I also found there people who worked in untraditional professions for Jews such as builders and specialists for building rural heaters (including one expert who was very famous in the area, and who received from the Soviet regime, in his old age, according to what I was told, an honorary title of "The Hero of Work").

After many petitions by the officials of the local authorities, under the initiative of "Tzeirei Tzion" ["Youths of Zion"] and following our meeting with the agronomist Luberski, the JCA people, whose center was in the neighboring colony of Novopoltavka, began to visit Yefeh- Nahar. They planned the planting of vineyards, established the seeding of oil seeds, and handled the improvements in the cowsheds. However, during that crazy period – with the frequent regime changes, the takeover of Ukraine by the Germans, the gangs of the Hatman, Reda, and Petliura and all other gangs and the "independent Republics" (the neighboring village of Bashtuka announced itself as an "independent Republic" and demanded from its neighboring villages, including Yefeh-Nahar to surrender) – the colony could not develop. When the Bolsheviks returned to power, "*communsemos*" (poor villages committees) were established and during the "military communism" period, they began to confiscate

*[Page 381]*

the harvests. The head of the "*communsemos*" was forced to lead the "confiscation battalions" into the farmers' homes. The work ceased and everyone developed an expertise in finding hiding places for their property.

When the Yevsketsia began to handle the Jewish colonies, I was forced to cease any ties with Yefeh-Nahar. I was told that a single Jewish kolkhoz was established there during the forced collectivization and later on, "for economic" reasons, the colony land was distributed among the neighboring villages, whose land bordered with the fields of Yefeh-Nahar. Two or three mixed kolkhozes were established, and Yefeh-Nahar ceased to exist as a Jewish colony. Most of its farmers immigrated before the war mainly to the cities. Sadly, only a few managed to make *Aliyah* to Eretz Israel.

## Dobroye

Dobroye was situated near the train station on the Nikolayev [Mykolaiv]– Kharkov line and served as the center for the export of crops from the neighboring Ukrainian villages. Many of its residents made a living from the crop trade. Based on the size of its population, Dobroye was considered the largest [Jewish] colony in the Kherson province. However, there were relatively only a few farms (about 170 – 180) there. Most of the residents worked in craftsmanship, trade, and in offices handling governmental affairs. The number of people who worked in occupation in white color jobs was larger than in other colonies. The colony had a number of physicians, pharmacists, nurses, midwives, office clerks, operation personnel, mail clerks, train station clerks (residents of the neighboring large Ukrainian village – Yavkino, were regular visitors in the colony), teachers (in three schools), and a large number of religious officials: rabbis, slaughterers, cantors, and about ten "melameds" who operated "*kheders*" [religious school for young boys].

Nevertheless, Dobroye was an agricultural colony, and its way of life was different from the one in Ukrainian towns. The attitude towards physical work was an attitude of respect. That fact can be attributed to the influence of the distinguished families, who were the leaders of the public life, the attitude of the colony's regime, which they also headed, and the customs of daily life. Dobroye was blessed with a village head who persisted from the days of the Czar, through all the revolutions and was always re-elected until the Bolsheviks took over. He was an intelligent and learned Jew who was liked by the public, and an old–

timer Zionist. During normal times, the public–social life was bustling. It contained essential institutions such as a supermarket, cooperative bank, drama club, and regular lectures.

In 1917, Dobroye served as a center for agriculture training for the "He'Khaluz" people. However, every regime change and every gang who operated in the area left deep wounds in the life of the colony. Dobroye and Novopoltavka (both situated near the railroad) experienced many pogroms. Luckily, clerks who worked in the train station had many friends among the colony's Jewish residents. Whenever a notice about a train, suspected of carrying a gang, was obtained from the nearest station

*[Page 382]*

they would quickly send a warning to the colony's Jewish residents, and they would prepare their wagons and horses for an escape to the fields, or to the more remote colony of Yefeh-Nahar. Dobroye was often left empty of its residents for several days at a time, therefore, if I am not mistaken, there were not that many people who were murdered as compared to Novopoltavka. Only the property was looted many times. Some of the farmers in the neighboring villages robbed most of the agricultural tools, and the gang members robbed everything they found in their homes. When the Soviet regime became established, Dobroye was left without the minimal means of sustenance. Most of the farmers did not have enough bread, and they lacked farm animals and tools. Thus, many left the colony, and despite the hunger that spread all over the country, they moved to the nearby cities to look for work.

During the "NEP" [Lenin's New Economic Program], when life returned to normal, more or less, many returned to the colony where young people who had remained in the colony, were skilled in establishing life anew. Many turned to agriculture. Those who owned a farm rebuilt it and others, who had not worked in agriculture before, turned to the local authority and received plots of land or abandoned farms (often against the opinion of the *cummunesmos*). For some reason, Dobroye, who had quite a few learned people from the older generation, has not been successful in instilling a passion for education among the youth. The number of students in high schools (even during the Kerensky period) was very small. Since my ties with Dobroye ceased, as I became an illegal activist, I do not know how the colony developed after the "NEP" period. There are almost no natives of Dobroye in Israel, except the Bar-Droma-Galilli family, whose father was a dedicated Zionist and managed to bring his whole family to Eretz Israel.

**David Tribman** (Tel Aviv)

*[Page 383]*

# The Rehabilitation of the Jewish Agricultural Colonies in Southern Ukraine

**Translated by** Moshe Kutten

**Edited by** Yocheved Klausner

### Sdeh-Menukha HaKtana, 7 September 1930

Following the destruction caused by the Makhno and Petliura gangs to the Jewish agricultural colonies in Southern Ukraine, the process of devastation continued due to the harsh drought of 1921. Most of the areas of Ukraine, except the province of Chernigov [Chernihiv] and its environs, did not harvest that year, did not even gather a single seed, and there was no pasture for the cattle and sheep. Masses of people died from hunger in the villages and towns, especially in the province of Kherson.

In the Jewish agricultural colonies, the cattle consumed the straw that covered the roofs of the houses, and in many houses, the roof boards were sold to buy sacks of flour. I saw hundreds of freight trains loaded with farmers and their belongings that arrived in the Chernigov province during the beginning of the summer of 1921 to exchange their belongings for flour or wheat seeds so that they could sustain their families. Also, some Jewish farmers from the colonies still had some valuables left. Among the people who suffered from the hunger calamity were all of the Jewish colonies in the province of Kherson – Dobroye, Novo-Poltavka, Yefeh-Nahar, Nahar-Tov, Romanovka, Bobrovy-Kut, Sdeh-Menukha HaGdola, Sdeh-Menukha HaKtana, Libovo, and Novo-Berislav, about 2500 families.

The disaster in the Jewish colonies worsened even more because, after the revolution, the regime discontinued the activity of the JCA [Jewish Charitable Association established in 1891 by Baron Hirsch], whose center was in France, and the association's leaders were helpless, particularly because they were suspect of collaborating with foreign companies. Some of the farmers tried to leave the colonies, but there was nowhere to go. Hunger and unemployment prevailed in the cities. During that tragic time, the "ORT" organization [the Society for Trades and Agricultural Labor, established in Russia in 1880], came to the rescue. The role of the "ORT" organization in Russia, especially in the Ukrainian cities, was to teach craftsmanship to the Jewish youth. For that purpose, the association established technical schools with workshops for children ages 13 – 14. The "ORT" organization continued its activity in Russia after the revolution; however, the authorities nominated Jewish communists to head the activities of the schools and the workshops. At that time, the center of the association was located in Berlin.

The agricultural department of "ORT" established its center in the Ukrainian capital of Kharkov, and its center of activity in the Jewish colonies was in Nikolayev, which became the province capital replacing Kherson. As the head of the department for assistance to the Jewish colonies, situated in Nikolayev, the authority nominated Elimelekh Eresh who was a communist but was removed from the

*[Page 384]*

ranks of the party due to his nationalistic tendencies. He was a clever man with a warm Jewish heart. Another member of the management was a communist by the name of Shmulevitz, a native of the colony of Yefeh-Nahar, who visited the meetings held once a month and was helping us [the Zionists] at the colonies and would frequently save us from snitching about preaching for Zionism. There was another member of the management, by the name of Schumakher, who was dedicated in his heart and soul. He was also active in the Jewish public in Nikolayev.

I was the agronomist of the association for its activity in the colonies and was tasked, along with the rest of the members of the management team, with the colonies' rehabilitation. As part of my role as an agronomist, I was moving from one colony to the other and was returning, at the end of each month, to the center in Nikolayev, where we held meetings and consultations with the members of the management. Equipped with resources and resolutions, I would return to the colonies for the entire month.

One of the activists at the center in Kharkov, was Golde, who was previously a member of Kvutzat (kibbutz) Kineret in Eretz Israel. I found out the "stain" in his past, from Ben-Tzion Israeli *z"l*, only when I came to Eretz Israel in 1927 when I visited Kvutzat Kineret.

The first activity at the end of the summer of 1922 was to provide seeds for autumn seeding. The settlers were reorganized, with the help of the "credit union" which was in operation in the early days of the J.C.A., under the assistance of which the fields were prepared for the autumn seeding. The seeds, which arrived from Romania, were distributed on credit, and the fields' owners would repay the price of the seeds through the credit union when their situation would allow.

The Berlin "ORT" association first sent the needed resources for the purchasing of horses – a horse per family, and sometimes a single horse for two families (while the actual requirement was a pair of horses per farm). Following that, the resources for acquiring the cows and seeds for the summer crops – wheat and barley, became available.

Due to a lack of agricultural know-how, and due to the desire to provide quick assistance, a large amount of vegetable seeds, tools for the cultivation of vegetable gardens, and machines for corn peeling were sent without consulting with us. These resources were never used or were hardly used.

At the end of the spring seeding period, the time has come to fix the roofs of the houses, namely – to arrange the wooden boards before the crops are harvested and straw from the threshing would become available to cover the roofs. We prepared lists and the "ORT" company ordered the boards, which arrived on time, before harvesting began.

After these initial urgent actions, we turned to improving the situation in the colonies. All the colonies, which were close to rivers and other sources of water, were supplied with Bulgarian water pumps to irrigate the vegetable gardens, which were prepared for the commercial market and were cultivated by the cooperatives, consisting of the members of the colonies. The production of yellow cheese which was sold in the big cities was reintroduced. The economic state of the colonies' farmers began to improve. One of the vital acts was to bring the farmers closer to their distanced lands.

[Page 385]

The number of families in the colony reached 400. The settlement was concentrated in a rather small area and its lands stretched out to distances of up to 18 – 20 kilometers from the houses. For that reason, the farmers were forced to remain in the fields and lodge there for weeks during the cultivation and seeding period and return home only for Shabbat. The main difficulty was transporting the crops and the hay from the distanced fields to the thresher in the yards, which lasted several weeks. At the end of the transporting effort, they turned to threshing and later on, rearranged the piles of straw in the shape of tall buildings with sloped roofs.

After consulting with the farmers' committees, it was decided to split the settlement in the large colonies into two parts, redistribute the lands, and establish new settlements consisting of half of the farmers, who would agree to re-build their houses and the farm structures at the center of their lands.

Based on our recommendation, the "ORT" organization agreed to provide the construction materials and resources for establishing the new settlements. Wells were repaired, and new wells were dug out. Plans were prepared and the redistribution of the lands was implemented, so that some of the plots that were close to the old settlement would be available to the farmers there, and the distanced plots would be concentrated around the new settlement.

Following two years of fruitful and effective activity of the "ORT" organization, which managed to substantially improve the state of the farmers in the colonies, the organization ceased its temporary operation in the spring of 1924 and handed over the responsibility to the people of the Agro-JOINT [The branch of the JOINT - Joint Distribution Committee in the Soviet Union, established after the revolution, aiming to settle "nonproductive" Jews]. In 1924, delegations on behalf of the American JOINT organization who were interested in the agricultural settlement of Jews from the cities of Russia began to visit southern Ukraine and Crimea.

The situation of the city Jews, most of whom were merchants, was very harsh. Representatives of groups of Jews would arrive, from time to time, at the office of "ORT" in Nikolayev asking to help them to transfer to agriculture, and thereby ensure sustenance for the families.

Fertile and productive lands, which remained after they had been confiscated from the large estate owners in Ukraine and northern Crimea, abounded. The buildings that remained in the estates could initially serve as a place of residence for people and animals and could accommodate the new settlers right away without many preparations, and they could begin to work as a collective. Later on, when the plans for the settlement became available and distributed, private homes were built on the settlers' lands.

The "ORT" people were forced to help groups of Jews, here and there, to settle on the land even earlier. However, that activity was incidental, since it was not included in the charter of the temporary agricultural activity of the "ORT" organization.

The Hakhshara [training] farms established by the HeKhalutz movement during the years 1922 – 1924 ("Tel Khai" ["Hill of Living"], "Ma'ayan" ["Wellspring"] and "Mishmar" ["Guard"]), served as evidence to the American JOINT's activists that the agricultural settlement in Crimea was possible and advantageous. These farms were profitable and operated on a high professional level thanks to the organization

*[Page 386]*

and dedication of their members – the members of the "HeKhalutz" movement who worked tirelessly, without receiving any compensation from the farm other than the minimal expenses needed for their sustenance. The largest among the "Hakhshara" farms – "Tel Khai," with an area of 20,000 *dunams* [about 4940 acres], developed the cultivation of seeds in cooperation with the Ukrainian company "The Seed." That farm was the one that was enhanced by selection and granted the Crimea agricultural market the wheat species called "*Cooperturka*" as well as the Sudanese hay.

A new settlement movement in Ukraine and Crimea commenced in the year 1925 by the Agro-JOINT. Tens of new settlements were established in Crimea, around the "HeKhalutz" farms, and in the Ukraine, in the area of the existing colonies. These new settlements served as a lever for a broader settlement enterprise in 1926.

In the winter of 1925 – 1926, a special committee was established in Crimea, consisting of three agronomists: a representative of the government, a representative of the "GEZERD" organization ["The Society for the Agricultural Organization of Working Class Jews in the USSR&148; ["OZET" in Russian and "GEZERD" in Yiddish], which cooperated with the "Agro-JOINT" organization, and the author of this article, as the representative of "Agro-JOINT." The committee was tasked to implement the settlement. An area, which was more or less contiguous and concentrated, of about 70,000 *disiyatins* (about 770,000 *dunams* [about 190,000 acres]) was selected. The area was approved following a difficult struggle and against the resistance by the Crimean-Tatarian regime. The *Yevsektsia's* representative H. Marzhin, did not get involved. When I explained to him that I selected a concentrated area to strengthen the defense capabilities of the settlement in case of pogroms, Merzhin responded that that was a Zionist political excuse. Despite his view, he did not dare to side with the Tatarian regime, which demanded to scatter the settlements.

In the spring of 1926, hundreds of settlers settled on the land. Every family received 30 *disiyatins* (330 *dunams* [81.5 acres]) for field crop cultivation and a large piece of land that could be used for a multi-sector farm. In Crimea, houses built from white stone (similar to Autoclaved Aerated Concrete Bricks), were built. The bricks were ordered in 1925 and arrived in time for construction in the spring of 1926.

Amid that operation, I was arrested and sent to Siberia. I did not have sufficient material to write about the continuation of the settlement enterprise in Crimea.

**Agronomist B. Gorshtein** (Tel Aviv)

*[Page 387]*

# From the Literature

*[Page 389]*

# A Jewish Colony in Russia in the Year 1823
## (Anonymous article in a Warsaw newspaper)

**Translated by** Moshe Kutten

**Edited by** Yocheved Klausner

A journal by the name "Der Beobakhter an der Weikhsel" ["The Observer from the Banks of the Vistula"] was published in Warsaw in 1922. The editor was Antony Eisenbaum. That was a bilingual Yiddish–Polish weekly journal, in which the editor himself authored most of the articles and the minority by other incidental participants. Nakhman Meizel, the editor of "Literarushe Bleter" ["Literacy Pages"], copied sections of letters by two anonymous Jewish women from that journal, changed their German–Yiddish linguistic to real Yiddish and published them in November 1931[1]. The two letters, with Nakhman Meizel's formulation and the Hebrew translation by Shimshon Meltzer, are brought up here.

## A

…Before completing the description of my journey, I must tell you about an odd incident that we have witnessed and which would most likely, amaze you. We saw a Jewish village with beautiful fields and fine pastures. That village is settled and built only by Jews. Would you believe that Jews, who are known disrespectfully throughout the world as loafers, can work the land so diligently and skillfully?

The village is called Yefeh-Nahar [Beautiful River]. It is located about 60 kilometers from Nikolayev, in the very beautiful area of the Ingulets River. The fifty families residing in that village cultivate their fields dedicatedly and diligently. Their wives and daughters are skillful in harvesting the crops and work diligently on the agricultural farm. There isn't even a single Christian farmer in the village.

Although they experience drought seasons often, as droughts are common in that area, their sustenance is assured from year to year. They are particularly successful with their cattle sector. There isn't even a single family in the village without at least five or six cows, several bulls, some horses, and several kinds of poultry. The butter and the cheese they produce are of very good quality and fetch better prices, even with Christian buyers, than the price obtained by other (non–Jewish) villages. The houses, which they built themselves, are small like peasants' huts; however, it can be said that their houses are much cleaner than those of other (non–Jewish) farmers.

*[Page 390]*

There are all sorts of agile craftsmen among them. They are now building a synagogue for themselves, for which they only employ Jewish builders and other craftsmen. They have a rule and a virtue in that they seldom drink liquor. There is only a single tavern in the village. Everyone is entitled to receive a passport from the "*Schultz*" (village elder and leader), who is Jewish, for three months (but not longer than that), if he behaves properly and is skilled in a craft. He could then work in his craft in the city or another town. This is only allowed after the harvest season. The rest of the Jewish residents study in a *Beit HaMidrash* [a Jewish study hall or a school].

The village women occupy themselves, during the winter time, in types of work common to peasant women. They look for among the city dwellers and perform the work at home in the village. To summarize, my dear friends, I was delighted when I realized how diligent these people are and how cordially they received us.

The person who amazed us the most was the unique and noble village elder – Mr. Nakhum Finkelshtein, who was born in Shklov, Lithuania. He was the initiator and the founder of the village. He managed his businesses in the city of Kherson when the news arrived sixteen years ago, about his brothers' hunger distress, which had already caused the death of many of them. He advised them to cultivate an available piece of land, not far from Nikolayev. He delivered a report to the Russian royal court, acted, and obtained 200 rubles for each family, a pair of oxen, one horse, and one cow. Since they were not used to that way of life, two-thirds of them died.

There are seven Jewish villages in existence here since 1808: Yefeh-Nahar, Nahar-Tov [Good River], Sdeh-Menukah [Field of Tranquility], Har-Shefer [Exquisite Mountain], Kaminka, and Izraelovka. This amazing Mr. Finkelshtein serves as the settlers' head "*Schultz*" (the head of the village elders), their representative, lawmaker, and friend. He always arouses their vigor and makes sure they remain sober. Although he is rich he accustoms his children to working the land, to encourage others. With admirable patience, he tolerates anything coming from these Jews, provided that he could make them into productive people.

We were very sorry not to be able to know this noble person personally. He now lives in Kherson, however, his son, who lives here with his family and brothers, received us cordially, served nice refreshments, and assisted us with all our needs. He refused to receive even very modest payment for his services.

It would be ungrateful if the name of this important man – Mr. Finkelshtein, would not remain in the memory of the Jews, although he does not run after any honor or glory. He considers his reward in the fact that people live a happy life because of him. May we hear, soon, the same good news about the situation of our own Jews.

*[Page 391]*

# B

You wanted to know what type of constitution these Russian Jewish settlers have and what type of political institutions exist in their villages. I could provide a single answer to both questions. It is sufficient to say that all of the settlers residing in the Russian provinces of Kherson, Ektaterinoslav, and Tavria, including Jews, Germans, Bulgarians, and Serbs have a single political constitution, without any exception. They are subject to the rule of a single office, located in Ekaterinoslvav. The office consists of six officials and one manager. In addition, there is a single supervisor, and General Iznov is currently serving in that role. For any issue connected to the settlers, whether it is a legal or any other affair he turns to that main office, which has the authority to decide, judge, allow, or punish. Even if one of the settlers has a claim against a person residing in another city, or the opposite, if a Russian citizen is suing a settler, all legal discussions must be held by the main office.

Every village has a village elder – a leader from among the residents. The village elder is authorized to punish any outlaw or a criminal to a jail time of two the five days. That village elder is the one who issues long–term passports, when work is not available at home, as well as travel certificates recognized throughout Russia. The village elder hand–signs and stamps it with a stamp he receives from the main office, and maintains a notebook in which he lists all the certificates he is issuing. There is one *"Kommissar"* [commissary] over five to six villages who receives the reports from the village–elders and handles their affairs in the main office, orders the necessities, and hands out and transfers everything to and from the main office.

Concerning the rest of your questions, my answer is that every Jewish village has *"melameds"* [religion teachers], cantors, caretakers [*"gabbais"*– synagogue administrators], and slaughterers who cultivate their fields during the working season if not entirely, at last partially, and also perform every required task. There are learned people among them who are able to religiously rule and conduct marriages. They also have public baths and *"mikvahs"* [ritual baths] in the larger villages and the residents of the smaller villages go to public baths in the larger ones.

You ask again whether the Jews go in the morning and at dusk to the *"Beit HaMidrash."* The answer is yes, my dear friend. During the harvest season, they conduct their prayers in *"minyan's"* [a group of a minimum number of 10 males, older than 13 required for a public Jewish prayer], in the fields and keep it short – they just pray "Barkhu" ["Let us praise" – A call to worship by the prayer leader at the beginning of the morning and evening services], *"Kdusha"* ["Holiness" – the sanctification of G–d's], and *"Kadish"* ["Holy" – a hymn of praises of G–d]. They come back home only on Shabbat. Their wives bring their meals to the field since they sleep there at night. In the wintertime, the Jewish farmers sit in Beit *HaMidrash*, study, and pray.

You ask again how the Jews handle themselves on Shabbat, where there are no Christian helpers. We have asked about it in detail and found out that they do not require any assistance, since during the summer, as well as in the winter, they light their candles an hour before sunset,

*[Page 392]*

and eat their dinner before it gets dark. They light the heater on Friday at dusk, and in the wintertime, they light it before Shabbat. They light it in such a way that the warmth lasts for twenty-four hours.

You ask again whether the settlers pay taxes, provide soldiers to the military, and whether there is anybody who handles these affairs for them. The answer is no, my dear friend. They are not bothered by these duties. Like all of the settlers in Russia, they are exempt from these duties for twenty years from the day they have become farmers. The Jews have been farmers for only fifteen – sixteen years. Despite that, The Tzar – Alexander, a friend of the people, has already promised to grant them an additional reprieve.

You wanted to know whether the Jews are marrying early there. The answer is yes, however, they do so for different reasons from those of all other Jews in Russia and Poland. The reason is that everyone wants to have a helpmate at home and on the farm. Their dowry fits the farmers' way of life, as they provide the young couple with oxen, cows, horses, sheep, and seeds. The matchmaker receives a good meal and fruit but no money.

### Translator's Note:

1. The article "Jews Who Work the Land" By Yosef Perl, pg 393, seems to be the unedited version mentioned above.

*[Page 393]*

# Jews who Work the Land
### A chapter from the satirical story "Bokhen Tzadik" [Testing a Righteous], [Prague], 1938

**by Yosef Perl**[1]

**Translated by** Moshe Kutten

**Edited by** Yocheved Klausner

### [A letter] from R' Ovadia to R' Kahana

The farmer kept his promise and agreed to go with me, during the last few days, to all the places where our people work the land, beginning with the year 5565 (1804/5). It was an extreme pleasure to be among them. I could not even begin to describe how delighted I was imagining being in a small Eretz Israel, particularly when I heard that the settlers named most of their settlements, most appropriately, in our sanctified language [Hebrew]. The name of one settlement is Sdeh Menukha [Field of Tranquility], which consists of two villages on two banks of the same river. The name of the other settlement is Yefeh-Nahar [Beautiful River, Effingar in Russian], and the third - Nahar-Tov [Good River]. The name of the fourth one is Har–Shefer [Exquisite Mountain], [also called River], and the fifth – is Ya'azor [Devine Help], [also called Israelovka]. Only one settlement has its name in another language [Russian] -Kaminka. Yefeh-Nahar was built on the bank of the Ingulets River, and close to fifty families reside in it. They work their land very diligently and very appropriately, from Sunday morning until lunchtime of Friday, the eve of the holy Shabbat. The wives and the daughters of those people, whose fields are far from the village, bring their food to the field. Wives and daughters help their husbands in the field, during the harvest season, and other farm tasks, in addition to doing their work at home. Although the entire area is subject to frequent droughts, these people do not suffer hunger. They also successfully grow cattle. There isn't any family who does not own five or six heads of cattle, a couple of oxen, a pair of horses, sheep, and plenty of poultry. The butter and cheese they produce are of high quality, and even the Christians are paying a higher price for these products than similar products bought from villagers of their faith. Their houses, which they have built by themselves, are small, typical of farmers' homes; however, inside their homes are exceptionally clean. I saw people skilled in various crafts, among them some who also own fields and farm animals like the other farmers, however, since they are busy with working in their crafts, the fieldwork and handling the farm animals are done by their wives and daughters.

I have not seen even a single Christian or a Jew from another location, for that matter, working in the construction of their synagogue, which is being built now. All the workers are local residents. They have one advantage over almost all other farmers in the country. While most of the other farmers are drunk, none of the locals like liquor, and the little they drink, they do it for their health. That is also the reason why there is only a single tavern in the village.

During the winter, when they do not have work to be done in the field or vineyard, the farmers

*[Page 394]*

revive their souls at the *Beit HaMidrsah* and those craftsmen who obey the law, obtain a permit from their leader (*Schultz*), who is also Jewish, to leave their home for a maximum of three months, and earn an additional income by working in neighboring towns and settlements. All the women do women's crafts at home for the residents of the neighboring cities. When I witnessed their tireless dedication to their work and their hospitality expressed by the fact that everything we asked for and not asked for they provided generously and joyfully, I said – "may people like them be more numerous among the Jews." When I asked for the reason for them coming here, they replied that there was a person, a native of the holy community of Shklov, whose name was R' Nakhum Finkelshtein, who advocated for them. It has been a few years since he started a business in Kherson, and he noticed that many available fields in the area were not cultivated by anybody. He knew that many of his people in the country were suffering from hunger, and he turned to the authorities to ask for help for his miserable brothers. The Czar agreed to allocate an amount of two hundred rubles, two oxen, a horse, and a cow for everyone who would be willing to become a farmer on the island of Crimea. R' Finkelshtein persuaded his people to become farmers and many people in Lithuania heeded his advice. Unfortunately, due to initial strains and troubles, the change of climate, and the difficult adaptation to life in the village two-thirds of these settlers died. The remaining third learned the work and adapted themselves to the way of life of farmers, albeit with great difficulty. Currently, they are accustomed to the farmers' way of life, enjoy their work, and are very knowledgeable in the fieldwork. I witnessed some people who have acquired a property worth several thousand rubles out of the insignificant amount they received initially. However, they are not boasting about their wealth, have not abandoned their fieldwork or their way of life as farmers, and continue to reside here.

The aforementioned R' Nakhum, who was their guide and supporter, has never had the need to become a farmer, since he was always a wealthy man. Nevertheless, he made his children work in the fields like the settlers. His sons and daughters live in the village of Yefeh-Nahar, and one of them received us very cordially and offered us from the bounty he was blessed to have by G–d, without accepting, even once, any compensation from us. I asked him about his father and he told me that his father lived together with the people who followed his advice, although they caused him dissatisfaction. He tolerated, patiently, their stubbornness and foolishness so that he could lead them to the state he envisioned. When he saw that his will and vision had been fulfilled and that the villagers were content with their lives, he left them and returned to Kherson. May G–d prolong his life, strengthen and support him. May he live to see the success and wealth of his children and grandchildren! May G–d promote and elevate all of his descendants and prolong their lives until the coming of the Messiah.

*[Page 395]*

## [A letter] from R' Kahana to R' Ovadia

I have received your second letter from the province of the Crimea peninsula. Please do not be angry with me for my harsh words in my last letter to you, in which I complained about your delay among the farmers in the above-mentioned province. We were too quick to urge you to hurry up and come back; we now realize that you have done well by your people to stay and delay your return. We now urge you to observe the way of life and activity of our people who reside there and describe your observations to us. This would serve as a shield and provide us with a proper response towards our enemies who claim that our people are lazy and that they are not willing to do physical work in craft or in the field, and therefore they only work in trade. With your description, our enemies can see that our brothers can be farmers and craftsmen if they are allowed to be. It would support our claim against the authorities that it was their fault in preventing us from working in crafts or in the field and thereby forcing us to look for our sustenance in trade and commerce. We could also state that if they open the gates for us to work in craft and labor, and support us as people who have not experienced labor for quite some time, then we are willing to burden ourselves with the physical work, like all other people in our country and sustain ourselves from the fruits of our work. This is why we are now eager to hear from you.

May peace be with you.

## [A letter] from R' Ovadia to R' Meir Kahana

I did not respond to your letter in which you were angry with me for being delayed here among the farmers, because I was sure that you have imagined the Jewish farmers to be like all other farmers in Poland. If you knew them, as well as I did, possessing this advantage that comes from their devotion to work and their flawless attributes, you would also want to get to know them better and spend affectionate time with them. Since I have read your last letter, in which you asked me to describe to you their life and customs, I am hurrying to respond to you and write about what I learned and saw.

An authority called *Galvana Kantara* [Guardian Bureau for Settlers] was established in each province of New Russia [Southern Ukraine] under a decree of the Russian Czar. The authority was put in charge of all the people who came to settle there from any nationality or location (colonists). The authority is responsible for all the financial and legal affairs of the settlers. Its main office is located in Ekaterinoslav and it consists of six officials headed by a director. The director, currently General Inzov, reports to the province governor. The director is authorized to judge, impose sentences, and handle any request

*[Page 396]*

by the people who report to him regarding legal issues, and any other affair between a settler and any other person, whether the person is the plaintiff or the defendant. Our brothers who settled in the Crimea peninsula are under the responsibility of that authority as well. Besides that authority, every village, which I named in my previous letter, elects one of the village residents to be the leader of the village, called the *Schultz*. The *Schultz* is authorized to punish all those who are idle. He is also authorized to impose punishments, such as jail time, or tying wooden restraints on one's feet, for small offenses.

The Guidance Bureau provides the *Schultz* with a stamp for stamping certificates (Reisenpaesse [Travel Permits]) for people who want to travel for a short time. The certificate must be listed in a special notebook, in Russian. If the *Schultz* does not know Russian, he must be helped by a person who does. I saw a *Schultz* by the name of Itzek, in the village of Yefeh-Nahar who has done everything he was tasked to do, very well.

A commissioner (Commissar) nominated over every five or six villages, is tasked with receiving from the *Schultz* all the reports about the affairs of the colonies, and issues between the colonies and the Bureau, and transferring them to the Guidance Bureau. R' Nakhum Finkelstein was the first person to be nominated for that role and was called *Ãœber–Schultz* [senior *Schultz*]. He was elected by all the Jewish villages but had to retire in his old age when he could no longer handle the load of the role.

I saw teachers, cantors, Jewish slaughters, and synagogue attendants in these villages, who were elected by their congregations. They serve voluntarily in addition to their regular work in the fields. There are also learned people among them who are able to rule based on Jewish law and teach. Their houses are filled with books, but their yards are filled with crops and grain. If a teacher needs to get paid for his work, then his fields are being cultivated, and the crops are being brought to his yard by the other farmers. They also have public baths in the larger villages, and the residents of the smaller villages go to take a bath there.

During the days when they do not work in the field, they pray in the synagogue every day, at dawn and dusk. In the field, they pray a short prayer (*Barkhu, Kedusha,* and *Kadish* [parts of the daily prayer]), in "*minyan's*" [10 males older than 13, required for every Jewish public prayer]. Their wives bring the food for their husbands working in the fields. All of the ceremonial work is performed by Jews since there are no Christians among them. Therefore, they light the candles on Friday evening one hour before sunset. They also eat dinner on Friday evening, and in the winter, they light the heater before the coming of Shabbat.

All the colonists, including the Jewish settlers, are exempt from taxes and property taxes for the first 20 years from the day they have settled. They marry their sons at a young age because they like to see their sons and grandsons helping them with the fieldwork. They award dowry like the other villagers according to their status; however, dowry is paid in oxen, sheep, horses, and grain, not as money.

***Translator's Notes:***

1. This story seems to be the source of the story "Jewish Colony in Russia in the Year 1823" (see 389), by its editor Antony Eisenbaum in his journal Beobachter an der Weichsel" ["The Observer from the Banks of the Vistula"], Warsaw, 1922.

---

*[Page 397]*

# The Kingship Gives Land to the Jews

## From his [short story] "BaYamim HaHem" ["In Those Days"], [1900]

## by Mendele Mokher Sfarim

### Translated by Moshe Kutten

### Edited by Yocheved Klausner

…And troubles and all sorts of calamities are looming and coming to the city K…, one after the other, like sea waves. Who, other than the Jews, are so accustomed to troubles that they bow their heads like stalks when a tidal wave is threatening to drown them in the angry sea and raise their heads again when the sea calms down? Blessed be He who said to the Jews: "Go through rivers, and thou would not drown. Go through the fire, and thou would not burn!" A decree issued [by the Czar] to get rid of the [women's] scarves – is certainly a bad decree. …And the Jews? The Jews get used to it. They push themselves a bit more, somewhat hungrier, somewhat more distressed, and make do with less, but trust that with the help of G–d, they would be able to live without scarves. A fire breaks out in the city. It is true – it is big trouble. But the Holy One, blessed be He – He is our Father, and the Jews are merciful. Letters are being written, and messengers are being sent, and the Jews wait and expect – but there is no savior. After all, the messengers are also people, made of flesh and blood. They too, have wives and children, and they, too, need to eat and drink like anybody else. The cold winter comes, so a temporary shelter outside would not do. So the Jews are forced to squeeze inside their small houses… and if the space is a bit too narrow – there is no problem. They all squeeze themselves more and are crowding brotherly together in unity. A contagious disease comes – and many die. A fast is announced and they recite the Psalms. Poverty is growing, and the number of the poor multiplies. Whoever desires and is able takes his cane and a bag and travels to the overseas countries and from there to the four corners of the world. The Holy One, blessed be He – His world is immense. Volhyn is a vast and delightful country. Being a "melamed" [Jewish religion teacher] is a good occupation there. Jews move there and become "melameds." Seemingly – peace on earth for them; however, a decree is dropped on them that it is forbidden to study except in government schools. The decree instills fear – they circumvent it and contrive a plot. The Holy one, blessed be He, will have mercy – and the "melameds" continue to teach.

This is how the people of the city K… spend the bad times that have befallen them.

During those days, the rumor about the colonies arrived at the city – the authorities were giving land to the Jews to settle and work it. That rumor spread like a flame and passed from mouth to ear. Many versions heaped on top of each other and got so twisted that they became impossible to untangle. What colonies? Where are these colonies? How do they give land?

The opinions were divided on this issue. Group after group of people fought with shrieking and angry voices, arguments, and curses.

– "Please, Rabbi Zelig," – pleads lame Khaikel, who would give his soul for the colonies –

*[Page 398]*

"you – the philosopher, the big awe-inspiring scholar with your 'blah–blah' and your humdrum, please tell me what it means, this thing, which can be a life-line for the Jews, a thing that you should not simply dismiss by frowning. Please talk to me in a regular spoken language, not in your usual "blah–blah" and humdrum language.

– "What would I say to you – Khaikel, if you are… please forgive me," – Rabbi Zelig responded, frowning, pinching a wisp from his flaky tobacco, and placing it in his nose – "You do not understand the meaning of things and their essence. They give away colonies? Why? People do not give away things for no reason. Khaikel goes and becomes a nobleman and estate owner? 'blah' and a hundred times 'blah'!"

– I tell the same things to my Feibush – Yekle, one of the "maggid's" [Jewish preacher] grandsons, joins our discussion – "You are asking to be an earl, Feibush? Isn't that so? This matter, I say, has the form of things that are foreign…" *goy* [Gentile]" … pagan, who absorbs forty [lashes], pardon your honor; and not only that, they say: for every negligence in working the land, or any other small offense, they would sentence the sinner to military service, or send him to the persecution country – Siberia. "Feibush," I say to him, you are a "melamed," and that is what you have done all of your life. Continue to be a "melamed" in the future. Your imagination that you have been impregnated last night, for example, and there is a goy in your womb, is nonsense. No, Feibush, the hands are Jacob's hands, not Esau's. [in Genesis 27:22 – "The voice is the voice of Jacob, but the hands are the hands of Esau"].

– "We do not want to go to these nearby provinces," – a voice is breaking out from another group gathered at the "Beit HaMidrash," "We do not want these provinces, even if they give us houses full of gold and silver. It is better if we go to those places – Ekaterinoslav and Kherson."

– "May it be as you say" – many voices can be heard coming from that group – "but the money, the money [where would that come from]?"

– The money – they give it…! There is money…! There will be money…! Be quiet, and let us hear what Rabbi Khaim has to say! …and what is Rabbi Khaim saying? He is saying that we need to call an assembly. Let us have an assembly!"

And that was what has been found out about the colonies at the assembly of the congregation:

Many of the Jews from "White Russia" [Belarus], and those who were expelled from the villages settled in 1806, as they requested. It was done with the kingship's support and money on its land in "New Russia" [southern Ukraine]. Subsequently, in 1810, a decree was issued that no more Jews would be sent there since the money to settle them had been exhausted. Jews were allowed to settle nine years later; however, all of the expenses were on their account. Four years later, the decree forbidding the Jews from settling has been renewed. According to the 1835 and 1847 laws, Jews were allowed to settle as farmers on public land, throughout the entire Pale of Settlement, particularly in the provinces of Ekaterinoslav and Kherson. The expenses of the settlers were borne by the Jewish public through the "meat tax." Since the Jewish population would have to cover the expenses of the settlers, the people left the matter of the settlement for a discussion in the following assembly.

Like all other gatherings, the following gatherings were a waste of time involving just futile talk without any real results. The settlement required money, but the congregation did not have any. Not only was it poor and deprived, it owed taxes and property taxes, which were collected forcibly. Every member, from the young to the old

[Page 399]

was filled with sorrow, and all were asking: "What would happen to us at the end?" In "*Beit HaMidrash*" Jews were discussing the coming of the "Messiah," calculating and announcing a new date of the coming, based on what a certain Rabbi, a Jewish great scholar, found in a phrase [which predicts the date]. That rumor calmed their spirit, and hope was shining in their eyes. They got stirred up and said: "Be strong, and we will be strengthened – the Jewish nation will survive!" The leaders of the communities would gather often, sitting and discussing the affairs of the congregation. At the end they would stand, sigh, and pray: "Please G–d – save your people – the Jews! Alas, their situation is poor and destitute!"

A story was told about the congregation leaders who gathered for a dinner, during a winter night, at the home of Rabbi Khaim. The frost was horrible during that night. The moon was shining in the sky, and the ice was sparkling like gems gracefully embellishing the new snow–gown that adorned the land, like a gift sent by the bright stars. That night was made solely for pleasure and lovers' outings. However, pleasure was not on the mind of the Jews of the city of K… Stillness and silence prevailed outside, and not a soul could be seen. The community leaders were sitting around the table beside a warm heater, and discussing the affairs of the congregation.

As they were talking, moaning, and groaning, the door opened, and a frozen stream like a dark-edged pillar of haze broke into the house. A sound of footsteps, with a peculiar creak, was heard, and a human figure emerged from the pillar of haze.

"Lippa"! – all said unanimously – "*Shalom Aleichem*," Lippa!"

Lippa was from among the homeowners. Forty-year-old, he was a clever and sharp man, diligent, and goodhearted, like those poor people who are happy even when they are oppressed. He treated people nicely and was loved by all the people in the city. When the rumor about the colonies arrived, he did not open his mouth in long-winded arguments or try to be wise like many others. Instead, he went to the district city and from there to the provincial city, to get informed and to learn about that matter and how he can become involved.

Lippa replied softly, to each and every one, flapping the wings of his cloak, shaking the frozen flakes of snow, and warming himself against the flaming fireplace. Everyone looked at him lovingly. All of a sudden, they all opened their mouths, smiling and pointing at his feet:

"Lippa, what are these?"

"*Laptis*" answered Lippa calmly.

"The days of Purim have not arrived yet, and here you are – wearing a costume and playing a game with us," – they said to him and laughed loudly.

They were not laughing without a reason. "*Laptis* were boots braided of reed that the simple peasants in Lithuania wore over pieces of rugs on their feet. The "boots" had strips that they tied around their lower leg from the knee to the ankle. A Jew, even the poorest of the poor, would rather walk with the back of his heel exposed or even go barefoot but would not ever wear *laptis*, as this would be like eating pork. A Jew would never wear "*laptis*" except during one of two joyful occasions – a joker who wears a peasant's costume on the holiday of Purim, or a comedian at a wedding bawl.

*[Page 400]*

"I am not wearing a costume. I am truly a farmer now," – responded Lippa, smiling cunningly: – To avoid bothering myself and announce it separately to every one of my town people and have a long discussion about it with everyone, I reconsidered and decided to wear *laptis* on my legs – "here, my Jewish brothers, observe and know who I am, and leave me be."

"If that is the case," says Rabbi Khaim, observing Lippa lovingly and earnestly – "tell us, Lippa, everything, in detail."

Lippa did not refuse, and he explained the issue of the colonies thoroughly, with all of its details and the laws associated with it. He told about everything he had experienced until he found friends he liked, and they established an association, planning to settle in one colony in the province of Kherson.

"And the money?" – asked the community leaders, extending puzzling and urging faces – "Where would you find the money? After all, the congregation cash box is empty."

– "Calm down"! – Lippa tells them calmly – "an angel does not perform two missions at the same time, but an agile Jew, does do many tasks at the same time. When I was busy dealing with the colonies' affairs, G–d made me an emissary in finding a match for the daughter of a certain person. I became a matchmaker and earned money. From that money, I gave some to my association's cash box, and a bit for the sustenance of my wife and daughter. I will take the rest, along with the money I will receive from selling my belongings and housewares – and if I need a little bit more money – I am sure my people that you would help me."

Sara offered the guests fatty delicacies, wine, and gels, and invited them to refresh themselves with the food.

– "For next year" – said Lippa with a friendly smile – "I will send you, G–d's willing, fat geese from my colony as a gift. As the song being sung today, over there:

G–d commanded the blessing to come, the grocery is not costly –
A goat for two *Zuzim* [1] and a chicken for a *Ksita* [2].

***Translator Notes:***

1. One *Zuz*, two *Zuzim*, an old Aramiac penny [A goat for two *Zuzim* taken from the song: "One Small Goat," sang at the conclusion of the Passover Seder.
2. *Ksita* – an old Aramaic currency.

———————

[Page 401]

# Jews who Work the Land

**From an article in the newspaper "HaShakhar," Seventh Year, Vienna, 5636 (1876)**

**by Aviezer Mi'Kandiya[1]**

**Translated by Moshe Kutten**

**Edited by Yocheved Klausner**

At the end of the article, the newspaper editor noted that the article was provided by the scholar Y. L. Gordon; however, the poet probably preferred to publish it under the aforementioned name.

It is very pleasant to see the spring in one of the colonies. Very early at dawn on Sunday, the people go out for their activities and work – plowing, seeding, or loosening the soil. Sunday follows the Shabbat, when the people rest and find serenity for their tired souls and bodies from the six days of hard work. Before leaving, the plowing convoys stand in the streets of the colony until they are loaded with the needed provisions. The plowing convoy consists of several elements. First in the convoy is a covered wagon laden with sacks of seeds, food and provisions, cooking wares, and field tools. Following it is the long wagon, filled with fodder and hay, and a big water barrel for the workers and their animals. The field plots of the colonies are narrow and long. Their width is about two *verstas* [an old Russian unit – about .663 miles], and their length is as long as twenty *verstas*. Not every plot contains a well, and there are colonies, such as "Tova" ["Good"] and "A'havat–Avoda" ["Love of Work"], that not only do not have wells in their fields but also the water from the well within the colony is too bitter and salty to drink. The residents in these colonies have to fill up on water from very deep wells located far from their colony. Hauling the water on a wagon pulled by horses, for themselves and for their animals, requires a substantial amount of effort. Next in the plowing convoy comes the plow and the four-wheel harrow with its three spades and the cultivation tools to loosen the soil and then pairs of riding horses (that could not be harnessed to a plow or a wagon), with Jewish riders driving them.

About twenty to thirty plowing convoys leave for the fields from each colony. The convoys are accompanied by the loud whistling of the farmers, their wives, and their children (which is a testimony to their joy about the fact that the days of fall and winter, days that nobody needs are gone, and to the hope in their heart that G–d would give his blessing to fill their barns with grain, the fruit of their land, as a compensation for the drought years). Also noisy is the rattling of the wheels and the neighing of the horses, which, for three whole months, have been standing by their managers, fattening themselves with barley seeds, idle from any work. Only at dusk could they gallop proudly in their run through the settlement's streets to the well to drink. Adding to the cacophony was the whistling of the sheep and the cattle, which had just given their udders' milk to the owners and were being driven out in herds to pasture in the field. The uproar of that commotion, mixed with the chirping of every poultry and house animal, sweetens the glorified spring splendor, like coming from a choir of divine poets.

During the harvest, crops ingathering, and threshing, the Jewish farmers are kept very busy. Whoever has not been a witness, with one's own eyes, to the diligence of these Jewish farmers, their agility and perseverance at these tasks, has never

*[Page 402]*

seen the diligence and perseverance of Jews. Husband and wife, father and sons maintain the counting of the required weeks to the harvest, ingathering and threshing; a youth of seventeen-year-old, is standing fully erect and powerful on the tall heap, and with a strong voice and a heart-warming laughter he calls those around him who stand on the wagons. They are holding long pitchforks, and streams of sweat are dripping down their faces like water. They lift up, with a lot of effort, one sheaf after the other. If the lifter misses its target, or if the load is too heavy due to the long leverage of the sheaf at the top of the pitchfork, the sheaf falls down and may take the lifter with it, throwing him down to the ground, crushing his or her skull. "Oh, come on you, weary people! Bring up sheaves! Why are you waiting?" With these sayings, the youth takes revenge over the lifters who, at the beginning, when they had laid down the foundations for the heap on the bottom, fed him the sheaves in a hurry and did not let him rest, even for a minute, until he lost the strength to stand on his feet. The lifters are boys and girls, thirteen-year-olds. They are already skilled in harnessing mighty horses, riding them, and performing other farm work.

It is difficult to believe that a Jewish boy, a thirteen-year-old, plows with horses or arranges a silo of hay as long as ten floors and as high as two or three, all of that with skilled hands of a craftsman. I was fortunate to witness these things when they occurred in the colonies, day by day. I heard that the Russian farmers were astonished at the diligence of the Jewish youths. They said: "It is difficult to find boys among us who are as agile at work as the Jewish children. Why would we speak badly of them or the older adults who work like an ox and a donkey carrying their load? The Jewish farmers perform the threshing in order and proper organization." The youth is standing at the center of the threshing surface, – which has been flattened by a circular roller, and drives the horses, harnessed to threshing stones, in the circle around it. His siblings and parents along with their hired workers, all are holding a three-tooth pitchfork or a rake, turning the upper layer of threshed crops, carrying the hay to the barn, and spreading the grain and the chaff into the winnowers. They work during the entire season of the ingathering and threshing, which lasts, in a good year, from the [Jewish] month of Av [July–August], until the winter. The noise of the wheels rumbling, the clatter of the winnowers, the shouts of the workers, and their whistling, which comes from all directions, can be heard all day and night, particularly during the day on Friday, when the workers are in a hurry to complete their work before the coming of the Shabbat. Even the delicate housewife leaves the cooking chores, and the "*Hatmana*" for Shabbat [covering a cooked food to keep it hot for Shabbat] to her younger daughter and hurries up to help complete the threshing and winnowing work, collect the chaff, and sweep the threshing floor before Shabbat, so that the crops would not be exposed on the threshing floor and be ruined by rain.

Although working the land is hard physical work involving sweat and effort, it is also satisfying and pleasant. If G–d blesses them with timely rains, their fields yield abundant food, their barns become filled with grain, and their wallets with money. However, years of drought and cattle diseases, which occur in that area, from time to time, cause havoc to their property and the fruits of their effort and decimate it.

These stories are not told for the sake of telling stories. Many real and wonderful activities, performed under the sun, serve as testimony and evidence of their truthfulness.

***Translator's Note:***

1.  Kandiya is the ancient name of Heraklion – the capital of Crete. Another famous Rabbi – Rabbi Yosef Shlomo Delmedigo is also known as the Yashar [honest in Hebrew] from Kandiya.

[Page 403]

# Appendices

*[Page 405]*

**Appendix A**

# Stopping the Settlement in the Western Provinces
# (In 1859)

**Translated by** Moshe Kutten

**Edited by** Yocheved Klausner

Czar Alexander the Second's manifest on the day of his coronation (26 August 1856) concerning the cancellation of the compulsory service weakened the settlement movement substantially.

Only 47 families settled in the Western Provinces in 1857, even though a substantial number of government land plots were available for settlement. On the other hand, 253 families left, either under the influence of the manifest or for other reasons. The total number of settlers in the Western Provinces reached 2827 families before 1858.

The character of the settlement in Kherson and Ekaterinoslav was different from the one in the 9 Western Provinces. The conditions in southern Ukraine were quite severe: frequent droughts, locusts, diseases, cattle plague, and a harsh climate. However, the concentration in large colonies, the supervision and guidance by the government (despite the bureaucratic flaws), the assistance by the government for the establishment of the farm, and the distance from the cities – all of these factors contributed to the colonies' agricultural character. Despite the distances between the colonies, they all had a uniform identity. In a journey of three to four hours, it was possible to reach the most distanced colony in the provinces of Kherson or Ekaterinoslav.

Contrary to that, the conditions in the Western Provinces were more favorable. The settlers could avoid the three-month torturing journey on foot. They were allowed to reside in their own homes until they could move to their settlements without suffering from the acclimatization difficulties in a new climate. They lived near their relatives and could be helped by them at a time of need. The ban on leaving the farms was enacted in the Western Provinces as well; however, the authorities were not very strict about that, and the settlers were, more or less, free in their movements.

Despite all these favorable conditions, the general picture, after 18 years of settlement in the Western Provinces, was quite bleak. The splitting into tiny settlements and the lack of connection between the settlements due to the distances contributed to the weakening of the settlement movement, which consisted of about three thousand families.

At the end of the 1850s, the criticism

*[Page 406]*

by the senior officials and their assistants in the bureaus against the Jewish settlement in the Western Provinces strengthened. The officials pointed at the lack of progress of the settlement movement and its bleak state, claiming that the Jews were not able to work the land and that they did not have any inclination for it. Yet, we cannot ignore the obstacles that were piled up in abundance in the way of the settlers: the bureaucratic foot-dragging and corruption, the inferior soil, lack of pasture lands, lack of resources, unfitting family status, lack of guidance, shortage of credit for the crops cycle's cash flow, being a minority among the Christian villages, and especially the hostile and alienating attitude within the Jewish public.

The Minister of State Assets – Moraviov, turned to the provincial authorities to report about the state of the settlers in every Province and to submit proposals for improvement.

The responses and reports of the provincial committees were quite bleak:

The Vilna [Vilnius] minister wrote: "Out of the 227 settlers in the province of Vilna – 121 are owners of good farms, as good as those of the Russian farmers. There are 71 failed farms and 35 families have not begun to establish their farms as of yet."

The Grodno's minister wrote: "Out of 201 settlers, there are only 72 established farms. All the other farms failed, among them, some farms are not cultivated at all."

The Kovno's [Kaunas] minister wrote: "The situation of the settlers in the province of Kovno is not good. Although it is important to introduce the Jews to agriculture, it is important to supervise them and concentrate them in special settlements."

The Mohilev's minister wrote: "Most of the settlers are negligent, and they neglect their farm. Many wander to the nearby cities to work as merchants. Those who do not have resources have not even started to establish their farm. The supervision over them is difficult. Wouldn't it be appropriate to discontinue the settlements throughout the province"?

The rest of the reports were written in a similar style.

We have a special interest in the review of Vasilchikov – Kiev's Provincial Minister. He too, counted the flaws of the settlement movement and said that, during the harvest, many farmers were not present on location. They were all scattered in the surrounding towns since they had leased their lands to the area's farmers in exchange for half of the harvest, as they had not yet established their farms and built their houses. The houses that were built were usually built without a plan and order and were quite narrow. The settlers did not obey the authority and the village leaders. The Jewish village leaders were not very good at managing public affairs, and the settlers treated them with contempt since they were not used to seeing one of their brothers in an authoritarian role. Vasilchikov was not content with the situation and offered a solution: Directing the Jews towards craftsmanship and handicraft. As a first step in that direction, he proposed to build a vocational school in every province and finance them from the cash collected from the "Meat Tax."

Vasilchikov also proposed to cease the settlement in the three provinces

[Page 407]

managed by him (Kiev, Podolia, and Vohlyn). Concerning the existing settlement, he proposed to improve it by efficient supervision.

Vasilchikov's plan was received favorably by Moraviov, the State Assets Minister, Lanski – the Interior Minister, and Bludov – the head of the "Committee for Jewish Affairs." It wasn't yet clear how to convert the Jews to craftsmanship. [They were numerous]. The ratio between the Jewish and the Christian population was as high as 1:10 and in Vilna – 1:8.5. Lanski did not think that the proposal could be accomplished. However, all three [of the ministers mentioned above] accepted the proposal to stop the Jewish settlement. The proposal was transferred to the assembly of the "Committee for Jewish Affairs," which was the highest authority for any Jewish affairs.

The "Committee for Jewish Affairs" expanded Vasilchikov's proposal and passed a resolution "to stop the Jewish settlement on government lands in the Western Provinces," and proposed to anybody interested in settlement to settle in Kherson and Ekaterinoslav, on the reserve areas slated for Jewish settlement. Jews were still allowed to settle in the Western Provinces on private lands acquired by them, but not on scattered individual plots, only in concentrated settlements containing at least 15 families.

The resolution was approved by Alexander the Second on October 22, 1859. According to the usual custom, the resolution should have been also submitted, formulated, and rationalized, to the Senate for publication. However, the Chief Procurator [the head of the senate], raised the question as to whether they should publish the reasons for stopping the settlement. At the end of 1850, public opinion still carried some value. The procedural question was discussed by the three ministers involved in that matter, and it was agreed that the reasons for stopping the settlement should not be published. Therefore, the law was issued as a senate regulation without detailed explanations and reasons.

That was how the end came to expanding the [Jewish] settlement in the Western Provinces beyond the borders of Kherson and Ekaterinoslav.

*[Page 408]*

## Appendix B

## The Agricultural Settlement throughout Russia in the Year 1856

In the year 1856, there were:

| Province | Colonies / Settlements | Families | People |
|---|---|---|---|
| Kherson | 19 Colonies | 1,929 | 14,523 |
| Ekaterinoslav | 14 Colonies | 427 | 9,596 |
| **Total in all of the Southern Provinces** | | 2356 | 24,114 |
| Podolia | 24 Settlements | 1,263 | 12,668 |
| Kiev [Kyiv] | 45 Settlements | 528 | 6,835 |
| Volyn | 28 Settlements | 231 | 2,435 |
| Minsk | 2 Settlements | 96 | 1,025 |
| Vilna [Vilnus] | 24 Settlements | 217 | 2,236 |

| | | | |
|---|---|---|---|
| Grodno [Hrodna] | 20 Settlements | 305 | 3,174 |
| Vitebsk | 33 Settlements | 130 | 1,139 |
| Kovno [Kaunas] | 8 Settlements | 110 | 1,708 |
| Mohilev | 2 Settlements | 159 | 1,684 |
| **[Total Western Provinces]** | | 3,036 | 32,274 |
| **[Total]** | | 5,395 | 56,393 |

Except for these colonies and settlements, hundreds purchased and settled in Tavria, Bessarabia, and Congressional Poland. We would not exaggerate if we would estimate their number at a round figure of 1600 families (about 10,000 people). We can, therefore, summarize that during the beginning of the reign of Alexander the Second (1855 – 60), the Jewish settlement included about 100 large colonies and about 300 small settlements in which 7 thousand families resided, altogether – 66 thousand families, out of an overall Jewish population in Russia (including Poland) of close to 3 million people.

*[Page 409]*

## Appendix C

## The Settlement in Kherson and Ekaterinoslav at the end of 1885

| Kherson Province | | | Ekaterinoslav | | |
|---|---|---|---|---|---|
| | Settlement | No. of Families | | Settlement | No. of Families |
| 1. | Sdeh-Menukha HHaGdola | 11 | 1. | Grafskoya | 26 |
| 2. | Sdeh-Menukha HHaKtana | 30 | 2. | Zelenopolya | 39 |
| 3. | Nahar-Tov hHaGdola | 83 | 3. | Nadezhnaya | 40 |
| 4. | Nahar–Tov–HaKtana | 26 | 4. | Sladkovodnaya | 28 |
| 5. | Bobrovy-Kut | 104 | 5. | Zatishya | 40 |
| 6. | Effingar [Yefeh-Nahar] | 87 | 6. | Rovnopol | 45 |
| 7. | Inguletz | 128 | 7. | Khlebodaravka | 21 |
| 8. | Kaminka | 51 | 8. | Novo-Zlatopol | 59 |
| 9. | Izlochista | 53 | 9. | Vesselaya | 27 |
| 10. | Novi-Berislav | 46 | 10. | Krasnoselka | 41 |

| 11. | Lvov | 91 | 11. | Mezherich | 37 |
| 12. | Novo-Poltavka | 97 | 12. | Trudoliubovka | 32 |
| 13. | Romanovka | 88 | 13. | Nechayevka | 21 |
| 14. | Novo-Vitebsk | 47 | 14. | Priyutnaya | 30 |
| 15. | Novo-Podolsk | 32 | 15. | Roskoshnoye | 26 |
| 16. | Novo-Kovna | 36 | 16. | Bogodrovka | 36 |
| 17. | Novo-Zhitomyr | 30 | 17. | Gorkaya | 26 |
| 18. | Dobroye | 102 | | | |
| 19. | Izraelovka | 76 | | | |
| 20. | Sehaidak | 35 | | | |
| 21. | Promukloya | 16 | | | |
| 22. | Volnaya | 24 | | | |
| | **Total no. families** <br> **Total no. people** | 1,393 <br> 10,299 | | **Total no. of families** <br> **Total no. of people** | 574 <br> 3,772 |

Altogether – in all the colonies – 1,967 families and about 14,071 people.

61,369 *disiyatins* [about 166,000 acres] land areas in the Jewish settlements.

*[Page 410]*

## Appendix D

# The State of the Jewish Settlement in the Western Provinces at the end of the 1880s

The conditions for the settlement in the Western Provinces were very difficult. The soil was soft and of poor quality. The pasture fields had already been distributed to the Christian farmers and were not allocated to the Jewish farmers. Transferring the plots to the settlers and reassigning them from the list of city dwellers to the one for farmers suffered from a prolonged "feet-dragging." The assistance from the fund of the "Meat Tax" was minuscule (initially 50 rubles and then 100 rubles), and was insufficient for the construction of the houses. An additional factor was the lack of knowledge in agriculture with all the blunders that resulted from it. Due to these difficulties, not all the settlers could proceed to receive their land, build houses, and establish farms. Even those who built houses and purchased the inventory, albeit with great efforts, did not see the fruits of their work very quickly. Under these circumstances, it was understandable that many of the settlers continued to work as small merchants and as craftsmen in the nearby towns.

As stated [See Appendix A], the government in Petersburg decided, in 1859, to stop the settlement of Jews on government land in the above-mentioned provinces. In 1864, a law was passed that forbade Jews to purchase [private] lands even using their own money. That law prevented the settlers who settled on private lands from purchasing additional land to enlarge their farms.

In 1865, a law was passed, allowing the Jewish settlers to transfer back from a status of an agriculturalist to a status of a city dweller. That law did not force the transferee to leave his land.

Although the Jews who transferred back to the status of city dwellers lost the right to be exempt from compulsory military service, they were released from their legal dependency on the "Volast" (a district council of several villages), which was authorized to impose physical punishment. In the colony of Sofyovka, in the province of Vohlyn, a Jewish farmer was sentenced to flogging because he did not cultivate his farm. That punishment angered all of the colony's farmers, and they transferred from the status of agriculturalists and listed themselves as city dwellers.

In 1866, the Ministry of State Assets ceased handling the Jewish settlements, and they were transferred to the ministry of the interior. As such, their rights were equalized with the rights of all other farmers, and they became subjects of a new regime and institutions which were established to handle all of Russia's farmers. They became entitled to elect and be elected to the local and regional institutions.

The larger colonies had their own local management, but the smaller settlements

*[Page 411]*

were joined with the neighboring Christian villages. They had, theoretically, the right to be elected to the local institutions, even to the position of a Justice of Peace; however, in practice, the residents of the small settlements did not enjoy that right because they were a minority.

In 1872 the government lands were distributed to the farmers permanently. Many injustices and errors of the previous distribution were corrected. However, that final distribution deprived the Jewish settlers cruelly. The institutions that supervised the distribution used a regulation that allowed banishing every Jew who did not cultivate his land. The assembly of the Christian village's farmers was authorized to determine, seemingly democratically, who among the Jewish farmers was cultivating his land, and who was leasing it. Their subjective tendency was, in most cases, to evict the Jews to gain additional land. If a certain Christian farmer testified that he had leased the land of a Jewish farmer, the Jew's land was taken away from him. In this "legal way," more than half of their fields (62.7%) were robbed from the Western Provinces' Jews, and many of them remained landless, except the half *disiyatin* [about 1.35 acres] a piece of land around the house which was only suitable for growing potatoes and other vegetables.

The farmers who were not expelled from their land persisted in cultivating their farms and acclimated to the life of working the land, and their children were born agriculturalists in every aspect. The farm sectors were cultivated and nurtured, not worse than those of their neighbors, the Russian farmers, and many of them, even excelled over the Russian farmers, although they also cultivated their farms using primitive methods.

The final blow to the Jewish settlement was landed with the "Constitution of the 3rd of May 1882," according to which it was prohibited for Jews to purchase or lease land throughout Russia (except for small plots in urban areas). Since that time, wealthy Jews couldn't settle on a permanently purchased or leased land. Furthermore, the rights of the Jews on the land they leased had expired, and according to the law they were banished from them. From that point, if a Jew wished to develop an agricultural sector and needed more land, he had to bypass the law by bribing, or leasing the land under a Christian name.

[Page 412]

## Appendix E

# The Jewish Settlement in Bessarabia

The province of Bessarabia was not initially among the provinces where the government allocated lands for Jewish settlement; however, purchasing private lands was not prohibited there. Many Jews, particularly from the cities of Shargorod, Kupygorov, and Proskurov [Khmelnytsky] in Podolia province, purchased land in the neighboring Bessarabia. Due to their limited resources and lack of experience in working the land, the first few years were difficult. They were happy when Jewish settlers from Bessarabia joined them. Some of these settlers were experts in growing sheep and others in growing tobacco. They served as guides for Podolia's Jews.

The government did not assist the Bessarabia's settlers, neither land nor loans. On the other hand, it did not impose any supervision upon the settlers. They were not forced to follow harsh regulations and not subjected to corrupt authority officials. They were free in their actions, efforts, initiatives, and mistakes. That independence instilled self-confidence in them.

During the initial stages of the settlement in Bessarabia, the attitude of the government circles towards the Jewish settlers was favorable and sympathetic. No special obstacles were placed in front of them. That was how 5 colonies were established on purchased land in the districts of Soroky [Soroca] and Bieltsy [Bălți] – Dombroveny, Lyublin, Vertyuzhany, Brichevo and Blalalo-Blad and 4 colonies on land leased for 50 years – Aleksandreny, Zguritza, Kapresht and Markuleshti. After the publication of the law forbidding the leasing of lands to Jews (May 3rd, 1882), the lease of three of these colonies was canceled, and only one of them, Markuleshti, continued to exist, bypassing the law using various tricks.

The colonies continued to develop – albeit by suffering many troubles, poverty, and distress – due to the nonintervention of the government, good climate, and plenty of water as well as the assistance of the local Jews who were always close to agriculture.

At the beginning of the 1860s, when the government's attitude towards the Jews, in general, and towards their settlement, in particular, was still liberal, wealthy Jews began to purchase small plots in their own localities for growing tobacco or vineyards. The more they became accustomed to agricultural work, and the more successful they were in doing that – the stronger the settlement process in Bessarabia became. The right to purchase lands permanently, or lease them, also helped in this process. One of the main agricultural sectors in Bessarabia was growing tobacco.

*[Page 413]*

[Agronomist] Akiva Ettinger visited Bessarabia at the end of the 1890s and the beginning of the 20th century, when he served as the local consultor for agricultural affairs on behalf of the J.C.A. His stories, written with a substantial love for the farmers in Bessarabia, contain very interesting material. We learn from these stories that the Turks introduced tobacco cultivation 150 years earlier and that the cultivation methods have been actually preserved since then. That continued until the sector was passed over slowly to the hands of the Jews, and they introduced several improvements, particularly in the methods of tobacco drying.

In 1889, the Russian scholar, Shcharbachov, published his research about tobacco cultivation in Russia for 25 years (1864 – 1889). According to him, 27 [%] of the tobacco areas were owned by Bessarabia Jews in 1864 and 62% in 1888. In 1888, 3431 Jews were working in tobacco-related jobs, and only 289 Christians, which means that 92% of the sector's workers were Jewish.

Initially, only the plot owners and some hired workers worked in the tobacco sector. However, over the years, the sector passed over to the hands of Jewish families who resided on tiny plots, as small as one *disiyatin* [about 2.7 acres] each. That limited area was cultivated during all the months of the year, by the family itself – the husband, wife, and children. Even the elderly found adequate work on the small farm, from among the many tasks available to them, starting from planting and ending in packaging.

Growing tobacco by self–work brought about 300 rubles annually, the average income for a working family. Families often also cultivated a vegetable garden for self–consumption.

The law of 1882, prohibiting the Jews from purchasing and leasing land, heavily burdened the tobacconists, who leased lands, and those who planned to purchase a plot for growing tobacco. The tobacconists bypassed the law by leasing plots under the name of a Christian person and by bribing the police. Despite the difficulties and the expenses, the Jewish tobacco growers did not abandon the sector.

A second agricultural sector that many Jews worked in was the cultivation of vineyards. Initially, this sector was more like a hobby or a second income occupation for the store owners. The first vineyards were cultivated primitively using methods that the Moldavians inherited from the Turks. The vines were not planted on straight lines but at equal distances. They were susceptible to diseases such as Oidium and Phylloxera. The first Jewish vineyard owners did not cultivate their vineyards by themselves and did not understand anything about the methods of trimming, names of the various varieties, etc. Over time, they learned to know the vine and some began to dedicate themselves to the sector and realized that well-cultivated vineyards could bring earnings at a level that was not lower than the income from a grocery store.

Over time, improvements have also been introduced in that sector, like in the other agricultural sectors in Russia. Akiva Ettinger, the agronomist and guide on behalf of J.C.A., helped tremendously in the progress of this sector.

There were some Jews who worked in growing sheep. They processed the milk into butter and cheese and marketed their products in the cities. These people were called "milkmen" by the public.

*[Page 414]*

In a census that was conducted by Ettinger in 1898, on behalf of the J.C.A., we find the following statistics:

536 households were registered in the Jewish colonies in Bessarabia, of them, 300 were working in general agriculture, 545 (251 people) worked in growing tobacco, 576 in cultivating vineyards, and 364 in milk production and sheep growing. Altogether, close to 2000 families from among Bessarabia's Jews (about 7.5% of the total Jewish population in that province) worked in agriculture toward the end of the 19th century.

Bessarabia's agriculturalists continued to develop their farms, along the lines that were drawn at the beginning of the 20th century, namely, along three main types of self–reliant farms as follows:

a.  A tobacco plantation of the size of 20 – 30 *dunams* [about 6 – 9 acres], which was cultivated by an average family, with three workers. On average, they produced an income of about 300 rubles annually, an amount which was sufficient for a comfortable life in a village.
b.  Vineyards of edible grapes and medicinal grapes were reestablished by grafting on American rootstock on an area of about 20 *dunams* [about 6 acres], on average. Self-work of the entire family and an investment of 800 rubles during the first three years, brought an income of 400–450 rubles annually per household. That amount allowed for a comfortable life near a city or town and in a settlement.
c.  A field crops farm on an area of 60-90 *disiyatins* [about 162 – 243 acres] each, with the addition of 2-3 cows, or 20-30 sheep or goats (in a common herd), which enabled modest sustenance for a household in a colony or a mixed village.

*[Page 415]*

## Appendix F

# A Review of the Agriculture in the Jewish Colonies in the Ukraine (Until 1926)

The lands of the old colonies in the regions of Kherson and Nikolayev [Mykolaiv] in Southern Ukraine stretched over a large region of more than 40,000 *disiyatins* (450,000 *dunams*) [108,000 acres] in the most fertile areas of the chernozem soil.

The agricultural farm in these colonies was mainly based on field crops. The Ukrainian's fertile "black soil" – chernozem, rich with humus, was capable of producing high yields even without the addition of fertilizers, provided that the number of precipitations was sufficient. There was no field irrigation in the colonies, and the yields were dependent on the "Grace of Heaven."

The amount of rain and its distribution throughout the season determined the yields. The average annual precipitation there was 500 millimeters. If the amount of rain was sufficient and its distribution was good, the yield of the winter crops – winter wheat and rye – per *disiyatin* (11 *dunams*) [2.7 acres] reached 200 *pods* [300 kilograms), and the yield of the summer crops – summer wheat, barley, and corn, reached 150 – 180 *pods* per *disiyatin* (about 200-500 kilograms per *dunam*). However, years with a sufficient amount of rain and a proper distribution were few and far between. Years with insufficient amounts of rain or improper distribution were more frequent, and the crops were actually lower. Some years, like 1921 and 1924 yielded very poor crops.

The area of a farm unit in the Jewish colonies was initially quite large – 30 *disiyatins* per farm. However, over the years, the lands were divided among the sons and the area of a farm unit became smaller and smaller. Many families reached the stage when the land was insufficient to sustain them. Some farmers leased additional areas and paid a third of the harvest for it, and the farm could not sustain the farmer's family. Some of the farmers turned to trade and craftsmanship.

After the end of the Civil War in Russia and the revolution, the Jewish colonies received, like the rest of the neighboring villages, additional land from the lands of the nearby estate owners. The number of farmers engaged in trade began to diminish anyway and was almost eliminated after the war. The Jewish farmers

[Page 416]

began to reestablish their farms and cultivate them on a proper level with the assistance of the organizations "ORT" and "JCA." According to the census of 1924, the following statistics were obtained about the occupations of the families residing in the colonies:

| Occupations | In Kherson's area | In Nikolayev's area |
|---|---|---|
| Agriculture | 77.4% | 75.9% |
| Agriculture with a secondary income (craftsmanship in the area during the winter) | 14.4% | 10.2% |
| Permanently occupied in craftsmanship (with agriculture as a secondary income) | 5.3% | 5.8% |
| People who did not seed at all | 8.6% | 2.4% |
| Total | 100% | 100% |

The Jewish agriculturists cultivated their fields by using a strict seed cycle which enabled considerable eradication of weeds and preservation of the humidity, at least in part of the soil. The cycle of seeds enabled rotation of the field cultivation, e.g. a fallow field, crops with rows of raised loose soil and autumn plowing for cultivation of summer crops.

The cycle of seeds was also aimed at enabling increased seeding of the winter crops, particularly winter wheat, which brought higher yields and higher income.

The development of farming and its progress in the Jewish settlements was influenced greatly by the agricultural school established by the J.C.A. organization near the colony of Novo-Poltavka. The school was headed by an agronomist of high stature and infinite dedication – Liubarski, who did a lot for the organization and advancement of agriculture in the colonies. The objectives of the school were:

a. To produce learned agriculturalists who would be able to serve as instructors and advanced farmers in every colony, and who would lead the way for the advancement of agricultural farming [in the Jewish colonies].
b. The school's farm demonstrated advanced farming in the following areas:
   o Fields, with various crops, cultivated properly, with proper tools and advanced methods

*[Page 417]*

- o Cattle – producing the highest yield, with proper maintenance and feeding
- o A milk sector and its proper usage, demonstrating the cleanliness of the milk farm and proper ways to prepare the produce for marketing
- o Clover and alfalfa fields
- o Vineyards and cultivation with trellising, the appropriate varieties of grapes, mainly Muscat and Shesla edible grapes

The advanced farming in these areas and others served as an example and model and thereby was an important means for the advancement of farming in the Jewish colonies.

That school was destroyed by the Makhno and Peliura gangs (after the Revolution) and was robbed and ransacked by the neighboring villagers. The wife of agronomist Liubarski, who lived in one of the school buildings, was shot by robbers when she tried to protect her husband with her own body. The school was abandoned and was not restored for many years.

## Milk Sector

The second most important sector of the agricultural farm in the colonies was the milk sector. Initially, it was established to provide milk for the families themselves, blessed with many children. Over time, the farmers increased the number of cows in the cowsheds, to produce and sell hard cheeses in the markets of the big cities.

After the Civil War, with the restoration of the colonies, the farmers organized and established cooperative milk and cheese factories, where they produced high-quality milk products, especially the cheeses of the variety "Bekshtin," which were sent to special warehouses in the cities where they were kept until they were cured and sold. The value of the cheese industry was very important. Most of the farmers in the colonies participated in it. The number of cows producing the milk reached thousands, and the yield of the best of them reached 3200 – 3500 liters per year.

## The Vegetable Gardens

In 1921, after the most difficult drought, when seeds of wheat, barley, and other crops had to be brought to the colonies from the outside, and only in very limited amounts, the value of the vegetable garden sector rose as a sector that could provide quick supply of food to the colonies, and could also provide employment and a nice income to the grower with a relatively low investment.

In the Jewish colonies located close to rivers, where it was possible to use the river water for irrigation, cooperative groups were formed to develop commercial vegetable gardens. The "ORT" organization provided "Bulgarian" water pumps that pumped the water from the rivers so that the gardens could be irrigated. Irrigated vegetable gardens developed and increased in number very quickly.

*[Page 418]*

In some of the colonies such as Yefe-Nahar and Sdeh-Menukha HaKtana, this sector played a major role in sustaining many families, especially during the first few years after the restoration of the colonies.

Over time, with the redevelopment of the other major farming sectors, the vegetable gardens sector declined slowly and lost its economic value in most of the colonies.

## The Vineyards

The J.C.A. organization introduced the first vineyards to the colony of Lvovo [Lvov] on the banks of the Dnieper as early as 1911. The varieties and the rootstocks conformed nicely to the soil conditions and the climate and the vineyards began to expand in the Jewish colonies. In 1914, commercial vineyards were also planted in Novo-Poltavka, the colony near the agricultural school, and in smaller areas in other colonies.

The commercial vineyards were planted in a concentrated manner in large enough areas for each farmer (about one *disiyatin*, or 11 *dunam*s [2.7 acres] per family). They had the potential to produce a nice income and became one of the major sectors on the farm. They enjoyed good and timely cultivation and proper care. Their owners specialized in this sector under continuous guidance from the school. Most of the fruit was processed as wine in the small cellars of the owners.

As customary in southern Ukraine, every house in the Jewish colonies had a cellar with a convex ceiling, dug deeply in the ground. The temperature in these cellars was cool in the summer and warm in the winter, and they served as warehouses for food accumulated during the summer and fall to feed the family members throughout the year, particularly during the long and cold winter months. These cellars served as private wineries for the production of wine from the grapes that grew in their vineyards and the wine was sold nicely bringing a high income.

With the restoration of the colonies after the Civil War and the harsh drought that followed, the planting of the vineyards in the colonies, on a commercial basis, began to widen again. In 1923, The J.C.A. organization sent American varieties of grapevine plants from France, and grapevines grafted on American rootstocks which were resistant to the grape disease – Phylloxera. "ORT" organized groups of farmers, guided them, and helped in planting a unified vineyard of 80 *disiyatins* [2160 acres] – a *disiyatin* for every farmer in the colony of Dobroye, and began to prepare additional planting in other colonies. According to the information we had, the planting of vineyards continued to expand in all of the Jewish colonies, and the vineyard sector became one of the most important of the agricultural farms there.

## The Fruit Tree Orchards

The only irrigated areas, before the vegetable gardens, were the fruit tree orchards in a few colonies. These orchards were planted along the banks of the Ingulets River, in the colonies of Sdeh-Menukha

*[Page 419]*

HaKtana and HaGdola [The Big Sdeh-Menukha and the small one] as well as in the colony of Bobrovy-Kut. The J.C.A. organization was the one who initiated that planting and implemented it in the years 1904 and 1907. The method of planting, keeping correct distances between the trees and matching the varieties, could serve as an example and a model for the whole region. As opposed to the orchards that had existed previously in the German as well as the other villages in the area, which were planted densely with summer fruit trees of a lower economic value – the orchards in the Jewish colonies had a higher commercial value (about 70%) with big apple varieties, which enabled easier cultivation and more efficient pest control.

The J.C.A. instructors brought more efficient methods from the orchards in France. Although they were not 100% suitable for the local conditions, they, nevertheless, helped in growing trees of higher value, which brought nice incomes to their owners.

In 1918 the above-mentioned colonies widened the areas of their orchards, corrected the errors made in the previous orchards, and increased the distances between the trees to 8 x 8 meters from 8 x 6. They fitted and further restricted the varieties of the apples and their owners saw a blessing in their yields.

With all of that, the fruits suffered from pest attacks, which were difficult to address without an overall organization of all of the local orchard owners.

## Growing Poultry and Bees

Like in all of the neighboring villages, primitive growing of poultry existed also in the Jewish colonies. Here and there some small hobbyists' beehives peeped through the trees. There were also a few bigger beehives – those which had a commercial value.

In summary[1] it can be said that the agricultural sectors in the Jewish colonies were more advanced than those in the neighboring villages, and some of them – such as the milk sector, vineyards, and fruit trees orchards, excelled and could easily serve as an example and model for the whole area.

Due to the continuous direction by guides and agronomists of the J.C.A organization during all of the years that the colonies existed and the dedicated and efficient work of the ORT organization and its agronomists in restoring

*[Page 420]*

the colonies after their destruction during the Civil War and the horrible drought of 1921, the agricultural farm in the Jewish colonies began to make its agricultural-cultural character more and more prominent.

During WWII, with the advance of Hitler's armies, the ax came down on the Jewish colonies. Most of the Jewish farmers were annihilated, and the rest spread throughout Russia. The colonies, with all of their advanced sectors, were destroyed.

May these lines serve as their eternal memorial.

———

***Author's Notes:***

1. This review details the status of the colonies until 1926. The author of this review made *Aliyah* to Eretz Israel in 1927, and his connection with the colonies stopped then.
   Agronomist B. Gurstein

———

[Page 421]

## Appendix G

## Birobidzhan – The autonomous Jewish District
## From the Encyclopedia of Social Study, Volume A, Sifriyat HaPoalim, 1962

Birobidzhan, known as the "Autonomous Jewish District," is located in the Khabarovsk province of the Soviet Union. A substantial part of its area stretched between the Bira and Bidzhan Rivers (and that is where the name came from). The total area of the district is 36,000 square kilometers and its population (according to the census from January 15, 1959) is 163,000 people including Jews, Russians, Ukrainians, Belarusians, Tatars, indigenous people (mainly Gulds and Tunguses), and other nationalities. On its southern and southeastern sides, along the Amur River, the district borders Manchuria (China). In its northern part, the Trans-Siberian Railroad crosses it from west to east.

The Jewish settlement in Birobidzhan began in May 1928, based on the resolution by the Central Executive Committee of the Soviet Union passed on March 28, 1928. According to this resolution, the region was handed over to the KOMZET ["The Committee for the Settlement of Toiling Jews on the Land of the Soviet Union"] for the exclusive settlement of Jews. In December 1934, the district was established, and its official name appeared in the Soviet Constitution (paragraph 22) as the "Autonomous Jewish District."

There were various motives for the resolution regarding the Jewish settlement in Birobidzhan: a) The intent of the authorities to settle and develop the Soviet Far East for economic and security reasons b) The desire the resolve the painful problem of the Soviet Union's Jewry, a substantial part of which has not integrated, as of yet, into the new Soviet economy c) The desire to divert the Soviet Jewish public opinion away from Eretz Israel and the Zionism d) The hope to win the empathy and financial support of the Jews abroad, similar to the support received by the Jewish settlement in Crimea and Southern Ukraine.

At the time, the Birobidzhan plan stirred up a storm in Jewish public opinion throughout the world and acquired both enthusiastic supporters and harsh opponents. Despite the effort and the vast amount of money invested in it, both by the Soviet regime and by Jewish organizations abroad (ICOR ["The Jewish Colonization Organization in the Soviet Union"], ORT, and others), the plan did not bring with it the desired outcomes. Natural disasters, lack of roads, organizational failures, climate problems, and especially the political instability during the 1930s fraught the progress of the settlement. After the elimination of KOMZET [Russian government's "Committee for Assisting Jewish Agriculture" and OZET ["Society for Settling Toiling Jews"] (in 1938) the flow of emigration weakened and ceased completely during the years of the Second World War.

[Page 422]

During the 33 years of the settlement, it is estimated that about 60 thousand Jews (about a thousand from countries abroad), came to Birobidzhan at the beginning of the 1930s; however, most of them left. The number of Jews there today has not been published by the authorities. It is estimated that the number reached 20 to 25 thousand people, concentrated in the two cities – Birobidzhan and Obluchye.

The number of Jewish agriculturalists in the district was very small. Only in one kolkhoz ("Illych's [Vladimir Lenin] Wills," previously "Waldheim"), most of the residents were Jewish. Theoretically, the

Yiddish language is one of the two formal languages of the district; however, all of the administration affairs are done in Russian. Not even one Jewish school has survived, and the Jewish theater was closed. The district Jewish newspaper – "Birobidzahnishe Shtern" ["Birobidzhan Star"] (2 pages), published three times a week, bi-lingual signs (Yiddish and Russian), a street named after Shalom Aleikhem, and a district library (mainly Russian books) also called after the Jewish author are virtually the only signs of the "Jewishness" of the district today.

The main reasons that led to the failure of the plan for the Jewish settlement in Birobidzhan were: a) lack of interest by the Jewish masses, for whom it was designed b) the political cleansing, which destroyed the little of what had been established as an autonomous unit.

The Soviet authorities have not shown any interest in continuing the settlement of Jews in Birobidzhan since 1948, although the Soviet Union's radio broadcasting in foreign languages, which is aimed towards listeners abroad, continued to emphasize the Jewish character of the "Jewish Autonomous District"

**Y. L.** [Livneh]

[Page 423]

# Maps

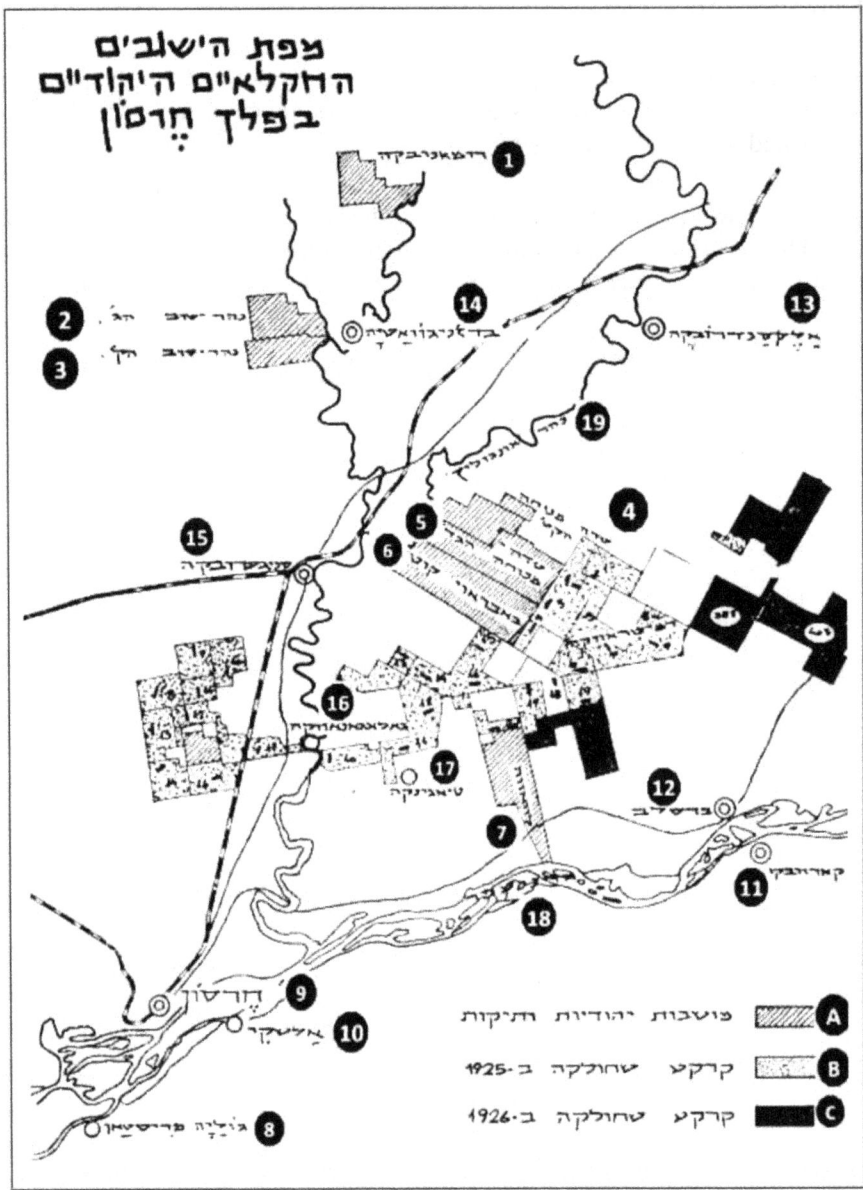

**Legend**

A  Established Jewish Settlements
B  Land distributed in 1925
C  Land Distributed in 1926

**Jewish Agricultural Settlements**

1  Romanovka
2  Nahar Tov Ha'ggola
3  Nahar Tov Ha'ktna
4  Sdeh Menukha Ha'ktana
5  Sdeh Menukha Ha'gdola
6  Bobrovy Kut
7  Lvova (Lvov)

**State cities, towns and villages**

8  G'olia Prystan (Hola Prystan)
9  Kherson
10  Oleshki
11  Kakhovka
12  Beryslav
13  Oleksanderovka
14  Berezhnguvate
15  Snigorivka (Snihuryvka)
16  Galagnivka
17  Tiagnka

**Rivers**

18  Inguletz River
19  Dnieper River

Map of the Jewish Settlements in the Kherson Province

[Page 424]

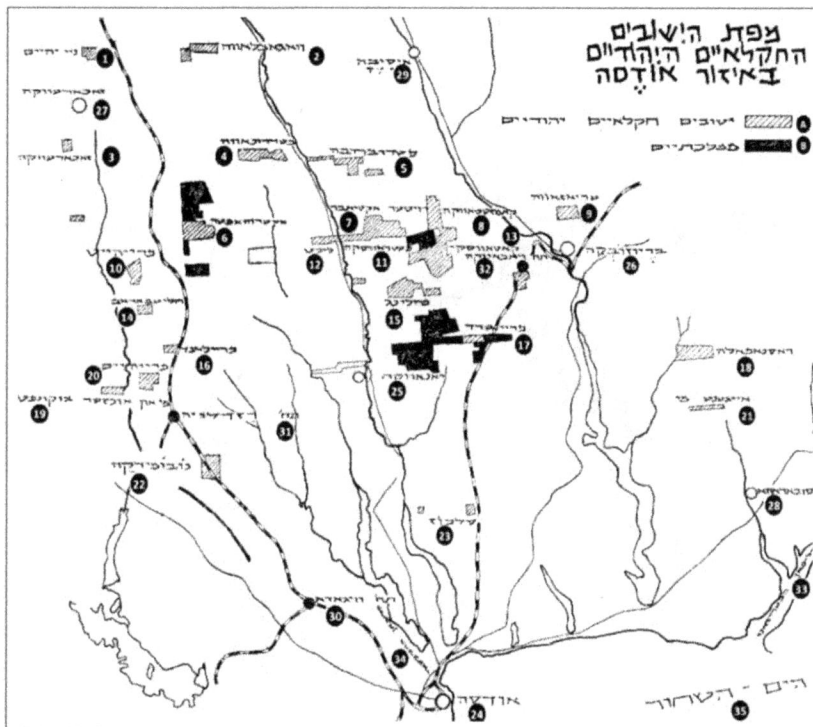

**Legend**

A  Jewish Agricultural Settlements
B  State Settlements

**Jewish Agricultural Settlements**

1  Nei Heim (New Home)
2  Vogotzlova
3  Zokhorveka
4  Beridnova
6  O?ed???apter
7  Roiter Oktiober (?) (Red October?)
8  Komzetovka
9  Eriozova
10  Freiheit (Freedom)
11  Petrovska
12  Likht (Light)
13  Katovsky
14  Friling (Spring)
15  Khliyebarov
16  Freiland (Happiness)
17  Frei Erd (Free Land)
18  Rosnopola
19  Mi on Unzer Tzukinft (Our Effort is Our Future)
20  Frie Heim (Free Home)
21  Eyegene Mi (Our Own Effort)
22  Novomirka
23  Selkhoz

**Cities and towns**

24  Odessa
25  Yanovka
26  Bryozovka (Berezivka)
27  Subarova
28  Zokhorevka
29  Isayeva

**Train Stations**

30  Vigoda Station
31  Razdelnia Station
32  Rakhovka Station

**Sea and estuaries**

33  The Berezani Estuary
34  The Khadzibey Estuary
35  The Black Sea

Map of the Jewish Agricultural Settlements in Odessa Region

*{page 425]*

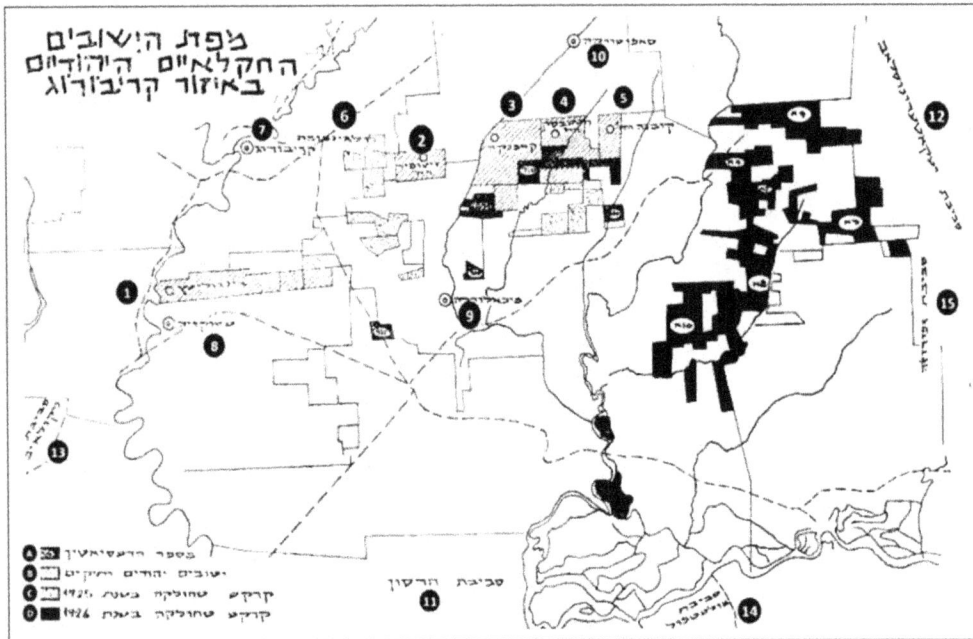

מפת הישובים
החקלאיים היהודים
באיזור קריבורוג

**Legend**

A   Number of disyatins
B   Established Jewish settlement
C   Land distributed in 1925
D   Land distributed in 1926

**Jewish Agricultural Settlements**

1   Inguletz
2   Novo Zhitomir (New Zhitomir)
3   Kamenka
4   Novo Vitebsk (New Vitebsk)
5   Novo Kovno (New Kovno)
6   Dolgintzova

**Cities and towns**

7   Krivoi-Rog (Krivvy -Rih)
8   Shidukoya
9   Mikhaelovka
10  Spitovka

**Bordering areas**

11  Kherson area
12  Ekareinoslav area
13  Nikolayev area
14  Moletelol area
15  Zmadrozha area

Map of the Jewish Agricultural Settlements in Krivoi-Rug (Krivvy-Rih) Region

*[Page 426]*

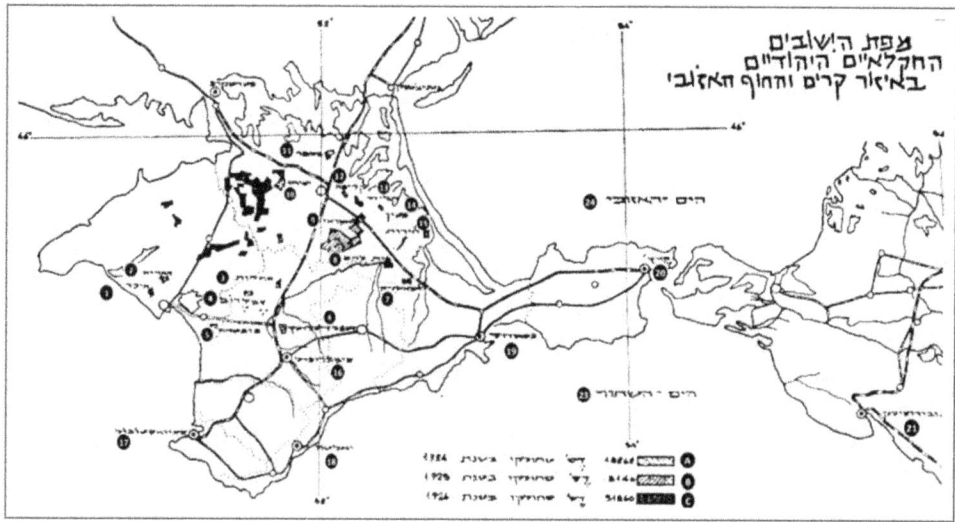

Map of the Jewish Agricultural Settlements in Regions of the Crimea and Azov Shore

**Legend**

A  Disyatins allocated in 1924
B  Disyatins allocated in 1925
C  Disyatins allocated in 1926

**Jewish Agricultural Settlements**

1  Ikar (Farmer)
2  Zorya (or Dorya)?
3  Akhdut (Unity)
4  Zemerov
5  Pobeda (Victory in Russian)
6  Zemliedieliyetz (worker of the land)
7  Rabotnik
8  Beit Lekhem
9  Khaklai (Agriculturalist)
10  Yetzira (Creation)
11  Mishmar (Guard)
12  Kadima (Forward)
13  Tel Khai (Hill of Living)
14  Ma'ayan (Spring)
15  Kherut (Freedom)

**State cities, towns and villages**

16  Simfropol
17  Sevastopol
18  Yalta
19  Fedodosi (Feodosya)
20  Krech
21  Novodrossysk
22  Henicheshin (Henichesk)

**Seas**

23  Black Sea
24  Azov Sea

*[Page 427]*

Map of the Jewish Agricultural Settlements in Regions of Zaprozheze and Mariopol

**Legend**

A  Ruined settlements
B  Land distributed in 1926
C  State settlements
D  Existing [Jewish] settlements

**Jewish Agricultural Settlements**

1  Bogodarovka
2  Rozkoshnoye
3  Gorykaya
4  Priyutnaya
5  Veslaya
6  NovoZlatopol
7  Krasnoselka
8  Mezehritch
9  Nadeshnaya
10  Zelenopole
11  Nechayebka
12  Truddoliubovka
13  Proletarskia (formally Grafskaya)
14  Khlebodarovka
15  Zatitya (Zatishye)
16  Rovnopol

**Cities and Towns**

17  Tsarakonstantinovka

**Bordering areas**

18  Orokhova Region in Zaporozhe district
19  Pikrova Region in Zaporozhe district

[Page 429]

# Bibliography

[for the article – "Toldot" by Tzvi Livneh pg. 13]

**Translated by** Moshe Kutten

**Edited by** Yocheved Klausner

The material used by the author for writing the historical chapters was vast, and it was a pleasant duty to list the books and authors that were used by the author either significantly or just marginally:

- N.Orshanski: "Русское Законодательство о Еевреяях" [Russian Legislation about Jews].
- Ettinger Akiva: "*Im Khaklaim Yehudim Batfutzot*" [With Jewish farmers in the Diaspora]. Sifriyat HaPoalim, Merkhahvia, 1942.
- Alek Julius: "Jüdische Kolonien in Russland" [Jewish Colonies in Russia], Berlin 1866.
- Erlich Asher: Collection in his memory named *"Asher Haya"* [What It Was] (containing the historical article by Yehoshua Bar Droma about the history of the colonies, pp. 49 – 57), Tel Aviv, 5719 [1958/59].
- Sh. Y. Borovoi (Bar-Rav-Hay): "Еврейская Земледельческая Колонизация в Старой России" [Jewish Agricultural Colonization in Old Russia], Moscow, 1928.
- Boris Brutzkus: "The Jewish Agriculture in Eastern Europe," Berlin 1926.
- Julius Gessen: "Гессен, Ю: Еврей в России, Ст П-бург" [The Jews in Russia], St. Petersburg 1906.
- Shim'on Dubnov: *"Divrei Yemei Am Olam"* [History of the Eternal People – Latest Generations], Volume 8, page 211 and on, Hebrew Ed.
- Dr. Arie Tartakower: *"Hityasvut HaYehudim Bagola"* [The Settlement of Jews in the Diaspora], 5719 [1958/9].
- Ya'akov Leshchinski: Articles and statistic material from his book: "The Jews in Soviet Russia," [Yiddishe Kempfer, New York, 1941].
- Professor Rafael Mahler – *"Divrei Yemei Yisrael – Dorot Akhronim"* [History of the Jewish Nation – Latest Generations], Volume 3, Sifriat Poalim, Merkhavia, 1955.
- Victor Nikitin:
  "Еврей Земледельцы (1807 - 1887)" [The Jewish farmers], St. Petersburg, 1887.
  "Еврейскии Поселения Северо ии Югозападных Губернии (1835 - 1890)" [Jewish settlements of the North and Southwest Provinces (1835 - 1890)], St. Petersburg, 1894.
- Dr. Arthur Rupin: "Hityashvut Hakhaklait Shel Hayehudim Berussia" [The Agricultural Settlement of the Jews in Russia], haPoel HaTzair, No. 12, Jan. 13, 1927.
- Rabbi A. Steinberg: "Поошрении Евреев к Земледелиию" [Attracting Jews to Agriculture], 1868.
- Various entries in Jewish encyclopedias (in Russian, English, and Hebrew) about the economic state of the Jews in Russia. 1904.
- Pamphlets, in Russian and Yiddish, that appeared in the 1920s, about the settlement enterprise, which took place during those years, mostly by officials and activists of the *Yevsektzia* [Jewish section in Russsian Communist Party]: Altman, Bronin, B. Y. Trotzki, Golde, Khavkin, Merezshin, Kirshner, B. Kahan and others.

*[Page 430]*

# Dates in the History of the Jewish Agricultural Settlement

**Translated by** Moshe Kutten

**Edited by** Yocheved Klausner

| | |
|---|---|
| 1789 | The beginning of the "Pale of Settlement" in Russia |
| 1800 | Derzhavin's memorandum which included the proposal for Jewish settlement in Novo-Russia |
| 1804 | The "Law for Remedying the State of the Jews" and the decree about the expulsion of Jews from the villages |
| 1807 | The establishment of the colonies: Bobrovy-Kut, Izraelovka, Sdeh-Menukha, and Dobroye |
| 1827 | The decree of the "Kantonists" – the compulsory military service of Jewish boys |
| 1835 | The establishment of the Jewish settlements in Bessarabia |
| 1837 | The failed program of Jewish settlement in Siberia |
| 1849 | The establishment of the colonies in the province of Ekaterinoslav: Novo-Zlatopol, Veselaya, Krasnoselka, Mezherich, Trudolyubovka, Nechaevaka |
| 1870 | The establishment of Mikve Israel by Karl Neter |
| 1877 | The establishment of Petakh Tikva |
| 1881 | "The Negev Storms" – the wave of pogroms in Southern Russia. The beginning of the immigration to America |
| 1882 | The "BILU *Aliyah*" and the establishment of the "Am Olam" movement |
| 1889 | The beginning of the Jewish settlement in Argentina |
| 1891 | The beginning of the activity of the J.C.A. organization in Argentina |
| 1914 | The establishment of the JOINT in the U.S. to help the victims of the war |
| 1918 | The establishment of the *Yevsektzia* in the Soviet Union |
| | The beginning of the "Third *Aliyah*," and the establishment of "HeKhalutz" in Russia |
| 1924 | The establishment of the "KOMZET" and "OZET" in the Soviet Union |
| | The peak in the momentum of the renewal of Jewish settlement |
| 1928 | The beginning of the [Jewish] settlement in Birobidzhan |

The elimination of "he'Khaluz" and its "hakhshara" [training] camps

1934    The declaration of Birobidzhan as an autonomous Jewish district

1941    The annihilation of the Jewish colonies at the beginning of the Nazi's conquest

**Please Note:** All page numbers in the following charts refer to the original book page nubers (Not the English edition page numbers)

# List of Pictures

**Prepared by** Moshe Kutten

| | |
|---|---|
| The educator, R' Moshe – Yevzory – Yevzrikhin, the grandfather of Asaf Simkhoni on his mother's side | |
| The grandson – Major General Asaf Simkhoni, the commander of the 1956 Sinai campaign who was killed [on the last day of] the war | |
| The memorial to the colonies' martyrs was built by the Holocaust survivors from Sdeh-Menukha The inscription on the memorial, in Russian and Yiddish says: "Here buried Soviet citizens from the village of Klininsk (Sdeh-Menukha), 1875 people, elderly, men, women, and children, who were tortured and murdered by the fascist executioners and the collaborators during the temporary occupation, on the 16 of September,1941." At the victims' mass grave on the memorial- day for the colonies' martyrs | 320/321 |
| Sdeh-Menukha HaGdola – the fruit tree orchard The harvest in the field (during the 1920s) Sdeh-Menukha HaGdola – in the orchard | 336/337 |
| R' Avraham Simongauz. One of the first settlers of Inguletz (one-hundred-year-old). Dovora–Gitle Tverdovsky (nee Medem) One of the first girls born in Novo-Poltavka (85-year-old) | 352/353 |

# Indices

**Prepared by** Moshe Kutten

## Name Index

| | | | | |
|---|---|---|---|---|
| | Ekaterina the 2nd | | Czaritza of Russia, also known as Catherine the Great | 19 |
| | Hershel | | the *"Klezmer"* in Sdeh Menukha | 188,214 |
| | Joseph the 2nd | | Emperor of Austria-Hungary empire | 16 |
| | Mar'el | | Atara Parag's brother | 281 |
| | Motl | | The *klezmer* | 279 |
| | Nekhama | | Rakhel Pnini's sister | 229 |
| | Nikolai (Nicolai) the 1st | | Russian Czar | 45, 50, 54 - 57, 61, 64, 66, 68, 70, 72, 75, 79, 84, 102, 150, 161, 163, 245, 248, 348 |
| | Nikolai (Nicolai) the 2nd | | Russian Czar | 239, 245, 298, 354 |
| | Pavel (Paul the 1st) | | Czar of Russia. also known as Czar Paul the 1st | 19, 21, 23 |
| | Ya'akov | | ben Khaviv | 232 |
| | Yehuda-Leib | | Rabbi, *klezmer* | 279 |
| | Yoelik | | slaughterer in Sdeh Menukha HaKtana | 214 |
| | Zalman | | Israel ben Eliyahu's uncle (Sdeh Menukha HaKtana) | 214 |
| ADLER | Feiga | | | 257 |
| A'HARONI | Aharon-Hirsh | | | 351 |

Jewish Farmers in Russia Fields

| A'HARONI | Malka | | | 350 |
|---|---|---|---|---|
| AHARONOVITZ-SHTEINBERG | Leizer | | | 376 |
| ALEIKHEM | Shalom | | Pen name of Solomon Naumovich Rabinovich | 247, 275, 352, 422 |
| ALEK | Julius | | | 429 |
| ALEXEYEV | | | Russian senator | 39 |
| ALKON | Leon | | | 23 |
| ALMOG (KOPELEVITZ) | Yehuda | | | 330 |
| ALTMAN | | | | 429 |
| ASTITAS | Meir | | | 257 |
| ASTITAS | Shmeul | | | 258 |
| AVIDOV | Nesya | yes | | 279 |
| AVIGAL (BEIGEL) | Moshe | | | 247 |
| BACKENDORF | | | Russian Minister of Police | 66, 67, 68, 69, 74 - 76, 78, 79 |
| BAKUNIN | | | Russian Mohilev Provincial Minister | 31 - 33 |
| BALFOUR | Arthur | | | 263, 310 |
| BALLIA | Shneor | | | 119 |
| BAR-COHEN | | | | 188 |
| BAR–DROMA–GALLILI | Tzipora | yes | | 342, 347, 382 |
| BAR-DROMAH | Yehushua | yes | | 343, 382 |
| BARINSKI | Ya'akov–Leib | | | 343, 344 |
| BAVLI | Khaim | | | 319 |
| BEIBILOV | Khaim | | | 209 |

| BRUTZKUS | Ber-Dov (Boris) | | | 122, 429 |
|---|---|---|---|---|
| BUDYONNY | Semyon Mikhailovich | | Red Army's general | 233, 318 |
| BUTRYMOWICZ | Mateusz | | Polish noble, Sejm representative from Pinsk | 17, 18 |
| CHEBERYAK | Vera | | witness in the anti-Semitic Beilis trial | 146 |
| CHERNOVITZ | Khaim | | Rabbi (nicknamed in Hebrew "Harav Hatzair -"The Young Rabbi) | 235 |
| CHIRKOVITZ | | | Russian senior official | 79 |
| COHEN | Israel-Dov | | Rabbi | 232, 235 |
| COHEN | Khaim | yes | | 234 |
| COHEN | Yanke (Ya'akov) | | *Melamed* | 243 |
| CORNIES | | | Mennonite. Head inspector of Jewish colonies in Ekaterinoslav | 88 |
| CZACKI | Tadeusz | | Polish noble, head of the Sejm finance commission | 18 |
| CZARTORYSKI (CHARTORINSKY) | Adam-Jerzy | | Polish noble,, Russian deputy foreign minister, a member of the Committee to Remedy the State of the Jews | 23, 27 |
| DANZIG | Avraham | | Rabbi | 348 |

Jewish Farmers in Russia Fields

| | | | | |
|---|---|---|---|---|
| DARBUSH | | | Russian general, commander of the Gendarmes Corps | 64, 65 |
| DASHKOVITZ | Shmuel | | | 235 |
| DAVIDOVSKI | | | | 298 |
| DE HIRSCH | Maurice | | Baron | 9, 118, 119, 121, 383 |
| DE RICHELIEU | | | Russian duke, Novo-Russia Provincial Minister | 32, 33, 37, 38, 42, 43 |
| DELON | Eliezer | | | 41 |
| DEMIDOV | | | Russian Deputy Novorossiya Provincial Minister | 72, 73, 75, 77 -79, 86, 92, 96 |
| DENIKIN | Anton | | Russian general | 197, 225, 274, 315, 355, 366, 367 |
| DERZHAVIN | | | Russian senator | 22, 195 |
| DINKIN | | | "White" Russian general | 233 |
| DIYAKOV | | | Russian general, Provincial Minister of Mohilev | 64, 67 |
| DOLGORUKOV | | | Russian Prince, Kharkov Provincial Minister | 73, 74 |
| DORFAMAN | Gitl Ekaterina-Moiseievna | | Doctor | 344 |
| DORFMAN | Moshe | | | 344 |
| DOR-SINAI | Zeev | yes | | 361 |

Jewish Farmers in Russia Fields

| | | | | |
|---|---|---|---|---|
| DRABKIN | | | Rabbi | 234 |
| DUBNOV | Shimon | | | 429 |
| DUBOVITS | | | | 164 |
| DUKHIN | Yehoshua | yes | | 285, 322 |
| DYERZHAVIN | Gavril-Romanovich | | Russian senator and Justice Minister, member of the Committee to Remedy the State of the Jews | 21 - 23, 25 - 27, 29 |
| EFRAT | | | | 95 |
| EISENBAUM | Antony | | | 389, 396 |
| ERESH | Elimelekh | | | 383 |
| EREV | Ya'akov | | | 194, 379 |
| EREZ | Yehuda | yes | | 375 |
| ERLICH | Asher | | | 429 |
| ETTINGER | Akiva | | | 122, 413, 414, 429 |
| FINKELSTEIN | Nakhum | | | 31 - 33, 394, 396 |
| FRUGG | Shimon | yes | | 8, 14, 170, 249, 273, 310, 312 |
| FRUMKIN | M. | | Member of the "KOMZET" state committee | 134 |
| GAAN | | | Russian head of settlers' Supervisory Committee, and later consultant and member of the Assets Ministry council | 87, 88, 90 - 92, 95, 96, 98, 104 |

Jewish Farmers in Russia Fields

| | | | | |
|---|---|---|---|---|
| GALITZIN | | | Russian Graf, Minister of Religions and Education | 42, 44, 45 |
| GAMM | | | Russian head of the colonies' Supervisory Committee | 105, 106 |
| GEBEL | | | Russian agronomist | 89 |
| GESEH | | | Russian Poltava Provincial Minister | 74 |
| GESSEN | Julius | | | 27, 28, 429 |
| GILBOT | Meir | | | 253 |
| GINSBURG, BARON | | | | 122 |
| GLADKII | | | Russian head of Ekaterinoslav department of state assets | 87 - 91, 95 |
| GLANZ | Ya'akov | | | 255 |
| GOLDA | V. | | Member of the "KOMZET" state committee | 134 |
| GOLDE | | | | 384 |
| GOLDE | | | | 429 |
| GOLOMB | Diklah | yes | | 4 |
| GORDIN | Ya'akov | | | 352 |
| GORSTEIN | B. | yes | | 386, 420 |
| GRIGORIEV [OR GRIGOROV] | Nikifor | | Ukrainian Hetman | 296, 233, 315, 317, 318, 346, 347, 356, 357, 376 |
| GRUZENBERG | | | | 122 |
| GRUZENBERG | Oscar | | | 271 |

| GUBER | Mordekhai | yes | | 257 |
|---|---|---|---|---|
| GUBER | Rivka | yes | | 256 |
| GUREVITZ | A. | yes | | 286 |
| GUROVITZ (OR GUREVITZ) | Herman-Bernard | | | 101, 109 |
| GUSAK | | | Rusiian G. O. P interrogator | 338 |
| GUZMAN | Yehudit | yes | | 277 |
| HALPERIN | Khayim | yes | | 4, 12, 272 |
| HARUSI | Imanuel | yes | | 4 |
| HAUSNER | Gideon | | | 248 |
| HAZAZ | Khaim | | | 248, 252 |
| HELLER | Israel | yes | | 370 |
| HERDER | Moshe | | | 119 |
| HERZL / HERTZL | Theodor | | | 9, 279, 300, 310. 311, 378 |
| HIRSZOWICZ | Avraham | | | 17, 18 |
| HOŁOWIŃSKI | | | Polish Sejm representative, member of the committee to improve the state of the Jews | 18 |
| HURVITZ | Itah | yes | | 291 |
| IGNATYEV | Nikolay Pavlovich | | Russian Interior Minister | 299 |
| INZOV | | | Russian general, head of the Guardian Bureau for the Settlers | 44, 45, 47 - 50, 52, 55 - 58, 60, 61, 69, 73, 395 |
| ISLAVIN | A. B. | | Personal secretary of Kisliyov - | 96, 97, 99, 100, 101, 108, 109, 110 |

Jewish Farmers in Russia Fields

| | | | | |
|---|---|---|---|---|
| | | | Russian Minister of State Assets | |
| ISRAELI | Bentzion | | | 384 |
| ITZEK | | | | 396 |
| IVANSCHINTZEV | | | Russian inspector of the "Jewish Settlement" - in 1880 | 113 - 115, 116 |
| IZAACKCHIK | Moshe | | | 249 |
| JEZIERSKI | | | Polish noble - head of committee to remedy the state of the Jews. | 18 |
| JOZEFOWICZ | Tzvi-Herszel | | Rabbi | 17 |
| KAFRI | Mikhael | | | 280 |
| KAHAN | B. | | | 429 |
| KAHANA | | | | 393, 394 |
| KAHANOV | Leibel | yes | | 194, 379 |
| KALGAORIA | | | Russian Ekaterinoslav Provincial Minister | 37 |
| KAMENEV | Lev | | Bolshevik leader | 285 |
| KAMINKER | Tzipora | yes | | 236 |
| KANKRIN | | | Russian Graf, Finance Minister | 63 - 66, 70 |
| KARINOV | | | Polish province-minister of Minsk | 19 |
| KARSON | L. | | Member of the "KOMZET" | 134 |

| | | | | |
|---|---|---|---|---|
| | | | state committee | |
| KARTZEV | | | Russian court advisor for special tasks | 84 - 86 |
| KATZENELSON | Yehudah-Leib Dr. | | Also known in his pen name as the author "Buki ben Yagli" | 122 |
| KERENSKY | Alexander-Fyodorovich | | A leader of the Russian revolution | 187, 224, 235, 311, 342, 379, 380, 382 |
| KESEH | Yona | | | 347 |
| KHALILI | Mordekhai | yes | Member of book's Initiating committee | 8, 226 |
| KHAVKIN | | | | 429 |
| KHOLONOVSKY | | | Russian member of the committee to remedy the state of the Jews. | 18 |
| KIRSHNER | | | | 429 |
| KISLIYOV | | | Russian Graf, Minister of State Assets | 69, 72 - 76, 84, 86 - 92, 95, 96, 101, 108 |
| KLAUS | | | Russian senior official of Novorossiya Settlement Department | 111, 112, 113 |
| KLAUSNER | Y. | | Doctor | 235 |
| KOCHUBEY | B. P | | Russian noble - noble, chair of the Committee to Remedy the | 23, 26, 27, 29, 31 - 36, 45, 46 |

| | | | State of the Jews and later Interior Minister, | |
|---|---|---|---|---|
| KOMAROV | Ben-Tzion | yes | | 198 |
| KOMAROV | | | Russian senior official in the Interior Ministry | 71 |
| KONDRENTZOV | | | Russian Novorossiya Deputy Provincial Minister, Demidov's replacement | 92 |
| KONTENIUS | | | Russian head judge in Novorossiya | 36, 37, 42, 43 |
| KOOK | Tzvi-Yehuda | | Rabbi | 266 |
| KOSOI | Berl | | | 347 |
| KOZODAVLEV | | | Russian vice-interior and interior minister | 39, 42, 44, 45 |
| KRASOLSHCHIK | Y. | | | 122 |
| KRIVESKY | | | Russian Inspector of the colonies | 75 |
| KULISHOV | | | | 87 - 89 |
| KURAKIN | | | Russian Interior Minister | 38 |
| KUTIN | Shlomo | | | 258 |
| LANSKY | | | Russian Office Manager and later the Interior Minister | 53, 55, 56 - 58, 407 |

| | | | | |
|---|---|---|---|---|
| LARIN | V. | | Member of the "KOMZET" state committee | 134 |
| LENIN | | | Soviet Union Communist Ruler | 382 |
| LENOV | | | | 42, 43 |
| LENPORT | Israel | | | 31 |
| LESHCHINSKI | Ya'akov | | | 140, 429 |
| LESHKROV | | | Russian government official | 43 |
| LEV | Leah | | | 249 |
| LEVINSOHN | V. | | Academic consultant of the rabbinical colleges in Vilna and Zhytomyr | 102 |
| LEVINSON [RIBAL] | Yitzkhak-Ber | | Rabbi | 80, 81 |
| LEVINSTEIN | | | | 343 |
| LEVISON | V. | | Professor, Curriculum advisor for the Jewish rabbinical and teaching college in Vilna | 102 |
| LIEBERMAN | | | | 32, 33, 188, 192 |
| LIKHTMAN | Breina | yes | | 259 |
| LILIENBLUM | Moshe-Leib | | | 118, 119 |
| LIPNOV | Y. P. | | Russian government's inspector | 37, 42 - 44 |
| LITVINOV | M. | | Member of the "KOMZET" | 134 |

| | | | state committee | |
|---|---|---|---|---|
| LIVNEH-LIEBERMAN | Tzvi | yes | | 4, 7, 13 |
| LUBARSKI / LIUBARSKI/ LOVARSKI | Sh. | | Agronomist | 122, 380, 416, 417 |
| LUBERSKI | | | | 380 |
| MAHLER | Rafael | | | 429 |
| MAKHNO | Batko | | Ukrainian gang leader | 129, 198, 200, 225, 239, 253, 261, 263, 315, 318, 319, 376, 377, 383, 417 |
| MANDELSHTAM | A. L | | Professor. Academic consultant of the rabbinical colleges in Vilna and Zhytomyr | 102 |
| MANEH | Mordekhai-Tzvi | | | 273 |
| MEDEM | Yehoshua | yes | | 262 |
| MELTZER | Shimshon | yes | | 4, 176 |
| MENDELSTAM | Benyamin | | | 80, 81 |
| MENDELSTAM | A. L. | | Curriculum advisor for the Jewish rabbinical and teaching college in Vilna | 102 |
| MENUKHI (NINBURG) | Yehuda | yes | | 197, 216 |
| MEREZSHIN / MARZHIN | H. | | Yevsektsia representative to committee for settling Jews in Crimea | 429, 386 |
| MERZHIN | A. | | | 134, 343 |

Jewish Farmers in Russia Fields

| | | | | |
|---|---|---|---|---|
| MESTCHEKIN | Yosi | yes | | 4, |
| MILMAN | Hershel-Aba | | | 232 |
| MIRKIN | | | Agronomist | 272 |
| MOKHER SFARIM | Mendele | | Pen name of Shalom Ya'akov Abramovitz | 275, 397 |
| MONETFIORY | | | Russian minister | 81 |
| MORADOV | | | | 369, 370 |
| MORAVIOV / MURAVYOV | | | Russian Minister of State Assets | 102, 104406, 407 |
| NEKHEMKIN | Arie | | | 250 |
| NIKITA | | | Russian Babkova Farm's Vice-Manager | 364 |
| NINBURG | Avraham-Moshe | | | 199, 379, 380 |
| NINBURG | Doba | | | 200 |
| NINBURG | Feiga | | | 199 |
| NINBURG | Shlomit | | | 199 |
| NINBURG | Shternah | yes | | 200 |
| NINBURG | Tuvia | | | 216 |
| NITKIN | Victor | | | 429 |
| NIVOKHOVITZ | Yehuda-Leib | | | 23, 28 |
| NOODLE | Aharon | | | 242 |
| NORDAU | Max | | | 310 |
| NOTKIN (SHKLOVER) | Neteh-Nathan | | | 20 - 23, 28, 29, 35, 80, 81 |
| NOVKOVSKY | Yehuda | | Rabbi | 352 |
| OBAROV | | | Russia's Secretary of Education | 102 |

| | | | | |
|---|---|---|---|---|
| OGIŃSKI | | | Lithuanian duke | 22 |
| ORSHANSKI | N | | | 429 |
| OSCHUK | | | Rusiian G. O. P interrogator | 336 |
| OSTROVSKI | G. | | Jewish estate owner in Ekaterinoslav | 115 |
| OSTROVSKI | Z. | | | 134 |
| OVADIA | | | | 393, 394 |
| OVOLYANOV | | | Russian attorney general | 22 |
| OVROV | | | Russian minister | 81 |
| OZSHIGOV | | | Russian Police Chief in the Kherson province | 75, 76 |
| PADYIEV | | | Russian assistant of General Inzov | 44, 47, 48, 50 - 53, 56, 60, 61 |
| PALKOV | Alter | | | 286 |
| PALKOV-LEV | Leah | yes | | 290 |
| PARAG | Atara | yes | | 282 |
| PARAG | Nakhman | yes | | 282 |
| PELN | | | Russian Baron, Courland Provincial Minister | 73 |
| PERES | Ya'akov | | | 81 |
| PERETZ | Avraham | | | 23, 27, 28 |
| PERETZ | Y. L. | | | 187, 247 |
| PERL | Yosef | yes | | 393 |

| Surname | Given name | | Role | Pages |
|---|---|---|---|---|
| PETLIURA | Symon | | Ukrainian gang leader | 225, 239, 274, 310, 315, 339, 355, 356, 380, 383, 417 |
| PINNES | Arye-Leib | | | 348 |
| PINSKER | Leon | | | 118 |
| PINSKI | David | | | 247 |
| PIODOROV | | | Russian Kherson's Provincial Minister | 90 |
| PITKIN | Mordekhai | yes | | 4, 177 |
| PIVNIAK | | | Rusiian G. O. P interrogator | 338 |
| PLUSHKIN | | | | 188 |
| PNINI | Khaim | | | 230 |
| PNINI | Rakhel | yes | | 229 |
| PNINI | Zisel | | | 230 |
| POLIASTRO | Bilha | | Doctor | 344 |
| PONIATOWSKI | Stanisław-August | | Polish king | 19 |
| POPKIN | Eliezer | | | 235, 237, 239 |
| POPOV | | | Russian government's Secret Advisor | 39, 41, 53 |
| POTYOMKIN | | | Russian prince | 27, 28 |
| PRANAITIS | Feiga | | witness in the anti-Semitic Bailys trial | 146 |
| PRIZEL | Adam | | Polish noble - Russian deputy Foreign Minister, a member of the Committee to Remedy the State of the Jews | 19, 20, 21, 23, 25, 26 |

| | | | | |
|---|---|---|---|---|
| RABINOWITZ | Ya'akov | | | 266 |
| RASPUTIN | Grigori Yefimovich | | | 311 |
| REBOSNIKOV | | | | 270 |
| REDA | | | A Ukrainian leader and a gang leader | 380 |
| ROSENTHAL | H. | | | 81 |
| ROTHSCHILD | Nathaniel Mayer | | Baron | 9, 118 |
| ROZHENSKI | Arye | yes | | 353 |
| ROZIN | Rakhel | | | 192 |
| RUDNITZKI | . | | Russia special envoy of the Ministry of State Assets | 102 - 105, 109 |
| RUPIN | Arthur | | | 429 |
| SAKHANOVSKI | Tzelik | | | 377 |
| SAMUELEV | | | father and Family | 270, 295, 297, 298, 301 |
| SAMUELEV | Sara | | Mother | 295 |
| SCHINDLER | | | Russian provincial physician | 73 |
| SCHNEERSOHN | Dov-Ber | | Admor, Rabbi | 80 |
| SCHNEERSOHN (SHNEUR) | Zalman | | Rabbi | 80, 351, 378 |
| SCHWALBIN | | | | 352 |
| SCHWARTZ | | | | 293, 298 |
| BOROVOI (BAR-RAV-HAY) | Sh. Y. | | | 429 |
| SHADMI | Sara | yes | | 193 |
| SHADMI | Tzvi | yes | | 190 |
| SHAPIRA | L. M. | | | 247 |

| | | | | |
|---|---|---|---|---|
| SHCHARBACHOV | | | | 413 |
| SHEIKEVITZ | Nakhum_Meir | | with the pen name SHEME"R | 192 |
| SHEPTELOVNITZ | Neteh | | Doctor | 28 |
| SHEVCHENKO | Taras Hryhorovych | | Ukranian poet | 310 |
| SHINMAN | A. | | Member of the "KOMZET" state committee | 134 |
| SHMULEVITZ | | | | 384 |
| SHTERNGES | | | | 258 |
| SHUMAKHER | | | | 384 |
| SIMKHONI | Asaf | | | 304 |
| SIMKHONI | Yehudit | yes | nee Yevzori-Yevzrikhin | 311, 314, 319, 379 |
| SIMKHONI | Yeshayahu | | | 319 |
| SIMKHONI (VESILNITZKI) | Mordekhai | yes | Member of book's Initiating committee | 8, 210, 216, 318, 319, 358 |
| SIMONGAUZ | Avraham | | | 350 - 353 |
| SIMONGAUZ | Khana–Stesya | | | 351 |
| SIMONGAUZ | Moshe | | | 351 |
| SIMONGAUZ | Shmuel | | | 350 |
| SIMOV | | | Russian general, Patron of the colonies | 272 |
| SIVIRIN-POTOCZKY | | | Polish noble - Russian minister and a member of the Committee to Remedy the State of the Jews | 23 |

Jewish Farmers in Russia Fields

| | | | | |
|---|---|---|---|---|
| SKOROPADSKY | | | Ukrainian leader | 346 |
| SLIOZBERG | Henri | | | 122 |
| SLUTZKI | Yehuda | yes | | 4 |
| SOKOLOV | Nakhum | | | 116, 118 |
| SOLOGUV | | | Russian head of Bobruisk office of the Ministry of State Assets - | 97 |
| SPERANSKY | Mikhail | | Russian manager of the interior ministry | 24, 27 |
| SPRANCHIK | | | | 32, 33 |
| STALIN | | | Soviet Union Communist ruler | 373 |
| STEIN | | | Doctor | 236 |
| STEINBERG | A. | | | 429 |
| STEMPEL | | | Baron, Russian Supervisory Committee's manager for the Jewish colonies in Kherson and Ekaterinoslav | 90 - 92, 95 |
| STEPHANOVKA | | | Estate noble owner in Ekaterinoslav | 115 |
| STERN | Betzalel (Bezilius) | | | 82 |
| STOREVELSKY | Yosef | | | 348 |
| STROKOV | | | Russian senior official in the Ministry of State Assets | 95 |

| | | | | |
|---|---|---|---|---|
| TAGAICHINOV | | | Russian Ekaterinoslav forest inspector | 89 |
| TARTAKOWER | Arie | | | 429 |
| TATIANES | Dunika | | | 215 |
| TCHERNIKHOVSKI | Shaul | | | 8, 205, 249 |
| TIKHAYEV | | | Russian provincial minister | 119, 120 |
| TIOMKIN | Zeev | | | 236, 302 |
| TOKARVITZ | Ya'akov | | Rabbi | 344 |
| TOREN | Avraham | yes | | 237 |
| TRIBMAN | David | yes | | 382 |
| TROKOV | | | Russian investigative commissioner | 95 |
| TROTSKY | Leon | | | 337 |
| TROTZKI | B. Y. | | | 429 |
| TRUMPLEDOR | Yoseph | | | 187, 329 |
| TVERDOVSKY / TVERDOVSKI | Avraham-Ber | | Mentioned in his pseudonym Ber'eh-Volf | 148, 149, 152, 157, 159, 160, 162, 163 |
| TVERDOVSKY / TVERDOVSKI | David | yes | | 4, 145 |
| TVERDOVSKY / TVERDOVSKI (NEE MEDEM) | Dvora-Gitl | | Also mentioned as a pseudonym as Dvora Zeisel | 147, 153, 175, 353 |
| TVERDOVSKY / TVERDOVSKI | Khaya | | | 145 |
| TVERDOVSKY / TVERDOVSKI | Moshe-Leib | | Mentioned in his pseudonym as R' Yehuda Leib | 145 - 175 |

Jewish Farmers in Russia Fields

| | | | | |
|---|---|---|---|---|
| TVERDOVSKY /TVERDOVSKI | Nakhman | | | 145 |
| TZEITLIN | Yehoshua | | | 27 |
| VASILCHIKOV | | | Russian Provincial Minister of Kiev | 406, 407 |
| VERLINSKY | Nakhum | | | 236 |
| VESLNITZKI | Zalman-Leib | | | 304 |
| VLADIMIROVITZ | Ivan | | Russian Babkova Farm's Manager | 364 |
| VON GRUBER | | | Russian inspector of the Jewish rabbinical colleges in Vilna Zhytomyr and teacher college in Vilna | 101, 102 |
| VORONTZOV | | | Russian Novorossiya Provincial Minister | 72, 73, 75 - 78, 81 - 83 |
| VOZNESENSKI | Sokolov | | Russian provincial minister | 159 |
| WELLER | M. | | | 122 |
| WILFNED | Yosef | yes | | 4 |
| WINOVER | M. | | | 122 |
| WRANGEL | Pyotr | | Russian White general | 225, 226, 318, 320 |
| YAFEH | Yitzkhak | | | 56 |
| YANKELEVITZ | Khana | | | 262 |
| [YAVETZ] | Yosef-Meir | | Rabbi | 242 |
| YEHUDAI | Rakhel | yes | | 266 |

Jewish Farmers in Russia Fields

| | | | | |
|---|---|---|---|---|
| YELIN | David | | | 301 |
| YEVZORI-YEVZRIKHIN | Benyamin | | | 319, 324, 325, 328 |
| YEVZORI-YEVZRIKHIN | David | | | 322, 327 |
| YEVZORI-YEVZRIKHIN | Leah | | | 322 |
| YEVZORI-YEVZRIKHIN | Moshe | yes | | 291, 301, 304, 314 |
| YEVZORI-YEVZRIKHIN | Yehuda | yes | | 311, 312, 316, 319 - 322, 341 |
| YEVZORI-YEVZRIKHIN | Zrubavel | | | 314, 318, 319, 321, 324 - 326, 328, 329 |
| YIEDANOV | | | Russian Head Inspector over the Jewish colonies | 48 |
| YIGNATIEV | | | Russian minister | 116 |
| YITZKHAKI (RASHI) | Shlomo | | Rabbi | 246, 254 |
| ZALMAN | Eliyahu ben Shlomo | | The Gaon from Vilna | 378 |
| ZEIDEL | | | | 234 |
| ZELENOI | A. A. | | Russian Minister of State Assets | 109 |
| ZELTZER | Eliezer | | | 233, 237, 239 |
| ZELTZER | Israel | yes | | 240 |
| ZELTZER | Shoshana | | | 233 |
| ZLIYONI | | | Ukrainian Hetman | 346 |
| ZOHAR | Tzvi | yes | | 4 |
| ZONENBERG | Zundil | | | 41 |
| ZONKOVSKII | | | Russian head of religions | 42 |

| | | | | |
|---|---|---|---|---|
| | | | and education ministry | |
| ZUBOV | A. V. | | Russian general, a member of the member of the Committee to Remedy the State of the Jews | 23 |
| ZUSMAN | | | | 350, 353 |

# Organizations of and for Jews

| Organization Name | Notes | Page(s) |
|---|---|---|
| "Agro-Joint" | A branch of the "Joint" for resettling Jews | 134, 135, 194, 385, 386 |
| "A'havat Tzion" | Literally - "The Love of Zion" Zionist organization | 302 |
| "Am Olam" | Literally - "Eternal People" - An organization for the establishment of socialist agricultural settlements in America | 10, 118, 121, 430 |
| "Bikur Kholim" | "Visiting the Sick," welfare organization | 351 |
| "BILU" ("Beit Ya'akov Lekhu Venelekha") | Literally - "House of Jacob, let us go," a movement for settling in Eretz Israel. | 10, 118, 209, 430 |

Jewish Farmers in Russia Fields

| "Bund" | General Jewish Worker Alliance Party | 243, 250, 343, 366 |
|---|---|---|
| "Central Committee for the Assistance to Jewish Refugees" | | 346 |
| "Central Committee in Petersburg" | JCA organization for helping Russian Jews to develop skills for productive occupations | 122, 123 |
| "Christian-Jewish Society" | Organization establish by Czar Alexander the 1st to convert Jews to Christianity | 45 |
| "Formanta Agraria" | A corporation for the development of the Jewish agriculture - in Argentina | 9 |
| "Fraternidad Agraria" | Financial center cooperative agriculture federations in Argentina | 9 |
| "Geulat Akhim" | Literally - "Brothers' Salvation," Zionist organization | 233 |
| "Hakhnasat Kallah" | Literally - "Bringing the bride under the bridal canopy", welfare organization to help poor brides | 232, 251 |
| "HaShomer" | Literaqlly - The Guard – a Jewish defense organization | 314 |

| "Hatkhiya" | Literally - "The Revival" - Zionist organization | 280 |
|---|---|---|
| "HeKhalutz BaMoshavot" | Literally - "The Pioneer in the Colonies," youth pioneer organization | 311, 314 |
| "HeKhalutz" | Literally - "The Pioneer," Zionist organization | 139, 187, 194, 197, 209, 224 - 226, 233, 259, 280, 281, 290, 313, 314, 318, 326, 328, 330, 331, 337, 342, 346, 347, 359, 360, 363, 366-370, 377, 379, 381, 385, 386, 430 |
| "He'Khaver" | "The Comrade' - the students' Zionist Union | 346 |
| "ICOR" | Organization for the Jewish Colonization in Russia (from Yiddish - Yiddishe Kolonizatsie Organizatsie in Rusland") | 421 |
| "JCA" ("Jewish Colonization Association") | Established by Baron de Hirsch | 9, 122, 123, 124 - 127, 135, 190, 201, 220, 244, 245, 262, 263, 266, 271, 273, 274, 291, 303, 342, 371, 376, 380, 383, 384, 413, 414. 416, 418, 419, 430 |
| "JDC" ("Joint") | "American Jewish Joint Distribution Committee" | 132, 134, 371, 385, 430 |
| "Jewish Colonial Bank" | | 303 |
| "JNF" ("Keren Kayement Le'Israel" or KKL) | The Jewish National Fund | 209, 233, 258, 279, 280, 286, 311 |
| "Khevrat Talmud Torah" | The organization of Jewish and Torah study | 232, 351 |
| "Khibat Tzion" | Literally - "Lovers of Zion" –the precursor to Zionism | 9, 118, 121 |

| | | |
|---|---|---|
| "Kol Israel Khaverim" ("Alliance Israélite Universelle" – or in short "The Alliance") | Jewish educational and social organization founded in France in 1860 | 116 |
| "KOMZET" (or KUMZET) | Russian government's "Committee for Assisting Jewish Agriculture" | 134 - 136, 138, 374, 421, 430 |
| "Lekhem Evionim" | Literally - "Bread for the Poor," welfare organization | 232, 351 |
| "Maccabi" | Zionist organization | 233 |
| "Ma'ot Khitin" | Literally "Pennies for Wheat," welfare organization | 251 |
| "OPE" – "Khevrat Mefitzei Haskala" | "Organization for the Dissemination of Education" | 189, 346 |
| "ORT" | "Association for the Promotion of Skilled Trades" | 118, 119, 132, 135, 383 - 385, 416 - 419, 421 |
| "OZET" | Society for Settling Toiling Jews ("GEZERD" in Yiddish) | 134 - 137, 374, 386, 421, 430 |
| "Poalei Tzion" | "Workers of Zion," Zionist organization | 366 |
| "Socialist Zionism movement" (S" Z) | | 261, 281 |
| "Tarbut" | Literally - "Culture," a secular organization for teaching Hebrew. | 342 |

| "Tzeirei Tzion' | Literally - "Youths of Zion" , Zionist organization | 187, 209, 233, 236, 237, 239, 346, 363, 369, 376, 377, 380 |
|---|---|---|
| "War Relief" | Jewish American wellfare union | 325 |
| "Yevsektzia" | Jewish section of the Communist Party | 137, 139, 254, 261, 328, 329, 352, 366, 368, 379, 381, 386, 430 |
| "Z" S Yugend" | "Zionist - Socialist Youth's | 329, 334, 335 |
| "Z" S" (or "S" Z") | "Zionist-Socialists" - Labor Zionist party | 261, 329, 330, 334, 376, 377, 379 |

# Jewish Colonies

| Jewish Colony | Location / Notes | Page(s) |
|---|---|---|
| A'havat Avoda | Ekaterinoslav province | 401 |
| Akhdut (Unity) | Crimea | 426 |
| Akhdut (Unity) | Crimea | 139 |
| Aleksandreny | Bessarabia | 412 |
| Avoda (Work) | Crimea | 139 |
| Beit Lekhem | Crimea | 139, 426 |
| Beit Lekhem Yehuda | USA | 10 |
| Beridnova | Odesa region | 424 |
| Blalalo–Blad | Bessarabia | 412 |
| Bobrovy-Kut | Kherson province | 11, 34, 103, 137, 187, 189, 192, 210, 229, 269, 273, 274, 294, 354, 355, 356, 357, 372, 383, 409, 419, 423, 429 |
| Bogodarovka | Ekaterinoslav province | 409, 427 |
| Brichevo | Bessarabia | 412 |

Jewish Farmers in Russia Fields

| Dobroye | Kherson province | 11, 34, 111, 129, 273, 293, 314, 316, 317, 320, 335, 341 - 347, 356, 381 - 383, 409, 418, 429 |
|---|---|---|
| Dolgintzova | Kherson province | 425 |
| Dombroveny | Bessarabia | 412 |
| Eriozova | Odesa region | 424 |
| Eyegene Mi (Our Own Effort) | Odesa region | 424 |
| Frei Erd (free land) | Odesa region | 424 |
| Freiheit (Freedom) | Odesa region | 424 |
| Freiland | Kherson province | 371 |
| Freiland (happiness) | Odesa region | 424 |
| FrieHeim (Free Home) | Odesa region | 424 |
| Friling (Spring) | Odesa region | 424 |
| Gil'ad | USA | 10 |
| Gorkaya | Ekaterinoslav province | 409, 427 |
| Grafskoya | Ekaterinoslav province | 112, 115, 409 |
| HaTikva (The Hope) | Crimea | 139 |
| Horostaipoli | Kiev Province | 374, 375 |
| Ikar (Farmer) | Crimea | 139, 426 |
| Inguletz (Har-Shefer) | Kherson province | 11, 34, 47, 350 - 353, 393, 409, 425 |
| Izraelovka (Ya'azor) | Kherson province | 11, 34, 103, 233, 234, 237, 238, 393, 409, 429 |
| Kadima (Forward) | Crimea | 426 |
| Kaminka (Kamenka) | Kherson province | 34, 36, 47, 393, 409, 425 |
| Kapresht | Bessarabia | 412 |

Jewish Farmers in Russia Fields

| | | |
|---|---|---|
| Petrovska | Odesa region | 424 |
| Pobeda (Victory in Russian) | Crimea | 426 |
| Poltavska | Kherson province | 78 |
| Priyutnoya | Ekaterinoslav province | 409, 427 |
| Promukloya | Kherson province | 409 |
| Rabattnik (?) | Crimea | 426 |
| Roiter Oktiober (?) (Red October?) | Odesa region | 424 |
| Romanovka | Kherson province | 78, 81, 82, 101, 109, 271, 273, 294, 314, 315, 383, 409, 423 |
| Roskoshnaye | Ekaterinoslav province | 409, 427 |
| Rosnopola | Odesa region | 424 |
| Rovnopol | Ekaterinoslav province | 409, 427 |
| Sdeh Menukha HaGdola (Tatarka, later Kalinindorf) | Kherson province | 11, 34, 38, 103, 137, 187 - 190, 192, 193, 201, 209, 210, 214, 227, 230, 238, 248, 269, 274, 294, 314, 318 - 321, 334, 336, 337, 354, 355, 357, 373, 378, 383, 393, 409, 419, 429 |
| Sdeh-Menukha-HaKtana (Nevel) | Kherson province | 11, 103, 176, 185, 188 - 230, 274, 304, 314, 320, 334, 354, 355, 371, 373, 378 - 380, 383, 393, 409, 418, 419, 423 |
| Sehaidek | Kherson province | 11, 231 - 240, 409 |
| Selkhoz | Odesa region | 424 |
| Shchedrin | Bobruisk Oblast, Belarus | 80 |
| Sicily Island | LA, USA | 10 |
| Sladkovodnaya | Ekaterinoslav province | 409 |
| Sofyovka | Vohlyn | 410 |
| Tel-Khai | Crimea, Hakhshara settlement for the HeKhalutz movement | 139, 277, 385, 426 |
| Touro | USA | 10 |

Jewish Farmers in Russia Fields

| | | |
|---|---|---|
| Tova | Ekaterinoslav province | 401 |
| Trudoliubovka | Ekaterinoslav province | 93, 112, 115, 129, 409, 427, 429 |
| Vertyuzhany | Bessarabia | 412 |
| Vesselaya | Ekaterinoslav province | 93, 112, 409, 427, 429 |
| Vogotzlova | Odesa region | 424 |
| Volnaya | Kherson province | 409 |
| Waldheim (later llych's Wills) | Birobidzhan | 422 |
| Yefeh-Nahar (Effingar) | Kherson province, On pages 145 - 176, it is mentioned in its pseudo name - Nahar Gilovka | 11, 34, 163, 192, 164, 145 - 176, 269, 272, 314, 317, 320, 335, 341 - 347, 371, 376, 380 - 384, 393, 394, 396, 409, 418 |
| Yetzira (Creation) | Crimea | 139, 426 |
| Yizluchistoye | | 49, 409 |
| Zatishe | Ekaterinoslav province | 409, 427 |
| Zelenopolya | Ekaterinoslav province | 409, 427 |
| Zemerov | Crimea | 426 |
| Zemliedieliyetz (worker of the land) | Crimea | 426 |
| Zguritza | Bessarabia | 412 |
| Zokhorveka | Odesa region | 424 |
| Zorya (or Dorya)? | Crimea | 426 |

1. **Note:** Exact translation: Jewish Agriculturalists on Russian Prairies

www.ingramcontent.com/pod-product-compliance
Lightning Source LLC
Chambersburg PA
CBHW082005150426

42814CB00005BA/236